# ConsumerReports®

# BUYING GUIDE 2014

THE EDITORS OF
CONSUMER REPORTS

# Contents

## Shop Smart in 2014

## Quick Guides & Product Ratings



## Autos 145

# Buying Advice at Your Fingertips

**The Consumer Reports Buying Guide for 2014 is your handy one-stop source for making informed, money-saving purchases. Consult it before you shop, then bring it to the store or keep it beside your computer to help you compare brands. Here's how to make the best use of this guide.**

If you are interested in squeezing the most value from every dollar you spend, this little book will be an invaluable shopping tool. It's packed with highlights from our exclusive buying advice and Ratings for more than 1,950 specific product models.

Preceding each Ratings chart, you'll find a Quick Guide to our buying advice. You can access our full buying advice by using your smart phone to scan QR codes provided with each Quick Guide (see page 11 for how to use QR codes), or by using the website address provided with each category.

But before you delve into the best stuff to buy, be sure to read about the best places to buy it—whether online or a walk-in store—in the **Comparing Retailers** section, starting on page 5. Based on valuable information provided to us by thousands of Consumer Reports readers, we discuss buying trends and provide information on the service, selection, and prices of dozens of retailers of appliances, computers, and many other electronics products.

After you've brushed up on your shopping savvy, turn to the **Product Ratings** section, starting on page 11, for guidance from the experts at Consumer Reports on 33 product categories, presented in alphabetical order. Along with the Ratings, you'll find a **brand repair history** for some products that reflects survey results from thousands of readers about repairs and problems they've had with various brands.

Are you in the market for a car? The **Autos** section, starting on page 145, has the latest **Ratings** and data on new and used models. In addition to reviews of the 2013-14 vehicles, there's a section on the best and worst used cars, and reliability Ratings for 230 models currently in the marketplace. The tires section includes 164 models.

So grab this handy little book whenever you shop. Whether you are shopping online or in a store, we're certain it will save you money and help you get the best value every time you pick it up.

# ConsumerReports®

WHO WE ARE

## About the CONSUMER REPORTS family of products

**Founded as a magazine in 1936, CONSUMER REPORTS now brings you its unbiased, trusted information in many formats. Products and publications include CONSUMER REPORTS magazine; buying guides, books, and special issues from Consumer Reports Publications Development; two newsletters—Consumer Reports on Health and Consumer Reports Money Adviser; ShopSmart magazine; and Consumer Reports TV News, a nationally syndicated consumer news service.**

**ConsumerReports.org** offers site subscribers a searchable version of our test findings and advice, as well as access to **Consumer Reports Mobile**. Auto prices and custom reports are available through the **Consumer Reports New Car Price Service, Consumer Reports Used Car Price Service,** and **ConsumerReports.org Cars Best Deals Plus.™** You can find prices, subscription rates, and more information on all these products and services at *ConsumerReports.org.* Go to "Consumer Reports Bookstore" at the bottom of the home page. For reporting on consumer news and issues, go to *Consumerist.com.*

**CONSUMER REPORTS** magazine specializes in head-to-head, brand-name comparisons of autos and household products. It also provides informed, impartial advice on a broad range of topics from health and nutrition to personal finance and travel.

**CONSUMER REPORTS** buys all the products it tests and accepts no free samples. We accept no advertising from outside entities nor do we let any company use our information or Ratings for commercial purposes.

**CONSUMER REPORTS** is an independent, nonprofit testing and information organization—the largest such organization in the world.

Since 1936, our mission has been to test products, inform the public, and protect consumers. Our income is derived solely from the sale of our publications and online information and services, and from nonrestrictive, noncommercial contributions, grants, and fees.

# Comparing Retailers

**Our product testers can tell you which refrigerator or computer delivers the most value. But then you have to find the lowest price and good service. To help you find the best places to shop, we survey tens of thousands of Consumer Reports subscribers annually about their experiences buying appliances, electronics, and computers in-store and online.**

## Where to buy appliances

Shoppers are increasingly going online to purchase appliances, especially smaller items such as coffeemakers and food processors. Compared to our findings from 2007, we also found more large appliances were being bought over the Internet. And online research is helping consumers find good deals. Those are some of the results of our exclusive appliance buying survey of almost 23,000 subscribers.

### RESEARCH CAN YIELD A GOOD PRICE

Low prices and sales were the top reasons people went to a specific retailer. And doing research in advance can help. In fact, 90 percent of our readers who tried that approach said it was useful. Price comparison websites topped their list of strategies, followed by retailer sites with buying advice and coupons.

And if you register an e-mail address with manufacturers or retailers, you may find benefits such as invitations to "family and friends" sales, which were common at several retailers.

### GETTING TO SATISFACTION

Appliance shoppers were relatively satisfied overall, even though no retailer earned perfect marks across the board. And survey respondents who bought small appliances were more critical about selection and service for several of the retailers.

No retailer had an excellent score for price, although some were very good in the measure. Selection and service were a sore spot for a few of the discounters in the small appliance category, in particular Costco, Sam's Club, and Walmart.

### SURVEY LISTS TOP RETAILERS

Abt Electronics was among the top choices of survey respondents for major appliances, along with independent stores. Abt, a store based in the Chicago area, had excellent scores for selection, product quality, service, checkout ease, and other measures.

Independent stores had excellent scores for service and checkout ease too. Amazon.com, QVC, and independent stores were among the top choices for small appliances. For our survey, subscribers told us about their overall satisfaction based on experiences buying more than 30,000 appliances.

### WHO PROVIDES THE BEST SUPPORT?

Purchasing an appliance is only one part of the equation. You need to figure out where to turn if it suddenly breaks down.

In a separate survey, subscribers were much more satisfied when they called an independent repair shop for service than when they called the manufacturer or major retailer. Though satisfaction was higher for independent repair shops, most outlets got only average scores for solving the problem.

## Where to buy electronics

Online retailers were among the best places to buy TVs, cameras, tablets, and other electronics, according to our readers. Our Ratings of places to buy major electronics are based on Consumer Reports' Annual Questionnaire. Online electronics shopping was more pleasing

## Appliance retailers

In order of highest reader score, within appliance type.

Better ⟵⟶ Worse: Excellent, Very good, Good, Fair, Poor

| Order | Retailer | Reader score (0–100) | Price | Selection | Product quality | Service | Checkout ease | Shipping | Installation | Haul-away |
|---|---|---|---|---|---|---|---|---|---|---|
| **A** | **MAJOR APPLIANCES** | | | | | | | | | |
| 1 | Abt Electronics | 93 | Very good | Excellent | Excellent | Excellent | Excellent | Excellent | Excellent | Excellent |
| 2 | Independents | 91 | Good | Good | Very good | Excellent | Excellent | Excellent | Excellent | Excellent |
| 3 | Pacific Sales | 88 | Good | Very good | Very good | Very good | Very good | Very good | Very good | Excellent |
| 4 | Lowe's | 87 | Good | Good | Very good | Good | Very good | Very good | Very good | Excellent |
| 5 | Home Depot | 86 | Good | Good | Very good | Good | Very good | Very good | Very good | Excellent |
| 6 | HHGregg | 84 | Very good | Good | Very good | Very good | Very good | Very good | Very good | Excellent |
| 7 | Sears | 84 | Good | Good | Very good | Good | Good | Very good | Very good | Very good |
| 8 | Best Buy | 83 | Very good | Good | Very good | Good | Good | Very good | Good | Very good |
| 9 | P.C. Richard & Son | 83 | Good | Good | Good | Good | Very good | Very good | Good | Very good |
| **B** | **SMALL APPLIANCES** | | | | | | | | | |
| 1 | Amazon.com | 94 | Very good | Excellent | Excellent | Very good | Excellent | Excellent | – | – |
| 2 | QVC | 92 | Very good | Good | Excellent | Very good | Excellent | Excellent | – | – |
| 3 | Independents | 91 | Good | Good | Excellent | Excellent | Excellent | Excellent | – | – |
| 4 | Costco | 91 | Very good | Poor | Very good | Poor | Good | – | – | – |
| 5 | Kohl's | 88 | Very good | Good | Very good | Good | Very good | – | – | – |
| 6 | Bed Bath & Beyond | 88 | Good | Good | Very good | Good | Very good | – | – | – |
| 7 | Macy's | 87 | Good | Good | Very good | Good | Very good | Excellent | – | – |
| 8 | Sam's Club | 85 | Very good | Poor | Very good | Poor | Fair | – | – | – |
| 9 | Lowe's | 85 | Good | Good | Good | Good | Good | Very good | – | – |
| 10 | Target | 83 | Good | Good | Good | Poor | Good | – | – | – |
| 11 | Home Depot | 83 | Good | Good | Good | Good | Good | Very good | – | – |
| 12 | Sears | 83 | Good | Good | Good | Good | Good | – | – | – |
| 13 | Best Buy | 82 | Good | Good | Good | Fair | Good | – | – | – |
| 14 | Walmart | 78 | Good | Fair | Good | Poor | Poor | – | – | – |

for our readers than shopping at walk-in stores, with convenience being a major reason for choosing to shop online.

Shopping at walk-in stores still has its place, notably for those who like to see products up close before they buy. And some of the better retailers in our Ratings are walk-in stores, although those standouts are mostly general retailers rather than chains that specialize in electronics. The retailer types described on this and the following page are listed in the order in which we think most people should consider buying from them.

### DEDICATED WEBSITES

No other category of store can match this one for pleasing customers in almost every respect, including selection, prices, and buying ease. The more innovative websites find ways to provide personal advice similar to what you'd get at a great walk-in store. Amazon.com offers among the largest number of user reviews. B&H's website was the only retailer that got our top rating for selection. Along with Newegg, it got the top rating for prices. Costco and Apple also ranked among the top online stores.

### INDEPENDENT STORES

Mom-and-pop independent stores should be your first stop if you need hand-holding for a major electronics purchase. With the exception of price, independents were above par in every respect. Prices were only average at independent stores, readers said. But try negotiating; readers were more successful in getting price reductions or extras at those stores than at big chain retailers.

### WAREHOUSE STORES

Don't expect a lot of selection in electronics products at a warehouse store. But price and quality at warehouse stores are above average. Costco, Sam's Club, and BJ's Wholesale Club are inferior choices if you have a specific model or brand in mind. Service was also below average at BJ's and Sam's.

### MAJOR ELECTRONICS CHAINS

Electronics chains are probably still your best option when you can't wait to buy an electronics item. While our

---

### Guide to the Ratings

Charts are based on 22,888 Consumer Reports subscribers who reported on 30,243 appliance-purchase experiences in the 2012 Consumer Reports National Research Center Appliance Shopper Satisfaction survey. (Respondents may not be representative of the U.S. population.) Major appliances include ranges, refrigerators, washers, and dryers; small appliances include coffeemakers, grills, and vacuum cleaners. **Reader score** reflects readers' assessments of their overall buying experience and is not limited to factors under **survey results**. A score of 100 would mean all respondents had been completely satisfied; 80, very satisfied, on average; 60, fairly well satisfied. Differences of fewer than 4 points aren't meaningful. Displayed scores are rounded; stores are listed in order of precise reader score. **Price, selection, product quality, service, checkout ease, shipping, installation,** and **haul-away** were rated on a scale from very poor to excellent. Scores for service are based on contact with company staff except for Amazon.com, which reflects customer ratings of website customer support. Small-appliance and major-appliance results aren't directly comparable because of differences in methodology. A dash (–) means not applicable or insufficient sample size.

readers found the major national names to be no better than middling in most respects, some regional chains scored better than average on a number of attributes. Some chains, including Best Buy, Walmart, and Staples let you order online and pick up at a store. As a result, you may be able to save on shipping charges.

### MASS MERCHANDISERS

Buying major electronics at a department store or discount chain no longer necessarily requires settling for a budget brand, but don't expect to be especially pleased with prices at any of those chains, our readers' experiences suggest.

### MANUFACTURERS' STORES

Apple stores receive top marks for customer service and product quality. But the Apple Store was also rated as mediocre in selection and below average for price.

### OFFICE-SUPPLY STORES

Staples was the sole such chain in our Ratings. According to our readers, the chain was average in most measures, although product quality was above average, as it was for most other walk-in stores.

## Where to buy computers

Even the lowest-rated retailer pleased most customers, according to our survey results. Apple's website stood out among the manufacturers' websites, which are the place to go if you want to customize a particular brand of computer. Return policies vary from store to store and site to site. Restocking fees can also be different from one place to another, but you'll usually pay 15 percent on returns of nondefective computers.

---

## Guide to the Ratings

**COMPUTER RETAILERS. Reader score** reflects respondents' satisfaction with their purchase experience and isn't limited to factors listed in the survey results. A score of 100 would mean all respondents were completely satisfied; 80 would mean very satisfied, on average; 60, fairly well satisfied. Differences in scores of fewer than 5 points aren't meaningful. Respondents rated vendors on their **selection** of computers, **prices**, and **service** (including knowledge and attentiveness of staff for walk-ins and usability for websites). These ratings are relative based on how each vendor compares with the others. Results are based on 16,353 responses from subscribers who bought new desktops and laptops from January 2011 through June 2012. Survey results might not reflect the U.S. population as a whole.

**ELECTRONICS RETAILERS.** Scores are based on 29,910 purchases of TVs, digital cameras, digital camcorders, DVD and Blu-ray players, GPS devices, video-game consoles, e-book readers, tablets, and MP3 players by 23,639 Consumer Reports readers between January 2011 and June 2012. Electronics retailers are among the highest-rated services in Consumer Reports National Research Center surveys. Results might not reflect the U.S. population. **Reader score** reflects overall satisfaction with the shopping experience and is not limited to the factors in the survey results. A score of 100 would mean all respondents were completely satisfied; 80, that respondents were very satisfied on average. Differences of fewer than 5 points are not meaningful. The scores under **survey results** reflect how each retailer did compared with the others. Scores for **customer service** and **buying ease** are not directly comparable between walk-in and online retailers. **Customer service** reflects online or phone support for websites and in-store sales help for walk-in stores. Online **buying ease** reflects using the website; in-store **buying ease,** fewer problems such as sale items being unavailable, long checkout lines, and crowded displays.

## Computer retailers

In order of highest reader score, within types.

Better ⟷ Worse: ⊜ ⊖ ○ ◒ ●

| Recommendation | Order | Retailer | Reader score (0–100) | Survey results: Selection | Price | Service |
|---|---|---|---|---|---|---|
| | | **A WEBSITES/CATALOGS** | | | | |
| ✓ | 1 | Costco.com | 90 | ○ | ⊜ | ⊖ |
| ✓ | 2 | Amazon.com | 90 | ⊜ | ⊖ | ⊜ |
| ✓ | 3 | Newegg.com | 90 | ⊜ | ⊜ | ⊜ |
| ✓ | 4 | TigerDirect.com | 89 | ⊖ | ⊖ | ⊖ |
| | 5 | Best Buy.com | 83 | ○ | ○ | ○ |
| | | **B MANUFACTURER WEBSITES/CATALOGS** | | | | |
| ✓ | 1 | Apple | 92 | ⊜ | ● | ⊜ |
| | 2 | Toshiba | 85 | ⊖ | ○ | ⊖ |
| | 3 | HP | 85 | ⊖ | ○ | ⊖ |
| | 4 | Lenovo | 84 | ⊜ | ○ | ○ |
| | 5 | Dell | 82 | ⊖ | ○ | ⊖ |
| | | **C WALK-IN STORES** | | | | |
| ✓ | 1 | Apple Store | 91 | ⊜ | ◒ | ⊜ |
| ✓ | 2 | Independents | 86 | ○ | ○ | ⊜ |
| ✓ | 3 | Micro Center | 86 | ⊖ | ⊖ | ⊜ |
| ✓ | 4 | Costco | 85 | ● | ⊖ | ◒ |
| | 5 | Staples | 81 | ○ | ○ | ⊖ |
| | 6 | Sam's Club | 81 | ● | ○ | ● |
| | 7 | Office Depot | 80 | ◒ | ○ | ○ |
| | 8 | Office Max | 80 | ◒ | ◒ | ○ |
| | 9 | Best Buy | 78 | ○ | ◒ | ○ |
| | 10 | Fry's Electronics | 78 | ⊖ | ○ | ◒ |
| | 11 | Walmart | 76 | ● | ○ | ● |

## Electronics retailers

In order of highest reader score, within types.

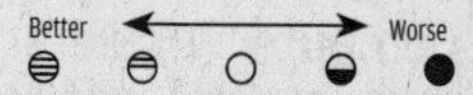


| Recommendation | Order | Retailer | Reader score (0–100) | Price | Customer service | Product quality | Selection | Buying ease | Returns (days) |
|---|---|---|---|---|---|---|---|---|---|
| | | **A ONLINE STORES** | | | | | | | |
| ✔ | 1 | Newegg.com | 95 | ⊜ | ⊖ | ⊜ | ⊖ | ⊜ | 30 [1] |
| ✔ | 2 | BHPhotoVideo.com | 95 | ⊜ | ⊖ | ⊜ | ⊜ | ⊜ | 30 |
| ✔ | 3 | Amazon.com | 94 | ⊖ | ⊖ | ⊖ | ⊖ | ⊜ | 30 |
| ✔ | 4 | Costco.com | 94 | ⊖ | ⊖ | ⊖ | ◒ | ⊖ | 90 |
| ✔ | 5 | Apple.com | 93 | ◒ | ⊖ | ⊜ | ○ | ⊜ | 14 [2] |
| | 6 | Walmart.com | 86 | ⊖ | ○ | ○ | ○ | ○ | [2] |
| | 7 | BestBuy.com | 86 | ⊖ | ◒ | ⊖ | ⊖ | ○ | 30 |
| | | **B WALK-IN STORES** | | | | | | | |
| ✔ | 1 | Apple Store | 92 | ◒ | ⊜ | ⊜ | ○ | ○ | 14 [2] |
| ✔ | 2 | Costco | 92 | ⊜ | ○ | ⊖ | ◒ | ○ | 90 |
| ✔ | 3 | Independents | 91 | ○ | ⊜ | ⊜ | ⊖ | ⊖ | [3] |
| | 4 | Army & Air Force Exchange | 89 | ⊖ | ⊖ | ⊜ | ○ | ○ | 30 [2] |
| | 5 | Sam's Club | 87 | ⊖ | ◒ | ⊖ | ◒ | ○ | [2] |
| | 6 | Staples | 87 | ○ | ○ | ⊖ | ○ | ○ | 14 |
| | 7 | Target | 86 | ○ | ○ | ⊖ | ◒ | ○ | 90 [2] |
| | 8 | HHGregg | 86 | ⊖ | ⊖ | ⊖ | ⊖ | ○ | 30 [1] |
| | 9 | BJ's Wholesale Club | 86 | ⊖ | ● | ⊖ | ● | ○ | [2] |
| | 10 | Sears | 85 | ○ | ○ | ⊖ | ○ | ○ | 30 [1] |
| | 11 | P.C. Richard & Son | 83 | ○ | ⊖ | ⊖ | ○ | ○ | 20 [1] |
| | 12 | Best Buy | 83 | ○ | ○ | ⊖ | ○ | ○ | 30 |
| | 13 | Fry's Electronics | 82 | ⊖ | ○ | ⊖ | ○ | ◒ | 30 [1] |
| | 14 | Walmart | 81 | ○ | ● | ○ | ◒ | ◒ | [2] |

[1] Some categories of products might be excluded from returns or subject to restocking fees. [2] Policies may differ for some products. [3] Policies vary by store.

# PRODUCT RATINGS AND BRAND RELIABILITY

**The Quick Guides, product Ratings, and brand reliability information that follow are designed to help you zero in on the model you want to buy. See the buying advice highlights in the Quick Guides to help you decide what you want from a product. Then go to the Ratings charts to get the big picture on performance.**

For some products you'll find full Ratings that include every currently available model we tested. For other products, the Ratings charts include only models recommended for most people in addition to models that we designated as Best Buys.

To obtain Ratings, we put all models within a category through weeks of testing, side by side, so that test results can be compared. We rank products by performance; products with equal scores are listed alphabetically.

Consumer Reports checked to make sure most products rated in this Buying Guide were still available when the book was published. However, depending on how long after publication you use this book, you may find a Rating for a product that is no longer available. Or, you may not find a Rating for a model that is available because it hadn't been tested as of publication.

Besides checking for similar models, you can also refer to the brand repair history charts for some products.

Every year we survey readers on repairs and other problems they encounter with household products. From their responses, we derive the percentage of a brand's products that have been repaired or had a serious problem. The reliability graphs that accompany the Ratings give brand repair rates for many of our product categories. Our findings have been consistent over the 30-plus years we've surveyed brand reliability, though they are not infallible predictors.

A brand's repair history includes data on many models, some of which may have been more or less reliable than others. And surveys of a brand's past models can't anticipate design or manufacturing changes. Still, you can improve your chances of getting a trouble-free product by going with a brand that has been reliable in the past.

## How to scan QR codes

Use your smart phone to access exclusive buying advice on Consumer Reports Mobile. If your phone didn't come with a QR code scanner installed, download one of the code-scanning apps available. Then scan the image of the QR code that appears with each product category on the following pages. Your phone will display the advice you'll need to get the best values. The code at right takes you to the Consumer Reports Mobile home page.

# Quick Guide BLU-RAY PLAYERS

**Blu-ray players can play high-definition Blu-ray discs, DVDs, and CDs, and many can stream video from Netflix and other online services. They're the perfect match for HDTVs.**

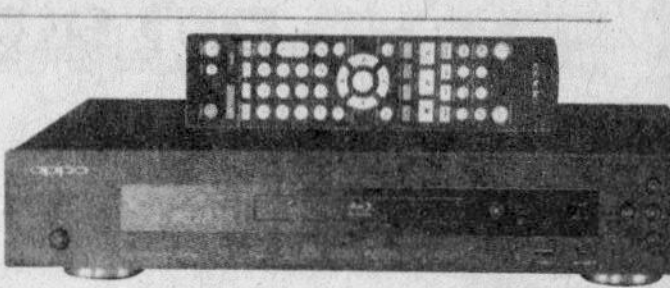

## Shopping tip

With most Blu-ray players, you won't have unlimited Web browsing, only access to specific sites as arranged by the manufacturer.

Scan this or see how, page 11

For more buying advice, go to *ConsumerReports.org/bluray*

### What to look for

- Wireless capability, which lets you hook up a player to a home network without running cables from your TV setup to a modem or router
- A 3D-capable player, if you have a 3D TV or may buy one soon

### What to skip

- A standard DVD player, if you have an HDTV, especially a 1080p model, which has enough resolution to display all the detail on a Blu-ray disc. The superior picture quality you'll get from a Blu-ray disc is worth the slight extra cost of the player
- A Blu-ray player, if you have a standard-def TV—which can't display Blu-ray's higher picture quality—and have no plans to buy an HDTV

### What you'll pay

Blu-ray players generally start at about $75, though you may find some models on sale for less. Many full-featured models from major brands cost $100 to $250. 3D players start at about $100, though some cost $400 or more.

**All tested models** In performance order, within types.

| Recommended | Rank | Brand & model | Price | Overall score (0–100; P \| F \| G \| VG \| E) | Test results: HD picture quality | DVD picture quality | Ease of use | Useful features | Blu-ray disc load time | DVD load time | Features: Blu-ray load time range (sec.) | DVD load time (sec.) | USB port | Web browsing | Memory card slot |
|---|---|---|---|---|---|---|---|---|---|---|---|---|---|---|---|
| **A 3D** | | | | | | | | | | | | | | | |
| ☑ | 1 | **Oppo** BDP-103 | $500 | 77 | ⊜ | ⊖ | ⊜ | ⊖ | ○ | ○ | 14-21 | 17 | 3 | | |
| ☑ | 2 | **LG** BP730 | 200 | 76 | ⊜ | ○ | ⊜ | ⊖ | ○ | ⊖ | 15-22 | 12 | 1 | • | |
| ✔ | 3 | **LG** BP530 | 120 | 75 | ⊜ | ○ | ⊖ | ⊖ | ○ | ⊖ | 13-21 | 13 | 1 | | |
| ✔ | 4 | **LG** BP620 | 140 | 74 | ⊜ | ⊖ | ⊖ | ⊖ | ○ | ⊖ | 12-21 | 15 | 1 | | |
| ☑ | 5 | **Panasonic** DMP-BDT330 | 190 | 73 | ⊜ | ⊖ | ⊖ | ⊖ | ○ | ⊖ | 10-24 | 15 | 1 | • | • |

| Recommended | Rank | Brand & model | Price | Overall score (0–100; P \| F \| G \| VG \| E) | Test results: HD picture quality | DVD picture quality | Ease of use | Useful features | Blu-ray disc load time | DVD load time | Features: Blu-ray load time range (sec.) | DVD load time (sec.) | USB port | Web browsing | Memory card slot |
|---|---|---|---|---|---|---|---|---|---|---|---|---|---|---|---|
| **A 3D continued** | | | | | | | | | | | | | | | |
| ✓ | 6 | **Yamaha** BD-S673 | $275 | 73 | Excellent | Very good | Excellent | Very good | Fair | Good | 26-36 | 18 | 2 | | |
| CR Best Buy | 7 | **Panasonic** DMP-BDT230 | 130 | 72 | Excellent | Very good | Very good | Very good | Good | Very good | 10-24 | 15 | 1 | • | • |
| ✓ | 8 | **Samsung** BD-F7500 | 250 | 72 | Excellent | Very good | Very good | Very good | Very good | Fair | 10-22 | 22 | 1 | • | |
| ✓ | 9 | **Samsung** BD-E5900 | 150 | 72 | Excellent | Very good | Very good | Very good | Good | Very good | 13-25 | 11 | 1 | • | |
| ✓ | 10 | **Panasonic** DMP-BDT500 | 280 | 71 | Excellent | Very good | Very good | Very good | Good | Good | 13-28 | 20 | 1 | • | • |
| ✓ | 11 | **Panasonic** DMP-BDT320 | 160 | 71 | Excellent | Very good | Very good | Very good | Good | Good | 12-28 | 20 | 1 | | • |
| CR Best Buy | 12 | **Sony** BDP-S5100 | 120 | 71 | Excellent | Very good | Very good | Very good | Good | Very good | 14-25 | 14 | 2 | • | |
| ✓ | 13 | **Sony** BDP-S790 | 250 | 69 | Excellent | Very good | Very good | Very good | Fair | Good | 21-32 | 20 | 2 | • | |
| ✓ | 14 | **Marantz** UD5007 | 600 | 67 | Excellent | Good | Very good | Good | Good | Good | 16-26 | 17 | 1 | | |
| ✓ | 15 | **Pioneer** Elite BDP-62FD | 380 | 67 | Excellent | Very good | Very good | Good | Good | Good | 16-23 | 19 | 2 | | |
| ✓ | 16 | **Panasonic** DMP-BBT01 | 230 | 67 | Excellent | Very good | Very good | Very good | Good | Good | 11-28 | 18 | 1 | • | • |
| ✓ | 17 | **Denon** DBT-1713UD | 500 | 67 | Excellent | Good | Very good | Good | Good | Good | 16-27 | 17 | 1 | | |
| | 18 | **Toshiba** BDX5300 | 100 | 66 | Excellent | Very good | Very good | Very good | Poor | Good | 28-40 | 17 | 1 | | |
| | 19 | **Pioneer** BDP-150 | 300 | 65 | Excellent | Very good | Very good | Good | Fair | Good | 24-32 | 18 | 2 | • | |
| | 20 | **Yamaha** BD-S473 | 185 | 65 | Excellent | Very good | Very good | Good | Fair | Good | 25-37 | 18 | 2 | | |
| | 21 | **Vizio** VBR135 | 100 | 62 | Excellent | Very good | Very good | Good | Good | Good | 16-24 | 19 | 1 | | |
| | 22 | **Pioneer** Elite BDP-52FD | 400 | 62 | Excellent | Good | Very good | Good | Poor | Very good | 32-42 | 12 | 2 | | |
| | 23 | **Onkyo** BD-SP809 | 400 | 61 | Excellent | Good | Very good | Good | Poor | Good | 24-46 | 18 | 1 | | |
| | 24 | **Sharp** BD-AMS20U | 150 | 60 | Excellent | Very good | Good | Good | Fair | Good | 16-36 | 18 | 2 | | |
| | 25 | **Sharp** BD-HP75U | 250 | 55 | Excellent | Good | Good | Good | Fair | Fair | 17-40 | 26 | 2 | | |

**Ratings Key** ⊜ Excellent ⊖ Very good ○ Good ◒ Fair ● Poor

☑ **CR Best Buy** These models offer the best combination of performance and price. All are recommended.

✓ **Recommended** These are high-performing models that stand out.

| Recommended | Rank | Brand & model | Price | Overall score (0–100; P \| F \| G \| VG \| E) | Test results: HD picture quality | DVD picture quality | Ease of use | Useful features | Blu-ray disc load time | DVD load time | Features: Blu-ray load time range (sec.) | DVD load time (sec.) | USB port | Web browsing | Memory card slot |
|---|---|---|---|---|---|---|---|---|---|---|---|---|---|---|---|
| **B STANDARD** | | | | | | | | | | | | | | | |
| ✓ | 1 | **LG** BP320 | $120 | 71 | Excellent | Very good | Very good | Very good | Good | Good | 11-24 | 17 | 1 | | |
| ✓ | 2 | **Sony** BDP-S3100 | 100 | 67 | Excellent | Very good | Very good | Very good | Good | Very good | 14-24 | 14 | 1 | • | |
| ✓ | 3 | **Panasonic** DMP-BD89 DMP-BD79 | 100 | 67 | Excellent | Very good | Very good | Good | Good | Good | 10-25 | 16 | 1 | | |
| | 4 | **Samsung** BD-F5100 | 85 | 65 | Excellent | Very good | Very good | Fair | Very good | Very good | 10-20 | 13 | 1 | | |
| | 5 | **Panasonic** DMP-BD77 | 170 | 62 | Excellent | Very good | Very good | Fair | Fair | Fair | 17-29 | 23 | 1 | | |
| | 6 | **Sony** BDP-S1100 | 90 | 58 | Excellent | Very good | Very good | Poor | Good | Very good | 13-23 | 14 | 1 | | |
| | 7 | **RCA** BRC11082 | 80 | 38 | Excellent | Very good | Fair | Poor | Fair | Very good | 15-56 | 15 | 1 | | |

**Ratings Key** ⊜ Excellent ⊖ Very good ○ Good ◒ Fair ● Poor

☑ **CR Best Buy** These models offer the best combination of performance and price. All are recommended.

✓ **Recommended** These are high-performing models that stand out.

## Guide to the Ratings

**Overall score** is based mainly on picture quality and ease of use. The displayed score is out of a total of 100 points. **HD** and **DVD picture quality** evaluate clarity and color accuracy from Blu-ray discs at 1080p and DVDs upconverted to 1080p. **Ease of use** pertains to the controls on the front panel and remote, and navigation through the player's menu. **Useful features** include audio/video outputs, Internet connectivity and services, and 3D capability. **Blu-ray disc** and **DVD load time** is the average time it took to load test discs. **Price** is approximate retail.

# Quick Guide CAMCORDERS

Camcorders are available in two main types: full-sized (HD) and action. Full-sized models are larger, include LCDs, and have lots of features. Action camcorders are smaller and lightweight, but have far fewer features; most don't even have LCDs.

## Shopping tip

Electronic viewfinders can help you shoot video in bright light situations.

Scan this or see how, page 11

## What to look for

- An LCD with very good quality, since most models don't include a viewfinder and you'll need to compose on the display
- Long battery life, since battery life varies greatly. Also, look for models that can be charged via a computer's USB port
- Although image quality is the most important factor in our tests, be sure to check for audio quality, which varies greatly

## What to skip

- Digital zoom, since this type of zoom degrades image quality

## What you'll pay

For full-sized HD camcorders, you'll spend $150 to $1,000. For action camcorders, you'll spend $100 to $400.

For more buying advice, go to *ConsumerReports.org/camcorders*

**Recommended models only** From 54 tested.

| Recommended | Rank | Brand & model (Similar models, in small type, are comparable to tested model.) | Price | Overall score (0–100; P \| F \| G \| VG \| E) | Picture quality | Low-light picture quality | Ease of use | Autofocus | Audio quality | Image stabilizer | Display quality | Versatility | Still camera | Battery life (min.) |
|---|---|---|---|---|---|---|---|---|---|---|---|---|---|---|
| **A HD** | | | | | | | | | | | | | | |
| ✔ | 1 | **Sony** HDR-TD20V | $1,000 | 77 | E | E | VG | E | VG | VG | E | VG | E | 220 |
| ✔ | 2 | **Sony** HDR-PJ790V | 1,600 | 75 | E | VG | VG | E | VG | VG | E | VG | E | 115 |
| ✔ | 3 | **Sony** HDR-PJ710V | 1,000 | 75 | E | E | VG | E | VG | E | E | VG | E | 110 |
| ✔ | 4 | **Sony** HDR-PJ580V | 650 | 73 | E | E | G | E | VG | VG | VG | VG | E | 120 |
| ✔ | 5 | **Sony** HDR-CX580V | 600 | 73 | E | E | VG | E | VG | VG | VG | VG | E | 120 |
| ✔ | 6 | **Sony** HDR-PJ650V | 1,100 | 71 | VG | VG | G | E | VG | VG | E | VG | E | 120 |
| ✔ | 7 | **Sony** HDR-TD30V | 1,000 | 69 | VG | VG | VG | E | VG | VG | E | VG | E | 105 |

| Recommended | Rank | Brand & model (Similar models, in small type, are comparable to tested model.) | Price | Overall score (0–100; P \| F \| G \| VG \| E) | Picture quality | Low-light picture quality | Ease of use | Autofocus | Audio quality | Image stabilizer | Display quality | Versatility | Still camera | Battery life (min.) |
|---|---|---|---|---|---|---|---|---|---|---|---|---|---|---|
| **A** | | **HD** continued | | | | | | | | | | | | |
| ✓ | 8 | **Canon** VIXIA HF M52 | $ 550 | 67 | E | E | VG | E | G | VG | E | G | VG | 120 |
| ✓ | 9 | **Canon** VIXIA HF M50 | 500 | 67 | E | E | VG | E | G | VG | E | G | VG | 115 |
| ✓ | 10 | **Canon** VIXIA HF G20 | 1,000 | 66 | VG | VG | VG | E | G | VG | E | VG | G | 110 |
| ✓ | 11 | **Panasonic** HC-V720 | 550 | 66 | VG | VG | VG | E | G | VG | E | G | VG | 85 |
| ✔ | 12 | **Panasonic** HC-V520 | 360 | 65 | VG | VG | VG | E | G | VG | E | G | G | 115 |
| ✓ | 13 | **Sony** HDR-PJ430V<br>HDR-CX430V | 850 | 64 | VG | VG | VG | E | G | VG | E | G | VG | 140 |
| ✓ | 14 | **Sony** HDR-PJ380 | 600 | 64 | VG | G | VG | E | G | G | E | G | VG | 155 |
| ✓ | 15 | **Sony** HDR-GW77V | 700 | 64 | E | E | VG | E | G | G | E | G | VG | 90 |
| ✔ | 16 | **Sony** HDR-CX290 | 350 | 62 | VG | G | VG | E | G | G | E | F | VG | 90 |
| ✓ | 17 | **JVC** Everio GC-PX100B | 1,000 | 61 | G | VG | G | VG | VG | G | VG | VG | E | 120 |
| ✔ | 18 | **Sony** HDR-CX380 | 450 | 61 | VG | G | VG | E | G | G | E | G | VG | 90 |

## Guide to the Ratings (HD)

**Overall score** mainly reflects picture quality and ease of use. The displayed score is out of a total of 100 points. **Picture quality** is based on recorded video images shot in good light at the highest quality setting available. **Low-light picture quality** is based on recorded video images shot in dim light at the highest quality setting available. **Ease of use** takes into account ergonomics of the controls and displays, and user manual readability. **Autofocus** takes into account speed and accuracy. **Audio quality** represents accuracy using the built-in microphone, plus freedom from noise. **Image stabilizer** reflects how well the model reduces the effects of camcorder shake. **Display quality** reflects image clarity, color accuracy, and contrast of the LCD. It also includes our judgment of the onscreen informational displays, video playback under bright sunlight, and (if applicable) touch-screen usability. **Versatility** indicates features that increase a camcorder's utility or capabilities. **Still camera** refers to overall quality of the photo functions of the camcorder, which includes picture quality and handling. **Battery life (min.)** is how long the camcorder can continuously record images with the LCD viewer in constant use and occasional use of other features such as the zoom lens. **Price** is approximate retail.

| Recommended | Rank | Brand & model | Price | Overall score (0–100; P \| F \| G \| VG \| E) | Picture quality | Ease of use | Audio quality | Image stabilizer | Autofocus | Display quality | Versatility | Still camera | Battery life, Wi-Fi off (min.) | Battery life, Wi-Fi on (min.) |
|---|---|---|---|---|---|---|---|---|---|---|---|---|---|---|
| **B ACTION** | | | | | | | | | | | | | | |
| Recommended | 1 | **Drift** HD Ghost | $400 | 63 | Fair | Good | Poor | NA | NA | Good | Good | Very good | 180 | NA |
| CR Best Buy | 2 | **GoPro** Hero3 White Edition | 200 | 61 | Good | Fair | Poor | NA | NA | NA | Good | Good | 150 | 126 |
| Recommended | 3 | **Sony** HDR-AS15 | 240 | 61 | Good | Fair | Poor | Very good | NA | NA | Fair | Fair | 140 | 126 |
| Recommended | 4 | **GoPro** Hero3 Black Edition | 400 | 60 | Good | Fair | Poor | NA | NA | NA | Good | Good | 90 | 66 |
| Recommended | 5 | **GoPro** Hero3 Silver Edition | 300 | 59 | Fair | Fair | Poor | NA | NA | NA | Good | Good | 120 | 100 |
| Recommended | 6 | **Polaroid** XS80 | 130 | 59 | Good | Fair | Poor | Very good | NA | Poor | Fair | Very good | 144 | NA |
| Recommended | 7 | **JVC** GC-XA1 Adixxion | 300 | 59 | Good | Good | Poor | Good | NA | Good | Good | Fair | 81 | 81 |
| CR Best Buy | 8 | **Polaroid** XS100 Extreme Edition | 160 | 59 | Fair | Fair | Poor | NA | NA | NA | Fair | Good | 150 | NA |
| CR Best Buy | 9 | **Contour** ROAM2 | 200 | 58 | Fair | Fair | Poor | NA | NA | NA | Fair | Good | 163 | NA |
| CR Best Buy | 10 | **Liquid** Image Model 727 the EGO | 180 | 53 | Fair | Fair | Poor | NA | NA | NA | Fair | Good | 130 | 29 |

**Ratings Key** Excellent Very good Good Fair Poor

**CR Best Buy** These models offer the best combination of performance and price. All are recommended.

**Recommended** These are high-performing models that stand out.

## Guide to the Ratings (Action)

**Overall score** mainly reflects picture quality and ease of use. **Picture quality** is based on image clarity, color accuracy, and contrast. **Ease of use** takes into account ergonomics of the controls and displays, and user manual readability. **Audio quality** represents accuracy using the built-in microphone, plus freedom from noise. **Image stabilizer** reflects how well the model reduces the effects of camcorder shake. "NA" indicates the model lacks this feature. **Autofocus** takes into account speed and accuracy. **Display quality** reflects image clarity, color accuracy, and contrast. **Versatility** indicates features that increase a camcorder's utility or capabilities. **Still camera** refers to overall quality of the photo functions of the camcorder, which includes picture quality and handling. **Battery life, Wi-Fi off (min.)** is how long the camcorder can continuously record images with Wi-Fi off. **Battery life, Wi-Fi on (min.)** is how long the camcorder can continuously record images with Wi-Fi on. **Price** is approximate retail.

# Quick Guide CHAIN SAWS

Gas chain saws cut quickest overall—a time-saver for after-storm cleanup and other extensive sawing. But corded electric saws require less upkeep and zero fueling, provided you have power or a home generator.

**What to look for**

- A chain brake, which stops the chain if the saw tip kicks back toward the operator
- A narrow-tipped bar and less-aggressive chain to help prevent kickback at its source
- Vibration dampening for gas saws
- Tools-free chain tensioning

**What to skip**

- Cordless, battery-powered electric saws, which cut slowest in our tests and offered short run times before their batteries needed recharging
- Large, heavy-duty saws if you're doing mostly light-duty work; light-duty gas and corded-electric saws should handle most tasks for less money

**What you'll pay**

Figure on $200 to $300 for the fastest gas models; $100 to $150 for a corded electric or lighter-duty gas model; $200 to $400 for a battery-powered saw.

**Shopping tip**

Buy a second chain to use while the first gets sharpened.

Scan this or see how, page 11

For more buying advice, go to *ConsumerReports.org/chainsaws*

**All tested models** In performance order, within types.

| Recommended | Rank | Brand & model (Similar models, in small type, are comparable to tested model.) | Price | Overall score (0–100; P \| F \| G \| VG \| E) | Cutting speed | Safety | Ease of use | Handling | Weight (lb.) | cc/amp | Bar length tested (in.) | Chain brake | Anti-vibration | Tool-free chain adjuster |
|---|---|---|---|---|---|---|---|---|---|---|---|---|---|---|
| **A** | | **BATTERY-POWERED** | | | | | | | | | | | | |
| | 1 | **Oregon** CS250S | $400 | 47 | ◒ | ⊜ | ⊖ | ⊖ | 12.3 | 40-volt | 12 | • | | • |
| | 2 | **Ryobi** RY40510 | 200 | 34 | ● | ⊖ | ⊖ | ⊖ | 8.5 | 40-volt | 12 | | | • |
| **B** | | **CORDED-ELECTRIC** | | | | | | | | | | | | |
| ✔ | 1 | **Worx** WG303.1 | 100 | 68 | ⊖ | ⊖ | ⊖ | ⊖ | 11 | 14.5-amp | 16 | • | | • |
| ✔ | 2 | **Worx** WG304.1 | 130 | 66 | ⊖ | ⊖ | ⊖ | ⊖ | 11.5 | 15-amp | 18 | • | | • |
| | 3 | **Makita** UC4030A | 230 | 60 | ○ | ○ | ⊖ | ⊖ | 11.5 | 14.5-amp | 16 | • | | • |
| | 4 | **Craftsman** 34119 P3516 | 80 | 57 | ○ | ⊜ | ○ | ⊖ | 9.5 | 12-amp | 16 | • | | • |

| Recommended | Rank | Brand & model<br>Similar models, in small type, are comparable to tested model. | Price | Overall score<br>0–100<br>P \| F \| G \| VG \| E | Test results: Cutting speed | Safety | Ease of use | Handling | Weight (lb.) | cc/amp | Bar length tested (in.) | Features: Chain brake | Anti-vibration | Tool-free chain adjuster |
|---|---|---|---|---|---|---|---|---|---|---|---|---|---|---|
| **B** | | **CORDED-ELECTRIC** continued | | | | | | | | | | | | |
| | 5 | **Green Works** 20032 | $100 | 54 | G | VG | G | VG | 11.8 | 13-amp | 18 | • | | • |
| | 6 | **Homelite** UT43122 | 75 | 52 | G | G | G | VG | 8.8 | 12-amp | 16 | | | • |
| | 7 | **Remington** RM1635W | 70 | 49 | F | VG | G | VG | 9.5 | 12-amp | 16 | | | |
| **C** | | **GASOLINE** | | | | | | | | | | | | |
| ✔ | 1 | **Stihl** MS 180 C-BE MS 181 C-BE | 230 | 81 | E | VG | E | VG | 11 | 32-cc | 16 | • | • | • |
| ✔ | 2 | **Husqvarna** 435 440E | 270 | 75 | E | G | VG | VG | 11.5 | 40.9-cc | 16 | • | • | |
| ✔ | 3 | **Echo** CS-352-16 | 270 | 75 | VG | VG | VG | E | 10.5 | 34-cc | 16 | • | • | |
| | 4 | **Echo** CS-400-18 | 300 | 74 | E | G | VG | VG | 12 | 40.2-cc | 18 | • | • | |
| | 5 | **Poulan** Pro PP4818 | 180 | 73 | E | G | VG | G | 15.3 | 48-cc | 18 | • | • | |
| | 6 | **Blue Max** 6595 | 180 | 69 | E | G | G | G | 13 | 45-cc | 18 | • | • | |
| | 7 | **Remington** RM5118R | 200 | 59 | E | F | F | G | 16 | 51-cc | 18 | • | • | |
| **D** | | **LIGHT-DUTY GASOLINE** | | | | | | | | | | | | |
| ✔ | 1 | **Craftsman** 34190 | 150 | 68 | VG | VG | G | VG | 13.8 | 42-cc | 18 | • | • | |
| | 2 | **Homelite** UT10589A UT10680A | 160 | 63 | VG | VG | VG | VG | 12 | 42-cc | 18 | • | • | |
| | 3 | **Earthquake** CS4116 | 170 | 55 | VG | G | F | G | 12 | 41-cc | 16 | • | • | |
| | 4 | **Poulan** P3816 | 140 | 54 | VG | VG | G | F | 12.8 | 38-cc | 16 | • | | |
| **E** | | **POWER LOPPERS** | | | | | | | | | | | | |
| ✔ | 1 | **Black & Decker** LP 1000 | 75 | 55 | G | E | F | E | 6.8 | 4.5-amp | 6 | | | |
| | 2 | **Worx** WG307 | 120 | 49 | F | E | VG | G | 8.8 | 5-amp | 6 | | | |

## Guide to the Ratings

**Overall score** is based on cutting speed, safety, ease of use, and handling. **Cutting speed** is how fast a saw cut through a 10-inch-square oak beam. **Safety** includes resistance to kickback and burn risk from hot mufflers, and whether saws have a bar or chain sheath or cover to prevent cuts during carrying or storage. **Ease of use** is primer or choke access, average number of pulls to start, checking and adding fuel, and air-filter and spark-plug access for gas saws, and ease of operation, chain adjustment, and checking bar oil for all saws. **Handling** reflects horizontal and vertical cutting, weight, and freedom from vibration. **Weight (lb.)** is to the nearest pound, for a fully assembled saw with bar and chain but without any gas or oil added. **cc/amp** is the engine cc (cubic centimeters), amps (for corded electric motors), and volts (for battery-powered electric motors), as stated by the manufacturer. **Bar length tested (in.)** is the length of the cutting surface to the nearest inch. **Price** is approximate retail.

# Quick Guide COMPUTERS, DESKTOP

**Windows 8 has brought new functionality to desktops, including touch screens and "tabletop" models that can run on batteries when you want to move around.**

## Shopping tip

Save money on your computer purchase by using coupon and forum sites such as Techbargains, FatWallet.com, and Ebates.

Scan this or see how, page 11

### What to look for

- For browsing the Web and checking e-mail, a low-end, dual-core processor such as the Intel Pentium Dual-Core or AMD Athlon/Turion X2
- Intel's fourth-generation Core processors for improved graphics performance, or AMD's Fusion processors for heavy-duty gaming
- At least 1TB of storage, especially if you have a lot of music, photos, and videos

For more buying advice, go to *ConsumerReports.org/computers*

### What to skip

- More than 4GB of memory, unless you're a heavy multitasker or video editor

### What you'll pay

You can get a very good all-in-one for $750 to $900, but many fuller-featured models cost more than $1,000.

All tested models in performance order, within types.

| Recommended | Rank | Brand & model | Price | Overall score (0–100; P \| F \| G \| VG \| E) | Test results: Performance | Versatility | Ergonomics | Display | Speakers | Features: Display size (in.) | Processor | Memory (GB) | Storage (GB) |
|---|---|---|---|---|---|---|---|---|---|---|---|---|---|
| **A ALL-IN-ONE** | | | | | | | | | | | | | |
| ✔ | 1 | **Dell** XPS 27 Touch | $1,600 | 84 | E | VG | VG | E | G | 27 | Core i5-4430S | 8 | 1000 |
| ✔ | 2 | **HP** ENVY 23-d150 | 1,250 | 77 | E | VG | VG | VG | G | 23 | Core i7-3770s | 8 | 2000 |
| ✔ | 3 | **Toshiba** PX35T-AST2G01 | 1,300 | 74 | E | VG | VG | VG | G | 23 | Core i7-4700MQ | 8 | 2000 |
| ✔ | 4 | **Sony** VAIO SVL24147CXB | 1,500 | 74 | VG | VG | VG | VG | G | 24 | Core i7-3630QM | 8 | 2000 |
| ✔ | 5 | **Sony** VAIO SVL24125CXW | 1,250 | 72 | VG | VG | VG | VG | G | 24 | Core i5-3210M | 8 | 2000 |
| ✔ | 6 | **Dell** XPS One 27 | 1,350 | 72 | VG | VG | VG | E | G | 27 | Core i5-3330S | 6 | 1000 |

| Recommended | Rank | Brand & model | Price | Overall score (0–100; P \| F \| G \| VG \| E) | Performance | Versatility | Ergonomics | Display | Speakers | Display size (in.) | Processor | Memory (GB) | Storage (GB) |
|---|---|---|---|---|---|---|---|---|---|---|---|---|---|
| **A** | | **ALL-IN-ONE** continued | | | | | | | | | | | |
| ✓ | 7 | **Samsung** DP700A7D-S03US | $1,650 | 69 | Very good | Very good | Very good | Very good | Fair | 27 | Core i7-3770T | 8 | 1000 |
| ✓ | 8 | **Vizio** CA27T-B1 | 1,450 | 69 | Excellent | Good | Good | Very good | Good | 27 | Core i7-3630QM | 8 | 1000 |
| ✓ | 9 | **Vizio** CA24T-B1 | 1,325 | 68 | Excellent | Good | Good | Very good | Good | 24 | Core i7-3630QM | 8 | 1000 |
| ✓ | 10 | **Asus** Transformer P1801-B037K | 1,300 | 67 | Excellent | Very good | Very good | Good | Good | 18.4 | Core i5-3350P | 8 | 1000 |
| ✓ | 11 | **Asus** ET2220IUTI-B019K | 950 | 67 | Excellent | Very good | Very good | Good | Good | 21.5 | Core i5-3330 | 8 | 1000 |
| ✓ | 12 | **Apple** iMac 27-inch MD095LL/A w/Fusion Drive | 2,050 | 66 | Excellent | Good | Good | Excellent | Good | 27 | Core i5 | 8 | 1000 |
| ✓ | 13 | **Toshiba** PX35T-A2300 | 900 | 66 | Very good | Very good | Very good | Very good | Good | 23 | Core i3-3120M | 6 | 2000 |
| ✓ | 14 | **Asus** ET2411IUKI-B008K | 750 | 65 | Very good | Very good | Very good | Very good | Fair | 23.6 | Core i3-3220 | 6 | 1000 |
| | 15 | **Vizio** CA27-A2 | 1,350 | 64 | Excellent | Good | Good | Very good | Fair | 27 | Core i7-3610QM | 8 | 1000 |
| | 16 | **Acer** Aspire A7600U-UR308 | 1,400 | 64 | Good | Very good | Very good | Very good | Poor | 27 | Core i5-3210M | 8 | 1000 |
| | 17 | **HP** Pavilion 23-f254 | 800 | 63 | Good | Very good | Very good | Very good | Good | 23 | A-6 6400K | 8 | 1000 |
| | 18 | **Samsung** DP700A3D-A01US | 950 | 63 | Very good | Very good | Very good | Very good | Good | 23.6 | Core i5-3470T | 6 | 1000 |
| | 19 | **Lenovo** IdeaCentre B540-57310058 | 850 | 62 | Very good | Very good | Very good | Very good | Good | 23 | Core i3-2130 | 4 | 1000 |
| | 20 | **Lenovo** C440-57317004 | 600 | 62 | Very good | Very good | Very good | Good | Fair | 21.5 | Pentium G2030 | 4 | 1000 |
| | 21 | **Lenovo** IdeaCentre Horizon | 1,500 | 60 | Good | Good | Very good | Very good | Fair | 27 | Core i5-3337U | 8 | 1000 |
| | 22 | **Apple** iMac 21.5-inch MD093LL/A | 1,300 | 60 | Excellent | Good | Good | Very good | Good | 21.5 | Core i5 | 8 | 1000 |
| | 23 | **Gateway** One ZX6980-UB15 | 725 | 60 | Good | Very good | Very good | Very good | Fair | 23 | Pentium G2020 | 6 | 500 |
| | 24 | **Samsung** DP500A2D-A01UB | 750 | 55 | Good | Good | Very good | Good | Fair | 21.5 | Core i3-3220T | 6 | 500 |
| | 25 | **Vizio** CA24T-B0 | 1,150 | 54 | Fair | Good | Good | Very good | Good | 24 | A-10 4600M | 8 | 1000 |

**Ratings Key** Excellent, Very good, Good, Fair, Poor

**CR Best Buy** These models offer the best combination of performance and price. All are recommended.

✓ **Recommended** These are high-performing models that stand out.

| Recommended | Rank | Brand & model | Price | Overall score (0–100; P \| F \| G \| VG \| E) | Test results: Performance | Versatility | Ergonomics | Display | Speakers | Features: Display size (in.) | Processor | Memory (GB) | Storage (GB) |
|---|---|---|---|---|---|---|---|---|---|---|---|---|---|
| **A** | | **ALL-IN-ONE** continued | | | | | | | | | | | |
| | 26 | **Sony** VAIO Tap 20 SVJ20215CXW | $ 800 | 52 | ◒ | ○ | ⊖ | ○ | ○ | 20 | Core i5-3317U | 4 | 750 |
| | 27 | **Dell** XPS 18 Touch | 1,000 | 50 | ○ | ○ | ⊖ | ○ | ○ | 18.4 | Core i3-3227U | 4 | 500 |
| **B** | | **COMPACT** | | | | | | | | | | | |
| ✓ | 1 | **Lenovo** H520s-57311365 | 500 | 66 | ⊖ | ⊖ | ⊖ | NA | NA | NA | Core i5-3330 | 6 | 1000 |
| | 2 | **Acer** Veriton L VL4620G-UI5333X | 650 | 60 | ⊖ | ○ | ⊖ | NA | NA | NA | Core i5-3330S | 4 | 500 |
| | 3 | **HP** Pavilion Slimline 400-034 | 400 | 59 | ⊖ | ⊖ | ⊖ | NA | NA | NA | Pentium G2020 | 4 | 1000 |
| | 4 | **Asus** Essentio M11BB-B05 | 550 | 48 | ◒ | ⊖ | ⊖ | NA | NA | NA | A-8 5500 | 12 | 1000 |
| **C** | | **FULL-SIZE** | | | | | | | | | | | |
| ✓ | 1 | **Dell** XPS 8700 Special Edition | 1,850 | 83 | ⊜ | ⊖ | ⊖ | NA | NA | NA | Core i7-4770 | 24 | 2000 |
| ✓ | 2 | **Dell** XPS 8700 | 800 | 77 | ⊖ | ⊖ | ⊖ | NA | NA | NA | Core i7-4770 | 8 | 1000 |
| ✔ | 3 | **Lenovo** IdeaCentre K450-57317212 | 600 | 73 | ⊖ | ⊖ | ⊖ | NA | NA | NA | Core i5-4430 | 8 | 1000 |
| ✔ | 4 | **HP** ENVY 700-010 | 600 | 72 | ○ | ⊖ | ⊖ | NA | NA | NA | A-10 6700 | 8 | 1000 |
| ✓ | 5 | **HP** ENVY 700-030qe | 1,000 | 70 | ⊖ | ⊖ | ⊖ | NA | NA | NA | Core i7-4770 | 12 | 2000 |
| ✓ | 6 | **Asus** Essentio M51AC-B07 | 900 | 70 | ⊖ | ⊖ | ⊖ | NA | NA | NA | Core i7-4770 | 16 | 2000 |
| ✓ | 7 | **Gateway** DX4870-UB318 | 500 | 66 | ⊖ | ⊖ | ⊖ | NA | NA | NA | Core i5-3330 | 8 | 1000 |
| | 8 | **Dell** Inspiron 660 | 600 | 62 | ⊖ | ⊖ | ⊖ | NA | NA | NA | Core i3-3220 | 6 | 1000 |

## Guide to the Ratings

**Overall score** reflects all the Ratings factors. Displayed scores are rounded; models are listed in order of precise score out of a total of 100. Scores are comparable between the full-size and compact categories. Scores for the all-in-one category are not comparable to any other category. **Performance** reflects speed while running productivity applications, multimedia applications, and 3D games. **Versatility** includes hardware, such as memory-card slots and A/V connections; software, such as security programs and productivity applications; and tech support and warranty provisions. **Ergonomics** represents the quality of the keyboard and pointing device, and accessibility of features. For all-in-ones, **display** is our judgment of clarity, color, brightness, and viewing angle. **Speakers** covers fidelity, bass response, and loudness. **Price** is approximate retail.

# OUR READERS RATE TECHNICAL SUPPORT

Apple bested its own scores from last year's survey and walloped other brand-name computer manufacturers, according to Consumer Reports National Research Center survey. It scored far higher than the other biggies for the elements that make for successful online and phone support: ease of contacting staff, clarity of advice, technical knowledge, patience, and time for follow-up. Whatever way readers asked for tech help—by phone (the most common way), online, or in person—Apple was also able to solve more than 80 percent of their computer problems. Independent shops that make custom computers came closest to Apple, with relatively high scores for phone support and problem solving.

Among makers of Windows-based computers, Dell was better than others at solving problems. As for the rest of the pack, Asus did better at satisfying readers than it did last year. The Acer/Gateway/eMachines group did worse, and its reader score was significantly lower than that of all other rated companies.

## Tech support

In order of reader score.

Better ⊜ ⊖ ○ ◒ ● Worse

| Manufacturer | Reader score (0–100) | Survey results: Phone support | Online support | Problems solved |
|---|---|---|---|---|
| Apple | 86 | ⊜ | ⊜ | 82% |
| Local independents | 78 | ⊜ | - | 71 |
| Lenovo | 63 | ◒ | ● | 54 |
| Asus | 62 | - | ● | 46 |
| Dell | 60 | ● | ● | 61 |
| Toshiba | 59 | ● | ● | 48 |
| HP/Compaq | 58 | ● | ● | 53 |
| Acer/Gateway/eMachines | 51 | ● | ● | 37 |

Ratings are based on responses from 6,313 owners of 7,571 desktop, laptop, and netbook computers. Data are based on respondents' most recent experience(s) contacting a manufacturer's technical support service, between January 2012 and January 2013. Reader score reflects overall satisfaction with manufacturer support. 100 means that respondents were completely satisfied; 80, very satisfied, on average; 60, fairly well satisfied; 40, somewhat dissatisfied. Reader score differences of fewer than 6 points aren't meaningful; problems solved differences of fewer than 10 points aren't meaningful. A dash (-) indicates insufficient data.

# Quick Guide COMPUTERS, LAPTOP

**Some laptops offer features and capabilities that rival those of traditional desktops. You'll find more thin-and-light laptops than ever, while touch screens and solid-state drives are becoming more common.**

### What to look for

- A convertible or detachable if you want a laptop/tablet combo
- An 11- to 13-inch model if you plan to carry the laptop around with you frequently
- A 14- to 16-inch screen for the ideal balance of performance, portability, and price
- A 17- to 18-inch model for an entertainment-oriented desktop replacement

### What to skip

- Shave off a little weight by skipping the built-in DVD or Blu-ray drive. You can add an external drive later if you find that it's necessary

### What you'll pay

A well-equipped, 15-inch laptop in the middle price range should cost about $700.

For more buying advice, go to *ConsumerReports.org/computers*

### Shopping tip

If you want to customize a model, order à la carte from the manufacturer's website.

Scan this or see how, page 11

**All tested models** In performance order, within types.

| Recommended | Rank | Brand & model | Price | Overall score (0–100; P \| F \| G \| VG \| E) | Test results: Ergonomics | Portability | Performance | Versatility | Display | Features: Battery life (hr.) | Weight (lb.) | Processor | Memory (GB) |
|---|---|---|---|---|---|---|---|---|---|---|---|---|---|
| | | **A 10- TO 13-INCH DETACHABLE** | | | | | | | | | | | |
| ☑ | 1 | **Samsung** ATIV Smart PC Pro XE700T1C-A01US | $1,100 | 69 | ⊖ | ⊖ | ⊜ | ○ | ⊖ | 7.25 | 3.5 | Core i5-3317U | 4 |
| ☑ | 2 | **Asus** Transformer Book TX300CA-DH71 Ultrabook | 1,450 | 66 | ⊖ | ○ | ⊜ | ○ | ⊖ | 5.5 | 4.2 | Core i7-3517U | 4 |
| ☑ | 3 | **Microsoft** Surface Pro | 920 | 65 | ○ | ⊖ | ⊜ | ○ | ⊖ | 5.75 | 2.5 | Core i5-3317U | 4 |
| | 4 | **HP** ENVY x2 11t-g010 | 650 | 64 | ⊖ | ⊜ | ◒ | ○ | ○ | 15.25 | 3.1 | Atom Z2760 | 2 |
| | 5 | **Lenovo** IdeaTab Lynx K3011 | 500 | 61 | ○ | ⊜ | ◒ | ○ | ⊖ | 13.25 | 2.9 | Atom Z2760 | 2 |

## A 10- TO 13-INCH DETACHABLE continued

| Recommended | Rank | Brand & model | Price | Overall score (0–100; P \| F \| G \| VG \| E) | Ergonomics | Portability | Performance | Versatility | Display | Battery life (hr.) | Weight (lb.) | Processor | Memory (GB) |
|---|---|---|---|---|---|---|---|---|---|---|---|---|---|
| | 6 | **HP** Split x2 13-m010dx | $ 700 | 60 | Excellent | Good | Excellent | Good | Good | 7 | 5 | Core i3-3229Y | 4 |
| | 7 | **Samsung** ATIV Smart PC XE500T1C-A01US | 700 | 60 | Very good | Excellent | Poor | Good | Very good | 11 | 3.2 | Atom Z2760 | 2 |
| | 8 | **Acer** Iconia W510-1422 | 600 | 57 | Good | Excellent | Fair | Good | Very good | 18.5 | 2.8 | Atom Z2760 | 2 |

## B 11- TO 13-INCH CONVERTIBLE

| Recommended | Rank | Brand & model | Price | Overall score (0–100; P \| F \| G \| VG \| E) | Ergonomics | Portability | Performance | Versatility | Display | Battery life (hr.) | Weight (lb.) | Processor | Memory (GB) |
|---|---|---|---|---|---|---|---|---|---|---|---|---|---|
| ✓ | 1 | **Dell** XPS 12 Convertible Touch Ultrabook | 1,100 | 75 | Excellent | Very good | Excellent | Good | Very good | 8 | 3.3 | Core i5-3317U | 4 |
| ✓ | 2 | **Sony** VAIO Duo 13 Ultrabook SVD13213CXB | 1,400 | 72 | Fair | Excellent | Excellent | Good | Very good | 9.25 | 2.9 | Core i5-4200U | 4 |
| ✓ | 3 | **Lenovo** IdeaPad Yoga 11S 59370508 | 750 | 66 | Good | Very good | Excellent | Good | Very good | 6.75 | 3 | Core i3-3229Y | 4 |
| | 4 | **Asus** Taichi 21-DH51 | 1,000 | 63 | Good | Very good | Excellent | Good | Very good | 4.75 | 2.8 | Core i5-3317U | 4 |
| | 5 | **Sony** VAIO Duo 11 Ultrabook | 1,150 | 61 | Fair | Very good | Excellent | Good | Very good | 6.5 | 2.8 | Core i5-3317U | 6 |
| | 6 | **Lenovo** Thinkpad Twist-33474HU | 900 | 59 | Very good | Good | Excellent | Good | Very good | 4.5 | 3.4 | Core i5-3317U | 4 |

## C 11-INCH

| Recommended | Rank | Brand & model | Price | Overall score (0–100; P \| F \| G \| VG \| E) | Ergonomics | Portability | Performance | Versatility | Display | Battery life (hr.) | Weight (lb.) | Processor | Memory (GB) |
|---|---|---|---|---|---|---|---|---|---|---|---|---|---|
| ✓ | 1 | **Acer** Aspire S7-191-6447 Ultrabook | 800 | 76 | Very good | Excellent | Excellent | Very good | Very good | 6.75 | 2.3 | Core i5-3337U | 4 |
| ✓ | 2 | **Apple** MacBook Air 11-inch MD711LL/A | 1,000 | 73 | Very good | Excellent | Very good | Fair | Very good | 12 | 2.4 | Core i5 1.3GHz | 4 |
| ✓ | 3 | **Sony** VAIO Pro SVP-11213CXB Ultrabook | 1,150 | 73 | Good | Excellent | Excellent | Good | Very good | 9.25 | 1.9 | Core i5-4200U | 4 |
| ✓ | 4 | **Apple** MacBook Air 11-inch MD223LL/A | 1,000 | 67 | Very good | Excellent | Very good | Fair | Very good | 7.25 | 2.4 | Core i5 1.7GHz | 4 |
| | 5 | **Acer** Aspire V5-171-9620 | 675 | 63 | Very good | Very good | Very good | Good | Good | 7.25 | 3.2 | Core i7-3517U | 6 |
| | 6 | **Asus** VivoBook X202E-DH31T Ultrabook | 600 | 50 | Good | Good | Good | Good | Good | 4.5 | 3.1 | Core i3-3217U | 4 |

**Ratings Key** Excellent, Very good, Good, Fair, Poor

**CR Best Buy** These models offer the best combination of performance and price. All are recommended.

**Recommended** These are high-performing models that stand out.

Overall score: 0–100 (P | F | G | VG | E)

## D 13-INCH

| Recommended | Rank | Brand & model | Price | Overall score | Ergonomics | Portability | Performance | Versatility | Display | Battery life (hr.) | Weight (lb.) | Processor | Memory (GB) |
|---|---|---|---|---|---|---|---|---|---|---|---|---|---|
| ✓ | 1 | **Sony** VAIO Pro SVP-13213CXS Ultrabook | $1,250 | 79 | G | E | E | G | VG | 10 | 2.3 | Core i5-4200U | 4 |
| ✓ | 2 | **Apple** MacBook Air 13-inch MD231LL/A | 1,000 | 74 | VG | E | VG | F | VG | 11.75 | 3 | Core i5 1.8GHz | 4 |
| ✓ | 3 | **Apple** MacBook Air 13-inch MD760LL/A | 1,100 | 73 | VG | E | G | F | VG | 15 | 2.9 | Core i5 1.3GHz | 4 |
| ✓ | 4 | **Toshiba** KIRAbook 13 | 1,600 | 73 | G | E | E | G | VG | 7.5 | 2.5 | Core i5-3337U | 8 |
| ✓ | 5 | **Apple** MacBook Pro 13-inch with Retina Display MD212LL/A | 1,500 | 72 | VG | VG | VG | F | E | 8.5 | 3.6 | Core i5 2.5GHz | 8 |
| ✓ | 6 | **Asus** Zenbook Prime UX32VD-DH71 Ultrabook | 1,300 | 67 | VG | VG | VG | G | VG | 6.5 | 3.3 | Core i7-3517U | 4 |
| ✓ | 7 | **Apple** MacBook Pro 13-inch MD101LL/A | 1,200 | 66 | VG | VG | VG | G | VG | 8.75 | 4.5 | Core i5 2.5GHz | 4 |
|  | 8 | **Lenovo** IdeaPad U310 59351642 Ultrabook | 550 | 58 | VG | VG | G | G | G | 6 | 3.7 | Core i3-3217U | 4 |
|  | 9 | **Acer** Aspire S3-391-6676 Ultrabook | 600 | 57 | VG | VG | G | G | G | 5.25 | 3 | Core i3-2377M | 4 |

## E 14-INCH

| Recommended | Rank | Brand & model | Price | Overall score | Ergonomics | Portability | Performance | Versatility | Display | Battery life (hr.) | Weight (lb.) | Processor | Memory (GB) |
|---|---|---|---|---|---|---|---|---|---|---|---|---|---|
| ✓ | 1 | **Lenovo** ThinkPad X1 Carbon Touch Ultrabook | 1,300 | 70 | E | VG | E | G | VG | 6 | 3.3 | Core i5-3247U | 4 |
| ✓ | 2 | **Vizio** CT14T-B1 | 1,300 | 69 | G | E | E | G | VG | 10.75 | 4.1 | Core i7-3635QM | 8 |
| ✓ | 3 | **Lenovo** ThinkPad X1 Carbon Ultrabook | 1,200 | 69 | VG | VG | E | G | VG | 5.75 | 2.9 | Core i5-3317U | 4 |
| ✓ | 4 | **Samsung** ATIV Book 5 NP540U4E-K01US | 900 | 69 | E | VG | E | G | G | 7.5 | 4.3 | Core i5-3337U | 4 |
| ✓ | 5 | **Lenovo** IdeaPad Y410p 59369921 | 825 | 65 | VG | G | E | VG | G | 5.75 | 5.4 | Core i7-4700MQ | 8 |
|  | 6 | **Vizio** CT14-A4 Ultrabook | 700 | 64 | G | VG | E | G | VG | 6 | 3.5 | Core i5-3317U | 4 |
|  | 7 | **Asus** VivoBook S400CA-DH51T Ultrabook | 750 | 59 | E | G | VG | G | G | 5 | 4.1 | Core i5-3317U | 4 |
|  | 8 | **Sony** VAIO Fit SVF14212CXW | 600 | 57 | VG | G | G | G | G | 5 | 4.3 | Core i3-3227U | 4 |
|  | 9 | **Dell** Inspiron 14R | 650 | 57 | VG | VG | G | VG | G | 9.75 | 5 | Core i3-3217U | 4 |
|  | 10 | **Lenovo** IdeaPad Z400 Touch-59365077 | 675 | 57 | VG | F | VG | VG | G | 5.25 | 5.3 | Core i5-3230M | 8 |

| Recommended | Rank | Brand & model | Price | Overall score (0–100; P, F, G, VG, E) | Test results: Ergonomics | Test results: Portability | Test results: Performance | Test results: Versatility | Test results: Display | Features: Battery life (hr.) | Features: Weight (lb.) | Features: Processor | Features: Memory (GB) |
|---|---|---|---|---|---|---|---|---|---|---|---|---|---|
| **E** | | **14-INCH** continued | | | | | | | | | | | |
| | 11 | **Acer** Aspire V5-471P-6605 | $ 550 | 55 | Very good | Good | Good | Very good | Good | 4.5 | 4.7 | Core i3-3227U | 4 |
| | 12 | **Sony** VAIO Fit SVF14213CXW | 700 | 55 | Very good | Good | Good | Very good | Good | 4.25 | 4.7 | Core i3-3227U | 4 |
| | 13 | **Lenovo** IdeaPad S400 59342932 | 525 | 52 | Very good | Good | Good | Good | Good | 4.25 | 3.5 | Core i3-3217U | 4 |
| | 14 | **HP** Pavilion Sleekbook 14-b010us | 550 | 51 | Very good | Good | Good | Good | Good | 4.75 | 4 | Core i3-2377M | 4 |
| | 15 | **Lenovo** IdeaPad S405 59342927 | 500 | 46 | Very good | Good | Fair | Good | Good | 4 | 3.5 | A8-4555M | 4 |
| | 16 | **HP** Pavilion Sleekbook 14-B110US | 500 | 39 | Very good | Good | Poor | Good | Good | 4.75 | 4 | A4-4355M | 4 |
| **F** | | **15- TO 16-INCH** | | | | | | | | | | | |
| ✓ | 1 | **Apple** MacBook Pro 15-inch with Retina display ME664LL/A | 2,200 | 78 | Very good | Excellent | Excellent | Fair | Excellent | 10 | 4.4 | Core i7 2.4GHz | 8 |
| ✓ | 2 | **Samsung** ATIV Book 8 NP880Z5E-X01UB | 1,200 | 77 | Very good | Excellent | Excellent | Very good | Very good | 10.25 | 5.7 | Core i7-3635QM | 8 |
| ✓ | 3 | **Apple** MacBook Pro 15-inch with Retina display MC975LL/A | 1,900 | 76 | Very good | Excellent | Excellent | Fair | Excellent | 12.5 | 4.5 | Core i7 2.3GHz | 8 |
| ✓ | 4 | **Acer** Aspire R7-571-6858 | 1,000 | 74 | Excellent | Very good | Excellent | Good | Excellent | 6.5 | 5.4 | Core i5-3337U | 6 |
| ✓ | 5 | **Vizio** CT15T-B1 Ultrabook | 1,300 | 73 | Very good | Excellent | Excellent | Good | Very good | 10.25 | 4.8 | Core i7-3635QM | 8 |
| ✓ | 6 | **Asus** Q550LF-BBI7T07 | 1,000 | 71 | Very good | Very good | Excellent | Very good | Very good | 7 | 5.6 | Core i7-4500U | 8 |
| ✓ | 7 | **Apple** MacBook Pro 15-inch MD103LL/A | 1,800 | 70 | Very good | Excellent | Very good | Good | Very good | 11.75 | 5.6 | Core i7 2.3GHz | 4 |
| ✓ | 8 | **Vizio** CN15-A5 | 1,000 | 69 | Good | Very good | Excellent | Good | Excellent | 5.5 | 5 | Core i7-3610QM | 8 |
| ✓ | 9 | **MSI** GT60 20C-022US | 1,325 | 69 | Very good | Good | Excellent | Very good | Very good | 6.75 | 7.5 | Core i7-4700MQ | 8 |
| ✓ | 10 | **Dell** Inspiron 15R | 850 | 68 | Very good | Very good | Very good | Very good | Good | 9.5 | 5.8 | Core i5-4200U | 8 |
| ✓ | 11 | **Toshiba** Satellite P50-AST2NX1 | 800 | 67 | Excellent | Very good | Excellent | Very good | Good | 5.5 | 4.7 | Core i5-4200U | 12 |

**Ratings Key** ⊜ Excellent ⊖ Very good ○ Good ◒ Fair ● Poor

☑ **CR Best Buy** These models offer the best combination of performance and price. All are recommended.

✓ **Recommended** These are high-performing models that stand out.

## F 15- TO 16-INCH continued

| Recommended | Rank | Brand & model | Price | Overall score (0–100; P \| F \| G \| VG \| E) | Test results: Ergonomics | Test results: Portability | Test results: Performance | Test results: Versatility | Test results: Display | Features: Battery life (hr.) | Features: Weight (lb.) | Features: Processor | Features: Memory (GB) |
|---|---|---|---|---|---|---|---|---|---|---|---|---|---|
| ✓ | 12 | **HP** ENVY TouchSmart Sleekbook m6-k015dx | $750 | 67 | Excellent | Very good | Very good | Good | Good | 8.75 | 5.7 | Core i5-4200U | 8 |
| ✓ | 13 | **Vizio** CT15-A4 Ultrabook | 800 | 67 | Good | Very good | Excellent | Good | Excellent | 5.25 | 4 | Core i5-3317U | 4 |
| ✓ | 14 | **Samsung** ATIV Book 4 NP470R5E-K02UB | 700 | 67 | Very good | Very good | Very good | Good | Good | 6.25 | 4.4 | Core i7-3537U | 8 |
| ✓ | 15 | **HP** ENVY TouchSmart 15t-j000 | 900 | 66 | Excellent | Very good | Excellent | Very good | Good | 6.25 | 5.7 | Core i7-4700MQ | 8 |
| ✓ | 16 | **Toshiba** Satellite L55-A5284NR | 675 | 66 | Very good | Very good | Excellent | Good | Good | 5.25 | 5 | Core i5-3337U | 8 |
| ✓ | 17 | **Toshiba** Satellite S55t-A5258NR | 950 | 65 | Excellent | Good | Excellent | Very good | Good | 4.75 | 5.3 | Core i7-4700MQ | 8 |
| ✓ | 18 | **Lenovo** IdeaPad U510 59347424 | 650 | 65 | Very good | Very good | Excellent | Very good | Good | 6 | 4.9 | Core i5-3317U | 6 |
| | 19 | **Asus** S56CA-DH51 Ultrabook | 550 | 63 | Excellent | Very good | Very good | Good | Good | 5.25 | 5 | Core i5-3317U | 6 |
| | 20 | **Acer** Aspire V3-571-9831 | 650 | 63 | Very good | Very good | Excellent | Very good | Good | 5.75 | 5.5 | Core i7-3632QM | 6 |
| | 21 | **Toshiba** Satellite C55-A5246NR | 525 | 63 | Very good | Very good | Very good | Good | Good | 6.25 | 5 | Core i3-3120M | 4 |
| | 22 | **Asus** K55A-DH71 | 650 | 62 | Very good | Good | Very good | Good | Good | 5.25 | 5.5 | Core i7-3630QM | 4 |
| | 23 | **Sony** VAIO Fit SVF15213CXB | 725 | 61 | Excellent | Good | Good | Very good | Very good | 4 | 5.3 | Core i3-3227U | 4 |
| | 24 | **Asus** VivoBook S500CA-DS51T | 625 | 61 | Excellent | Very good | Very good | Good | Good | 4.75 | 4.8 | Core i5-3317U | 6 |
| | 25 | **Acer** Aspire E1-571-6680 | 400 | 59 | Very good | Very good | Good | Good | Good | 6.75 | 5.2 | Core i3-3110M | 4 |
| | 26 | **Dell** Inspiron 15 | 550 | 58 | Very good | Very good | Good | Good | Good | 8.25 | 5.8 | Core i3-3227U | 4 |
| | 27 | **Acer** Aspire V5-571P-6407 | 625 | 56 | Excellent | Good | Good | Very good | Good | 4.25 | 5.4 | Core i3-3227U | 6 |
| | 28 | **HP** Pavilion 15-e016nr | 400 | 56 | Very good | Very good | Good | Good | Good | 6.5 | 5.1 | A4-5150M | 4 |
| | 29 | **Gateway** NE56R41u | 325 | 55 | Very good | Very good | Good | Good | Good | 6 | 5.3 | Pentium B960 | 4 |
| | 30 | **HP** ENVY Sleekbook m6-k010dx | 600 | 55 | Excellent | Very good | Fair | Good | Good | 6 | 4.7 | A10-5745M | 6 |
| | 31 | **HP** Pavilion g6-2211nr | 450 | 54 | Very good | Very good | Fair | Good | Good | 6.5 | 5.2 | A4-4300M | 4 |

**Ratings Key** ⊜ Excellent ⊖ Very good ○ Good ◒ Fair ● Poor

☑ **CR Best Buy** These models offer the best combination of performance and price. All are recommended.

✓ **Recommended** These are high-performing models that stand out.

| Recommended | Rank | Brand & model | Price | Overall score (0–100; P \| F \| G \| VG \| E) | Test results: Ergonomics | Portability | Performance | Versatility | Display | Features: Battery life (hr.) | Weight (lb.) | Processor | Memory (GB) |
|---|---|---|---|---|---|---|---|---|---|---|---|---|---|
| **F** | | **15- TO 16-INCH** continued | | | | | | | | | | | |
| | 32 | **HP** ENVY Sleekbook 6-1110us | $ 625 | 51 | ⊖ | ⊖ | ◒ | ○ | ○ | 7 | 4.5 | A8-4555M | 4 |
| | 33 | **Toshiba** Satellite L855D-S5117 | 400 | 50 | ⊖ | ⊖ | ◒ | ○ | ○ | 6 | 5.2 | A8-4500M | 4 |
| | 34 | **Acer** Aspire V3-551-8458 | 425 | 49 | ⊖ | ○ | ◒ | ⊖ | ○ | 5.25 | 5.6 | A8-4500M | 6 |
| | 35 | **HP** Pavilion TouchSmart Sleekbook 15-b150us | 650 | 39 | ⊖ | ○ | ● | ○ | ○ | 4.5 | 5.5 | A8-4555M | 6 |
| **G** | | **17- TO 18-INCH** | | | | | | | | | | | |
| ✓ | 1 | **HP** ENVY TouchSmart m7-j010dx | 1,000 | 76 | ⊜ | ○ | ⊜ | ⊖ | ⊖ | 5.5 | 7.1 | Core i7-4700QM | 8 |
| ✓ | 2 | **MSI** GT70 20C-065US | 1,400 | 75 | ⊖ | ○ | ⊜ | ⊖ | ⊜ | 6.75 | 8.2 | Core i7-4700MQ | 8 |
| ✓ | 3 | **Toshiba** Qosmio X75-A7295 | 1,350 | 72 | ⊖ | ○ | ⊜ | ⊖ | ⊖ | 4.75 | 7.4 | Core i7-4700MQ | 16 |
| ✓ | 4 | **Toshiba** Satellite S75-A7270 | 725 | 70 | ⊖ | ○ | ⊜ | ⊖ | ○ | 4.5 | 6 | Core i5-3230M | 8 |
| ✓ | 5 | **Samsung** NP700G7C-S02US | 1,900 | 69 | ⊖ | ◒ | ⊜ | ⊖ | ⊖ | 3.5 | 8.8 | Core i7-3630QM | 16 |
| | 6 | **HP** Pavilion 17-e021nr | 600 | 61 | ⊖ | ○ | ⊖ | ⊖ | ○ | 5.5 | 6 | Core i3-3110M | 6 |
| | 7 | **Toshiba** Satellite L75D-A7268NR | 600 | 59 | ⊖ | ○ | ○ | ⊖ | ○ | 4.5 | 6 | A8-5550M | 6 |
| | 8 | **Dell** Inspiron 17 | 500 | 57 | ⊖ | ○ | ○ | ○ | ○ | 5 | 6.1 | Core i3-3227U | 4 |
| | 9 | **Asus** X75A-DH31 | 525 | 57 | ⊖ | ○ | ○ | ○ | ○ | 4.75 | 6.6 | Core i3-2350M | 4 |
| | 10 | **Toshiba** Satellite C75D-A7265NR | 500 | 53 | ⊖ | ⊖ | ○ | ○ | ○ | 5.25 | 5.9 | A6-5200 | 4 |

## Guide to the Ratings

**Overall score** reflects all the Ratings factors. Displayed scores are rounded; models are listed in order of precise score, out of a total of 100. **Ergonomics** represents the quality of the keyboard and pointing device, and accessibility of features. **Portability** score is based on battery life and weight. **Performance** is based on performance while running productivity applications, multimedia applications, and 3D games. **Versatility** includes hardware such as memory-card slots and A/V connections, software such as security programs and productivity applications, and tech support and warranty provisions. **Display** covers display size, clarity, color, contrast, brightness, and glare. **Battery life (hr.)** is estimated in hours while running productivity applications. **Weight (lb.)** is the weight of the laptop as you would carry it around, including the battery but without the power adapter. **Price** is approximate retail.

## Most & Least Reliable

### DESKTOPS

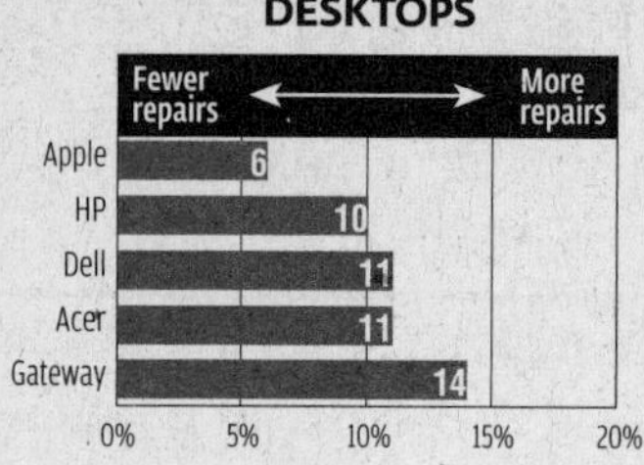


Apple was the least repair-prone brand of desktop computers. That's what we found when we asked readers who bought 15,892 desktops from 2010 through the first half of 2013 about their experiences. The graph shows the percentage of models from each brand that were repaired or had a serious problem. Differences of fewer than four points were not meaningful, and data are adjusted to eliminate differences due to the age of the desktop. Models within a brand may vary, and design and manufacturing changes may affect future reliability. Still, choosing a brand with a good repair history can improve your odds of getting a reliable brand.

Source: Annual Product Reliability Survey, Consumer Reports National Research Center.

### LAPTOPS

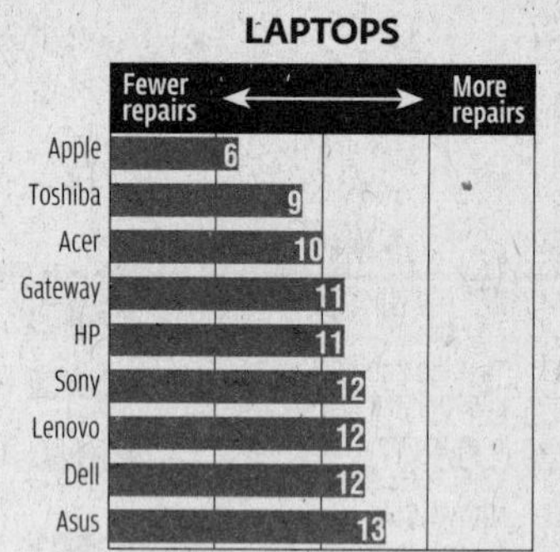


Apple was among the more reliable brands of laptop computers. That's what we found when we asked over 24,000 readers who bought a full-size laptop between 2010 and 2013 about their experiences. The graph shows the percentage of models from each brand that were repaired or had a serious problem. Differences of less than 4 points aren't meaningful, and we've adjusted the data to eliminate differences linked to the age and use of the laptops. Models within a brand may vary, and design or manufacture changes may affect future reliability. Still, choosing a brand with a good repair history can improve your odds of getting a reliable model.

# Quick Guide COOKTOPS

Cooktops can be placed wherever counter space allows, including an island, so you can interact with others instead of staring at a wall. While gas and smoothtop electric cooktops dominate, prices are dropping for induction, which speeds cooking using an electromagnetic field.

### What to look for

- A gas cooktop if you want the visual confirmation of a flame, a smoothtop electric for easy cleaning
- An induction model for quick heating; some now cost just over $1,000, though you can still pay far more
- At least one high-powered gas burner or electric element for quick heating

### What to skip

- Buying by Btu. Short for British Thermal Unit, this merely indicates gas used and heat generated and doesn't guarantee better or faster cooking
- Models with recipe databases and other pricey features if you just want good cooking

### What you'll pay

You'll probably pay $1,300 or more for a separate cooktop and wall oven, while some high-performing electric and gas ranges sell for less than half that amount.

For more buying advice, go to *ConsumerReports.org/cooktops*

### Shopping tip

More 30-inch gas cooktops have five burners instead of four, though using all five at once may require some maneuvering.

Scan this or see how, page 11

**Recommended models only** From 61 tested.

| Recommended | Rank | Brand & model (Similar models, in small type, are comparable to tested model.) | Price | Overall score (0–100; P \| F \| G \| VG \| E) | Test results: High heat | Test results: Low heat | Features: High-power burners | Medium-power burners | Low-power burners | Stainless steel | Glass ceramic | Porcelain enamel | Continuous grates |
|---|---|---|---|---|---|---|---|---|---|---|---|---|---|
| **A 30-INCH GAS** | | | | | | | | | | | | | |
| ✔ | 1 | **Bosch** NGM8054UC | $1,100 | 79 | ○ | ⊜ | 1 | 2 | 2 | • | | | • |
| ✔ | 2 | **Kenmore** 32353 | 1,200 | 76 | ○ | ⊜ | 2 | 2 | 1 | • | | | • |
| ✔ | 3 | **LG** LSCG306ST LCG3091ST | 1,100 | 73 | ⊖ | ⊖ | 1 | 3 | 1 | • | | | • |
| **B 36-INCH GAS** | | | | | | | | | | | | | |
| ✔ | 1 | **Thermador** SGSX365FS | 1,900 | 81 | ⊖ | ⊜ | 3 | 2 | 0 | • | | | • |
| ✔ | 2 | **GE** Monogram ZGU385NSMSS | 1,400 | 80 | ○ | ⊜ | 3 | 2 | 0 | • | | | • |

## B 36-INCH GAS continued

| Recommended | Rank | Brand & model (Similar models, in small type, are comparable to tested model.) | Price | Overall score (0–100; P \| F \| G \| VG \| E) | Test results: High heat | Test results: Low heat | Features: High-power burners | Features: Medium-power burners | Features: Low-power burners | Features: Stainless steel | Features: Glass ceramic | Features: Porcelain enamel | Features: Continuous grates |
|---|---|---|---|---|---|---|---|---|---|---|---|---|---|
| ✓ | 3 | **GE** Profile JGP975WEKWW | $1,200 | 80 | ○ | ⊜ | 1 | 2 | 2 | | | • | • |
| ✓ | 4 | **GE** Café CGP650SETSS<br>Profile PGP986SETSS | 1,300 | 77 | ○ | ⊜ | 1 | 3 | 1 | • | | | • |
| ✓ | 5 | **Electrolux** EW36GC55GS | 1,300 | 74 | ○ | ⊜ | 2 | 2 | 1 | • | | | • |
| ✓ | 6 | **LG** LCG3691ST | 1,300 | 74 | ⊖ | ⊖ | 2 | 2 | 1 | • | | | • |
| ✓ | 7 | **Bosch** NGM8654UC | 1,200 | 70 | ○ | ⊖ | 4 | 0 | 1 | • | | | • |
| ✓ | 8 | **Kenmore** 32313 32333 | 1,100 | 69 | ⊖ | ⊖ | 2 | 2 | 1 | • | | | • |

## C 30-INCH ELECTRIC SMOOTHTOP

| Recommended | Rank | Brand & model (Similar models, in small type, are comparable to tested model.) | Price | Overall score (0–100; P \| F \| G \| VG \| E) | Test results: High heat | Test results: Low heat | Features: High-power elements | Features: Medium-power elements | Features: Low-power elements | Features: Expandable elements | Features: Touch controls |
|---|---|---|---|---|---|---|---|---|---|---|---|
| ✓ | 1 | **KitchenAid** KECC604BBL | $ 900 | 94 | ⊜ | ⊜ | 2 | 0 | 2 | • | |
| ✓ | 2 | **Maytag** MEC7430WS<br>MEC7630W | 800 | 94 | ⊜ | ⊜ | 2 | 0 | 2 | | |
| ✓ | 3 | **Kenmore** 44273 | 1,150 | 93 | ⊜ | ⊜ | 2 | 1 | 1 | • | • |
| ✔ | 4 | **Kenmore** 42733 | 640 | 91 | ⊜ | ⊜ | 2 | 0 | 2 | • | |
| ✓ | 5 | **Frigidaire** Professional FPEC3085KS [1] | 950 | 90 | ⊖ | ⊜ | 1 | 3 | 0 | • | |
| ✓ | 6 | **GE** Café CP350STSS | 1,200 | 90 | ⊖ | ⊜ | 1 | 1 | 3 | • | |
| ✓ | 7 | **Electrolux** Icon E30EC65ESS [3] | 1,200 | 88 | ⊖ | ⊜ | 1 | 2 | 2 | • | |
| ✓ | 8 | **LG** LCE3081ST | 1,000 | 87 | ⊖ | ⊜ | 1 | 1 | 2 | • | • |
| ✔ | 9 | **Whirlpool** G7CE3034XP | 700 | 86 | ⊖ | ⊜ | 2 | 0 | 2 | • | |
| ✓ | 10 | **GE** Profile PP945BMBB | 950 | 86 | ⊖ | ⊜ | 2 | 0 | 2 | • | • |
| ✓ | 11 | **Bosch** NET5054UC | 900 | 85 | ⊖ | ⊜ | 1 | 2 | 1 | • | • |

| Recommended | Rank | Brand & model<br>Similar models, in small type, are comparable to tested model. | Price | Overall score<br>0 100<br>P \| F \| G \| VG \| E | Test results: High heat | Test results: Low heat | Features: High-power elements | Features: Medium-power elements | Features: Low-power elements | Features: Expandable elements | Features: Touch controls |
|---|---|---|---|---|---|---|---|---|---|---|---|
| **D** | | **36-INCH ELECTRIC SMOOTHTOP** | | | | | | | | | |
| ✔ | 1 | **Maytag** MEC7536W [2] | $ 830 | 94 | Excellent | Excellent | 2 | 0 | 3 | | |
| ✔ | 2 | **Maytag** MEC7636W [2] | 1,100 | 94 | Excellent | Excellent | 2 | 0 | 3 | • | |
| ✔ | 3 | **Frigidaire** Professional FPEC3685KS | 1,000 | 90 | Very good | Excellent | 1 | 3 | 1 | • | |
| **E** | | **30-INCH INDUCTION** | | | | | | | | | |
| ✔ | 1 | **Kenmore** 43820 | 1,600 | 99 | Excellent | Excellent | 3 | 1 | 0 | | • |
| ✔ | 2 | **GE** Profile PHP900DMBB | 1,400 | 99 | Excellent | Excellent | 2 | 2 | 0 | | • |
| ✔ | 3 | **Kenmore** 43800 | 1,300 | 97 | Excellent | Excellent | 3 | 1 | 0 | | • |
| ✔ | 4 | **Bosch** NIT5065UC | 1,800 | 97 | Excellent | Excellent | 2 | 0 | 2 | | • |
| ✔ | 5 | **Electrolux** Icon E30IC75FSS | 2,000 | 97 | Excellent | Excellent | 3 | 1 | 0 | | • |
| ✔ | 7 | **KitchenAid** KICU500XB | 1,400 | 95 | Excellent | Excellent | 2 | 2 | 0 | | • |
| ✔ (CR Best Buy) | 8 | **Whirlpool** GCI3061XB | 1,200 | 95 | Excellent | Excellent | 2 | 0 | 2 | | • |
| ✔ | 9 | **LG** LCE30845 | 1,800 | 93 | Excellent | Excellent | 1 | 2 | 1 | | • |

[1] Performance is equivalent to the tested version in the 36-inch size category. [2] Performance is equivalent to the tested version in the 30-inch size category. [3] On Oct. 21, 2010, the Consumer Product Safety Commission announced a recall of Electrolux Icon E30EC65ESS smoothtop cooktops because liquids can pool under the control knobs and cause the surface heating element to turn on unexpectedly, heat to temperatures other than expected, and not turn off.

**Ratings Key** ⊜ Excellent ⊖ Very good ○ Good ◒ Fair ● Poor

**CR Best Buy** These models offer the best combination of performance and price. All are recommended.

**Recommended** These are high-performing models that stand out.

## Guide to the Ratings

**Overall score** reflects cooktop performance at high and low heat. The displayed score is out of a total of 100 points. **High heat** reflects how quickly the highest-powered element heated a large pot of water to near-boiling. **Low heat** reflects how well the lowest-powered element melted and held chocolate without scorching and how the most powerful element, set to low, held tomato sauce below a boil. **Price** is approximate retail.

## Most & Least Reliable

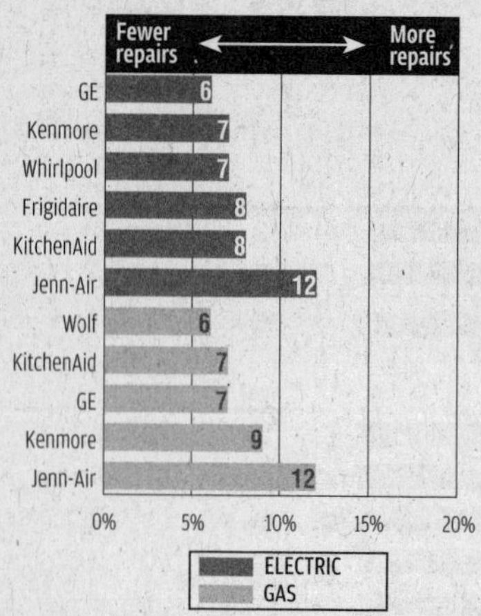


Jenn-Air was among the more repair-prone brands of electric and gas cooktops. That's what we found when we asked readers to report on 11,788 cooktops purchased from 2008 through the first half of 2012 about their experiences. The graph shows the percentages of models from each brand that were repaired or had serious problems. Differences of fewer than five points were not meaningful, and data were adjusted to eliminate differences due to the age of the cooktop. Induction cooktops were excluded from this repair history analysis. Models within a brand may vary, and design and manufacturing changes may affect future reliability. Still, choosing a brand with a good repair history can improve your odds of getting a reliable brand.

Source: Annual Product Reliability Survey, Consumer Reports National Research Center.

# Quick Guide CORDLESS DRILLS

Drills with enough speed and power for most jobs start as low as $100, and many come with smart chargers that work quickly, getting you back to work in a half hour or less.

**Shopping tip**

Drill batteries cost up to $80, but you can cut costs by using them in other tools from the same manufacturer.

Scan this or see how, page 11

**What to look for**

- Drills with two batteries for use in tandem
- Chargers that recharge in an hour or less
- Multiple speeds
- A meter that indicates the remaining charge

**What to skip**

- Buying strictly by voltage; some 14.4- and 15.6-volt models had more oomph and staying power in our tests than some with 18 volts or more
- The maximum power and run time of a drill powered by lithium-ion or nickel-metal-hydride batteries if you're simply hanging pictures; consider a less-expensive, nickel-cadmium-powered drill for lighter-duty chores

**What you'll pay**

Models with 15.6 to 18 volts typically offer the best balance of power and light weight, and cost $180 on average.

For more buying advice, go to *ConsumerReports.org/drills*

Recommended models only From 81 tested.

| Recommended | Rank | Brand & model | Price | Overall score (0–100; P \| F \| G \| VG \| E) | Speed | Power | Run time | Charge time | Handling | Noise at ear | Weight (lb.) | Volts | Battery type | Battery recharge time (min.) | Speed ranges |
|---|---|---|---|---|---|---|---|---|---|---|---|---|---|---|---|
| **A CORDLESS IMPACT DRIVER** | | | | | | | | | | | | | | | |
| ✓ | 1 | **Ryobi** P236 | $70 | 78 | ⊖ | ⊜ | ⊜ | ⊖ | ⊖ | ● | 4.3 | 18 | Li-ion | 60 | 1 |
| ✓ | 2 | **Hitachi** WH18DSAL | 160 | 74 | ⊖ | ⊜ | ⊖ | ⊜ | ⊜ | ● | 3.2 | 18 | Li-ion | 40 | 1 |
| ✓ | 3 | **DeWalt** DCF885C2 | 220 | 74 | ⊖ | ⊜ | ○ | ⊜ | ⊜ | ● | 2.9 | 20 | Li-ion | 30 | 1 |
| **B CORDLESS SCREWDRIVER** | | | | | | | | | | | | | | | |
| ✓ | 1 | **Milwaukee** 2401-22 | 100 | 66 | ⊜ | ◒ | ◒ | ⊜ | ⊜ | ⊖ | 2.1 | 12 | Li-ion | 30 | 1 |
| **C GENERAL USE DRILL/DRIVER** | | | | | | | | | | | | | | | |
| ✓ | 1 | **Hitachi** DS18DSAL | 170 | 78 | ⊜ | ⊜ | ○ | ⊜ | ⊜ | ○ | 3.4 | 18 | Li-ion | 40 | 2 |
| ✓ | 2 | **Makita** LXFD01CW | 200 | 77 | ⊜ | ⊜ | ○ | ⊜ | ⊖ | ○ | 3.3 | 18 | Li-ion | 15 | 2 |
| ✓ | 3 | **Ridgid** R86008K | 180 | 77 | ⊜ | ⊖ | ⊖ | ⊜ | ⊖ | ○ | 4 | 18 | Li-ion | 25 | 2 |

| Recommended | Rank | Brand & model | Price | Overall score (0–100; P \| F \| G \| VG \| E) | Test results: Speed | Power | Run time | Charge time | Handling | Noise at ear | Weight (lb.) | Volts | Features: Battery type | Battery recharge time (min.) | Speed ranges |
|---|---|---|---|---|---|---|---|---|---|---|---|---|---|---|---|
| **C** | | **GENERAL USE DRILL/DRIVER** continued | | | | | | | | | | | | | |
| ✓ | 4 | **DeWalt** DCD780C2 | $220 | 75 | E | E | F | E | VG | G | 3.5 | 20 | Li-ion | 30 | 2 |
| ✓ | 5 | **Panasonic** EY6432GQKW | 200 | 75 | E | VG | E | VG | G | G | 4.9 | 15.6 | NiMH | 55 | 2 |
| ✓ | 6 | **DeWalt** DCD760KL | 220 | 74 | E | VG | G | E | VG | G | 3.9 | 18 | Li-ion | 30 | 2 |
| ✔ | 7 | **Ridgid** R9600 | 180 | 72 | E | E | F | E | VG | F | 4 | 18 | Li-ion | 40 | 2 |
| ✔ | 8 | **Craftsman** 17310 | 100 | 72 | VG | VG | G | E | VG | G | 3.8 | 19.2 | Li-ion | 30 | 2 |
| ✓ | 9 | **Bosch** DDS181-02 | 200 | 71 | E | VG | G | E | VG | F | 3.4 | 18 | Li-ion | 30 | 2 |
| ✓ | 10 | **Kobalt** KT200A | 160 | 71 | E | E | F | E | VG | G | 3.9 | 18 | Li-ion | 20 | 2 |
| **D** | | **LIGHT USE DRILL/DRIVER** | | | | | | | | | | | | | |
| ✔ | 1 | **Hitachi** DS14DSFL | 140 | 70 | E | VG | G | E | VG | G | 3.3 | 14.4 | Li-ion | 40 | 2 |
| ✔ | 2 | **Black & Decker** LDX220SBFC | 90 | 66 | VG | VG | F | E | E | G | 3.1 | 20 | Li-ion | 35 | 2 |
| ✓ | 3 | **DeWalt** DCD710S2 | 160 | 66 | VG | G | F | E | E | G | 2.5 | 12 | Li-ion | 30 | 2 |
| ✓ | 4 | **Milwaukee** 2410-22 | 160 | 63 | VG | G | P | E | VG | G | 2.6 | 12 | Li-ion | 30 | 2 |
| ✓ | 5 | **Ridgid** R92009 | 140 | 58 | VG | G | P | E | G | G | 2.6 | 12 | Li-ion | 30 | 2 |
| ✓ | 6 | **Porter-Cable** PCL120DDC | 90 | 56 | G | G | P | E | E | G | 2.3 | 12 | Li-ion | 30 | 2 |
| ✓ | 7 | **DeWalt** DC742KA | 140 | 55 | VG | G | P | VG | VG | G | 3.8 | 12 | NiCd | 60 | 2 |
| ✓ | 8 | **Skil** 2895-01 | 100 | 55 | VG | G | F | G | G | G | 4.7 | 18 | NiCd | 60 | 2 |
| **E** | | **TOUGHER JOB DRILL/DRIVER** | | | | | | | | | | | | | |
| ✓ | 1 | **Makita** BHP454 | 280 | 84 | E | E | E | E | F | G | 5 | 18 | Li-ion | 30 | 2 |
| ✓ | 2 | **Milwaukee** 2603-22 | 280 | 83 | E | E | E | VG | VG | F | 5 | 18 | Li-ion | 30 | 2 |
| ✓ | 3 | **DeWalt** DCD 940KX | 280 | 81 | E | E | E | VG | G | G | 6.1 | 18 | NiCd | 60 | 2 |

## Guide to the Ratings

**Overall score** is based on speed, power, run and charge times, handling, and noise. The displayed score is out of a total of 100 points. **Speed** is for drilling holes and driving screws. **Power** is twisting force. **Run time** is work per battery charge. **Charge time** is for a fully discharged battery. **Handling** is based on the drill's weight, balance, and effort to position head. **Noise at ear** denotes sound pressure, measured in decibels. **Weight (lb.)** includes the drill and battery pack. **Volts** is as specified for the battery pack. Under **battery type**, Li-ion is Lithium-ion, NiMH is nickel-metal-hydride, and NiCd is nickel cadmium. **Price** is approximate retail.

# Quick Guide DECK STAINS

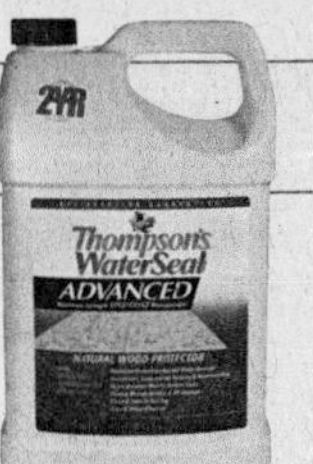


Some deck treatments can lighten your workload by lasting longer before they need to be reapplied. The best we tested not only kept their looks for at least three years outdoors; they also resisted cracking, dirt, and mildew.

**Shopping tip**

Need to buy 5 gallons? Buy the stain in one 5-gallon bucket. You'll save as much as $30 and get more consistent color.

Scan this or see how, page 11

**What to look for**

- A mildew-resistant stain for shady areas, and a fade-resistant one for sunny spots
- Opaque, or solid, stains for a long-lasting finish
- Clear finishes to show off natural color and grain—provided you're willing to reapply them each year
- Semitransparent stains for a reasonable compromise

**What to skip**

- Buying strictly by brand; different products from the same manufacturer often performed differently

**What you'll pay**

You'll need about a gallon of solid stain ($30–$45) for a 350-foot deck that's been previously stained, twice as much for two coats on a new deck. Double the amounts for semitransparent stains ($25-$45) or clear sealers ($18–$38), which tend to soak into the wood.

For more buying advice, go to *ConsumerReports.org/stains*

All tested models In performance order, within types.

| Recommended | Rank | Brand & model | Price per gallon | Overall score (0–100; P \| F \| G \| VG \| E) | Test results: Appearance after 3 years | Appearance after 6 years | Appearance after 9 years | Features: Resists cracking | Resists color change | Resists dirt | Resists mildew | VOCs (grams/liter) |
|---|---|---|---|---|---|---|---|---|---|---|---|---|
| | | **A CLEAR SEALER** | | | | | | | | | | |
| ✓ | 1 | **Thompson's** WaterSeal Advanced Waterproofer | $23 | 31 | ○ | NA | NA | • | | | | 250 |
| | 2 | **Thompson's** WaterSeal Waterproofer Plus Clear Wood Protector | 19 | 28 | ◒ | NA | NA | • | | | • | 100 |
| | 3 | **Olympic** Maximum Waterproofing Sealant (Lowe's) | 33 | 22 | ◒ | NA | NA | • | | | | 230 |

| Recommended | Rank | Brand & model | Price per gallon | Overall score (0–100; P \| F \| G \| VG \| E) | Test results: Appearance after 3 years | Test results: Appearance after 6 years | Test results: Appearance after 9 years | Features: Resists cracking | Features: Resists color change | Features: Resists dirt | Features: Resists mildew | Features: VOCs (grams/liter) |
|---|---|---|---|---|---|---|---|---|---|---|---|---|
| | | **A CLEAR SEALER** continued | | | | | | | | | | |
| | 4 | **Wolman** RainCoat Clear Water Repellent | $18 | 21 | Fair | NA | NA | • | | | | 250 |
| | 5 | **Benjamin Moore** Waterproofer | 24 | 18 | Fair | NA | NA | • | | | | 250 |
| | 6 | **Sherwin-Williams** Deckscapes Clear Sealer | 38 | 15 | Fair | NA | NA | | | | • | 311 |
| | | **B SEMI-TRANSPARENT** | | | | | | | | | | |
| ✓ | 1 | **Behr** Premium Semi-Transparent Weatherproofing Wood Stain (Home Depot) | 37 | 65 | Excellent | Excellent | NA | • | • | • | • | 100 |
| | 2 | **Cabot** Semi-Transparent Deck & Siding | 38 | 46 | Excellent | Fair | NA | • | | | • | 250 |
| | 3 | **Behr** Semi-Transparent Waterproofing Wood Stain (Home Depot) | 29 | 41 | Excellent | Fair | NA | | | | | 100 |
| | 4 | **Sherwin-Williams** Deckscapes Semi-Transparent | 46 | 38 | Excellent | Fair | NA | | | | | 170 |
| | 5 | **Flood** TWF-SEMI Semi-Transparent Wood Stain | 29 | 38 | Excellent | Fair | NA | | | | | 250 |
| | 6 | **Ace** Wood Royal Semi-Transparent Deck & Siding | 31 | 35 | Excellent | Fair | NA | | | | • | 100 |
| | 7 | **Thompson's** WaterSeal Deck & House Semi-Transparent Latex | 25 | 32 | Excellent | Fair | NA | | | | • | 100 |
| | 8 | **Wolman** DuraStain Semi-Transparent Stain | 30 | 32 | Fair | Fair | NA | | | | | 250 |
| | 9 | **Sikkens** Cetol Cetol SRD Semi-Transparent | 43 | 31 | Good | Fair | NA | | | | | 250 |
| | 10 | **Olympic** Maximum Deck, Fence & Siding Semi-Transparent Stain (Lowe's) | 36 | 31 | Good | Fair | NA | | | | • | 233 |
| | 11 | **Sherwin-Williams** Woodscapes Semi-Transparent Stain | 46 | 21 | Fair | Poor | NA | | | | | 79 |

**Ratings Key** Excellent, Very good, Good, Fair, Poor

**CR Best Buy** These models offer the best combination of performance and price. All are recommended.

✓ **Recommended** These are high-performing models that stand out.

| Recommended | Rank | Brand & model | Price per gallon | Overall score (0–100; P \| F \| G \| VG \| E) | Test results: Appearance after 3 years | Appearance after 6 years | Appearance after 9 years | Features: Resists cracking | Resists color change | Resists dirt | Resists mildew | VOCs (grams/liter) |
|---|---|---|---|---|---|---|---|---|---|---|---|---|
| **C SOLID WOOD** | | | | | | | | | | | | |
| ✔ | 1 | **Behr** Solid Color Waterproofing Wood Stain (Home Depot) | $29 | 80 | ⊜ | ⊜ | ⊖ | • | • | • | • | 100 |
| ✔ | 2 | **Benjamin Moore** Arborcoat Deck & Siding Solid | 46 | 68 | ⊜ | ⊖ | ○ | • | • | | | 100 |
| ✔ | 3 | **Wolman** DuraStain Solid | 33 | 66 | ⊖ | ⊖ | ○ | • | • | | | 100 |
| ✔ | 4 | **Sears** Weatherbeater Deck, Fence & Siding Solid | 32 | 64 | ⊖ | ⊖ | ○ | • | | | | 90 |
| | 5 | **Sherwin-Williams** Woodscapes Solid | 48 | 62 | ⊜ | ○ | ○ | • | • | | | 136 |
| | 6 | **Olympic** Maximum Deck, Fence & Siding Solid Stain (Lowe's) | 36 | 62 | ⊖ | ⊖ | ○ | • | • | • | | 166 |
| | 7 | **Behr** Premium Solid Color Weatherproofing Wood Stain (Home Depot) | 37 | 61 | ⊖ | ⊖ | ○ | • | • | | • | 100 |
| | 8 | **Sherwin-Williams** Deckscapes Solid | 46 | 61 | ⊜ | ○ | ○ | • | • | | | 122 |
| | 9 | **Flood** SWF-SOLID Solid Wood Stain | 29 | 56 | ⊜ | ⊖ | ◒ | • | | | | 250 |
| | 10 | **Cabot** Solid Color Decking Stain | 38 | 55 | ⊜ | ○ | ◒ | | • | | | 100 |
| | 11 | **Sikkens** Rubbol Solid Siding Finish | 41 | 41 | ⊖ | ○ | ● | | | | | 200 |
| | 12 | **Woodsman** Solid Color Deck Stain | 30 | 27 | ○ | ◒ | ● | | | | | 250 |

## Guide to the Ratings

**Overall score** is a weighted average of each year's appearance for up to 3 years of testing. Scores for previously tested products may have changed because of changes in tabulations. **Appearance after 3 years** summarizes performance after 1 year of our accelerated weathering (i.e., equivalent to 1 year on a deck or 3 years on a vertical surface). Testing stops when appearance falls to Fair or Poor, at which time the product must be reapplied. **Appearance after 6 years** summarizes performance after 2 years of our accelerated weathering (i.e., equivalent to 2 years on a deck or 6 years on a vertical surface). Testing stops when appearance falls to Fair or Poor, at which time the product must be reapplied. **Appearance after 9 years** summarizes performance after 3 years of our accelerated weathering (i.e., equivalent to 3 years on a deck or 9 years on a vertical surface). Products that at this point still rate at least Good for appearance are considered superior products. **VOCs (grams/liter)** is the maximum level of volatile organic compounds stated on the can. **Price** is approximate retail per gallon.

# Quick Guide DIGITAL CAMERAS, ADVANCED

**Consumers are placing increasing demands on cameras, and manufacturers are meeting these needs by adding more capabilities, especially wireless features.**

SLR-likes (also called mirrorless) lack the mirror found in SLRs, so they can be built thinner and smaller.

Scan this or see how, page 11

### What to look for

- Wide-angle capability, with some models able to go as wide as 24 mm
- Extended zoom ranges from 5x to 42x
- An SLR or SLR-like model with interchangeable lenses for the most versatility
- Wi-Fi features for quickly uploading images and video
- A viewfinder is a plus, though not a necessity

### What to skip

- An extended warranty, because digital cameras have been among the most reliable products overall in our subscriber surveys

### What you'll pay

For advanced point-and-shoots, expect to spend $450 to $1,300. For SLR-like cameras, expect to spend $300 to $1,500. For SLRs, expect to spend $450 to $1,700.

For more buying advice, go to *ConsumerReports.org/cameras*

**All tested models** in performance order, within types.

| Recommended | Rank | Brand & model | Price | Overall score (0–100; P \| F \| G \| VG \| E) | Megapixels | Weight (oz.) | Image quality | Flash photos | Video quality | Ease of use | LCD quality | Viewfinder | Test lens |
|---|---|---|---|---|---|---|---|---|---|---|---|---|---|
| **A** | | **ADVANCED POINT-AND-SHOOT** | | | | | | | | | | | |
| Recommended | 1 | **Nikon** Coolpix A | $1,100 | 71 | 16.1 | 12 | Very good | Very good | Very good | Very good | Excellent | NA | 28mm |
| Recommended | 2 | **Fujifilm** X100S | 1,300 | 69 | 16 | 17 | Very good | Very good | Very good | Very good | Very good | Excellent | 35mm |
| Recommended | 3 | **Ricoh** GR | 800 | 69 | 16 | 9 | Very good | Good | Good | Very good | Very good | NA | 28mm |
| Recommended | 4 | **Panasonic** Lumix DMC-FZ200 | 600 | 69 | 12 | 22 | Very good | Very good | Very good | Very good | Very good | Very good | 25-600mm |
| CR Best Buy | 5 | **Panasonic** Lumix DMC-LF1 | 500 | 68 | 12 | 7 | Very good | Very good | Very good | Good | Excellent | Very good | 28-200mm |

**Ratings Key** Excellent, Very good, Good, Fair, Poor

**CR Best Buy** These models offer the best combination of performance and price. All are recommended.

**Recommended** These are high-performing models that stand out.

| Recommended | Rank | Brand & model | Price | Overall score (0–100; P \| F \| G \| VG \| E) | Megapixels | Weight (oz.) | Image quality | Flash photos | Video quality | Ease of use | LCD quality | Viewfinder | Test lens |
|---|---|---|---|---|---|---|---|---|---|---|---|---|---|
| | | **A ADVANCED POINT-AND-SHOOT** continued | | | | | | | | | | | |
| ✔ | 6 | **Panasonic** Lumix DMC-LX7 | $ 500 | 66 | 10 | 11 | ⊖ | ⊖ | ⊖ | ○ | ⊖ | NA | 24-90mm |
| ✔ | 7 | **Canon** PowerShot G15 | 500 | 65 | 12 | 13 | ⊖ | ○ | ⊖ | ○ | ⊖ | ◒ | 28-140mm |
| ☑ | 8 | **Fujifilm** X20 | 600 | 65 | 12 | 14 | ⊖ | ⊖ | ○ | ⊖ | ⊖ | ⊜ | 28-112mm |
| ✔ | 9 | **Pentax** MX-1 | 450 | 65 | 12 | 15 | ○ | ⊖ | ⊖ | ⊖ | ⊜ | NA | 28-112mm |
| ☑ | 10 | **Leica** X Vario | 2,850 | 64 | 16 | 24 | ⊖ | ⊖ | ○ | ○ | ⊜ | NA | 28-70mm |
| ☑ | 11 | **Olympus** Stylus XZ-2 | 600 | 64 | 12 | 14 | ⊖ | ⊖ | ⊖ | ○ | ⊖ | NA | 28-112mm |
| ☑ | 12 | **Sony** Cyber-shot DSC-RX100 | 650 | 62 | 20 | 9 | ⊖ | ⊖ | ⊖ | ○ | ⊖ | NA | 28-100mm |
| | 13 | **Fujifilm** FinePix X-S1 | 700 | 61 | 12 | 35 | ○ | ⊖ | ○ | ○ | ⊖ | ⊖ | 24-624mm |
| | 14 | **Canon** PowerShot SX50 HS | 430 | 61 | 12 | 22 | ○ | ○ | ○ | ⊖ | ⊖ | ○ | 24-1200mm |
| | 15 | **Nikon** Coolpix P7700 | 450 | 60 | 12 | 15 | ⊖ | ○ | ○ | ○ | ⊖ | NA | 28-200mm |
| | 16 | **Samsung** EX2F | 450 | 59 | 12 | 12 | ⊖ | ⊖ | ⊖ | ○ | ⊖ | NA | 24-80mm |
| | 17 | **Canon** PowerShot G1 X | 700 | 59 | 14 | 20 | ⊖ | ○ | ⊖ | ○ | ⊜ | ◒ | 28-112mm |
| | 18 | **Fujifilm** FinePix HS50EXR | 480 | 54 | 16 | 30 | ○ | ○ | ◒ | ⊖ | ⊖ | ⊖ | 24-1000mm |
| | 19 | **Sigma** DP2 Merill | 950 | 44 | 15 | 14 | ○ | ⊜ | ◒ | ○ | ◒ | NA | 45mm |
| | | **B SLR** | | | | | | | | | | | |
| ✔ | 1 | **Canon** EOS Rebel T5i | 900 | 73 | 18 | 30 | ⊖ | ⊖ | ⊖ | ⊖ | ⊖ | ⊖ | 18-55mm (1.6) |
| ☑ | 2 | **Nikon** D7100 | 1,500 | 72 | 24 | 44 | ⊖ | ⊜ | ⊜ | ⊖ | ⊖ | ⊜ | 18-105mm (1.5) |
| ☑ | 3 | **Canon** EOS 60D | 1,050 | 71 | 18 | 36 | ⊖ | ⊜ | ⊖ | ⊖ | ⊖ | ⊜ | 18-55mm (1.6) |
| ✔ | 4 | **Canon** EOS Rebel SL1 | 800 | 71 | 18 | 23 | ⊖ | ⊖ | ⊖ | ⊖ | ⊖ | ⊖ | 18-55mm (1.6) |
| ☑ | 5 | **Olympus** E-5 | 1,700 | 70 | 12 | 49 | ⊖ | ⊖ | ⊖ | ⊖ | ⊖ | ⊜ | 14-54mm (2.0) |
| ☑ | 6 | **Nikon** D7000 | 1,100 | 70 | 16 | 44 | ⊖ | ○ | ⊖ | ○ | ⊖ | ⊜ | 18-105mm (1.5) |
| ✔ | 7 | **Canon** EOS Rebel T3i | 650 | 70 | 18 | 29 | ⊖ | ⊖ | ⊖ | ⊖ | ⊖ | ⊜ | 18-55mm (1.6) |
| ☑ | 8 | **Canon** EOS 7D Digital | 1,700 | 69 | 18 | 50 | ⊖ | ⊖ | ⊖ | ⊖ | ⊖ | ⊖ | 18-135mm (1.6) |
| ☑ | 9 | **Canon** EOS Rebel T4i | 750 | 69 | 18 | 29 | ⊖ | ○ | ○ | ⊖ | ⊖ | ⊖ | 18-55mm (1.6) |
| ✔ | 10 | **Canon** EOS Rebel T3 | 600 | 67 | 12 | 26 | ⊖ | ○ | ⊖ | ⊖ | ○ | ⊜ | 18-55mm (1.6) |
| ☑ | 11 | **Nikon** D5200 | 900 | 66 | 24 | 20 | ⊖ | ⊖ | ○ | ⊖ | ⊖ | ⊜ | 18-55mm (1.5) |
| ✔ | 12 | **Nikon** D3200 | 600 | 66 | 24 | 29 | ⊖ | ○ | ○ | ○ | ⊖ | ⊖ | 18-55mm (1.5) |

| Recommended | Rank | Brand & model | Price | Overall score (0–100; P \| F \| G \| VG \| E) | Megapixels | Weight (oz.) | Image quality | Flash photos | Video quality | Ease of use | LCD quality | Viewfinder | Test lens |
|---|---|---|---|---|---|---|---|---|---|---|---|---|---|
| | **B** | **SLR** continued | | | | | | | | | | | |
| ✅ | 13 | **Nikon** D3100 | $ 450 | 65 | 14 | 29 | ⊖ | ⊖ | ⊖ | ○ | ○ | ⊖ | 18-55mm (1.5) |
| ☑ | 14 | **Pentax** K-30 | 850 | 65 | 16 | 33 | ⊖ | ○ | ○ | ⊖ | ○ | ⊜ | 18-55mm (1.5) |
| ☑ | 15 | **Pentax** K-5 | 1,050 | 65 | 16 | 36 | ⊖ | ○ | ○ | ⊖ | ○ | ⊖ | 18-55mm (1.5) |
| ✅ | 16 | **Nikon** D5100 | 750 | 65 | 16 | 31 | ⊖ | ○ | ⊖ | ○ | ⊖ | ⊖ | 18-55mm (1.5) |
| | 17 | **Pentax** K-5 II | 1,350 | 61 | 16 | 37 | ○ | ○ | ◒ | ⊖ | ⊖ | ⊖ | 18-55mm (1.5) |
| | 18 | **Sigma** SD15 | 950 | 37 | 14 | 42 | ◒ | ○ | NA | ○ | ○ | ⊜ | 18-50mm (1.7) |
| | **C** | **SLR-LIKE** | | | | | | | | | | | |
| ☑ | 1 | **Panasonic** Lumix DMC-GH3 | 1,300 | 72 | 16 | 32 | ⊖ | ⊖ | ⊖ | ⊖ | ⊖ | ⊜ | 12-35mm (2.0) |
| ☑ | 2 | **Panasonic** Lumix DMC-G6K | 750 | 70 | 16 | 15 | ⊖ | ⊖ | ⊖ | ⊖ | ⊜ | ⊜ | 14-42mm (2.0) |
| ☑ | 3 | **Panasonic** Lumix DMC-G5K | 800 | 69 | 16 | 21 | ⊖ | ⊖ | ⊖ | ⊖ | ⊖ | ⊜ | 14-42mm (2.0) |
| ☑ | 4 | **Olympus** OM-D E-M5 | 1,000 | 68 | 16 | 25 | ⊖ | ○ | ⊖ | ⊖ | ⊖ | ⊖ | 12-50mm (2.0) |
| ☑ | 5 | **Samsung** NX300 | 750 | 68 | 20 | 20 | ⊖ | ⊜ | ⊖ | ○ | ⊜ | NA | 18-55mm (1.5) |
| ✅ | 6 | **Panasonic** Lumix DMC-GF6K | 600 | 68 | 16 | 16 | ○ | ⊖ | ⊖ | ⊖ | ⊖ | NA | 14-42mm (2.0) |
| ☑ | 7 | **Sony** SLT-A57K | 600 | 68 | 16 | 31 | ⊖ | ⊖ | ○ | ⊖ | ⊖ | ⊖ | 18-55mm (1.5) |
| ✅ | 8 | **Sony** NEX-3NL | 450 | 67 | 16 | 14 | ⊖ | ○ | ⊖ | ⊖ | ⊖ | NA | 16-50mm (1.5) |
| ☑ | 9 | **Nikon** 1 J2 | 700 | 66 | 10 | 14 | ⊖ | ○ | ○ | ⊖ | ○ | NA | 11-27.5mm (2.7) |
| ☑ | 10 | **Samsung** NX20 | 1,000 | 66 | 20 | 23 | ⊖ | ⊖ | ○ | ⊖ | ⊖ | ⊖ | 18-55mm (1.5) |
| ☑ | 11 | **Sony** SLT-A65VK | 800 | 65 | 24 | 31 | ○ | ⊖ | ⊖ | ⊖ | ⊖ | ⊖ | 18-55mm (1.5) |

## Guide to the Ratings

**Overall score** is based mainly on image quality, the presence of useful features, battery life, and weight. **Megapixels** is the sensor's pixel count, in millions. **Weight (oz.)** is with battery and memory card. **Image quality** combines several tests, including regular photos, low-light photos, and flash photos as well as resolution, macro, veiling glare, vignetting, and color and geometric distortion tests. **Flash photos** tests the quality of the built-in flash's light output and evenness of illumination. **Video quality** mostly reflects footage shot in regular and low light, with audio quality and macro (close-up) capability also considered. **Ease of use** is our evaluation of the camera's controls, manual, response time, and focusing. **LCD quality** is a judgment of images viewed under various lighting conditions. **Viewfinder** is our evaluation of its quality, including accuracy in displaying the framing of the image that will be recorded. **Test lens** is the kit lens tested. To calculate its 35-mm-equivalent focal range, multiply the minimum and maximum settings shown, respectively, by the magnification factor, if shown (in parentheses). **Price** is approximate retail.

| Recommended | Rank | Brand & model | Price | Overall score (0–100; P \| F \| G \| VG \| E) | Megapixels | Weight (oz.) | Image quality | Flash photos | Video quality | Ease of use | LCD quality | Viewfinder | Test lens |
|---|---|---|---|---|---|---|---|---|---|---|---|---|---|
| **C** | | **SLR-LIKE** continued | | | | | | | | | | | |
| ☑ Recommended | 12 | **Olympus** Pen E-P5 | $1,250 | 65 | 16 | 16 | Very good | Very good | Good | Very good | Very good | NA | 14-42mm (2.0) |
| ☑ Recommended | 13 | **Sony** NEX-7K | 1,150 | 65 | 24 | 20 | Very good | Good | Very good | Good | Very good | Very good | 18-55mm (1.5) |
| ■ CR Best Buy | 14 | **Sony** NEX-F3K | 500 | 65 | 16 | 19 | Very good | Good | Very good | Good | Very good | NA | 18-55mm (1.5) |
| ☑ Recommended | 15 | **Sony** SLT-A77V | 1,000 | 65 | 24 | 36 | Good | Very good | Very good | Very good | Very good | Very good | 18-55mm (1.5) |
| ■ CR Best Buy | 16 | **Olympus** E-PM2 | 500 | 64 | 16 | 15 | Very good | Good | Very good | Very good | Very good | NA | 14-42mm (2.0) |
| ☑ Recommended | 17 | **Sony** NEX-6L | 900 | 64 | 16 | 17 | Very good | Good | Very good | Good | Very good | Very good | 16-50mm (1.5) |
| ■ CR Best Buy | 18 | **Samsung** NX1100 | 350 | 64 | 20 | 15 | Very good | Good | Good | Good | Very good | NA | 20-50mm (1.5) |
| ☑ Recommended | 19 | **Sony** SLT-A58K | 600 | 63 | 20 | 30 | Good | Good | Good | Very good | Good | Excellent | 18-55mm (1.5) |
| ☑ Recommended | 20 | **Panasonic** Lumix DMC-GF5X | 750 | 63 | 12 | 14 | Very good | Good | Good | Very good | Very good | NA | 14-42mm (2.0) |
| ☑ Recommended | 21 | **Samsung** NX210 | 900 | 63 | 20 | 19 | Very good | Very good | Fair | Very good | Very good | NA | 18-55mm (1.5) |
| | 22 | **Panasonic** Lumix DMC-GX1X | 700 | 61 | 16 | 16 | Very good | Good | Very good | Very good | Very good | NA | 14-42mm (2.0) |
| | 23 | **Samsung** NX2000 | 650 | 61 | 20 | 15 | Very good | Very good | Fair | Very good | Very good | NA | 20-50mm (1.5) |
| | 24 | **Olympus** Pen Lite E-PL5 | 700 | 60 | 16 | 18 | Very good | Good | Good | Very good | Good | NA | 14-42mm (2.0) |
| | 25 | **Nikon** 1 J1 | 500 | 60 | 10 | 15 | Very good | Good | Very good | Very good | Good | NA | 10-30mm (2.7) |
| | 26 | **Nikon** 1 J3 | 600 | 60 | 14 | 13 | Very good | Good | Good | Good | Very good | NA | 10-30mm (2.7) |
| | 27 | **Samsung** NX1000 | 550 | 60 | 20 | 16 | Very good | Very good | Fair | Good | Very good | NA | 20-50mm (1.5) |
| | 28 | **Fujifilm** X-E1 | 1,400 | 59 | 16 | 24 | Very good | Very good | Good | Good | Very good | Very good | 18-55mm (1.5) |
| | 29 | **Nikon** 1 S1 | 500 | 59 | 10 | 12 | Very good | Very good | Good | Good | Very good | NA | 11-27.5mm (2.7) |
| | 30 | **Nikon** 1 V2 | 1,000 | 58 | 14 | 17 | Very good | Good | Good | Very good | Good | Good | 10-30mm (2.7) |
| | 31 | **Sony** NEX-5NK | 700 | 57 | 16 | 18 | Good | Very good | Good | Good | Very good | NA | 18-55mm (1.5) |
| | 32 | **Sony** NEX-5RK | 650 | 57 | 16 | 18 | Good | Very good | Good | Good | Very good | NA | 18-55mm (1.5) |
| | 33 | **Canon** EOS M | 900 | 55 | 18 | 22 | Very good | Good | Good | Good | Very good | NA | 18-55mm (1.6) |
| | 34 | **Pentax** Q10 | 600 | 54 | 12 | 11 | Good | Good | Good | Good | Very good | NA | 5-15mm (5.5) |
| | 35 | **Pentax** Q | 400 | 54 | 12 | 11 | Good | Good | Good | Good | Very good | NA | 5-15mm (5.5) |
| | 36 | **Fujifilm** X-Pro1 | 1,200 | 52 | 16 | 24 | Good | Excellent | Fair | Good | Excellent | Very good | 35mm (1.5) |
| | 37 | **Pentax** K-01 | 1,000 | 50 | 16 | 28 | Good | Good | Fair | Good | Good | NA | 18-55mm (1.5) |

**Ratings Key** ⊜ Excellent ⊖ Very good ○ Good ◒ Fair ● Poor

■ **CR Best Buy** These models offer the best combination of performance and price. All are recommended.

☑ **Recommended** These are high-performing models that stand out.

# Quick Guide DIGITAL CAMERAS, BASIC

Most of the models we tested offer Good or Very Good overall performance and image quality. Most get 200 to 350 shots per battery charge and many have a 3-inch display.

**What to look for**

- A wide-angle end of the zoom range as low as 28mm, 24mm or wider, for more panoramic landscapes or group portraits
- An LCD that can swivel for hard-to-reach shots
- A touch screen for easy interaction with menus
- An optical or electronic viewfinder, which can help you compose when bright light washes out your LCD
- A dedicated video button, which lets you record video when you're shooting photos

**What to skip**

- Buying a camera solely based on its megapixel count, since higher resolution doesn't necessarily produce better photographs

**What you'll pay**

For basic point-and-shoots, expect to spend $90 to $500.

For more buying advice, go to *ConsumerReports.org/cameras*

**Shopping tip**

When looking for a basic camera, only consider optical zoom. Disregard digital zoom; it degrades image quality.

Scan this or see how, page 11

**Recommended models only** From 130 tested.

| Recommended | Rank | Brand & model | Price | Overall score (0–100; P \| F \| G \| VG \| E) | Megapixels | Weight (oz.) | Image quality | Flash photos | Video quality | Ease of use | LCD quality | Widest angle (mm) | Battery life (shots) |
|---|---|---|---|---|---|---|---|---|---|---|---|---|---|
| **A COMPACT** | | | | | | | | | | | | | |
| ✔ | 1 | **Olympus** Stylus XZ-10 | $400 | 65 | 12 | 8 | ⊖ | ⊖ | ○ | ○ | ⊖ | 26 | 240 |
| ✔ | 2 | **Nikon** Coolpix P310 | 250 | 60 | 16 | 7 | ⊖ | ⊖ | ○ | ○ | ○ | 24 | 230 |
| ✔ | 3 | **Nikon** Coolpix S8200 | 330 | 57 | 16 | 8 | ⊖ | ○ | ○ | ○ | ○ | 25 | 250 |
| ✔ | 4 | **Fujifilm** XF1 | 450 | 57 | 12 | 8 | ⊖ | ○ | ○ | ○ | ○ | 25 | 300 |
| ✔ (CR Best Buy) | 5 | **Nikon** Coolpix L610 | 150 | 57 | 16 | 9 | ⊖ | ⊖ | ◒ | ○ | ○ | 25 | 120 |
| ✔ | 6 | **Canon** PowerShot S110 | 400 | 55 | 12 | 7 | ⊖ | ○ | ○ | ○ | ⊖ | 24 | 200 |

| Recommended | Rank | Brand & model | Price | Overall score (0–100; P \| F \| G \| VG \| E) | Megapixels | Weight (oz.) | Image quality | Flash photos | Video quality | Ease of use | LCD quality | Widest angle (mm) | Battery life (shots) |
|---|---|---|---|---|---|---|---|---|---|---|---|---|---|
| **B SUBCOMPACT** | | | | | | | | | | | | | |
| ✓ | 1 | **Nikon** Coolpix P330 | $350 | 63 | 12 | 7 | Very good | Very good | Very good | Good | Very good | 24 | 200 |
| ✓ | 2 | **Nikon** Coolpix S800c | 250 | 60 | 16 | 6 | Very good | Good | Very good | Good | Good | 25 | 140 |
| ✓ | 3 | **Sony** Cyber-shot DSC-WX70 | 190 | 59 | 16 | 4 | Very good | Good | Very good | Good | Good | 25 | 240 |
| ✓ | 4 | **Nikon** Coolpix S6500 | 200 | 57 | 16 | 5 | Very good | Good | Good | Good | Good | 25 | 150 |
| ✓ | 5 | **Canon** PowerShot ELPH 110 HS | 230 | 57 | 16 | 5 | Good | Good | Very good | Good | Good | 24 | 170 |
| | 6 | **Canon** PowerShot N | 300 | 56 | 12 | 7 | Very good | Poor | Good | Good | Very good | 28 | 200 |
| ✓ | 7 | **Panasonic** Lumix DMC-3D1 | 400 | 56 | 12 | 7 | Very good | Good | Very good | Good | Good | 25 | 200 |
| ✓ | 8 | **Panasonic** Lumix DMC-SZ1 | 140 | 56 | 16 | 5 | Good | Good | Good | Good | Good | 25 | 250 |
| ✓ | 9 | **Panasonic** Lumix DMC-SZ5 | 200 | 56 | 14 | 5 | Good | Good | Good | Good | Good | 25 | 250 |
| ✓ (CR Best Buy) | 10 | **Panasonic** Lumix DMC-FH8 | 150 | 55 | 16 | 4 | Good | Good | Very good | Good | Good | 24 | 260 |
| **C SUPERZOOM** | | | | | | | | | | | | | |
| ✓ | 1 | **Canon** PowerShot SX280 HS | 300 | 64 | 12 | 8 | Very good | Very good | Good | Good | Very good | 25 | 210 |
| ✓ | 2 | **Panasonic** Lumix DMC-ZS30 | 400 | 64 | 18 | 7 | Very good | Good | Good | Very good | Very good | 24 | 300 |
| ✓ | 3 | **Sony** Cyber-Shot DSC-HX50V | 450 | 63 | 20 | 10 | Very good | Very good | Very good | Good | Very good | 24 | 400 |
| ✓ | 4 | **Olympus** Stylus SH-50 iHS | 270 | 63 | 16 | 10 | Very good | Good | Very good | Very good | Very good | 25 | 300 |
| ✓ | 5 | **Sony** Cyber-shot DSC-HX300 | 500 | 63 | 20 | 23 | Very good | Good | Very good | Good | Very good | 24 | 310 |
| ✓ | 6 | **Olympus** Stylus SP-820UZ | 330 | 62 | 14 | 19 | Very good | Good | Good | Good | Good | 22 | NA |
| ✓ | 7 | **Fujifilm** FinePix F900EXR | 370 | 60 | 16 | 8 | Very good | Good | Fair | Very good | Good | 25 | 260 |

**Ratings Key** Excellent, Very good, Good, Fair, Poor

✓ **CR Best Buy** These models offer the best combination of performance and price. All are recommended.

✓ **Recommended** These are high-performing models that stand out.

| Recommended | Rank | Brand & model | Price | Overall score (0–100; P \| F \| G \| VG \| E) | Megapixels | Weight (oz.) | Image quality | Flash photos | Video quality | Ease of use | LCD quality | Widest angle (mm) | Battery life (shots) |
|---|---|---|---|---|---|---|---|---|---|---|---|---|---|
| **C SUPERZOOM** continued | | | | | | | | | | | | | |
| ✓ | 8 | **Olympus** SZ-31MR iHS | $400 | 60 | 16 | 9 | ○ | ⊖ | ○ | ◒ | ○ | 25 | NA |
| ✓ | 9 | **Nikon** Coolpix S9500 | 330 | 59 | 18 | 7 | ⊖ | ○ | ○ | ○ | ○ | 25 | 230 |
| ✓ | 10 | **Nikon** Coolpix S9400 | 280 | 59 | 18 | 7 | ⊖ | ○ | ⊖ | ○ | ⊖ | 25 | 230 |
| ✔ | 11 | **Olympus** Stylus SZ-16 iHS | 230 | 59 | 16 | 8 | ⊖ | ⊖ | ○ | ○ | ○ | 25 | 270 |
| ✓ | 12 | **Nikon** Coolpix P520 | 430 | 59 | 18 | 21 | ⊖ | ⊖ | ○ | ○ | ⊖ | 24 | 200 |
| ✔ | 13 | **Nikon** Coolpix L820 | 250 | 59 | 16 | 18 | ⊖ | ○ | ⊖ | ○ | ⊖ | 23 | 320 |
| ✔ | 14 | **Panasonic** Lumix DMC-ZS8 | 280 | 59 | 14 | 7 | ⊖ | ○ | ○ | ○ | ○ | 24 | 340 |
| ✓ | 15 | **Leica** V-Lux 40 | 700 | 59 | 14 | 7 | ⊖ | ○ | ○ | ○ | ○ | 24 | 260 |
| ✓ | 16 | **Sony** Cyber-shot DSC-WX300 | 330 | 58 | 18 | 6 | ⊖ | ○ | ⊖ | ○ | ○ | 25 | 500 |
| ✓ | 17 | **Panasonic** Lumix DMC-FZ60 | 350 | 58 | 16 | 18 | ○ | ⊖ | ⊖ | ○ | ⊖ | 25 | 450 |
| ✓ | 18 | **Panasonic** Lumix DMC-ZS20 | 300 | 57 | 14 | 7 | ⊖ | ○ | ○ | ○ | ○ | 24 | 260 |
| ✓ | 19 | **Fujifilm** FinePix S8400W | 315 | 57 | 16 | 25 | ⊖ | ⊖ | ◒ | ○ | ⊖ | 24 | 300 |
| ✓ | 20 | **Fujifilm** FinePix F770EXR | 260 | 57 | 16 | 8 | ⊖ | ◒ | ◒ | ○ | ○ | 25 | 300 |
| ✓ | 21 | **Samsung** WB850F | 340 | 56 | 16 | 9 | ⊖ | ○ | ○ | ○ | ○ | 23 | NA |
| ✓ | 22 | **Sony** Cyber-shot DSC-HX20V | 300 | 56 | 18 | 9 | ○ | ○ | ⊖ | ○ | ⊖ | 25 | 320 |
| ✓ | 23 | **Leica** V-Lux 30 | 650 | 56 | 14 | 8 | ○ | ○ | ⊖ | ○ | ○ | 24 | NA |
| ✔ | 24 | **Panasonic** Lumix DMC-ZS15 | 280 | 56 | 12 | 7 | ○ | ○ | ⊖ | ○ | ○ | 24 | 260 |
| ✓ | 25 | **Sony** Cyber-shot DSC-HX10V | 300 | 55 | 18 | 8 | ○ | ○ | ⊖ | ○ | ○ | 24 | 340 |
| ✓ | 26 | **Sony** Cyber-shot DSC-HX200V | 415 | 55 | 18 | 22 | ○ | ○ | ⊖ | ○ | ⊖ | 27 | 450 |
| **D RUGGED & WATERPROOF** | | | | | | | | | | | | | |
| ✓ | 1 | **Panasonic** Lumix DMC-TS5 | 400 | 58 | 16 | 8 | ⊖ | ○ | ⊖ | ○ | ⊖ | 28 | 370 |
| ✓ | 2 | **Olympus** Stylus TG-830 iHS | 230 | 57 | 16 | 8 | ⊖ | ○ | ○ | ○ | ⊖ | 28 | NA |
| ✓ | 3 | **Nikon** Coolpix AW110 | 330 | 56 | 16 | 7 | ⊖ | ○ | ⊖ | ○ | ⊖ | 28 | 250 |

| Recommended | Rank | Brand & model | Price | Overall score (0–100; P / F / G / VG / E) | Megapixels | Weight (oz.) | Image quality | Flash photos | Video quality | Ease of use | LCD quality | Widest angle (mm) | Battery life (shots) |
|---|---|---|---|---|---|---|---|---|---|---|---|---|---|
| **D** | | **RUGGED & WATERPROOF** continued | | | | | | | | | | | |
| ✓ | 4 | **Panasonic** Lumix DMC-TS4 | $300 | 56 | 12 | 7 | Very good | Good | Good | Good | Good | 28 | 310 |
| ✓ | 5 | **Sony** Cyber-Shot DSC-TX30 | 350 | 56 | 18 | 5 | Good | Very good | Very good | Good | Good | 26 | 250 |
| ✓ | 6 | **Fujifilm** FinePix XP200W | 280 | 56 | 16 | 8 | Good | Good | Good | Good | Good | 28 | 300 |
| ✓ | 7 | **Olympus** Stylus TG-2 iHS | 330 | 53 | 12 | 9 | Very good | Good | Good | Good | Good | 25 | 300 |
| ✓ | 8 | **Canon** PowerShot D20 | 350 | 53 | 12 | 8 | Good | Good | Good | Good | Good | 28 | 280 |
| ✓ | 9 | **Olympus** Tough TG-1 iHS | 350 | 52 | 12 | 8 | Good | Very good | Good | Good | Very good | 25 | 350 |
| CR Best Buy | 10 | **Olympus** Stylus TG-630 iHS | 170 | 52 | 12 | 6 | Good | Very good | Fair | Very good | Good | 28 | 270 |
| CR Best Buy | 11 | **Panasonic** Lumix DMC-TS20 | 180 | 50 | 16 | 5 | Good | Good | Fair | Good | Good | 25 | 250 |

**Ratings Key** Excellent · Very good · Good · Fair · Poor

**CR Best Buy** These models offer the best combination of performance and price. All are recommended.

**Recommended** These are high-performing models that stand out.

## Guide to the Ratings

**Overall score** is based mainly on image quality, ease of use, and versatility, plus LCD, flash, and video quality. **Megapixels** is the number of pixels, in millions, on the sensor. **Weight (oz.)** is with battery, memory card, and strap. **Image quality** combines several tests, including regular photos, low-light photos, and flash photos as well as color tests, among others. **Flash photos** tests the quality of the built-in flash's light output and evenness of illumination. **Video quality** mostly reflects footage shot in regular and low light, with audio quality and macro (close-up) capability also considered. **Ease of use** is our evaluation of the camera's controls, manual, response time, and focusing. **LCD quality** is a judgment of images viewed under various lighting conditions. For **widest angle (mm)**, the lower the number, the broader the vista the camera can capture. **Battery life (shots)** is as the manufacturer states. **Price** is approximate retail.

## Most & Least Reliable

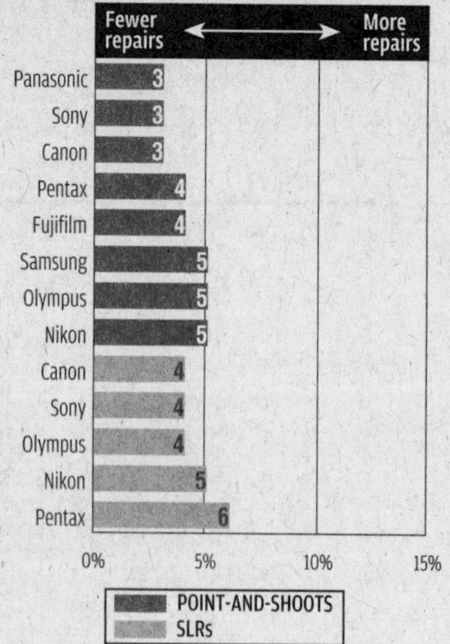


Most cameras are very reliable, and few differences exist among brands. That's what we found when we asked more than 126,000 readers who bought a digital camera between 2008 and 2012 about their experiences. The graph shows the percentage of models for each brand that were repaired or had a serious problem. Differences of less than 3 points aren't meaningful, and we've adjusted the data to eliminate differences linked solely to the age of the digital camera. Models within a brand can vary, and design or manufacture changes might affect future reliability. Still, choosing a brand with a good repair history can improve your odds of getting a reliable model.

Source: Annual Product Reliability Survey, Consumer Reports National Research Center.

# Quick Guide DISHWASHERS

Thanks to tougher federal standards, new dishwashers use less energy and water. Those we recommend aced our washing tests and are quiet.

**Shopping tip**

The three basic cycles—light, normal, and heavy—should be enough for most chores, even for baked-on food.

Scan this or see how, page 11

### What to look for

- Adjustable racks and other loading aids for flexibility
- A soil sensor to adjust the cycle's time and water use, improving efficiency
- A rinse/hold cycle, to prevent soil from setting while you wait for a full load

### What to skip

- Drawer models, which are expensive and tend to use more energy and water than regular models
- A self-cleaning filter, if noise is a concern; look for a model with a manual-clean filter

### What you'll pay

You can pay $1,500 or more for a dishwasher with hidden controls, interactive digital displays, and special grime-fighting cycles. But for clean dishes, sparkling performance starts at about $600.

For more buying advice, go to *ConsumerReports.org/dishwashers*

**All tested models** In performance order, within types.

| Recommended | Rank | Brand & model<br>**Similar models,** in small type, are comparable to tested model. | Price | Overall score<br>0–100<br>P \| F \| G \| VG \| E | Test results: Washing | Energy use | Noise | Ease of use | Cycle time (min.) | Features: Sensor | Self-cleaning filter | Stainless-steel tub | Hidden controls | Ample flatware slots | Adjustable upper rack |
|---|---|---|---|---|---|---|---|---|---|---|---|---|---|---|---|
| **A** | | **CONVENTIONAL** | | | | | | | | | | | | | |
| ✔ | 1 | **Kenmore** Elite 12793<br>Elite 12803 | $1,350 | 85 | ⊜ | ⊜ | ⊜ | ⊖ | 145 | • | | • | Some | • | • |
| ✔ | 2 | **Kenmore** Elite 12783<br>Elite 12763, Elite 12773 | 1,200 | 82 | ⊜ | ⊜ | ⊜ | ⊖ | 135 | • | | • | Some | • | • |
| ✔ | 3 | **Bosch** Ascenta SHX-3AR7[5]UC<br>Ascenta SHE3AR7[ ]UC, Ascenta SHE3ARF[ ]UC (Lowe's), Ascenta SHX3AR5[ ]UC | 700 | 81 | ⊜ | ⊜ | ⊖ | ⊖ | 95 | • | | | All | • | • |
| ✔ | 4 | **Bosch** SHX98M0[9]UC | 1,550 | 81 | ⊜ | ⊖ | ⊜ | ⊖ | 115 | • | | • | Some | • | • |
| ✔ | 5 | **KitchenAid** KDFE454CSS | 1,500 | 81 | ⊜ | ⊜ | ⊜ | ○ | 140 | • | | • | | • | • |
| ✔ | 6 | **Thermador** Topaz Series DWHD640JFM<br>Sapphire Series DWHD650JFM, Sapphire Series DWHD650JFP, Topaz Series DWHD640JFP | 1,500 | 80 | ⊜ | ⊖ | ⊜ | ⊖ | 125 | • | | • | All | • | • |

| Recommended | Rank | Brand & model<br>Similar models, in small type, are comparable to tested model. | Price | Overall score<br>0–100<br>P \| F \| G \| VG \| E | Test results: Washing | Energy use | Noise | Ease of use | Cycle time (min.) | Features: Sensor | Self-cleaning filter | Stainless-steel tub | Hidden controls | Ample flatware slots | Adjustable upper rack |
|---|---|---|---|---|---|---|---|---|---|---|---|---|---|---|---|
| | | **A CONVENTIONAL** continued | | | | | | | | | | | | | |
| ✓ | 7 | **Bosch** 800 Series SHE68R5[2]UC<br>800 Series SHX68R5[ ]UC, 800 Series SHV68R5[3]UC | $ 900 | 80 | Excellent | Excellent | Very good | Very good | 115 | • | | • | Some | • | • |
| ✓ | 8 | **Bosch** 800 Plus Series SHX7PT55UC<br>800 Plus Series SHE7PT55UC, 800 Plus Series SHP7PT55UC, 800 Plus SHX8PT55UC, 800 Plus Series SHV7PT53UC | 1,300 | 80 | Excellent | Excellent | Very good | Very good | 125 | • | | • | All | • | • |
| ✓ | 9 | **Bosch** 500 Series SHP65T55UC<br>500 Series SHX65T55UC, 500 Series DLX SHP65TL5UC, 500 Series SHE65T55UC | 900 | 80 | Excellent | Excellent | Very good | Very good | 125 | • | | • | All | • | • |
| | 10 | **LG** Steam LDF7932[ST] | 1,000 | 80 | Excellent | Very good | Very good | Excellent | 130 | • | • | • | Some | • | • |
| ✓ | 11 | **Miele** Futura Dimension G5575SCSF<br>Futura Dimension G5575SCVi, Futura Dimension Plus G5775SC[ ], Futura Dimension Plus G5705[ ], Futura Dimension G5505[ ] | 1,950 | 80 | Excellent | Excellent | Very good | Very good | 150 | • | | • | All | • | • |
| ✓ | 12 | **Bosch** 300 Series DLX SHX53TL5UC<br>300 Series SHE53T55UC, 300 Series DLX SHE53TL5UC, 300 Series SHP53T55UC, 300 Series DLX SHP53TL5UC, 300 Series DLX SHV53TL3UC, 300 Series SHX53T55UC, 300 Series SHV53T53UC | 850 | 80 | Excellent | Excellent | Good | Very good | 125 | • | | • | All | • | • |
| ✓ | 13 | **KitchenAid** KUDE50CX[SS]<br>KUDE20FX[ ], KUDE40FX[ ], KUDE48FX[ ], KUDE20IX[ ] | 1,350 | 79 | Excellent | Excellent | Good | Very good | 125 | • | | • | | • | • |
| ✓ | 14 | **KitchenAid** KUDE50FBSS | 1,500 | 79 | Excellent | Very good | Excellent | Good | 145 | • | | • | Some | • | • |
| ✓ | 15 | **Bosch** 800 Plus Series SHX9ER5[5]UC<br>800 Plus Series SHV9ER5[3]UC, 800 Plus Series SHE9ER5[5]UC | 1,800 | 79 | Excellent | Very good | Excellent | Very good | 120 | • | | • | All | • | • |
| ✓ | 16 | **Bosch** Evolution 500 SHE55M1[2]UC | 850 | 79 | Excellent | Excellent | Very good | Very good | 110 | • | | • | | • | • |

**Ratings Key** Excellent, Very good, Good, Fair, Poor

**CR Best Buy** These models offer the best combination of performance and price. All are recommended.

✓ **Recommended** These are high-performing models that stand out.

## A CONVENTIONAL continued

| Recommended | Rank | Brand & model<br>Similar models, in small type, are comparable to tested model. | Price | Overall score<br>0–100<br>P \| F \| G \| VG \| E | Test results: Washing | Energy use | Noise | Ease of use | Cycle time (min.) | Features: Sensor | Self-cleaning filter | Stainless-steel tub | Hidden controls | Ample flatware slots | Adjustable upper rack |
|---|---|---|---|---|---|---|---|---|---|---|---|---|---|---|---|
| ✔ | 17 | **Bosch** 800 Series SHE68T55UC 800 Series DLX SHX68TL5UC, 800 Series DLX SHE68TL5UC, 800 Series SHX68T55UC, 800 Series SHV68T53UC | $ 950 | 79 | ⊜ | ⊜ | ⊖ | ⊖ | 125 | • | | • | | • | • |
| | 18 | **LG** LDF6920[WW] | 700 | 79 | ⊜ | ⊖ | ⊖ | ⊖ | 125 | • | • | • | All | • | • |
| | 19 | **Whirlpool** WDF735PABB | 600 | 78 | ⊜ | ⊜ | ○ | ⊖ | 130 | • | | | | • | • |
| | 20 | **Thermador** Emerald Series DWHD440MFM | 1,300 | 78 | ⊖ | ⊜ | ⊖ | ⊖ | 130 | • | | • | All | • | • |
| | 21 | **Kenmore** 1328[3] 1304[ ], 1327[ ] | 650 | 77 | ⊜ | ⊜ | ○ | ⊖ | 120 | • | | | All | • | • |
| | 22 | **Frigidaire** Gallery FGHD2472PF | 700 | 76 | ⊜ | ⊖ | ⊖ | ⊜ | 130 | • | • | • | All | • | • |
| | 23 | **Bosch** 500 Series SHX55R5[5]UC 500 Series SHV55R5[3]UC, 500 Series SHE55R5[ ]UC | 900 | 76 | ⊜ | ⊜ | ⊖ | ⊖ | 110 | • | | • | All | • | • |
| | 24 | **Thermador** DWHD-651JFP DWHD651JFM | 2,200 | 76 | ⊖ | ⊖ | ⊖ | ⊖ | 120 | • | | • | All | • | • |
| | 25 | **KitchenAid** KUDE70FX[SS] KUDE60FX[ ], KUDE60HX[ ] | 1,600 | 76 | ⊜ | ⊜ | ○ | ⊖ | 115 | • | | • | All | • | • |
| | 26 | **Maytag** MDB8959SBS | 800 | 75 | ⊜ | ⊖ | ○ | ⊖ | 115 | • | • | • | All | • | • |
| | 27 | **KitchenAid** KUDS30SX[SS] | 950 | 75 | ⊜ | ⊖ | ○ | ⊖ | 115 | • | • | • | Some | • | • |
| | 28 | **GE** GDT550HSDSS | 650 | 74 | ⊜ | ⊜ | ⊖ | ⊖ | 155 | • | | | Some | • | • |
| | 29 | **Bosch** 300 Series SHX33RL[5]UC 300 Series SHX33RF[ ]UC (Lowe's), 300 Series SHE43RF[ ]UC (Lowe's), 300 Series SHE43RL[ ]UC, 300 Series SHX43R5[ ]UC, 300 Series SHX43RL[5]UC, 300 Series SHE43R5[ ]UC | 720 | 74 | ⊜ | ⊜ | ⊖ | ○ | 110 | • | | • | All | • | • |
| | 30 | **Kenmore** 15693 | 850 | 74 | ⊜ | ⊜ | ⊖ | ○ | 130 | • | | • | All | • | • |
| | 31 | **Miele** Futura Crystal G5105SC Futura Crystal G5175SC | 1,530 | 74 | ⊜ | ⊖ | ○ | ⊖ | 145 | • | | • | | • | • |
| | 32 | **Kenmore** Elite 1396[3] | 1,000 | 73 | ⊜ | ⊜ | ⊖ | ○ | 135 | • | | • | All | • | • |
| | 33 | **LG** LDF7551[ST] LDF7561[ST] | 900 | 72 | ⊖ | ⊖ | ⊖ | ⊖ | 145 | • | | • | All | • | • |

| Recommended | Rank | Brand & model<br>Similar models, in small type, are comparable to tested model. | Price | Overall score<br>0–100<br>P \| F \| G \| VG \| E | Test results: Washing | Energy use | Noise | Ease of use | Cycle time (min.) | Features: Sensor | Self-cleaning filter | Stainless-steel tub | Hidden controls | Ample flatware slots | Adjustable upper rack |
|---|---|---|---|---|---|---|---|---|---|---|---|---|---|---|---|
| **A** | | **CONVENTIONAL** continued | | | | | | | | | | | | | |
| | 34 | **Bosch** Integra 800 Plus SHX58E2[5]UC 800 Plus Series SHV7ER5[ ]UC, 800 Plus Series SHE7ER5[ ]UC, 800 Plus Series SHX7ER5[ ]UC, 800 Plus Series SHX8ER5[ ]UC, 800 Plus Series SHE8ER5[ ]UC | $1,500 | 72 | Very good | Very good | Very good | Very good | 125 | • | | • | All | • | • |
| | 35 | **LG** LDF8072[ST] LDF8574[ST] | 1,100 | 72 | Very good | Very good | Very good | Very good | 145 | • | | • | All | • | • |
| | 36 | **Samsung** DMT800RH[W] | 750 | 72 | Excellent | Very good | Good | Excellent | 120 | • | • | • | All | • | • |
| | 37 | **LG** LDS5540ST | 800 | 71 | Very good | Very good | Very good | Excellent | 145 | • | • | • | | • | • |
| | 38 | **Dacor** Renaissance RDW24S Distinctive DDW24S | 1,700 | 71 | Excellent | Very good | Good | Very good | 150 | • | | • | All | | |
| | 39 | **GE** GDF540HSD[SS] GDF540HGD[ ] | 600 | 71 | Very good | Very good | Very good | Good | 150 | • | | | | • | • |
| | 40 | **GE** GDWT668V[SS] GDWT368V[SS], GDWT308V[ ], GDWT608V[ ], GDWT708V[ ] | 800 | 70 | Very good | Very good | Good | Very good | 135 | • | • | • | All | • | |
| | 41 | **GE** Profile DWT580V[SS] Monogram ZBD8900V[ ], Profile PDWT500V[ ], Profile PDWT 480V[SS], Cafe CDWT980V[SS], Monogram ZBD6900V[ ], Monogram ZBD6920V[SS], Monogram ZBD7920V[SS], Monogram ZBD8920V[SS] | 1,450 | 70 | Very good | Very good | Very good | Excellent | 110 | • | • | • | All | • | • |
| | 42 | **KitchenAid** KUDS30FX[SS] KUDS30CX[ ], KUDC10IX[ ], KUDC10FX[ ], KUDS30IX[ ] | 850 | 70 | Excellent | Very good | Good | Very good | 115 | • | • | • | All | • | • |
| | 43 | **Miele** Futura Classic G4205SC | 1,000 | 70 | Excellent | Very good | Very good | Good | 145 | • | | • | | • | • |
| | 44 | **GE** Profile PDWT200V[WW] Profile PDWT380V[SS], Profile PDWT300V[ ], Profile PDWT180V[SS], Profile PDWT100V[ ], Profile PDWT280V[SS], Cafe CDWT280V[SS] | 850 | 69 | Very good | Very good | Good | Very good | 140 | • | • | • | All | • | |
| | 45 | **Asko** D5894XXL[HS] | 2,400 | 69 | Very good | Excellent | Very good | Very good | 130 | • | | • | All | • | • |

**Ratings Key** Excellent, Very good, Good, Fair, Poor

☑ **CR Best Buy** These models offer the best combination of performance and price. All are recommended.

✓ **Recommended** These are high-performing models that stand out.

| Recommended | Rank | Brand & model<br>Similar models, in small type, are comparable to tested model. | Price | Overall score<br>0–100<br>P \| F \| G \| VG \| E | Test results: Washing | Energy use | Noise | Ease of use | Cycle time (min.) | Features: Sensor | Self-cleaning filter | Stainless-steel tub | Hidden controls | Ample flatware slots | Adjustable upper rack |
|---|---|---|---|---|---|---|---|---|---|---|---|---|---|---|---|
| **A** | | **CONVENTIONAL** continued | | | | | | | | | | | | | |
| | 46 | **GE** GDF520PSD[SS]<br>GDF510PGD[ ], GDT530PSD[SS], GDF-520PGD[ ], GDF510PSD[SS], GDF510PMD[SA] | $ 500 | 69 | ⊖ | ⊖ | ⊖ | ○ | 150 | • | | | | • | |
| | 47 | **Asko** D5634XXL[HS] | 1,350 | 68 | ⊜ | ⊖ | ○ | ⊖ | 150 | • | | • | Some | | |
| | 48 | **Whirlpool** Gold WDT770PAY[M] | 700 | 68 | ⊖ | ⊜ | ○ | ⊖ | 115 | • | | | All | • | • |
| | 49 | **Miele** Futura Diamond G5975SCSF<br>Futura Diamond G5915SCi | 2,700 | 67 | ⊖ | ⊜ | ⊖ | ⊖ | 130 | • | | • | All | • | • |
| | 50 | **GE** GDWF100V[WW]<br>GHDT108V[ ] (Home Depot), GHDT168V[SS] (Home Depot), GDWF160V[ ] | 600 | 67 | ⊖ | ⊖ | ○ | ○ | 110 | • | • | • | | • | |
| | 51 | **Frigidaire** Gallery FGHD2465N[F]<br>Professional FPHD2485N[F] | 600 | 66 | ⊖ | ⊖ | ○ | ⊖ | 130 | • | • | | Some | | • |
| | 53 | **Jenn-Air** Trifecta JDB8700AW[P] | 1,550 | 66 | ⊜ | ⊖ | ⊖ | ○ | 170 | • | | • | All | • | • |
| | 54 | **Frigidaire** Gallery FGBD2431K[W] | 350 | 66 | ⊜ | ○ | ○ | ○ | 155 | | • | | | | |
| | 55 | **Frigidaire** Gallery FGBD2432K[W] Gallery BBBD2432K[ ] (Best Buy), Gallery LGBD2432K[ ] (Lowe's), Gallery DGBD2432K[ ] | 400 | 66 | ⊖ | ⊖ | ○ | ⊖ | 145 | • | • | | | | |
| | 56 | **Scholtes** LFDS3XL60HZ | 1,400 | 66 | ⊖ | ⊜ | ⊖ | ⊖ | 105 | • | | • | All | • | • |
| | 57 | **Frigidaire** Gallery FGBD2445N[F] | 550 | 65 | ⊖ | ⊖ | ○ | ⊖ | 120 | • | • | | | | • |
| | 58 | **Kenmore** 1326[3]<br>1325[ ], 1329[ ] | 750 | 65 | ⊖ | ⊜ | ○ | ⊖ | 130 | • | | • | | • | • |
| | 59 | **Smeg** STA8614XU | 1,000 | 65 | ⊖ | ⊜ | ⊖ | ⊖ | 120 | • | | • | All | • | • |
| | 60 | **Bosch** Ascenta DLX SHX4AT75UC<br>Ascenta SHX4AT55UC | 700 | 64 | ⊜ | ⊜ | ⊖ | ⊖ | 120 | • | | • | All | • | • |
| | 61 | **Whirlpool** WDL785SAAM | 875 | 64 | ⊖ | ⊜ | ○ | ⊖ | 135 | • | | • | | • | • |
| | 62 | **Maytag** MDB4709PA[M]<br>MDB6769PA[ ] | 550 | 64 | ⊖ | ⊖ | ○ | ○ | 105 | • | • | | | • | |
| | 63 | **Whirlpool** Gold WDF530PAY[W]<br>Gold WDT710PAY[ ] | 440 | 63 | ⊖ | ⊜ | ○ | ○ | 105 | • | | | | • | |

| Recommended | Rank | Brand & model<br>Similar models, in small type, are comparable to tested model. | Price | Overall score<br>0–100<br>P \| F \| G \| VG \| E | Test results: Washing | Test results: Energy use | Test results: Noise | Test results: Ease of use | Test results: Cycle time (min.) | Features: Sensor | Features: Self-cleaning filter | Features: Stainless-steel tub | Features: Hidden controls | Features: Ample flatware slots | Features: Adjustable upper rack |
|---|---|---|---|---|---|---|---|---|---|---|---|---|---|---|---|
| | | **A CONVENTIONAL** continued | | | | | | | | | | | | | |
| | 64 | **GE** Monogram ZBD9900R[II] | $1,800 | 62 | Very good | Very good | Very good | Good | 180 | • | | • | All | | • |
| | 65 | **Samsung** DW7933LRA[SR] | 600 | 62 | Very good | Very good | Good | Very good | 150 | • | • | • | | • | • |
| | 66 | **LG** LDF9932[ST] | 1,300 | 62 | Very good | Very good | Very good | Very good | 140 | • | • | • | All | • | • |
| | 67 | **Jenn-Air** Trifecta JDB8200AW[S] | 1,200 | 61 | Very good | Very good | Very good | Good | 170 | • | | • | All | • | • |
| | 68 | **Whirlpool** Gold WDF730PAY[M] | 600 | 61 | Very good | Excellent | Good | Very good | 115 | • | | | | • | • |
| | 69 | **Viking** D3 Series RDDB301[SS]<br>D3 Series RDDB201[ ], Professional VDB301[ ] | 1,450 | 61 | Very good | Very good | Good | Very good | 155 | | | • | All | | |
| | 70 | **Viking** Professional VDB451[SS] FDB451 | 1,950 | 61 | Excellent | Very good | Very good | Very good | 205 | | | • | All | • | |
| | 71 | **Frigidaire** Gallery FGHD2433K[F] | 450 | 61 | Very good | Very good | Good | Very good | 135 | • | • | | Some | • | • |
| | 72 | **Samsung** DMT300RF[W] | 500 | 60 | Very good | Very good | Good | Very good | 170 | • | • | • | | • | • |
| | 73 | **Frigidaire** Professional FPHD2491K[F] | 650 | 60 | Very good | Good | Good | Very good | 180 | • | | • | All | • | • |
| | 74 | **Electrolux** Wave-Touch EWDW6505G[S] | 1,200 | 59 | Very good | Very good | Very good | Excellent | 135 | • | • | • | All | • | • |
| | 75 | **Jenn-Air** JDB3200AW[W] | 1,100 | 59 | Very good | Excellent | Very good | Good | 125 | • | | • | All | • | |
| | 76 | **Maytag** MDB4409PA[W] | 380 | 58 | Very good | Very good | Fair | Good | 115 | • | • | | | • | |
| | 77 | **GE** GLD5766V[SS]<br>GLD5606V[ ], GLD5666V[SS], GLD5708V[ ], GLD5604V[ ] | 520 | 58 | Very good | Very good | Good | Good | 140 | • | • | | All | • | |
| | 78 | **Electrolux** IQ EIDW5905J[S] | 1,000 | 57 | Very good | Excellent | Good | Very good | 90 | • | • | • | All | | • |
| | 79 | **Frigidaire** Gallery FGBD2438PF | 500 | 57 | Very good | Very good | Good | Fair | 130 | | | | | | |
| | 80 | **Fagor** LFA-086XL | 1,300 | 55 | Very good | Very good | Good | Very good | 120 | • | | • | All | • | • |
| | 81 | **Frigidaire** Gallery FGBD2434PF | 400 | 55 | Very good | Very good | Good | Fair | 125 | | | | | | |

**Ratings Key** ⊜ Excellent ⊖ Very good ○ Good ◒ Fair ● Poor

☑ **CR Best Buy** These models offer the best combination of performance and price. All are recommended.

☑ **Recommended** These are high-performing models that stand out.

| Recommended | Rank | Brand & model<br>Similar models, in small type, are comparable to tested model. | Price | Overall score<br>0 100<br>P \| F \| G \| VG \| E | Test results: Washing | Energy use | Noise | Ease of use | Cycle time (min.) | Features: Sensor | Self-cleaning filter | Stainless-steel tub | Hidden controls | Ample flatware slots | Adjustable upper rack |
|---|---|---|---|---|---|---|---|---|---|---|---|---|---|---|---|
| **A** | | **CONVENTIONAL** continued | | | | | | | | | | | | | |
| | 82 | **Amana** ADB1100AWW | $ 300 | 54 | ⊖ | ⊖ | ◒ | ◒ | 160 | | | | | | |
| | 83 | **Electrolux** Icon EDW7505HP[S] | 1,400 | 54 | ○ | ⊖ | ⊖ | ⊜ | 125 | • | • | • | All | • | • |
| | 84 | **Blomberg** DWT57500[SS] | 1,000 | 53 | ○ | ⊜ | ○ | ⊖ | 125 | • | | • | All | • | • |
| | 85 | **Frigidaire** Gallery FGBD2435N[W] | 400 | 53 | ⊖ | ⊖ | ○ | ○ | 135 | • | • | | | | |
| | 86 | **Frigidaire** FFBD2409L[S] | 380 | 52 | ⊖ | ⊖ | ○ | ○ | 125 | • | • | | | | |
| | 87 | **Ikea** Nutid | 650 | 52 | ⊖ | ⊖ | ◒ | ○ | 125 | • | • | • | All | | |
| | 88 | **Summit** DW2432SS | 650 | 48 | ○ | ⊜ | ○ | ○ | 110 | • | | • | | • | • |
| | 89 | **Haier** DWL3225SD[SS] DWL2825DD[ ] | 480 | 45 | ○ | ⊖ | ○ | ○ | 120 | • | • | • | | • | • |
| | 90 | **Haier** DWL7075MC[SS] DWL4035MC[ ] | 750 | 44 | ○ | ○ | ○ | ○ | 120 | • | • | • | All | • | • |
| | 91 | **Viking** Professional VDB450E[SS] Designer Series DFB450E | 1,800 | 44 | ○ | ⊖ | ○ | ⊖ | 170 | • | | • | All | • | |
| | 92 | **Blomberg** DWT55100[SS] | 850 | 44 | ○ | ⊜ | ○ | ⊖ | 125 | • | | • | All | • | • |
| | 94 | **Kenmore** 15112 | 300 | 43 | ○ | ⊜ | ○ | ◒ | 110 | | | | | | |
| | 95 | **Whirlpool** Gold WDT910SAY[M] Gold WDF-750SAY[ ], Gold WDT790SAY[ ] | 800 | 43 | ○ | ⊜ | ⊜ | ⊖ | 125 | • | | • | All | • | • |
| | 96 | **Blomberg** DWT24100[SS] | 600 | 43 | ○ | ⊖ | ○ | ⊖ | 110 | • | | • | | • | • |
| | 97 | **Ikea** Renlig 802.222.43 | 500 | 43 | ○ | ⊜ | ◒ | ◒ | 120 | • | | | | • | |
| | 98 | **Hotpoint** HDA3600DWW | 380 | 38 | ○ | ⊜ | ◒ | ◒ | 110 | | • | | | | |

## Guide to the Ratings

**Overall score** is mostly washing performance and includes noise, energy and water use, and loading. The displayed score is out of a total of 100 points. **Washing** is normal-cycle results with a very dirty full load. **Energy use** is energy and water use for a normal cycle. **Noise** covers listener judgments during fill, wash, and drain. **Ease of use** considers convenience of controls and the ability to hold extra place settings and oversized items. **Cycle time (min.)** is based on a normal cycle, including heated dry, where that feature is available. Under **brand & model**, bracketed letters or numbers mean color code. **Price** is approximate retail.

| Recommended | Rank | Brand & model / Similar models, in small type, are comparable to tested model. | Price | Overall score (0–100; P \| F \| G \| VG \| E) | Test results: Washing | Energy use | Noise | Ease of use | Cycle time (min.) | Features: Sensor | Self-cleaning filter | Stainless-steel tub | Hidden controls | Ample flatware slots | Adjustable upper rack |
|---|---|---|---|---|---|---|---|---|---|---|---|---|---|---|---|
| | | **A CONVENTIONAL** continued | | | | | | | | | | | | | |
| | 99 | **Whirlpool** WDF310PAA[W] <br> WDF310PLA[ ], WDF310PCA[ ] | $ 350 | 35 | ◒ | ⊜ | ◒ | ◒ | 115 | • | | | | | |
| | 100 | **Frigidaire** FBD2400KS | 310 | 34 | ○ | ⊜ | ◒ | ◒ | 90 | | | | | | |
| | 101 | **Amana** ADB1400PY[S] | 380 | 34 | ◒ | ⊜ | ◒ | ○ | 115 | • | | | | • | |
| | 102 | **Amana** ADB1000AWW | 260 | 23 | ◒ | ⊜ | ● | ◒ | 80 | | • | | | | |
| | | **DON'T BUY: PERFORMANCE PROBLEM** This model repeatedly drenched our floor with water while operating. | | | | | | | | | | | | | |
| ✗ | | **Fagor** LFA-65SS | 1,000 | | NA | NA | NA | NA | 0 | • | | • | • | | • |
| | | **B DISHWASHER DRAWERS** | | | | | | | | | | | | | |
| | 1 | **Fisher & Paykel** DD24DCTX7 | 1,300 | 66 | ⊜ | ⊜ | ○ | ○ | 110 | • | | | Some | • | |
| | 2 | **KitchenAid** KUDD03DT[WH] | 1,550 | 43 | ⊜ | ○ | ○ | ○ | 125 | • | | | All | • | |

## Most & Least Reliable

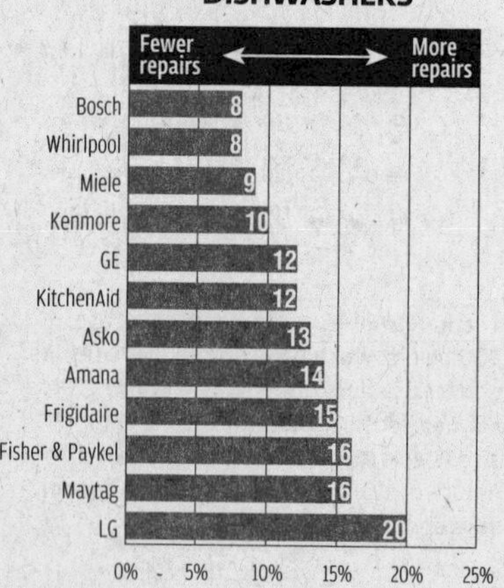


Choosing a dishwasher with a good repair history can improve your odds of getting a reliable model. So each year we survey thousands of our readers about their experiences. LG was the least reliable dishwasher brand in our latest survey. We lacked enough data to include Samsung and Electrolux in the chart, but our analysis shows both brands have been repair-prone. Our findings are based on more than 86,000 dishwashers readers bought new between 2008 and 2012. Differences of fewer than 4 points aren't meaningful. Data are adjusted to eliminate differences linked solely to the dishwasher's age and use. Note that models within a brand may vary, and design or manufacturing changes may affect future reliability.

Source: Annual Product Reliability Survey, Consumer Reports National Research Center.

# Quick Guide DRYERS

**Though washers have become more efficient, dryers haven't changed much. Touchpad controls and stainless steel tubs look impressive, but don't improve performance. Gas and electric dryers perform similarly in our tests.**

### What to look for

- A moisture sensor, to cut down on energy costs and avoid overdrying clothes
- An extended-tumble setting without heat, to prevent wrinkles when you don't remove clothes immediately

### What to skip

- Extra large, super, and super-plus dryer capacity, because the differences aren't meaningful for everyday use
- Steam setting, which left shirts wrinkled in our tests, though it did remove odors better than regular dryers

### What you'll pay

Gas dryers cost about $80 to $150 more than comparable electric models, but the likely savings in fuel costs should more than make up the difference in the long run.

For more buying advice, go to *ConsumerReports.org/dryers*

**Shopping tip**

Look for a dryer that scored a Very Good for noise if it will be near a bedroom.

Scan this or see how, page 11

**Recommended models only** From 259 tested.

| Recommended | Rank | Brand & model<br>Similar models, in small type, are comparable to tested model. | Price | Overall score<br>0–100<br>P \| F \| G \| VG \| E | Test results: Drying performance | Test results: Capacity | Test results: Convenience | Test results: Noise | Features: Stainless-steel drum | Features: Porcelain top | Features: Drying rack | Features: Custom programs | Features: Steam option |
|---|---|---|---|---|---|---|---|---|---|---|---|---|---|
| **A ELECTRIC** | | | | | | | | | | | | | |
| ✓ | 1 | **Samsung** DV50F9A8EVP | $1,100 | 83 | ⊜ | ⊜ | ⊖ | ⊜ | • | | • | • | • |
| ✓ | 2 | **GE** GFDR485EFMC | 1,400 | 81 | ⊜ | ⊜ | ⊜ | ⊖ | • | | • | • | • |
| ✓ | 3 | **Maytag** Maxima XL MED8000AG | 1,450 | 79 | ⊜ | ⊜ | ⊖ | ⊜ | • | | | | • |
| ✓ | 4 | **Kenmore** Elite 81073 | 1,350 | 79 | ⊜ | ⊜ | ⊜ | ⊖ | • | • | • | • | • |
| ✓ | 5 | **LG** DLEX3470[W] | 1,000 | 79 | ⊜ | ⊜ | ⊖ | ⊜ | • | | • | • | • |
| ✓ | 6 | **Samsung** DV456EWHD[WR] | 900 | 78 | ⊜ | ⊜ | ⊖ | ⊖ | | | | • | |
| ✓ | 7 | **Whirlpool** Duet WED96HEAW | 1,300 | 78 | ⊜ | ⊜ | ⊖ | ⊜ | • | | | | • |
| ✓ | 8 | **Maytag** Bravos X MEDX700AG | 900 | 78 | ⊜ | ⊜ | ⊖ | ⊖ | | | | | |
| ✓ | 9 | **Kenmore** Elite 6152[2] | 1,000 | 78 | ⊜ | ⊜ | ⊖ | ⊖ | • | | • | • | • |

| Recommended | Rank | Brand & model<br>Similar models, in small type, are comparable to tested model. | Price | Overall score<br>0–100<br>P \| F \| G \| VG \| E | Test results: Drying performance | Test results: Capacity | Test results: Convenience | Test results: Noise | Features: Stainless-steel drum | Features: Porcelain top | Features: Drying rack | Features: Custom programs | Features: Steam option |
|---|---|---|---|---|---|---|---|---|---|---|---|---|---|
| **A** | | **ELECTRIC** continued | | | | | | | | | | | |
| ✓ | 10 | **LG** DLEX8000[V] | $1,350 | 78 | ⊜ | ⊜ | ⊖ | ⊖ | • | • | • | • | • |
| ✓ | 11 | **GE** GFDS260EFWW | 1,100 | 78 | ⊜ | ⊜ | ⊖ | ⊖ | • | | | • | • |
| ✓ | 12 | **LG** Smart ThinQ DLEX6001V | 1,500 | 78 | ⊜ | ⊜ | ⊖ | ⊖ | • | | • | • | • |
| ✓ | 13 | **LG** DLEX5170[W] | 900 | 78 | ⊜ | ⊜ | ⊖ | ⊜ | • | | • | • | • |
| ✓ | 14 | **Kenmore** 8137[2] | 950 | 78 | ⊜ | ⊜ | ⊖ | ⊖ | • | | • | • | • |
| ✓ | 15 | **Whirlpool** Cabrio WED5700AC | 900 | 78 | ⊜ | ⊜ | ⊖ | ⊖ | | | | | |
| ✓ | 16 | **Samsung** DV457EVGS[GR] | 1,550 | 78 | ⊜ | ⊜ | ⊖ | ⊖ | • | | • | • | • |
| ✓ | 17 | **Whirlpool** Duet WEL98HEBU | 1,500 | 77 | ⊜ | ⊜ | ⊖ | ⊜ | • | | | • | • |
| ✓ | 18 | **Kenmore** 8117[2] | 720 | 77 | ⊜ | ⊖ | ⊖ | ⊜ | | | | | |
| ✓ | 19 | **LG** DLEX3360[W] | 900 | 77 | ⊜ | ⊜ | ⊖ | ⊖ | • | | • | • | • |
| ✓ | 20 | **LG** DLEX4070W | 1,200 | 77 | ⊜ | ⊜ | ⊖ | ⊖ | • | | • | • | • |
| ✓ | 21 | **Kenmore** 6800[2] | 800 | 77 | ⊜ | ⊜ | ⊖ | ⊖ | | | • | | |
| ✓ | 22 | **Whirlpool** Duet WED94HEAW<br>Duet WED88HEAW | 1,100 | 77 | ⊜ | ⊜ | ⊖ | ⊖ | • | | | | • |
| ✓ | 23 | **Samsung** DV520AE[P] | 1,400 | 77 | ⊜ | ⊜ | ⊖ | ⊖ | • | | • | • | • |
| ✓ | 24 | **LG** DLE4870W | 800 | 77 | ⊜ | ⊜ | ⊖ | ⊖ | | | | • | |
| **B** | | **GAS** | | | | | | | | | | | |
| ✓ | 1 | **Samsung** DV50F9A8GVP | $1,200 | 83 | ⊜ | ⊜ | ⊖ | ⊜ | • | | • | • | • |
| ✓ | 2 | **GE** GFDR485GFMC | 1,500 | 81 | ⊜ | ⊜ | ⊜ | ⊖ | • | | • | • | • |
| ✓ | 3 | **Maytag** Maxima XL MGD8000AG | 1,550 | 79 | ⊜ | ⊜ | ⊖ | ⊜ | • | | | | • |
| ✓ | 4 | **Kenmore** Elite 91073 | 1,450 | 79 | ⊜ | ⊜ | ⊜ | ⊖ | • | • | • | • | • |
| ✓ | 5 | **LG** DLGX3471[W] | 1,200 | 79 | ⊜ | ⊜ | ⊖ | ⊜ | • | | • | • | • |
| ✓ | 6 | **Samsung** DV456GWHDWR | 1,000 | 78 | ⊜ | ⊜ | ⊖ | ⊖ | | | | • | |
| ✓ | 7 | **Samsung** DV5451AG[W] | 1,000 | 78 | ⊜ | ⊜ | ⊖ | ⊖ | | | • | | • |
| ✓ | 8 | **Whirlpool** Duet WGD96HEAW | 1,400 | 78 | ⊜ | ⊜ | ⊖ | ⊜ | • | | | | • |
| ✓ | 9 | **Maytag** Bravos X MGDX700AG | 1,000 | 78 | ⊜ | ⊜ | ⊖ | ⊖ | | | | | |
| ✓ | 10 | **Kenmore** Elite 71522 | 1,100 | 78 | ⊜ | ⊜ | ⊖ | ⊖ | • | | • | • | • |
| ✓ | 11 | **LG** DLGX3886[W] DLGX3876[ ] | 1,480 | 78 | ⊜ | ⊜ | ⊖ | ⊖ | • | • | • | • | • |
| ✓ | 12 | **LG** DLGX8001[V] | 1,440 | 78 | ⊜ | ⊜ | ⊖ | ⊖ | • | • | • | • | • |
| ✓ | 13 | **GE** GFDS260GFWW | 1,200 | 78 | ⊜ | ⊜ | ⊖ | ⊖ | • | | | • | • |

| Recommended | Rank | Brand & model<br>Similar models, in small type, are comparable to tested model. | Price | Overall score<br>0–100<br>P \| F \| G \| VG \| E | Test results: Drying performance | Test results: Capacity | Test results: Convenience | Test results: Noise | Features: Stainless-steel drum | Features: Porcelain top | Features: Drying rack | Features: Custom programs | Features: Steam option |
|---|---|---|---|---|---|---|---|---|---|---|---|---|---|
| **B** | | **GAS** continued | | | | | | | | | | | |
| ✓ | 14 | **LG** Smart ThinQ DLEX6002V | $1,600 | 78 | Excellent | Excellent | Very good | Very good | • | | • | • | • |
| ✓ | 15 | **LG** DLGX5171[W] | 1,050 | 78 | Excellent | Excellent | Very good | Excellent | • | | • | • | • |
| ✓ | 16 | **Kenmore** 9137[2] | 1,100 | 78 | Excellent | Excellent | Very good | Very good | • | | • | • | • |
| ✓ | 17 | **Whirlpool** Cabrio WGD5700AC | 1,000 | 78 | Excellent | Excellent | Very good | Very good | | | | | |
| ✓ | 18 | **Samsung** DV5471AG[W] | 1,150 | 78 | Excellent | Excellent | Very good | Very good | • | | • | | • |
| ✓ | 19 | **Samsung** DV457GVGS[GR] | 1,700 | 78 | Excellent | Excellent | Very good | Very good | • | | • | • | • |
| ✓ | 20 | **LG** DLGX5002[W] DLG5002[ ] | 1,080 | 77 | Excellent | Excellent | Very good | Very good | • | | • | • | • |
| ✓ | 21 | **Kenmore** 9117[2] | 900 | 77 | Excellent | Very good | Very good | Excellent | | | | | |
| ✓ | 22 | **LG** DLGX3361[W] | 980 | 77 | Excellent | Excellent | Very good | Very good | • | | • | • | • |
| ✓ | 23 | **LG** DLGX4071W | 1,300 | 77 | Excellent | Excellent | Very good | Very good | • | | • | • | • |
| ✓ | 24 | **LG** DLGX2551[W] | 1,180 | 77 | Excellent | Excellent | Very good | Very good | | | • | • | • |
| CR Best Buy | 25 | **Kenmore** 7800[2] | 900 | 77 | Excellent | Excellent | Very good | Very good | | | • | | |
| ✓ | 26 | **Whirlpool** Duet WGD94HEAW<br>Duet WGD88HEAW | 1,200 | 77 | Excellent | Excellent | Very good | Very good | • | | | | • |
| ✓ | 27 | **Samsung** DV520AG[P] | 1,480 | 77 | Excellent | Excellent | Very good | Very good | • | | • | • | • |
| ✓ | 28 | **LG** DLG4871W | 900 | 77 | Excellent | Excellent | Very good | Very good | | | | • | |

**Ratings Key** Excellent · Very good · Good · Fair · Poor

**CR Best Buy** These models offer the best combination of performance and price. All are recommended.

✓ **Recommended** These are high-performing models that stand out.

## Guide to the Ratings

**Overall score** is based primarily on drying performance, drum volume, and noise. The displayed score is out of a total of 100 points. **Drying performance** is measured for multiple fabrics and load sizes. **Capacity** refers to the drum volume of models we tested, which varied from about 6 to 8 cu. ft. **Convenience** takes into account controls and ergonomics, such as ease of loading and unloading, servicing the lint filter, whether the door could clear a tall basket, and whether the machine has a raised edge to contain spills. **Noise** reflects panelists' judgments. Under Features, a **stainless-steel drum** is likely to resist damage better than plastic and painted metal drums. A **porcelain top** resists scratching better than a painted one but generally adds to a dryer's cost. **Drying rack** attaches inside the drum to keep items such as sneakers or sweaters from tumbling. **Custom programs** allows you to save your favorite settings. Generally, a water hook-up is required with the **steam option** feature. In this cycle, a small amount of water is sprayed into the drum while tumbling with heat. It helps to reduce wrinkles and odors, but it is intended for only a few garments at a time. **Price** is approximate retail for models in white.

## Most & Least Reliable

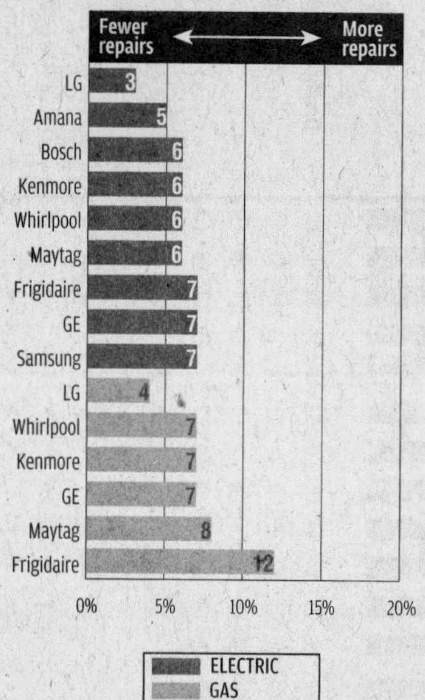


LG was among the least repair-prone brands of electric clothes dryer, and it was the least repair-prone brand of gas clothes dryer. Frigidaire was the most repair-prone brand of gas dryer. That's what we found when we asked almost 80,000 readers who bought a dryer between 2008 and 2012 about their experiences. The graph shows the percentage of machines for each brand that needed a repair or had a serious problem. Differences of less than 3 points aren't meaningful, and we've adjusted the data to eliminate differences linked solely to age and use of the dryer. Models within a brand may vary, and design or manufacture changes may affect future reliability. Still, choosing a brand with a good repair history can improve your odds of getting a reliable model.

Source: Annual Product Reliability Survey, Consumer Reports National Research Center.

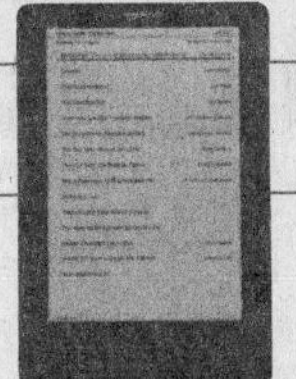

# Quick Guide E-BOOK READERS

**Light weight, long battery life, and crisp type make e-book readers the best device for reading e-books.**

### What to look for

- A 6-inch screen, for the best balance of screen size and portability for most people
- Touch capability to help you easily select content and turn the pages

### What to skip

- 3G access to the Internet; while that offers the most flexibility for obtaining new content, models with Wi-Fi-only access suit most users and generally cost less
- Color capability. For the most part, you're better off buying a tablet to get this

### What you'll pay

Prices typically range from $100 to $200, though some cost less than $100.

For more buying advice, go to *ConsumerReports.org/ebooks*

### Shopping tip

Some e-readers allow you to borrow e-books from public libraries.

Scan this or see how, page 11

**All tested models** In performance order, within types.

| Recommended | Rank | Brand & model<br>**Similar models,** in small type, are comparable to tested model. | Price | Overall score<br>0–100<br>P \| F \| G \| VG \| E | Readability | Versatility | Responsiveness | Page turn | Navigation | File support | Touch screen |
|---|---|---|---|---|---|---|---|---|---|---|---|
| | | **A 8-INCH OR LARGER** | | | | | | | | | |
| ☑ | 1 | **Amazon** Kindle DX (3rd Gen) | $380 | 71 | ⊜ | ○ | ⊜ | ○ | ⊜ | ⊖ | |
| | 2 | **Ectaco** jetBook Color | 500 | 47 | ○ | ○ | ○ | ◒ | ⊖ | ⊜ | • |
| | | **B 6- TO 7-INCH** | | | | | | | | | |
| ☑ | 1 | **Barnes & Noble** Nook Simple Touch with GlowLight | 120 | 83 | ⊜ | ⊖ | ⊜ | ⊜ | ⊜ | ⊖ | • |
| ✅ | 2 | **Barnes & Noble** Nook Simple Touch | 100 | 82 | ⊜ | ⊖ | ⊜ | ⊜ | ⊜ | ⊖ | • |
| ☑ | 3 | **Amazon** Kindle Paperwhite 3G with Special Offers<br>Kindle Paperwhite 3G without Special Offers | 180 | 82 | ⊜ | ⊖ | ⊖ | ⊜ | ⊜ | ⊖ | • |
| ☑ | 4 | **Amazon** Kindle Paperwhite with Special Offers<br>Kindle Paperwhite without Special Offers | 120 | 81 | ⊜ | ○ | ⊖ | ⊜ | ⊜ | ⊖ | • |

| Recommended | Rank | Brand & model<br>Similar models, in small type, are comparable to tested model. | Price | Overall score (0–100; P \| F \| G \| VG \| E) | Test results: Readability | Versatility | Responsiveness | Page turn | Navigation | File support | Touch screen |
|---|---|---|---|---|---|---|---|---|---|---|---|
| **B 6- TO 7-INCH continued** | | | | | | | | | | | |
| Recommended | 5 | **Amazon** Kindle Keyboard 3G with Special Offers<br>Kindle Keyboard 3G without Special Offers | $140 | 79 | Excellent | Very good | Excellent | Excellent | Very good | Very good | |
| CR Best Buy | 6 | **Kobo** eReader Touch Edition | 100 | 75 | Very good | Very good | Excellent | Very good | Very good | Very good | • |
| CR Best Buy | 7 | **Amazon** Kindle with Special Offers<br>Kindle without Special Offers | 70 | 74 | Excellent | Good | Excellent | Very good | Very good | Very good | |
| Recommended | 8 | **Sony** Reader PRS-T2 | 130 | 74 | Excellent | Very good | Very good | Good | Excellent | Excellent | • |
| Recommended | 9 | **Kobo** Vox eReader | 180 | 66 | Very good | Very good | Good | Excellent | Excellent | Good | • |
| | 10 | **Bookeen** Cybook Orizon | 150 | 54 | Good | Good | Very good | Fair | Very good | Very good | • |
| Recommended | 11 | **Aluratek** LIBRE Touch (AEBK08FB) | 150 | 50 | Fair | Good | Good | Good | Very good | Very good | • |
| | 12 | **Kobo** Wireless eReader | 70 | 48 | Good | Good | Good | Fair | Fair | Very good | |
| **C 5-INCH OR SMALLER** | | | | | | | | | | | |
| | 1 | **Ectaco** jetBook mini | 120 | 43 | Good | Fair | Fair | Excellent | Good | Fair | |

**Ratings Key** Excellent Very good Good Fair Poor

**CR Best Buy** These models offer the best combination of performance and price. All are recommended.

**Recommended** These are high-performing models that stand out.

## Guide to the Ratings

**Overall score** is in performance order, based on display readability, e-book reader versatility, performance, page turn, navigation, and file versatility. The displayed score is out of a total of 100 points. **Readability** is a measurement of how well the e-book reader can be viewed in various lighting conditions. **Versatility** mainly includes characteristics that aid in usefulness and convenience. **Responsiveness** is a speed measurement of how quickly an e-book reader can turn on from full off, resume from sleep, open an e-book, and transfer an e-book from a computer via USB. **Page turn** measures how quickly an e-book reader can turn to the next page of an e-book. **Navigation** includes the reader's ability to rotate to landscape and portrait mode, automatically and manually bookmark a page, search for an e-book, search through an online bookstore, and the presence of an accelerometer. **File support** is a Rating of typical e-book formats supported as well as other typical file formats you may want to read on an e-book reader. The following formats are rated: EPUB, PDF, MOBI, Word documents, TXT, RTF, JPEG, and GIF. **Touch screen** is a full touch-sensitive display that responds to light contact with a stylus, finger, or both. **Price** is approximate retail.

# Quick Guide GAS GRILLS

You don't have to spend a fortune to get great-tasting grilled food, and many lower-priced grills now have side burners and other perks once found only on the priciest of grills.

### What to look for

- Burners made of high-quality stainless steel, cast iron, or cast brass, which typically carry a 10-year or longer warranty
- Stainless-steel and cast-iron grates for sturdiness and rust-resistance (you'll need to oil uncoated cast grates)
- A battery-powered electronic igniter, usually easier and more reliable than push-button or rotary starters
- Side burners to handle the veggies while the burgers cook; some can sear meat

### What to skip

- Buying by Btu, because more Btu/hr. doesn't guarantee faster preheating or better searing and cooking

### What you'll pay

Figure on $300 to $600 for a grill that can handle most of your cooking needs; some include stainless trim at that price. Several midsized grills that cost less than $600 outcooked models that cost hundreds of dollars more.

For more buying advice, go to *ConsumerReports.org/grills*

### Shopping tip

Large grills fit 30 or more burgers; a medium fits 16 to 30, based on our measurements of main cooking area.

Scan this or see how, page 11

**Recommended models only** From 165 tested.

| Recommended | Rank | Brand & model (Similar models, in small type, are comparable to tested model.) | Price | Overall score (0–100; P \| F \| G \| VG \| E) | Test results: Preheat performance | High temp evenness | Low temp evenness | Indirect cooking | Convenience | Features: Stainless-steel grates | Coated-cast-iron grates | All or mostly stainless | Long-warranty burners | Side burner |
|---|---|---|---|---|---|---|---|---|---|---|---|---|---|---|
| **A LARGE** | | | | | | | | | | | | | | |
| ✔ | 1 | **Jenn-Air** 720-0709 (Sam's Club) 720-0709B (Sam's Club) | $950 | 77 | Very good | Excellent | Very good | Very good | Good | • | | • | | • |
| ✔ | 2 | **KitchenAid** 720-0709C (Sam's Club) | 800 | 77 | Very good | Excellent | Very good | Very good | Good | • | | • | | • |
| ✔ | 3 | **Grand Hall** Grand Tech | 500 | 76 | Very good | Excellent | Very good | Very good | Very good | | • | | • | |

**Ratings Key** ⊜ Excellent ⊖ Very good ○ Good ◒ Fair ● Poor

✔ **CR Best Buy** These models offer the best combination of performance and price. All are recommended.

✔ **Recommended** These are high-performing models that stand out.

| Recommended | Rank | Brand & model<br>**Similar models,** in small type, are comparable to tested model. | Price | Overall score<br>0–100<br>P \| F \| G \| VG \| E | Test results: Preheat performance | Test results: High temp evenness | Test results: Low temp evenness | Test results: Indirect cooking | Test results: Convenience | Features: Stainless-steel grates | Features: Coated-cast-iron grates | Features: All or mostly stainless | Features: Long-warranty burners | Features: Side burner |
|---|---|---|---|---|---|---|---|---|---|---|---|---|---|---|
| | | **B MIDSIZE** | | | | | | | | | | | | |
| ✓ | 1 | **Weber** Spirit SP-320 46700401<br>Spirit SP-310 46500401 | $600 | 83 | ⊖ | ⊜ | ⊜ | ⊜ | ⊜ | • | | • | • | • |
| ✓ | 2 | **Vermont** Castings Signature Series VCS300SSP<br>Signature Series VCS323SSP | 950 | 80 | ⊖ | ⊜ | ⊜ | ⊜ | ○ | | • | • | • | |
| ✓ | 3 | **Weber** Genesis S-330<br>Genesis S-310 | 950 | 79 | ⊖ | ⊜ | ⊜ | ○ | ⊜ | • | | • | • | • |
| ✓ | 4 | **Char-Broil** Red 463250511 (Home Depot) Gourmet TRU-Infrared 463251713 (Home Depot) | 400 | 78 | ⊖ | ⊜ | ⊜ | ⊜ | ○ | | • | | • | • |
| ✓ | 5 | **Weber** Spirit E-320 46710001<br>Spirit E-310 46510001 | 820 | 77 | ⊖ | ⊖ | ⊜ | ⊖ | ⊜ | | • | | • | • |
| ✓ | 6 | **Brinkmann** 810-2545-C (Walmart)<br>810-2546-C (Walmart) | 260 | 76 | ⊖ | ⊜ | ⊖ | ⊖ | ○ | | • | | | • |
| ✓ | 7 | **Weber** Genesis E-330<br>Genesis E-320, Genesis E-310 | 800 | 75 | ⊖ | ⊜ | ⊜ | ○ | ⊜ | | • | | • | • |
| ✓ | 8 | **Kenmore** 16142 | 350 | 74 | ⊖ | ⊖ | ⊜ | ⊖ | ○ | | • | • | | • |
| | | **C PORTABLE OR SMALL** | | | | | | | | | | | | |
| ✓ | 1 | **Weber** Spirit E-220 46310001 Spirit S-210 46110001, Spirit E-210 46110001 | 450 | 79 | ⊖ | ⊜ | ⊜ | ⊖ | ⊜ | | • | | • | • |
| ✓ | 2 | **Napoleon** Terrace SE325PK | 600 | 72 | ⊖ | ⊖ | ⊜ | ⊖ | ○ | | • | • | • | |

## Guide to the Ratings

**Overall score** is based on performance, convenience, and features. The displayed score is out of a total of 100 points. **Preheat performance** indicates how hot the grill's surface is, and how quickly and evenly it reached that temperature after 10 minutes of preheating. **High-temp** and **low-temp evenness** is measured across the grill's surface using thermocouples. **Indirect cooking** indicates how well the grill will slow-cook food when only some of the burners are on and the food isn't placed directly over the flames. **Convenience** is an evaluation of construction, materials, and features. **Price** is approximate retail. Not every model with a rotisserie burner comes with a rotisserie motor and spit.

# Quick Guide GENERATORS

**Some of the best portable generators can power a houseful of lights and appliances for well under $1,000. But a larger stationary model can power everything with far less fuss.**

**What to look for**

- Enough wattage for your needs. Figure on 5,000 to 7,000 watts for most home items; 10,000 watts or more for central AC, a washer and dryer, and an electric range
- A propane or natural-gas hookup. It saves the storage and potential sourcing hassles of gasoline and is found on all stationary models and some portables
- Automatic low-oil shutoff, which protects the engine from damage. All stationary models and some portables have it
- Electric start for portables, to eliminate yanking on a starter cord

**What to skip**

- Big surge-watt promises; models that scored well in our tests were up to the higher watts motorized appliances draw when they cycle on

**What you'll pay**

Figure on $600 to $1,500 for most 5,000- to 7,000-watt portables; $1,800 to $3,200 for a similar-wattage stationary model; roughly $3,500 for higher-watt models.

**Shopping tip**

Factor in another $500 to $900 for a transfer switch to safely power your home's electrical box.

Scan this or see how, page 11

For more buying advice, go to *ConsumerReports.org/generators*

**Recommended models only** From 27 tested.

| Recommended | Rank | Brand & model | Price | Overall score (0–100; P \| F \| G \| VG \| E) | Test results: Ease of use | Power delivery | Noise | Power quality | Run time range (hr.) | Features: Claimed output (watts) | Fuel type | Electric start | Fuel gauge |
|---|---|---|---|---|---|---|---|---|---|---|---|---|---|
| **A PORTABLE** | | | | | | | | | | | | | |
| ✓ | 1 | **Troy-Bilt** XP7000 30477 | $900 | 72 | ⊖ | ⊜ | ◒ | ○ | 12-18 | 7000 | gas | • | • |
| ✓ | 2 | **Honda** EM6500SXK2 | 2,800 | 70 | ⊖ | ⊜ | ○ | ⊖ | 8-13 | 5500 | gas | • | • |
| ✓ | 3 | **Briggs & Stratton** 30470 | 900 | 69 | ⊖ | ⊜ | ◒ | ⊖ | 8-12 | 7000 | gas | • | • |
| ✓ | 4 | **Honda** EU6500iS | 4,500 | 69 | ⊜ | ○ | ⊜ | ⊜ | 5-11 | 5500 | gas | • | • |

| Recommended | Rank | Brand & model | Price | Overall score (0–100; P \| F \| G \| VG \| E) | Test results: Ease of use | Test results: Power delivery | Test results: Noise | Test results: Power quality | Test results: Run time range (hr.) | Features: Claimed output (watts) | Features: Fuel type | Features: Electric start | Features: Fuel gauge |
|---|---|---|---|---|---|---|---|---|---|---|---|---|---|
| **A** | | **PORTABLE** continued | | | | | | | | | | | |
| CR Best Buy | 5 | **Predator** 68530 | $ 600 | 68 | Very good | Excellent | Fair | Very good | 8-13 | 7000 | gas | • | • |
| CR Best Buy | 6 | **Generac** GP5500 5939 | 700 | 67 | Very good | Excellent | Fair | Very good | 8-14 | 5500 | gas | | • |
| Recommended | 7 | **NorthStar** 165603 | 1,500 | 66 | Very good | Excellent | Good | Good | 8-12 | 6600 | gas | | |
| Recommended | 8 | **Champion** 41537 | 1,000 | 66 | Very good | Excellent | Fair | Very good | 7-11 | 7500 | gas | • | • |
| Recommended | 9 | **Troy-Bilt** 6000 30475 | 700 | 65 | Good | Excellent | Good | Very good | 9-16 | 6000 | gas | | • |
| **B** | | **LARGE STATIONARY** | | | | | | | | | | | |
| Recommended | 1 | **Kohler** 14RESAL | 3,700 | 93 | Excellent | Excellent | Very good | Excellent | 134-230 | NG 12000 LPG 14000 | LPG/NG | • | |
| Recommended | 2 | **Generac** 6241 | 3,500 | 91 | Excellent | Excellent | Good | Excellent | 120-236 | NG 13000 LPG 14000 | LPG/NG | • | |
| **C** | | **SMALL STATIONARY** | | | | | | | | | | | |
| Recommended | 1 | **Kohler** 8.5 RES-QS7 | 3,200 | 92 | Excellent | Excellent | Very good | Excellent | 196-252 | NG 7000 LPG 8500 | LPG/NG | • | NA |
| CR Best Buy | 2 | **Generac** 6237 | 2,250 | 91 | Excellent | Excellent | Good | Excellent | 265-408 | NG 7000 LPG 8000 | LPG/NG | • | |
| Recommended | 3 | **Generac** CorePower 5837 | 1,800 | 77 | Excellent | Very good | Good | Very good | 226-366 | NG 6000 LPG 7000 | LPG/NG | • | NA |

**Ratings Key** Excellent, Very good, Good, Fair, Poor

**CR Best Buy** These models offer the best combination of performance and price. All are recommended.

**Recommended** These are high-performing models that stand out.

## Guide to the Ratings

**Overall score** is based on power delivery, power quality, run time, noise, and ease of use. **Ease of use** includes starting, transport (for portables), and helpful features such as fuel shutoff. **Power delivery** indicates how much wattage models delivered and how well they handled surges in power demand over various loads. **Noise** was measured at 23 and 50 feet from the generator. **Power quality** evaluates a generator's ability to deliver power smoothly, with consistent voltage. **Run time range (hr.)** is our average of how long a generator ran, over various loads, on a full tank of fuel. In features, under **claimed output (watts)** and **fuel type,** LPG=propane and NG=natural gas. **Price** is approximate retail.

# Quick Guide LAWN MOWERS

You don't have to spend $600 to get a great mower: Some top-rated self-propelled Hondas start at about $400, while some top Toros and Troy-Bilts cost even less.

Mowers with multiple drive speeds cost more than single-speed mowers, but can save time with added flexibility.

Scan this or see how, page 11

**What to look for**

- An electric push-type mower (corded or cordless) for small, level lawns
- A gas-powered mower for larger lawns and long or thick grass and weeds
- Side-discharge capability for when grass is too tall to mulch or bag effectively
- Rear-wheel drive for slopes
- A blade-brake clutch, which stops only the blade when you release the handlebar lever
- A washout port that accepts a hose for easy cleaning

**What to skip**

- A larger engine, which doesn't necessarily mean higher-quality mowing

**What you'll pay**

Figure on $300 to $600 for top-scoring gas self-propelled mowers, $400 for battery-powered models, and $200 to $250 for a capable push gas or corded-electric mower.

For more buying advice, go to *ConsumerReports.org/mowers*

Recommended models only From 79 tested.

| Recommended | Rank | Brand & model (Similar models, in small type, are comparable to tested model.) | Price | Overall score (0–100; P \| F \| G \| VG \| E) | Test results: Mulching | Bagging | Side discharging | Handling | Ease of use | Features: Forward speeds | Drive wheels | Deck size (in.) | Engine size | Electric start | Blade brake clutch |
|---|---|---|---|---|---|---|---|---|---|---|---|---|---|---|---|
| **A ELECTRIC-BATTERY SELF-PROPELLED** | | | | | | | | | | | | | | | |
| ✔ | 1 | **Black & Decker** SPCM1936 | $450 | 61 | ⊖ | ○ | ⊖ | ⊖ | ⊖ | var. | rear | 19 | 36 volts | • | NA |
| **B GAS MULTIPLE SPEEDS SELF-PROPELLED** | | | | | | | | | | | | | | | |
| ✔ | 1 | **Honda** HRX217VKA | 600 | 83 | ⊜ | ⊜ | ⊖ | ⊜ | ⊖ | var. | rear | 21 | 190 | | |
| ✔ | 2 | **Honda** HRR2169VLA | 500 | 83 | ⊜ | ⊜ | ⊖ | ⊜ | ⊜ | var. | rear | 21 | 160 | • | |
| ✔ | 3 | **Toro** 20381 20382 | 520 | 82 | ⊜ | ⊜ | ⊜ | ⊜ | ⊖ | var. | rear | 21 | 159 | | |

| Recommended | Rank | Brand & model (Similar models, in small type, are comparable to tested model.) | Price | Overall score (0–100; P \| F \| G \| VG \| E) | Test results: Mulching | Bagging | Side discharging | Handling | Ease of use | Features: Forward speeds | Drive wheels | Deck size (in.) | Engine size | Electric start | Blade brake clutch |
|---|---|---|---|---|---|---|---|---|---|---|---|---|---|---|---|
| **B GAS MULTIPLE SPEEDS SELF-PROPELLED** continued | | | | | | | | | | | | | | | |
| Recommended | 4 | **Honda** HRR2169VYA | $480 | 82 | Excellent | Excellent | Very good | Excellent | Very good | var. | rear | 21 | 160 | | • |
| CR Best Buy | 5 | **Honda** HRR2169VKA | 400 | 81 | Excellent | Excellent | Very good | Excellent | Very good | var. | rear | 21 | 160 | | |
| Recommended | 6 | **Toro** Recycler 20333 Recycler 20334 | 400 | 75 | Excellent | Very good | Very good | Very good | Very good | var. | rear | 22 | 190 | | • |
| CR Best Buy | 7 | **Troy-Bilt** TB-280ES 12AGA26G | 340 | 73 | Very good | Very good | Very good | Very good | Very good | var. | front | 21 | 190 | • | |
| CR Best Buy | 8 | **Toro** Recycler 20332 | 360 | 73 | Excellent | Very good | Very good | Very good | Good | var. | rear | 22 | 190 | | |
| CR Best Buy | 9 | **Troy-Bilt** TB-320 12AVC35U | 330 | 72 | Very good | Very good | Very good | Very good | Very good | var. | rear | 21 | 190 | | |
| Recommended | 10 | **Ariens** Razor 911179 | 400 | 70 | Very good | Excellent | Good | Good | Very good | var. | rear | 21 | 159 | • | |
| **C GAS SINGLE SPEED SELF-PROPELLED** | | | | | | | | | | | | | | | |
| CR Best Buy | 1 | **Toro** 20370 | 280 | 66 | Excellent | Very good | Very good | Fair | Good | 1 | front | 22 | 149 | | |
| Recommended | 2 | **Toro** 20371 | 300 | 65 | Excellent | Very good | Very good | Fair | Good | 1 | front | 22 | 149 | | |
| Recommended | 3 | **Yard Man** 12A-18M7 | 250 | 60 | Very good | Good | Very good | Fair | Very good | 1 | rear | 19 | 173 | • | |

| Recommended | Rank | Brand & model (Similar models, in small type, are comparable to tested model.) | Price | Overall score (0–100; P \| F \| G \| VG \| E) | Test results: Mulching | Bagging | Side discharging | Handling | Ease of use | Features: Can bag | Can mulch | Can side discharge | Deck size (in.) | Engine size |
|---|---|---|---|---|---|---|---|---|---|---|---|---|---|---|
| **D ELECTRIC-BATTERY PUSH** | | | | | | | | | | | | | | |
| Recommended | 1 | **Black & Decker** CM1936 CM1936ZF2 | $400 | 59 | Very good | Good | Good | Good | Very good | • | • | • | 19 | 36 volts |
| Recommended | 2 | **Black & Decker** CMM1200 | 430 | 58 | Very good | Good | Good | Good | Very good | • | • | • | 19 | 24 volts |
| Recommended | 3 | **Toro** 20360 | 420 | 56 | Very good | Fair | NA | Good | Very good | • | • | | 20 | 36 volts |

**Ratings Key** Excellent · Very good · Good · Fair · Poor

**CR Best Buy** These models offer the best combination of performance and price. All are recommended.

**Recommended** These are high-performing models that stand out.

| Recommended | Rank | Brand & model<br>Similar models, in small type, are comparable to tested model. | Price | Overall score<br>0–100<br>P \| F \| G \| VG \| E | Test results: Mulching | Bagging | Side discharging | Handling | Ease of use | Features: Can bag | Can mulch | Can side discharge | Deck size (in.) | Engine size |
|---|---|---|---|---|---|---|---|---|---|---|---|---|---|---|
| **E** | | **ELECTRIC-CORDED PUSH** | | | | | | | | | | | | |
| ☑ | 1 | **Black & Decker** MM875 | $240 | 56 | ⊖ | ⊖ | ○ | ◒ | ⊖ | • | • | • | 19 | 12 amps |
| **F** | | **GAS PUSH** | | | | | | | | | | | | |
| ✔ | 1 | **Cub** Cadet SC100 11A-A92J | 250 | 71 | ⊖ | ⊖ | ⊖ | ⊖ | ⊖ | • | • | • | 21 | 159 |
| ✔ | 2 | **Craftsman** 37432 | 220 | 67 | ⊖ | ○ | ⊖ | ⊖ | ⊖ | • | • | • | 21 | 149 |
| ✔ | 3 | **Yard Machines** 11A-B96N | 240 | 67 | ⊖ | ⊖ | ⊜ | ⊖ | ○ | • | • | • | 21 | 190 |
| ☑ | 4 | **Ariens** Razor 911173 | 350 | 65 | ⊖ | ⊜ | ○ | ◒ | ⊖ | • | • | • | 21 | 159 |

## Guide to the Ratings

**Overall score** is based mainly on cutting performance, handling, and ease of use. The displayed score is out of a total of 100 points. **Mulching** is how evenly clippings were cut and distributed. **Bagging** is filling evenness and capacity with full bag(s), including clogged chutes. **Side-discharging** is how evenly clippings were dispersed. **Handling** is ease of using drive controls, pushing, pulling, U-turns, and other maneuvers. **Ease of use** is ease of starting, using blade-stopping controls, changing speeds, and adjusting cut height. For gas-powered mowers, **engine size** is in cubic centimeters; electric models are rated in volts for cordless or amperes for corded. **Price** is approximate retail for mowers and attachments.

## Most & Least Reliable

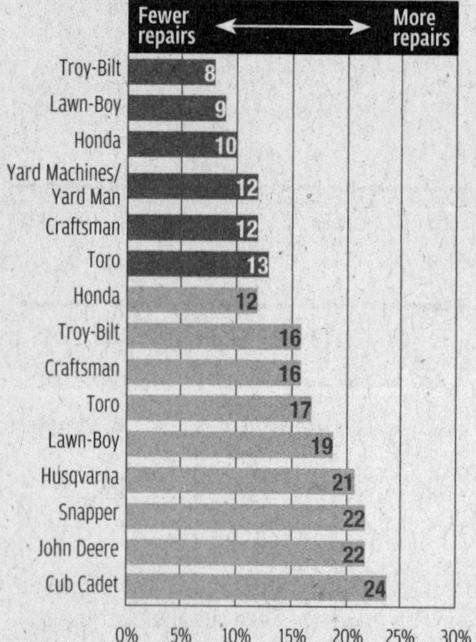


Choosing a mower brand with a good repair history can improve your odds of getting a reliable model. So each year we survey thousands of our readers about their experiences. While we found no standouts for push mowers, Cub Cadet, John Deere, Snapper, and Husqvarna were among the most repair-prone brands—and Honda among the least—for self-propelled mowers. As of 2013, Snapper mowers are being made by the company that makes Craftsman and Troy-Bilt models; we'll see if Snapper's reliability improves.

Our findings are based on 9,149 push and 34,032 self-propelled mowers readers bought new from 2008 through the first half of 2012. Differences of fewer than 5 points aren't meaningful, and data are adjusted to eliminate differences linked to mower age and use. Models within a brand may vary, and changes in design or manufacture may affect future reliability.

Source: Annual Product Reliability Survey, Consumer Reports National Research Center.

# Quick Guide LAWN TRACTORS

Front-engine lawn tractors are still the riding mower of choice for most buyers. But tight-turning, zero-turn-radius models are gaining fast, despite being pricier and harder to control on steep slopes.

**What to look for**

- A high-back seat for added comfort and support
- Variable drive speeds you control with a foot pedal
- A washout port that accepts a hose for cleaning beneath
- Electric power takeoff to engage and disengage the blades without a lever
- A visible fuel gauge

**What to skip**

- Zero-turn-radius riders for steep slopes, where riders can be hard to steer and stop
- Small rear-engine riders, which typically take a 30-inch bite but can cost as much as a wider-cutting lawn tractor
- Pricey bagging systems; mulch kits cost far less and often yield comparable results

**What you'll pay**

About $1,500 to $1,800 for tractors; $2,200-plus for many zero-turn riders.

For more buying advice, go to *ConsumerReports.org/tractors*

**Shopping tip**

Check our scores for the mowing mode you prefer before deciding on any tractor or riding mower.

Scan this or see how, page 11

Recommended models only From 63 tested.

| Recommended | Rank | Brand & model (Similar models, in small type, are comparable to tested model.) | Price | Overall score (0–100; P \| F \| G \| VG \| E) | Test results: Side discharging | Mulching | Bagging | Handling | Ease of use | Features: Deck size (in.) | Engine power (hp) |
|---|---|---|---|---|---|---|---|---|---|---|---|
| **A** | | **LAWN TRACTORS** | | | | | | | | | |
| CR Best Buy | 1 | **Snapper** NXT2346 | $2,800 | 76 | Very good | Very good | Very good | Excellent | Excellent | 46 | 23 |
| Recommended | 2 | **John Deere** X310 | 4,000 | 75 | Very good | Very good | Excellent | Excellent | Excellent | 42 | 18.5 |
| Recommended | 3 | **John Deere** X304 | 3,600 | 75 | Very good | Very good | Excellent | Excellent | Very good | 42 | 18.5 |
| CR Best Buy | 4 | **John Deere** D110 D130, D120 | 1,700 | 74 | Very good | Very good | Very good | Excellent | Very good | 42 | 19.5 |
| CR Best Buy | 5 | **Husqvarna** YTH21K46 | 1,600 | 73 | Very good | Very good | Very good | Excellent | Very good | 46 | 21 |

**Ratings Key** Excellent, Very good, Good, Fair, Poor

**CR Best Buy** These models offer the best combination of performance and price. All are recommended.

**Recommended** These are high-performing models that stand out.

| Recommended | Rank | Brand & model<br>Similar models, in small type, are comparable to tested model. | Price | Overall score<br>0–100<br>P \| F \| G \| VG \| E | Test results: Side discharging | Mulching | Bagging | Handling | Ease of use | Features: Deck size (in.) | Engine power (hp) |
|---|---|---|---|---|---|---|---|---|---|---|---|
| **A** | | **LAWN TRACTORS** continued | | | | | | | | | |
| Recommended | 6 | **John Deere** X300 | $3,000 | 73 | Very good | Very good | Excellent | Very good | Very good | 42 | 18.5 |
| CR Best Buy | 7 | **Craftsman** 28856 | 1,600 | 72 | Very good | Very good | Excellent | Excellent | Very good | 42 | 24 |
| CR Best Buy | 8 | **Craftsman** 28885 | 1,300 | 70 | Very good | Very good | Very good | Very good | Good | 46 | 21 |
| **B** | | **ZERO-TURN-RADIUS RIDERS** | | | | | | | | | |
| CR Best Buy | 1 | **Troy-Bilt** Mustang 42" 17WFCACS RZT L42 | 2,300 | 82 | Excellent | Excellent | Excellent | Very good | Excellent | 42 | 22 |
| CR Best Buy | 2 | **Troy-Bilt** Mustang 50" 17WFCACP RZT L50 | 2,800 | 79 | Very good | Excellent | 0 | Very good | Excellent | 50 | 25 |
| Recommended | 3 | **John Deere** Z235 | 2,500 | 73 | Very good | Very good | Excellent | Very good | Excellent | 42 | 20 |
| CR Best Buy | 4 | **Craftsman** 25001 | 2,300 | 72 | Very good | Very good | Very good | Very good | Very good | 42 | 24 |
| Recommended | 5 | **Toro** TimeCutter SS4235 74627 TimeCutter SS4235 74624 | 2,600 | 71 | Very good | Very good | Very good | Very good | Excellent | 42 | 20 |
| Recommended | 6 | **Husqvarna** RZ4623 | 2,600 | 70 | Very good | Very good | Very good | Very good | Very good | 46 | 23 |
| **C** | | **LAWN TRACTORS (WIDE DECK)** | | | | | | | | | |
| CR Best Buy | 1 | **John Deere** D140 D160, D150 | 2,000 | 69 | Good | Very good | Very good | Excellent | Excellent | 48 | 22 |
| Recommended | 2 | **Craftsman** 28861 | 2,800 | 68 | Good | Good | Excellent | Excellent | Very good | 54 | 26 |
| CR Best Buy | 3 | **Craftsman** 28858 | 2,000 | 68 | Good | Good | Excellent | Excellent | Very good | 54 | 26 |
| **D** | | **REAR-ENGINE RIDER** | | | | | | | | | |
| Recommended | 1 | **Troy-Bilt** TB30R 13BC26JD | 1,000 | 58 | Very good | Very good | Fair | Fair | Very good | 30 | 11.5 |

**Ratings Key** Excellent, Very good, Good, Fair, Poor
**CR Best Buy** These models offer the best combination of performance and price. All are recommended.
**Recommended** These are high-performing models that stand out.

## Guide to the Ratings

**Overall score** is based mainly on cutting performance, handling, and ease of use. The displayed score is out of a total of 100 points. **Side discharging** is how evenly clippings were dispersed from the side-discharge chute. **Mulching** is how evenly clippings were cut and distributed. **Bagging** is filling evenness and capacity with full bag(s), including clogged chutes. **Handling** includes clutching or drive engagement, braking, steering, turn radius, and stability. **Ease of use** includes leg room, seat and steering-wheel comfort, ease of blade and brake engagement, cut-height adjustment, bag removal, and cutting-mode changes. **Deck size (in.)** is the manufacturer's claimed cutting width, or swatch, in inches. **Engine power (hp)** is the manufacturer's claimed horsepower. **Price** is approximate retail.

## Most & Least Reliable

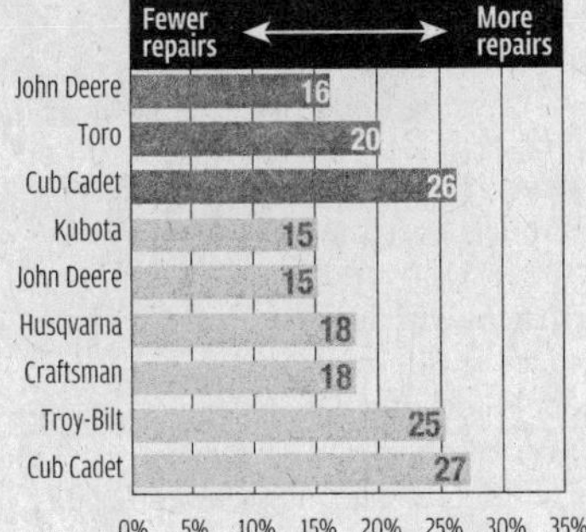


Choosing a brand of lawn tractor or zero-turn-radius riding mower with a good repair history can improve your odds of getting a reliable model. So each year we survey thousands of our readers about their experiences. Troy-Bilt and Cub Cadet were the most repair-prone brands for tractors; Cub Cadet was also the most repair-prone for zero-turn-radius mowers. Our findings are based on 18,697 lawn tractors and 2,397 zero-turn-radius mowers readers bought new from 2008 through the first half of 2012. Differences of fewer than 6 points aren't meaningful, and data are adjusted to eliminate differences linked to the age and use of the mower. Also note that models within a brand may vary, and changes in design or manufacture may affect future reliability.

Source: Annual Product Reliability Survey, Consumer Reports National Research Center.

# Quick Guide MICROWAVES

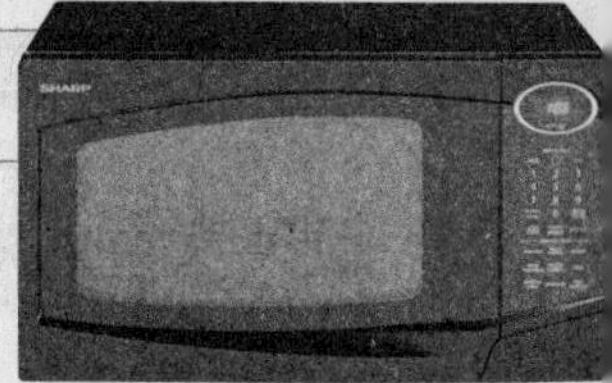


Earlier microwaves had just an automatic popcorn setting and perhaps a few others. Many now have auto settings for oatmeal, pasta, stew, and grits, as well as for reheating or defrosting.

### What to look for

- A sensor, which helps prevent over- or undercooking by measuring emitted steam to gauge when food is done
- Convection, speed-cook, and grilling features if you want to use your microwave as a second oven—and are willing to pay more

### What to skip

- A raft of preprogrammed shortcut keys if you're mostly defrosting and popping corn

### What you'll pay

Countertop models cost the least (about $80 to $300) and are best for kitchens with lots of counter space. Midsized and large models add capacity and features, with midsized models selling the most overall. Over-the-range microwaves ($300 to $900) save space but don't vent as well as a capable range hood.

For more buying advice, go to *ConsumerReports.org/microwaves*

### Shopping tip

More watts typically mean more cooking power. But differences of 100 watts or so don't matter much.

Scan this or see how, page 11

**Recommended models only** From 67 tested.

| Recommended | Rank | Brand & model (Similar models, in small type, are comparable to tested model.) | Price | Overall score (0–100; P \| F \| G \| VG \| E) | Test results: Heating evenness | Defrosting evenness | Speed of heating | Microwaving noise | Ease of use | Venting | Usable capacity (cu. ft.) | Features: Claimed capacity (cu. ft.) | Watts |
|---|---|---|---|---|---|---|---|---|---|---|---|---|---|
| **A** | | **MIDSIZED COUNTERTOP** | | | | | | | | | | | |
| ✔ | 1 | **Kenmore** 6633[9] | $140 | 79 | ⊖ | ⊜ | ⊖ | ⊖ | ⊜ | NA | 0.8 | 1.2 | 1,000 |
| ✔ | 2 | **Kenmore** 6325[2] 6912[ ] | 130 | 76 | ⊖ | ⊜ | ⊖ | ⊖ | ⊜ | NA | 0.9 | 1.2 | 1,200 |
| ☑ | 3 | **Sharp** R-323TKC | 140 | 74 | ⊖ | ⊜ | ⊖ | ⊖ | ⊖ | NA | 0.7 | 1 | 1,100 |
| ☑ | 4 | **Panasonic** Genius Prestige NN-SD681S | 180 | 71 | ⊖ | ⊜ | ⊖ | ○ | ⊜ | NA | 0.7 | 1.2 | 1,200 |
| **B** | | **LARGE COUNTERTOP** | | | | | | | | | | | |
| ✔ | 1 | **Whirlpool** MT4155SP[B] | 185 | 76 | ⊖ | ⊜ | ⊖ | ⊖ | ⊜ | NA | 0.9 | 1.5 | 1,200 |
| ☑ | 2 | **GE** Profile PEB2060DM[BB] | 270 | 76 | ⊖ | ⊖ | ⊜ | ⊖ | ⊜ | NA | 1.2 | 2 | 1,200 |

| Recommended | Rank | Brand & model (Similar models, in small type, are comparable to tested model.) | Price | Overall score (0–100; P \| F \| G \| VG \| E) | Test results: Heating evenness | Defrosting evenness | Speed of heating | Microwaving noise | Ease of use | Venting | Usable capacity (cu. ft.) | Features: Claimed capacity (cu. ft.) | Watts |
|---|---|---|---|---|---|---|---|---|---|---|---|---|---|
| | | **B LARGE COUNTERTOP** continued | | | | | | | | | | | |
| ✓ | 3 | **Panasonic** Inverter NN-H965BF | $180 | 76 | Very good | Excellent | Very good | Good | Excellent | NA | 1.4 | 2.2 | 1,250 |
| ✓ | 4 | **Whirlpool** Gold GT4175SP[B] | 280 | 76 | Very good | Very good | Very good | Very good | Excellent | NA | 1.1 | 1.7 | 1,200 |
| ✓ | 5 | **Kenmore** Elite 7915[9] | 150 | 76 | Very good | Excellent | Very good | Very good | Very good | NA | 0.9 | 1.5 | 1,200 |
| ✓ | 6 | **GE** Profile JES2251SJ[SS] | 280 | 75 | Excellent | Very good | Very good | Very good | Excellent | NA | 1.5 | 2.2 | 1,200 |
| ✓ | 7 | **LG** LCRT2010[ST] | 200 | 75 | Very good | Very good | Very good | Very good | Excellent | NA | 1.2 | 2 | 1,200 |
| ✓ | 8 | **GE** JES2051SN[SS] | 250 | 72 | Very good | Very good | Very good | Very good | Excellent | NA | 1.2 | 2 | 1,200 |
| CR Best Buy | 9 | **Oster** OGG61403 | 100 | 72 | Very good | Excellent | Very good | Very good | Excellent | NA | 0.8 | 1.4 | 1,200 |
| ✓ | 10 | **Maytag** UMC5200BA[B] | 270 | 72 | Very good | Excellent | Very good | Very good | Very good | NA | 1.1 | 2 | 1,100 |
| ✓ | 11 | **Sharp** R426LS | 170 | 71 | Very good | Very good | Very good | Very good | Very good | NA | 0.8 | 1.4 | 1,100 |
| ✓ | 12 | **LG** LCRT1510SV | 190 | 71 | Good | Very good | Very good | Very good | Very good | NA | 0.9 | 1.5 | 1,200 |
| | | **C OVER-THE-RANGE** | | | | | | | | | | | |
| ✓ | 1 | **Kenmore** Elite 8852[2] | 550 | 80 | Very good | Excellent | Good | Very good | Excellent | Excellent | 1.4 | 2 | 1,000 |
| ✓ | 2 | **Panasonic** Genius Prestige NN-SD297[SR] | 430 | 73 | Very good | Excellent | Good | Good | Excellent | Excellent | 0.8 | 2 | 1,200 |

**Ratings Key** Excellent · Very good · Good · Fair · Poor

**CR Best Buy** These models offer the best combination of performance and price. All are recommended.

**Recommended** These are high-performing models that stand out.

## Guide to the Ratings

**Overall score** is based mainly on evenness of heating, ease of use, and auto-defrosting ability. The displayed score is out of a total of 100 points. **Heating evenness** reflects how evenly a model reheated a dish of cold mashed potatoes. **Defrosting evenness** is based on how well the automatic-defrost program defrosted a pound of frozen ground beef. **Speed of heating** is based on the temperature rise of water heated in the microwave. **Microwaving noise** reflects how quiet the oven is while microwaving on high and how loud the vent fan is when operating at its highest setting. **Ease of use** includes how easy it is to set the microwave without referring to the instructions. **Venting** is based on the volume of air drawn in by the microwave's internal fan on the highest setting. **Usable capacity (cu.ft.)** is the usable space based on our measurements, and excludes the corner spaces for models with rotating turntables. Note that most over-the-range models allow you to turn the rotation off to fit large dishes. (A few countertop models also offer that feature.) With the rotation off, measured capacity approximates claimed. But food might require extra tending and stirring. **Price** is approximate retail.

## Most & Least Reliable

### MICROWAVES (OTR)

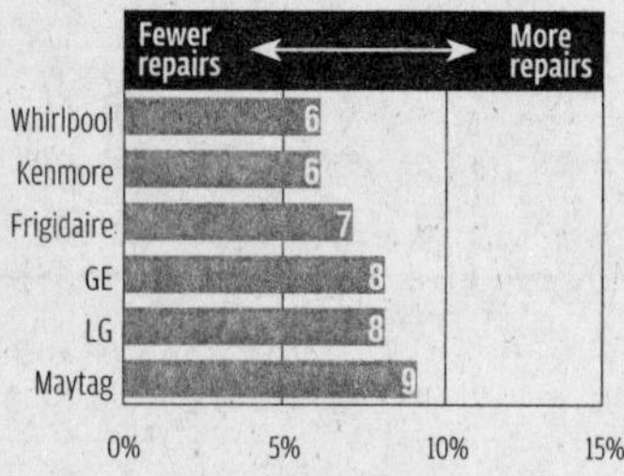


Source: Annual Product Reliability Survey, Consumer Reports National Research Center.

There were only minor differences in brand repair rates for over-the-range (OTR) microwave ovens. That's what we found when we asked almost 12,500 readers who bought an OTR microwave oven between 2008 and 2012. While we lacked sufficient historical data to include Samsung, our data indicated that it has been as reliable as the brands that appear in the graph. The graph shows the percentage of brands that were repaired or had a serious problem. Differences of less than 3 points aren't meaningful, and we've adjusted the data to eliminate differences linked solely to the age of the microwaves. Models within a brand may vary, and design or manufacture changes may affect future reliability. Still, choosing a brand with a good repair history can improve your odds of getting a reliable model.

# Quick Guide PAINTS, EXTERIOR

**Home centers are the go-to place for top paints, with Home Depot's Behr and Lowe's Valspar leading our Ratings. But independent brands like Benjamin Moore and Sherwin-Williams also make our recommended list.**

**Shopping tip**

Pros often get special rates from independent retailers, but make sure the brand they like aced our tests.

Scan this or see how, page 11

### What to look for

- Flat and satin finishes for siding. Flat hides flaws while satin adds a touch of gloss
- Shinier semi-gloss for doors, windows, trim, and shutters for visual contrast
- Mildew resistance for shady spots; fade resistance for sunny ones; dirt resistance for urban areas

### What to skip

- Economy grades of paints, which don't weather as well as top-of-the-line products from the same brand . Many top paints are low-priced
- Buying strictly by brand, since manufacturers often reformulate paints to comply with tougher regulations

### What you'll pay

The best values range from about $25 to $40 per gallon; buying 5-gallon containers can save you even more.

For more buying advice, go to *ConsumerReports.org/paint*

All tested models In performance order, within types.

| Recommended | Rank | Brand & model | Price | Overall score (0–100; P \| F \| G \| VG \| E) | Test results: Appearance after 3 years | Appearance after 6 years | Appearance after 9 years | Features: Resists cracking | Resists color change | Resists dirt | Resists mildew | VOCs (grams/liter) |
|---|---|---|---|---|---|---|---|---|---|---|---|---|
| **A** | | **FLAT** | | | | | | | | | | |
| ✓ | 1 | **Behr** Premium Plus Ultra Flat Enamel (Home Depot) | $37 | 80 | ⊜ | ⊜ | ⊖ | • | • | | • | 100 |
| ✓ | 2 | **California Paints** Fres-Coat Velvet Flat | 44 | 79 | ⊜ | ⊜ | ⊖ | • | • | • | | 100 |
| ✓ | 3 | **Sherwin-Williams** Duration Flat | 67 | 79 | ⊜ | ⊜ | ⊖ | • | • | | | 92 |
| ✓ | 4 | **Glidden** Spred Flat | 25 | 77 | ⊜ | ⊖ | ⊖ | • | • | | | 100 |
| ✓ | 5 | **Glidden** Premium Flat (Home Depot) | 22 | 77 | ⊜ | ⊖ | ⊖ | • | • | | • | 100 |

| Recommended | Rank | Brand & model | Price | Overall score (0–100; P \| F \| G \| VG \| E) | Test results: Appearance after 3 years | Test results: Appearance after 6 years | Test results: Appearance after 9 years | Features: Resists cracking | Features: Resists color change | Features: Resists dirt | Features: Resists mildew | Features: VOCs (grams/liter) |
|---|---|---|---|---|---|---|---|---|---|---|---|---|
| **A FLAT** continued | | | | | | | | | | | | |
| CR Best Buy | 6 | **Behr** Premium Plus Flat (Home Depot) | $26 | 76 | Excellent | Very good | Very good | • | • | • | • | 100 |
| | 7 | **Valspar** Ultra Flat (Lowe's) | 28 | 75 | Excellent | Very good | Very good | • | • | | | 100 |
| | 8 | **Valspar** DuraMax Flat (Lowe's) | 37 | 74 | Excellent | Very good | Very good | • | • | | | 100 |
| | 9 | **Sherwin-Williams** Resilience Flat | 59 | 70 | Very good | Very good | Very good | • | • | | | 48 |
| **B SATIN** | | | | | | | | | | | | |
| Recommended | 1 | **Behr** Premium Plus Ultra Satin Enamel (Home Depot) | 39 | 82 | Excellent | Excellent | Very good | • | • | • | • | 50 |
| CR Best Buy | 2 | **Behr** Premium Plus Satin Enamel (Home Depot) | 28 | 79 | Excellent | Very good | Very good | • | • | • | • | 100 |
| Recommended | 3 | **Benjamin Moore** Aura Low Lustre | 68 | 79 | Excellent | Very good | Very good | • | • | | • | 50 |
| Recommended | 4 | **Sherwin-Williams** Duration Satin | 68 | 78 | Excellent | Excellent | Very good | • | • | | | 107 |
| CR Best Buy | 5 | **Glidden** Premium Satin (Home Depot) | 25 | 75 | Excellent | Very good | Very good | • | • | • | | 50 |
| CR Best Buy | 6 | **Glidden** Spred Satin | 27 | 75 | Excellent | Very good | Very good | • | • | • | | 50 |
| | 7 | **Valspar** DuraMax Satin (Lowe's) | 39 | 72 | Very good | Very good | Very good | • | • | • | | 150 |
| | 8 | **California Paints** Fres-Coat Satin Gloss | 48 | 72 | Excellent | Very good | Very good | • | • | • | • | 150 |
| | 9 | **Sears** WeatherBeater Ultra Satin | 44 | 71 | Very good | Very good | Very good | • | • | | | 53 |
| | 10 | **Sherwin-Williams** Resilience Satin | 63 | 70 | Very good | Very good | Good | • | • | | | 48 |
| | 11 | **Valspar** Ultra Satin (Lowe's) | 30 | 70 | Excellent | Very good | Good | • | • | • | | 150 |
| | 12 | **Kilz** Casual Colors Satin | 30 | 63 | Excellent | Very good | Fair | | • | | • | 50 |

**Ratings Key** Excellent, Very good, Good, Fair, Poor

**CR Best Buy** These models offer the best combination of performance and price. All are recommended.

**Recommended** These are high-performing models that stand out.

| Recommended | Rank | Brand & model | Price | Overall score (0–100; P \| F \| G \| VG \| E) | Test results: Appearance after 3 years | Test results: Appearance after 6 years | Test results: Appearance after 9 years | Features: Resists cracking | Features: Resists color change | Features: Resists dirt | Features: Resists mildew | Features: VOCs (grams/liter) |
|---|---|---|---|---|---|---|---|---|---|---|---|---|
| **C** | | **SEMI-GLOSS** | | | | | | | | | | |
| ✓ | 1 | **Valspar** DuraMax Semi-Gloss (Lowe's) | $40 | 80 | ⊜ | ⊖ | ⊖ | • | • | • | | 50 |
| ✓ | 2 | **Behr** Premium Plus Ultra Semi-Gloss Enamel (Home Depot) | 40 | 79 | ⊜ | ⊖ | ⊖ | • | • | | | 50 |
| ✓ | 3 | **Sherwin-Williams** Duration Semi-Gloss | 69 | 76 | ⊜ | ⊖ | ⊖ | • | • | | | 41 |
| ✓ | 4 | **Behr** Premium Plus Semi-Gloss Enamel (Home Depot) | 29 | 75 | ⊜ | ⊖ | ⊖ | • | • | • | • | 150 |
| ✓ | 5 | **Glidden** Spred Semi-Gloss | 28 | 74 | ⊜ | ⊖ | ⊖ | • | • | | | 50 |
| | 6 | **Benjamin Moore** Aura Semi-Gloss | 68 | 70 | ⊜ | ⊖ | ⊖ | • | • | | | 50 |
| | 7 | **Glidden** Premium Semi-Gloss (Home Depot) | 27 | 69 | ⊖ | ⊖ | ⊖ | • | • | | | 50 |
| | 8 | **Valspar** Ultra Semi-Gloss (Lowe's) | 31 | 66 | ⊖ | ⊖ | ○ | • | • | | | 150 |
| | 9 | **Kilz** Casual Colors Semi-Gloss | 31 | 63 | ⊜ | ⊖ | ◒ | | • | | | 50 |

## Guide to the Ratings

**Overall score** is a weighted average of each year's appearance for up to 3 years of testing. **Appearance after 3 years** summarizes performance after 1 year of our accelerated weathering (i.e., equivalent to 3 years on a vertical wall). Testing stops when appearance falls to Fair or Poor, at which time the product must be reapplied. **Appearance after 6 years** summarizes performance after 2 years of our accelerated weathering (i.e., equivalent to 6 years on a vertical wall). Testing stops when appearance falls to Fair or Poor, at which time the product must be reapplied. **Appearance after 9 years** summarizes performance after 3 years of our accelerated weathering (i.e., equivalent to 9 years on a vertical wall). Testing stops after 3 years, regardless of whether appearance falls to Fair or Poor. Products that at this point still rate at least Good for appearance are considered superior products. **VOCs (grams/liter)** indicates the level of volatile organic compounds as stated on the can. **Price** is approximate retail per gallon.

# Quick Guide PAINTS, INTERIOR

Many recommended paints are self-priming, so you can paint directly over old finishes and wallboard. While one coat might do, a second coat will give a richer, more even finish.

### What to look for

- Flat paint for a formal living room, dining room, or other space that doesn't see heavy use, because it isn't the most stain resistant
- Eggshell or satin for family rooms, kitchens, bathrooms, kids' rooms, hallways, and the like
- Semi-gloss for windowsills, trim, and other woodwork to add contrast. (While typically stain resistant, many semigloss paints will dull when cleaned.)

### What to skip

- Bright greens and yellows for sun-drenched rooms, because these colors tend to fade a lot; whites and browns are better choices

### What you'll pay

About $20 to $68 per gallon. Each gallon covers about 400 square feet of smooth wall; rougher surfaces will require a bit more paint.

For more buying advice, go to *ConsumerReports.org/paint*

### Shopping tip

Manufacturer and retailer websites offer color-choosing tools, rebates, and deals.

Scan this or see how, page 11

**Recommended models only** From 65 tested.

| Recommended | Rank | Brand & model | Price | Overall score (0–100; P \| F \| G \| VG \| E) | Test results: Hiding | Staining | Gloss change | Scrubbing | Surface smoothness | Features: Resists mildew | Resists sticking | Resists fading | Claimed VOCs (grams/liter) |
|---|---|---|---|---|---|---|---|---|---|---|---|---|---|
| **A** | | **FLAT & MATTE** | | | | | | | | | | | |
| ✓ | 1 | **Valspar** Signature Matte (Lowe's) | $32 | 82 | ⊜ | ⊜ | ○ | ⊜ | ⊜ | • | | • | 50 |
| ✓ | 2 | **Behr** Premium Plus Ultra Flat Enamel (Home Depot) | 32 | 82 | ⊖ | ⊜ | ⊖ | ⊜ | ⊜ | • | • | | 50 |
| ✓ | 3 | **Benjamin Moore** Aura Matte | 68 | 77 | ⊖ | ⊖ | ○ | ⊜ | ⊖ | • | • | | 50 |
| ✔ | 4 | **Behr** Premium Plus Flat Enamel (Home Depot) | 26 | 76 | ⊖ | ⊜ | ⊜ | ⊜ | ⊖ | • | | | 0 |

| Recommended | Rank | Brand & model | Price | Overall score (0–100; P \| F \| G \| VG \| E) | Test results: Hiding | Test results: Staining | Test results: Gloss change | Test results: Scrubbing | Test results: Surface smoothness | Features: Resists mildew | Features: Resists sticking | Features: Resists fading | Features: Claimed VOCs (grams/liter) |
|---|---|---|---|---|---|---|---|---|---|---|---|---|---|
| **A FLAT & MATTE** continued | | | | | | | | | | | | | |
| Recommended | 5 | **Benjamin Moore** Natura Flat | $57 | 75 | Very good | Very good | Very good | Excellent | Good | • | • | • | 0 |
| Recommended | 6 | **Clark + Kensington** Flat Enamel (Ace) | 30 | 75 | Very good | Excellent | Good | Excellent | Very good | – | • | • | 50 |
| CR Best Buy | 7 | **Olympic** One Flat Enamel (Lowe's) | 25 | 75 | Very good | Excellent | Good | Excellent | Good | • | • | – | 50 |
| CR Best Buy | 8 | **Valspar** Ultra Flat (Lowe's) | 25 | 74 | Very good | Very good | Fair | Excellent | Very good | • | • | • | 0 |
| CR Best Buy | 9 | **Glidden** Premium Flat (Home Depot) | 20 | 73 | Very good | Good | Excellent | Good | Very good | • | • | – | 50 |
| **B SATIN & EGGSHELL** | | | | | | | | | | | | | |
| Recommended | 1 | **Clark + Kensington** Satin Enamel (Ace) | 32 | 86 | Excellent | Excellent | Very good | Excellent | Excellent | – | • | • | 50 |
| Recommended | 2 | **Benjamin Moore** Aura Satin | 68 | 84 | Excellent | Excellent | Very good | Excellent | Very good | • | – | • | 50 |
| Recommended | 3 | **Kilz** Casual Colors Satin | 30 | 82 | Excellent | Excellent | Very good | Excellent | Good | • | • | – | 50 |
| CR Best Buy | 4 | **Glidden** Premium Satin (Home Depot) | 24 | 80 | Very good | Excellent | Excellent | Excellent | Good | • | • | – | 50 |
| Recommended | 5 | **Behr** Premium Plus Ultra Satin Enamel (Home Depot) | 34 | 77 | Very good | Excellent | Good | Excellent | Very good | • | • | – | 50 |
| CR Best Buy | 6 | **Olympic** One Satin Enamel (Lowe's) | 27 | 77 | Very good | Excellent | Excellent | Excellent | Good | • | – | – | 50 |
| CR Best Buy | 7 | **Glidden** Duo Eggshell | 26 | 76 | Very good | Excellent | Excellent | Excellent | Fair | • | – | • | 50 |
| Recommended | 8 | **Valspar** Signature Satin (Lowe's) | 34 | 75 | Very good | Excellent | Good | Excellent | Good | – | – | – | 50 |
| Recommended | 9 | **Benjamin Moore** Regal Select Eggshell | 51 | 75 | Very good | Excellent | Very good | Excellent | Fair | • | – | • | 50 |
| CR Best Buy | 10 | **Ace** Royal Interiors Satin | 27 | 74 | Very good | Excellent | Good | Excellent | Excellent | • | – | – | 50 |
| Recommended | 11 | **Valspar** + Satin (Lowe's) | 42 | 74 | Very good | Excellent | Excellent | Excellent | Good | – | – | – | 0 |

**Ratings Key** Excellent, Very good, Good, Fair, Poor

**CR Best Buy** These models offer the best combination of performance and price. All are recommended.

**Recommended** These are high-performing models that stand out.

| Recommended | Rank | Brand & model | Price | Overall score (0–100; P \| F \| G \| VG \| E) | Test results: Hiding | Staining | Gloss change | Scrubbing | Surface smoothness | Features: Resists mildew | Resists sticking | Resists fading | Claimed VOCs (grams/liter) |
|---|---|---|---|---|---|---|---|---|---|---|---|---|---|
| **C** | | **SEMI-GLOSS** | | | | | | | | | | | |
| ✓ | 1 | **Clark + Kensington** Semi-Gloss Enamel (Ace) | $33 | 85 | ⊜ | ⊜ | ○ | ⊜ | ⊜ | • | • | • | 50 |
| ✓ | 2 | **Behr** Premium Plus Ultra Semi-Gloss Enamel (Home Depot) | 34 | 84 | ⊖ | ⊜ | ⊜ | ⊜ | ⊜ | • | | | 50 |
| ✓ | 3 | **Valspar** Signature Semi-Gloss (Lowe's) | 35 | 82 | ⊜ | ⊜ | ◒ | ⊜ | ⊖ | • | • | | 50 |
| ✓ | 4 | **Benjamin Moore** Aura Semi-Gloss | 68 | 80 | ⊜ | ⊜ | ○ | ⊜ | ⊖ | • | | | 50 |
| ✔ | 5 | **Ace** Royal Interiors Semi-Gloss | 28 | 77 | ⊖ | ⊜ | ⊖ | ⊜ | ⊖ | • | | | 50 |
| ✔ | 6 | **Glidden** Brilliance Semi-Gloss (Walmart) | 26 | 77 | ⊜ | ⊜ | ⊖ | ⊜ | ○ | | | • | 0 |
| ✔ | 7 | **Glidden** Premium Semi-Gloss (Home Depot) | 26 | 76 | ⊖ | ⊜ | ○ | ⊜ | ○ | • | • | | 50 |
| ✔ | 8 | **Better Homes and Gardens** Semi-Gloss (Walmart) | 26 | 76 | ⊖ | ⊜ | ⊜ | ⊜ | ◒ | | | • | 0 |
| ✔ | 9 | **Glidden** Duo Semi-Gloss | 27 | 75 | ⊖ | ⊜ | ⊜ | ⊜ | ○ | | | • | 50 |
| ✓ | 10 | **Benjamin Moore** Natura Semi-Gloss | 57 | 75 | ⊖ | ⊜ | ○ | ⊜ | ⊜ | • | | | 0 |

## Guide to the Ratings

**Overall score** is mainly hiding, surface smoothness, and resistance to staining, scrubbing, gloss change, sticking, mildew, and fading. Volatile organic compounds aren't scored. Most results reflect white, pastel, and medium-tint bases. **Hiding** is coverage of contrasting color with one and two coats (with one-coat coverage weighted most heavily). **Staining** is resistance to greasy stains. **Gloss change** is appearance after cleaning with an abrasive cleaner. **Scrubbing** is ability to resist abrasive cleaner. **Surface smoothness** is the absence of roller marks when dry. **Resists mildew** is the ability to inhibit mildew growth. **Resists sticking** indicates lack of tackiness when dry. **Resists fading** is the ability to maintain color in strong sunlight. **Claimed VOCs (grams/liter)** is the manufacturer's stated level of volatile organic compounds in the untinted base coat measured in grams per liter. **Price** is approximate retail.

# Quick Guide PRINTERS, ALL-IN-ONE

**If all you do is print, you can save money and space by purchasing a dedicated printer. But if you want to copy or scan, or even fax, it's worth investigating an all-in-one.**

### What to look for

- If you don't need to print in color or scan color photos, an all-in-one laser for superior quality, faster print speed, and a lower cost per page
- An all-in-one inkjet, if you want color printing and a model that excels at printing your photos
- Printers with low monthly costs (ink and paper)

### What to skip

- High ink- or toner-cartridge costs, which can make a bargain-priced printer a bad deal in the long run
- An inkjet with a single color cartridge, because separate color cartridges may be more economical, depending on your photos

### What you'll pay

All-in-ones are actually getting less expensive and more versatile. Inkjets cost $60 and up.

For more buying advice, go to *ConsumerReports.org/printers*

### Shopping tip

If you're printing photos, a memory card reader or PictBridge compatibility can be helpful.

Scan this or see how, page 11

**All tested models** In performance order, within types.

| Recommended | Rank | Brand & model | Price | Overall score (0–100; P \| F \| G \| VG \| E) | Ink cost/month ($) | Maintenance ink use | Photo quality | 4x6 photo time | 8x10 photo time | Text quality | Text speed | Graphics quality | Convenience | Scan quality | Copy quality | Power saving | Versatility |
|---|---|---|---|---|---|---|---|---|---|---|---|---|---|---|---|---|---|
| **A** | | **BLACK-AND-WHITE LASER** | | | | | | | | | | | | | | | |
| ✓ | 1 | **Canon** imageCLASS MF4890dw | $300 | 76 | 5.4 | ⊜ | NA | NA | NA | ⊜ | ⊜ | ⊖ | ⊖ | ⊖ | ⊜ | ⊜ | ◒ |
| ✔ | 2 | **Canon** imageCLASS MF4770n | 200 | 76 | 5.4 | ⊜ | NA | NA | NA | ⊜ | ⊜ | ⊖ | ⊖ | ⊖ | ⊜ | ⊜ | ● |
| ✔ | 3 | **Samsung** SCX-3405FW | 150 | 76 | 5.8 | ⊜ | NA | NA | NA | ⊜ | ⊜ | ⊖ | ○ | ⊖ | ⊜ | ⊜ | ◒ |
| ✓ | 4 | **Canon** imageCLASS MF5950dw | 400 | 76 | 3.8 | ⊜ | NA | NA | NA | ⊜ | ⊜ | ⊖ | ○ | ⊖ | ⊜ | ⊖ | ◒ |
| ✓ | 5 | **HP** LaserJet Pro 400 MFP M425dn | 350 | 76 | 2.7 | ⊜ | NA | NA | NA | ⊜ | ⊜ | ⊖ | ○ | ⊖ | ⊖ | ⊖ | ○ |
| ✓ | 6 | **Dell** 2355dn | 400 | 75 | 0.1 | ⊜ | NA | NA | NA | ⊜ | ⊜ | ○ | ⊖ | ⊜ | ⊜ | ○ | ○ |

| Recommended | Rank | Brand & model | Price | Overall score (0–100; P \| F \| G \| VG \| E) | Ink cost/month ($) | Maintenance ink use | Photo quality | 4x6 photo time | 8x10 photo time | Text quality | Text speed | Graphics quality | Convenience | Scan quality | Copy quality | Power saving | Versatility |
|---|---|---|---|---|---|---|---|---|---|---|---|---|---|---|---|---|---|
| **A BLACK-AND-WHITE LASER** continued | | | | | | | | | | | | | | | | | |
| Recommended | 7 | **Samsung** SL-M2875FW | $300 | 75 | 4.65 | Excellent | NA | NA | NA | Excellent | Excellent | Very good | Good | Very good | Very good | Very good | Fair |
| CR Best Buy | 8 | **Brother** MFC-7360N | 200 | 74 | 0.1 | Excellent | NA | NA | NA | Excellent | Excellent | Good | Very good | Excellent | Excellent | Excellent | Fair |
| CR Best Buy | 9 | **Brother** DCP-7060D | 160 | 72 | 0.1 | Excellent | NA | NA | NA | Excellent | Excellent | Good | Very good | Excellent | Excellent | Excellent | Fair |
| Recommended | 10 | **Brother** MFC-7860DW | 300 | 72 | 2.7 | Excellent | NA | NA | NA | Very good | Excellent | Good | Very good | Very good | Excellent | Excellent | Good |
| | 11 | **Dell** B1265dnf | 200 | 69 | 4.6 | Excellent | NA | NA | NA | Excellent | Excellent | Good | Very good | Very good | Very good | Excellent | Good |
| | 12 | **Canon** imageCLASS MF3010 | 150 | 69 | 4.9 | Excellent | NA | NA | NA | Excellent | Excellent | Good | Good | Very good | Excellent | Excellent | Poor |
| | 13 | **OKI** MB471w | 480 | 67 | 1.3 | Excellent | NA | NA | NA | Excellent | Excellent | Good | Good | Good | Excellent | Very good | Good |
| | 14 | **Panasonic** KX-MB1520 | 140 | 64 | 5.2 | Excellent | NA | NA | NA | Very good | Excellent | Good | Good | Very good | Excellent | Very good | Poor |
| | 15 | **Panasonic** KX-MB2030 | 200 | 63 | 0.3 | Excellent | NA | NA | NA | Very good | Excellent | Very good | Good | Good | Very good | Very good | Fair |
| | 16 | **Panasonic** KX-MB2000 | 140 | 62 | 0.5 | Excellent | NA | NA | NA | Very good | Excellent | Very good | Good | Good | Very good | Very good | Fair |
| **B COLOR LASER** | | | | | | | | | | | | | | | | | |
| Recommended | 1 | **Dell** 2155cn | 360 | 71 | 11.7 | Excellent | Good | NA | Excellent | Excellent | Excellent | Excellent | Very good | Very good | Very good | Good | Fair |
| | 2 | **Dell** C1765nfw | 280 | 69 | 20.1 | Excellent | Very good | NA | Excellent | Excellent | Very good | Excellent | Good | Very good | Very good | Very good | Fair |
| | 3 | **Brother** MFC-9970CDW | 700 | 67 | 5.6 | Excellent | Fair | Excellent | Excellent | Excellent | Excellent | Excellent | Good | Very good | Very good | Very good | Good |
| | 4 | **Samsung** CLX-4195FW | 350 | 66 | 7.9 | Excellent | Fair | NA | Excellent | Excellent | Excellent | Excellent | Good | Very good | Very good | Very good | Fair |
| | 5 | **Samsung** CLX-3305FW | 380 | 65 | 14.9 | Excellent | Fair | NA | Excellent | Excellent | Excellent | Very good | Good | Very good | Very good | Very good | Fair |
| | 6 | **HP** LaserJet Pro 200 color MFP M276nw | 500 | 62 | 9.7 | Excellent | Fair | NA | Excellent | Excellent | Very good | Very good | Very good | Very good | Very good | Very good | Fair |
| | 7 | **Brother** MFC-9325CW | 400 | 55 | 9.6 | Excellent | Poor | Excellent | Excellent | Excellent | Excellent | Very good | Good | Very good | Very good | Good | Fair |

**Ratings Key** Excellent · Very good · Good · Fair · Poor

**CR Best Buy** These models offer the best combination of performance and price. All are recommended.

**Recommended** These are high-performing models that stand out.

| Recommended | Rank | Brand & model | Price | Overall score (0–100; P \| F \| G \| VG \| E) | Ink cost/month ($) | Maintenance ink use | Photo quality | 4x6 photo time | 8x10 photo time | Text quality | Text speed | Graphics quality | Convenience | Scan quality | Copy quality | Power saving | Versatility |
|---|---|---|---|---|---|---|---|---|---|---|---|---|---|---|---|---|---|
| **C** | | **INKJET** | | | | | | | | | | | | | | | |
| ✓ | 1 | **HP** Photosmart 7520 | $200 | 78 | 6.4 | F | VG | E | VG | VG | VG | E | G | E | VG | E | VG |
| ✓ | 2 | **Epson** Expression Premium XP-800 | 180 | 76 | 7.5 | E | E | VG | G | VG | E | VG | VG | VG | VG | E | E |
| ✓ (shaded) | 3 | **Epson** Expression Premium XP-600 | 100 | 73 | 8 | E | VG | VG | G | VG | VG | VG | VG | VG | VG | E | E |
| ✓ | 4 | **HP** Photosmart 6520 | 120 | 72 | 6.5 | F | F | VG | VG | VG | VG | E | G | VG | VG | E | VG |
| ✓ (shaded) | 5 | **Canon** Pixma MG3220 | 70 | 72 | 7.3 | VG | VG | VG | G | VG | VG | VG | VG | VG | VG | E | G |
| ✓ | 6 | **Canon** Pixma MG6320 | 150 | 72 | 7.6 | NA | E | E | VG | E | E | VG | G | VG | VG | E | E |
| ✓ | 7 | **Canon** Pixma MG5420 | 150 | 71 | 6.9 | G | E | E | VG | E | E | VG | G | VG | VG | E | E |
| ✓ | 8 | **Canon** Pixma MX922 | 200 | 71 | 6.5 | F | E | E | VG | E | E | VG | VG | VG | VG | E | VG |
| ✓ (shaded) | 9 | **Brother** DCP-J140W | 100 | 71 | 7.2 | E | E | G | G | F | G | F | VG | VG | G | E | G |
| ✓ | 10 | **HP** Officejet Pro 8600 Plus | 220 | 71 | 4.2 | P | VG | E | E | VG | E | VG | VG | VG | VG | E | VG |
| ✓ | 11 | **Brother** MFC-J6910DW | 300 | 70 | 5.4 | NA | VG | VG | VG | G | VG | F | VG | VG | G | E | E |
| ✓ | 12 | **Brother** MFC-J5910DW | 200 | 70 | 5.8 | NA | VG | VG | VG | G | VG | G | VG | VG | VG | E | E |
| ✓ | 13 | **Canon** Pixma MX892 | 200 | 70 | 8.8 | NA | VG | E | E | VG | VG | VG | VG | VG | VG | E | E |
| ✓ (shaded) | 14 | **Canon** Pixma MG2220 | 60 | 70 | 7.3 | VG | VG | VG | G | VG | VG | VG | VG | VG | VG | E | F |
| ✓ | 15 | **Canon** Pixma MX512 | 150 | 70 | 6.6 | NA | VG | VG | VG | VG | VG | VG | VG | VG | VG | E | VG |
| | 16 | **Epson** Expression Photo XP-850 | 300 | 69 | 10.9 | F | VG | VG | G | G | VG | G | VG | VG | VG | G | E |
| | 17 | **Dell** V525w | 100 | 69 | 11.2 | NA | VG | E | VG | VG | VG | VG | VG | VG | VG | VG | VG |
| | 18 | **HP** Officejet 6600 | 120 | 68 | 5.5 | NA | VG | VG | VG | VG | E | VG | G | VG | VG | E | G |
| | 19 | **Brother** MFC-J625DW | 130 | 68 | 5.1 | NA | VG | VG | E | G | VG | G | E | VG | G | E | E |
| | 20 | **HP** Officejet Pro 8600 | 150 | 68 | 4 | NA | VG | E | E | VG | VG | VG | VG | VG | VG | E | VG |
| | 21 | **HP** Officejet 4620 | 100 | 68 | 6.4 | NA | VG | VG | G | VG | VG | VG | G | VG | VG | E | G |
| | 22 | **Brother** MFC-J4310DW | 170 | 68 | 4 | E | VG | E | VG | G | E | F | VG | VG | G | E | E |
| | 23 | **Epson** Workforce Pro WP-4540 | 400 | 68 | 4.6 | NA | VG | VG | VG | VG | E | VG | VG | VG | VG | VG | G |

## C INKJET continued

| Recommended | Rank | Brand & model | Price | Overall score (0–100; P \| F \| G \| VG \| E) | Ink cost/month ($) | Maintenance ink use | Photo quality | 4x6 photo time | 8x10 photo time | Text quality | Text speed | Graphics quality | Convenience | Scan quality | Copy quality | Power saving | Versatility |
|---|---|---|---|---|---|---|---|---|---|---|---|---|---|---|---|---|---|
| | 24 | **Canon** Pixma MX432 | $100 | 66 | 6.9 | NA | VG | VG | VG | VG | VG | VG | VG | VG | VG | E | G |
| | 25 | **HP** Officejet Pro 276dw | 400 | 66 | 4.46 | F | F | E | VG | VG | E | G | VG | VG | G | E | VG |
| | 26 | **Dell** V725w | 170 | 66 | 10.8 | NA | F | E | E | E | VG | VG | VG | VG | VG | VG | VG |
| | 27 | **Brother** MFC-J4710DW | 250 | 66 | 4.3 | E | G | E | VG | G | E | F | VG | VG | G | E | E |
| | 28 | **HP** Officejet 6700 Premium | 140 | 65 | 5.3 | NA | VG | VG | VG | F | E | G | G | VG | VG | E | G |
| | 29 | **Epson** Workforce WF-3540 | 150 | 65 | 6.1 | G | F | G | F | VG | E | VG | VG | VG | VG | G | E |
| | 30 | **HP** Envy 120 | 200 | 65 | 7.8 | E | VG | VG | F | E | VG | VG | G | VG | VG | VG | G |
| | 31 | **Canon** Pixma MG4220 | 130 | 64 | 7.5 | VG | VG | VG | G | VG | VG | VG | VG | VG | G | E | VG |
| | 32 | **Brother** MFC-J4410DW | 180 | 64 | 4.2 | VG | G | E | VG | VG | VG | G | G | E | G | E | E |
| | 33 | **Brother** MFC-J4510DW | 150 | 64 | 4 | VG | VG | E | VG | G | E | G | G | E | G | E | E |
| | 34 | **Canon** Pixma MX522 | 150 | 64 | 7.5 | VG | G | VG | G | VG | VG | VG | VG | VG | VG | E | G |
| | 35 | **Epson** Workforce WF-3520 | 150 | 64 | 5.1 | G | F | G | F | VG | E | G | VG | VG | VG | E | E |
| | 36 | **Brother** MFC-J6510DW | 230 | 63 | 5.7 | NA | E | G | G | G | VG | G | VG | VG | G | VG | E |
| | 37 | **Canon** Pixma MX452 | 100 | 62 | 7.4 | VG | G | VG | G | VG | VG | VG | VG | VG | VG | E | F |
| | 38 | **HP** Officejet Pro X476DN | 650 | 61 | 3.6 | G | F | E | E | G | E | G | G | E | VG | VG | G |
| | 39 | **Canon** Pixma MX392 | 70 | 61 | 7.2 | VG | G | VG | G | VG | VG | VG | VG | E | VG | E | F |
| | 40 | **Epson** Workforce WF-2540 | 100 | 60 | 9.6 | E | G | G | P | VG | VG | G | VG | G | G | E | G |
| | 41 | **Epson** Workforce WF-2530 | 80 | 59 | 9.9 | E | G | G | P | VG | VG | G | VG | VG | VG | E | G |
| | 42 | **HP** Officejet Mobile 150 | 400 | 50 | 10.3 | VG | G | G | F | E | VG | VG | G | F | VG | VG | G |

## Guide to the Ratings

**Overall score** is based on speed and quality of print, scan, and copy functions, plus ease of use. The displayed score is out of a total of 100 points. **Ink cost/month ($)** is estimated cost (in dollars) for ink or toner in a month of typical use. For inkjets: 23 text pages, 9 graphics pages, 2.4 large photos, 3.6 small photos, and 3.5 photos on plain paper. For lasers: 62 text pages, 24 graphics pages, 1.7 large photos, 1.9 small photos, and 2.3 photos on plain paper. **Maintenance ink use** reflects the amount of extra ink used by an inkjet printer to maintain its print heads. "NA" indicates an older model that did not undergo this test. **Photo quality** reflects a photo's appearance. The **4x6 photo time** score reflects how quickly the model can print one 4x6 photo on photo-quality paper. One minute or less is excellent; 1 to 2 minutes is very good; 2 to 4 minutes is good; 4 to 6 minutes is fair; and longer than 6 minutes is poor. The **8x10 photo time** score reflects how quickly the model can print one 8x10 photo on photo-quality paper. Two minutes or less is excellent; 2 to 4 minutes is very good; 4 to 6 minutes is good; 6 to 8 minutes is fair; and longer than 8 minutes is poor. **Text quality** assesses clarity and crispness of black text. **Text speed** reflects how quickly the model can print text on five pages of plain, letter-sized pages. Thirty seconds or less is excellent; 31 to 60 seconds is very good; 61 to 90 seconds is good; 91 to 120 seconds is fair; and longer than 120 seconds is poor. **Graphics quality** assesses the appearance of color graphics produced by the printer. Black-and-white lasers were judged on black-and-white graphics. **Convenience** measures the ease of carrying out a series of common activities with the printer. **Scan quality** is for color photos, graphics, and text scanned at each model's default settings. **Copy quality** is for graphics and text. **Power saving** indicates how well the printer conserves power between uses. **Versatility** indicates features that increase a printer's utility or capabilities. **Price** is approximate retail.

# Quick Guide PRINTERS, REGULAR

**Inkjet and laser printers have become more affordable and increasingly full featured.**

**Shopping tip**

A printer with an Energy Star label will consume very little power when not printing.

Scan this or see how, page 11

### What to look for

- A laser printer, if you want fast, low-cost, top-quality black-and-white text
- An inkjet, if you want the most versatile printer. You can print color photos and graphics, as well as text
- Features such as a memory-card reader, PictBridge support, or a wireless interface, if you want to print photos without a computer

### What to skip

- Color laser printers, which are more costly than their monochrome counterparts and unsuited for photos
- Snapshot printers, most of which didn't provide the photo quality of the best regular inkjets in our tests

### What you'll pay

Color inkjets can cost as little as $50, and monochrome laser printers less than $80.

For more buying advice, go to *ConsumerReports.org/printers*

All tested models in performance order, within types.

| Recommended | Rank | Brand & model | Price | Overall score (0–100; P \| F \| G \| VG \| E) | Ink cost/month ($) | Maintenance ink use | 4x6 photo cost ($) | 8x10 photo cost ($) | Text cost (cents) | Photo quality | 4x6 photo time | 8x10 photo time | Text quality | Text speed | Graphics quality | Power saving |
|---|---|---|---|---|---|---|---|---|---|---|---|---|---|---|---|---|
| **A** | | **BLACK-AND-WHITE LASER** | | | | | | | | | | | | | | |
| ☑ | 1 | **HP** LaserJet Pro P1606dn | $180 | 78 | 1.2 | ⊜ | NA | NA | 4.1 | NA | NA | NA | ⊜ | ⊜ | ○ | ⊜ |
| ✅ | 2 | **HP** LaserJet Pro P1102w | 130 | 78 | 1.4 | ⊜ | NA | NA | 5.2 | NA | NA | NA | ⊜ | ⊜ | ◓ | ⊜ |
| ☑ | 3 | **HP** LaserJet Pro 400 M401dw | 380 | 77 | 2.7 | ⊜ | NA | NA | 2.3 | NA | NA | NA | ⊜ | ⊜ | ◓ | ◓ |
| ☑ | 4 | **Samsung** ML-2955DW | 150 | 75 | 3.4 | ⊜ | NA | NA | 3.4 | NA | NA | NA | ⊜ | ⊜ | ○ | ⊜ |
| ☑ | 5 | **Samsung** SL-M2825DW | 150 | 74 | 2.98 | ⊜ | NA | NA | 2.3 | NA | NA | NA | ⊜ | ⊜ | ◓ | ⊜ |
| ✅ | 6 | **Brother** HL-2270DW | 140 | 73 | 0.6 | ⊜ | NA | NA | 1.9 | NA | NA | NA | ⊜ | ⊜ | ○ | ⊜ |

| Recommended | Rank | Brand & model | Price | Overall score (0–100; P \| F \| G \| VG \| E) | Ink cost/month ($) | Maintenance ink use | 4x6 photo cost ($) | 8x10 photo cost ($) | Text cost (cents) | Photo quality | 4x6 photo time | 8x10 photo time | Text quality | Text speed | Graphics quality | Power saving |
|---|---|---|---|---|---|---|---|---|---|---|---|---|---|---|---|---|
| **A BLACK-AND-WHITE LASER** continued | | | | | | | | | | | | | | | | |
| CR Best Buy | 7 | **Samsung** ML-2165W | $130 | 73 | 5.6 | Excellent | NA | NA | 5.3 | NA | NA | NA | Excellent | Excellent | Good | Excellent |
| | 8 | **Dell** B2360dn | 230 | 68 | 2.3 | Excellent | NA | NA | 1.8 | NA | NA | NA | Excellent | Excellent | Very good | Very good |
| | 9 | **Samsung** ML-3712DW | 300 | 68 | 2.3 | Excellent | NA | NA | 1.7 | NA | NA | NA | Excellent | Excellent | Good | Excellent |
| | 10 | **Dell** B1160w | 110 | 67 | 5.2 | Excellent | NA | NA | 4.4 | NA | NA | NA | Excellent | Excellent | Very good | Excellent |
| **B COLOR LASER** | | | | | | | | | | | | | | | | |
| Recommended | 1 | **Dell** C1660w | 180 | 67 | 22 | Excellent | NA | 1.35 | 12.3 | Very good | NA | Excellent | Excellent | Very good | Excellent | Very good |
| Recommended | 2 | **Samsung** CLP-365w | 230 | 66 | 12.7 | Excellent | NA | 1.2 | 3.1 | Fair | NA | Excellent | Excellent | Excellent | Very good | Very good |
| | 3 | **Brother** HL-4570CDW | 500 | 64 | 1.3 | Excellent | 0.15 | 0.5 | 1.3 | Fair | Excellent | Excellent | Excellent | Excellent | Excellent | Very good |
| | 4 | **Brother** HL-3170CDW | 280 | 64 | 7.3 | Excellent | 0.15 | 0.55 | 2.7 | Good | NA | Excellent | Very good | Excellent | Very good | Excellent |
| | 5 | **Samsung** CLP-415NW | 300 | 62 | 9.2 | Excellent | NA | 0.85 | 3.2 | Fair | NA | Excellent | Excellent | Excellent | Excellent | Very good |
| | 6 | **Konica** Minolta Magicolor 1600W | 200 | 59 | 1.9 | Excellent | NA | 0.65 | 3 | Good | NA | Excellent | Excellent | Excellent | Very good | Good |
| **C INKJET** | | | | | | | | | | | | | | | | |
| Recommended | 1 | **Epson** Workforce Pro WP-4010 | 200 | 70 | 4.4 | NA | 0.45 | 1.45 | 2.1 | Very good | Excellent | Excellent | Very good | Excellent | Very good | Excellent |
| Recommended | 2 | **HP** Officejet Pro 251dw | 230 | 69 | 4.4 | Fair | 0.25 | 0.75 | 1.6 | Very good | Excellent | Very good | Very good | Excellent | Good | Excellent |
| CR Best Buy | 3 | **Canon** Pixma iP7220 | 80 | 69 | 6.9 | NA | 0.5 | 1.7 | 6.1 | Excellent | Excellent | Very good | Excellent | Excellent | Very good | Excellent |
| Recommended | 4 | **Epson** Stylus Photo R2000 | 600 | 69 | 7.5 | NA | 0.5 | 1.7 | 7.8 | Excellent | Excellent | Very good | Very good | Poor | Very good | Very good |
| CR Best Buy | 5 | **HP** Officejet 6100 | 80 | 69 | 5.2 | NA | 0.25 | 0.9 | 3.4 | Very good | Very good | Very good | Very good | Excellent | Very good | Excellent |
| Recommended | 6 | **Canon** Pixma iX6520 | 200 | 65 | 3.1 | NA | 0.55 | 1.85 | 6.8 | Very good | Excellent | Excellent | Very good | Excellent | Good | Excellent |
| Recommended | 7 | **HP** Officejet Pro 8100 | 100 | 65 | 3.9 | NA | 0.25 | 0.85 | 1.6 | Good | Very good | Excellent | Very good | Excellent | Good | Excellent |

**Ratings Key** Excellent · Very good · Good · Fair · Poor

**CR Best Buy** These models offer the best combination of performance and price. All are recommended.

**Recommended** These are high-performing models that stand out.

| Recommended | Rank | Brand & model | Price | Overall score (0–100; P \| F \| G \| VG \| E) | Ink cost/month ($) | Maintenance ink use | 4x6 photo cost ($) | 8x10 photo cost ($) | Text cost (cents) | Photo quality | 4x6 photo time | 8x10 photo time | Text quality | Text speed | Graphics quality | Power saving |
|---|---|---|---|---|---|---|---|---|---|---|---|---|---|---|---|---|
| **C** | | **INKJET** continued | | | | | | | | | | | | | | |
| | 8 | **HP** Officejet Pro X451DN | $450 | 61 | 3.5 | ○ | 0.2 | 0.75 | 1.5 | ◒ | ⊜ | ⊜ | ○ | ⊜ | ○ | ⊖ |
| | 9 | **Epson** Artisan 50 | 230 | 61 | 5.6 | NA | 0.65 | 2.2 | 4.5 | ⊖ | ○ | ⊖ | ○ | ○ | ⊖ | ⊜ |
| | 10 | **Epson** WorkForce 30 | 70 | 55 | 4.4 | NA | 0.5 | 1.7 | 4.8 | ○ | ○ | ○ | ⊖ | ⊜ | ⊖ | ⊜ |
| | 11 | **Epson** Stylus Photo R2880 | 600 | 47 | 6.4 | NA | 0.5 | 1.7 | 3.9 | ⊜ | ○ | ⊖ | ◒ | ● | ⊖ | ⊜ |

## Guide to the Ratings

**Overall score** is based mainly on speed and text/photo quality. The displayed score is out of a total of 100 points. **Ink cost/month ($)** is estimated cost (in dollars) for ink or toner in a month of typical use. For inkjets: 23 text pages, 9 graphics pages, 2.4 large photos, 3.6 small photos, and 3.5 photos on plain paper. For lasers: 62 text pages, 24 graphics pages, 1.7 large photos, 1.9 small photos, and 2.3 photos on plain paper. **Maintenance ink use** reflects the amount of extra ink used by an inkjet printer to maintain its print heads. "NA" indicates an older model that did not undergo these tests. **4x6 photo cost ($), 8X10 photo cost ($),** and **text cost (cents)** indicates the cost per print. **Photo quality** reflects a photo's appearance. The **4x6 photo time** score reflects how quickly the model can print one 4x6 photo on photo-quality paper. One minute or less is excellent; 1 to 2 minutes is very good; 2 to 4 minutes is good; 4 to 6 minutes is fair; and longer than 6 minutes is poor. The **8x10 photo time** score reflects how quickly the model can print one 8x10 photo on photo-quality paper. Two minutes or less is excellent; 2 to 4 minutes is very good; 4 to 6 minutes is good; 6 to 8 minutes is fair; and longer than 8 minutes is poor. **Text quality** assesses clarity and crispness of black text. **Text speed** reflects how quickly the model can print text on five pages of plain, letter-sized pages. Thirty seconds or less is excellent; 31 to 60 seconds is very good; 61 to 90 seconds is good; 91 to 120 seconds is fair; and longer than 120 seconds is poor. **Graphics quality** assesses the appearance of color graphics produced by the printer, or black-and-white graphics for black-and-white lasers. **Power saving** indicates how well the printer conserves power between uses. **Price** is approximate retail.

# Quick Guide RANGES

Electric smoothtops are the most popular and blend high performance and value. Pro-style gas and dual-fuel ranges are the most expensive, with style the big draw.

### What to look for

- On electric and gas ranges, at least one high-heat element or burner to heat large quantities of food quickly
- Dual ovens if you want to cook two meals at once
- Induction, which uses a magnetic field to heat more quickly and efficiently. Prices are dropping, though you'll need magnetic cookware
- At least five oven-rack positions for flexibility

### What to skip

- Dual-fuel models, which blend a gas cooktop with an electric oven. Our tests did not find an advantage to this combination

### What you'll pay

About $400 to $600 for coil; $700 to $1,700 for smoothtop; $1,700 to $2,700 for induction; $600 to $2,000 for gas; $3,000-plus for pro-style.

For more buying advice, go to *ConsumerReports.org/ranges*

### Shopping tip

Induction models are about 25 percent faster than electric smoothtops in our tests and even faster than gas models.

Scan this or see how, page 11

**All tested models** In performance order, within types.

Similar models, in small type, are comparable to tested model. Overall score: 0–100; P | F | G | VG | E

**A COIL TOP, SINGLE OVEN (30-INCH)**

| Recommended | Rank | Brand & model | Price | Overall score | Cooktop high | Cooktop low | Baking | Broiling | Oven capacity | Self-cleaning | High-power burners | Medium-power burners | Low-power burners | Convection mode | Double oven | Cooking drawer | Slide-in | Stainless steel available |
|---|---|---|---|---|---|---|---|---|---|---|---|---|---|---|---|---|---|---|
| ✔ | 1 | **Kenmore** 90212 | $430 | 81 | VG | E | VG | G | E | E | 2 | 0 | 2 | | | | | • |
| | 2 | **Frigidaire** FFEF3015LW | 450 | 78 | VG | E | VG | G | E | E | 2 | 0 | 2 | | | | | • |
| | 3 | **Hotpoint** RB757DPWH | 400 | 76 | VG | E | VG | VG | VG | VG | 2 | 0 | 2 | | | | | |
| | 4 | **Whirlpool** RY160LXTQ | 800 | 75 | VG | E | VG | G | VG | E | 2 | 0 | 2 | | | | • | • |
| | 5 | **Amana** AER5523XAW AER5524XA | 450 | 69 | VG | E | G | G | VG | E | 2 | 0 | 2 | | | | | |
| | 6 | **Whirlpool** RF263LXTQ | 400 | 65 | VG | E | VG | F | VG | E | 2 | 0 | 2 | | | | | • |

| Recommended | Rank | Brand & model (Similar models, in small type, are comparable to tested model.) | Price | Overall score (0–100; P \| F \| G \| VG \| E) | Test results: Cooktop high | Cooktop low | Baking | Broiling | Oven capacity | Self-cleaning | Features: High-power burners | Medium-power burners | Low-power burners | Convection mode | Double oven | Cooking drawer | Slide-in | Stainless steel available |
|---|---|---|---|---|---|---|---|---|---|---|---|---|---|---|---|---|---|---|
| **A** | | **COIL TOP, SINGLE OVEN (30-INCH)** continued | | | | | | | | | | | | | | | | |
| | 7 | **Kenmore** 90313 | $ 600 | 65 | Very good | Excellent | Good | Excellent | Excellent | Excellent | 2 | 0 | 2 | • | | | | • |
| | 8 | **Whirlpool** WFC310S0AW | 500 | 63 | Very good | Excellent | Very good | Fair | Very good | Excellent | 2 | 0 | 2 | | | | | • |
| | 9 | **GE** JBP35DDWW | 600 | 57 | Excellent | Good | Good | Very good | Excellent | Excellent | 2 | 0 | 2 | | | | | • |
| | 10 | **Kenmore** 90112 | 400 | 54 | Good | Good | Good | Excellent | Good | NA | 2 | 0 | 2 | | | | | • |
| | 11 | **Whirlpool** WFC340S0AW | 700 | 44 | Very good | Excellent | Very good | Poor | Very good | Very good | 2 | 0 | 2 | | | | | • |
| **B** | | **INDUCTION SMOOTHTOP, SINGLE OVEN (30-INCH)** | | | | | | | | | | | | | | | | |
| ✔ | 1 | **GE** Profile PHB925STSS | 2,700 | 90 | Excellent | Excellent | Very good | Excellent | Excellent | Excellent | 3 | 1 | 0 | • | | | | • |
| ✔ | 2 | **Kenmore** Elite 97203 | 2,500 | 89 | Excellent | Excellent | Excellent | Excellent | Excellent | Excellent | 3 | 1 | 0 | • | | | | • |
| ✔ | 3 | **Samsung** FTQ307NWGX | 2,000 | 89 | Excellent | Excellent | Excellent | Excellent | Excellent | Very good | 2 | 2 | 0 | • | | | | • |
| | 4 | **Samsung** NE595N0PBSR | 1,700 | 77 | Excellent | Excellent | Very good | Very good | Excellent | Very good | 2 | 0 | 2 | • | | | | • |
| | 5 | **Electrolux** EW30IS65JS | 3,200 | 73 | Excellent | Very good | Good | Excellent | Good | Excellent | 3 | 1 | 0 | • | | • | • | • |
| | 6 | **Maytag** MIR8890AS | 1,800 | 67 | Excellent | Excellent | Very good | Good | Excellent | Poor | 2 | 0 | 2 | • | | | | • |
| **C** | | **SMOOTHTOP, DOUBLE OVEN (30-INCH)** | | | | | | | | | | | | | | | | |
| ✔ | 1 | **GE** Profile PS978STSS | 2,800 | 86 | Very good | Excellent | Excellent | Very good | Excellent | Excellent | 2 | 1 | 1 | • | • | | • | • |
| ✔ | 2 | **Maytag** MET8885XS | 1,700 | 83 | Excellent | Excellent | Excellent | Good | Excellent | Good | 2 | 0 | 2 | • | • | | | • |
| ✔ | 3 | **Frigidaire** FGEF302TNF | 1,400 | 82 | Excellent | Excellent | Very good | Very good | Excellent | Excellent | 2 | 0 | 2 | | • | | | • |
| ✔ | 4 | **Frigidaire** FGEF308TNF | 1,800 | 81 | Very good | Excellent | Very good | Very good | Excellent | Excellent | 1 | 2 | 1 | • | • | | | • |
| ✔ | 5 | **LG** LDE3015ST | 1,300 | 81 | Excellent | Excellent | Very good | Excellent | Excellent | Very good | 2 | 0 | 2 | | • | | | • |
| | 6 | **KitchenAid** Architect Series II KERS507XSS | 1,600 | 77 | Very good | Excellent | Very good | Good | Excellent | Good | 2 | 0 | 2 | • | • | | | • |
| | 7 | **Kenmore** 98053 | 1,600 | 76 | Excellent | Very good | Very good | Good | Very good | Very good | 2 | 0 | 2 | • | • | | | • |

**Ratings Key** Excellent · Very good · Good · Fair · Poor

**CR Best Buy** These models offer the best combination of performance and price. All are recommended.

✔ **Recommended** These are high-performing models that stand out.

Ratings key (overall score scale 0–100): P | F | G | VG | E

| Recommended | Rank | Brand & model (Similar models, in small type, are comparable to tested model.) | Price | Overall score | Cooktop high | Cooktop low | Baking | Broiling | Oven capacity | Self-cleaning | High-power burners | Medium-power burners | Low-power burners | Convection mode | Double oven | Cooking drawer | Slide-in | Stainless steel available |
|---|---|---|---|---|---|---|---|---|---|---|---|---|---|---|---|---|---|---|
| **C** | | **SMOOTHTOP, DOUBLE OVEN (30-INCH)** continued | | | | | | | | | | | | | | | | |
| | **8** | **Frigidaire** FGEF301DNW | $1,300 | 75 | E | VG | VG | G | E | E | 2 | 0 | 2 | | • | | | • |
| | **9** | **GE** JB850DTWW | 1,150 | 75 | E | E | VG | G | E | VG | 2 | 0 | 2 | | • | | | • |
| | **10** | **Samsung** FE710DRS | 1,400 | 73 | E | VG | VG | VG | E | VG | 2 | 0 | 2 | • | • | | | • |
| | **11** | **GE** PB975STSS | 1,400 | 72 | VG | VG | VG | VG | E | VG | 1 | 2 | 1 | • | • | | | • |
| | **12** | **Whirlpool** GGE388LXQ | 1,100 | 71 | VG | E | G | VG | E | G | 2 | 0 | 2 | | • | | | • |
| | **13** | **LG** LDE3017ST | 1,300 | 69 | VG | E | G | E | E | E | 2 | 0 | 2 | • | • | | | • |
| | **14** | **Frigidaire** FGEF304DKW | 1,500 | 67 | VG | E | G | VG | VG | E | 2 | 0 | 2 | • | • | | | • |
| | **15** | **Frigidaire** FGEF306TM | 1,300 | 57 | VG | E | F | VG | E | VG | 2 | 0 | 2 | • | • | | | • |
| | **16** | **LG** LDE3035ST | 1,400 | 49 | E | E | P | E | E | E | 2 | 0 | 2 | | • | | | • |
| **D** | | **SMOOTHTOP, SINGLE OVEN (30-INCH)** | | | | | | | | | | | | | | | | |
| ✓ | **1** | **Kenmore** 92163 | 1,550 | 87 | E | E | VG | E | E | E | 2 | 0 | 2 | • | | | | • |
| ✓ | **2** | **GE** JB705STSS | 1,000 | 86 | E | E | VG | VG | E | E | 2 | 0 | 2 | • | | | | • |
| ✓ | **3** | **LG** LRE3023S | 1,000 | 86 | E | E | VG | E | E | VG | 2 | 0 | 2 | • | | | | • |
| ✓ | **4** | **GE** Café CS980SNSS | 2,800 | 86 | VG | E | E | E | E | G | 1 | 2 | 2 | • | | • | | • |
| ✓ | **5** | **LG** LRE3025S | 1,250 | 86 | E | E | E | VG | E | VG | 2 | 0 | 2 | • | | | | • |
| ✓ | **6** | **GE** PB920STSS | 1,800 | 85 | E | E | VG | VG | E | E | 1 | 2 | 1 | • | | | | • |
| ✓ | **7** | **Electrolux** EI30EF35JS | 1,600 | 85 | E | E | E | G | VG | E | 2 | 1 | 1 | • | | | | • |
| ✓ | **8** | **Kenmore** 92803 | 850 | 84 | E | E | VG | E | E | E | 2 | 0 | 2 | • | | | | • |
| ✓ | **9** | **GE** JB650DTWW<br>JB655DTWW | 800 | 81 | E | E | VG | VG | E | E | 2 | 0 | 2 | | | | | • |
| ✓ | **10** | **LG** LRE3012ST | 850 | 81 | E | E | VG | VG | E | VG | 2 | 0 | 2 | | | | | • |
| | **11** | **LG** LSE3092ST | 2,200 | 80 | E | E | VG | VG | E | VG | 2 | 0 | 2 | • | | • | • | • |
| | **12** | **Samsung** FE-R300SB | 550 | 80 | VG | E | VG | G | E | G | 2 | 0 | 2 | | | | | • |
| | **13** | **Frigidaire** FFE-F3018LW<br>FFEF3020LW | 600 | 79 | VG | E | VG | G | E | E | 2 | 0 | 2 | | | | | • |
| | **14** | **GE** JSP42DNWW | 1,200 | 79 | VG | E | VG | VG | VG | G | 1 | 2 | 1 | | | | • | • |
| | **15** | **GE** JSP46DNWW<br>JSP46DPWW | 1,450 | 78 | VG | E | E | E | VG | F | 1 | 2 | 1 | • | | | • | • |

## D SMOOTHTOP, SINGLE OVEN (30-INCH) continued

| Recommended | Rank | Brand & model (Similar models, in small type, are comparable to tested model.) | Price | Overall score (0–100; P \| F \| G \| VG \| E) | Test results: Cooktop high | Cooktop low | Baking | Broiling | Oven capacity | Self-cleaning | Features: High-power burners | Medium-power burners | Low-power burners | Convection mode | Double oven | Cooking drawer | Slide-in | Stainless steel available |
|---|---|---|---|---|---|---|---|---|---|---|---|---|---|---|---|---|---|---|
| | 16 | **LG** LRE30453SB | $ 730 | 78 | Very good | Excellent | Very good | Excellent | Excellent | Very good | 2 | 0 | 2 | • | | | | • |
| | 17 | **Samsung** NE594R0ABSR | 850 | 77 | Excellent | Excellent | Very good | Very good | Excellent | Very good | 2 | 0 | 2 | • | | | | • |
| | 18 | **Electrolux** EW30ES65GW | 2,200 | 77 | Excellent | Excellent | Very good | Very good | Good | Good | 2 | 1 | 2 | • | | • | • | • |
| | 19 | **Maytag** MER8770WW | 800 | 76 | Excellent | Excellent | Very good | Good | Excellent | Very good | 2 | 0 | 2 | • | | | | • |
| | 20 | **Whirlpool** WFE371LVB | 550 | 76 | Very good | Very good | Very good | Very good | Excellent | Good | 2 | 0 | 2 | | | | | • |
| | 21 | **LG** LRE30955ST | 1,600 | 76 | Good | Excellent | Very good | Very good | Excellent | Very good | 1 | 2 | 1 | • | | | | • |
| | 22 | **Frigidaire** Professional FPEF3081MF | 900 | 76 | Very good | Excellent | Very good | Very good | Very good | Very good | 1 | 2 | 1 | • | | | | • |
| | 23 | **Frigidaire** Gallery FGEF3031KW | 650 | 76 | Very good | Excellent | Good | Excellent | Excellent | Good | 2 | 0 | 2 | | | | | • |
| | 24 | **Samsung** NE597R0ABSR | 1,200 | 75 | Excellent | Very good | Very good | Very good | Excellent | Very good | 2 | 0 | 2 | • | | | | • |
| | 25 | **GE** JB750DFWW | 1,000 | 75 | Very good | Very good | Very good | Good | Excellent | Excellent | 1 | 2 | 1 | • | | | | • |
| | 26 | **Kenmore** 92603 | 780 | 74 | Excellent | Excellent | Good | Excellent | Excellent | Excellent | 2 | 0 | 2 | | | | | • |
| | 27 | **Frigidaire** Gallery FGEF3032MF | 675 | 74 | Excellent | Excellent | Good | Excellent | Very good | Very good | 2 | 0 | 2 | • | | | | • |
| | 28 | **KitchenAid** Architect Series KERS807SSS | 2,000 | 71 | Very good | Excellent | Very good | Good | Good | Very good | 2 | 2 | 0 | • | | | | • |
| | 29 | **Jenn-Air** JER8885RAS | 1,600 | 70 | Very good | Excellent | Good | Good | Very good | Excellent | 2 | 0 | 2 | • | | | | • |
| | 30 | **Samsung** FTQ353IWUX | 800 | 70 | Very good | Good | Very good | Very good | Excellent | Very good | 2 | 0 | 2 | • | | | | • |
| | 31 | **Maytag** MER7765WW | 600 | 69 | Very good | Excellent | Very good | Good | Very good | Good | 2 | 0 | 2 | • | | | | • |
| | 32 | **Whirlpool** GFE461LVQ | 800 | 68 | Very good | Excellent | Very good | Fair | Very good | Good | 2 | 0 | 2 | • | | | | • |
| | 33 | **Whirlpool** Gold GY399LXUQ | 1,500 | 68 | Very good | Excellent | Good | Very good | Good | Very good | 2 | 0 | 2 | • | | | • | |
| | 34 | **Samsung** FTQ387LWGX | 1,000 | 67 | Very good | Good | Very good | Very good | Excellent | Very good | 2 | 0 | 2 | • | | | | • |

**Ratings Key** Excellent · Very good · Good · Fair · Poor

**CR Best Buy** These models offer the best combination of performance and price. All are recommended.

**Recommended** These are high-performing models that stand out.

| Recommended | Rank | Brand & model<br>Similar models, in small type, are comparable to tested model. | Price | Overall score<br>0–100<br>P \| F \| G \| VG \| E | Test results: Cooktop high | Cooktop low | Baking | Broiling | Oven capacity | Self-cleaning | Features: High-power burners | Medium-power burners | Low-power burners | Convection mode | Double oven | Cooking drawer | Slide-in | Stainless steel available |
|---|---|---|---|---|---|---|---|---|---|---|---|---|---|---|---|---|---|---|
| **D** | | **SMOOTHTOP, SINGLE OVEN (30-INCH)** continued | | | | | | | | | | | | | | | | |
| | 35 | **Whirlpool** WFE720H0AS | $1,100 | 66 | ⊜ | ⊜ | ⊖ | ○ | ⊜ | ● | 2 | 0 | 2 | • | | | | • |
| | 36 | **KitchenAid** KERS206XWH | 850 | 65 | ⊖ | ○ | ○ | ⊖ | ⊜ | ⊖ | 2 | 0 | 2 | • | | | | • |
| | 37 | **Whirlpool** WFE330W0AW | 700 | 64 | ⊖ | ⊜ | ⊖ | ◒ | ⊖ | NA | 1 | 1 | 2 | | | | | • |
| | 38 | **Whirlpool** WFE510S0AW | 600 | 64 | ⊖ | ⊜ | ⊖ | ◒ | ⊖ | ⊜ | 2 | 0 | 2 | | | | | • |
| | 39 | **Whirlpool** WFE520C0AW | 700 | 63 | ⊖ | ⊜ | ⊖ | ◒ | ⊖ | ⊜ | 2 | 0 | 2 | | | | | • |
| | 40 | **Maytag** MER8674AS | 850 | 62 | ⊜ | ⊜ | ○ | ○ | ⊜ | ● | 2 | 0 | 2 | | | | | • |
| | 41 | **Whirlpool** WFE361LVQ | 450 | 62 | ⊖ | ⊖ | ⊖ | ◒ | ⊖ | ⊖ | 2 | 0 | 2 | | | | | • |
| | 42 | **Amana** AER5830VAB<br>AER5844VAW | 550 | 56 | ⊖ | ⊜ | ⊖ | ◒ | ⊖ | ⊜ | 2 | 0 | 2 | | | | | • |
| | 43 | **Kenmore** 91312 | 500 | 56 | ⊖ | ○ | ○ | ⊜ | ○ | NA | 1 | 1 | 2 | | | | | • |
| | 44 | **Maytag** MER8880AS | 1,100 | 54 | ⊖ | ○ | ⊖ | ○ | ⊜ | ● | 1 | 2 | 1 | • | | | | • |
| | 45 | **Amana** AER5823XAW | 450 | 52 | ○ | ⊜ | ⊖ | ◒ | ⊖ | NA | 0 | 2 | 2 | | | | | • |
| | 46 | **Frigidaire** FFEF3013LS | 500 | 48 | ⊖ | ⊜ | ◒ | ○ | ○ | NA | 2 | 0 | 2 | | | | | • |
| **E** | | **GAS AND DUAL-FUEL, DOUBLE OVEN (30-INCH)** | | | | | | | | | | | | | | | | |
| ✔ | 1 | **LG** LDG3037ST | 1,900 | 75 | ○ | ⊜ | ⊜ | ⊖ | ⊖ | ◒ | 2 | 2 | 1 | • | • | | | • |
| ✔ | 2 | **KitchenAid** KDRS505XSS Dual-fuel | 2,000 | 71 | ○ | ⊜ | ⊖ | ⊖ | ⊜ | ○ | 1 | 2 | 2 | • | • | | | • |
| ✔ | 3 | **LG** LDG3016ST | 1,800 | 70 | ○ | ⊜ | ⊖ | ○ | ⊖ | ○ | 2 | 2 | 1 | • | • | | | • |
| | 4 | **GE** JGB870SETSS | 1,500 | 61 | ⊖ | ⊜ | ⊖ | ◒ | ⊜ | ○ | 1 | 2 | 2 | • | • | | | • |
| | 5 | **Kenmore** 78013 | 1,650 | 58 | ⊖ | ○ | ⊖ | ◒ | ⊜ | ⊖ | 2 | 1 | 1 | | • | | | • |
| | 6 | **Jenn-Air** JGR8890ADP | 1,850 | 58 | ○ | ⊖ | ○ | ○ | ⊜ | ⊖ | 2 | 2 | 0 | • | • | | | • |
| | 7 | **LG** LDG3035ST | 1,600 | 57 | ○ | ⊜ | ⊖ | ◒ | ⊖ | ◒ | 2 | 2 | 1 | | • | | | • |
| | 8 | **LG** LDG3015ST | 1,500 | 57 | ○ | ⊖ | ○ | ○ | ⊜ | ◒ | 2 | 2 | 1 | | • | | | • |

| Recommended | Rank | Brand & model<br>Similar models, in small type, are comparable to tested model. | Price | Overall score<br>0 100<br>P \| F \| G \| VG \| E | Test results: Cooktop high | Cooktop low | Baking | Broiling | Oven capacity | Self-cleaning | Features: High-power burners | Medium-power burners | Low-power burners | Convection mode | Double oven | Cooking drawer | Slide-in | Stainless steel available |
|---|---|---|---|---|---|---|---|---|---|---|---|---|---|---|---|---|---|---|
| **E** | | **GAS AND DUAL-FUEL, DOUBLE OVEN (30-INCH)** continued | | | | | | | | | | | | | | | | |
| | 9 | **GE** Café CGS990SETSS | $2,900 | 57 | ⊖ | ⊜ | ○ | ◒ | ⊜ | ◒ | 2 | 2 | 1 | • | • | | | • |
| | 10 | **Whirlpool** GGG388LXQ | 1,100 | 57 | ○ | ⊜ | ○ | ◒ | ⊜ | ○ | 1 | 2 | 1 | | • | | | • |
| | 11 | **Frigidaire** FGGF304DLF FGGF301DNF | 1,600 | 51 | ⊖ | ○ | ○ | ◒ | ⊖ | ⊖ | 2 | 2 | 1 | • | • | | | • |
| | 12 | **Maytag** MGT8885XS | 1,500 | 43 | ○ | ⊜ | ⊖ | ● | ⊜ | ○ | 1 | 2 | 2 | • | • | | | • |
| **F** | | **GAS AND DUAL-FUEL, SINGLE OVEN (30-INCH)** | | | | | | | | | | | | | | | | |
| ☑ | 1 | **LG** LRG3097ST | 1,900 | 74 | ⊖ | ⊜ | ⊖ | ⊖ | ⊜ | ○ | 2 | 2 | 1 | • | | | | • |
| ☑ | 2 | **LG** LRG3095ST | 1,500 | 72 | ○ | ⊜ | ⊖ | ⊖ | ⊜ | ○ | 2 | 2 | 1 | • | | | | • |
| ✅ | 3 | **Frigidaire** Gallery FGGF3032MW | 775 | 71 | ○ | ⊜ | ⊖ | ○ | ⊖ | ○ | 2 | 2 | 1 | • | | | | • |
| ☑ | 4 | **LG** LRG3091SW | 1,000 | 71 | ○ | ⊜ | ⊖ | ○ | ⊜ | ○ | 2 | 2 | 1 | | | | | • |
| | 5 | **Maytag** MGR8772WW | 1,000 | 68 | ○ | ⊜ | ⊖ | ○ | ⊖ | ⊖ | 2 | 3 | 0 | • | | | | • |
| | 6 | **GE** JGBS23SETSS | 800 | 68 | ○ | ⊖ | ⊖ | ○ | ⊜ | NA | 1 | 2 | 1 | | | | | • |
| | 7 | **Frigidaire** Gallery FGGF3031KW | 700 | 68 | ⊖ | ○ | ⊜ | ○ | ⊖ | ○ | 2 | 2 | 1 | | | | | • |
| | 8 | **Maytag** MGR7665WB | 700 | 66 | ○ | ⊖ | ⊜ | ○ | ⊖ | ○ | 2 | 1 | 1 | | | | | • |
| | 9 | **Whirlpool** Gold GW399LXUQ | 1,400 | 66 | ○ | ⊜ | ⊖ | ○ | ○ | ○ | 2 | 1 | 1 | • | | | • | • |
| | 10 | **Frigidaire** FGF368GS | 500 | 65 | ○ | ⊜ | ⊖ | ◒ | ⊖ | ○ | 1 | 2 | 1 | | | | | • |
| | 11 | **Electrolux** EI30GF35JS | 1,500 | 65 | ⊖ | ⊜ | ⊖ | ◒ | ⊖ | ⊖ | 2 | 2 | 1 | • | | | | • |
| | 12 | **Samsung** FX710BGS FX510BGS | 1,500 | 65 | ⊖ | ○ | ⊖ | ○ | ⊜ | ◒ | 2 | 2 | 1 | • | | | | • |
| | 13 | **GE** JGB600SETSS | 800 | 65 | ⊖ | ⊜ | ⊜ | ◒ | ⊖ | ○ | 1 | 2 | 2 | • | | | | • |
| | 14 | **Frigidaire** FGF382HS | 700 | 64 | ○ | ⊖ | ⊖ | ○ | ○ | ○ | 1 | 2 | 1 | | | | | • |
| | 15 | **GE** Café CGS980SEMSS | 2,700 | 63 | ○ | ⊜ | ⊖ | ◒ | ⊖ | ○ | 2 | 1 | 2 | • | | • | | • |
| | 16 | **Kenmore** 72402 | 600 | 63 | ○ | ⊜ | ⊖ | ◒ | ⊖ | ⊜ | 1 | 2 | 1 | | | | | • |
| | 17 | **Maytag** MGR7661WW | 500 | 63 | ○ | ⊜ | ⊖ | ◒ | ⊖ | ⊖ | 1 | 2 | 1 | | | | | • |

| Recommended | Rank | Brand & model<br>Similar models, in small type, are comparable to tested model. | Price | Overall score<br>0–100<br>P \| F \| G \| VG \| E | Test results: Cooktop high | Cooktop low | Baking | Broiling | Oven capacity | Self-cleaning | Features: High-power burners | Medium-power burners | Low-power burners | Convection mode | Double oven | Cooking drawer | Slide-in | Stainless steel available |
|---|---|---|---|---|---|---|---|---|---|---|---|---|---|---|---|---|---|---|
| **F** | | **GAS AND DUAL-FUEL, SINGLE OVEN (30-INCH)** continued | | | | | | | | | | | | | | | | |
| | 18 | **GE** Café C2S980SEMSS Dual-fuel | $2,800 | 62 | Good | Excellent | Very good | Fair | Very good | Good | 2 | 1 | 2 | • | | • | | • |
| | 19 | **Samsung** NX583G0VBSR | 900 | 62 | Very good | Good | Excellent | Fair | Excellent | Good | 2 | 2 | 1 | • | | | | • |
| | 20 | **GE** Café CGS985SETSS | 2,700 | 61 | Very good | Excellent | Very good | Fair | Very good | Fair | 2 | 2 | 1 | • | | • | | • |
| | 21 | **Jenn-Air** JDS8860BDP Dual-fuel | 2,400 | 61 | Good | Good | Very good | Good | Good | Very good | 2 | 1 | 1 | • | | | • | • |
| | 22 | **GE** JGBP-28DEMBB | 700 | 60 | Good | Very good | Very good | Good | Very good | Fair | 2 | 1 | 1 | | | | | • |
| | 23 | **Frigidaire** Gallery FGGF3054KW | 850 | 60 | Very good | Very good | Excellent | Fair | Very good | Good | 2 | 2 | 1 | • | | | | • |
| | 24 | **Amana** AGR6011VDS | 900 | 60 | Fair | Excellent | Excellent | Good | Excellent | Good | 1 | 2 | 1 | • | | | | • |
| | 25 | **GE** JGB800SEPSS<br>JGB810SETSS | 1,100 | 60 | Very good | Excellent | Very good | Fair | Very good | Good | 2 | 2 | 1 | | | | | • |
| | 26 | **GE** JGB296SETSS | 800 | 60 | Very good | Very good | Excellent | Fair | Very good | Good | 1 | 2 | 2 | • | | | | • |
| | 27 | **Electrolux** EW30GS65GW | 2,200 | 59 | Good | Excellent | Very good | Fair | Good | Good | 2 | 1 | 1 | • | | | • | • |
| | 28 | **Kenmore** 72703 | 850 | 59 | Very good | Very good | Very good | Fair | Very good | Very good | 2 | 2 | 1 | | | | | • |
| | 29 | **KitchenAid** KGRS206XWH | 850 | 59 | Very good | Very good | Very good | Fair | Very good | Good | 2 | 2 | 1 | • | | | | • |
| | 30 | **GE** PGS975SEMSS | 2,100 | 58 | Good | Excellent | Very good | Fair | Good | Good | 1 | 2 | 1 | • | | | • | • |
| | 31 | **GE** JGB281SERSS | 700 | 57 | Good | Excellent | Very good | Fair | Very good | Good | 1 | 2 | 1 | | | | | • |
| | 32 | **Whirlpool** WFG510S0AS | 600 | 56 | Good | Good | Excellent | Fair | Very good | Very good | 1 | 2 | 1 | | | | | • |
| | 33 | **Kenmore** 72313 | 1,100 | 55 | Very good | Good | Very good | Fair | Very good | Very good | 2 | 2 | 1 | • | | | | • |
| | 34 | **Whirlpool** WFG520S0AS | 600 | 54 | Good | Good | Excellent | Fair | Very good | Very good | 2 | 1 | 1 | | | | | • |
| | 35 | **Kenmore** 72903 | 1,000 | 54 | Very good | Good | Very good | Fair | Good | Very good | 2 | 2 | 1 | • | | | | • |
| | 36 | **Frigidaire** FFGF3023LS | 700 | 53 | Good | Excellent | Excellent | Poor | Very good | Excellent | 1 | 2 | 1 | | | | | • |
| | 37 | **Kenmore** 72503 | 700 | 53 | Good | Good | Very good | Fair | Very good | Very good | 1 | 2 | 1 | | | | | • |

**Ratings Key** Excellent, Very good, Good, Fair, Poor

☑ **CR Best Buy** These models offer the best combination of performance and price. All are recommended.

✓ **Recommended** These are high-performing models that stand out.

| Recommended | Rank | Brand & model (Similar models, in small type, are comparable to tested model.) | Price | Overall score (0–100; P \| F \| G \| VG \| E) | Test results: Cooktop high | Cooktop low | Baking | Broiling | Oven capacity | Self-cleaning | Features: High-power burners | Medium-power burners | Low-power burners | Convection mode | Double oven | Cooking drawer | Slide-in | Stainless steel available |
|---|---|---|---|---|---|---|---|---|---|---|---|---|---|---|---|---|---|---|
| | **F** | **GAS AND DUAL-FUEL, SINGLE OVEN (30-INCH)** continued | | | | | | | | | | | | | | | | |
| | 38 | **Frigidaire** Professional FPG3081KF | $1,000 | 52 | ○ | ○ | ⊖ | ◒ | ⊖ | ⊖ | 2 | 2 | 1 | • | | | | • |
| | 39 | **GE** Café C2S985SETSS Dual-fuel | 2,700 | 51 | ⊖ | ⊜ | ◒ | ○ | ⊖ | ◒ | 2 | 2 | 1 | • | | • | | • |
| | 40 | **Whirlpool** WFG540H0AH | 900 | 51 | ○ | ○ | ⊜ | ◒ | ⊖ | ● | 2 | 2 | 1 | • | | | | • |
| | 41 | **Hotpoint** RGB790DERWW | 500 | 51 | ○ | ⊖ | ○ | ◒ | ⊖ | ◒ | 1 | 2 | 1 | | | | | • |
| | 42 | **Whirlpool** WFG361LVQ | 450 | 51 | ○ | ⊖ | ⊖ | ◒ | ⊖ | ○ | 1 | 2 | 1 | | | | | • |
| | 43 | **Maytag** MGR8880AS | 1,100 | 50 | ○ | ○ | ⊖ | ◒ | ⊖ | ● | 2 | 2 | 1 | • | | | | • |
| | 44 | **Maytag** MGR8674AS | 850 | 49 | ○ | ○ | ⊖ | ◒ | ⊖ | ● | 2 | 2 | 1 | | | | | • |
| | 45 | **Kenmore** 70602 | 600 | 48 | ◒ | ⊖ | ⊖ | ⊖ | ○ | NA | 1 | 3 | 1 | | | | | • |
| | 46 | **Frigidaire** FFGF3017LW | 550 | 46 | ○ | ⊖ | ○ | ◒ | ○ | NA | 1 | 2 | 1 | | | | | • |
| | 47 | **Kenmore** 70502 | 500 | 42 | ○ | ◒ | ⊖ | ⊖ | ○ | NA | 1 | 3 | 0 | | | | | • |
| | 48 | **KitchenAid** Architect Series KGRS807SSS | 1,700 | 31 | ○ | ● | ⊖ | ⊖ | ○ | ○ | 2 | 0 | 2 | • | | | | • |
| | **G** | **PRO-STYLE GAS AND DUAL-FUEL (30-INCH)** | | | | | | | | | | | | | | | | |
| ✓ | 1 | **KitchenAid** KDRS407VSS<br>KDRU707VSS Dual-fuel | 4,000 | 72 | ⊖ | ⊜ | ⊖ | ○ | ○ | ⊖ | 3 | 0 | 1 | • | | | | • |
| | 2 | **Wolf** DF304 Dual-fuel | 6,400 | 68 | ○ | ⊖ | ⊖ | ⊖ | ○ | ◒ | 3 | 1 | 0 | • | | | | • |
| | 3 | **Dacor** DR30G | 3,100 | 66 | ○ | ⊜ | ○ | ○ | ⊖ | NA | 3 | 1 | 0 | • | | | | • |
| | 4 | **GE** Monogram ZGP304NRSS | 5,000 | 65 | ○ | ⊜ | ⊖ | ○ | ⊜ | ○ | 1 | 3 | 0 | • | | | | • |
| | 5 | **Kenmore** Pro 79523 Dual-fuel | 3,800 | 65 | ⊖ | ⊖ | ⊖ | ⊖ | ⊖ | ⊖ | 1 | 2 | 1 | • | | | | • |
| | 6 | **Jenn-Air** JGRP430WP | 4,000 | 62 | ○ | ⊜ | ⊜ | ◒ | ○ | ⊖ | 3 | 0 | 1 | • | | | | • |
| | 7 | **DCS** RGU-305 | 3,700 | 62 | ○ | ⊜ | ○ | ⊖ | ○ | NA | 5 | 0 | 0 | • | | | | • |
| | 8 | **NXR** DRGB3001 | 2,000 | 60 | ○ | ⊜ | ○ | ○ | ○ | NA | 4 | 0 | 0 | • | | | | • |
| | 9 | **DCS** RGTC305SS | 4,700 | 58 | ⊖ | ⊜ | ⊖ | ◒ | ◒ | ◒ | 5 | 0 | 0 | • | | | • | • |

| Recommended | Rank | Brand & model<br>Similar models, in small type, are comparable to tested model. | Price | Overall score<br>0–100<br>P \| F \| G \| VG \| E | Test results: Cooktop high | Cooktop low | Baking | Broiling | Oven capacity | Self-cleaning | Features: High-power burners | Medium-power burners | Low-power burners | Convection mode | Double oven | Cooking drawer | Slide-in | Stainless steel available |
|---|---|---|---|---|---|---|---|---|---|---|---|---|---|---|---|---|---|---|
| **G** | | **PRO-STYLE GAS AND DUAL-FUEL (30-INCH)** continued | | | | | | | | | | | | | | | | |
| | 10 | **Dacor** Epicure ER30GSCH | $3,600 | 58 | ○ | ⊜ | ○ | ○ | ○ | NA | 3 | 1 | 0 | • | | | | • |
| | 11 | **Viking** VDSC-530SS Dual-fuel | 5,500 | 52 | ○ | ⊜ | ○ | ⊖ | ⊖ | ○ | 4 | 0 | 0 | • | | | • | • |
| | 12 | **Thermador** PRG304GH | 4,500 | 52 | ⊖ | ⊜ | ◒ | ◒ | ○ | NA | 4 | 0 | 0 | • | | | | • |
| | 13 | **Dacor** Epicure ER30D Dual-fuel | 5,300 | 51 | ○ | ⊜ | ○ | ○ | ○ | ◒ | 3 | 1 | 0 | • | | | • | • |
| | 14 | **Viking** VGSC5304BSS | 5,000 | 46 | ⊖ | ⊜ | ◒ | ⊖ | ◒ | ◒ | 4 | 0 | 0 | • | | | | • |
| | 15 | **Bertazzoni** PRO304GASX | 3,100 | 45 | ⊖ | ⊖ | ◒ | ○ | ◒ | NA | 1 | 1 | 2 | • | | | | • |
| | 16 | **Wolf** GR304 | 4,900 | 45 | ○ | ⊜ | ◒ | ◒ | ○ | NA | 3 | 1 | 0 | • | | | | • |
| | 17 | **American Range** ARR304 | 3,600 | 32 | ⊖ | ● | ○ | ◒ | ⊖ | NA | 3 | 1 | 0 | • | | | | • |
| | 18 | **Blue Star** RNB304BV1SS | 3,700 | 31 | ⊖ | ● | ⊖ | ● | ⊖ | NA | 3 | 1 | 0 | • | | | | • |
| | 19 | **Bertazzoni** A30 4GGV XE<br>A30 4GGV XS | 2,400 | 24 | ○ | ● | ◒ | ○ | ◒ | NA | 1 | 1 | 2 | • | | | | • |
| **H** | | **PRO-STYLE GAS AND DUAL-FUEL (36-INCH)** | | | | | | | | | | | | | | | | |
| ✔ | 1 | **KitchenAid** KDRU763VSS Dual-fuel<br>KDRU767VSS, KDRS-463VSS, KDRS467VSS, KDRS462VSS | 6,000 | 74 | ⊖ | ⊜ | ⊖ | ⊖ | ⊖ | ⊖ | 3 | 0 | 1 | • | | | | • |
| ✔ | 2 | **GE** Monogram ZDP364NDPSS Dual-fuel | 7,500 | 72 | ○ | ⊜ | ⊖ | ○ | ⊖ | ⊖ | 4 | 0 | 0 | • | | | | • |
| | 3 | **Thermador** PRG366JG<br>PRG364JDG | 7,500 | 68 | ⊖ | ⊜ | ⊖ | ○ | ⊜ | ● | 6 | 0 | 0 | • | | | | • |
| | 4 | **Viking** VGSC536-4G | 7,200 | 68 | ⊖ | ⊜ | ⊖ | ⊖ | ○ | ◒ | 4 | 0 | 0 | • | | | | • |
| | 5 | **Wolf** GR366 | 6,000 | 59 | ○ | ⊜ | ○ | ◒ | ⊖ | NA | 5 | 1 | 0 | • | | | | • |
| | 6 | **NXR** DRGB3602 | 3,000 | 56 | ○ | ⊜ | ○ | ○ | ○ | NA | 6 | 0 | 0 | • | | | | • |
| | 7 | **Kenmore** Pro 79623 Dual-fuel | 5,500 | 52 | ⊖ | ○ | ○ | ○ | ⊜ | ⊖ | 2 | 4 | 0 | • | | | | • |
| | 8 | **Jenn-Air** JGRP436WP | 5,200 | 43 | ○ | ⊜ | ⊖ | ● | ⊖ | ⊖ | 5 | 0 | 1 | • | | | | • |

## Guide to the Ratings

**Overall score** reflects cooktop speed and simmer performance, and oven capacity, baking, broiling, and self-cleaning. The displayed score is out of a total of 100 points. **Cooktop high** is how quickly the most powerful element heated water to near-boil. **Cooktop low** is how well the lowest-powered element melted and held chocolate without scorching and how well the most powerful element, set on low, held tomato sauce below a boil. **Baking** reflects even browning of cakes and cookies in multi-rack baking tests. **Broiling** is even browning of a pan of burgers and high-heat searing. **Oven capacity** is our evaluation of usable space. **Self-cleaning** is the self-cleaning cycle's effectiveness after the oven is coated with a mixture of eggs, cheese, pie filling, and other ingredients. **Price** is approximate retail.

## Most & Least Reliable

### ELECTRIC RANGES

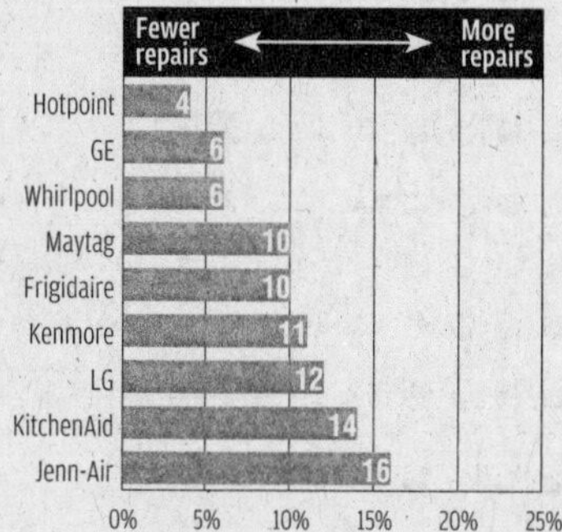


### GAS/DUAL-FUEL RANGES

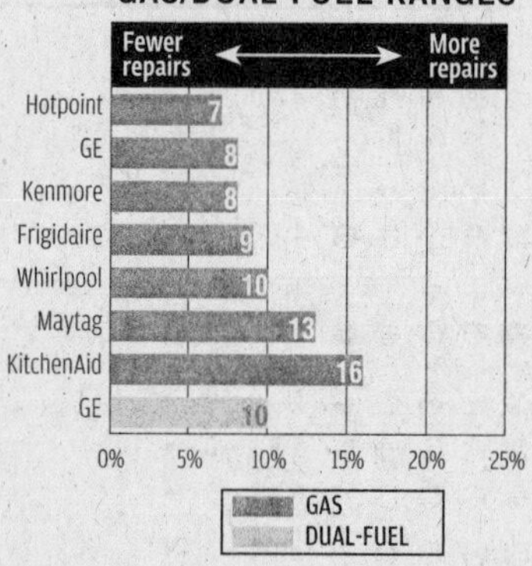


Hotpoint, General Electric, and Whirlpool were the least repair prone brands of electric ranges and KitchenAid and Jenn-Air were among the more repair prone brands of electric ranges. For gas ranges, KitchenAid was the most repair-prone brand; Maytag was also repair-prone. We lacked enough data to include Kenmore dual-fuel and Jenn-Air ranges in the repair graphs. But data we have indicate that Kenmore dual-fuel ranges have been reliable and Jenn-Air dual-fuel and gas ranges have been repair-prone. That's what we found when we asked more than 67,000 readers who bought electric ranges between 2007 and 2012 and gas ranges between 2006 and 2012 about their experiences. The graph shows the percentage of models for each brand that were repaired or had a serious problem. Differences of fewer than 3 points aren't meaningful, and we've adjusted the data to eliminate differences linked solely to age of the range. Models within a brand can vary, and design or manufacture changes might affect future reliability. Still, choosing a brand with a good repair history can improve your odds of getting a reliable model.

Source: Annual Product Reliability Survey, Consumer Reports National Research Center.

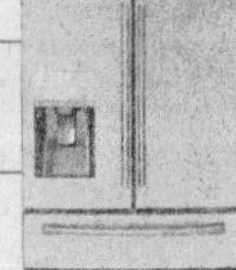

# Quick Guide REFRIGERATORS

Refrigerators are available in more sizes and configurations than ever. New features include hot-water dispensers and slim ice makers that fit in the door.

**Shopping tip**

Width is the key dimension if your new fridge will fill an existing opening; height matters too if there are cabinets overhead.

Scan this or see how, page 11

### What to look for

- Print-resistant stainless steel or faux-stainless finishes for busy kitchens (also consider classic white or black)
- Temperature-controlled drawers to keep meat, fish, cold cuts, and other foods at lower temperatures
- Split shelves to make space for taller items as needed
- Adjustable door bins and shelves, to make the most of available storage space

### What to skip

- Fancy climate controls. Many manufacturers claim special freshness technologies, but refrigerators that maintain consistent temperatures are best at keeping your food fresh. Dual evaporators help as well by maintaining optimal humidity levels

### What you'll pay

Figure on $1,600 to $3,000 for French-door models. Capable top-freezers start at under $1,000. Side-by-sides are around $1,500, and cabinet-depths cost $2,500 to $3,500.

For more buying advice, go to *ConsumerReports.org/refrigerators*

Recommended models only From 296 tested.

| Recommended | Rank | Brand & model<br>Similar models, in small type, are comparable to tested model. | Price | Overall score | Test results: Temperature performance | Energy efficiency | Noise | Ease of use | Energy cost/yr. ($) | Total usable capacity (cu. ft.) | Fridge usable capacity (cu. ft.) | Freezer usable capacity (cu. ft.) | Exterior height (in.) | Exterior width (in.) | Exterior depth (in.) |
|---|---|---|---|---|---|---|---|---|---|---|---|---|---|---|---|
| **A** | | **TOP FREEZER** | | | | | | | | | | | | | |
| ✔ | 1 | **GE** Profile PTS22LHS[WW]<br>Profile PTS22SHS[ ] | $1,400 | 69 | ⊜ | ⊖ | ○ | ○ | 64 | 17.1 | 11.8 | 5.3 | 68 | 33 | 32 |
| ✔ | 2 | **Whirlpool** WRT771REY[W] | 1,100 | 67 | ⊖ | ⊜ | ⊖ | ○ | 54 | 17.7 | 11.6 | 6.1 | 66 | 33 | 34 |
| ✔ | 3 | **Haier** HT21TS45SW | 900 | 65 | ⊖ | ⊜ | ⊖ | ● | 53 | 17.5 | 12.7 | 4.8 | 67 | 32 | 32 |
| ✔ | 4 | **LG** LTC22350[SW] | 1,000 | 65 | ⊖ | ⊜ | ○ | ◒ | 55 | 17.3 | 12.1 | 5.2 | 68 | 33 | 33 |
| ✔ | 5 | **Frigidaire** Gallery FGHT2144K[F]<br>Gallery FGHT2134K[ ] | 800 | 64 | ⊖ | ⊜ | ○ | ◒ | 57 | 16.7 | 12 | 4.7 | 70 | 30 | 33 |

| Recommended | Rank | Brand & model<br>**Similar models,** in small type, are comparable to tested model. | Price | Overall score | Test results: Temperature performance | Energy efficiency | Noise | Ease of use | Energy cost/yr. ($) | Total usable capacity (cu. ft.) | Fridge usable capacity (cu. ft.) | Freezer usable capacity (cu. ft.) | Exterior height (in.) | Exterior width (in.) | Exterior depth (in.) |
|---|---|---|---|---|---|---|---|---|---|---|---|---|---|---|---|
| | | **A TOP FREEZER** continued | | | | | | | | | | | | | |
| ✔ | 6 | **Haier** HT21TS77SP | $ 700 | 63 | ⊖ | ⊜ | ○ | ◒ | 47 | 17.6 | 12.7 | 4.9 | 67 | 32 | 32 |
| ✔ | 7 | **Haier** HT18TS77SP | 600 | 63 | ⊖ | ⊜ | ○ | ◒ | 41 | 15.4 | 11 | 4.4 | 66 | 30 | 31 |
| ✓ | 8 | **Frigidaire** LFHT2117L[W] (Lowe's) FFHT2117L[W] | 700 | 62 | ⊖ | ⊜ | ⊖ | ◒ | 55 | 17.1 | 12.3 | 4.8 | 69 | 30 | 34 |
| ✓ | 9 | **Kenmore** 78892 | 700 | 62 | ⊖ | ⊜ | ○ | ● | 52 | 15.1 | 11.5 | 3.6 | 66 | 30 | 31 |
| ✓ | 10 | **Maytag** M1TXEGMY[W] | 770 | 62 | ⊖ | ⊜ | ○ | ◒ | 59 | 16.7 | 10.9 | 5.8 | 66 | 33 | 31 |
| ✓ | 11 | **Kenmore** 79433 | 1,400 | 62 | ○ | ⊜ | ⊖ | ◒ | 54 | 19.4 | 13.8 | 5.6 | 69 | 33 | 32 |
| | | **B CONVENTIONAL BOTTOM-FREEZER** | | | | | | | | | | | | | |
| ✓ | 1 | **Whirlpool** Gold GB2FHDXW[Q] | 1,200 | 73 | ⊜ | ⊜ | ◒ | ◒ | 52 | 15.3 | 11.1 | 4.2 | 70 | 33 | 31 |
| ✔ | 2 | **Amana** ABB2221WE[W] ABB2224WE[ ] | 1,000 | 73 | ⊜ | ⊜ | ○ | ◒ | 56 | 16.5 | 11.4 | 5.1 | 70 | 33 | 32 |
| ✓ | 3 | **Maytag** MBF2258XE[W] MBL2258XE[ ], MBR2258XE[ ] | 1,100 | 73 | ⊜ | ⊜ | ○ | ◒ | 52 | 15.4 | 11.3 | 4.1 | 70 | 33 | 31 |
| ✓ | 4 | **Maytag** MBF1958XE[W] | 1,150 | 72 | ⊜ | ⊖ | ○ | ◒ | 50 | 12.8 | 9.2 | 3.6 | 67 | 30 | 31 |
| | | **C FOUR-DOOR FRENCH-DOOR BOTTOM-FREEZER** | | | | | | | | | | | | | |
| ✓ | 1 | **Samsung** RF31FMESBSR | 2,900 | 79 | ⊜ | ⊜ | ⊖ | ⊖ | 69 | 19 | 13 | 6 | 69 | 36 | 36 |
| | | **D THREE-DOOR FRENCH-DOOR BOTTOM-FREEZER** | | | | | | | | | | | | | |
| ✓ | 1 | **LG** LFX28991[ST] | 3,000 | 85 | ⊜ | ⊜ | ⊜ | ○ | 54 | 18.4 | 12.5 | 5.9 | 69 | 36 | 34 |
| ✓ | 2 | **Samsung** RF261BIAESR | 2,100 | 84 | ⊜ | ⊜ | ⊖ | ⊖ | 48 | 18.8 | 13.5 | 5.3 | 70 | 36 | 33 |
| ✓ | 3 | **Kenmore** Elite 72093 | 3,400 | 83 | ⊜ | ⊜ | ⊜ | ⊖ | 71 | 22.5 | 15.8 | 6.7 | 69 | 36 | 35 |
| ✔ | 4 | **Kenmore** 7160[3] | 1,700 | 83 | ⊜ | ⊜ | ⊜ | ○ | 52 | 17.5 | 12.5 | 5 | 69 | 36 | 32 |
| ✓ | 5 | **LG** LFX33975ST | 3,000 | 83 | ⊜ | ⊜ | ⊜ | ⊖ | 71 | 22.3 | 15.6 | 6.7 | 69 | 36 | 35 |
| ✔ | 6 | **Whirlpool** Gold GX5FHTXV[Q] Gold GX5FHDXV[ ] | 1,700 | 82 | ⊜ | ⊜ | ○ | ⊖ | 60 | 16.2 | 11.6 | 4.6 | 70 | 36 | 33 |

| Recommended | Rank | Brand & model (Similar models, in small type, are comparable to tested model.) | Price | Overall score | Temperature performance | Energy efficiency | Noise | Ease of use | Energy cost/yr. ($) | Total usable capacity (cu. ft.) | Fridge usable capacity (cu. ft.) | Freezer usable capacity (cu. ft.) | Exterior height (in.) | Exterior width (in.) | Exterior depth (in.) |
|---|---|---|---|---|---|---|---|---|---|---|---|---|---|---|---|
| | | **D THREE-DOOR FRENCH-DOOR BOTTOM-FREEZER** continued | | | | | | | | | | | | | |
| Recommended | 7 | **Samsung** RFG298HD[RS] (Lowe's) RFG297HD[ ], RFG296HD[ ] | $2,800 | 81 | Excellent | Very good | Excellent | Very good | 74 | 18.6 | 12.7 | 5.9 | 69 | 36 | 35 |
| Recommended | 8 | **LG** LFC25776[SW] | 1,750 | 81 | Excellent | Excellent | Excellent | Good | 51 | 18 | 13 | 5 | 70 | 36 | 33 |
| Recommended | 9 | **Samsung** RF323TEDB[SR] | 3,300 | 80 | Excellent | Excellent | Very good | Good | 73 | 21.8 | 14.7 | 7.1 | 69 | 36 | 36 |
| Recommended | 10 | **LG** LFX28979[ST] | 2,850 | 79 | Excellent | Excellent | Excellent | Good | 66 | 18.2 | 12.5 | 5.7 | 69 | 36 | 34 |
| Recommended | 11 | **Kenmore** Elite 7103[2] | 2,500 | 79 | Excellent | Very good | Excellent | Good | 67 | 16.9 | 11.8 | 5.1 | 70 | 33 | 33 |
| Recommended | 12 | **LG** LFX31925[ST] | 3,200 | 79 | Excellent | Excellent | Excellent | Very good | 73 | 19.4 | 13.4 | 6 | 69 | 36 | 34 |
| Recommended | 13 | **GE** Café CFE29TSDSS | 3,000 | 78 | Excellent | Very good | Very good | Very good | 72 | 19.6 | 13.2 | 6.4 | 69 | 36 | 36 |
| Recommended | 14 | **Samsung** RF261BEAE[SR] | 2,100 | 78 | Excellent | Excellent | Good | Very good | 57 | 18.6 | 13.4 | 5.2 | 69 | 36 | 35 |
| CR Best Buy | 15 | **Kenmore** 7201[2] | 1,550 | 78 | Excellent | Excellent | Very good | Good | 60 | 16.9 | 12 | 4.9 | 70 | 36 | 33 |
| Recommended | 16 | **LG** LFC25765[ST] | 1,900 | 78 | Excellent | Excellent | Excellent | Good | 60 | 17.9 | 12.6 | 5.3 | 69 | 33 | 34 |
| Recommended | 17 | **Kenmore** Elite 7205[3] | 3,200 | 78 | Excellent | Very good | Excellent | Very good | 75 | 19.4 | 13.4 | 6 | 71 | 36 | 35 |
| Recommended | 18 | **LG** LFX28978[SW] | 2,700 | 78 | Excellent | Excellent | Excellent | Good | 66 | 18.3 | 12.5 | 5.8 | 70 | 36 | 33 |
| Recommended | 19 | **LG** LFX25991[ST] | 3,400 | 77 | Excellent | Very good | Excellent | Very good | 60 | 14 | 9.5 | 4.5 | 69 | 36 | 29 |
| Recommended | 20 | **Kenmore** Elite 7230[3] | 1,920 | 76 | Excellent | Very good | Excellent | Good | 64 | 17.5 | 12.4 | 5.1 | 69 | 33 | 33 |
| | | **E SIDE-BY-SIDE** | | | | | | | | | | | | | |
| CR Best Buy | 1 | **Samsung** RS265TD[WP] RS263TD[ ], RS267TD[ ] | 1,300 | 76 | Very good | Very good | Excellent | Very good | 73 | 18.1 | 11.6 | 6.5 | 70 | 36 | 34 |
| Recommended | 2 | **KitchenAid** KSF26C6X[YY] | 1,950 | 75 | Excellent | Very good | Good | Very good | 75 | 18.6 | 12.2 | 6.4 | 69 | 36 | 34 |
| Recommended | 3 | **Bosch** Linea 800 B22CS80SN[S] B22CS50SN[ ] | 2,700 | 74 | Very good | Very good | Excellent | Very good | 75 | 14.5 | 9.5 | 5 | 69 | 36 | 28 |
| CR Best Buy | 4 | **Maytag** MSD2559XE[W] | 1,250 | 73 | Very good | Very good | Very good | Good | 67 | 15.9 | 10.4 | 5.5 | 70 | 36 | 33 |

**Ratings Key** Excellent Very good Good Fair Poor

**CR Best Buy** These models offer the best combination of performance and price. All are recommended.

**Recommended** These are high-performing models that stand out.

## E SIDE-BY-SIDE continued

| Recommended | Rank | Brand & model (Similar models, in small type, are comparable to tested model.) | Price | Overall score | Temperature performance | Energy efficiency | Noise | Ease of use | Energy cost/yr. ($) | Total usable capacity (cu. ft.) | Fridge usable capacity (cu. ft.) | Freezer usable capacity (cu. ft.) | Exterior height (in.) | Exterior width (in.) | Exterior depth (in.) |
|---|---|---|---|---|---|---|---|---|---|---|---|---|---|---|---|
| ✓ | 5 | **DCS** RX215PJX1 | $2,500 | 73 | ⊜ | ⊖ | ○ | ○ | 62 | 15.7 | 10.1 | 5.6 | 70 | 36 | 28 |
| ✓ | 6 | **Kenmore** Elite 5118[3] | 2,000 | 72 | ⊖ | ⊜ | ⊖ | ⊖ | 72 | 21.2 | 13.1 | 8.1 | 69 | 36 | 35 |
| ✓ | 7 | **Frigidaire** Gallery FGUS2676L[P] Gallery FGUS2632L[ ], Gallery FGUS2647L[ ], Gallery FGUS2645L[ ], Gallery FGUS2642L[ ] | 1,200 | 72 | ⊜ | ⊖ | ○ | ⊖ | 72 | 16.9 | 11.6 | 5.3 | 70 | 36 | 33 |

## F BUILT-IN

| Recommended | Rank | Brand & model | Price | Overall score | Temperature performance | Energy efficiency | Noise | Ease of use | Energy cost/yr. ($) | Total usable capacity (cu. ft.) | Fridge usable capacity (cu. ft.) | Freezer usable capacity (cu. ft.) | Exterior height (in.) | Exterior width (in.) | Exterior depth (in.) |
|---|---|---|---|---|---|---|---|---|---|---|---|---|---|---|---|
| ✓ | 1 | **Thermador** Freedom Collection T36BB820SS | 7,400 | 80 | ⊜ | ⊖ | ⊜ | ⊖ | 59 | 14.3 | 9.8 | 4.5 | 84 | 36 | 25 |
| ✓ | 2 | **Jenn-Air** JS42PPDUDB[SS] | 7,200 | 80 | ⊖ | ⊜ | ⊜ | ⊖ | 73 | 17.3 | 12 | 5.3 | 84 | 42 | 26 |
| ✓ | 3 | **Bosch** Integra 800 Series B36BT830NS | 7,500 | 78 | ⊜ | ○ | ⊜ | ⊖ | 64 | 13.8 | 9.2 | 4.6 | 84 | 36 | 25 |
| ✓ | 4 | **Thermador** Freedom Collection T36BT810NS | 8,000 | 78 | ⊜ | ○ | ⊜ | ⊖ | 64 | 13.8 | 9.2 | 4.6 | 84 | 36 | 25 |
| ✓ | 5 | **Thermador** KBUDT4265E[S] | 8,750 | 77 | ⊖ | ⊖ | ⊜ | ⊖ | 78 | 16 | 10.6 | 5.4 | 84 | 42 | 26 |
| ✓ | 6 | **Sub-Zero** BI42S[S] | 8,000 | 76 | ⊜ | ⊖ | ⊖ | ⊖ | 79 | 18.3 | 12.3 | 6 | 84 | 42 | 26 |
| ✓ | 7 | **Miele** KF1901Vi | 7,200 | 76 | ⊜ | ○ | ⊜ | ⊖ | 65 | 14 | 10.6 | 3.4 | 83 | 36 | 24 |

## Guide to the Ratings

**Overall score** is based primarily on temperature performance and energy efficiency. Noise and ease of use are also considered. The displayed score is out of a total of 100 points. **Temperature performance** denotes performance at different room temperatures, including high heat, and how uniformly each maintained 37° F in the refrigerator and 0° F in the freezer. **Energy efficiency** is energy consumption per cubic foot of measured usable storage space. **Noise** is with compressors running. **Ease of use** assesses features and design including layout, controls, and lighting. **Energy cost/yr. ($)** is the estimated cost in dollars, based on the current year's average national electricity rate. Your cost will vary depending on the rate for electricity in your area. **Total usable capacity (cu.ft.)** is our measurement of total usable interior space. **Fridge/Freezer usable capacity (cu.ft.)** is our measurement of usable refrigerator/freezer space. **Exterior height, width,** and **depth** are without handle, rounded up to the nearest inch (37-inch-wide freestanding models fit in 36-inch openings). Under brand & model, bracketed letters or numbers are color codes. **Price** is approximate retail.

## Most & Least Reliable

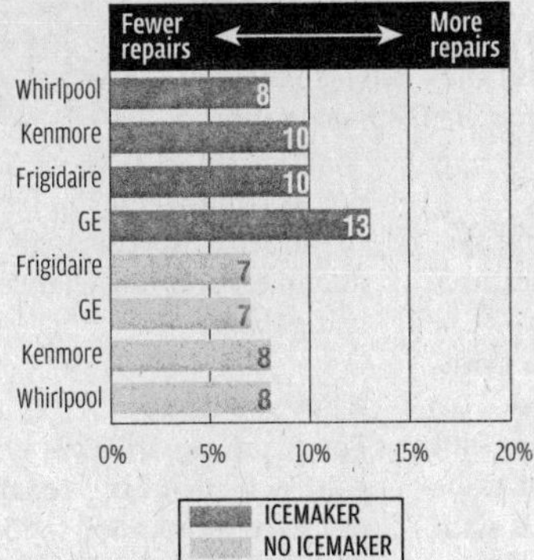


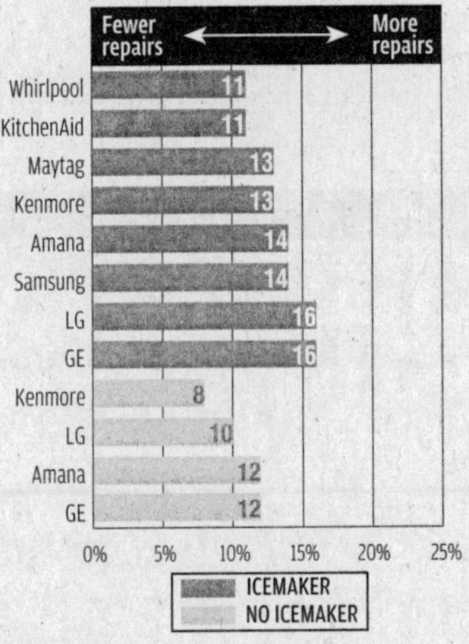


Choosing a refrigerator with a good repair history can improve your odds of getting a reliable model. So each year we survey thousands of readers about their experiences. Though no top-freezer or bottom-freezer brand stood out, LG has been the most repair-prone brand of side-by-side refrigerators with icemakers. Our findings are based on more than 82,000 freestanding refrigerators that readers bought new between 2008 and 2012. Differences of fewer than 4 points aren't meaningful. Data are adjusted to eliminate differences linked solely to age. Models within a brand may vary, and design and manufacture changes may affect future reliability.

Source: Annual Product Reliability Survey, Consumer Reports National Research Center.

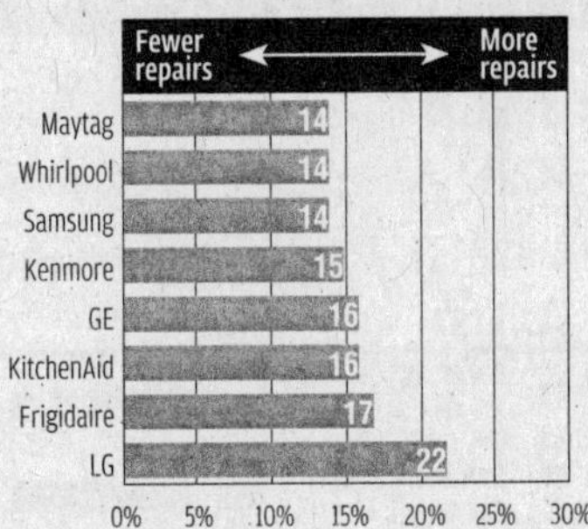

# Quick Guide SMART PHONES

**Smart phones are getting smarter every day. They're not only great for texting, e-mail, and social networking, but they can also play music, shoot photos and video, and direct you via GPS navigation.**

## Shopping tip

Make sure you can read the phone's display in bright sunlight, especially for texting and Web surfing.

Scan this or see how, page 11

### What to look for

- The phone's operating system, which dictates its features and capabilities
- How many apps are available and what they cost
- The keyboard—phones with virtual keyboards tend to be less bulky than models with physical keyboards, but it's easier to type on a physical keyboard without looking

### What to skip

- Phone insurance and extended warranties, which are not worth it when you factor in the extra expense, high deductibles, and low chance of using them

### What you'll pay

Phone prices with a two-year contract, including rebates, range from about $50 to $300. Smart phones purchased unlocked without a contract can cost significantly more, starting at $500.

For more buying advice, go to *ConsumerReports.org/cellphones*

**All tested models** In performance order, within types.

| Recommended | Rank | Brand & model (Similar models, in small type, are comparable to tested model.) | Price | Overall score (0–100; P \| F \| G \| VG \| E) | Ease of use | Messaging | Web browsing | Display quality | Voice quality | Phoning | Battery life | Camera: Image quality | Camera: Video quality | Portability | Display diagonal size (in.) | Operating system |
|---|---|---|---|---|---|---|---|---|---|---|---|---|---|---|---|---|
| **A** | | **AT&T** | | | | | | | | | | | | | | |
| ✓ | 1 | **Samsung** Galaxy S 4 (16GB) Galaxy S 4 (32GB) | $200 | 81 | ⊜ | ⊜ | ⊜ | ⊜ | ○ | ⊜ | ⊜ | ⊜ | ○ | ⊖ | 5 | And. |
| ✓ | 2 | **Samsung** Galaxy S 4 Active | 200 | 80 | ⊜ | ⊜ | ⊜ | ⊜ | ○ | ⊜ | ⊜ | ⊜ | ○ | ⊖ | 5 | And. |
| ✓ | 3 | **LG** Optimus G | 50 | 79 | ⊜ | ⊜ | ⊜ | ⊜ | ○ | ⊖ | ⊜ | ⊖ | ◒ | ⊖ | 4.7 | And. |
| ✓ | 4 | **HTC** One (32GB) One (64GB) | 200 | 79 | ⊜ | ⊜ | ⊜ | ⊜ | ○ | ⊖ | ⊜ | ○ | ◒ | ⊖ | 4.7 | And. |
| ✓ | 5 | **Samsung** Galaxy S III (16GB) | 100 | 78 | ⊜ | ⊜ | ⊜ | ⊜ | ○ | ⊜ | ⊖ | ⊖ | ○ | ⊖ | 4.8 | And. |
| ✓ | 6 | **Apple** iPhone 5 (16GB) iPhone 5 (32GB), iPhone 5 (64GB) | 200 | 77 | ⊜ | ⊖ | ⊜ | ⊜ | ○ | ⊖ | ○ | ⊜ | ⊖ | ⊜ | 4 | iOS |

| Recommended | Rank | Brand & model<br>Similar models, in small type, are comparable to tested model. | Price | Overall score<br>0–100<br>P \| F \| G \| VG \| E | Test results: Ease of use | Messaging | Web browsing | Display quality | Voice quality | Phoning | Battery life | Camera: Image quality | Camera: Video quality | Portability | Display diagonal size (in.) | Operating system |
|---|---|---|---|---|---|---|---|---|---|---|---|---|---|---|---|---|
| | | **A AT&T continued** | | | | | | | | | | | | | | |
| ✓ | 7 | **Nokia** Lumia 1020 | $300 | 77 | Excellent | Excellent | Excellent | Excellent | Good | Very good | Excellent | Very good | Good | Good | 4.5 | WP |
| ✓ | 8 | **Pantech** Discover | 50 | 77 | Excellent | Excellent | Excellent | Excellent | Good | Very good | Excellent | Very good | Fair | Very good | 4.8 | And. |
| ✓ | 9 | **HTC** One X+ | 200 | 77 | Excellent | Excellent | Excellent | Excellent | Good | Very good | Excellent | Good | Fair | Very good | 4.7 | And. |
| ✓ | 10 | **HTC** One VX | 50 | 77 | Excellent | Excellent | Excellent | Very good | Good | Very good | Excellent | Good | Good | Very good | 4.5 | And. |
| ✓ | 11 | **Samsung** Galaxy Note II (16GB) | 300 | 77 | Excellent | Excellent | Excellent | Excellent | Good | Good | Excellent | Excellent | Very good | Fair | 5.5 | And. |
| ✓ | 12 | **LG** Optimus G Pro | 100 | 77 | Excellent | Excellent | Excellent | Excellent | Good | Good | Excellent | Very good | Good | Fair | 5.5 | And. |
| ✓ | 13 | **HTC** Windows Phone 8X (16GB)<br>Windows Phone 8X (8GB) | 100 | 76 | Excellent | Excellent | Excellent | Excellent | Good | Very good | Very good | Very good | Very good | Very good | 4.3 | WP |
| ✓ | 14 | **Nokia** Lumia 920 | 100 | 76 | Excellent | Excellent | Excellent | Excellent | Good | Very good | Very good | Excellent | Good | Good | 4.4 | WP |
| ✓ | 15 | **BlackBerry** Z10 | 200 | 75 | Excellent | Excellent | Excellent | Very good | Good | Very good | Very good | Very good | Good | Very good | 4.2 | BB |
| ✓ | 16 | **Apple** iPhone 4S (16GB) | 100 | 74 | Excellent | Very good | Very good | Excellent | Good | Very good | Good | Very good | Very good | Excellent | 3.5 | iOS |
| ✓ | 17 | **Pantech** Flex | 0 | 72 | Excellent | Very good | Excellent | Excellent | Good | Very good | Very good | Good | Fair | Very good | 4.3 | And. |
| ✓ | 18 | **Samsung** Galaxy Rugby Pro | 100 | 72 | Very good | Very good | Excellent | Very good | Good | Very good | Excellent | Good | Fair | Good | 4 | And. |
| ✓ | 19 | **BlackBerry** Q10 | 200 | 71 | Very good | Very good | Very good | Excellent | Good | Very good | Excellent | Very good | Good | Very good | 3.1 | BB |
| ✓ | 20 | **HTC** First | 0 | 70 | Good | Very good | Excellent | Excellent | Good | Very good | Excellent | Good | Fair | Excellent | 4.3 | And. |
| | 21 | **Apple** iPhone 4 (8GB) | 0 | 69 | Excellent | Very good | Good | Excellent | Good | Very good | Good | Good | Very good | Excellent | 3.5 | iOS |
| | 22 | **BlackBerry** Torch 9810 | 10 | 66 | Very good | Excellent | Very good | Excellent | Good | Very good | Good | Good | Good | Very good | 3.2 | BB |
| | | **B SPRINT** | | | | | | | | | | | | | | |
| ✓ | 1 | **Samsung** Galaxy S 4 (16GB) | 150 | 79 | Excellent | Excellent | Excellent | Excellent | Good | Excellent | Very good | Excellent | Good | Very good | 5 | And. |
| ✓ | 2 | **LG** Optimus G | 0 | 77 | Excellent | Excellent | Excellent | Excellent | Good | Very good | Very good | Very good | Fair | Very good | 4.7 | And. |
| ✓ | 3 | **HTC** One (32GB) | 100 | 77 | Excellent | Excellent | Excellent | Excellent | Fair | Very good | Very good | Good | Fair | Very good | 4.7 | And. |
| ✓ | 4 | **Samsung** Galaxy S III (16GB)<br>Galaxy S III (32GB) | 100 | 76 | Excellent | Excellent | Excellent | Excellent | Good | Excellent | Good | Very good | Good | Very good | 4.8 | And. |
| ✓ | 5 | **Apple** iPhone 5 (16GB) iPhone 5 (64GB), iPhone 5 (32GB) | 100 | 75 | Excellent | Very good | Excellent | Excellent | Good | Very good | Good | Excellent | Very good | Excellent | 4 | iOS |

**Ratings Key** Excellent · Very good · Good · Fair · Poor

**CR Best Buy** These models offer the best combination of performance and price. All are recommended.

✓ **Recommended** These are high-performing models that stand out.

| Recommended | Rank | Brand & model (Similar models, in small type, are comparable to tested model.) | Price | Overall score (0–100; P \| F \| G \| VG \| E) | Test results: Ease of use | Messaging | Web browsing | Display quality | Voice quality | Phoning | Battery life | Camera: Image quality | Camera: Video quality | Portability | Display diagonal size (in.) | Operating system |
|---|---|---|---|---|---|---|---|---|---|---|---|---|---|---|---|---|
| | | **B SPRINT** continued | | | | | | | | | | | | | | |
| ✓ | 6 | **Samsung** Galaxy Note II (16GB) | $250 | 75 | E | E | E | E | G | G | VG | E | VG | F | 5.5 | And. |
| ✓ | 7 | **LG** Optimus F3 | 0 | 73 | E | VG | VG | E | G | VG | E | G | G | E | 4 | And. |
| ✓ | 8 | **HTC** Evo 4G LTE | 0 | 73 | E | E | E | E | G | VG | G | F | G | VG | 4.7 | And. |
| ✓ | 9 | **Motorola** Photon Q 4G LTE | 100 | 73 | E | E | E | E | G | VG | G | VG | G | G | 4.3 | And. |
| ✓ | 10 | **HTC** 8XT | 100 | 73 | E | E | E | E | F | VG | G | VG | VG | VG | 4.3 | WP |
| ✓ | 11 | **Sprint** Vital | 0 | 73 | E | E | E | E | F | VG | VG | G | F | VG | 5 | And. |
| ✓ | 12 | **Samsung** Galaxy Victory 4G LTE | 50 | 71 | E | VG | E | VG | G | VG | G | G | G | VG | 4 | And. |
| ✓ | 13 | **LG** Viper | 0 | 69 | E | E | E | VG | F | VG | G | G | F | VG | 4 | And. |
| ✓ | 14 | **Kyocera** Torque | 0 | 68 | VG | VG | E | VG | F | VG | E | G | F | F | 4 | And. |
| ✓ | 15 | **Apple** iPhone 4S (16GB) | 100 | 67 | E | VG | G | E | G | VG | G | VG | VG | E | 3.5 | iOS |
| | 16 | **Sprint** Force | 0 | 66 | VG | VG | E | VG | F | G | G | G | P | VG | 4 | And. |
| | 17 | **Kyocera** Hydro Edge | 20 | 58 | VG | VG | G | VG | F | VG | VG | G | F | VG | 4 | And. |
| | 18 | **LG** Optimus Elite | 0 | 58 | VG | VG | G | VG | G | G | G | F | F | E | 3.5 | And. |
| | 19 | **ZTE** Fury | 0 | 56 | VG | VG | G | VG | G | VG | G | G | P | VG | 3.5 | And. |
| | 20 | **Kyocera** Rise | 0 | 55 | VG | VG | G | VG | G | VG | G | F | P | VG | 3.5 | And. |
| | | **C T-MOBILE** | | | | | | | | | | | | | | |
| ✓ | 1 | **Samsung** Galaxy S 4 (16GB) | 0 | 81 | E | E | E | E | G | E | E | E | G | VG | 5 | And. |
| ✓ | 2 | **HTC** One (32GB) | 0 | 79 | E | E | E | E | G | VG | E | G | F | VG | 4.7 | And. |
| ✓ | 3 | **Samsung** Galaxy S III (16GB) | 0 | 78 | E | E | E | E | G | E | VG | VG | G | VG | 4.8 | And. |
| ✓ | 4 | **Apple** iPhone 5 (16GB) iPhone 5 (32GB), iPhone 5 (64GB) | 150 | 77 | E | VG | E | E | G | VG | G | E | VG | E | 4 | iOS |
| ✓ | 5 | **Samsung** Galaxy Note II (16GB) | 0 | 77 | E | E | E | E | G | G | E | E | VG | F | 5.5 | And. |
| ✓ | 6 | **Sony** Xperia Z | 0 | 77 | E | E | E | E | G | VG | VG | VG | G | VG | 5 | And. |
| ✓ | 7 | **Nokia** Lumia 925 | 0 | 77 | E | E | E | E | G | VG | VG | VG | G | VG | 4.5 | WP |
| ✓ | 8 | **Google** Nexus 4 (16GB) | 0 | 76 | E | E | E | E | G | VG | VG | G | G | VG | 4.7 | And. |

## C T-MOBILE continued

| Recommended | Rank | Brand & model (Similar models, in small type, are comparable to tested model.) | Price | Overall score (0–100; P \| F \| G \| VG \| E) | Ease of use | Messaging | Web browsing | Display quality | Voice quality | Phoning | Battery life | Camera: Image quality | Camera: Video quality | Portability | Display diagonal size (in.) | Operating system |
|---|---|---|---|---|---|---|---|---|---|---|---|---|---|---|---|---|
| ✔ | 9 | **LG** Optimus L9 | $0 | 76 | E | E | E | E | G | VG | VG | G | F | E | 4.5 | And. |
| ✔ | 10 | **BlackBerry** Z10 | 0 | 75 | E | E | E | VG | G | VG | VG | VG | G | VG | 4.2 | BB |
| ✔ | 11 | **Samsung** Galaxy S II | 0 | 75 | E | E | E | E | G | E | G | VG | G | VG | 4.5 | And. |
| ✔ | 12 | **Apple** iPhone 4S (16GB) | 70 | 74 | E | VG | VG | E | G | VG | G | VG | VG | E | 3.5 | iOS |
| ✔ | 13 | **Samsung** Galaxy Exhibit | 0 | 71 | E | VG | E | VG | G | VG | G | G | F | E | 3.8 | And. |
| ✔ | 14 | **BlackBerry** Q10 | 0 | 71 | VG | VG | VG | E | G | VG | E | VG | G | VG | 3.1 | BB |
| ✔ | 15 | **Nokia** Lumia 521 | 0 | 71 | VG | E | E | E | G | VG | VG | G | F | VG | 4 | WP |
|  | 16 | **T-Mobile** myTouch Q | 0 | 63 | VG | VG | VG | E | G | VG | G | F | P | G | 4 | And. |
|  | 17 | **T-Mobile** Prism II | 0 | 60 | G | VG | G | VG | G | VG | VG | G | F | VG | 3.5 | And. |

## D VERIZON

| Recommended | Rank | Brand & model | Price | Overall score | Ease of use | Messaging | Web browsing | Display quality | Voice quality | Phoning | Battery life | Camera: Image quality | Camera: Video quality | Portability | Display diagonal size (in.) | Operating system |
|---|---|---|---|---|---|---|---|---|---|---|---|---|---|---|---|---|
| ✔ | 1 | **Samsung** Galaxy S 4 (16GB) | 200 | 79 | E | E | E | E | G | E | VG | E | G | VG | 5 | And. |
| ✔ | 2 | **Motorola** Droid Razr Maxx HD | 150 | 79 | E | E | E | E | G | VG | E | VG | G | VG | 4.7 | And. |
| ✔ | 3 | **Motorola** Droid Razr HD | 50 | 77 | E | E | E | E | G | VG | VG | VG | G | VG | 4.7 | And. |
| ✔ | 4 | **Motorola** Droid Razr M | 0 | 75 | E | E | E | E | G | VG | G | VG | G | E | 4.3 | And. |
| ✔ | 5 | **Apple** iPhone 5 (16GB) iPhone 5 (64GB), iPhone 5 (32GB) | 200 | 75 | E | VG | E | E | G | VG | G | E | VG | E | 4 | iOS |
| ✔ | 6 | **Samsung** Galaxy Note II (16GB) | 250 | 75 | E | E | E | E | G | G | VG | E | VG | F | 5.5 | And. |
| ✔ | 7 | **Nokia** Lumia 928 | 100 | 75 | E | E | E | E | G | VG | VG | VG | G | G | 4.4 | WP |
| ✔ | 8 | **BlackBerry** Z10 | 100 | 74 | E | E | E | VG | F | VG | G | VG | G | VG | 4.2 | BB |
| ✔ | 9 | **LG** Spectrum 2 | 0 | 74 | E | E | E | E | F | E | G | VG | F | VG | 4.7 | And. |
| ✔ | 10 | **Pantech** Perception | 0 | 73 | E | E | E | E | F | E | VG | G | F | VG | 4.8 | And. |
| ✔ | 11 | **HTC** Droid DNA | 50 | 73 | E | E | E | E | F | VG | G | G | F | G | 5 | And. |
| ✔ | 12 | **LG** Lucid 2 | 20 | 73 | E | E | E | E | G | VG | VG | F | F | E | 4.3 | And. |
| ✔ | 13 | **Nokia** Lumia 822 | 20 | 73 | E | E | E | E | G | VG | G | VG | F | VG | 4.3 | WP |

| Recommended | Rank | Brand & model<br>Similar models, in small type, are comparable to tested model. | Price | Overall score<br>0–100<br>P \| F \| G \| VG \| E | Test results: Ease of use | Messaging | Web browsing | Display quality | Voice quality | Phoning | Battery life | Camera: Image quality | Camera: Video quality | Portability | Display diagonal size (in.) | Operating system |
|---|---|---|---|---|---|---|---|---|---|---|---|---|---|---|---|---|
| | **D** | **VERIZON** continued | | | | | | | | | | | | | | |
| ✓ | 14 | **HTC** Windows Phone 8X (16GB) | $50 | 73 | ⊜ | ⊜ | ⊜ | ⊜ | ◒ | ⊖ | ○ | ⊖ | ⊖ | ⊖ | 4.3 | WP |
| ✓ | 15 | **Motorola** Droid 4 | 100 | 73 | ⊜ | ⊜ | ⊜ | ⊖ | ○ | ⊖ | ○ | ⊖ | ○ | ○ | 4 | And. |
| ✓ | 16 | **Samsung** ATIV Odyssey | 0 | 71 | ⊜ | ⊜ | ⊜ | ⊜ | ◒ | ⊖ | ○ | ○ | ○ | ⊜ | 4 | WP |
| ✓ | 17 | **Casio** G'zOne Commando 4G LTE | 100 | 71 | ⊜ | ⊜ | ⊜ | ⊖ | ◒ | ⊖ | ○ | ○ | ○ | ○ | 4 | And. |
| ✓ | 18 | **Samsung** Galaxy Stellar | 0 | 71 | ⊜ | ⊜ | ⊜ | ⊜ | ◒ | ⊜ | ○ | ◒ | ◒ | ⊖ | 4 | And. |
| ✓ | 19 | **Samsung** Galaxy Stratosphere II | 50 | 70 | ⊜ | ⊜ | ⊜ | ⊖ | ◒ | ⊜ | ○ | ○ | ◒ | ○ | 4 | And. |
| ✓ | 20 | **BlackBerry** Q10 | 200 | 69 | ⊖ | ⊖ | ⊖ | ⊜ | ◒ | ⊖ | ⊖ | ⊖ | ○ | ⊖ | 3.1 | BB |
| ✓ | 21 | **LG** Intuition | 0 | 68 | ⊜ | ⊜ | ⊜ | ⊜ | ○ | ◒ | ○ | ○ | ○ | ◒ | 5 | And. |
| ✓ | 22 | **Apple** iPhone 4S (16GB) | 100 | 67 | ⊜ | ⊖ | ○ | ⊜ | ○ | ⊖ | ○ | ⊖ | ⊖ | ⊜ | 3.5 | iOS |
| | 23 | **Apple** iPhone 4 (8GB) | 0 | 65 | ⊜ | ⊖ | ○ | ⊜ | ○ | ⊖ | ○ | ○ | ⊖ | ⊜ | 3.5 | iOS |
| | 24 | **Pantech** Marauder | 0 | 65 | ⊖ | ⊖ | ⊜ | ⊖ | ◒ | ⊖ | ○ | ○ | ◒ | ○ | 3.7 | And. |
| | 25 | **Casio** G'zOne Commando | 50 | 60 | ⊖ | ⊖ | ○ | ⊖ | ○ | ⊖ | ⊖ | ○ | ◒ | ○ | 3.6 | And. |
| | 26 | **BlackBerry** Bold 9930 | 100 | 59 | ⊖ | ⊖ | ○ | ⊜ | ◒ | ⊖ | ○ | ◒ | ◒ | ⊜ | 2.8 | BB |
| | 27 | **Jitterbug** Touch | 150 | 50 | ○ | ⊖ | ◒ | ○ | ○ | ⊖ | ○ | ◒ | ● | ⊖ | 3 | And. |

## Guide to the Ratings

**Overall score** is based mainly on test results. **Ease of use** indicates how easy it is to access features and modes, such as phoning, messaging, Web browsing, the camera, the music player, applications, and other multimedia content. **Messaging** assesses keyboard ergonomics, e-mail readability, attachment capabilities, and text-messaging features. **Web browsing** assesses browser capabilities. **Display quality** represents overall picture quality, contrast in normal and bright lighting, and color accuracy. **Voice quality** incorporates listening and talking in noisy and quiet settings using live phone calls. **Phoning** considers the step-saving functions for making and receiving calls, speed dialing, and more. **Battery life** was tested under strong and weak cell network signals, and considers tasks that involve voice, data, standby, and other factors. **Camera: Image quality** evaluates resolution, dynamic range, color accuracy, and visual noise. **Camera: Video quality** judges recorded video images shot at the highest quality setting available. **Portability** represents our judgment based on the best combination of size and weight. **Display diagonal size (in.)** is to the nearest tenth of an inch. Under **operating system,** And.=Android; BB=BlackBerry; iOS=iOS; WP=Windows Phone. **Price** is approximate retail.

# Quick Guide SNOW BLOWERS

Our tests of nearly 50 snow blowers show that some of the best can quickly clear even the heavy stuff for as little as $700.

**What to look for**

- A wide (28-inch plus) two-stage gasoline snow blower, with driven wheels and an impeller for farther throwing, for larger driveways or heavier snow
- A compact two-stage or single-stage gas model for lighter-duty work
- A plug-in electric model solely for small areas and decks with very light snowfall

**What to skip**

- Any single-stage model for gravel driveways; the auger that scoops snow and propels the machine will also pick up and hurl the gravel
- The smallest plug-in models for anything but the lightest-duty work

**What you'll pay**

Figure on $1,000 to $2,000 for large two-stage models, $700 to $900 for smaller models; $500 to $700 for single-stage gas models, $200 to $400 for single-stage electrics.

For more buying advice, go to *ConsumerReports.org/snowblowers*

**Shopping tip**

Single-handle controls and a joystick for the chute are handy for gas models.

Scan this or see how, page 11

Recommended models only From 89 tested.

| Recommended | Rank | Brand & model (Similar models, in small type, are comparable to tested model.) | Price | Overall score (0–100; P \| F \| G \| VG \| E) | Width (in.) | Removal speed | Plow pile removal | Throwing distance | Surface cleaning | Handling | Noise | Controls | Engine size | Electric start | Multiple speeds |
|---|---|---|---|---|---|---|---|---|---|---|---|---|---|---|---|
| **A** | | **COMPACT TWO-STAGE GAS** | | | | | | | | | | | | | |
| ✓ | 1 | **Craftsman** 88173 524SWE 31AM53TR, 98536, Gold 31AM63KE | $ 680 | 73 | 24 | VG | E | G | VG | VG | G | VG | 208 cc | • | • |
| ✓ | 2 | **Toro** Power Max 724 OE 37770 | 800 | 69 | 24 | VG | E | VG | VG | VG | G | VG | 205 cc | • | • |
| ✓ | 3 | **Sno-Tek** 920402 | 600 | 66 | 24 | G | VG | VG | VG | VG | F | VG | 208 cc | • | • |
| ✓ | 4 | **Honda** HS724WA | 2,200 | 65 | 24 | E | G | E | VG | F | F | VG | 196 cc | | • |

| Recommended | Rank | Brand & model (Similar models, in small type, are comparable to tested model.) | Price | Overall score (0–100; P \| F \| G \| VG \| E) | Width (in.) | Removal speed | Plow pile removal | Throwing distance | Surface cleaning | Handling | Noise | Controls | Engine size | Electric start | Multiple speeds |
|---|---|---|---|---|---|---|---|---|---|---|---|---|---|---|---|
| **B** | | **SINGLE-STAGE GAS** | | | | | | | | | | | | | |
| CR Best Buy | 1 | **Toro** Power Clear 621 38458 Power Clear 621 38459 | $ 650 | 70 | 21 | Very good | Very good | Good | Excellent | Excellent | Fair | Very good | 163 cc | | |
| CR Best Buy | 2 | **Cub Cadet** 221 LHP 31AM2T6D 88782 | 550 | 67 | 21 | Good | Very good | Fair | Very good | Excellent | Fair | Excellent | 208 cc | • | |
| CR Best Buy | 3 | **Toro** Power Clear 621 38451 Power Clear 621 38452 | 500 | 65 | 21 | Very good | Very good | Good | Excellent | Excellent | Fair | Good | 163 cc | | |
| **C** | | **TWO-STAGE GAS** | | | | | | | | | | | | | |
| Recommended | 1 | **Cub Cadet** 930SWE 31AH95SU | 1,600 | 89 | 30 | Excellent | Excellent | Excellent | Excellent | Very good | Fair | Excellent | 357 cc | • | • |
| CR Best Buy | 2 | **Craftsman** 88396 98539, Storm 3090XP 31AH55R | 1,200 | 88 | 30 | Excellent | Excellent | Very good | Very good | Excellent | Fair | Excellent | 357 cc | • | • |
| Recommended | 3 | **Ariens** 921013 | 1,400 | 86 | 30 | Excellent | Excellent | Excellent | Very good | Excellent | Fair | Very good | 305 cc | • | • |
| CR Best Buy | 4 | **Ariens** 921022 | 1,000 | 85 | 28 | Excellent | Excellent | Excellent | Very good | Excellent | Fair | Very good | 250 cc | • | • |
| Recommended | 5 | **Toro** Power Max 828 OXE 38634 | 1,500 | 84 | 28 | Excellent | Excellent | Very good | Excellent | Very good | Fair | Excellent | 250 cc | • | • |
| Recommended | 6 | **John Deere** 1695812 | 1,500 | 83 | 30 | Excellent | Excellent | Very good | Excellent | Good | Fair | Excellent | 342 cc | • | • |
| Recommended | 7 | **John Deere** 1028E | 1,300 | 82 | 28 | Excellent | Excellent | Excellent | Very good | Very good | Fair | Excellent | 305 cc | • | • |

**Ratings Key** Excellent, Very good, Good, Fair, Poor

**CR Best Buy** These models offer the best combination of performance and price. All are recommended.

**Recommended** These are high-performing models that stand out.

## Guide to the Ratings

**Overall score** is based mainly on removal speed, distance, surface cleaning, controls, and handling. **Width (in.)** is the clearing width, or swath, in inches. **Removal speed** indicates how quickly models could remove snow without laboring. **Plow pile removal** is how fast the snow thrower can remove a simulated pile of snow left by a plow at the end of a driveway. **Throwing distance** is how far snow was dispersed straight ahead, left, and right with the discharge chute set for maximum distance. **Surface cleaning** indicates how much snow was left on our blacktop surface after clearing with the skid shoes and/or scraper set for best clearing. **Handling** denotes ease of pushing, pulling, and steering. **Noise** measures sound pressure in the operator's ear. Hearing protection is strongly advised for a Rating of less than Good. **Controls** include ease of discharge chute adjustment, handle height and comfort, engine controls, and speed selection. **Price** is approximate retail.

# Quick Guide SOUND BARS

A sound bar speaker system is an easy way to improve your TV's sound. Most are 2.1-channel systems that include a bar-shaped enclosure with an array of speakers, plus a subwoofer.

**Shopping tip**

A 2.1-channel system with virtual surround-sound can create a multichannel effect without rear speakers.

Scan this or see how, page 11

### What to look for

- Enough inputs—both audio and video—if you'll be connecting components to the sound bar rather than to your TV. And make sure they're the right type
- A powered sound bar that contains its own amplification, unless you'll be using a receiver or a separate amp
- A model with a separate powered subwoofer, which can often produce deeper, more powerful bass

### What to skip

- A model with a built-in disc player if you already have one

### What you'll pay

Sound bar prices vary widely, from about $100 to $750. Some can cost as much as $2,000.

For more buying advice, go to *ConsumerReports.org/theater*

All tested models in performance order, within types.

| Recommended | Rank | Brand & model | Price | Overall score (0–100; P \| F \| G \| VG \| E) | Test results: Sound quality | Ease of use | Versatility | Number of channels | Number of speakers supplied | Features: Active subwoofer | Wireless subwoofer |
|---|---|---|---|---|---|---|---|---|---|---|---|
| | | **SOUND BARS** | | | | | | | | | |
| ✔ | 1 | **Sonos** Playbar | $ 700 | 61 | ⊖ | ⊖ | ◒ | 5.1 | 1 | NA | Optional |
| ✔ | 2 | **Sony** HT-CT260 | 300 | 59 | ⊖ | ⊖ | ◒ | 2.1 | 1.1 | • | • |
| ✔ | 3 | **Vizio** VHT215 | 180 | 58 | ⊖ | ⊖ | ◒ | 2.1 | 1.1 | • | • |
| | 4 | **Atlantic** Technology H-PAS PowerBar PB-235 | 900 | 53 | ⊖ | ○ | ◒ | 2.1 | 1 | NA | NA |
| | 5 | **Toshiba** SBX4250 | 300 | 53 | ○ | ⊖ | ◒ | 2.1 | 1.1 | • | • |
| | 6 | **Vizio** SB4021M-A1 | 200 | 53 | ○ | ○ | ● | 2.1 | 1.1 | • | • |
| | 7 | **Sony** HT-CT660 | 400 | 52 | ○ | ⊖ | ◒ | 2.1 | 1.1 | • | • |
| | 8 | **Sharp** HT-SB60 | 500 | 51 | ○ | ○ | ◒ | 2.1 | 1.1 | • | • |
| | 9 | **Yamaha** YAS-101 | 250 | 50 | ○ | ○ | ● | 2.1 | 1 | NA | NA |

| Recommended | Rank | Brand & model | Price | Overall score (0–100; P \| F \| G \| VG \| E) | Test results: Sound quality | Ease of use | Versatility | Number of channels | Number of speakers supplied | Features: Active subwoofer | Wireless subwoofer |
|---|---|---|---|---|---|---|---|---|---|---|---|
| | | **SOUND BARS** continued | | | | | | | | | |
| | 10 | **Harman/Kardon** SB 30 | $ 800 | 50 | ⊖ | ○ | ● | 11.1 | 1.1 | • | • |
| | 11 | **Samsung** HW-F750 | 800 | 50 | ○ | ○ | ◒ | 2.1 | 1.1 | • | • |
| | 12 | **ZVOX** Z-Base V320 | 250 | 49 | ○ | ○ | ● | 2 | 1 | NA | NA |
| | 13 | **Harman/Kardon** SB 16 | 600 | 49 | ○ | ⊖ | ● | 2.1 | 1.1 | • | • |
| | 14 | **JBL** Cinema SB 400 | 550 | 47 | ○ | ○ | ◒ | 2.1 | 1.1 | • | • |
| | 15 | **LG** NB3730A | 400 | 47 | ○ | ⊖ | ○ | 2.1 | 1.1 | • | • |
| | 16 | **Bose** CineMate 1 SR | 1,500 | 47 | ○ | ◒ | ● | 5.1 | 1.1 | • | • |
| | 17 | **JBL** SB 300 | 500 | 46 | ○ | ◒ | ● | 2.1 | 1.1 | • | • |
| | 18 | **Klipsch** HD Theater SB 3 | 800 | 45 | ○ | ○ | ● | 2.1 | 1.1 | • | • |
| | 19 | **Bose** Solo TV sound system | 400 | 44 | ○ | ◒ | ● | 2 | 1 | NA | |
| | 20 | **Energy** Power Bar | 400 | 43 | ○ | ○ | ● | 2.1 | 1.1 | • | • |
| | 21 | **ZVOX** Z-Base 555 | 400 | 43 | ○ | ○ | ● | 2.1 | 1 | NA | |
| | 22 | **Boston** Acoustics TVee Model 25 | 300 | 43 | ○ | ○ | ● | 2.1 | 1.1 | • | • |
| | 23 | **Polk** Audio SurroundBar 5000 IHT | 400 | 43 | ○ | ○ | ● | 2.1 | 1.1 | • | • |
| | 24 | **Vizio** VSB211 | 130 | 40 | ○ | ○ | ● | 2.1 | 1.1 | | |
| | 25 | **Polk** Audio SurroundBar 6000 Instant Home Theater | 500 | 39 | ○ | ○ | ● | 2.1 | 1.1 | • | • |
| | 26 | **Samsung** HW-F550 | 360 | 39 | ◒ | ○ | ◒ | 2.1 | 1.1 | • | • |
| | 27 | **SpeakerCraft** CS3 | 600 | 39 | ⊖ | ● | ● | 2 | 1 | NA | NA |
| | 28 | **Boston** Acoustics TVee 10 | 200 | 37 | ◒ | ○ | ● | 2 | 1 | NA | NA |
| | 29 | **Coby** CSMP95 | 100 | 31 | ◒ | ◒ | ● | 2.1 | 1.1 | • | • |
| | 30 | **Coby** CSMP91 | 100 | 29 | ◒ | ◒ | ◒ | 2.1 | 1 | NA | |
| | 31 | **RCA** RTS736W | 100 | 29 | ◒ | ○ | ◒ | 2 | 1 | NA | NA |
| | 32 | **Sharp** HT-SL75 | 150 | 26 | ◒ | ○ | ● | 2.1 | 1.1 | • | |

## Guide to the Ratings

**Overall score** is based mainly on sound quality; ease of use and versatility are also factored in. The displayed score is out of a total of 100 points. **Sound quality** represents tonal accuracy and ability to reproduce fine sonic detail. **Ease of use** refers to setup and use of controls. **Versatility** is based on useful features. **Number of channels** refers to audio signal channels supplied by the system. **Number of speakers supplied** are those that come with the system. **Price** is approximate retail.

# Quick Guide STREAMING MEDIA PLAYERS

**One of the easiest, least expensive ways to add Internet capability to a TV, a streaming media player connects to your TV via an HDMI input, and to your home network via built-in Wi-Fi.**

## Shopping tip

Social-media junkies can access Facebook and Twitter through some streaming media players. Some let you use your smart phone or tablet as a remote control.

Scan this or see how, page 11

### What to look for

- A player that has all the streaming services you want right out of the box. Additional services may be added later, but don't assume that the one you want will be among them
- A player that has analog video connections, such as composite or component video, if you'll be using the player with an older TV that lacks HDMI inputs
- A player that supports the media formats of content—music, videos, and photos—you already own
- A Google TV-powered player if you want a full Web browser and access to Google Play for movies, books, games, apps, and more
- An Apple TV media player if you have a lot of content stored in iTunes, on a Mac computer, or on Apple's iCloud

### What to skip

- A pricier model with tons of content if all you really want is Netflix

### What you'll pay

From $50 to $100 for a basic model, or from $75 to $170 for a player that uses the Google TV platform.

For more buying advice, go to *ConsumerReports.org/streamingmediaplayers*

**All tested models** In performance order, within types.

| Recommended | Rank | Brand & model | Price | Overall score (0–100; P \| F \| G \| VG \| E) | Test results: Features | Everyday use | Connectivity | First time setup | Picture quality | Features: App or channel store | Streaming video services | USB ports |
|---|---|---|---|---|---|---|---|---|---|---|---|---|
| **A ADVANCED** | | | | | | | | | | | | |
| ☑ | 1 | **Sony** NSZ-GS7 | $170 | 67 | ⊖ | ○ | ○ | ⊜ | ⊜ | GP | N, A, V, HBO, P, S | 2 |
| ☑ | 2 | **Hisense** Pulse w/ Google TV (GX1200V) | 75 | 67 | ⊖ | ⊖ | ○ | ⊜ | ⊜ | GP | N, V, HBO, P | 1 |
| ☑ | 3 | **Netgear** NeoTV Prime w/ Google TV (GTV100) | 100 | 67 | ⊖ | ○ | ○ | ⊜ | ⊜ | GP | N, A, V, HBO, P | 1 |

| Recommended | Rank | Brand & model | Price | Overall score (0–100; P \| F \| G \| VG \| E) | Test results: Features | Test results: Everyday use | Test results: Connectivity | Test results: First time setup | Test results: Picture quality | Features: App or channel store | Features: Streaming video services | Features: USB ports |
|---|---|---|---|---|---|---|---|---|---|---|---|---|
| **A ADVANCED** continued | | | | | | | | | | | | |
| | 4 | **Vizio** Co-Star w/ Google TV (VAP430) | $100 | 65 | Very good | Good | Good | Excellent | Excellent | GP | N, A, V, M-Go, P | 1 |
| | 5 | **Asus** CUBE w/ Google TV | 140 | 62 | Very good | Good | Good | Excellent | Excellent | GP | N, HBO, P | 2 |
| **B BASIC** | | | | | | | | | | | | |
| CR Best Buy | 1 | **Western** Digital WD TV Play Media Player | 65 | 68 | Very good | Very good | Very good | Very good | Excellent | None | N, V, HP, C | 1 |
| Recommended | 2 | **Roku** 3 | 100 | 62 | Very good | Good | Good | Good | Excellent | Roku | N, A, V, HP, B, HBO | 1 |
| Recommended | 3 | **Panasonic** DMP-MST60 | 90 | 61 | Very good | Fair | Good | Excellent | Excellent | Viera | N, A, V, HP, C | 1 |
| | 4 | **Panasonic** DMP-MS10 | 70 | 57 | Good | Fair | Good | Excellent | Excellent | None | N, V, HP, C | 1 |
| | 5 | **Boxee** Cloud DVR (DSM-382) | 110 | 55 | Good | Good | Very good | Fair | Excellent | None | N, V | 2 |
| | 6 | **Roku** Streaming Stick | 90 | 54 | Very good | Good | Fair | Good | Excellent | Roku | N, A, V, HP, B, HBO | 0 |
| | 7 | **D-Link** MovieNite Plus (DSM-312) | 65 | 53 | Good | Good | Fair | Very good | Excellent | Vudu, MN | N, V | 0 |
| | 8 | **Apple** TV (3rd gen) | 100 | 51 | Good | Good | Good | Good | Excellent | None | N, HP, HBO, iTunes | 0 |
| | 9 | **Magnavox** HD Streaming Video Player TB600MG2F | 50 | 51 | Good | Good | Fair | Good | Excellent | Vudu Apps | N, V, HP, F | 0 |
| | 10 | **D-Link** MovieNite (DSM-310) | 50 | 47 | Good | Good | Fair | Very good | Excellent | None | N, V | 0 |
| | 11 | **Favi** SmartStick (4 GB) | 50 | 44 | Good | Fair | Fair | Good | Very good | GP, SS | N, HBO, P | 1 |

**Ratings Key** Excellent, Very good, Good, Fair, Poor

**CR Best Buy** These models offer the best combination of performance and price. All are recommended.

**Recommended** These are high-performing models that stand out.

## Guide to the Ratings

**Overall score** is based mainly on the number of features and how easy the player is to use, but also includes its picture quality performance. The displayed score is out of a total of 100 points. **Features** reflects the presence or absence of features, including the number of streaming video services, other Internet services, and the ability to play media files. **Everyday use** evaluates how easy it is to use on a normal basis. **Connectivity** is the amount and type of connections that will make the player more versatile. **First time setup** evaluates how easy it is to set up the product out of the box. **Picture quality** includes image clarity, color accuracy, and contrast of streaming video. In features, under **streaming video services**, A=Amazon Instant Video, B=Blockbuster, C=CinemaNow, F=Film Fresh, HBO=HBO Go, HP=Hulu Plus, iTunes=iTunes Store, M-Go=M-Go, N=Netflix, P=Play Movies & TV, S=Sony Video Unlimited, and V=Vudu. **Price** is approximate retail.

# Quick Guide TABLETS

Lightweight and highly portable, tablets are made to be carried wherever you go. Most have 7- to 10-inch screens.

### What to look for

- A 10-inch screen for better Web surfing, video, and gaming; a 7-inch screen for better portability
- A display with a wide viewing angle
- An operating system that can be upgraded
- Ability to access a rich variety of apps authorized by the OS manufacturer

### What to skip

- A 3G or 4G model, unless you need "everywhere access" and are willing to pay extra for it

### What you'll pay

You'll spend about $400 for a good, 10-inch Android tablet with 16GB of memory that's Wi-Fi-only. An equivalent iPad costs $500. Smaller Android tablets that we recommend start as low as $200.

For more buying advice, go to *ConsumerReports.org/tablets*

**Shopping tip**

Tablets can double as e-readers and movie viewers, and a wide variety of inexpensive apps is available.

Scan this or see how, page 11

**All tested models** In performance order, within types.

| Recommended | Rank | Brand & model (Similar models, in small type, are comparable to tested model.) | Price | Overall score (0–100; P \| F \| G \| VG \| E) | Test results: Portability | Ease of use | Display | Versatility | Touch response | Features: Battery life (hr.) | Weight (lb.) | Operating system |
|---|---|---|---|---|---|---|---|---|---|---|---|---|
| | **A** | **7- TO 8-INCH WITH 3G/4G+WI-FI** | | | | | | | | | | |
| ✓ | 1 | **Apple** iPad Mini (Wi-Fi, 4G, 16GB) iPad Mini (Wi-Fi, 4G, 32GB), iPad Mini (Wi-Fi, 4G, 64GB) | $460 | 84 | Excellent | Excellent | Very good | Very good | Excellent | 11.3 | 0.7 | iOS 6 |
| ✓ | 2 | **Samsung** Galaxy Note 8.0 (Wi-Fi, 4G, 16GB) | 500 | 84 | Excellent | Excellent | Very good | Excellent | Excellent | 10 | 0.8 | And. 4.1 |
| ✓ | 3 | **Samsung** Galaxy Tab 7.7 (Wi-Fi, 4G, 16GB) | 350 | 78 | Very good | Excellent | Very good | Very good | Excellent | 8.3 | 0.8 | And. 3.2 |
| CR Best Buy | 4 | **Google** Nexus 7 (Wi-Fi, 4G, 32GB) | 300 | 77 | Very good | Excellent | Very good | Very good | Excellent | 8.9 | 0.8 | And. 4.2 |

**Ratings Key** Excellent, Very good, Good, Fair, Poor

**CR Best Buy** These models offer the best combination of performance and price. All are recommended.

**Recommended** These are high-performing models that stand out.

| Recommended | Rank | Brand & model<br>Similar models, in small type, are comparable to tested model. | Price | Overall score<br>0–100<br>P \| F \| G \| VG \| E | Test results: Portability | Test results: Ease of use | Test results: Display | Test results: Versatility | Test results: Touch response | Features: Battery life (hr.) | Features: Weight (lb.) | Features: Operating system |
|---|---|---|---|---|---|---|---|---|---|---|---|---|
| **A** | | **7- TO 8-INCH WITH 3G/4G+WI-FI** continued | | | | | | | | | | |
| ☑ | 5 | **Samsung** Galaxy Tab 2 (7.0) (Wi-Fi, 4G, 8GB) | $300 | 72 | VG | VG | VG | VG | E | 8.3 | 0.8 | And. 4 |
| ☑ | 6 | **Motorola** Droid Xyboard 8.2 (Wi-Fi, 4G, 32GB) | 530 | 72 | G | VG | VG | VG | E | 5.2 | 0.9 | And. 3.2 |
| ☑ | 7 | **T-Mobile** SpringBoard (Wi-Fi, 4G, 16GB) | 390 | 71 | G | VG | VG | VG | E | 6.1 | 0.9 | And. 4 |
| | 8 | **Lenovo** IdeaTab A2107 (Wi-Fi, 3G, 16GB) | 200 | 61 | VG | VG | F | VG | E | 8.5 | 0.9 | And. 4 |
| **B** | | **7- TO 8-INCH, WI-FI-ONLY** | | | | | | | | | | |
| ☑ | 1 | **Samsung** Galaxy Note 8.0 (Wi-Fi, 16GB) | 400 | 85 | E | E | VG | E | E | 10 | 0.8 | And. 4.1 |
| ☑ | 2 | **Samsung** Galaxy Tab 3 8.0 (Wi-Fi, 16GB) | 300 | 84 | E | E | VG | E | E | 11.8 | 0.7 | And. 4.2 |
| ☑ | 3 | **Apple** iPad Mini (Wi-Fi, 16GB) iPad Mini (Wi-Fi, 32GB), iPad Mini (Wi-Fi, 64GB) | 330 | 80 | E | E | VG | VG | E | 10.5 | 0.7 | iOS 6 |
| ✅ | 4 | **Samsung** Galaxy Tab 3 7.0 (Wi-Fi, 8GB) | 200 | 80 | E | E | VG | VG | E | 9.7 | 0.7 | And. 4.1 |
| ✅ | 5 | **Google** Nexus 7 (Wi-Fi, 16GB) Nexus 7 (Wi-Fi, 32GB) | 200 | 76 | VG | E | VG | G | E | 9.5 | 0.7 | And. 4.2 |
| ✅ | 6 | **Wikipad** 7 (Wi-Fi, 16GB) | 250 | 71 | VG | VG | VG | VG | E | 8.4 | 0.7 | And. 4.1 |
| ✅ | 7 | **Samsung** Galaxy Tab 2 (7.0) (Wi-Fi, 8GB) | 200 | 71 | VG | E | VG | G | E | 8.3 | 0.8 | And. 4.1 |
| ✅ | 8 | **Kobo** Arc (Wi-Fi, 32GB) Arc (Wi-Fi, 64GB), Arc (Wi-Fi, 16GB) | 250 | 68 | VG | VG | VG | G | E | 9.3 | 0.8 | And. 4 |
| | 9 | **Acer** Iconia Tab W3-810 (Wi-Fi, 32GB) Iconia Tab W3-810 (Wi-Fi, 64GB) | 380 | 64 | VG | VG | F | VG | E | 11.3 | 1.1 | Wind. 8 |
| | 10 | **Lenovo** IdeaTab A1000 (Wi-Fi, 16GB) | 150 | 63 | VG | VG | F | G | E | 10.3 | 0.8 | And. 4.1 |
| | 11 | **HP** Slate 7 (Wi-Fi, 8GB) | 170 | 62 | VG | VG | G | G | E | 7.2 | 0.8 | And. 4.1 |
| | 12 | **Lenovo** IdeaTab A2107 (Wi-Fi, 8GB) | 150 | 58 | VG | VG | F | G | VG | 9.4 | 0.9 | And. 4 |
| | 13 | **Acer** Iconia Tab A110 (Wi-Fi, 8GB) | 200 | 58 | VG | VG | F | G | E | 6.9 | 0.9 | And. 4.1 |
| | 14 | **Asus** MeMO Pad ME172V (Wi-Fi, 16GB) | 150 | 55 | VG | VG | F | G | VG | 7 | 0.8 | And. 4.1 |
| | 15 | **Archos** GamePad (Wi-Fi, 8GB) | 180 | 53 | G | VG | F | G | E | 5 | 0.7 | And. 4.1 |
| | 16 | **Coby** MID7065-8 (Wi-Fi, 8GB) | 130 | 52 | G | VG | F | G | E | 4.7 | 0.7 | And. 4 |
| | 17 | **Coby** MID8065-8 (Wi-Fi, 8GB) | 160 | 52 | G | VG | F | G | E | 6 | 1 | And. 4 |

| Recommended | Rank | Brand & model<br>Similar models, in small type, are comparable to tested model. | Price | Overall score<br>0–100<br>P \| F \| G \| VG \| E | Test results: Portability | Ease of use | Display | Versatility | Touch response | Features: Battery life (hr.) | Weight (lb.) | Operating system |
|---|---|---|---|---|---|---|---|---|---|---|---|---|
| | | **C 7- TO 9-INCH, SPECIALTY** | | | | | | | | | | |
| ✔ Recommended | 1 | **Amazon** Kindle Fire HD 8.9 (Wi-Fi, 4G, 32GB) Kindle Fire HD 8.9 (Wi-Fi, 4G, 64GB) | $410 | 78 | Very good | Very good | Excellent | Very good | Excellent | 9.1 | 1.2 | And. 4 |
| ✔ Recommended | 2 | **Amazon** Kindle Fire HD 8.9 (Wi-Fi, 16GB) Kindle Fire HD 8.9 (Wi-Fi, 32GB) | 280 | 75 | Very good | Very good | Excellent | Good | Excellent | 9.1 | 1.2 | And. 4 |
| ✔ CR Best Buy | 3 | **Amazon** Kindle Fire HD (Wi-Fi, 16GB) Kindle Fire HD (Wi-Fi, 32GB) | 210 | 74 | Excellent | Very good | Very good | Good | Excellent | 10.7 | 0.9 | And. 4 |
| ✔ CR Best Buy | 4 | **Barnes & Noble** Nook HD+ (Wi-Fi, 16GB) Nook HD+ (Wi-Fi, 32GB) | 150 | 66 | Very good | Very good | Very good | Good | Excellent | 9 | 1.1 | And. 4 |
| ✔ CR Best Buy | 5 | **Barnes & Noble** Nook HD (Wi-Fi, 16GB) Nook HD (Wi-Fi, 8GB) | 150 | 66 | Very good | Very good | Very good | Good | Excellent | 8.8 | 0.7 | And. 4 |
| | 6 | **Amazon** Kindle Fire (Wi-Fi, 8GB) (2nd gen) | 170 | 62 | Very good | Very good | Very good | Fair | Excellent | 7.6 | 0.9 | And. 4 |
| | | **D 9- TO 12-INCH WITH 3G/4G+WI-FI** | | | | | | | | | | |
| ✔ Recommended | 1 | **Apple** iPad (Wi-Fi, 4G, 16GB) (4th gen) iPad (Wi-Fi, 4G, 128GB) (4th gen), iPad (Wi-Fi, 4G, 32GB) (4th gen), iPad (Wi-Fi, 4G, 64GB) (4th gen) | 630 | 85 | Excellent | Excellent | Excellent | Very good | Excellent | 11.7 | 1.5 | iOS 6 |
| ✔ Recommended | 2 | **Samsung** Galaxy Note 10.1 (Wi-Fi, 4G, 16GB) | 600 | 83 | Excellent | Excellent | Very good | Very good | Excellent | 11.4 | 1.3 | And. 4.1 |
| ✔ Recommended | 3 | **Asus** VivoTab RT TF600T (Wi-Fi, 4G, 32GB) | 700 | 82 | Excellent | Very good | Excellent | Excellent | Excellent | 10.7 | 1.2 | Wind. RT |
| ✔ Recommended | 4 | **Samsung** Galaxy Tab 2 (10.1) (Wi-Fi, 4G, 16GB) | 500 | 81 | Excellent | Excellent | Very good | Very good | Excellent | 11.5 | 1.3 | And. 4.1 |
| ✔ Recommended | 5 | **Dell** Latitude 10 (Wi-Fi, 3G, 64GB) | 750 | 81 | Very good | Very good | Excellent | Excellent | Excellent | 11.3 | 1.5 | Wind. 8 |
| ✔ Recommended | 6 | **Apple** iPad 2 (Wi-Fi, 3G, 16GB) | 530 | 80 | Excellent | Excellent | Very good | Very good | Excellent | 11.6 | 1.3 | iOS 6 |
| ✔ Recommended | 7 | **Samsung** Galaxy Tab 10.1 (Wi-Fi, 4G, 16GB) Galaxy Tab 10.1 (Wi-Fi, 4G, 32GB) | 500 | 77 | Very good | Very good | Very good | Very good | Excellent | 8.9 | 1.3 | And. 3.1 |
| | 8 | **Asus** Transformer Pad TF300TL (Wi-Fi, 4G, 32GB) | 500 | 74 | Very good | Very good | Very good | Very good | Excellent | 7.8 | 1.4 | And. 4 |

**Ratings Key** Excellent · Very good · Good · Fair · Poor

✔ **CR Best Buy** These models offer the best combination of performance and price. All are recommended.

✔ **Recommended** These are high-performing models that stand out.

| Recommended | Rank | Brand & model<br>Similar models, in small type, are comparable to tested model. | Price | Overall score<br>0–100<br>P \| F \| G \| VG \| E | Test results: Portability | Ease of use | Display | Versatility | Touch response | Features: Battery life (hr.) | Weight (lb.) | Operating system |
|---|---|---|---|---|---|---|---|---|---|---|---|---|
| **E** | | **9- TO 12-INCH, WI-FI-ONLY** | | | | | | | | | | |
| ✔ | 9 | **Google** Nexus 10 (Wi-Fi, 16GB) Nexus 10 (Wi-Fi, 32GB) | $400 | 83 | ⊜ | ⊜ | ⊜ | ⊖ | ⊜ | 11 | 1.3 | And. 4.2 |
| ✓ | 10 | **Apple** iPad (Wi-Fi, 16GB) (4th gen) iPad (Wi-Fi, 32GB) (4th gen), iPad (Wi-Fi, 64GB) (4th gen), iPad (Wi-Fi, 128GB) (4th gen) | 500 | 83 | ⊜ | ⊜ | ⊜ | ⊖ | ⊜ | 12.9 | 1.5 | iOS 6 |
| ✔ | 11 | **Samsung** Galaxy Tab 3 10.1 (Wi-Fi, 16GB) | 400 | 82 | ⊜ | ⊜ | ⊖ | ⊖ | ⊜ | 9.6 | 1.1 | And. 4.2 |
| ✓ | 12 | **Samsung** Galaxy Note 10.1 (Wi-Fi, 16GB) Galaxy Note 10.1 (Wi-Fi, 32GB) | 500 | 81 | ⊜ | ⊜ | ⊖ | ⊖ | ⊜ | 11.1 | 1.3 | And. 4.1 |
| ✓ | 13 | **Asus** VivoTab RT TF600T (Wi-Fi, 32GB) VivoTab RT TF600T (Wi-Fi, 64GB) | 550 | 81 | ⊜ | ⊖ | ⊜ | ⊖ | ⊜ | 10.7 | 1.2 | Wind. RT |
| ✓ | 14 | **Samsung** ATIV Smart PC (Wi-Fi, 64GB) | 700 | 80 | ⊜ | ⊖ | ⊖ | ⊜ | ⊜ | 13.4 | 1.6 | Wind. 8 |
| ✔ | 15 | **Samsung** Galaxy Tab 2 (10.1) (Wi-Fi, 16GB) | 350 | 80 | ⊜ | ⊖ | ⊖ | ⊖ | ⊜ | 12.4 | 1.3 | And. 4.1 |
| ✔ | 16 | **Microsoft** Surface with Windows RT (Wi-Fi, 32GB) Surface with Windows RT (Wi-Fi, 64GB) | 350 | 79 | ⊖ | ⊖ | ⊜ | ⊖ | ⊜ | 10.6 | 1.5 | Wind. RT |
| ✓ | 17 | **Dell** Latitude 10 (Wi-Fi, 64GB) Latitude 10 (Wi-Fi, 32GB) | 650 | 79 | ⊜ | ⊖ | ⊜ | ⊜ | ⊜ | 11.5 | 1.5 | Wind. 8 |
| ✓ | 18 | **Dell** Latitude 10 Essentials (Wi-Fi, 32GB) Latitude 10 Essentials (Wi-Fi, 64GB) | 500 | 79 | ⊜ | ⊖ | ⊜ | ⊖ | ⊜ | 12.6 | 1.4 | Wind. 8 |
| ✓ | 19 | **Sony** Xperia Tablet Z (Wi-Fi, 16GB) Xperia Tablet Z (Wi-Fi, 32GB) | 500 | 79 | ⊜ | ⊖ | ⊜ | ⊖ | ⊜ | 9.7 | 1.1 | And. 4.1 |
| ✓ | 20 | **Asus** Transformer Pad Infinity TF700T (Wi-Fi, 32GB) Transformer Pad Infinity TF700T (Wi-Fi, 64GB) | 500 | 78 | ⊖ | ⊜ | ⊖ | ⊖ | ⊜ | 8 | 1.3 | And. 4 |
| ✓ | 21 | **Apple** iPad 2 (Wi-Fi, 16GB) | 400 | 77 | ⊜ | ⊜ | ⊖ | ○ | ⊜ | 11.6 | 1.3 | iOS 6 |
| ✓ | 22 | **Dell** XPS 10 (Wi-Fi, 32GB) XPS 10 (Wi-Fi, 64GB) | 450 | 77 | ⊜ | ⊖ | ⊖ | ⊖ | ⊜ | 10.9 | 1.4 | Wind. RT |
| ✓ | 23 | **Acer** Iconia W510 (Wi-Fi, 64GB) | 570 | 77 | ⊜ | ⊖ | ⊖ | ⊖ | ⊜ | 10 | 1.3 | Wind. 8 |
| ✓ | 24 | **Lenovo** IdeaTab Lynx K3011 (Wi-Fi, 64GB) | 500 | 76 | ⊜ | ⊖ | ⊖ | ⊖ | ⊜ | 10.9 | 1.4 | Wind. 8 |
| ✓ | 25 | **Acer** Iconia Tab A700 (Wi-Fi, 32GB) | 450 | 76 | ⊖ | ⊖ | ⊖ | ⊖ | ⊜ | 9.5 | 1.5 | And. 4 |
| ✓ | 26 | **Asus** Transformer Pad TF300T (Wi-Fi, 16GB) Transformer Pad TF300T (Wi-Fi, 32GB) | 350 | 76 | ⊖ | ⊖ | ⊖ | ⊖ | ⊜ | 8.9 | 1.4 | And. 4.2 |
| ✓ | 27 | **Toshiba** Excite 10 SE (Wi-Fi, 16GB) Excite 10 SE (Wi-Fi, 32GB) | 300 | 75 | ⊖ | ⊖ | ⊖ | ⊖ | ⊜ | 10.5 | 1.4 | And. 4.1 |

| Recommended | Rank | Brand & model<br>Similar models, in small type, are comparable to tested model. | Price | Overall score<br>0–100<br>P \| F \| G \| VG \| E | Test results: Portability | Ease of use | Display | Versatility | Touch response | Features: Battery life (hr.) | Weight (lb.) | Operating system |
|---|---|---|---|---|---|---|---|---|---|---|---|---|
| | | **E 9- TO 12-INCH, WI-FI-ONLY** continued | | | | | | | | | | |
| | 28 | **Lenovo** IdeaTab S2110 (Wi-Fi, 16GB) IdeaTab S2110 (Wi-Fi, 32GB) | $400 | 74 | Excellent | Very good | Very good | Good | Very good | 10.8 | 1.2 | And. 4 |
| | 29 | **Asus** MeMO Pad Smart ME301T (Wi-Fi, 16GB) | 300 | 73 | Very good | Very good | Very good | Very good | Excellent | 8.4 | 1.2 | And. 4.1 |
| | 30 | **HP** ENVY x2 (Wi-Fi, 64GB) | 650 | 72 | Very good | Very good | Very good | Very good | Excellent | 8.5 | 1.5 | Wind. 8 |
| | 31 | **Acer** Iconia Tab A200 (Wi-Fi, 16GB) Iconia Tab A200 (Wi-Fi, 32GB) | 300 | 69 | Very good | Excellent | Good | Very good | Excellent | 9.6 | 1.6 | And. 4 |
| | 32 | **Acer** Iconia Tab A210 (Wi-Fi, 16GB) | 350 | 69 | Very good | Very good | Good | Very good | Excellent | 8.8 | 1.5 | And. 4.1 |
| | 33 | **Microsoft** Surface Pro (Wi-Fi, 64GB) Surface Pro (Wi-Fi, 128GB) | 900 | 67 | Fair | Very good | Excellent | Very good | Excellent | 5.9 | 2.1 | Wind. 8 |
| | 34 | **Samsung** ATIV Smart PC Pro (Wi-Fi, 128GB) | 1,130 | 66 | Good | Very good | Very good | Very good | Excellent | 6.1 | 2 | Wind. 8 |
| | 35 | **Coby** MID1065-8 (Wi-Fi, 8GB) | 230 | 63 | Good | Very good | Very good | Good | Excellent | 6.5 | 1.4 | And. 4 |
| | 36 | **Razer** Edge (Wi-Fi, 64GB) | 1,000 | 53 | Fair | Very good | Very good | Very good | Excellent | 4.2 | 2.2 | Wind. 8 |
| | 37 | **Coby** MID9740-8 (Wi-Fi, 8GB) | 180 | 46 | Good | Good | Fair | Good | Excellent | 5.6 | 1.4 | And. 4 |
| | | **F 10- TO 12-INCH-SCREEN CONVERTIBLE WITH KEYBOARD** | | | | | | | | | | |
| ✔ | 1 | **Lenovo** IdeaPad Yoga 11 (Wi-Fi, 32GB) | 550 | 71 | Good | Very good | Very good | Very good | Excellent | 15.2 | 2.7 | Wind. RT |

**Ratings Key** Excellent, Very good, Good, Fair, Poor

☑ **CR Best Buy** These models offer the best combination of performance and price. All are recommended.

✔ **Recommended** These are high-performing models that stand out.

## Guide to the Ratings

**Overall score** is based on ease of use, display, touch response, versatility, battery life, and weight. **Portability** is based on size, weight, and battery life. **Ease of use** considers reading books, playing media, and using e-mail and the Web. **Display** score reflects color, viewing angle, brightness, and amount of glare. **Versatility** reflects the presence of useful features. **Touch response** indicates responsiveness of the touch screen when selecting and moving objects or typing. **Battery life (hr.)** indicates the time it takes to deplete a fully charged battery while the tablet loads a sequence of Web pages over Wi-Fi. **Weight (lb.)** is without a case or cover. In features, under **operating system:** And.=Android, iOS=iOS, and Wind.=Windows. **Price** is approximate retail.

# Quick Guide TVs

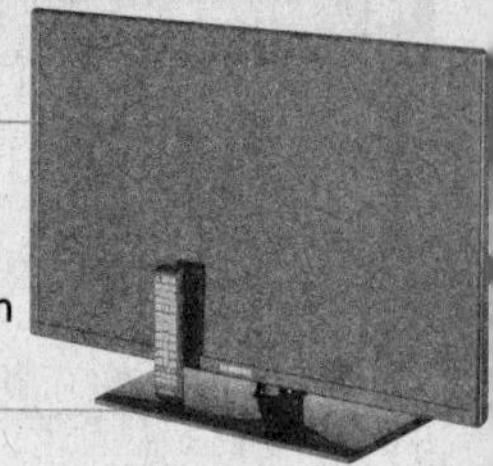

**Both LCD and plasma TVs offer slim designs and provide excellent HD picture quality. Many new models have Wi-Fi capability and can stream video from Internet services such as Netflix and Amazon Instant Video.**

### Shopping tip

Most new LCD sets have LED backlights. They use less energy than other LCD TVs and plasmas but don't necessarily have a better picture.

Scan this or see how, page 11

### What to look for

- An LCD set if you have a very bright room or want a wider choice of screen sizes
- A plasma TV if you want the widest viewing angle and no issue with motion blur

### What to skip

- Pricey HDMI cables; those costing a few dollars are fine
- An extended warranty; major-brand LCD and plasma sets have been very reliable
- Internet connectivity if your Blu-ray player, game system, or set-top box can stream the services you want

### What you'll pay

40- to 42-inch sets start at about $400, 47- to 50-inch sets at about $600, and 60-inch sets at about $1,500. 3D and Internet features might add a few hundred dollars to the price.

For more buying advice, go to *ConsumerReports.org/tvs*

All tested models in performance order, within types.

| Recommended | Rank | Brand & model | Price | Overall score (0–100; P \| F \| G \| VG \| E) | Test results: Display type (Backlight) | Screen size (in.) | HD picture quality | 3D performance | Viewing angle | Sound quality | Remote ease of use | On-screen menu ease of use | Versatility | Energy cost/yr. ($) |
|---|---|---|---|---|---|---|---|---|---|---|---|---|---|---|
| **A** | | **29-INCH AND SMALLER** | | | | | | | | | | | | |
| ✓ | 1 | **Samsung** UN26EH4000 | $300 | 64 | LCD (LED) | 26 | ⊜ | NA | ○ | ○ | ⊜ | ⊜ | ◒ | 7 |
| ✓ | 2 | **Samsung** UN29F4000 | 280 | 60 | LCD (LED) | 29 | ⊜ | NA | ○ | ◒ | ⊜ | ⊜ | ◒ | 10 |
| ✓ | 3 | **Vizio** E291i-A1 | 250 | 58 | LCD (LED) | 29 | ⊖ | NA | ◒ | ◒ | ○ | ⊖ | ○ | 9 |
| ✓ | 4 | **LG** 29LN4510 | 250 | 58 | LCD (LED) | 29 | ⊖ | NA | ○ | ◒ | ⊖ | ⊜ | ◒ | 8 |
| ✓ | 5 | **Toshiba** 29L1350U | 200 | 58 | LCD (LED) | 29 | ⊖ | NA | ◒ | ○ | ⊖ | ⊜ | ◒ | 8 |
| ✓ | 6 | **Philips** 26PFL4907 | 300 | 56 | LCD (LED) | 26 | ⊖ | NA | ○ | ○ | ○ | ○ | ○ | 6 |

| Recommended | Rank | Brand & model | Price | Overall score (0–100; P \| F \| G \| VG \| E) | Display type (Backlight) | Screen size (in.) | HD picture quality | 3D performance | Viewing angle | Sound quality | Remote ease of use | On-screen menu ease of use | Versatility | Energy cost/yr. ($) |
|---|---|---|---|---|---|---|---|---|---|---|---|---|---|---|
| **A** | | **29-INCH AND SMALLER** continued | | | | | | | | | | | | |
| | 7 | **Philips** 29PFL4508 | $250 | 54 | LCD (LED) | 29 | Very good | NA | Fair | Fair | Very good | Very good | Fair | 6 |
| | 8 | **Magnavox** 29ME403V | 280 | 52 | LCD (LED) | 29 | Very good | NA | Fair | Fair | Very good | Very good | Fair | 6 |
| | 9 | **Coby** LEDTV2916 | 230 | 52 | LCD (LED) | 29 | Very good | NA | Fair | Fair | Good | Very good | Fair | 7 |
| | 10 | **Insignia** NS-28E200NA14 | 220 | 51 | LCD (LED) | 28 | Very good | NA | Fair | Fair | Very good | Excellent | Fair | 6 |
| | 11 | **Magnavox** 26MF321B | 230 | 43 | LCD (CCFL) | 26 | Good | NA | Fair | Fair | Good | Very good | Fair | 12 |
| **B** | | **32-INCH** | | | | | | | | | | | | |
| ✔ | 1 | **Samsung** UN32EH5000 | 300 | 66 | LCD (LED) | 32 | Excellent | NA | Good | Good | Excellent | Excellent | Fair | 8 |
| ✔ | 2 | **Samsung** UN32F6300 | 600 | 65 | LCD (LED) | 32 | Excellent | NA | Good | Fair | Very good | Excellent | Very good | 17 |
| | 3 | **Vizio** E320i-A0 | 300 | 64 | LCD (LED) | 32 | Excellent | NA | Fair | Good | Good | Very good | Good | 10 |
| | 4 | **Samsung** UN32F5000 | 370 | 63 | LCD (LED) | 32 | Excellent | NA | Good | Good | Excellent | Excellent | Fair | 14 |
| | 5 | **Sony** Bravia KDL-32R400A | 300 | 62 | LCD (LED) | 32 | Excellent | NA | Good | Good | Very good | Excellent | Fair | 9 |
| | 6 | **Sony** Bravia KDL-32W650A | 650 | 62 | LCD (LED) | 32 | Excellent | NA | Good | Fair | Very good | Very good | Good | 10 |
| | 7 | **Philips** 32PFL4907 | 300 | 61 | LCD (LED) | 32 | Very good | NA | Very good | Good | Good | Good | Good | 8 |
| | 8 | **Magnavox** 32ME402V | 230 | 61 | LCD (LED) | 32 | Very good | NA | Very good | Good | Very good | Very good | Fair | 6 |
| | 9 | **LG** 32LN530B | 280 | 60 | LCD (LED) | 32 | Very good | NA | Very good | Good | Very good | Excellent | Fair | 9 |
| | 10 | **LG** 32LN5300 | 350 | 60 | LCD (LED) | 32 | Very good | NA | Very good | Good | Very good | Excellent | Fair | 12 |
| | 11 | **Toshiba** 32L2300U | 280 | 57 | LCD (LED) | 32 | Very good | NA | Good | Fair | Very good | Excellent | Fair | 10 |
| | 12 | **Vizio** M321i-A2 | 380 | 57 | LCD (LED) | 32 | Very good | NA | Good | Fair | Very good | Good | Good | 8 |
| | 13 | **Panasonic** Viera TC-L32C5 | 320 | 57 | LCD (CCFL) | 32 | Very good | NA | Fair | Good | Very good | Excellent | Fair | 18 |
| | 14 | **Insignia** NS-32D200NA14 | 230 | 56 | LCD (LED) | 32 | Very good | NA | Good | Fair | Very good | Excellent | Fair | 5 |
| | 15 | **Panasonic** Viera TC-L32XM6 | 300 | 55 | LCD (LED) | 32 | Very good | NA | Fair | Fair | Very good | Excellent | Fair | 7 |
| | 16 | **Magnavox** 32ME303V | 300 | 55 | LCD (LED) | 32 | Very good | NA | Very good | Fair | Very good | Very good | Fair | 7 |

**Ratings Key** Excellent, Very good, Good, Fair, Poor

**CR Best Buy** These models offer the best combination of performance and price. All are recommended.

**Recommended** These are high-performing models that stand out.

| Recommended | Rank | Brand & model | Price | Overall score (0–100; P \| F \| G \| VG \| E) | Display type (Backlight) | Screen size (in.) | HD picture quality | 3D performance | Viewing angle | Sound quality | Remote ease of use | On-screen menu ease of use | Versatility | Energy cost/yr. ($) |
|---|---|---|---|---|---|---|---|---|---|---|---|---|---|---|
| **B** | | **32-INCH** continued | | | | | | | | | | | | |
| | 17 | **Haier** LE32D32200 | $230 | 54 | LCD (LED) | 32 | Very good | NA | Good | Fair | Very good | Very good | Fair | 6 |
| | 18 | **JVC** EM32T | 250 | 53 | LCD (LED) | 32 | Very good | NA | Fair | Fair | Very good | Very good | Poor | 6 |
| | 19 | **Sanyo** DP32242 | 210 | 52 | LCD (LED) | 32 | Very good | NA | Fair | Good | Good | Very good | Fair | 10 |
| | 20 | **Sceptre** X322BV-HD | 180 | 52 | LCD (CCFL) | 32 | Good | NA | Very good | Good | Good | Very good | Fair | 14 |
| | 21 | **Sanyo** DP32642 | 200 | 51 | LCD (CCFL) | 32 | Very good | NA | Fair | Good | Very good | Good | Fair | 12 |
| | 22 | **Element** ELCFW329 | 200 | 50 | LCD (CCFL) | 32 | Very good | NA | Fair | Fair | Good | Excellent | Fair | 14 |
| | 23 | **Sharp** Aquos LC-32LE450U | 260 | 48 | LCD (LED) | 32 | Good | NA | Fair | Fair | Very good | Excellent | Fair | 7 |
| | 24 | **Dynex** DX-32L200NA14 | 180 | 45 | LCD (CCFL) | 32 | Good | NA | Good | Fair | Good | Excellent | Fair | 14 |
| | 25 | **Coby** LEDTV3226 | 270 | 43 | LCD (LED) | 32 | Good | NA | Fair | Poor | Very good | Very good | Poor | 1 |
| **C** | | **37- TO 39-INCH** | | | | | | | | | | | | |
| | 1 | **Toshiba** 39L4300U | 500 | 63 | LCD (LED) | 39 | Excellent | NA | Good | Good | Very good | Very good | Very good | 12 |
| | 2 | **LG** 39LN5700 | 550 | 63 | LCD (LED) | 39 | Excellent | NA | Good | Fair | Very good | Excellent | Very good | 12 |
| | 3 | **Magnavox** 39MF412B | 330 | 62 | LCD (CCFL) | 39 | Excellent | NA | Fair | Good | Very good | Very good | Fair | 23 |
| | 4 | **Westinghouse** EW39T6MZ | 250 | 60 | LCD (LED) | 39 | Very good | NA | Fair | Good | Very good | Very good | Poor | 12 |
| | 5 | **Magnavox** 39ME413V | 360 | 59 | LCD (LED) | 39 | Excellent | NA | Good | Fair | Very good | Very good | Fair | 9 |
| | 6 | **Vizio** E370-A0 | 350 | 58 | LCD (LED) | 37 | Very good | NA | Very good | Good | Good | Very good | Fair | 9 |
| | 7 | **Panasonic** Viera TC-L39EM60 | 500 | 56 | LCD (LED) | 39 | Very good | NA | Good | Good | Very good | Excellent | Fair | 9 |
| | 8 | **Insignia** NS-39E400NA14 | 320 | 53 | LCD (LED) | 39 | Very good | NA | Good | Fair | Very good | Excellent | Fair | 10 |
| | 9 | **Sanyo** FVM3982 | 300 | 52 | LCD (CCFL) | 39 | Very good | NA | Fair | Good | Very good | Fair | Fair | 19 |
| | 10 | **Coby** TFTV3925 | 450 | 43 | LCD (CCFL) | 39 | Good | NA | Fair | Poor | Very good | Very good | Poor | 21 |

**Ratings Key** Excellent · Very good · Good · Fair · Poor

**CR Best Buy** These models offer the best combination of performance and price. All are recommended.

**Recommended** These are high-performing models that stand out.

| Recommended | Rank | Brand & model | Price | Overall score (0–100; P \| F \| G \| VG \| E) | Display type (Backlight) | Screen size (in.) | HD picture quality | 3D performance | Viewing angle | Sound quality | Remote ease of use | On-screen menu ease of use | Versatility | Energy cost/yr. ($) |
|---|---|---|---|---|---|---|---|---|---|---|---|---|---|---|
| | | **D 40- TO 43-INCH** | | | | | | | | | | | | |
| ✓ | 1 | **Samsung** PN43E450 | $ 420 | 68 | Plasma | 43 | ⊖ | NA | ⊜ | ○ | ⊜ | ⊜ | ◒ | 27 |
| ✓ | 2 | **LG** 42GA6400 | 850 | 67 | LCD (LED) | 42 | ⊖ | ⊖ | ⊖ | ○ | ⊖ | ⊖ | ⊖ | 15 |
| ✓ | 3 | **Samsung** UN40EH6000 | 600 | 67 | LCD (LED) | 40 | ⊜ | NA | ○ | ○ | ⊜ | ⊜ | ◒ | 15 |
| ✓ | 4 | **Panasonic** Viera TC-L42E60 | 700 | 66 | LCD (LED) | 42 | ⊜ | NA | ○ | ○ | ⊖ | ⊖ | ⊖ | 11 |
| | 5 | **Panasonic** Viera TC-P42S60 | 500 | 66 | Plasma | 42 | ⊜ | NA | ⊜ | ○ | ⊖ | ⊖ | ○ | 37 |
| ✓ | 6 | **Samsung** UN40F5500 | 530 | 65 | LCD (LED) | 40 | ⊜ | NA | ○ | ○ | ⊖ | ⊜ | ⊖ | 20 |
| ✓ | 7 | **Sony** Bravia KDL-40EX640 | 900 | 65 | LCD (LED) | 40 | ⊜ | NA | ○ | ○ | ⊖ | ⊖ | ⊖ | 18 |
| | 8 | **Vizio** E420i-A0 | 480 | 63 | LCD (LED) | 42 | ⊖ | NA | ⊖ | ○ | ○ | ⊖ | ○ | 17 |
| | 9 | **Sony** Bravia KDL-40R450A | 450 | 63 | LCD (LED) | 40 | ⊜ | NA | ○ | ○ | ⊖ | ⊜ | ◒ | 15 |
| | 10 | **Samsung** PN43F4500 | 400 | 62 | Plasma | 43 | ⊖ | NA | ⊜ | ◒ | ⊜ | ⊜ | ◒ | 33 |
| | 11 | **LG** 42LN5400 | 550 | 62 | LCD (LED) | 42 | ⊖ | NA | ⊖ | ○ | ⊖ | ⊜ | ◒ | 15 |
| | 12 | **LG** 42PN4500 | 400 | 62 | Plasma | 42 | ⊖ | NA | ⊜ | ○ | ⊖ | ⊜ | ◒ | 34 |
| | 13 | **Panasonic** Viera TC-P42X60 | 400 | 61 | Plasma | 42 | ⊖ | NA | ⊜ | ○ | ⊖ | ⊜ | ◒ | 29 |
| | 14 | **Sony** Bravia KDL-40BX450 | 500 | 60 | LCD (CCFL) | 40 | ⊜ | NA | ○ | ○ | ⊖ | ⊖ | ◒ | 26 |
| | 15 | **Sceptre** X405BV-FHD3 | 320 | 55 | LCD (CCFL) | 40 | ⊖ | NA | ◒ | ◒ | ○ | ⊜ | ◒ | 16 |
| | 16 | **RCA** LED42C45RQ | 420 | 53 | LCD (LED) | 42 | ⊖ | NA | ◒ | ◒ | ○ | ⊜ | ◒ | 15 |
| | 17 | **TCL** LE40FHDE3000 | 360 | 53 | LCD (LED) | 40 | ⊖ | NA | ○ | ◒ | ○ | ⊜ | ◒ | 13 |
| | 18 | **Element** ELEFT406 | 350 | 51 | LCD (LED) | 40 | ⊖ | NA | ◒ | ◒ | ○ | ⊜ | ◒ | 13 |
| | 19 | **Hitachi** Ultravision LE42S606 | 500 | 49 | LCD (LED) | 42 | ○ | NA | ◒ | ◒ | ⊖ | ⊜ | ◒ | 14 |
| | | **E 46- TO 52-INCH** | | | | | | | | | | | | |
| ✓ | 1 | **Samsung** PN51F8500 | 1,600 | 75 | Plasma | 51 | ⊜ | ⊖ | ⊜ | ○ | ⊖ | ⊜ | ⊜ | 63 |
| ✓ | 2 | **Samsung** PN51E490 | 720 | 72 | Plasma | 51 | ⊖ | ⊖ | ⊜ | ○ | ⊜ | ⊜ | ◒ | 29 |
| ✓ | 3 | **LG** 47LA6900 | 1,050 | 71 | LCD (LED) | 47 | ⊖ | ⊖ | ⊖ | ⊖ | ⊖ | ⊖ | ⊖ | 16 |
| | 4 | **Samsung** UN46ES6600 | 1,200 | 70 | LCD (LED) | 46 | ⊖ | ○ | ◒ | ⊖ | ⊜ | ⊜ | ⊖ | 21 |

## E 46- TO 52-INCH continued

| Recommended | Rank | Brand & model | Price | Overall score (0–100; P \| F \| G \| VG \| E) | Display type (Backlight) | Screen size (in.) | HD picture quality | 3D performance | Viewing angle | Sound quality | Remote ease of use | On-screen menu ease of use | Versatility | Energy cost/yr. ($) |
|---|---|---|---|---|---|---|---|---|---|---|---|---|---|---|
| ✓ | 5 | **Panasonic** Viera TC-L47WT60 | $2,500 | 69 | LCD (LED) | 47 | Very good | Very good | Very good | Fair | Very good | Very good | Very good | 24 |
| ✓ | 6 | **Samsung** UN46EH5300 | 650 | 68 | LCD (LED) | 46 | Excellent | NA | Good | Very good | Excellent | Excellent | Very good | 17 |
| ✓ | 7 | **LG** 47LA6200 | 800 | 68 | LCD (LED) | 47 | Very good | Good | Very good | Good | Very good | Excellent | Very good | 17 |
| ✓ | 8 | **Panasonic** Viera TC-P50S60 | 700 | 67 | Plasma | 50 | Excellent | NA | Excellent | Good | Very good | Very good | Good | 46 |
| ✓ | 9 | **Sony** Bravia KDL-47W802A | 1,100 | 66 | LCD (LED) | 47 | Very good | Good | Very good | Good | Very good | Very good | Very good | 12 |
| ✓ (CR Best Buy) | 10 | **LG** 50PN6500 | 600 | 66 | Plasma | 50 | Very good | NA | Excellent | Good | Very good | Excellent | Fair | 44 |
| ✓ (CR Best Buy) | 11 | **Samsung** PN51F5300 | 650 | 66 | Plasma | 51 | Excellent | NA | Excellent | Good | Excellent | Excellent | Fair | 51 |
| ✓ | 12 | **Panasonic** Viera TC-L50ET60 | 1,300 | 66 | LCD (LED) | 50 | Very good | Good | Very good | Fair | Very good | Very good | Very good | 13 |
| ✓ | 13 | **Vizio** E500d-A0 | 650 | 66 | LCD (LED) | 50 | Very good | Good | Very good | Good | Good | Very good | Good | 17 |
| ✓ (CR Best Buy) | 14 | **Samsung** UN46EH5000 | 600 | 65 | LCD (LED) | 46 | Excellent | NA | Good | Good | Excellent | Excellent | Fair | 11 |
| ✓ | 15 | **Toshiba** 50L7300U | 850 | 65 | LCD (LED) | 50 | Excellent | NA | Good | Fair | Very good | Excellent | Very good | 16 |
|  | 16 | **LG** 50LN5700 | 850 | 64 | LCD (LED) | 50 | Very good | NA | Very good | Good | Very good | Excellent | Very good | 19 |
|  | 17 | **Sharp** Aquos LC-50LE650U | 850 | 61 | LCD (LED) | 50 | Very good | NA | Good | Fair | Very good | Very good | Good | 16 |
|  | 18 | **Vizio** E470i-A0 | 600 | 60 | LCD (LED) | 47 | Very good | NA | Very good | Good | Good | Very good | Very good | 18 |
|  | 19 | **Insignia** NS-46E440NA14 | 550 | 59 | LCD (LED) | 46 | Very good | NA | Good | Good | Very good | Excellent | Fair | 15 |
|  | 20 | **Vizio** E500i-A1 | 540 | 59 | LCD (LED) | 50 | Very good | NA | Good | Good | Good | Very good | Good | 28 |
|  | 21 | **Samsung** PN51F4500 | 500 | 58 | Plasma | 51 | Very good | NA | Excellent | Fair | Excellent | Excellent | Fair | 40 |
|  | 22 | **Philips** 50PFL3908 | 730 | 58 | LCD (LED) | 50 | Excellent | NA | Fair | Fair | Very good | Good | Good | 23 |
|  | 23 | **Toshiba** 50L2200U | 700 | 57 | LCD (LED) | 50 | Very good | NA | Good | Good | Very good | Excellent | Fair | 20 |
|  | 24 | **Sanyo** DP46142 | 400 | 54 | LCD (LED) | 46 | Very good | NA | Good | Good | Good | Very good | Fair | 20 |
|  | 25 | **Sanyo** FVM5082 | 480 | 54 | LCD (CCFL) | 50 | Very good | NA | Good | Good | Very good | Good | Fair | 34 |
|  | 26 | **Element** ELEFT466 | 500 | 52 | LCD (LED) | 46 | Very good | NA | Fair | Fair | Good | Excellent | Fair | 14 |

**Ratings Key** Excellent · Very good · Good · Fair · Poor

✓ (filled) **CR Best Buy** These models offer the best combination of performance and price. All are recommended.

✓ **Recommended** These are high-performing models that stand out.

| Recommended | Rank | Brand & model | Price | Overall score (0–100; P \| F \| G \| VG \| E) | Display type (Backlight) | Screen size (in.) | HD picture quality | 3D performance | Viewing angle | Sound quality | Remote ease of use | On-screen menu ease of use | Versatility | Energy cost/yr. ($) |
|---|---|---|---|---|---|---|---|---|---|---|---|---|---|---|
| | | **E 46- TO 52-INCH** continued | | | | | | | | | | | | |
| | 27 | **Element** ELDFT465J | $ 500 | 50 | LCD (CCFL) | 46 | G | NA | F | VG | G | E | F | 37 |
| | 28 | **TCL** LE48FHDF3310 | 550 | 48 | LCD (LED) | 48 | G | NA | G | F | G | VG | F | 11 |
| | 29 | **Sanyo** FVM4612 | 480 | 47 | LCD (LED) | 46 | G | NA | G | F | G | E | F | 16 |
| | 30 | **Sanyo** DP50843 | 500 | 46 | LCD (CCFL) | 50 | G | NA | F | F | VG | G | P | 35 |
| | 31 | **Seiki** SE50UY04 | 1,300 | 46 | LCD (LED) | 50 | G | NA | G | F | G | E | F | 24 |
| | 32 | **RCA** LED52B45RQ | 600 | 40 | LCD (LED) | 52 | F | NA | G | F | G | E | F | 24 |
| | | **F 55- TO 59-INCH** | | | | | | | | | | | | |
| ✓ | 1 | **LG** 55GA7900 | 1,500 | 74 | LCD (LED) | 55 | E | G | VG | VG | VG | VG | VG | 17 |
| ✓ | 2 | **Samsung** UN55ES8000 | 2,100 | 74 | LCD (LED) | 55 | VG | VG | G | VG | E | E | E | 21 |
| ✓ | 3 | **Sony** Bravia XBR-55X900A | 4,000 | 74 | LCD (LED) | 55 | E | G | G | VG | VG | VG | VG | 35 |
| ✓ | 4 | **LG** 55LA7400 | 1,500 | 73 | LCD (LED) | 55 | VG | VG | VG | VG | VG | VG | VG | 17 |
| ✓ | 5 | **Panasonic** Viera TC-P55ST60 | 1,350 | 72 | Plasma | 55 | E | VG | E | F | VG | VG | VG | 56 |
| ✓ | 6 | **Samsung** UN55ES6500 | 1,400 | 72 | LCD (LED) | 55 | VG | VG | F | VG | E | E | VG | 25 |
| ✓ | 7 | **Samsung** UN55F7100 | 1,500 | 69 | LCD (LED) | 55 | VG | VG | G | G | G | E | VG | 23 |
| ✓ | 8 | **Sony** Bravia KDL-55W900A | 2,300 | 69 | LCD (LED) | 55 | E | F | G | F | VG | VG | VG | 17 |
| ✓ | 9 | **Samsung** UN55F6400 | 1,300 | 67 | LCD (LED) | 55 | VG | G | G | G | G | E | VG | 26 |
| ✓ | 10 | **Toshiba** 58L7350U | 1,300 | 67 | LCD (LED) | 58 | E | F | G | F | E | VG | VG | 20 |
| ✔ | 11 | **JVC** JLE55SP4000 | 1,100 | 66 | LCD (LED) | 55 | VG | G | VG | G | VG | VG | VG | 16 |
| | 12 | **Vizio** M551d-A2R | 1,100 | 62 | LCD (LED) | 55 | VG | G | VG | G | VG | VG | G | 25 |
| | 13 | **Philips** 55PFL5907 | 1,100 | 60 | LCD (LED) | 55 | VG | NA | F | G | G | G | G | 25 |
| | 14 | **RCA** LED55C55R120Q | 800 | 56 | LCD (LED) | 55 | VG | NA | G | F | G | E | F | 25 |
| | 15 | **Insignia** NS-55L260A13 | 550 | 56 | LCD (CCFL) | 55 | VG | NA | VG | F | VG | E | F | 40 |
| | 16 | **TCL** LE55FHDF3300Z | 730 | 54 | LCD (LED) | 55 | VG | NA | G | G | G | E | F | 18 |
| | 17 | **Sanyo** FVD5833 | 750 | 49 | LCD (LED) | 58 | VG | NA | G | F | VG | G | F | 26 |

## G 60-INCH AND LARGER

| Recommended | Rank | Brand & model | Price | Overall score (0–100; P \| F \| G \| VG \| E) | Display type (Backlight) | Screen size (in.) | HD picture quality | 3D performance | Viewing angle | Sound quality | Remote ease of use | On-screen menu ease of use | Versatility | Energy cost/yr. ($) |
|---|---|---|---|---|---|---|---|---|---|---|---|---|---|---|
| Recommended | 1 | **LG** 60LA8600 | $2,300 | 76 | LCD (LED) | 60 | Excellent | Very good | Very good | Very good | Good | Very good | Excellent | 25 |
| Recommended | 2 | **Samsung** PN64F5500 | 1,800 | 74 | Plasma | 64 | Excellent | Excellent | Excellent | Good | Good | Excellent | Very good | 81 |
| Recommended | 3 | **Panasonic** Viera TC-P65VT60 | 3,100 | 73 | Plasma | 65 | Excellent | Very good | Excellent | Fair | Very good | Very good | Very good | 84 |
| Recommended | 4 | **Panasonic** Viera TC-P60ZT60 | 3,300 | 73 | Plasma | 60 | Excellent | Very good | Excellent | Fair | Very good | Very good | Very good | 79 |
| Recommended | 5 | **Samsung** PN64F8500 | 2,900 | 73 | Plasma | 64 | Excellent | Very good | Excellent | Good | Good | Excellent | Excellent | 86 |
| Recommended | 6 | **Samsung** UN60F7500 | 2,200 | 72 | LCD (LED) | 60 | Excellent | Very good | Good | Good | Good | Excellent | Excellent | 25 |
| CR Best Buy | 7 | **Panasonic** Viera TC-P60ST60 | 1,500 | 72 | Plasma | 60 | Excellent | Very good | Excellent | Fair | Very good | Very good | Very good | 60 |
| CR Best Buy | 8 | **LG** 60PH6700 | 1,050 | 72 | Plasma | 60 | Excellent | Very good | Excellent | Good | Very good | Very good | Very good | 67 |
| Recommended | 9 | **Sharp** Aquos LC-60LE857U | 2,000 | 72 | LCD (LED) | 60 | Very good | Good | Good | Very good | Very good | Very good | Very good | 17 |
| Recommended | 10 | **Samsung** PN64E550 | 2,100 | 71 | Plasma | 64 | Very good | Very good | Excellent | Very good | Excellent | Excellent | Very good | 90 |
| CR Best Buy | 11 | **Samsung** PN60F5500 | 1,200 | 71 | Plasma | 60 | Very good | Excellent | Excellent | Good | Good | Excellent | Very good | 45 |
| Recommended | 12 | **Samsung** UN65F8000 | 3,000 | 70 | LCD (LED) | 65 | Excellent | Good | Good | Good | Very good | Excellent | Excellent | 24 |
| Recommended | 13 | **Panasonic** Viera TC-L60DT60 | 2,800 | 69 | LCD (LED) | 60 | Very good | Very good | Very good | Fair | Very good | Very good | Very good | 23 |
| CR Best Buy | 14 | **Sony** Bravia KDL-60R550A | 1,500 | 68 | LCD (LED) | 60 | Excellent | Fair | Good | Very good | Very good | Very good | Very good | 31 |
| CR Best Buy | 15 | **Vizio** M601d-A3R | 1,400 | 67 | LCD (LED) | 60 | Excellent | Fair | Good | Good | Very good | Very good | Good | 24 |
| Recommended | 16 | **Sharp** Aquos LC-70C7500U | 2,200 | 65 | LCD (LED) | 70 | Excellent | NA | Good | Good | Very good | Very good | Very good | 31 |
|  | 17 | **Sharp** Aquos LC-60C6500U | 1,060 | 64 | LCD (LED) | 60 | Very good | NA | Good | Good | Very good | Excellent | Very good | 22 |
|  | 18 | **LG** 60PN6500 | 900 | 64 | Plasma | 60 | Very good | NA | Excellent | Good | Very good | Excellent | Fair | 63 |
|  | 19 | **Vizio** E601i-A3 | 1,000 | 63 | LCD (LED) | 60 | Excellent | NA | Fair | Good | Very good | Very good | Very good | 29 |
|  | 20 | **Insignia** NS-65D260A13 | 1,100 | 51 | LCD (LED) | 65 | Good | NA | Very good | Fair | Very good | Excellent | Fair | 34 |

**Ratings Key** Excellent, Very good, Good, Fair, Poor

**CR Best Buy** These models offer the best combination of performance and price. All are recommended.

**Recommended** These are high-performing models that stand out.

## Guide to the Ratings

**Overall score** is based mainly on test results. **Display type (Backlight)** indicates the type of technology used (LCD or plasma) and backlight type. **Screen size (in.)** is the size of the television's screen, measured diagonally in inches. **HD picture quality** assesses detail, color accuracy, and contrast, using signals from a Blu-ray player, cable box, and professional broadcast equipment and meters. All signals are routed through an HDMI input. **3D performance** evaluates the TV's ability to reproduce realistic 3D images. **Viewing angle** evaluates picture quality at various horizontal and vertical viewing angles. **Sound quality** is measured from the set's built-in speakers using computer driven test equipment, with additional subjective testing by a listening panel. **Remote ease of use** assesses the usability of the TV's remote control, considering button layout, backlighting, labeling, and practical features. **On-screen menu ease of use** considers the menu's interaction with the remote, menu layout, and practical features. **Versatility** indicates features that increase a TV's utility or capabilities, including 3D capability, access to Internet and Web browsing, number of HD and USB inputs, support for various media, and other useful features. **Energy cost/yr. ($)** is the estimated cost per year in dollars, calculated for 5 hours per day turned on and 19 hours in the off mode. Your usage and local rates will affect your costs. **Price** is approximate retail.

### Most & Least Reliable

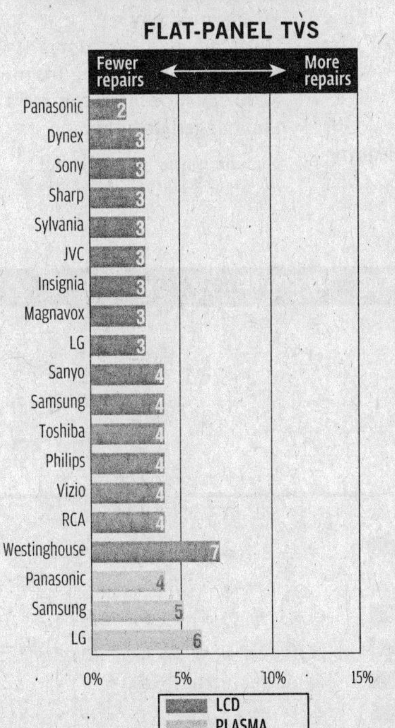


Westinghouse is the most repair-prone brand of flat panel LCD TVs. That's what we found when we asked about more than 161,000 flat panel LCD and plasma TVs purchased by our readers between 2009 and 2013. The graph shows the percentage of models for each brand that were repaired or had a serious problem. Differences of less than 3 points aren't meaningful, and we've adjusted the data to eliminate differences linked solely to the age of the TV. Models within a brand can vary, and design or manufacture changes might affect future reliability. Still, choosing a brand with a good repair history can improve your odds of getting a reliable model.

Source: Annual Product Reliability Survey, Consumer Reports National Research Center.

# Quick Guide VACUUM CLEANERS

**The best upright models, especially with a bag, deliver the most power for deep-cleaning carpets. But you might want to give up a little oomph and opt for a canister, which is easier to maneuver and quieter to run.**

**Shopping tip**

Check prices online. Still, brick-and-mortar stores might offer the best deal due to price-matching policies targeting "showrooming."

Scan this or see how, page 11

### What to look for

- Easy pushing, pulling, lifting, and carrying; be sure you try before you buy
- An upright, if carpet deep-cleaning is important
- A canister for cleaning drapes, upholstery, on stairs, and under furniture, since you move mostly the hose and wand instead of the entire machine

### What to skip

- Splurging on extra cleaning tools, when the basic tools that come standard should suffice for most cleaning jobs
- Bagless models if you have asthma or allergies, because emptying their bin is typically a dusty, messy chore

### What you'll pay

Capable bagless uprights start at about $50; figure on $200-plus for most canisters and bagged uprights.

For more buying advice, go to *ConsumerReports.org/vacuums*

**All tested models** In performance order, within types.

| Recommended | Rank | Brand & model<br>Similar models, in small type, are comparable to tested model. | Price | Overall score (0–100; P \| F \| G \| VG \| E) | Test results: Carpet | Bare floors | Tool airflow | Noise | Emissions | Handling | Pet hair | Features: Bag | Brush on/off | Easy on/off | Manual pile adjust |
|---|---|---|---|---|---|---|---|---|---|---|---|---|---|---|---|
| **A** | | **BAGGED UPRIGHT** | | | | | | | | | | | | | |
| ✔ | 1 | **Hoover** WindTunnel Anniversary Edition U6485-900 TurboPower WindTunnel Anniversary Edition UH50000 | $ 230 | 73 | E | E | E | F | E | G | VG | • | • | • | • |
| ✔ | 2 | **Miele** S 7210 Twist | 475 | 72 | E | VG | VG | VG | E | G | E | • | • | • | |
| ✔ | 3 | **Kirby** Sentria | 1,350 | 72 | E | E | E | F | E | F | E | • | • | • | • |
| ✔ | 4 | **Miele** S 7260 Cat & Dog | 715 | 72 | E | E | VG | VG | E | G | E | • | • | • | |
| ✔ | 5 | **Kenmore** Intuition 31100 | 250 | 71 | VG | VG | E | G | E | G | E | • | • | • | • |

| Recommended | Rank | Brand & model — Similar models, in small type, are comparable to tested model. | Price | Overall score (0–100; P \| F \| G \| VG \| E) | Test results: Carpet | Bare floors | Tool airflow | Noise | Emissions | Handling | Pet hair | Features: Bag | Brush on/off | Easy on/off | Manual pile adjust |
|---|---|---|---|---|---|---|---|---|---|---|---|---|---|---|---|
| **A BAGGED UPRIGHT** continued | | | | | | | | | | | | | | | |
| CR Best Buy | 6 | **Kenmore** Progressive 31069 | $200 | 71 | Very good | Excellent | Excellent | Good | Excellent | Good | Excellent | • | • | • | • |
| CR Best Buy | 7 | **Hoover** WindTunnel Max UH30600 | 180 | 70 | Very good | Excellent | Very good | Good | Excellent | Good | Excellent | • | • | • | • |
| Recommended | 8 | **Hoover** Platinum Bagged UH30010COM | 300 | 70 | Excellent | Excellent | NA | Good | Very good | Very good | Excellent | • | | • | |
| Recommended | 9 | **Kenmore** Intuition 31200 | 300 | 69 | Very good | Excellent | Excellent | Good | Excellent | Fair | Fair | • | • | • | • |
| Recommended | 10 | **Kenmore** Intuition 31810 | 270 | 69 | Very good | Excellent | Very good | Good | Excellent | Good | Fair | • | • | • | • |
| Recommended | 11 | **Miele** S 7580 Bolero Swing | 880 | 69 | Excellent | Very good | Very good | Very good | Excellent | Good | Excellent | • | • | • | |
| Recommended | 12 | **Miele** S 7280 Jazz Salsa | 600 | 69 | Excellent | Very good | Good | Very good | Excellent | Good | Excellent | • | • | • | |
| CR Best Buy | 13 | **Eureka** Boss Smart Vac 4870[ ] | 160 | 67 | Very good | Excellent | Good | Good | Excellent | Fair | Excellent | • | • | | • |
| Recommended | 14 | **Sebo** Felix Premium | 600 | 66 | Very good | Excellent | Good | Good | Excellent | Very good | Excellent | • | • | • | • |
| Recommended | 15 | **Hoover** WindTunnel T-Series Pet UH30310 | 150 | 65 | Very good | Excellent | Very good | Good | Excellent | Very good | Excellent | • | • | • | • |
| Recommended | 16 | **Hoover** WindTunnel T-Series UH30300 | 140 | 65 | Very good | Excellent | Very good | Good | Excellent | Very good | Excellent | • | • | • | • |
| | 17 | **Panasonic** MC-UG471 | 150 | 63 | Good | Excellent | Excellent | Good | Excellent | Good | Excellent | • | | • | |
| | 18 | **Eureka** AirSpeed ABS AS1050A (Walmart) | 130 | 61 | Very good | Excellent | Good | Fair | Excellent | Very good | Excellent | • | | • | • |
| | 19 | **Riccar** Supralite RSL4 Freedom F3600 | 470 | 59 | Excellent | Excellent | NA | Fair | Excellent | Very good | Excellent | • | | • | |
| | 20 | **Riccar** Brilliance Premium Synchrony Premium | 900 | 59 | Excellent | Excellent | Fair | Fair | Very good | Fair | Excellent | • | • | • | • |
| | 21 | **Oreck** Magnesium | 500 | 57 | Very good | Excellent | NA | Good | Excellent | Excellent | Very good | • | | | |
| | 22 | **Lindhaus** Diamante 380 | 930 | 50 | Good | Excellent | Fair | Very good | Excellent | Fair | Excellent | • | • | | • |
| | 23 | **Dirt Devil** Featherlite Bagged M085590 | 50 | 49 | Good | Excellent | Good | Fair | Good | Good | Excellent | • | | • | |
| | 24 | **Sebo** automatic X5 | 700 | 48 | Good | Excellent | Fair | Good | Very good | Good | Very good | • | | • | |
| | 25 | **Oreck** Graphite | 350 | 47 | Good | Excellent | NA | Fair | Excellent | Good | Very good | • | | • | |
| | 26 | **Aerus** FreshEra | 500 | 44 | Good | Very good | NA | Fair | Excellent | Very good | Excellent | • | | • | |
| | 27 | **Royal** Eminence MRY9750 | 600 | 43 | Good | Fair | Good | Good | Excellent | Good | Excellent | • | • | • | |
| | 28 | **Cirrus** Performance Pet CR99 | 500 | 41 | Good | Fair | Very good | Fair | Excellent | Good | Excellent | • | • | • | |

**Ratings Key** Excellent, Very good, Good, Fair, Poor

**CR Best Buy** These models offer the best combination of performance and price. All are recommended.

**Recommended** These are high-performing models that stand out.

| Recommended | Rank | Brand & model<br>Similar models, in small type, are comparable to tested model. | Price | Overall score<br>0–100<br>P \| F \| G \| VG \| E | Test results: Carpet | Bare floors | Tool airflow | Noise | Emissions | Handling | Pet hair | Features: Bag | Brush on/off | Easy on/off | Manual pile adjust |
|---|---|---|---|---|---|---|---|---|---|---|---|---|---|---|---|
| | | **B BAGLESS UPRIGHT** | | | | | | | | | | | | | |
| ✓ | 1 | **LG** Kompressor LuV350P | $400 | 70 | E | E | G | G | E | VG | VG | | • | • | |
| **✓** | 2 | **Hoover** WindTunnel T-Series Rewind Bagless UH70120 WindTunnel T-Series Rewind Bagless UH70110 | 130 | 69 | VG | E | E | G | E | VG | E | | | • | • |
| ✓ | 3 | **LG** Kompressor Total Care LuV400T | 500 | 68 | E | E | G | G | E | G | E | | • | • | • |
| ✓ | 4 | **Kenmore** Intuition 31040 | 250 | 66 | VG | E | G | G | E | G | E | | • | • | • |
| **✓** | 5 | **Eureka** AirSpeed AS1000A AirSpeed AS1001A Gold, AirSpeed AS1002A (Target) | 120 | 66 | VG | E | VG | G | E | VG | VG | | | • | • |
| ✓ | 6 | **Hoover** Platinum Bagless UH70015 | 270 | 65 | VG | E | G | G | E | G | E | | • | • | • |
| ✓ | 7 | **Shark** Rotator Professional Lift-Away NV501 | 250 | 65 | VG | E | G | VG | E | VG | F | | • | | |
| ✓ | 8 | **LG** Kompressor LuV200R | 300 | 64 | VG | E | VG | VG | VG | F | VG | | • | • | • |
| **✓** | 9 | **Bissell** CleanView Helix Deluxe 71V9 CleanView Helix Deluxe 71V9-2 (Lowe's) | 100 | 64 | VG | E | VG | G | E | VG | E | | | | • |
| ✓ | 10 | **Shark** Navigator Lift-Away NV352 Navigator Lift-Away NV351 (Walmart) | 200 | 63 | VG | E | G | G | E | VG | F | | • | | |
| | 11 | **Panasonic** MC-UL815 | 200 | 62 | VG | VG | G | G | VG | G | E | | • | • | |
| | 12 | **Shark** Navigator Profes-sional Lift-Away NV356E | 200 | 62 | VG | E | G | G | E | VG | F | | • | | |
| | 13 | **Hoover** WindTunnel Pet Rewind UH70210 | 160 | 61 | G | E | VG | G | E | G | E | | • | • | • |
| | 14 | **Hoover** WindTunnel T-Series Purely Clean UH70202 | 130 | 61 | G | E | VG | G | E | G | VG | | • | • | • |
| | 15 | **Bissell** Momentum 82G71 | 100 | 60 | VG | VG | VG | G | E | G | VG | | | | • |
| | 16 | **Hoover** WindTunnel Rewind Plus UH70205 | 150 | 59 | G | VG | G | G | E | G | E | | • | • | • |
| | 17 | **Panasonic** MC-UL915 | 230 | 59 | G | E | G | G | VG | G | E | | • | | |
| | 18 | **Panasonic** MC-UL810 | 170 | 58 | VG | VG | VG | G | G | G | E | | | • | |
| | 19 | **Shark** Navigator NV22L | 150 | 58 | G | E | G | VG | VG | VG | E | | • | | |
| | 20 | **Hoover** WindTunnel Max UH70600 | 220 | 57 | VG | VG | G | F | E | G | G | | • | • | • |
| | 21 | **Electrolux** Nimble EL8602[ ] Nimble EL8605[ ] (Lowe's) | 300 | 57 | G | E | G | G | E | G | E | | • | • | |

| Recommended | Rank | Brand & model<br>Similar models, in small type, are comparable to tested model. | Price | Overall score<br>0–100<br>P \| F \| G \| VG \| E | Test results: Carpet | Bare floors | Tool airflow | Noise | Emissions | Handling | Pet hair | Features: Bag | Brush on/off | Easy on/off | Manual pile adjust |
|---|---|---|---|---|---|---|---|---|---|---|---|---|---|---|---|
| | | **B BAGLESS UPRIGHT** continued | | | | | | | | | | | | | |
| | 22 | **Bissell** Pet Hair Eraser 87B4 Pet Hair Eraser 87B4-3 (Best Buy), Pet Hair Eraser 87B4-2 (Lowe's) | $150 | 57 | Very good | Good | Good | Good | Very good | Good | Very good | | | | • |
| | 23 | **Panasonic** JetForce MC-UL427 | 170 | 57 | Good | Excellent | Very good | Good | Good | Very good | Excellent | | • | • | |
| | 24 | **Dyson** DC41 Animal | 600 | 56 | Good | Excellent | Very good | Good | Excellent | Very good | Good | | • | • | |
| | 25 | **Eureka** Whirlwind+ Pet Lover 3276[ ] | 100 | 56 | Very good | Good | Very good | Good | Excellent | Good | Excellent | | | | • |
| | 26 | **Bissell** PowerClean 16N5-9 | 200 | 56 | Good | Excellent | Good | Fair | Very good | Good | Good | | • | • | • |
| | 27 | **Bissell** Healthy Home 16N5-F | 200 | 56 | Good | Excellent | Good | Fair | Very good | Good | Good | | • | • | • |
| | 28 | **Eureka** SuctionSeal Pet AS1104A | 160 | 55 | Good | Excellent | Very good | Good | Fair | Good | Excellent | | • | • | • |
| | 29 | **Eureka** AirSpeed Zuum AS5203A | 100 | 55 | Very good | Excellent | Fair | Good | Excellent | Very good | Excellent | | | • | • |
| | 30 | **LG** Kompressor LuV250C | 250 | 54 | Good | Very good | Fair | Good | Excellent | Good | Fair | | • | • | • |
| | 31 | **Hoover** WindTunnel Pet Cyclonic UH70085 | 200 | 52 | Good | Very good | Good | Good | Excellent | Good | Excellent | | • | • | • |
| | 32 | **Bissell** Total Floors Pet 61C5W | 140 | 52 | Good | Excellent | Good | Fair | Good | Good | Excellent | | • | | • |
| | 33 | **Bissell** Lift-Off Multi Cyclonic Pet 89Q9 Lift-Off Multi Cyclonic Pet 89Q9-4 (Kohl's), Lift-Off Multi Cyclonic Pet 89Q9-6 (Bed Bath & Beyond), Lift-Off Multi Cyclonic Pet 18Z6 (Target) | 180 | 52 | Good | Excellent | Good | Good | Very good | Good | Fair | | • | | • |
| | 34 | **Electrolux** Versatility EL8505 Versatility EL8502 | 270 | 52 | Very good | Good | Fair | Good | Very good | Good | Very good | | • | • | |
| | 35 | **Hoover** WindTunnel Air UH70400 | 180 | 50 | Good | Excellent | Good | Good | Excellent | Very good | Good | | • | • | |
| | 36 | **Electrolux** Precision BrushRoll Clean EL8807A Precision BrushRoll Clean EL8805A | 300 | 49 | Good | Excellent | Fair | Good | Excellent | Very good | Excellent | | • | | • |
| | 37 | **Bissell** ProLite Multi Cyclonic 17G5 ProLite Multi Cyclonic 17G5-2 (Lowe's) | 150 | 48 | Good | Excellent | Good | Good | Fair | Good | Fair | | • | • | |
| | 38 | **Bissell** OptiClean Pet 30C7T (Target) | 150 | 48 | Good | Excellent | Good | Fair | Good | Good | Very good | | • | | • |

**Ratings Key** Excellent  Very good  Good  Fair  Poor

☑ **CR Best Buy** These models offer the best combination of performance and price. All are recommended.

☑ **Recommended** These are high-performing models that stand out.

| Recommended | Rank | Brand & model<br>**Similar models,** in small type, are comparable to tested model. | Price | Overall score<br>0–100<br>P \| F \| G \| VG \| E | Test results: Carpet | Bare floors | Tool airflow | Noise | Emissions | Handling | Pet hair | Features: Bag | Brush on/off | Easy on/off | Manual pile adjust |
|---|---|---|---|---|---|---|---|---|---|---|---|---|---|---|---|
| | | **B BAGLESS UPRIGHT** continued | | | | | | | | | | | | | |
| | 39 | **Oreck** VersaVac | $ 250 | 48 | G | E | NA | G | E | VG | F | | • | | |
| | 40 | **Dyson** DC40 Multi Floor | 500 | 45 | F | E | G | F | E | VG | F | | • | • | |
| | 41 | **Dyson** DC24 Ball Multi Floor | 430 | 44 | G | E | P | VG | E | VG | F | | • | | |
| | 42 | **Shark** Navigator Light NV100 | 150 | 43 | G | E | P | G | E | E | E | | • | | |
| | 43 | **Hoover** WindTunnel Pet Rewind Plus UH70086 | 165 | 41 | F | G | G | G | E | G | VG | | • | • | • |
| | 44 | **Eureka** AirExcel NLS 5403A | 100 | 40 | F | G | VG | G | F | VG | E | | | • | • |
| | 45 | **Eureka** Endeavor NLS 5400A (Walmart) | 80 | 33 | P | VG | VG | G | VG | VG | VG | | | • | • |
| | | **C BAGGED CANISTER** | | | | | | | | | | | | | |
| ✓ | 1 | **Kenmore** Intuition 28014 | 500 | 72 | VG | E | E | VG | E | G | E | • | • | • | • |
| ✓ | 2 | **Kenmore** Progressive 21714 | 400 | 72 | VG | E | VG | G | E | G | E | • | • | • | • |
| ✓ | 3 | **Miele** S 5281 Callisto | 990 | 71 | VG | E | E | VG | E | G | VG | • | • | • | • |
| ✔ | 4 | **Kenmore** Progressive 21614 | 300 | 70 | VG | E | VG | G | E | G | E | • | • | • | • |
| ✔ | 5 | **Kenmore** Progressive 21514 | 250 | 68 | VG | E | G | G | VG | G | G | • | • | • | • |
| | 6 | **Hoover** WindTunnel S3670 | 250 | 68 | VG | E | VG | G | E | F | VG | • | • | • | |
| | 7 | **Electrolux** UltraOne EL7070A | 800 | 67 | G | E | E | VG | E | F | E | • | • | • | • |
| | 8 | **Electrolux** UltraSilencer DeepClean EL7060[ ]<br>UltraSilencer DeepClean EL7061[ ] (Lowe's) | 500 | 65 | VG | E | G | E | E | F | E | • | • | • | • |
| ✔ | 9 | **Panasonic** MC-CG902 | 250 | 65 | VG | VG | VG | G | E | G | G | • | • | • | • |
| | 10 | **Miele** S 2181 Titan | 660 | 63 | G | E | E | VG | E | G | E | • | • | • | |
| | 11 | **Panasonic** MC-CG983 | 500 | 63 | VG | VG | VG | G | E | G | G | • | • | • | • |
| | 12 | **Panasonic** MC-CG917 | 300 | 63 | VG | G | E | G | E | G | E | • | • | • | • |
| | 13 | **Riccar** Immaculate Premier Gusto | 1,400 | 63 | G | E | VG | F | E | G | E | • | • | • | • |
| | 14 | **Electrolux** JetMaxx Green EL4040[ ] | 400 | 61 | G | E | G | G | E | G | E | • | • | • | |
| | 15 | **Miele** S 2121 Olympus | 330 | 58 | G | E | VG | VG | E | G | VG | • | NA | • | NA |
| | 16 | **Miele** S 2121 Delphi | 550 | 56 | G | E | VG | VG | E | G | F | • | • | • | |

| Recommended | Rank | Brand & model (Similar models, in small type, are comparable to tested model.) | Price | Overall score (0–100; P \| F \| G \| VG \| E) | Test results: Carpet | Bare floors | Tool airflow | Noise | Emissions | Handling | Pet hair | Features: Bag | Brush on/off | Easy on/off | Manual pile adjust |
|---|---|---|---|---|---|---|---|---|---|---|---|---|---|---|---|
| | | **C BAGGED CANISTER** continued | | | | | | | | | | | | | |
| | 17 | **Electrolux** UltraSilencer EL6986A | $ 300 | 55 | Good | Excellent | Good | Excellent | Excellent | Fair | Excellent | • | NA | • | • |
| | 18 | **Miele** S 6270 Topaz | 800 | 55 | Good | Excellent | Very good | Very good | Excellent | Good | Very good | • | • | • | |
| | 19 | **Aerus** Lux Legacy | 1,300 | 55 | Good | Excellent | Very good | Good | Excellent | Good | Excellent | • | • | • | |
| | 20 | **Aerus** Lux Guardian Ultra | 1,500 | 52 | Good | Excellent | Good | Good | Excellent | Good | Excellent | • | • | • | |
| | 21 | **Sebo** Air Belt C3.1 | 900 | 51 | Good | Excellent | Good | Very good | Excellent | Good | Fair | • | | • | |
| | 22 | **Sebo** Air Belt K3 Volcano | 880 | 51 | Good | Excellent | Good | Very good | Excellent | Good | Excellent | • | | • | |
| | 23 | **Miele** S 6290 Jasper | 520 | 48 | Fair | Excellent | Very good | Excellent | Excellent | Good | Fair | • | NA | • | • |
| | | **D BAGLESS CANISTER** | | | | | | | | | | | | | |
| ✔ | 1 | **LG** Kompressor LcV900B | 400 | 69 | Very good | Excellent | Very good | Very good | Excellent | Fair | Fair | | • | • | • |
| | 2 | **Hoover** Platinum S3865 | 400 | 65 | Very good | Excellent | Good | Good | Excellent | Fair | Excellent | | • | • | • |
| | 3 | **Rainbow** E-series E2 | 1,350 | 54 | Good | Excellent | Very good | Good | Excellent | Fair | Excellent | | • | | • |
| | 4 | **Dyson** DC39 Animal | 500 | 51 | Fair | Excellent | Very good | Very good | Excellent | Good | Fair | | • | • | |
| | 5 | **Hoover** Elite Cyclonic S3825 | 200 | 51 | Good | Excellent | Good | Good | Very good | Fair | Very good | | • | • | |
| | 6 | **Electrolux** UltraActive DeepClean EL4300A | 450 | 50 | Very good | Excellent | Poor | Good | Excellent | Fair | Excellent | | • | • | • |
| | 7 | **Hoover** Multi-Cyclonic SH40060 | 150 | 49 | Good | Excellent | Good | Good | Excellent | Good | Fair | | • | • | |
| | 8 | **Hoover** Zen Whisper SH40080 | 250 | 44 | Fair | Excellent | Very good | Very good | Very good | Fair | Fair | | • | • | |
| | 9 | **Samsung** Electric Blue VCC88P0H1B | 350 | 43 | Good | Excellent | Poor | Very good | Excellent | Good | Very good | | • | • | • |
| | 10 | **Samsung** Champagne VCC96P0H1G | 450 | 42 | Good | Excellent | Poor | Very good | Excellent | Good | Very good | | • | • | • |
| | 11 | **Dirt Devil** Vision M082750 | 170 | 37 | Fair | Excellent | Poor | Fair | Excellent | Fair | Fair | | • | • | • |
| | 12 | **Dyson** DC26 City Multi floor | 400 | 31 | Poor | Excellent | Poor | Good | Excellent | Very good | Good | | • | • | |

**Ratings Key** Excellent, Very good, Good, Fair, Poor

**CR Best Buy** These models offer the best combination of performance and price. All are recommended.

✔ **Recommended** These are high-performing models that stand out.

## Guide to the Ratings

**Overall score** is based mainly on cleaning performance and ease of use. The displayed score is out of a total of 100 points. **Carpet** indicates how much embedded talc and sand a vacuum lifted from a medium-pile carpet. **Bare floors** shows how well a vacuum picked up sand without dispersing it on bare floors. **Tool airflow** indicates the strength of airflow through the hose. **Noise** is based on measurements in decibels. **Emissions** indicates our measurement of the quantity of wood-flour particles a vacuum released under two conditions: when only the motor was turned on and while vacuuming. **Handling** reflects how easy it is to push, pull, and carry a vacuum. **Pet hair** reflects how well a vacuum picks up pet hair from medium-pile carpet. **Price** is approximate retail.

## Most & Least Reliable

### VACUUMS

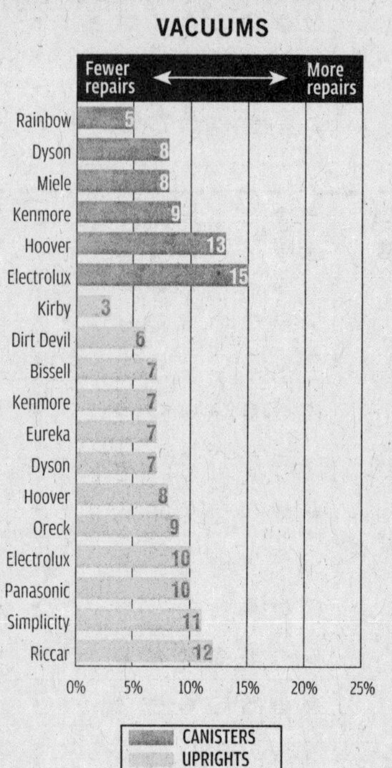


Choosing a vacuum with a good repair history can improve your odds of getting a reliable model. So each year we survey thousands of our readers about their experiences. Kirby was among the least repair-prone brands of upright vacuums in our latest survey. Rainbow was among the least repair-prone brands of canister vacuums, and Hoover and Electrolux were the most repair-prone in that category. Our findings are based on more than 102,000 vacuums readers bought new between 2008 and 2012. Differences of fewer than 4 points aren't meaningful. Data are adjusted to eliminate differences linked to the age and use of the vacuum. Models within a brand may vary, and design or manufacture changes may affect future reliability.

Source: Annual Product Reliability Survey, Consumer Reports National Research Center.

# Quick Guide WALL OVENS

The cooktop and wall oven combination offers more design flexibility and can come in handy when more than one person is cooking.

## Shopping Tip

Front-mounted touchpad controls are easy to bump and reset by accident. Be sure that they're well-placed.

Scan this or see how, page 11

### What to look for

- Control lockout, if the control panel will be within a young child's reach
- Smooth cover or floor over the bottom baking element, which can help with easier cleanup of spills
- Five or more oven rack positions, for more flexibility in arranging racks and bakeware

### What to skip

- A small oven window, which won't give a full view to the interior
- Menu databases and other perks if you want to save

### What you'll pay

You can get an electric cooktop and wall oven for as little as $1,300 or so, though capable ranges cost far less.

For more buying advice, go to *ConsumerReports.org/ovens*

All tested models in performance order, within types.

| Recommended | Rank | Brand & model (Similar models, in small type, are comparable to tested model.) | Price | Overall score (0–100; P \| F \| G \| VG \| E) | Test results: Baking | Broiling | Oven capacity | Self-cleaning | Features: Width (in.) | Covered element | Convection mode | Temperature probe |
|---|---|---|---|---|---|---|---|---|---|---|---|---|
| | | **A DOUBLE ELECTRIC** | | | | | | | | | | |
| ✓ | 1 | **Whirlpool** WOD93EC0AS | $2,500 | 80 | ⊖ | ⊜ | ⊜ | ⊜ | 30 | • | • | |
| ✓ | 2 | **Maytag** MEW9630A | 2,700 | 80 | ⊖ | ⊜ | ⊜ | ⊜ | 30 | • | • | |
| ✓ | 3 | **KitchenAid** KEBS209BSP | 3,500 | 79 | ⊖ | ⊜ | ⊜ | ⊖ | 30 | • | • | • |
| ✓ | 4 | **GE** PT9550FSSS | 3,600 | 73 | ⊖ | ⊖ | ⊖ | ⊖ | 30 | • | • | • |
| ✓ | 5 | **Whirlpool** WOD51EC0A | 2,000 | 72 | ⊖ | ⊜ | ⊜ | ⊜ | 30 | • | | |
| ✓ | 6 | **Maytag** MEW7630A | 1,700 | 72 | ⊖ | ⊜ | ⊜ | ⊜ | 30 | • | | |
| ✓ | 7 | **Bosch** HBL5650UC | 2,805 | 72 | ⊖ | ⊖ | ⊖ | ⊖ | 30 | • | • | • |

| Recommended | Rank | Brand & model (Similar models, in small type, are comparable to tested model.) | Price | Overall score (0–100; P \| F \| G \| VG \| E) | Test results: Baking | Test results: Broiling | Test results: Oven capacity | Test results: Self-cleaning | Features: Width (in.) | Features: Covered element | Features: Convection mode | Features: Temperature probe |
|---|---|---|---|---|---|---|---|---|---|---|---|---|
| | | **A DOUBLE ELECTRIC** continued | | | | | | | | | | |
| ✔ Recommended | 8 | **Bosch** HBL8650UC | $3,115 | 72 | Very good | Very good | Very good | Very good | 30 | • | • | • |
| | 9 | **Electrolux** EI30EW45JS | 3,200 | 70 | Very good | Very good | Very good | Excellent | 30 | • | • | |
| | 10 | **Electrolux** EW30EW65GS | 3,500 | 70 | Very good | Very good | Very good | Excellent | 30 | • | • | • |
| | 11 | **GE** JT5500SFSS | 2,900 | 70 | Very good | Very good | Excellent | Very good | 30 | • | • | |
| | 12 | **LG** LWD3010ST | 2,700 | 65 | Good | Excellent | Very good | Good | 30 | • | • | |
| | 13 | **Frigidaire** FFET3025L | 1,700 | 64 | Very good | Good | Good | Excellent | 30 | | | |
| | 14 | **Thermador** ME302JS | 4,000 | 63 | Very good | Very good | Good | Very good | 30 | • | • | • |
| | 15 | **Kenmore** 42003 | 3,300 | 61 | Good | Very good | Very good | Excellent | 30 | • | • | • |
| | 16 | **GE** CT959STSS | 3,200 | 60 | Very good | Good | Very good | Excellent | 30 | • | • | • |
| | 17 | **GE** JT3500FSSS | 2,200 | 58 | Good | Very good | Excellent | Very good | 30 | • | | |
| | 18 | **Frigidaire** FPET3085KF | 3,200 | 56 | Good | Very good | Good | Excellent | 30 | • | • | |
| | 19 | **Wolf** DO30-2F/S | 6,300 | 55 | Good | Excellent | Good | Fair | 30 | • | • | • |
| | | **B SINGLE ELECTRIC** | | | | | | | | | | |
| ✔ CR Best Buy | 1 | **Whirlpool** WOS92EC0AH | 1,500 | 80 | Very good | Excellent | Excellent | Excellent | 30 | • | • | |
| ✔ CR Best Buy | 2 | **Maytag** MEW9530AW | 1,400 | 80 | Very good | Excellent | Excellent | Excellent | 30 | • | • | |
| ✔ Recommended | 3 | **KitchenAid** KEBS109BWW | 2,000 | 79 | Very good | Excellent | Excellent | Very good | 30 | • | • | • |
| ✔ Recommended | 4 | **GE** PT9050FSSS<br>PT7050FSSS | 2,600 | 73 | Very good | Very good | Very good | Very good | 30 | • | • | • |
| ✔ CR Best Buy | 5 | **Whirlpool** WOS51EC0AS | 1,300 | 72 | Very good | Excellent | Excellent | Excellent | 30 | • | | |
| ✔ CR Best Buy | 6 | **Maytag** MEW7530AW | 1,000 | 72 | Very good | Excellent | Excellent | Excellent | 30 | • | | |
| ✔ Recommended | 7 | **Bosch** HBL5450UC | 1,900 | 72 | Very good | Very good | Very good | Very good | 30 | • | • | • |
| | 8 | **Electrolux** EI30EW35KS | 1,700 | 70 | Very good | Very good | Very good | Excellent | 30 | • | • | |
| | 9 | **GE** JT5000FSSS | 1,800 | 70 | Very good | Very good | Excellent | Very good | 30 | • | • | |

**Ratings Key** Excellent Very good Good Fair Poor

✔ **CR Best Buy** These models offer the best combination of performance and price. All are recommended.

✔ **Recommended** These are high-performing models that stand out.

| Recommended | Rank | Brand & model<br>**Similar models,** in small type, are comparable to tested model. | Price | Overall score<br>0–100<br>P \| F \| G \| VG \| E | Test results: Baking | Test results: Broiling | Test results: Oven capacity | Test results: Self-cleaning | Features: Width (in.) | Features: Covered element | Features: Convection mode | Features: Temperature probe |
|---|---|---|---|---|---|---|---|---|---|---|---|---|
| | | **B SINGLE ELECTRIC** continued | | | | | | | | | | |
| | 10 | **Viking** Professional VESO130SS | $2,900 | 69 | G | E | VG | G | 30 | • | • | |
| | 11 | **Electrolux** Icon E30EW75ESS<br>Icon E30EW75GSS | 2,200 | 67 | E | VG | F | E | 30 | • | • | |
| | 12 | **Viking** VESO5302SS | 3,600 | 66 | VG | VG | G | VG | 30 | • | • | • |
| | 13 | **LG** LWS3081ST | 2,000 | 65 | G | E | VG | G | 30 | • | • | • |
| | 14 | **GE** Profile PT925DNBB | 2,500 | 65 | VG | VG | E | F | 30 | | • | • |
| | 15 | **Frigidaire** FFEW3025S | 1,700 | 64 | VG | G | G | E | 30 | | | |
| | 16 | **GE** Profile PT916SRSS | 1,900 | 64 | G | E | VG | E | 30 | • | • | • |
| | 17 | **Thermador** ME301JS | 2,900 | 63 | VG | VG | G | VG | 30 | • | • | • |
| | 18 | **GE** JTP70SMSS | 1,500 | 62 | G | VG | VG | VG | 30 | • | • | |
| | 19 | **Kenmore** Pro 41003 | 2,400 | 61 | G | VG | VG | E | 30 | • | • | • |
| | 20 | **GE** Café CT918STSS | 2,200 | 60 | VG | G | VG | E | 30 | • | • | • |
| | 21 | **KitchenAid** KEBK101BBL | 1,800 | 60 | G | E | E | VG | 30 | • | | |
| | 22 | **GE** JT3000FSSS | 1,400 | 58 | G | VG | E | VG | 30 | • | | |
| | 23 | **Frigidaire** Professional FPEW3085KF | 1,700 | 56 | G | VG | G | E | 30 | • | • | |
| | 24 | **Wolf** E-Series SO30-2F/S L-Series SO30U/S, L-Series SO30F/S, E-Series SO30-2U/S | 4,000 | 55 | G | E | G | F | 30 | • | • | • |
| | 25 | **Frigidaire** FGEW3065KF | 1,500 | 54 | G | VG | G | E | 30 | • | • | |
| | 26 | **GE** JTP30DPBB | 1,200 | 54 | VG | F | VG | VG | 30 | • | | |
| | 27 | **Kenmore** 48839 | 1,000 | 52 | G | G | G | E | 30 | • | | |
| | 28 | **KitchenAid** KEBS107SSS | 2,000 | 49 | G | G | G | VG | 30 | • | • | • |
| | 29 | **Kenmore** Elite 48093 | 2,300 | 47 | G | G | G | E | 30 | • | • | • |
| | 30 | **Dacor** DO130 | 2,200 | 45 | G | G | G | G | 30 | • | • | • |
| | 31 | **GE** Monogram ZET1SMSS<br>Monogram ZET1PMSS, Monogram ZET1RMSS | 3,400 | 45 | VG | F | G | E | 30 | • | • | • |
| | 32 | **Fagor** 5HA-780X | 2,100 | 44 | G | G | F | E | 30 | • | • | |

## Guide to the Ratings

**Overall score** reflects oven capacity and baking, broiling, and self-cleaning ability. The displayed score is out of a total of 100 points. **Baking** reflects whether cakes and cookies baked on two racks were evenly browned. **Broiling** is based on even browning of a pan of burgers, and high-heat searing ability. **Oven capacity** measures usable space. **Self-cleaning** gauges the self-cleaning cycle's effectiveness. **Price** is approximate retail.

## Most & Least Reliable

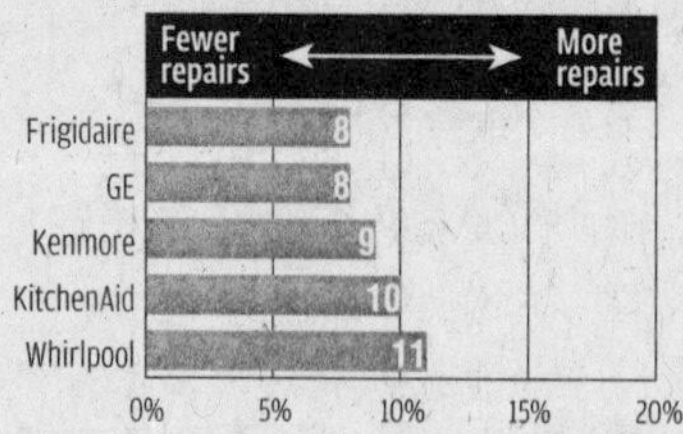


Choosing a brand with a good repair history can improve your odds of getting a reliable model. So each year we survey thousands of our readers about their experiences. Whirlpool has been less reliable than Frigidaire and GE. Although we lacked sufficient historical data for all years to include Jenn-Air in the graph, our data indicate that it has been a repair-prone brand. Our findings are based on the more than 13,000 wall ovens readers bought new between 2007 and 2012. Differences of fewer than 3 points aren't meaningful. Data are adjusted to eliminate differences linked solely to the wall oven's age. Note that models within a brand may vary, and design or manufacturing changes may affect future reliability.

Source: Annual Product Reliability Survey, Consumer Reports National Research Center.

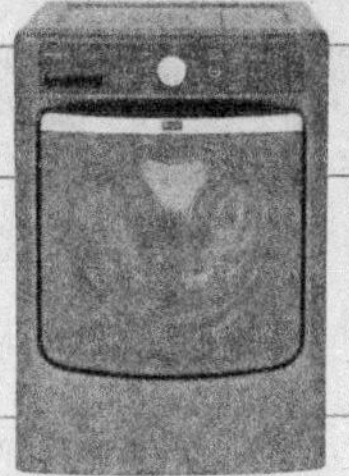

# Quick Guide WASHERS

Some front-loaders now wash faster than top-loaders without sacrificing cleaning or gentleness. You'll also find more programmable wash menus and even built-in USB ports that allow for future software upgrades.

**Shopping tip**

Moving laundry to an upper level? Have a pro confirm that floor joists can support the weight and vibrations.

Scan this or see how, page 11

### What to look for

- A porcelain top or lid, which resists scratching better than painted metal
- A stainless-steel or porcelain tub, which won't rust
- An extra rinse cycle, if you or others in your home are sensitive to detergent residue
- Dial controls, generally easier to use than some touch-pad or digital controls

### What to skip

- Customized programs, because basic cycles and settings can handle most washing needs
- Steam settings—the steam models we've tested cleaned well even when we didn't use the steam option

### What you'll pay

Capable machines that combine performance and value start at well under $1,000.

For more buying advice, go to *ConsumerReports.org/washers*

Recommended models only From 99 tested.

| Recommended | Rank | Brand & model (Similar models, in small type, are comparable to tested model.) | Price | Overall score (0–100; P \| F \| G \| VG \| E) | Test results: Washing performance | Energy efficiency | Water efficiency | Capacity | Gentleness | Noise | Vibration | Cycle time (min.) | Features: Energy star | Stainless-steel tub | Auto temp. control | Auto bleach dispenser |
|---|---|---|---|---|---|---|---|---|---|---|---|---|---|---|---|---|
| **A FRONT LOADER** | | | | | | | | | | | | | | | | |
| ✓ | 1 | **Maytag** Maxima XL MHW8000AW | $1,300 | 93 | ⊜ | ⊜ | ⊜ | ⊜ | ⊖ | ⊖ | ⊖ | 50 | • | • | • | • |
| ✓ | 2 | **Maytag** Maxima XL MHW7000AW<br>Maxima XL MHW6000AW | 1,150 | 90 | ⊜ | ⊜ | ⊜ | ⊜ | ⊖ | ⊖ | ⊜ | 45 | • | • | • | • |
| ✓ | 3 | **Whirlpool** Duet WFL98HEBU | 1,500 | 90 | ⊜ | ⊜ | ⊜ | ⊜ | ⊖ | ⊖ | ⊖ | 75 | • | • | • | • |
| ✓ | 4 | **Whirlpool** Duet WFW86HEBC<br>Duet WFW80HEBW | 1,100 | 90 | ⊜ | ⊜ | ⊜ | ⊜ | ⊖ | ○ | ⊖ | 45 | • | • | • | • |

## A FRONT LOADER continued

| Recommended | Rank | Brand & model (Similar models, in small type, are comparable to tested model.) | Price | Overall score (0–100; P \| F \| G \| VG \| E) | Test results: Washing performance | Energy efficiency | Water efficiency | Capacity | Gentleness | Noise | Vibration | Cycle time (min.) | Features: Energy star | Stainless-steel tub | Auto temp. control | Auto bleach dispenser |
|---|---|---|---|---|---|---|---|---|---|---|---|---|---|---|---|---|
| Recommended | 5 | **Kenmore** Elite 41073 | $1,500 | 90 | Excellent | Excellent | Excellent | Excellent | Very good | Very good | Very good | 95 | • | • | • | • |
| Recommended | 6 | **Whirlpool** Duet WFW88HEAW | 1,000 | 90 | Excellent | Excellent | Excellent | Excellent | Very good | Very good | Very good | 45 | • | • | • | • |
| CR Best Buy | 7 | **Whirlpool** Duet WFW70HEBW | 800 | 89 | Excellent | Excellent | Excellent | Excellent | Excellent | Very good | Very good | 45 | • | • | • | • |
| Recommended | 8 | **Samsung** WF457ARGS[GR] WF455ARGSWR | 1,550 | 89 | Excellent | Excellent | Excellent | Excellent | Good | Very good | Excellent | 100 | • | • | • | • |
| Recommended | 9 | **LG** WM8000H[V]A | 1,350 | 89 | Excellent | Excellent | Excellent | Excellent | Very good | Very good | Very good | 100 | • | • | • | • |
| Recommended | 10 | **LG** WM3470H[W]A | 1,100 | 88 | Excellent | Excellent | Excellent | Excellent | Very good | Very good | Very good | 85 | • | • | • | • |
| Recommended | 11 | **Whirlpool** Duet WFW96HEA[W] | 1,300 | 87 | Excellent | Excellent | Excellent | Excellent | Excellent | Very good | Very good | 50 | • | • | • | • |
| Recommended | 12 | **Samsung** WF435ATGJ[WR] WF433BTGJ[ ] | 1,300 | 87 | Excellent | Excellent | Excellent | Excellent | Good | Good | Very good | 105 | • | • | • | • |
| Recommended | 13 | **Whirlpool** Duet WFW94HEX[W] Duet WFW95HEX[ ], Duet WFW97HEX[ ] | 1,100 | 87 | Excellent | Excellent | Excellent | Excellent | Very good | Very good | Very good | 75 | • | • | • | • |
| Recommended | 14 | **Kenmore** Elite 4147[2] | 1,100 | 87 | Excellent | Excellent | Excellent | Excellent | Excellent | Very good | Very good | 85 | • | • | • | • |
| Recommended | 15 | **Kenmore** 4137[2] | 1,050 | 87 | Excellent | Excellent | Excellent | Excellent | Very good | Good | Very good | 85 | • | • | • | • |
| CR Best Buy | 16 | **LG** WM3070H[W]A | 900 | 87 | Excellent | Excellent | Excellent | Excellent | Very good | Very good | Very good | 85 | • | • | • | • |
| Recommended | 17 | **Samsung** WF511AB[W] | 1,300 | 86 | Excellent | Excellent | Excellent | Excellent | Very good | Good | Excellent | 80 | • | • | • | • |
| Recommended | 18 | **Kenmore** Elite 4157[2] | 1,200 | 86 | Excellent | Excellent | Excellent | Excellent | Very good | Excellent | Very good | 90 | • | • | • | • |
| Recommended | 19 | **Samsung** WF405ATPA[WR] | 1,100 | 86 | Excellent | Excellent | Excellent | Excellent | Very good | Good | Good | 100 | • | • | • | • |

**Ratings Key** Excellent · Very good · Good · Fair · Poor

**CR Best Buy** These models offer the best combination of performance and price. All are recommended.

**Recommended** These are high-performing models that stand out.

| Recommended | Rank | Brand & model<br>Similar models, in small type, are comparable to tested model. | Price | Overall score (0–100; P \| F \| G \| VG \| E) | Test results: Washing performance | Energy efficiency | Water efficiency | Capacity | Gentleness | Noise | Vibration | Cycle time (min.) | Features: Energy star | Stainless-steel tub | Auto temp. control | Auto bleach dispenser |
|---|---|---|---|---|---|---|---|---|---|---|---|---|---|---|---|---|
| **B** | | **TOP LOADER** | | | | | | | | | | | | | | |
| CR Best Buy | 1 | **LG** WT1101CW | $ 700 | 82 | Excellent | Excellent | Excellent | Excellent | Very good | Very good | Excellent | 75 | • | • | • | |
| CR Best Buy | 2 | **Samsung** WA422PRHD[WR] | 800 | 82 | Excellent | Very good | Excellent | Excellent | Good | Very good | Excellent | 75 | • | • | • | |
| Recommended | 3 | **LG** WT5070C[W] | 1,000 | 81 | Very good | Excellent | Excellent | Excellent | Very good | Very good | Excellent | 65 | • | • | • | • |
| Recommended | 4 | **Samsung** WA484DSHA[WR] | 1,000 | 81 | Very good | Excellent | Excellent | Excellent | Good | Very good | Excellent | 75 | • | • | • | • |
| CR Best Buy | 5 | **GE** GTWN7450DWW | 800 | 80 | Very good | Very good | Excellent | Excellent | Very good | Very good | Excellent | 60 | • | • | • | • |
| Recommended | 6 | **LG** Smart ThinQ WT6001HV | 1,600 | 79 | Very good | Excellent | Excellent | Excellent | Very good | Very good | Excellent | 80 | • | • | • | |
| Recommended | 7 | **Samsung** WA50F9A6DSW<br>WA50F9A7DSW | 1,000 | 79 | Very good | Excellent | Excellent | Excellent | Good | Good | Excellent | 75 | • | • | • | |
| Recommended | 8 | **Samsung** WA50F9A8DSP | 1,200 | 79 | Very good | Excellent | Excellent | Excellent | Good | Good | Excellent | 75 | • | • | • | |
| Recommended | 9 | **Maytag** Bravos XL MVWB750Y[W] | 850 | 79 | Very good | Excellent | Excellent | Excellent | Very good | Good | Excellent | 65 | • | • | • | • |
| CR Best Buy | 10 | **Samsung** WA400PJHD[WR] | 700 | 78 | Excellent | Very good | Excellent | Excellent | Good | Good | Excellent | 75 | • | • | • | |
| Recommended | 11 | **LG** WT5170H[W] | 1,100 | 78 | Very good | Excellent | Excellent | Excellent | Very good | Good | Excellent | 70 | • | • | • | • |
| Recommended | 12 | **Samsung** WA456DRHD[WR] | 850 | 78 | Very good | Very good | Excellent | Excellent | Good | Very good | Excellent | 75 | • | • | • | • |
| Recommended | 13 | **GE** Adora GHWN8350DWS (Home Depot)<br>GTWN8250DWS, GTWS8450DWS | 1,000 | 77 | Very good | Very good | Excellent | Excellent | Very good | Good | Excellent | 60 | • | • | • | • |
| Recommended | 14 | **LG** WT4870C[W] | 800 | 77 | Very good | Very good | Excellent | Excellent | Very good | Very good | Excellent | 75 | • | • | • | |
| Recommended | 15 | **Maytag** Bravos XL MVWB950Y[W] | 1,000 | 76 | Very good | Excellent | Excellent | Excellent | Very good | Good | Excellent | 70 | • | • | • | • |
| Recommended | 16 | **Whirlpool** Vantage WTW7990X[G] | 1,700 | 75 | Very good | Very good | Excellent | Excellent | Good | Very good | Excellent | 80 | • | • | • | • |

**Ratings Key** Excellent Very good Good Fair Poor

**CR Best Buy** These models offer the best combination of performance and price. All are recommended.

**Recommended** These are high-performing models that stand out.

## Guide to the Ratings

**Overall score** is based mainly on washing ability, capacity, efficiency, and noise. The displayed score is out of a total of 100 points. **Washing performance** reflects the degree of color change to swatches of fabric using the most aggressive normal cycle. **Energy efficiency** is based on the energy needed to heat the water using a warm wash and cold rinse. **Water efficiency** is based on total water used for multiple loads. For top-loaders, **capacity** is based on how well the washer agitates increasingly large loads. For front-loaders, the score is based on our judgment of the maximum-sized load that the washer holds. Models that earned lower scores for **gentleness** are more likely to treat your clothes roughly, causing wear and tear. **Noise** reflects panelists' judgments during the fill, agitate, and spin cycles. **Vibration** reflects usage on a suspended wooden floor. **Cycle time (min.)** is rounded to the nearest 5 minutes. **Price** is approximate retail.

## Most & Least Reliable

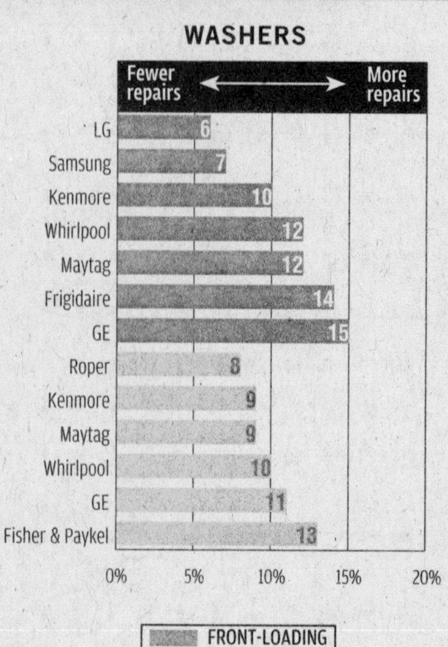


Fisher & Paykel was among the most repair-prone brands of top-loader washers. For front-loaders, LG and Samsung were the most reliable; GE and Frigidaire were among the most repair-prone brands. That's what we found when we asked more than 92,000 readers who bought a clothes washer between 2008 and 2012 about their experiences. The graph shows the percentage of models for each brand that were repaired or had a serious problem. Differences of less than 3 points aren't meaningful, and we've adjusted data to eliminate differences linked solely to a washer's usage and age. Models within a brand may vary, and changes in design or manufacture may affect future reliability. Still, choosing a brand with a good repair history can improve your odds of getting a reliable model.

Source: Annual Product Reliability Survey, Consumer Reports National Research Center.

# Autos

# RATING THE 2013-2014 MODELS

Included here are Ratings on nearly 300 vehicles that CR has recently tested. Within each category, they are ranked by their overall road-test score.

To earn our Recommendation (✓) vehicles must perform well in our road tests; have average or better reliability; and perform adequately if included in safety tests conducted by the Insurance Institute for Highway Safety (IIHS) and the National Highway Traffic Safety Administration (NHTSA).

Because of a NHTSA mandate, electronic stability control (ESC), a proven lifesaving feature, has been included as standard equipment on all light vehicles since the 2012 model year.

Scan this or see how, page 11

**Survey results** include predicted reliability, our forecast of how well a new car is likely to hold up, based on data from our 2012 Annual Auto Survey. Owner satisfaction also comes from our annual survey; it is based on a question where we ask subscribers if they would definitely buy or lease their vehicle again.

**Owner cost** is a Rating of the five-year projected cost to own a vehicle, including depreciation, fuel, interest, insurance, maintenance/repair, and sales tax.

**Fuel economy** is the overall mileage a vehicle achieved in our real-world tests, based on results from several tests, and reflects a realistic mix of city and highway driving.

An asterisk (*) means the powertrain has changed since the last test.

For more Buying Advice, go to *www.ConsumerReports.org/cars*

| Rec. | Make & model | Price as tested | Overall road-test score (0–100; P \| F \| G \| VG \| E) | Survey results: Predicted reliability | Survey results: Owner satisfaction | Owner cost | Fuel economy: Overall MPG |
|---|---|---|---|---|---|---|---|
| | **ELECTRIC CARS: LIMITED-RANGE** | | | | | | |
| | **Ford Focus** Electric | $40,990 | 69 | NA | NA | NA | 107 [1] |
| ✓ | **Nissan Leaf** SL | 35,430 | 69 | ⊜ | ⊜ | NA | 106 [1] |
| | **Mitsubishi i-MiEV** SE | 33,630 | 31 | NA | NA | NA | 111 [1] |
| | **SUBCOMPACT: SEDANS** | | | | | | |
| ✓ | **Kia Rio** EX | $17,275 | 67 | ⊖ | ○ | ⊜ | 30 |
| ✓ | **Hyundai Accent** GLS | 16,050 | 65 | ○ | ○ | ⊜ | 31 |

[1] Miles-per-gallon equivalent (MPGe).

**Ratings Key** Better ⟷ Worse: ⊜ ⊖ ○ ◒ ●  ✓ Recommended

| Rec. | Make & model | Price as tested | Overall road-test score (0–100; P \| F \| G \| VG \| E) | Survey results: Predicted reliability | Survey results: Owner satisfaction | Owner cost | Fuel economy: Overall MPG |
|---|---|---|---|---|---|---|---|
| | **SUBCOMPACT: SEDANS** continued | | | | | | |
| ✔ | **Chevrolet Sonic** LT (1.8) | $17,290 | 65 | ○ | ○ | ⊜ | 28 |
| | **Ford Fiesta** SE | 16,595 | 61 | ◒ | ○ | ⊜ | 33 |
| | **Nissan Versa** SV | 15,490 | 53 | ● | ● | ⊜ | 32 |
| | **SUBCOMPACT: HATCHBACKS** | | | | | | |
| ✔ | **Honda Fit** Sport (MT) | $17,850 | 76 | ⊜ | ⊖ | ⊜ | 33 |
| ✔ | **Hyundai Accent** SE (MT) | 16,695 | 72 | ○ | ○ | ⊜ | 32 |
| ✔ | **Honda Fit** (base) | 16,915 | 68 | ⊜ | ⊖ | ⊜ | 30 |
| | **Ford Fiesta** SES (MT) | 17,795 | 65 | ◒ | ○ | ⊜ | 32 |
| ✔ | **Mazda2** Sport (MT) | 14,770 | 64 | ⊖ | ◒ | ⊜ | 33 |
| ✔ | **Kia Rio** EX | 17,475 | 63 | ⊖ | ○ | ⊜ | 29 |
| ✔ | **Scion XD** (MT) | 15,820 | 62 | ⊜ | ○ | ⊜ | 34 |
| ✔ | **Mazda2** Touring | 17,075 | 60 | ⊖ | ◒ | ⊜ | 30 |
| ✔ | **Scion xD** | 16,620 | 60 | ⊜ | ○ | ⊜ | 29 |
| | **Chevrolet Sonic** LTZ (1.4T, MT) | 19,870 | 59 | ○ | ○ | ⊜ | 30 |
| | **Honda Insight** EX | 21,790 | 54 | ⊖ | ◒ | ⊜ | 38 |
| | **Toyota Prius** C Two | 20,850 | 53 | ⊜ | ⊜ | ⊜ | 43 |
| | **Toyota Yaris** LE | 17,290 | 41 | NA | NA | ⊜ | 32 |
| | **Chevrolet Spark** 1LT | 15,420 | 34 | new | new | ⊜ | 32 |
| | **Scion iQ** | 16,205 | 29 | NA | NA | ⊜ | 34 |
| | **Smart ForTwo** Passion | 15,355 | 28 | NA | NA | ⊜ | 39 |
| | **COMPACT: SEDANS** | | | | | | |
| ✔ | **Subaru Impreza** Premium | $21,345 | 82 | ⊜ | ⊖ | ⊖ | 27 |
| | **Kia Forte** LX | 19,570 | 81 | new | new | ⊜ | 28 |
| ✔ | **Hyundai Elantra** GLS | 19,410 | 80 | ⊖ | ⊖ | ⊜ | 29 |
| | **Volkswagen Jetta** Hybrid SE | 28,055 | 79 | new | new | ⊜ | 37 |
| | **Ford Focus** SE SFE | 21,650 | 77 | ● | ○ | ⊜ | 31 |
| ✔ | **Chevrolet Cruze** Eco | 21,775 | 72 | ○ | ⊖ | ⊖ | 27 |
| | **Ford Focus** SE | 20,280 | 71 | ● | ○ | ⊜ | 28 |
| ✔ | **Honda Civic** EX | 21,605 | 71 | ⊖ | ○ | ⊜ | 29 |
| ✔ | **Chevrolet Cruze** 1LT (1.4T) | 20,530 | 70 | ○ | ⊖ | ⊖ | 26 |
| | **Chevrolet Cruze** Turbo Diesel | 27,300 | 70 | new | new | ⊖ | 33 |

| Rec. | Make & model | Price as tested | Overall road-test score (0–100; P \| F \| G \| VG \| E) | Survey results: Predicted reliability | Survey results: Owner satisfaction | Owner cost | Fuel economy: Overall MPG |
|---|---|---|---|---|---|---|---|
| | **COMPACT: SEDANS** continued | | | | | | |
| ✓ | **Chevrolet Cruze** LS (1.8) | $18,375 | 69 | G | G | VG | 26 |
| ✓ | **Volkswagen Jetta** TDI | 25,100 | 68 | G | VG | E | 34 |
| ✓ | **Honda Civic** Hybrid | 25,140 | 66 | VG | F | E | 40 |
| | **Dodge Dart** SXT (2.0L) | 20,680 | 64 | new | new | VG | 27 |
| | **Nissan Sentra** SV | 20,570 | 64 | new | new | E | 29 |
| | **Mitsubishi Lancer** ES | 17,515 | 62 | NA | NA | VG | 25 |
| | **Dodge Dart** Rallye (1.4T) | 24,490 | 61 | new | new | VG | 29 |
| | **COMPACT: HATCHBACKS/WAGONS** | | | | | | |
| ✓ | **Volkswagen Golf** TDI (MT) | $25,730 | 88 | G | E | E | 38 |
| ✓ | **Mazda5** Grand Touring | 24,820 | 88 | E | VG | VG | 23 |
| ✓ | **Volkswagen Golf** (2.5) | 20,565 | 85 | VG | G | E | 24 |
| | **Ford C-MAX** Hybrid SE | 26,685 | 83 | new | new | E | 37 |
| ✓ | **Volkswagen Jetta SportWagen** TDI (MT) | 28,085 | 81 | G | E | E | 36 |
| ✓ | **Toyota Prius** V Three | 28,217 | 80 | VG | E | E | 41 |
| ✓ | **Toyota Prius** Four | 29,230 | 79 | E | E | E | 44 |
| ✓ | **Subaru Impreza** Sport Premium | 22,345 | 79 | E | VG | VG | 26 |
| ✓ | **Volkswagen Jetta SportWagen** SE (2.5) | 26,755 | 78 | VG | G | VG | 23 |
| ✓ | **Mazda3** s Grand Touring | 22,795 | 77 | E | G | E | 25 |
| | **Ford Focus** SE | 22,185 | 74 | P | G | VG | 28 |
| ✓ | **Toyota Prius** Plug-in Advanced | 40,510 | 71 | E | E | E | 67[1] /43[2] |
| ✓ | **Scion xB** | 18,360 | 68 | E | G | E | 23 |
| ✓ | **Hyundai Elantra** GT | 20,445 | 68 | VG | VG | VG | 27 |
| ✓ | **Chevrolet Volt** | 43,700 | 68 | VG | E | NA | 99[1] /32[2] |
| | **Nissan Cube** 1.8S | 16,790 | 64 | G | G | E | 28 |
| | **Mini Cooper** Clubman | 24,700 | 64 | E | G | E | 29 |
| | **SEDANS: MIDSIZED** | | | | | | |
| ✓ | **Toyota Camry** Hybrid XLE | $29,052 | 93 | E | E | E | 38 |
| ✓ | **Toyota Camry** XLE (V6) | 32,603 | 92 | VG | VG | VG | 26 |

[1] Miles-per-gallon equivalent (MPGe). [2] Miles per gallon while running on gas engine.

## SEDANS: MIDSIZED continued

| Rec. | Make & model | Price as tested | Overall road-test score (0–100; P \| F \| G \| VG \| E) | Survey results: Predicted reliability | Survey results: Owner satisfaction | Owner cost | Fuel economy: Overall MPG |
|---|---|---|---|---|---|---|---|
| ✓ | **Honda Accord** LX (4-cyl.) | $23,270 | 90 | ⊖ | ⊖ | ⊜ | 30 |
| ✓ | **Honda Accord** EX-L (V6) | 30,860 | 90 | ⊖ | ⊖ | ⊖ | 26 |
| | **Hyundai Sonata** Limited (2.0T) | 28,090 | 89 | ● | ⊖ | ⊖ | 25 |
| ✓ | **Hyundai Sonata** GLS (2.4) | 21,800 | 89 | ○ | ⊖ | ⊜ | 27 |
| | **Chevrolet Malibu** 2LTZ (2.0T) | 33,865 | 89 | new | new | ○ | 24 |
| ✓ | **Subaru Legacy** 3.6R Limited | 30,094 | 88 | ○ | ○ | ○ | 22 |
| ✓ | **Toyota Camry** LE (4-cyl.) | 23,830 | 88 | ⊜ | ⊖ | ⊜ | 27 |
| | **Ford Fusion** SE Hybrid | 28,290 | 87 | new | new | ⊜ | 39 |
| ✓ | **Mazda6** Sport | 23,590 | 85 | ⊖ | new | ⊜ | 32 |
| | **Chevrolet Malibu** 1LT (2.5L) | 26,030 | 84 | new | new | ⊖ | 26 |
| ✓ | **Nissan Altima** 3.5 SL | 31,610 | 84 | ⊖ | new | ○ | 24 |
| ✓ | **Kia Optima** SX (2.0T) | 29,050 | 84 | ⊖ | ⊖ | ○ | 24 |
| | **Ford Fusion** SE (1.6T) | 25,585 | 82 | new | new | ⊖ | 25 |
| | **Volkswagen Passat** SEL Premium (V6) | 33,720 | 82 | NA | NA | ◒ | 23 |
| ✓ | **Kia Optima** LX (2.4) | 21,885 | 81 | ○ | ⊖ | ⊖ | 25 |
| ✓ | **Nissan Altima** 2.5 S | 23,410 | 81 | ⊖ | new | ⊜ | 31 |
| ✓ | **Subaru Legacy** 2.5i Premium | 24,189 | 81 | ⊖ | ⊖ | ⊖ | 26 |
| ✓ | **Volkswagen Passat** TDI SE | 28,665 | 80 | ⊖ | ⊜ | ⊜ | 37 |
| | **Ford Fusion** Titanium (2.0T) | 33,180 | 78 | new | new | ◒ | 22 |
| | **Chevrolet Malibu** Eco | 28,285 | 76 | new | new | ⊖ | 29 |
| ✓ | **Volkswagen Passat** SE (2.5) | 25,595 | 76 | ⊖ | ⊖ | ⊖ | 25 |
| | **Hyundai Sonata** Hybrid | 26,695 | 69 | ◒ | ○ | ⊜ | 33 |
| | **Chrysler 200** Limited (V6) | 27,825 | 52 | ◒ | ⊖ | ○ | 21 |
| | **Dodge Avenger** SXT (4-cyl.) | 22,290 | 43 | NA | NA | ⊖ | 21 |

## SEDANS: LARGE

| Rec. | Make & model | Price as tested | Overall road-test score | Predicted reliability | Owner satisfaction | Owner cost | Overall MPG |
|---|---|---|---|---|---|---|---|
| | **Chevrolet Impala** 2LTZ (3.6) | $39,110 | 95 | new | new | ○ | 22 |
| ✓ | **Hyundai Genesis** 3.8 | 39,850 | 92 | ○ | ⊖ | ◒ | 22 |
| ✓ | **Toyota Avalon** Hybrid Limited | 42,501 | 86 | ⊖ | ⊖ | ○ | 36 |
| | **Kia Cadenza** | 39,030 | 86 | new | new | ◒ | 22 |
| ✓ | **Toyota Avalon** Limited (V6) | 40,670 | 85 | ⊖ | ⊖ | ○ | 24 |
| ✓ | **Chrysler 300** Limited (V6) | 38,335 | 83 | ○ | ⊜ | ◒ | 22 |

| Rec. | Make & model | Price as tested | Overall road-test score (0–100; P \| F \| G \| VG \| E) | Survey results: Predicted reliability | Survey results: Owner satisfaction | Owner cost | Fuel economy: Overall MPG |
|---|---|---|---|---|---|---|---|
| | **SEDANS: LARGE** continued | | | | | | |
| ✓ | **Nissan Maxima** 3.5 SV | $33,700 | 83 | ⊖ | ○ | ◒ | 22 |
| | **Chrysler 300** C | 44,730 | 82 | ● | ⊜ | ◒ | 18 |
| | **Lincoln MKZ** Hybrid | 41,915 | 82 | new | new | ◒ | 34 |
| | **Hyundai Azera** | 37,185 | 81 | NA | NA | ◒ | 23 |
| | **Lincoln MKZ** 2.0 EcoBoost | 41,365 | 81 | new | new | ● | 23 |
| | **Buick LaCrosse** (Leather, eAssist) | 34,935 | 78 | ◒ | ○ | ○ | 26 |
| | **Dodge Charger** SXT Plus (V6) | 34,510 | 75 | ● | ⊜ | ◒ | 22 |
| | **Buick LaCrosse** Touring (V6) | 37,555 | 74 | ● | ○ | ◒ | 20 |
| | **Ford Taurus** Limited (3.5, V6) | 37,885 | 64 | ○ | ○ | ◒ | 21 |
| | **CARS: LUXURY COMPACT** | | | | | | |
| ✓ | **Infiniti G37** Journey | $37,225 | 95 | ⊜ | ⊖ | ◒ | 21 |
| ✓ | **BMW 328i** | 43,195 | 86 | ⊜ | ⊖ | ◒ | 28 |
| ✓ | **Mercedes-Benz C250** | 40,705 | 85 | ⊖ | ⊖ | ◒ | 24 |
| ✓ | **Acura TSX** (4-cyl.) | 29,675 | 84 | ⊖ | ⊖ | ⊖ | 25 |
| ✓ | **Volkswagen CC** Sport (2.0T) | 32,800 | 81 | ○ | ○ | ○ | 26 |
| ✓ | **Buick Regal** CXL (turbo)* | 32,135 | 79 | ○ | ○ | ○ | 23 |
| ✓ | **Acura ILX** (2.0L) | 30,095 | 77 | ⊖ | new | ⊖ | 28 |
| ✓ | **Volvo S60** T5 | 35,100 | 77 | ○ | ⊖ | ○ | 23 |
| ✓ | **Audi A4** Premium Quattro | 35,895 | 76 | ⊖ | ⊖ | ○ | 25 |
| | **Cadillac ATS** Luxury (turbo) | 43,295 | 76 | new | new | ◒ | 23 |
| | **Buick Verano** Leather (2.4) | 27,750 | 73 | ● | ⊖ | ⊖ | 24 |
| ✓ | **Lexus CT** 200h Premium | 32,012 | 71 | ⊜ | ⊖ | ⊖ | 40 |
| | **SEDANS: LUXURY MIDSIZED** | | | | | | |
| ✓ | **Audi A6** 3.0 Premium Plus Quattro | $56,295 | 93 | ○ | ⊜ | ● | 22 |
| ✓ | **Infiniti Q70** (3.7) | 53,825 | 93 | ○ | ⊖ | ● | 21 |
| ✓ | **Hyundai Genesis** 4.6* | 43,800 | 87 | ○ | ⊜ | ◒ | 20 |
| ✓ | **Mercedes-Benz E350** | 57,965 | 86 | ⊖ | ⊖ | ● | 21 |
| ✓ | **Lexus GS** 350 | 58,858 | 84 | ⊖ | ⊜ | ● | 21 |
| | **Infiniti Q70** Hybrid | 58,655 | 83 | NA | NA | ● | 25 |
| ✓ | **Acura TL** (base) | 36,465 | 82 | ⊖ | ⊖ | ○ | 24 |
| ✓ | **Lexus ES** 300h | 44,017 | 82 | ⊖ | ⊖ | ○ | 36 |

| Rec. | Make & model | Price as tested | Overall road-test score (0–100; P \| F \| G \| VG \| E) | Survey results: Predicted reliability | Survey results: Owner satisfaction | Owner cost | Fuel economy: Overall MPG |
|---|---|---|---|---|---|---|---|
| | **SEDANS: LUXURY MIDSIZED** continued | | | | | | |
| ✔ | **BMW 535i** | $58,375 | 81 | ○ | ⊖ | ● | 23 |
| ✔ | **Lexus ES** 350 | 43,702 | 80 | ⊖ | ⊖ | ◒ | 25 |
| | **Jaguar XF** 3.0 (AWD) | 59,645 | 79 | new | ○ | ● | 21 |
| | **Cadillac XTS** Premium | 57,200 | 79 | new | new | ● | 22 |
| | **Acura RLX** Tech | 55,345 | 74 | ⊖ | new | ● | 23 |
| | **Volvo S80** 3.2 | 45,305 | 70 | ⊖ | ○ | ◒ | 20 |
| | **Lincoln MKS** (base, 3.7) | 50,070 | 60 | ○ | ○ | ● | 20 |
| | **SEDANS: LUXURY LARGE** | | | | | | |
| | **Tesla Model** S (base, 85 kWh) | $89,650 | 99 | new | new | NA | 84 [1] |
| ✔ | **Lexus LS** 460L | 82,504 | 92 | ⊖ | ⊜ | ● | 21 |
| | **Audi A8** L* | 91,275 | 91 | NA | NA | ● | 21 |
| | **Porsche Panamera** S* | 105,110 | 84 | NA | NA | ● | 20 |
| | **Jaguar XJL** Portfolio* | 81,575 | 83 | ● | ⊖ | ● | 19 |
| ✔ | **Hyundai Equus** Signature* | 58,900 | 82 | ○ | ⊜ | ● | 19 |
| | **BMW 750Li*** | 97,525 | 74 | ● | ⊖ | ● | 18 |
| | **SPORTS CARS: HIGH-PERFORMANCE** Equipped with manual transmission | | | | | | |
| ✔ | **BMW 135i** | $37,650 | 97 | ○ | ⊖ | ◒ | 23 |
| ✔ | **Subaru Impreza** WRX STi | 37,640 | 89 | ○ | ⊖ | ◒ | 21 |
| ✔ | **Nissan 370Z** Coupe Touring | 38,565 | 86 | ⊖ | NA | ◒ | 23 |
| | **Mitsubishi Lancer** Evolution GSR | 38,078 | 83 | NA | NA | ● | 21 |
| | **Ford Mustang** GT Premium (V8) | 36,310 | 83 | ◒ | ⊜ | ○ | 22 |
| ✔ | **Ford Mustang** Premium (V6) | 28,880 | 76 | ○ | ⊖ | ⊖ | 24 |
| ✔ | **Chevrolet Camaro** 2SS (V8) | 35,425 | 71 | ○ | ⊜ | ◒ | 18 |
| | **Hyundai Genesis Coupe** Grand Touring (V6)* | 28,375 | 70 | ◒ | ○ | ⊖ | 23 |
| | **Dodge Challenger** R/T (V8) | 35,015 | 67 | ◒ | ⊜ | ◒ | 19 |
| | **Chevrolet Camaro** 2LT (V6) | 28,195 | 60 | ○ | ⊖ | ⊖ | 21 |
| | **SPORTY CARS** Equipped with manual transmission | | | | | | |
| | **Volkswagen GTI** (4-door) | $27,504 | 85 | ● | ⊜ | ⊖ | 27 |
| ✔ | **Subaru Impreza** WRX | 26,088 | 84 | ○ | ⊖ | ○ | 24 |

[1] Miles-per-gallon equivalent (MPGe).

| Rec. | Make & model | Price as tested | Overall road-test score (0–100; P \| F \| G \| VG \| E) | Survey results: Predicted reliability | Survey results: Owner satisfaction | Owner cost | Fuel economy: Overall MPG |
|---|---|---|---|---|---|---|---|
| | **SPORTY CARS** continued | | | | | | |
| ✓ | **Scion FR-S** | $25,025 | 83 | ◒ | new | ⊖ | 30 |
| | **Subaru BRZ** Premium | 27,117 | 82 | ● | new | ⊖ | 30 |
| ✓ | **Mini Cooper** (base) | 21,700 | 81 | ○ | ⊖ | ⊜ | 33 |
| | **Volkswagen Jetta** GLI Autobahn | 26,835 | 76 | NA | NA | ⊖ | 27 |
| | **Ford Focus** ST | 28,270 | 74 | ● | new | ○ | 25 |
| | **Mini Cooper** S | 26,400 | 74 | ● | ⊜ | ⊜ | 30 |
| | **Mitsubishi Lancer** Ralliart (AT) | 28,344 | 72 | NA | NA | ◒ | 20 |
| ✓ | **Hyundai Veloster** (base) | 20,340 | 71 | ⊖ | ⊖ | ⊜ | 31 |
| | **Fiat 500** Abarth | 26,050 | 71 | NA | ⊖ | ⊖ | 28 |
| ✓ | **Honda Civic** Si | 23,175 | 70 | ○ | ⊖ | ⊖ | 29 |
| | **Scion tC** | 19,165 | 63 | NA | NA | ⊜ | 28 |
| | **Fiat 500** Sport | 18,600 | 61 | ○ | ⊖ | ⊜ | 33 |
| | **Volkswagen Beetle** 2.5L | 20,835 | 60 | ● | NA | ⊜ | 26 |
| | **Honda CR-Z** EX | 21,510 | 57 | ⊜ | ○ | ⊜ | 35 |
| | **ROADSTERS** Equipped with manual transmission | | | | | | |
| | **Porsche Boxster** 2.7 | $59,600 | 89 | new | new | ● | 23 |
| ✓ | **Mazda MX-5** Miata Grand Touring | 31,150 | 89 | ⊖ | ⊜ | ⊖ | 28 |
| | **Mercedes-Benz SLK250** | 48,045 | 81 | NA | NA | ◒ | 26 |
| | **Audi TT** Premium Plus (DSG) | 45,300 | 80 | NA | NA | ◒ | 25 |
| | **BMW Z4** sDrive28i | 55,225 | 76 | NA | NA | ◒ | 28 |
| | **CONVERTIBLES: FOUR-SEAT** | | | | | | |
| ✓ | **Volkswagen Eos** Lux | $35,829 | 78 | ○ | ⊖ | ○ | 25 |
| | **Infiniti Q60** (base) | 48,715 | 77 | ● | ○ | ● | 20 |
| | **Mini Cooper** S (MT) | 32,850 | 77 | ● | ⊜ | ⊖ | 30 |
| | **Ford Mustang** GT Premium (V8) | 43,880 | 75 | ◒ | ⊜ | ◒ | 23 |
| | **Jaguar XK** Convertible* | 85,635 | 74 | NA | NA | ● | 19 |
| ✓ | **Audi A5** Premium Plus (2.0T)* | 49,300 | 74 | ⊖ | ⊖ | ● | 22 |
| ✓ | **Chevrolet Camaro** 2SS (V8) | 43,510 | 65 | ○ | ⊜ | ◒ | 17 |
| | **Fiat 500C** Pop (MT) | 21,000 | 59 | ○ | ⊜ | ⊜ | 34 |

**Ratings Key** Better ⟵⟶ Worse: ⊜ ⊖ ○ ◒ ●

✓ **Recommended**

| Rec. | Make & model | Price as tested | Overall road-test score (0–100; P \| F \| G \| VG \| E) | Survey results: Predicted reliability | Survey results: Owner satisfaction | Owner cost | Fuel economy: Overall MPG |
|---|---|---|---|---|---|---|---|
| | **MINIVANS** | | | | | | |
| ✔ | **Honda Odyssey** EX-L | $38,055 | 86 | ○ | ⊖ | ○ | 21 |
| ✔ | **Nissan Quest** SL | 39,040 | 81 | ⊖ | ⊖ | ◒ | 19 |
| ✔ | **Toyota Sienna** XLE (FWD) | 35,810 | 80 | ⊖ | ⊖ | ○ | 20 |
| ✔ | **Toyota Sienna** XLE (AWD) | 38,201 | 79 | ⊖ | ⊖ | ◒ | 19 |
| ✔ | **Kia Sedona** EX | 33,990 | 77 | ◒ | ◒ | ◒ | 18 |
| | **Chrysler Town & Country** Touring-L | 37,505 | 74 | ◒ | ⊖ | ◒ | 17 |
| | **Dodge Grand Caravan** R/T | 37,295 | 74 | ◒ | ○ | ◒ | 17 |
| | **SUVs: SMALL** | | | | | | |
| ✔ | **Subaru Forester** 2.5i Premium | $26,814 | 88 | ⊖ | ⊖ | ⊖ | 26 |
| | **Ford Escape** Titanium (2.0T) | 36,600 | 79 | new | new | ◒ | 22 |
| ✔ | **Honda CR-V** EX | 26,455 | 77 | ⊜ | ⊖ | ⊖ | 23 |
| ✔ | **Volkswagen Tiguan** SEL | 37,020 | 76 | ○ | ○ | ◒ | 21 |
| ✔ | **Mazda CX-5** Touring (2.5L) | 28,090 | 76 | ⊜ | ⊜ | ⊖ | 25 |
| ✔ | **Toyota RAV4** XLE | 26,802 | 75 | ⊖ | ⊖ | ⊖ | 24 |
| | **Ford Escape** SE (1.6T) | 28,040 | 75 | new | new | ⊖ | 22 |
| ✔ | **Subaru XV Crosstrek** Premium | 24,215 | 75 | ⊖ | new | ⊖ | 26 |
| ✔ | **Mazda CX-5** Sport (2.0L) | 25,300 | 74 | ⊜ | ⊜ | ⊖ | 25 |
| ✔ | **Nissan Rogue** SV | 25,850 | 73 | ⊖ | ◒ | ⊖ | 22 |
| ✔ | **Kia Sportage** SX (2.0T) | 31,440 | 72 | ⊜ | ○ | ○ | 21 |
| ✔ | **Kia Sportage** LX | 24,400 | 70 | ⊜ | ○ | ⊖ | 22 |
| ✔ | **Hyundai Tucson** GLS | 24,920 | 70 | ○ | ◒ | ⊖ | 22 |
| ✔ | **Mitsubishi Outlander Sport** SE | 24,520 | 65 | ⊜ | NA | ⊖ | 23 |
| ✔ | **Nissan Juke** SV | 24,840 | 65 | ○ | ○ | ⊖ | 24 |
| | **Mitsubishi Outlander** SE (4-cyl.) | 27,180 | 57 | ⊖ | new | ○ | 23 |
| | **Jeep Patriot** Latitude* | 24,440 | 52 | ⊖ | ◒ | ⊖ | 21 |
| | **Jeep Compass** Latitude* | 24,985 | 49 | ◒ | ◒ | ⊖ | 22 |
| | **SUVs: MIDSIZED** | | | | | | |
| ✔ | **Toyota Highlander** Hybrid Limited | $47,255 | 89 | ⊖ | ⊖ | ◒ | 27 |
| | **Hyundai Santa Fe** GLS (V6) | 36,290 | 83 | new | new | ◒ | 20 |

| Rec. | Make & model | Price as tested | Overall road-test score (0–100; P \| F \| G \| VG \| E) | Survey results: Predicted reliability | Survey results: Owner satisfaction | Owner cost | Fuel economy: Overall MPG |
|---|---|---|---|---|---|---|---|
| | **SUVs: MIDSIZED** continued | | | | | | |
| ✓ | **Toyota Highlander** Limited (V6) | $38,578 | 81 | ⊜ | ⊖ | ◒ | 18 |
| ✓ | **Nissan Murano** SL | 36,330 | 78 | ⊖ | ⊖ | ◒ | 19 |
| ✓ | **Toyota Venza** (V6) | 34,209 | 77 | ⊖ | ○ | ○ | 20 |
| ✓ | **Jeep Grand Cherokee** Limited (V6) | 41,375 | 77 | ○ | ⊖ | ◒ | 18 |
| | **Kia Sorento** EX (V6) | 37,950 | 76 | new | new | ○ | 20 |
| ✓ | **Mazda CX-9** Grand Touring | 38,615 | 76 | ⊜ | ○ | ◒ | 16 |
| | **Hyundai Santa Fe Sport** (4-cyl.) | 28,370 | 74 | new | new | ⊖ | 23 |
| ✓ | **Honda Pilot** EX-L | 36,980 | 73 | ⊖ | ⊖ | ◒ | 18 |
| ✓ | **Subaru Outback** 2.5i Limited | 34,698 | 73 | ⊜ | ⊜ | ⊖ | 24 |
| | **Subaru Tribeca** Limited | 34,270 | 70 | NA | NA | ◒ | 16 |
| | **Nissan Pathfinder** SL | 40,470 | 69 | new | new | ◒ | 18 |
| | **Ford Edge** SEL (FWD, 2.0 EcoBoost) | 36,910 | 69 | ● | ○ | ○ | 21 |
| ✓ | **Chevrolet Equinox** LTZ (V6) | 36,925 | 66 | ⊖ | ○ | ○ | 18 |
| ✓ | **GMC Terrain** SLT2 (V6) | 36,675 | 66 | ⊖ | ○ | ○ | 18 |
| ✓ | **Chevrolet Equinox** 1LT (4-cyl.) | 26,350 | 66 | ○ | ○ | ⊖ | 21 |
| ✓ | **GMC Terrain** SLE1 (4-cyl.) | 26,745 | 66 | ○ | ○ | ⊖ | 21 |
| | **Ford Explorer** XLT (V6) | 39,275 | 65 | ● | ○ | ◒ | 18 |
| | **Ford Edge** SEL (3.5) | 37,625 | 63 | ● | ○ | ◒ | 18 |
| | **Honda Crosstour** EX-L (V6) | 34,730 | 62 | ○ | ○ | ○ | 21 |
| | **Dodge Journey** Crew (V6) | 36,975 | 61 | ● | ○ | ◒ | 16 |
| | **Nissan Xterra** S | 28,000 | 60 | ○ | ○ | ○ | 17 |
| | **Toyota 4Runner** SR5 (V6) | 37,425 | 55 | ⊜ | ○ | ◒ | 18 |
| | **Toyota FJ Cruiser** | 30,881 | 36 | ⊜ | ⊖ | ○ | 17 |
| | **Jeep Wrangler** Unlimited Sahara | 36,340 | 20 | ◒ | ⊖ | ◒ | 17 |
| | **SUVs: LARGE** | | | | | | |
| ✓ | **Chevrolet Traverse** LT | $39,920 | 80 | ○ | ○ | ◒ | 16 |
| ✓ | **GMC Acadia** SLT2 | 39,630 | 80 | ○ | ○ | ◒ | 16 |
| ✓ | **Ford Flex** SEL | 38,460 | 69 | ○ | ⊖ | ◒ | 18 |
| ✓ | **Dodge Durango** Crew (V8)* | 47,375 | 66 | ○ | ⊜ | ● | 14 |
| ✓ | **Toyota Sequoia** Limited (5.7) | 54,005 | 66 | ⊜ | ⊖ | ● | 15 |
| ✓ | **Chevrolet Suburban** LT3 (5.3) | 51,940 | 66 | ○ | ⊖ | ● | 14 |

| Rec. | Make & model | Price as tested | Overall road-test score (0–100; P \| F \| G \| VG \| E) | Survey results: Predicted reliability | Survey results: Owner satisfaction | Owner cost | Fuel economy: Overall MPG |
|---|---|---|---|---|---|---|---|
| | **SUVs: LARGE** continued | | | | | | |
| ✔ | **GMC Yukon** XL SLT3 (5.3) | $52,285 | 66 | ○ | ⊖ | ● | 14 |
| ✔ | **Dodge Durango** Crew (V6)* | 43,785 | 65 | ○ | ⊜ | ● | 17 |
| ✔ | **Ford Expedition** EL Eddie Bauer | 48,730 | 65 | ○ | ⊖ | ● | 13 |
| | **Nissan Armada** Platinum | 55,400 | 61 | ● | ◒ | ● | 13 |
| | **Chevrolet Tahoe** LTZ (5.3) | 57,435 | 58 | ○ | ⊖ | ● | 14 |
| | **GMC Yukon** SLT2 (5.3) | 56,625 | 58 | ○ | ⊖ | ● | 14 |
| | **Chevrolet Tahoe** Hybrid | 55,585 | 57 | NA | NA | ● | 19 |
| | **GMC Yukon** Hybrid | 56,045 | 57 | NA | NA | ● | 19 |
| | **SUVs: LUXURY COMPACT** | | | | | | |
| | **BMW X3** xDrive28i (2.0T) | $44,595 | 80 | new | ⊖ | ◒ | 23 |
| ✔ | **Audi Allroad** 2.0T Premium | 43,570 | 79 | ⊖ | ⊖ | ◒ | 22 |
| ✔ | **Acura RDX** | 36,605 | 79 | ○ | new | ◒ | 22 |
| ✔ | **Infiniti QX50** Journey* | 39,425 | 78 | ⊖ | ○ | ◒ | 18 |
| ✔ | **Mercedes-Benz GLK350** | 44,995 | 77 | ○ | ○ | ● | 21 |
| ✔ | **Audi Q5** Premium Plus (2.0T) | 41,075 | 77 | ○ | ⊖ | ◒ | 21 |
| | **BMW X1** xDrive28i (2.0T) | 38,795 | 74 | new | new | ◒ | 23 |
| ✔ | **Volvo XC60** T6 | 42,245 | 70 | ○ | ⊖ | ◒ | 17 |
| | **Mini Cooper Countryman** S | 32,500 | 66 | ● | ⊖ | ⊖ | 26 |
| | **Buick Encore** Leather | 30,555 | 64 | new | new | ◒ | 23 |
| | **Cadillac SRX** Luxury | 43,085 | 62 | ◒ | ◒ | ● | 18 |
| | **Land Rover Range Rover Evoque** Pure | 45,745 | 58 | NA | NA | ● | 21 |
| | **SUVs: LUXURY MIDSIZED** | | | | | | |
| ✔ | **Lexus RX** 450h | $53,576 | 88 | ⊜ | ⊖ | ● | 26 |
| | **Volkswagen Touareg** TDI Sport | 49,505 | 82 | ● | ⊖ | ● | 24 |
| ✔ | **Lexus RX** 350 | 47,381 | 79 | ⊜ | ⊖ | ● | 21 |
| ✔ | **Acura MDX** Tech | 49,460 | 79 | ⊖ | ⊖ | ● | 20 |
| ✔ | **Infiniti QX60** (3.5) | 51,920 | 78 | ⊖ | new | ● | 19 |
| ✔ | **Volvo XC70** | 42,560 | 77 | ⊖ | ⊖ | ◒ | 18 |
| | **Porsche Cayenne** (base, V6) | 63,805 | 76 | ◒ | ⊜ | ● | 19 |
| | **Mercedes-Benz ML350** | 56,960 | 76 | ◒ | ⊖ | ● | 18 |
| | **Land Rover LR4** | 54,010 | 73 | NA | NA | ● | 15 |

| Rec. | Make & model | Price as tested | Overall road-test score (0–100; P \| F \| G \| VG \| E) | Survey results: Predicted reliability | Survey results: Owner satisfaction | Owner cost | Fuel economy: Overall MPG |
|---|---|---|---|---|---|---|---|
| | **SUVs: LUXURY MIDSIZED** continued | | | | | | |
| ✓ | **Infiniti QX70** (V6)* | $51,635 | 71 | ○ | ○ | ● | 18 |
| ✓ | **Lexus GX** 460 | 58,428 | 69 | ○ | ⊖ | ● | 17 |
| | **Lincoln MKX** (3.7) | 50,235 | 64 | ● | ○ | ● | 18 |
| | **Volvo XC90** 3.2 | 49,850 | 58 | ◒ | ◒ | ● | 17 |
| | **SUVs: LUXURY LARGE** | | | | | | |
| | **Mercedes-Benz GL350** BlueTec | $73,020 | 81 | new | new | ● | 20 |
| ✓ | **Buick Enclave** CXL | 43,260 | 77 | ○ | ○ | ◒ | 15 |
| | **Toyota Land Cruiser** | 67,707 | 69 | NA | NA | ● | 14 |
| ✓ | **Infiniti QX80** | 63,395 | 67 | ○ | ⊖ | ● | 15 |
| ✓ | **Lincoln Navigator** Ultimate | 59,015 | 65 | ○ | ⊖ | ● | 13 |
| | **Cadillac Escalade** (base) | 64,905 | 61 | ○ | NA | ● | 13 |
| | **PICKUPS: COMPACT** | | | | | | |
| ✓ | **Honda Ridgeline** RTS | $30,825 | 79 | ⊖ | ⊖ | ◒ | 15 |
| ✓ | **Nissan Frontier** SV (V6) | 30,110 | 67 | ⊖ | ○ | ○ | 15 |
| | **Toyota Tacoma** (V6) | 33,119 | 50 | ○ | ⊖ | ○ | 17 |
| | **PICKUPS: FULL-SIZED** | | | | | | |
| | **Chevrolet Silverado** 1500 LT (5.3L V8) | $42,070 | 81 | new | new | ◒ | 16 |
| | **GMC Sierra** 1500 SLE (5.3L V8) | 43,200 | 81 | new | new | ◒ | 16 |
| ✓ | **Ram 1500** Big Horn (5.7L V8) | 42,810 | 78 | ○ | ⊖ | ◒ | 15 |
| | **Ford F-150** XLT (3.5L EcoBoost V6) | 40,410 | 70 | ◒ | ⊜ | ◒ | 15 |
| ✓ | **Ford F-150** XLT (5.0L V8) | 39,355 | 70 | ○ | ⊖ | ◒ | 15 |
| ✓ | **Toyota Tundra** SR5 (5.7L V8) | 34,738 | 69 | ⊖ | ⊖ | ◒ | 15 |
| | **Nissan Titan** SV (5.6L V8) | 36,905 | 66 | ● | ○ | ◒ | 14 |
| | **PICKUPS: HEAVY DUTY DIESEL** | | | | | | |
| | **Chevrolet Silverado** 2500 LTZ (6.6L, V8) | $55,755 | 69 | ◒ | ⊜ | ● | 14 |
| | **GMC Sierra** 2500 (6.6L, V8) | 55,755 | 69 | ◒ | ⊜ | ● | 14 |
| | **Ford F-250** Lariat (6.7L, V8) | 54,765 | 65 | ● | ⊜ | ● | 16 |

# REVIEWS OF THE 2013-14 MODELS

This rundown of all the major 2013-14 models can start you on your search for a new car, minivan, SUV, or pick-up. You'll find a summary of each model, often based on recent road tests that are applicable to this year's models.

Most models include Consumer Reports' predicted reliability rating, an indication of how problematic we expect a model to be. It is based on our 2012 Annual Auto Survey, where we asked owners about any serious problems they've had with their vehicles in the previous 12 months. These data allow us to predict how well new cars are likely to hold up.

Recommended models (☑) must perform well in our road tests; have average or better reliability; and perform adequately if included in safety tests conducted by the Insurance Institute for Highway Safety (IIHS) and the National Highway Traffic Safety Administration (NHTSA).

Entries include, where available, the date of the last road test for that model published in Consumer Reports magazine. These road-test reports are also available to subscribers of our website, at *ConsumerReports.org.*

| | Model | Predicted reliability | Description/with last road-test date |
|---|---|---|---|
| ☑ | **Acura ILX** | ⊖ | This upscale version of the Honda Civic offers three four-cylinder engines. Transmission choices are six-speed manual or five-speed automatic, and a CVT with the hybrid. The ILX offers a variety of luxury features. **Nov. 2012** |
| ☑ | **Acura MDX** | ⊖ | The redesigned 2014 MDX is easy to live with. It's comfortable and quieter than its predecessor, but isn't as sporty. The tight third-row gives it room for seven. The 3.5-liter V6 and six-speed transmission provide competitive acceleration and 20 mpg overall—among the best of any three-row or luxury SUV. **Oct. 2013** |
| ☑ | **Acura RDX** | ○ | Well equipped for the money, the RDX has a smooth, capable V6 that got a respectable 22 mpg overall. Handling is sound if not especially agile, and the ride is a little stiff. Cabin ambience is a bit plain, but the controls are simple to use. **Sep. 2012** |
| | **Acura RLX** | ⊖ | Acura's largest sedan falls short in driving dynamics, especially in ride and handling. It has a slick V6 powertrain and a comfy, spacious interior with a host of electronic features. The AWD hybrid uses electric motors to power the rear wheels. **Sep. 2013** |
| ☑ | **Acura TL** | ⊖ | The TL returned a good 23 mpg overall. Handling is taut and the ride compliant, but the vague steering lacks feedback. Road noise stands out in the otherwise quiet interior. The rear seat is tight and the well-finished interior is cluttered with buttons. AWD is available. **Nov. 2011** |
| ☑ | **Acura TSX** | ⊖ | The TSX's smooth four-cylinder gets 25 mpg overall, and the slick transmission and agile handling make it enjoyable, but the steering is vague. The front seats are well-shaped, but rear-seat room is tight. A wagon and a V6 are available. **Jun. 2009** |

**Ratings Key** **Better** ⟵⟶ **Worse** ⊜ ⊖ ○ ◒ ● ☑ **Recommended**

| | Model | Predicted reliability | Description/with last road-test date |
|---|---|---|---|
| | **Audi A3** | New | A new sedan version arrives in early 2014 with gas turbo and diesel engines. Hybrid and performance versions arrive later. The car is longer than the old A3 hatch, bringing more interior room. |
| ☑ | **Audi A4** | ⊖ | The A4 has a firm, yet supple and controlled ride, with agile handling. The responsive four-cylinder turbo engine is mated to a super smooth eight-speed automatic. AWD is optional. The interior has excellent fit and finish, but the rear seat is tight. The driver-interaction system is complicated. **Jul. 2011** |
| ☑ | **Audi A5** | ⊖ | The base A5 is powered by a four-cylinder turbo engine. Handling is agile. The cabin is quiet and nicely furnished. The S5 uses a 3.0-liter supercharged V6, and there is a V8-powered RS 5. The rear seats are snug for two adults. **May 2010** |
| ☑ | **Audi A6** | ○ | The A6 is one of our top-rated cars, quick, agile, and comfortable. Engines include a 2.0-liter turbo four-cylinder with front- or all-wheel drive and a 3.0-liter supercharged V6 with all-wheel drive. A diesel is new for 2014. **Jan. 2012** |
| | **Audi A7** | ⊜ | This sporty, coupe-like hatchback offers V6, V8, and diesel engines. The interior is very luxurious and features an available heads-up display. Audi has added some optional functionality to the MMI radio interface with touch pad controls as well. |
| | **Audi A8** | NA | The A8 boasts strong engines and a slick eight-speed automatic transmission. It also has plenty of high-tech and safety features. The revised control interface is still complex, and includes a touch pad near the shifter for handwritten inputs. **Dec. 2011** |
| ☑ | **Audi Allroad** | ⊖ | This A4 wagon has SUV-like styling and extra ground clearance. Agile handling makes it fun to drive and the quiet cabin is beautifully finished. A spunky, four-cylinder turbo and slick eight-speed automatic provide competitive fuel economy. **Dec. 2012** |
| ☑ | **Audi Q5** | ○ | Stylish and sporty, the Q5 SUV is almost as much fun to drive as a sports sedan. It rides well and has a comfortable, quiet, and well-finished cabin. Rear-seat and cargo space are fairly modest. The turbo four-cylinder returned a commendable 21 mpg overall. A supercharged V6 and a diesel are available. **Sep. 2012** |
| | **Audi Q7** | NA | Audi's luxury SUV offers a tight third-row seat. A supercharged V6 and 3.0-liter V6 turbodiesel are the only engines offered. Handling is fairly nimble but the Q7 doesn't shine at its limits. |
| | **Audi TT** | NA | The TT has responsive—but not very sporty—handling. The turbo four-cylinder engine is punchy enough. The excellent S-tronic manumatic works well and is the only transmission. A higher-performance TTS is available. **Jun. 2013** |
| ☑ | **BMW 1 Series** | ○ | The 1 Series two-door coupe offers 3.0-liter six-cylinder and a twin-turbo six-cylinder. It is spectacular to drive, with excellent steering. Although snug, the interior features high levels of fit and finish. A 135is boosts performance a bit. **Oct. 2008** |
| ☑ | **BMW 3 Series** | ⊜ | The excellent 3 Series sedan has impressive handling, ride comfort, quietness, and interior quality. The four-cylinder turbo performs well and averaged 28 mpg overall. A 3.0-liter six-cylinder turbo is available. A GT hatchback arrives this fall. **Aug. 2012** |
| | **BMW 4 Series** | New | The new 3 Series coupe becomes the 4 Series, with an added image of luxury and exclusivity. The new coupe is longer, lower, and less angular than the old 3 Series coupe. AWD will be available. |

|  | Model | Predicted reliability | Description/with last road-test date |
|---|---|---|---|
| ✔ | **BMW 5 Series** | ○ | The 5 Series is refined and relatively fuel efficient. Our turbo six-cylinder had strong acceleration and the eight-speed automatic is slick. The ride is impressive, but steering is slow and vague and the car understeers easily, making handling disappointing. Fit and finish is excellent. AWD and a diesel are available. **Nov. 2010** |
|  | **BMW 6 Series** | NA | The posh 6 Series coupe and convertible deliver strong performance. Power comes from a V8 mated with either an eight-speed automatic or a six-speed manual. Acceleration is ferocious and handling is sharper than the 5 Series. |
|  | **BMW 7 Series** | ● | The 7 Series is not the crisp, sporty car of yore. Handling lacks agility and while the ride is steady and supple, it is still a bit stiff. We found the turbo V8 smooth, refined, and punchy. Controls are complex and frustrating to use. The roomy cabin is super quiet and impeccably finished and seat comfort is tops. **Dec. 2011** |
|  | **BMW i3** | New | The new i3 is an all-electric hatchback that offers a small motorcycle engine acting as a generator, doubling the electric-only range of 80 to 100 miles. Charge times are said to be 3 hours on 240-volts. Price will start at $41,350 before tax credit. |
|  | **BMW X1** | New | The X1 compact SUV uses a turbo six-cylinder with a six-speed automatic or a turbo four-cylinder with an eight-speed automatic. It's sporty to drive but the ride is stiff, the steering is heavy at low speeds, and the cabin is snug. **May 2013** |
|  | **BMW X3** | New | The X3 boasts a well-finished, quiet, and comfortable cabin. The taut ride is borderline stiff, but well controlled. Handling is sports-sedan-like. The base 2.0-liter turbo four-cylinder got a very good 23 mpg overall in our tests. A 3.0-liter turbo six-cylinder is optional. Both use a smooth eight-speed automatic. **Sep. 2012** |
|  | **BMW X5** | New | 2014 brings a new X5 that is available in rear- or all-wheel drive. Six-cylinder gas and diesel engines are available, with the top model using a 4.4-liter turbo V8. Comprehensive safety gear includes new self-parking and driver-assist systems. |
|  | **BMW X6** | NA | Based on the old X5 SUV, the X6 features standard AWD. It is a coupe-like SUV, but with four doors. Most versions are powered by a 3.0-liter turbo six-cylinder. A 4.4-liter V8 is also offered. A high-performance M version and a hybrid are available. |
|  | **BMW Z4** | NA | The sleek Z4 looks sharp but is unimpressive as a sports car. The vague steering, jittery ride, and understeer undermine its fun factor. The turbo four-cylinder is powerful and got 28 mpg overall, but has a diesel-like clatter. **Jun. 2013** |
| ✔ | **Buick Enclave** | ○ | This large SUV can seat up to eight adults. It has a smooth 3.6-liter V6 and six-speed automatic. We found the ride comfortable and quiet. Handling is agile and secure. The third-row seat is roomy and fit and finish is excellent. **Jul. 2009** |
|  | **Buick Encore** | New | The Encore is a subcompact SUV. Good points include a quiet interior, compliant ride, and great maneuverability. But its small four-cylinder feels weak and the well-appointed cabin is narrow and cramped. **Aug. 2013** |

**Ratings Key** Better ⟵⟶ Worse ⊜ ⊖ ○ ◒ ●  ✔ **Recommended**

| | Model | Predicted reliability | Description/with last road-test date |
|---|---|---|---|
| | **Buick LaCrosse** | ◒ | The LaCrosse features a base four-cylinder with the eAssist mild hybrid system. The refined 3.6-liter V6 is powerful. Rear-seat room and interior fit and finish are impressive, and AWD is available. The ride is steady and supple and handling is responsive. However, visibility is not a strong suit. **Oct. 2012** |
| ✓ | **Buick Regal** | ○ | The Regal's turbo 2.0-liter four-cylinder is quick and fairly quiet. Handling is agile and the car steers well. The ride is supple and controlled and wind noise is well suppressed. The interior is nicely furnished with good seats but the rear is rather tight. **Jul. 2011** |
| | **Buick Verano** | ● | The entry-level Verano is based on the Cruze but with more upscale trimmings. Engine choices are a 2.4-liter four-cylinder and a 2.0-liter turbo four-cylinder. The car is quiet, with a comfortable ride and responsive, but not sporty, handling. The cabin is tight and details like manual seat recline are chintzy. **Nov. 2012** |
| | **Cadillac ATS** | New | Offered in rear- and all-wheel drive, the ATS handles nimbly, but its turbo four-cylinder doesn't feel overly powerful, and got just 23-mpg overall. The six-speed automatic is adequate. A taut ride and good brakes are positives, but the CUE infotainment system is convoluted. **May 2013** |
| | **Cadillac CTS** | New | A new CTS sedan arrives this fall. It is longer and wider than the old car, and offers a 3.6-liter V6, a turbo V6, and a 2.0-liter turbo four-cylinder. Based on the ATS, it will better compete with the Audi A6 and BMW 5 Series. The wagon, coupe, and CTS-V carry on with the old platform for now. |
| | **Cadillac ELR** | New | The ELR is a slightly more powerful, luxury cousin of the Chevrolet Volt, with the same plug-in electric/gasoline backup engine setup. It can run on electricity alone for up to 35 miles before its 1.4-liter turbo four-cylinder extends the range to 300 or so miles. The instruments feature the distracting CUE infotainment system. |
| | **Cadillac Escalade** | ○ | The luxurious Escalade uses a powerful 6.2-liter V8 engine. Acceleration is strong, even when towing, but fuel economy is just 13 mpg. The interior is quiet and the ride is comfortable, but handling is clumsy and braking distances are long. **Nov. 2006** |
| | **Cadillac SRX** | ◒ | The SRX has agile and sporty handling, but the ride is too firm at low speeds. Its 3.6-liter V6 and smooth six-speed automatic got 18 mpg overall. The interior is well finished and the front seats are supportive, but the rear seat is snug. The revised interior includes the frustrating CUE infotainment system. **Jun. 2013** |
| | **Cadillac XTS** | New | This large sedan's ride is somewhat jittery and the engine sounds coarse when prodded. Handling is sound but unexceptional. The interior is very roomy and has comfortable seats, but the CUE infotainment interface is unintuitive. Visibility is impaired, due in part to the high rear deck. **Jan. 2013** |
| ✓ | **Chevrolet Camaro** | ○ | The Camaro's base 3.6-liter V6 is powerful, and the 6.2-liter, V8-powered SS is very quick. Handling is capable, but so-so steering and the car's weight hurt its agility. The ride is taut and controlled. The styling impedes practicality and visibility and some controls are hard to decipher. The Z/28 trimline returns for 2014. **Oct. 2009** |

| | Model | Predicted reliability | Description/with last road-test date |
|---|---|---|---|
| | **Chevrolet Corvette** | New | The sleekly styled new Corvette has more power, sharper handling, and a better-dressed interior. Power comes from a 455-hp V8. The engine is teamed with a choice of a six-speed automatic or seven-speed manual. |
| ✔ | **Chevrolet Cruze** | ○ | Chevy's small Cruze sedan handles well and has a sound ride, but we averaged just 26 mpg with the 1.8- and 1.4-liter engines. The Eco trim gets 27 mpg, and the diesel got an impressive 49 mpg highway in our tests. The well-finished cabin is spacious up front but cramped in the rear. **May 2011** |
| ✔ | **Chevrolet Equinox** | ○ | The spacious Equinox SUV has easy access and it rides and handles OK, but feels dated and sluggish despite a lively new 3.6-liter V6. Fuel economy is so-so from both the V6 (18 mpg) and the base four-cylinder (21 mpg). The MyLink infotainment system is easy to use, a modest plus. **Aug. 2013** |
| | **Chevrolet Impala** | New | The redesigned 2014 Impala is now a contemporary large, upscale sedan that's roomy, comfortable, quiet, refined, and enjoyable to drive. The ride is cushy and controlled. Engine choices include a V6 and two four-cylinders. The V6 version performs capably, with secure and responsive handling. **Sep. 2013** |
| | **Chevrolet Malibu** | New | The Malibu is comfortable and quiet, with a cushy ride. Handling is sound, but feels soggy at its limits. In our tests the punchy 2.0-liter turbo got 24 mpg overall; the mild-hybrid 29 mpg; and the 2.5-liter got 26 mpg. The well-finished interior has simple controls but the backseat is cramped. **Jun. 2013** |
| | **Chevrolet Silverado 1500** | New | Chevy's good-performing new Silverado has revised styling and powertrains and many new safety features. We got 16 mpg overall with the tested 5.3-liter V8 and standard six-speed automatic. The Silverado's cabin stays impressively quiet and the ride is tolerable. **Nov. 2013** |
| ✔ | **Chevrolet Sonic** | ○ | The subcompact Sonic is fairly quick and quiet for the class. Handling is responsive, but the steering is darty. The 1.8-liter four-cylinder performs well; the turbo 1.4-liter is modestly quicker and thriftier. The sedan has a huge trunk but the hatchback is more versatile; both have a cramped rear seat. **May 2012** |
| | **Chevrolet Spark** | New | Chevrolet's smallest car isn't a good deal. Its dinky 84-hp, 1.2-liter four-cylinder and jerky four-speed automatic combine to provide slow acceleration and just 32 mpg overall. The cabin is cramped and noisy and the ride is stiff and jittery. The Spark is exceptionally easy to park, and the rear seat is usable by adults. **Jan. 2013** |
| | **Chevrolet SS** | New | The rear-drive SS is borrowed from GM's Australian brand, Holden. A 415-hp, 6.2-liter V8 and six-speed automatic are standard. The SS includes a long list of luxury and advanced safety features, and is the basis for a new generation of police cars. |
| ✔ | **Chevrolet Suburban** | ○ | The Suburban can tow a heavy trailer and swallow tons of cargo. There is room for up to nine. The third-row seat is low and uncomfortable. The standard 5.3-liter V8 is just adequate and returned 14 mpg overall. Look for a new Suburban in 2014. **Feb. 2011** |
| | **Chevrolet Tahoe** | ○ | The Tahoe's ride is supple, but handling and braking are so-so. There is little cargo space behind the cramped third-row seat. We got just 14 mpg in our tests with the 5.3-liter V8. Look for a new Tahoe in 2014. **Feb. 2011** |

| | Model | Predicted reliability | Description/with last road-test date |
|---|---|---|---|
| ✔ | **Chevrolet Traverse** | ○ | Chevrolet's version of GM's large, car-based SUVs can seat seven or eight people comfortably. Handling is responsive, the ride is comfortable, and the well-finished interior is quiet. The 3.6-liter V6 engine returned 16 mpg overall, but the six-speed automatic sometimes hesitates to downshift when needed. **Jun. 2013** |
| ✔ | **Chevrolet Volt** | ⊖ | Overall the Volt is quick, quiet, and responsive, typically covering 35 miles on an electric charge. The 1.4-liter gas engine extends the range to about 315 miles. As a four-seater, practicality is compromised. Recharge times are about 5 hours with a 220-volt supply and twice that with 110 volts. **Oct. 2011** |
| | **Chrysler 200** | ◒ | The aging 200 has a compliant ride and the optional V6 is strong and smooth. But the four-cylinder is noisy and unrefined. Both engines get 21 mpg overall. The six-speed automatic doesn't shift smoothly or quickly, the suspension is soft, and handling is underwhelming even at moderate speeds. **Aug. 2011** |
| ✔ | **Chrysler 300** | ○ | The 300's 3.6-liter V6 is smooth and powerful, and the eight-speed automatic helped it get a good 22 mpg overall. The cabin is roomy and nicely trimmed, and the Uconnect infotainment system is one of the best available. The 5.7-liter V8 gets only 18 mpg; the SRT8 uses a potent 6.4-liter V8. **Oct. 2012** |
| | **Chrysler Town & Country** | ◒ | While the Town & Country has a very comfortable and settled ride and a quiet, well-equipped cabin, fuel economy is unimpressive and the transmission shifts slowly. Handling is sound in everyday driving but sloppy when pushed to the limits. **Aug. 2011** |
| | **Dodge Avenger** | NA | The uninspiring Avenger has a compliant ride and the optional V6 is strong and smooth, but the four-cylinder is noisy and unrefined. Both engines get 21 mpg overall. The six-speed automatic doesn't shift smoothly or quickly, the suspension is soft, and handling is underwhelming even at moderate speeds. **Aug. 2011** |
| | **Dodge Challenger** | ◒ | The large, heavy Challenger comes up a bit short on sporty credentials. It is very quick in a straight line and is a fairly comfortable and effortless cruiser. Handling lacks agility but the Dodge is ultimately secure. Good controls, decent interior quality, and the ability to seat five are pluses. **Aug. 2012** |
| | **Dodge Charger** | ● | High points for the Charger include responsive handling and a steady, comfortable ride. The spacious cabin has good-quality materials and the touchscreen is easy to use. The V6 performs well and uses a slick eight-speed automatic; a V8 is optional. Visibility has been improved but is still not great. **Oct. 2012** |
| | **Dodge Dart** | New | The Dart's thrashy-sounding 1.6-liter turbo makes decent power, but the automated manual is unrefined. The base 2.0-liter is underpowered and its six-speed automatic upshifts too quickly, a fuel-saving but performance-robbing strategy. Handling is good and the ride is composed. The rear seat is tight. **Jan. 2013** |
| ✔ | **Dodge Durango** | ○ | The Durango boasts a spacious, quiet cabin with a usable third-row seat. Cargo and trailer-towing capacities are generous. The muscular V8 returns just 14 mpg. The V6 is smooth, refined, and more economical but feels a bit sluggish. Handling is relatively responsive and ultimately secure. **Aug. 2011** |

**Ratings Key** Better ⊜ ⊖ ○ ◒ ● Worse ✔ Recommended

| Model | Predicted reliability | Description/with last road-test date |
|---|---|---|
| **Dodge Grand Caravan** | ◒ | While the Grand Caravan has a very comfortable and settled ride, and a quiet, well-equipped cabin, fuel economy is unimpressive and the transmission shifts slowly. Handling is sound in everyday driving but sloppy when pushed to the limits. **Aug. 2011** |
| **Dodge Journey** | ● | Dodge's midsized SUV seats five, and offers a tiny third row. The 3.6-liter V6 got only 16 mpg in our tests; FWD versions get a noisy 2.4-liter four. Despite updates through the years the Journey is still mediocre. It rides well and is quiet, but its lack of agility makes it feel larger than it is. **Aug. 2011** |
| **Dodge SRT Viper** | New | The new SRT Viper is powered by a 640-hp, 8.4-liter V10 with a standard six-speed manual. It has a more upscale interior and controls. Two versions are offered: the base and the fancier GTS. The new chassis is said to markedly improve handling. |
| **Fiat 500** | ○ | The Fiat 500 is a tiny, fun-to-drive hatchback. The 1.4-liter four doesn't pack a lot of power but delivers sufficient thrust. Expect about 33 mpg overall. The five-speed manual and clutch are smooth. Handling is very agile and secure. The high-performance Abarth is quick, corners well, and sounds good. **Oct. 2011** |
| **Fiat 500L** | New | This small people mover is significantly larger than the 500. It's rather narrow, but can seat five. Rear-seat room is generous, access is extremely easy, and visibility is excellent. Interior materials are a bit basic, but there is a sense of style. Power comes from the Abarth's 1.4-liter turbo four-cylinder. |
| **Ford C-MAX** | New | This is a clever, well-finished, and practical five-passenger car that rides well and handles with agility. The regenerative braking system makes pedal feel a bit touchy. The 2.0-liter four-cylinder and electric motor deliver smooth, adequate acceleration, and we got 37 mpg overall in our tests. **Mar. 2013** |
| **Ford Edge** | ● | The Edge's MyFord Touch controls are distracting, lacking tactile feedback and requiring too much attention. The 3.5-liter V6 and six-speed automatic returned 18 mpg overall. But the powertrain lacks refinement, and the transmission isn't the smoothest. The ride is a bit jittery and road noise is pronounced. **Feb. 2011** |
| **Ford Escape** | New | The Escape drives very well, with agile handling, a composed ride, and a solid feel. Both four-cylinder engines, the 1.6-liter turbo and the quieter 2.0-liter turbo, get about 22 mpg overall. The footwells are narrow and the base-level cloth seats lack support and comfort. Many controls are needlessly complex. **Nov. 2012** |
| ☑ **Ford Expedition** | ○ | The Expedition has a spacious interior and the independent suspension allows the comfy third-row seat to fold flat into the floor. The noisy V8 felt sluggish and returned 13 mpg overall. Handling is responsive, and towing capacity is generous. **Aug. 2007** |
| **Ford Explorer** | ● | The roomy Explorer has a versatile interior and a usable third-row seat. Handling is secure but not particularly agile. The 3.5-liter V6 is punchy enough though a bit rough when revved. A 2.0-liter turbo four is available with FWD. The interior is well-finished but the MyFord Touch system is distracting. **Jun. 2011** |
| ☑ **Ford F-150** | ○ | The F-150's 5.0-liter V8 and V6 turbo make the truck quick and delivered 15 mpg overall. The crew-cab is very roomy, but step-in is high. Handling is a bit clumsy but secure enough, and the ride is tolerable. The interior is quiet and quite refined. **Sep. 2011** |

| Model | Predicted reliability | Description/with last road-test date |
|---|---|---|
| **Ford Fiesta** | ◒ | This subcompact drives nicely, with agile handling and a supple, controlled ride. Wind, road, and engine noise are well suppressed. Interior fit and finish are impressive, with soft-touch dash materials and Ford's SYNC multimedia system. However, the rear seat is extremely cramped. A sporty ST is available. **Jan. 2011** |
| ☑ **Ford Flex** | ○ | The Flex has SUV-like versatility and car-like driving dynamics. We got 18 mpg overall with the 3.5-liter V6 and six-speed automatic. The turbo V6 is quick. The vast interior is very roomy and nicely finished. The ride is comfortable and quiet, and handling is responsive and secure but not particularly agile. **Nov. 2012** |
| **Ford Focus** | ● | The sporty yet quiet Focus is fun to drive, and its solid interior makes it feel substantial. We got 28 mpg overall in SE and SEL trims, and 31 mpg in the SFE. The rear seat is tight and the radio controls are confusing. The EV can go about 80 miles on a charge. The sporty ST is a fun hatchback. **Sep. 2011** |
| **Ford Fusion** | New | All versions of the stylish Fusion have a supple ride, agile handling, and sharp steering. The cabin is nicely furnished and has decent interior room. The Hybrid can go short distances in electric only mode, while the plug-in hybrid can run for about 20 miles on electricity. **Mar. 2013** |
| ☑ **Ford Mustang** | ○ | The Mustang's 3.7-liter V6 is refined and punchy, and returns 24 mpg, while the powerful 5.0-liter V8 is a scorcher. The manual is a short-throw six-speed gearbox. The ride is a bit jiggly, but not punishing. Handling is nimble, braking is good, and the Mustang steers well. **Oct. 2010** |
| **Ford Taurus** | ○ | The plush, quiet Taurus is cramped for a big car and hard to see out of. Improvements gave the 3.5 V6 more power and fuel economy of 21 mpg. AWD is available with the V6. A turbo four-cylinder is also available, as is the super-quick SHO. Handling is responsive but dull. **Oct. 2012** |
| **Ford Transit Connect** | New | Ford's second-generation Transit Connect will seat five or seven passengers. A 2.5-liter four-cylinder with a six-speed automatic is standard; a 1.6-liter turbo is optional. The wagon has sliding doors and flat-folding second and third rows. Optional features include a rear-view camera and SYNC with MyFord Touch. |
| ☑ **GMC Acadia** | ○ | GMC's version of the large, car-based GM SUVs can seat seven or eight people comfortably. Handling is responsive, the ride is comfortable, and the well-finished interior is quiet. The 3.6-liter V6 engine returned 16 mpg overall, but the six-speed automatic sometimes hesitates to downshift when needed. **Jun. 2013** |
| **GMC Sierra 1500** | New | GMC's new Sierra has revised styling and powertrains, and many new safety features. We got 16 mpg overall with the tested 5.3-liter V8 and standard six-speed automatic in our tested Silverado. The cabin stays quiet and the ride is tolerable. **Nov. 2013** |
| ☑ **GMC Terrain** | ○ | The spacious Terrain has easy access and it rides and handles OK, but feels dated and sluggish despite a lively 3.6-liter V6. Fuel economy is so-so from both the V6 (18 mpg) and the base four-cylinder (21 mpg). The MyLink infotainment system is easy to use, a modest plus. **Aug. 2013** |

**Ratings Key** **Better** ⟵⟶ **Worse** ⊜ ◓ ○ ◒ ●  ☑ **Recommended**

| | Model | Predicted reliability | Description/with last road-test date |
|---|---|---|---|
| ✓ | **GMC Yukon XL** | ○ | This twin of the Chevrolet Suburban is a longer version of the Yukon. Handling and braking are OK, and the ride is supple. Interior quality is very good. It can seat up to nine with cargo space left over and tow a heavy trailer. Look for a new Yukon/Yukon XL in 2014. **Feb. 2011** |
| ✓ | **Honda Accord** | ⊖ | The Accord's 2.4-liter four-cylinder and CVT got an impressive 30 mpg overall; the V6 and six-speed automatic got a very good 26 mpg. Handling is agile and the ride is supple. The rear bench is snug for three, and top-trim models have a fussy radio. Both plug-in and regular hybrids are available. **Feb. 2013** |
| ✓ | **Honda Civic** | ⊖ | The Civic has a comfortable ride and responsive handling, with decent braking performance. Inside is a relatively quiet and well-trimmed interior. All of the powertrains are smooth and unobtrusive, although the Si can get loud. The rear seat provides decent room. All versions have a standard backup camera. **May 2013** |
| | **Honda Crosstour** | ○ | The Crosstour, a raised hatchback based on the old Accord, seats five and offers AWD. We like the comfortable seats, wide cabin, and strong V6 powertrain. But frustratingly convoluted controls, clumsy handling, and lousy view to the rear kill our enthusiasm. A four-cylinder is available with front-drive versions. **Nov. 2013** |
| ✓ | **Honda CR-V** | ⊜ | The sensible CR-V has a smooth, responsive four-cylinder and five-speed automatic. Despite the slightly vague steering, handling is responsive in ordinary driving. The ride is absorbent and composed but road noise is pronounced. The rear seat is roomy, but the small rear windows restrict the view aft. **Jun. 2012** |
| | **Honda CR-Z** | ⊜ | The CR-Z two-seat hybrid uses a 1.5-liter four-cylinder gas engine. The electric power is used to enhance performance. We got 35 mpg overall in our tests, not terribly impressive for a hybrid. Handling isn't very sporty and the ride is jumpy. Rear visibility is compromised. **Jan. 2011** |
| ✓ | **Honda Fit** | ⊜ | This small four-door hatchback offers easy access and very good visibility, and has an amazing amount of interior room. While not overly powerful, the Fit feels responsive, with a smooth and willing engine, and agile handling. The ride is a bit choppy. An electric version is available in limited numbers for lease. **Mar. 2009** |
| | **Honda Insight** | ⊖ | The Insight got 38 mpg overall in our tests. It is somewhat snug and rear-seat access is awkward. The ride is stiff and choppy and road noise is pronounced. Handling lacks agility and can be tricky at the limits. **Aug. 2009** |
| ✓ | **Honda Odyssey** | ○ | The family-friendly Odyssey has a supple ride and responsive handling. It gets 21 mpg overall with the standard six-speed automatic. The spacious interior is well finished and has a flat-folding third-row seat. **Nov. 2013** |
| ✓ | **Honda Pilot** | ⊖ | The Pilot offers seating for eight. The powertrain is smooth and ride and handling sound. However, acceleration, braking, and interior fit and finish aren't very impressive. Road noise is very pronounced. **Sep. 2012** |
| ✓ | **Honda Ridgeline** | ⊖ | This crew-cab pickup has a supple and steady ride and agile handling. Its 5-foot-long composite cargo bed features an all-weather, lockable trunk. The 3.5-liter V6 engine is quiet, smooth, and responsive, and it can tow 5,000 pounds. **Jul. 2005** |

| | Model | Predicted reliability | Description/with last road-test date |
|---|---|---|---|
| ☑ | **Hyundai Accent** | ○ | Hyundai's entry-level sedan and hatchback handle responsively and use a smooth 1.6-liter four-cylinder, mated to either a six-speed manual or automatic. We got 31 mpg with the auto, 32 mpg with the manual hatchback. The front cabin is roomy but the rear is snug and the ride is jittery. **May 2012** |
| | **Hyundai Azera** | NA | The Azera is stylish and refined, with a quiet and spacious cabin that has room for five. Its smooth 3.3-liter V6 and six-speed automatic provide strong performance and an impressive 23 mpg overall. But the ride is too stiff, handling lacks agility, and the heavy steering feels artificial. **Oct. 2012** |
| ☑ | **Hyundai Elantra** | ⊖ | The Elantra's 1.8-liter four-cylinder and six-speed automatic returned a very good 29 mpg overall. The ride is compliant and handling is responsive and secure, but road noise is pronounced. The interior is nice and has decent rear-seat room. The GT hatchback is competent but not a standout. **May 2011** |
| ☑ | **Hyundai Equus** | ○ | Hyundai's flagship has a comfortable ride, but motions can be a bit busy and handling is less than agile. It is more stately than sporty. A 5.0-liter V8 and eight-speed automatic are the sole powertrain. The interior is spacious and well finished. **Dec. 2011** |
| ☑ | **Hyundai Genesis** | ○ | The Genesis is very impressive, especially for the price. The refined V6 delivers quick acceleration and gets 22 mpg overall with the 8-speed automatic. But the optional V8 doesn't add much. Handling is responsive and secure, but the ride is still unrefined. The roomy interior is very quiet and well finished. **Nov. 2011** |
| | **Hyundai Genesis Coupe** | ◒ | This coupe has very capable and nimble handling, and the 3.8-liter V6 is punchy and powerful. The 2.0-liter turbo is somewhat noisy. But the car is really let down by an imprecise manual transmission and a stiff, unsettled ride. **Oct. 2009** |
| | **Hyundai Santa Fe** | New | Both the three-row Santa Fe and two-row Santa Fe Sport are versatile, with a nice interior and roomy cabin. But the three-row version handles and rides better. The Sport's 2.4-liter four-cylinder got 23 mpg overall; the smooth 3.3-liter V6 in the larger Santa Fe delivered a class-leading 20 mpg. **Sep. 2013** |
| ☑ | **Hyundai Sonata** | ○ | The Sonata has a comfortable ride, responsive handling, and a well-finished cabin. The four-cylinder and six-speed automatic returned 27 mpg in our tests. The quicker and stronger four-cylinder turbo returns 25 mpg overall. Road noise is evident and rear-seat access is awkward. A hybrid is also available. **Aug. 2010** |
| ☑ | **Hyundai Tucson** | ○ | The Tucson handles securely and responsively, but the ride is stiff and road noise is pronounced. Its smooth 2.4-liter, four-cylinder returns 22 mpg, and the six-speed automatic is responsive. The interior is spacious but the low rear seat lacks thigh support. The styling robs cargo space and hurts the rear view. **Jul. 2010** |
| ☑ | **Hyundai Veloster** | ⊖ | This sporty hatchback has a rear door only on the right-hand side. Power comes from a 1.6-liter, four-cylinder and both a manual and a dual-clutch automated manual six-speed are offered. A more powerful turbo four and six-speed automatic are available. The interior has a funky, high-tech look. **Jul. 2012** |

| | Model | Predicted reliability | Description/with last road-test date |
|---|---|---|---|
| ☑ | **Infiniti G37** | ⊜ | Agile and quick, the G37 is fun to drive. A price reduction for 2014 makes it a budget alternative to the Q50. Power comes from a strong but thirsty 328-hp, 3.7-liter V6. Controls are simple but the cabin and trunk are a bit snug. Rear- or all-wheel drive is available. **Jun. 2009** |
| | **Infiniti Q50** | ⊖ | Infiniti's new Q50 sports sedan supersedes the G37 and offers a 328-hp 3.7-liter V6 or new hybrid powertrain. Buyers can choose from rear- or all-wheel drive. The redesign debuts Infiniti's InTouch infotainment system and new safety technologies. |
| ☑ | **Infiniti Q70** | ○ | The Q70, formerly the M, is very quick and handles responsively. Its 330-hp 3.7-liter V6 and seven-speed automatic deliver decent fuel economy. The cabin is quiet, although engine noise comes through at high revs. The transitions between electric and gas mode in the Hybrid are rather abrupt. **Nov. 2010** |
| ☑ | **Infiniti QX50** | ⊖ | This small pseudo-SUV has agile handling and a steady ride. The rear seat is very snug and the cargo area is tiny. Styling has compromised rear visibility, but the interior is nicely finished and the controls are logical enough. The sole engine is Infiniti's rather nice 3.7-liter V6. **Sep. 2008** |
| ☑ | **Infiniti QX60** | ⊖ | A three-row SUV with less bulk than a full-size model, the QX60 has a spacious, luxurious, quiet, and well-finished interior. Available in either FWD or AWD, the V6 and CVT deliver smooth acceleration and 19-mpg overall on premium fuel. Handling lacks agility. A hybrid version is available. **Nov. 2012** |
| ☑ | **Infiniti QX70** | ○ | The QX70 has an eager 3.7-liter V6 and responsive handling. The ride is quite stiff. Well-finished and fairly roomy, the stylish cabin is quiet. Outward visibility isn't great, though, and cargo capacity is modest. **Jul. 2009** |
| ☑ | **Infiniti QX80** | ○ | Infiniti's full-sized QX80 is plush, with a quiet cabin and very smooth and strong performance. But it gobbles premium fuel, and the handling, cumbersome even in everyday driving, can be disconcerting when pushed to its limits. **Feb. 2011** |
| | **Jaguar F-Type** | New | Jaguar's new F-Type is a two-seat roadster positioned below the XK. Three supercharged engines are available: two V6s and a V8. The eight-speed automatic facilitates manual overrides with paddles on the steering wheel. |
| | **Jaguar XF** | NA | The midsized XF is a pleasure to drive. It has a stylish, quiet interior that's unfortunately a little cramped, especially in back. An eight-speed automatic is standard and AWD is optional. The supercharged 3.0-liter V6 proved very quick and agile. Low-slung, coupe-like styling takes a toll on access and visibility. **Sep. 2013** |
| | **Jaguar XJ** | ● | The XJ is a capable, luxurious sports sedan. Its 5.0-liter V8 makes it very quick, but the car also handles with grace and delivers a supple and steady ride. The trunk is quite small for a large sedan. The touch screen for the climate, audio, and navigation systems is rather complex and responds slowly. **Dec. 2011** |
| | **Jaguar XK** | NA | The XK has a powerful V8 and smooth six-speed automatic. Handling is athletic and capable. The ride is very supple and controlled. The convertible roof is well-insulated. The touch screen washes out in sunlight and responds very slowly. **Oct. 2006** |

| | Model | Predicted reliability | Description/with last road-test date |
|---|---|---|---|
| | **Jeep Cherokee** | New | The Cherokee shares its platform with the Dodge Dart, itself based on an Alfa Romeo platform. It is offered in front- and all-wheel drive. The base engine is a 2.4-liter four-cylinder, with a new optional 3.2-liter V6. Both use a new nine-speed automatic. |
| | **Jeep Compass** | ◒ | The Compass has secure handling but is not agile, particularly at its limits. The low-speed ride is composed. The sluggish, guttural-sounding 2.4-liter four-cylinder got just 22 mpg overall. The front seats are uncomfortable and the cabin is cramped. Rear styling restricts visibility aft. **Aug. 2011** |
| ✔ | **Jeep Grand Cherokee** | ○ | This versatile SUV has a well-trimmed cabin, a supple ride, and relatively agile handling. Powertrain choices include V6 and V8 gas engines, a new diesel, and a high-performance SRT8 version. The eight-speed automatic is smooth and responsive. Talents as a tow vehicle or off-roader add to the appeal. **Aug. 2013** |
| | **Jeep Patriot** | ⊖ | This small SUV has a compliant ride but handling lacks agility. The 2.4-liter four-cylinder is noisy, the spongy front seats offer little lateral support, and the narrow cabin, wide center console, and small windows give the car a closed-in feeling. **Aug. 2011** |
| | **Jeep Wrangler** | ◒ | The Wrangler's 3.6-liter V6 and five-speed automatic give it better refinement and fuel economy than earlier Wranglers. While as good as it's ever been and great for off-roading, the Jeep is outdated for on-road use. IIHS side-crash-test results without the optional side air bags are poor. **Mar. 2012** |
| | **Kia Cadenza** | New | The Cadenza, derived from the Hyundai Azera, is a large front-wheel-drive sedan powered by a slick, responsive 3.3-liter V6 and six-speed automatic. The interior is luxurious and quiet, and boasts a roomy backseat. Controls are simple and straightforward, and the ride is quite civilized. **Oct. 2013** |
| | **Kia Forte** | New | This cousin of the Hyundai Elantra brings a spacious and quiet interior, simple controls, and a very nice ride. Handling is OK but not super agile. Our base LX averaged 28 mpg with its 1.8-liter four and six-speed automatic. EX models are powered by a 2.0-liter four. The Forte5 hatchback is new as well. **Sep. 2013** |
| ✔ | **Kia Optima** | ○ | The Optima handles very securely, and its standard 2.4-liter four-cylinder performs well. Top-level trims get an economical and powerful turbo, and a hybrid is available. The front seats are comfortable and the interior is refined. The styling hurts rear visibility and cabin access, and the rear seat is a bit low. **Jun. 2011** |
| ✔ | **Kia Rio** | ⊖ | The Rio is similar to the Hyundai Accent sedan and hatchback. Power comes from a 1.6-liter four-cylinder that got just 29 mpg overall in the hatchback and 30 mpg in the sedan, both with an automatic. The car feels solid, and the stiff ride and noise are par for the class. **May 2012** |
| | **Kia Sedona** | ◒ | The aging Sedona's ride and handling fall short. Controls are simple and fit and finish is good. The 3.5-liter V6 and six-speed automatic provide spirited acceleration and decent fuel economy. Handling is secure but not agile and the ride is stiff. While it seats seven, getting to the third row is a chore. **Mar. 2011** |
| | **Kia Sorento** | New | We like the Sorento for its convenient size, comfortable accommodations, and long list of up-to-date accessory features. Its new V6 gets a decent 20 mpg. An adequate four-cylinder is available. The ride is acceptable but a little jiggly, and handling, though secure, isn't exactly sporty. A tiny third row is optional. **Aug. 2013** |

| | Model | Predicted reliability | Description/with last road-test date |
|---|---|---|---|
| | **Kia Soul** | New | Kia's all-new Soul has more passenger and cargo room, with claimed improvements to ride, handling, and visibility. Two four-cylinder engines, a 1.6-liter, and a 2.0-liter will be available. The outgoing Soul had very easy access, abundant head room, and a surprisingly spacious rear seat. |
| ✔ | **Kia Sportage** | ⊜ | The Sportage is far more stylish inside and out than the similar Hyundai Tucson, but that comes at the expense of visibility. Cabin appointments are basic but nicely fitted. Its four-cylinder and V6 engines are civilized and returns reasonably good fuel economy. **Mar. 2011** |
| | **Land Rover LR2** | NA | The LR2 provides good off-road ability. The ride is firm but steady and the car benefits from good steering. In our accident avoidance test, however, the LR2 disconcertingly lifted two wheels at its handling limits, reducing driver confidence. The controls are confusing. |
| | **Land Rover LR4** | NA | Land Rover's LR4 is roomy and quiet, with a luxurious, well-appointed interior. The new V6 supercharged and eight-speed automatic will make it more fuel efficient. The LR4 has strong off-road ability and is able to traverse rough terrain easily. Handling is ultimately secure. Controls can be confusing. **Jun. 2010** |
| | **Land Rover Range Rover** | New | The redesigned Range Rover is roomier and even more luxurious than before and shed some weight to benefit fuel economy. Interior materials have been upgraded, and the redesign looks more streamlined. An eight-speed automatic is standard, and the supercharged engines deliver strong performance. |
| | **Land Rover Range Rover Evoque** | NA | The Evoque offers 2-door and 4-door versions, both with a 2.0-liter turbo four-cylinder and a new nine-speed automatic transmission. Acceleration and braking are commendable, but handling becomes disconcerting at the limits, and the ride is rather choppy. Interior room and visibility were sacrificed for styling. **Mar. 2012** |
| | **Land Rover Range Rover Sport** | New | The redesigned Sport has a unibody frame and aluminum construction. Power comes from new supercharged six- and eight-cylinder engines mated to an eight-speed automatic. Expect it to be sportier than the regular Range Rover but with the same level of opulence and high-tech safety features. |
| ✔ | **Lexus CT 200h** | ⊜ | The CT gets an impressive 40 mpg overall, but acceleration is leisurely. The ride is stiff, and engine and road noise are noticeable. Handling is capable but the steering is vague on-center. The cabin is snug with a tight backseat and tiny cargo capacity. The interior is nice but falls short of being luxurious. **Oct. 2011** |
| ✔ | **Lexus ES** | ⊖ | Our ES with the 3.5-liter V6 and automatic got 25 mpg overall; our tested hybrid averaged 36 mpg. The ride is decent, but not luxurious and handling is sloppy at its limits. The very quiet cabin looks good but there is evidence of cost cutting throughout. The infotainment system is distracting and convoluted. **Jan. 2013** |
| ✔ | **Lexus GS** | ⊖ | The GS is engaging to drive, with a sporty ride and handling. A 3.5-liter V6 and six-speed automatic is the standard powertrain. AWD is optional, and a hybrid is available. Interior space is now par for the class and the cabin is nicely furnished. **Dec. 2012** |

**Ratings Key** Better ⊜ ⊖ ○ ◒ ● Worse    ✔ **Recommended**

| | Model | Predicted reliability | Description/with last road-test date |
|---|---|---|---|
| ✓ | **Lexus GX** | ○ | The bulky GX is very quiet, quick, good for towing, and capable off-road. Handling is ungainly but ultimately secure. The powertrain is slick and refined, the ride is comfortable, and the cabin is plush. The 4.6-liter V8 gets 17 mpg overall. The third row seat is tiny but folds neatly into the floor when not in use. **Jun. 2010** |
| | **Lexus IS** | ⊖ | The new IS comes with 2.5- and 3.5-liter V6 engines. A six-speed automatic is standard, with the rear-drive IS 350 offering an eight-speed automatic. The seats are supposed to deliver improved comfort and support. The wheelbase has been stretched by 3 inches, but this is still a snug car. |
| ✓ | **Lexus LS** | ⊖ | The LS is luxurious and highly refined, with a comfortable and serene ride. The spacious cabin is exceptionally quiet, and controls are user-friendly. Handling has been improved, but the LS is still not an engaging driver's car. The powertrain is very smooth and responsive. A hybrid is available. **May 2013** |
| | **Lexus LX** | NA | This luxury SUV is plush, quiet, and upscale. The LX's 5.7-liter V8 is strong, but we got only 14 mpg overall in the similar Toyota Land Cruiser. The ride is comfortable and the Toyota was very impressive off-road. The power-folding third-row seat folds up to the sides of the interior, limiting cargo space. |
| ✓ | **Lexus RX** | ⊜ | The RX rides comfortably and has a very well-finished, roomy interior. Handling is lackluster and the steering gives little feedback. The 3.5-liter V6 provides strong acceleration and an impressive 21 mpg overall. The RX 450h hybrid delivered an impressive 26 mpg overall. **Jul. 2009** |
| | **Lincoln MKS** | ○ | This large sedan, based on the Ford Taurus, has a 3.7-liter V6 that provides good power but isn't particularly refined. Top-level models use a direct-injection, turbo V6 rather than a V8. Front- and all-wheel drive are available. The ride is comfortable but not always settled. Handling is secure but lacks agility. **Jan. 2013** |
| | **Lincoln MKT** | ● | Lincoln's version of the Ford Flex has a very roomy interior and offers many luxury amenities, but visibility is compromised. Base models are powered by a 3.7-liter V6, while the uplevel engine is a turbo V6. The ride is comfortable but stiffer than in the Flex. Handling lacks agility, and is cumbersome at its limits. |
| | **Lincoln MKX** | ● | This upscale version of the Ford Edge uses a fairly powerful 3.7-liter, V6 engine and six-speed automatic. Fuel economy is unimpressive. The ride is reasonably comfortable but handling lacks agility. Interior materials are disappointing and many buttons are difficult to read at night. **Feb. 2011** |
| | **Lincoln MKZ** | New | Good looks, sharp handling, a composed ride, and a luxurious interior make the MKZ appealing. But the touch-activated controls and compromised rear-seat room and cabin access are detractions. Powertrains include a four-cylinder turbo, a strong V6, and a hybrid that returned 34 mpg overall in our tests. **Jul. 2013** |
| ✓ | **Lincoln Navigator** | ○ | The Navigator comes in standard and long versions, the latter 15 inches longer for increased cargo space. The V8 is sluggish and thirsty. The third-row seat is power operated, folds flat into the floor, and is as comfortable as the second-row seats. **Jul. 2007** |

**Ratings Key** Better ⟷ Worse: ⊜ ⊖ ○ ◒ ●    ✓ **Recommended**

| | Model | Predicted reliability | Description/with last road-test date |
|---|---|---|---|
| ✓ | **Mazda CX-5** | ⊜ | The CX-5 has taut and agile handling and quick, well weighted steering. But we found the ride choppy and road and wind noise are pronounced. Both four-cylinder engines returned an impressive 25 mpg overall. The six-speed automatic is fairly smooth; a six-speed manual is available on FWD versions. **Jun. 2013** |
| ✓ | **Mazda CX-9** | ⊜ | The CX-9 has a small but easy-to-access third-row seat. The 3.7-liter V6 is smooth and refined. Handling is taut and agile, and the ride is firm and steady, yet comfortable. Braking performance is better in the Grand Touring model. The blind-spot system works well. **Nov. 2008** |
| ✓ | **Mazda MX-5 Miata** | ⊖ | With its 2.0-liter four-cylinder and standard six-speed manual, the Miata is a joy to drive. A six-speed automatic is optional. Operating the manual top is a breeze, and a hard top is available. Handling is super agile, and steering is quick and precise. The ride is reasonably comfortable but the cabin is noisy. **May 2010** |
| ✓ | **Mazda2** | ⊖ | The Mazda2 subcompact is a five-door hatchback with a 1.5-liter four-cylinder engine. A five-speed manual transmission is standard, and a four-speed automatic is optional. Handling is quite nimble, and the ride is tolerable, but the cabin is noisy. Rear-seat room is relatively good. **Jan. 2011** |
| | **Mazda3** | ⊖ | An all-new Mazda3 is on sale, with two four-cylinder engines, six-speed manual and automatic transmissions, and a braking system that stores energy to power the car's electrical system. A novel heads-up display is optional. |
| ✓ | **Mazda5** | ⊜ | The Mazda5 microvan is a compact wagon that seats six. Its 2.5-liter four-cylinder engine can be overtaxed on hills or when carrying a full load. Elevated noise levels make it feel less substantial than some larger alternatives. On the other hand, it is agile and fun to drive and has good visibility. **Dec. 2011** |
| ✓ | **Mazda6** | ⊖ | The Mazda6 is sporty, stylish, and delivered an impressive 32 mpg overall from the 2.5-liter four-cylinder. The six-speed automatic is smooth and responsive. We found the 6 agile and capable in the corners. The ride is steady but on the firm side, especially at low speeds. A diesel engine is available. **Jun. 2013** |
| ✓ | **Mercedes-Benz C-Class** | ⊖ | Mercedes' small sedan is agile, quiet, and comfortable. The front seats are excellent; the rear is a little tight. The punchy turbo four-cylinder in the C250 is very smooth and returned 24 mpg overall. Other engines include stronger V6s and a 450-hp V8. All-wheel drive is available only with the 3.0-liter V6. **Aug. 2012** |
| | **Mercedes-Benz CLA** | New | The new CLA is a compact, swoopy FWD sedan that starts at under $30,000. Power comes from a new 208-hp, 2.0-liter turbo four-cylinder mated to a seven-speed automated manual. An all-wheel-drive version will also be available for about $3,000 more. |
| | **Mercedes-Benz CLS** | NA | The CLS is a coupe-like four-door sedan with a swoopy roof and seating for just four passengers. Rear-seat room is tight, and the angle of the roof limits head room. The sedan is luxurious and comfortable, with strong performance and agile handling. |
| ✓ | **Mercedes-Benz E-Class** | ⊖ | The E-Class is very quiet and fit and finish is impressive. But the steering lacks communication. The 3.5-liter V6 is smooth and quiet, and mated to a seven-speed automatic. A four-cylinder diesel is new. Handling is capable and secure. The seats are comfortable and supportive. **Dec. 2012** |

| | Model | Predicted reliability | Description/with last road-test date |
|---|---|---|---|
| | **Mercedes-Benz GL-Class** | New | This seven-passenger SUV has a luxurious interior and roomy third row, with the most comfortable ride of any SUV we've tested. Handling is responsive but very clumsy at the limit. We got 20 mpg overall from the turbodiesel V6; three turbo V8s are available and all use a seven-speed automatic. **Oct. 2013** |
| ✔ | **Mercedes-Benz GLK-Class** | ○ | The GLK's 3.5-liter V6 delivers quick acceleration and 21 mpg overall. It rides well, except on rough pavement. Handling is fairly nimble. The high seating position gives a good view out. While the front seats are firm, rear leg room is stingy. A four-cylinder diesel is also available. **May 2013** |
| | **Mercedes-Benz M-Class** | ◒ | The M-Class has a smooth, powerful gasoline V6, as well as a turbodiesel V6, a V8, and an AMG version. Handling is responsive but let down by vague steering. The ride is firm, but steady and supple. It has an impressively quiet cabin and meticulous fit and finish. **Jun. 2012** |
| | **Mercedes-Benz S-Class** | New | A new S-Class debuted with a powerful 4.6-liter turbo V8 as the base engine. A 5.5-liter turbo S63 AMG 4Matic version will be available in a few months. The new car brings a whole host of advanced technology. |
| | **Mercedes-Benz SL** | New | The latest SL uses a 4.6-liter turbo V8 instead of the previous 5.4-liter. A start-stop system that shuts the engine off at stops saves some gas. It looks a lot like the old two-seat roadster with its retractable hardtop. But it's slightly longer and wider. It is full of new high-tech features and safety equipment. |
| | **Mercedes-Benz SLK** | NA | The SLK is fun with its energetic four-cylinder and a six-speed manual. This combination returned 26 mpg overall in our tests. A V6 and seven-speed automatic are available. The ride is firm but civilized, and the narrow cabin is well finished. **Jun. 2013** |
| ✔ | **Mini Cooper** | ○ | Agile handling and quick, precise steering make the Mini fun to drive, but the ride is choppy. The base engine has adequate response, but the turbo engine in the S is quicker. Rear-seat room is tight and most controls are confusing to use. Fuel economy ranges from 29 to 33 mpg depending on the version. **Sep. 2008** |
| | **Mini Cooper Countryman** | ● | The four-door Countryman is still a small car. The quirky interior has four well shaped, comfortable seats. The quick steering and fantastic agility make it fun to drive. But the controls are frustrating and the ride is choppy. Power comes from a 1.6-liter four-cylinder engine. The S version offers all-wheel-drive. **Jan. 2012** |
| | **Mini Paceman** | New | The Mini family expands with the addition of the Paceman, essentially a two-door version of the Countryman. The Paceman four-seater offers a 1.6-liter four-cylinder with front-wheel drive, but all-wheel-drive versions get a more powerful turbo four-cylinder and the JCW version an even stronger version. |
| | **Mitsubishi i-MiEV** | NA | The electric i-MiEV uses a 16 kwh lithium-ion battery and takes 6-7 hours to charge on a 240-volt charger, or 21 hours on a 110-volt charger. We got about 56 miles on a charge. Although it is one of the cheapest all-electric cars available, the trade-off is that it's slow, clumsy, stiff riding, and Spartan inside. **Mar. 2013** |
| | **Mitsubishi Lancer** | NA | Overall the Lancer is unimpressive. While agile, with a decent ride, its 2.0-liter engine is sluggish and moans at high revs. Fuel economy is uncompetitive. The interior is furnished with drab plastics and subpar fit and finish. **Oct. 2007** |

| | Model | Predicted reliability | Description/with last road-test date |
|---|---|---|---|
| | **Mitsubishi Mirage** | New | Mitsubishi's new four-door hatchback subcompact will have fuel economy rated at 37/44 mpg city/highway and 40 mpg combined, thanks to a tiny 74-hp, three-cylinder engine with a CVT. A five-speed manual will be available. The Mirage will come with a long list of standard and optional equipment. |
| | **Mitsubishi Outlander** | ⊖ | With its tight, kids-only third-row seat the Outlander is the only small SUV with seating for seven. But that can't offset its many shortcomings. It handles clumsily, the ride is fairly stiff, and the engine's sluggish acceleration is accompanied by raucous noise. Overall, we see little reason to consider the Outlander. **Oct. 2013** |
| ✔ | **Mitsubishi Outlander Sport** | ⊜ | Despite the name the Outlander Sport is not fun to drive. It has limited rear-seat and cargo space. Handling isn't particularly nimble and acceleration from the 2.0-liter engine is adequate at best. All-wheel drive bumps the price up to where it competes with many better SUVs. **Mar. 2011** |
| ✔ | **Nissan Altima** | ⊖ | The Altima is a well-rounded, roomy sedan that delivers excellent fuel economy with its four-cylinder. Both the revised 2.5-liter four-cylinder and the carryover 3.5-liter V6 use a CVT that works well. Handling is rather ordinary, though ultimately secure. Blind-spot and lane-departure warnings are available. **Dec. 2012** |
| | **Nissan Armada** | ● | This large SUV has seating for eight. It is quick, thanks to its smooth-revving but noisy 5.6-liter V8 and slick five-speed automatic. Handling is relatively responsive, but the ride is quite stiff. Interior quality is so-so. It is difficult for children to reach the high-mounted exterior rear-door handles. **Jun. 2012** |
| | **Nissan Cube** | ○ | This small car holds five passengers in a surprisingly roomy interior. It's powered by a 1.8-liter four-cylinder engine mated to either a CVT or a six-speed manual. Handling is rather clumsy and the steering is vague. Wind and road noise are pronounced. Fit and finish is on the cheap side. **Nov. 2009** |
| ✔ | **Nissan Frontier** | ⊖ | We found the Frontier quick and nimble, with a stiff but tolerable ride. The powerful 4.0-liter V6 revs smoothly. Base models use a 2.5-liter four-cylinder. Rear-seat room is tight in the crew cab. A longer bed is a new option. **Jul. 2005** |
| ✔ | **Nissan Juke** | ○ | The funky-looking Juke has the raised ride height and optional all-wheel drive of an SUV but the steeply raked rear quarter of a hatchback. Power comes from a 1.6-liter turbo four-cylinder. A six-speed manual is available on front-wheel-drive models; the AWD versions employ a CVT. **Mar. 2011** |
| ✔ | **Nissan Leaf** | ⊜ | The Leaf five-seat, electric-powered hatchback has a 75-mile typical range. A full charge from a 220-volt home outlet takes 6 hours, or twice as long on a 110-volt outlet. At low speeds the Leaf feels quick and it is quiet and rides comfortably. Cabin access is easy, and the rear seat is fairly roomy. **Nov. 2011** |
| ✔ | **Nissan Maxima** | ⊖ | The highlight of the Maxima is its smooth, powerful 3.5-liter V6 that is mated to a CVT. Acceleration is very quick. The steering is overly light at low speeds and firms up rather abruptly, which takes away from the car's handling. The ride is comfortable enough and the cabin is quiet. **Feb. 2009** |

**Ratings Key** Better ⟷ Worse: ⊜ ⊖ ○ ◒ ●    ✔ **Recommended**

| | Model | Predicted reliability | Description/with last road-test date |
|---|---|---|---|
| ✓ | **Nissan Murano** | ⊖ | The Murano has a nice, quiet interior and a comfortable ride. The 3.5-liter V6 is powerful and delivers a respectable 19 mpg overall. The CVT is one of the best on the market. Handling remains responsive and secure. The interior is stylish and functional. But the limited rear visibility is a notable drawback. **Sep. 2008** |
| | **Nissan Pathfinder** | New | The Pathfinder's third-row seat is tight, but access is possible even with a child seat in the second row. The ride is comfortable enough, but handling lacks agility. Power comes from a 3.5-liter V6. The cabin is quiet and spacious, and the controls are fairly easy to master. A hybrid version is available. **May 2013** |
| ✓ | **Nissan Quest** | ⊖ | The Quest is a luxurious minivan, with a plush and quiet interior and a supple, compliant ride. Just don't expect sporty handling to go with its smooth and powerful 3.5-liter V6. The top-line LE version comes with a blind-spot warning system and a power-folding third-row seat. **Dec. 2011** |
| ✓ | **Nissan Rogue** | ⊖ | Based on the old Sentra sedan, the outgoing small Nissan Rogue SUV is compact, pleasant, and competitive in its class. The 170-hp, 2.5-liter engine gets a bit raspy at high revs. The ride is supple and handling is fairly nimble and secure. A redesign, with an optional third-row seat, is coming out in late fall. **Aug. 2008** |
| | **Nissan Sentra** | New | In our test of the roomy redesigned Sentra we got 29 mpg overall from the noisy 1.8-liter four-cylinder and CVT. The car feels underpowered and is obnoxiously loud. The ride seems compliant at first, but it's jumpy and abrupt over pavement imperfections. Handling lacks agility but is secure at its limits. **May 2013** |
| | **Nissan Titan** | ● | The Titan is powerful and has a comfortable ride. It's relatively agile and the cabin is large. The engine is strong but loud. The cargo bed is smaller than competing trucks, but the payload capacity, once meager, has been increased. **May 2012** |
| | **Nissan Versa** | ● | Nissan's subcompact Versa sedan is disappointing, with a noisy and cheap interior. The engine drones as revs increase, and the CVT accentuates engine noise. Handling lacks agility. The ride is compliant but jumpy. The rear cabin is relatively roomy and fuel economy is commendable at 32 mpg overall. **May 2012** |
| | **Nissan Versa Note** | New | The Note is the new hatchback version of the Versa sedan. Nissan claims best-in-class cargo space and fuel economy, with a rating of 31 mpg city, 40 mpg highway, and 35 mpg combined. Power comes from a 1.6-liter, four-cylinder engine mated to a CVT transmission. Pricing starts at $13,990. |
| | **Nissan Xterra** | ○ | The Xterra has good off-road capability and is relatively civilized on the road. The 4.0-liter V6 delivers quick acceleration but just 17 mpg. The 4WD system is still part-time. The interior looks rugged and is well-assembled. **Aug. 2005** |
| ✓ | **Nissan Z** | ⊖ | The Z two-seater uses a wonderfully strong and smooth V6. The six-speed manual shifter is a bit notchy but is easy to use. Its well finished, upscale interior is a relatively enjoyable place to be, but road and tire noise are constant and the cabin is cramped. A convertible version is also available. **Oct. 2009** |

**Ratings Key** **Better** ⟵⟶ **Worse** ⊜ ⊖ ○ ◒ ●   ✓ **Recommended**

| | Model | Predicted reliability | Description/with last road-test date |
|---|---|---|---|
| | **Porsche 911** | NA | The 911 offers a variety of powerful engines, but the base 3.4-liter six-cylinder boxer and the 3.8-liter six-cylinder in the Carrera S, both matched to a seven-speed manual transmission, easily get the job done. Features to help with fuel efficiency include automatic engine start-stop and electro-hydraulic power steering. |
| | **Porsche Boxster** | New | The Boxster's 2.7-liter six-cylinder is very responsive and the six-speed manual is smooth and crisp. Handling is still excellent despite some loss of steering feedback, and the ride is not punishing. It's a tremendous car to drive, and the S version is even more powerful. A seven-speed automatic is optional. **Jun. 2013** |
| | **Porsche Cayenne** | ◒ | The midsized Cayenne is a very sporty, agile SUV, with gas, diesel, and hybrid engines. All use a supersmooth eight-speed automatic. The ride is supple and steady, but stiff at low speeds. The front and rear seats are comfortable. Interior fit and finish is impeccable, but the controls are confusing. **Feb. 2011** |
| | **Porsche Cayman** | New | Based on the Boxster, the Cayman uses the same midmounted, 2.7-liter, flat-six engine. The higher-performance Cayman S has a 3.4-liter, six-cylinder engine. The fixed-roof coupe seats two passengers and uses a hatchback design that brings more rear storage area than the Boxster has. |
| | **Porsche Panamera** | NA | Porsche's four-door luxury car delivers strong performance, with comfort for four adults. Handling is agile, capable, and enjoyable, with excellent steering and lots of cornering grip. The ride is firm. The luxurious interior is dominated by a button-filled center stack for radio, climate, and other controls. **Nov. 2012** |
| ☑ | **Ram 1500** | ○ | The Ram combines full-size truck capabilities with a cushioned ride, competent handling, and a luxuriously quiet cabin. The best powertrain choice is probably the effortless 5.7-liter V8 and new slick eight-speed automatic. The conventional V6 is also good. A V6 diesel, the first for this class, arrives soon. **Nov. 2013** |
| | **Scion FR-S** | ◒ | Developed with Subaru, the FR-S features a 2.0-liter four-cylinder and a choice of a six-speed manual or automatic. It has super-agile handling and good balance at its limits. In corners the car turns in promptly with virtually no body lean. The steering is well weighted, with decent feedback. **Oct. 2012** |
| | **Scion iQ** | NA | The tiny iQ four-seat hatchback is slow, noisy, and uncomfortable. Its few pluses include nimbleness, ease of parking, and a very good 34-mpg overall. Several similarly priced competitors are just as economical and much better cars. **Aug. 2012** |
| | **Scion tC** | NA | The tC's 2.5-liter engine got a very good 28 mpg overall with the six-speed manual. An automatic is available. It's fairly nimble and pleasing to drive and the cabin is relatively spacious. However, the ride, build quality, and visibility are so-so. The newly revised tC may be better. **May 2011** |
| ☑ | **Scion xB** | ⊜ | The xB's 2.4-liter, four-cylinder delivers good performance but returns just 23 mpg overall. The ride is compliant, and handling is responsive. The radio controls are a bit confusing. The rear seat and cargo area are enormous and cabin access is easy. Low windows and thick roof pillars hurt visibility. **Oct. 2007** |

| | Model | Predicted reliability | Description/with last road-test date |
|---|---|---|---|
| ☑ | **Scion xD** | ⊜ | The small xD is nimble, but has a jittery, unsettled ride. The 1.8-liter four-cylinder delivers only adequate performance, but a miserly 29 mpg overall with the automatic and 34 with the manual. The cabin is noisy and the driving position is awkward, particularly for taller drivers. The rear is roomy for two adults. **Jun. 2008** |
| | **Smart ForTwo** | NA | This tiny two-seater features a 1.0-liter, three-cylinder engine that does a decent job putting along with traffic. We measured 39 mpg overall. The Smart has a harsh ride, clumsy handling, and an automated manual transmission that shifts slowly, causing the car to pause and heave. Cabin access is easy. **Nov. 2008** |
| | **Subaru BRZ** | ● | Developed with Toyota, the BRZ features a 2.0-liter four-cylinder and a six-speed manual or automatic. It has super-agile handling and good balance at its limits. In corners the car turns in promptly with virtually no body lean. The steering is well weighted, with decent feedback. **Oct. 2012** |
| ☑ | **Subaru Forester** | ⊖ | The 2014 redesign brought easy access, great sight lines, abundant interior space, simple controls, and impressive fuel economy. The ride is OK but could be better, and handling isn't very agile. The infotainment system is rudimentary. **Jul. 2013** |
| ☑ | **Subaru Impreza** | ⊜ | The Impreza has a very absorbent and controlled ride. Handling is responsive and secure. Acceleration is good, and fuel economy of 27 mpg overall for the sedan is impressive given the standard AWD. The CVT exacerbates engine noise. **May 2012** |
| ☑ | **Subaru Impreza WRX/STi** | ○ | The WRX has a powerful turbo engine, a well-tuned suspension, and standard AWD. The STi is more powerful and sportier. Look for a redesigned WRX in spring 2014. **Oct. 2009** |
| ☑ | **Subaru Legacy** | ⊖ | The Legacy is a roomy sedan that rides and handles well and gets good fuel economy. But ride quality isn't impressive. The 2.5-liter four-cylinder engine now gets 26 mpg overall. The CVT accentuates engine noise, particularly on the highway. The 3.6-liter six-cylinder uses a five-speed automatic. **Feb. 2013** |
| ☑ | **Subaru Outback** | ⊜ | The Outback's updated 2.5-liter four-cylinder engine now produces 173 hp. It got 24 mpg overall in our tests with the CVT. Suspension tweaks made the ride considerably stiffer, but did tidy up the sloppy on-limit handling a bit. The 3.6-liter six-cylinder and five-speed automatic are carried over. **Dec. 2012** |
| | **Subaru Tribeca** | NA | The Tribeca has an impressive ride and handling balance. The six-cylinder engine and automatic make a decent powertrain. But the second- and third-row seats are cramped. It's a long reach to the navigation system's touch screen. The styling makes some controls difficult to see. **Jan. 2008** |
| ☑ | **Subaru XV Crosstrek** | ⊖ | Mechanically the same as the Impreza, the Crosstrek has an eight-inch higher ride height. The cabin is rather noisy, the ride is stiff, and the four-cylinder has to work hard, but fuel economy is a gratifying 26 mpg. The quieter and cheaper Impreza hatch makes more sense. A hybrid is now on sale. **Feb. 2013** |
| | **Tesla Model S** | New | The Model S is a super agile, quick, and quiet luxury hatchback. With its largest available battery, range varies from about 180 to 225 miles, depending on the weather. A huge iPad-like center screen controls almost all accessory functions. Demerits include tight access and a restricted view out. **Jul. 2013** |

| | Model | Predicted reliability | Description/with last road-test date |
|---|---|---|---|
| | **Toyota 4Runner** | ⊜ | The 4Runner is good for towing and off-roading, but is not the best family vehicle. The rough-sounding 4.0-liter V6 is powerful and relatively fuel-efficient. The ride is unsettled and handling is mediocre at best. A Trail version is meant for serious off-road use. Only Limited trims get full-time 4WD. **Dec. 2010** |
| ✓ | **Toyota Avalon** | ⊖ | The Avalon's redesign brought mixed results. It's still a very good car, with a spacious, comfortable, and well-equipped interior. But the excellent ride has been stiffened too much on models with the 18-inch wheel package. Handling has been sharpened, but the controls are complicated. **Jul. 2013** |
| ✓ | **Toyota Camry** | ⊜ | The Camry is refined, comfortable, and roomy. Handling is relatively responsive and interior materials are good overall. Fuel economy for all three engines is impressive. Bluetooth is standard, and Toyota's Entune smartphone integration is available. **Feb. 2012** |
| | **Toyota Corolla** | ⊖ | The redesigned 2014 Corolla has a lengthened wheelbase for a more spacious interior. Most versions get the 1.8-liter four-cylinder. The new Eco version is claimed to get more than 40 mpg on the highway. Upper trim levels will benefit from a new CVT, and a six-speed manual is available. |
| | **Toyota FJ Cruiser** | ⊜ | The FJ is superb off road. But visibility is compromised by the thick roof pillars and small windows, and the rear doors are awkward to use. The V6 gets just 17 mpg. The FJ scores too low in our testing to be recommended. **Jan. 2007** |
| ✓ | **Toyota Highlander** | ⊜ | The Highlander has a cushy ride and a comfortable cabin. The 3.5-liter V6 delivers solid performance and 18 mpg overall. A 2.7-liter four-cylinder is available on FWD versions. The Hybrid got an impressive 27 mpg overall. A redesign arrives in early 2014. **Jan. 2008** |
| | **Toyota Land Cruiser** | NA | Toyota's Land Cruiser is quick, quiet, comfortable, and refined, but not agile. It rides very nicely and the interior is roomy and well finished. Off-road performance is terrific, partly because its crawl mode helps navigate steep slopes. **Dec. 2008** |
| ✓ | **Toyota Prius** | ⊜ | The Prius averaged 44 mpg overall in our tests and can quietly propel itself on electric power up to 25 mph. The ride is firm yet steady, and handling is sound and secure although not particularly agile. The interior is roomy but some controls take a bit of getting used to. **Nov. 2009** |
| | **Toyota Prius C** | ⊜ | The Prius C is a smaller and less expensive Prius. It gets 43 mpg overall, 1 mpg less than the regular Prius. Its harsh ride, noisy engine and cabin, and slow acceleration resulted in a road test score too low for us to recommend the car. **Jul. 2012** |
| ✓ | **Toyota Prius V** | ⊖ | This Prius wagon has a very roomy rear seat and a generous cargo area. The extra weight and a less aerodynamic shape take a small toll on fuel economy, but the V still got an excellent 41 mpg overall in our tests. It drives similarly to the standard Prius, but rear visibility is better than the smaller car's. **Mar. 2012** |

**Ratings Key** Better ⟵⟶ Worse: ⊜ ⊖ ○ ◒ ●    ✓ **Recommended**

| | Model | Predicted reliability | Description/with last road-test date |
|---|---|---|---|
| ✓ | **Toyota RAV4** | ⊖ | The latest RAV4 has a smooth 2.5-liter four-cylinder and six-speed automatic that got 24 mpg overall with AWD. Handling is nimble and the ride is firm and settled. Inside the cabin are clear controls, but a number of cheap details are still apparent. A rear-view camera is standard. **Jun. 2013** |
| ✓ | **Toyota Sequoia** | ⊜ | In our tests, the eight-passenger Sequoia returned 15 mpg overall with the 5.7-liter V8 and six-speed automatic. Rear-wheel and selectable full-time 4WD are available. The third-row seat folds flat. The ride is firm, and handling is clumsy but secure. The interior is very roomy. **Nov. 2008** |
| ✓ | **Toyota Sienna** | ⊖ | The Sienna rides comfortably, but handling is lackluster. The V6 returned 20 mpg overall with the six-speed automatic. The AWD version is a bit quicker and sacrifices just 1 mpg. Interior fit and finish is mediocre and the cabin is noisy. **Sep. 2010** |
| | **Toyota Tacoma** | ○ | The Tacoma has competitive fuel economy, but clumsy handling makes it a chore to drive. The 4.0-liter V6 provides strong performance but is noisy. Its constantly jiggly ride is fatiguing. The cabin's high floor and low roof makes access tricky and the driving position is too low and uncomfortable. **May 2012** |
| ✓ | **Toyota Tundra** | ⊖ | The Tundra has relatively responsive handling, but the ride with the TRD package is stiff. The 5.7-liter V8 is very powerful. The tailgate is easy to raise and lower. A 4.6-liter V8 is also available. 2014 brings some exterior and interior updates. **Sep. 2007** |
| ✓ | **Toyota Venza** | ⊖ | The Venza fits in between a station wagon and a SUV. Assets include easy cabin access, a quiet interior, and a roomy rear seat. The rear hatch and large cargo floor aid cargo flexibility. The refined 3.5-liter V6 engine provides plenty of power. A 2.7-liter four-cylinder engine is available. **Jun. 2009** |
| | **Toyota Yaris** | NA | Toyota's least expensive car has excellent fuel economy of 32 mpg overall and a relatively roomy rear seat. But it is very Spartan and noisy inside, with an awkward driving position. The Yaris scores too low to be recommended. **May 2012** |
| | **Volkswagen Beetle** | ● | While roomy and decent to drive, the Beetle suffers from cost-cutting. The ride is compliant but unsettled. Handling is responsive but sloppy in demanding conditions. The standard five-cylinder engine sounds gruff and unrefined. Wind noise is excessive, and rear visibility is limited. **Jul. 2012** |
| ✓ | **Volkswagen CC** | ○ | Stylish and sleek, the CC is a four-door coupe with agile handling. Power comes from a responsive turbocharged four-cylinder, which returned 26 mpg overall, or a strong V6. The ride is good and cabin finish is first-rate. But the rear seat is tight. All-wheel drive is optional. **Nov. 2012** |
| ✓ | **Volkswagen Eos** | ○ | The Eos' folding metal hard top offers a sunroof-only position. Power comes from a 2.0-liter, turbo four-cylinder, which delivers strong acceleration and a good 25 mpg overall. The DSG automated manual is smooth and shifts quickly. **May 2008** |
| ✓ | **Volkswagen Golf** | ⊖ | The Golf is agile, with responsive steering. Its 2.5-liter five-cylinder gets a mediocre 24 mpg overall, while the manual diesel got an impressive 38 mpg. The ride is supple and controlled. Interior quality is impressive. The front seats are supportive, but the rear is cramped. A redesign arrives in 2014. **Mar. 2010** |

| | Model | Predicted reliability | Description/with last road-test date |
|---|---|---|---|
| | **Volkswagen GTI** | ● | The GTI is agile and quick, with a gutsy turbo 2.0-liter four-cylinder that sounds good, all of which make it fun to drive but not at the expense of comfort. A redesign arrives in 2014. **May 2010** |
| ✔ | **Volkswagen Jetta** | ○ | The Jetta sedan's handling lacks agility and interior fit and finish is unimpressive, but the rear seat is roomy. The TDI diesel gets an impressive 34 mpg overall but the DSG transmission is jerky at low speeds. The hybrid gets 37 mpg overall. The sporty GLI is quick, agile, and enjoyable to drive. **Oct. 2011** |
| ✔ | **Volkswagen Jetta SportWagen** | ○ | The Jetta wagon has a quiet, composed ride and responsive handling, but it is less agile than the similar Golf hatchback. Acceleration is a bit leisurely with the diesel, but with readily available power at low revs most will find it adequate. **Jan. 2011** |
| ✔ | **Volkswagen Passat** | ⊖ | The Passat offers lots of room. The base engine is a lackluster 2.5-liter five-cylinder. In our test the diesel got an impressive 37 mpg overall. A powerful 3.6-liter V6 is available. The Passat is quiet and rides comfortably, with responsive handling, but the car falls short on grip when pushed to its limits. **Feb. 2012** |
| ✔ | **Volkswagen Tiguan** | ○ | The Tiguan has a roomy rear seat and excellent fit and finish. Handling is agile and secure. The ride can be stiff with the low profile tires. The turbo four-cylinder is smooth and strong, and it yielded 21 mpg overall in our tests. AWD is available. **Mar. 2012** |
| | **Volkswagen Touareg** | ● | This agile, solid, and well-finished SUV has comfortable seats and a plush interior. The V6 diesel and eight-speed automatic returned 24 mpg overall in our tests. The cabin is quiet, and access is easy. A hybrid is the top-of-the-line version. **Jun. 2011** |
| ✔ | **Volvo S60** | ○ | The S60's five-cylinder can sound gruff but provides lively acceleration and respectable fuel economy. The ride is taut and steady. The top-level AWD T6 is agile and refined. The interior is quiet and nicely laid out, and the front seats are comfortable, although the rear is tight and the trunk is small. **Jul. 2011** |
| | **Volvo S80** | ⊖ | The S80 doesn't deliver the performance or luxury expected in this class. Rear-seat room is cramped and rear access is compromised. FWD S80s get a 3.2-liter six-cylinder, which delivered 20 mpg overall in our testing. A turbocharged six-cylinder is available on the AWD version. **Nov. 2007** |
| ✔ | **Volvo XC60** | ○ | The XC60 SUV is pleasant to drive but not very sporty. The ride is a little stiff, but handling is responsive and secure at its limits. Wind and road noise are well suppressed. The interior is nicely finished with high-quality materials. The seats are nicely shaped and comfortable but rear leg room is a bit tight. **Sep. 2009** |
| ✔ | **Volvo XC70** | ⊖ | The XC70 AWD wagon has a raised ride height. The pleasant 3.2-liter six-cylinder and six-speed automatic deliver adequate performance, but got just 18 mpg. A more powerful, turbocharged engine is available. The ride is fairly stiff, and handling is secure. Inside, the cabin is quiet and nicely trimmed. **Sep. 2008** |
| | **Volvo XC90** | ◒ | The best features of the outdated XC90 include a flexible interior, seven-passenger seating, and impressive safety features. An adequate 3.2-liter six-cylinder is standard. The ride is stiff and unsettled, and handling, although secure, lacks agility. **Jun. 2012** |

**Ratings Key** Better ⟵⟶ Worse: ⊜ ⊖ ○ ◒ ●   ✔ **Recommended**

# USED CARS: THE MOST RELIABLE MODELS & THE ONES TO AVOID

**BEST OF THE BEST** These are the top used sedans, wagons, and SUVs available in four different price ranges. Each performed well in our testing when they were new and have been consistently reliable over time. All of them come with standard Electronic Stability Control (ESC) during the model years listed. **WORST OF THE WORST** These are used-cars that have had multiple years of much-worse-than-average reliability among the 2003-2012 models. All of the vehicles are listed alphabetically.

## Best of the Best

### Less than $10,000

**>SMALL CARS**

**Pontiac Vibe 2009** This sensible wagon's 2009 redesign brought standard ESC and stronger, more fuel-efficient engines. A twin of the Toyota Matrix, it has a flat load floor. Pontiac's demise means you can find the Vibe at a cheap price.

**>SEDANS**

**Hyundai Sonata (4-cyl.) 2008 and Acura TSX 2004** The economical and efficient Sonata has a decent ride, secure handling, and a four-cylinder that returned 23 mpg overall. The TSX is a more upscale and sportier alternative.

**>SUVs**

**Toyota RAV4 (4-cyl.) 2004** The RAV4 was redesigned in 2001, but it wasn't until 2004 that it got standard antilock brakes and ESC. It has nimble handling, good brakes, easy cabin access, and a strong engine. 21 mpg overall is decent for an AWD SUV.

### $10,000-$15,000

**>SMALL CARS**

**Honda Fit 2011 and Mazda3 2011** The Fit is an excellent choice among hatchbacks. It has amazing space utilization; responsive, agile handling; and an efficient four-cylinder that returns 30 mpg overall with an automatic transmission. For a bit more refinement, look for a Mazda3 hatchback or sedan.

**>SEDANS**

**Honda Accord (V6) 2006-07 and Acura TL 2005-06** An excellent choice among used cars, the Accord's smooth V6 is economical and strong, the ride is comfortable and compliant, and reliability is excellent. The four-cylinder version is nice but didn't get ESC until 2008. A more luxurious option is the Acura TL.

**>SMALL SUVs**

**Toyota RAV4 (4-cyl.) 2006-08 and Honda CR-V 2005-07** The 2006 RAV4 gained more interior room, a V6, and an optional third-row seat. The four-cylinder has nimble handling, very good 23 mpg overall, and a versatile cabin. The CR-V is a sportier, if somewhat noisier, alternative.

**>MIDSIZED/LARGE SUVs**

**Toyota Highlander (V6)**

Honda Fit 2011

**2004-07 and Infiniti FX 2003-04**
The Highlander is quiet and comfortable. We got 19 mpg overall with the V6. The interior is roomy and the controls are easy to use. A third-row seat was optional and a hybrid version was added in 2006. The Infiniti FX is a sportier two-row alternative.

### $15,000-$20,00

**>SMALL CARS**
**Toyota Prius 2010-11 and Hyundai Elantra (sedan) 2011-12**
At 44 mpg overall, the Prius delivers the best gas mileage of any non-plug-in, five-passenger vehicle. The 2010 redesign brought more room, better brakes, and sound but not agile handling. For a more enjoyable driving experience, look for a Hyundai Elantra sedan.

**>SEDANS**
**Toyota Camry (4-cyl.) 2010-12 and Infiniti M 2006-07**
Expect impressive 26 to 27 mpg overall with the four-cylinder Camry in addition to a roomy cabin and superb reliability. If a powerful engine and luxurious interior move you, opt for the Infiniti M V6.

**>SUVs**
**Honda Pilot 2007-08 and Mazda CX-9 2009**
The Pilot combines a roomy cabin, good driving dynamics, seating for eight, and respectable fuel economy in a package that isn't too big to fit in your garage. But road noise is a bit pronounced. The CX-9 is more agile and has a roomier third-row seat.

### $20,000-$25,000

**>SEDANS**
**BMW 328i 2009, Infiniti G 2009, and Toyota Avalon 2010**
The 3 Series combines agile handling, a taut ride, good brakes, and powerful six-cylinder engines in a comfortable, if slightly snug, interior. The Infiniti G is a similarly sporty alternative. Look for the Toyota Avalon if you want a roomy interior and lots of comfort.

**>SUVs**
**Acura MDX 2007-08 and Lexus RX 2008**
The Acura MDX is a well-rounded, family-friendly SUV. It has a strong and refined V6 powertrain that gets 17 mpg overall, a firm but pleasant ride, a well-appointed cabin, comfortable front seats, and a third-row seat. The Lexus RX is a smaller two-row option that's quieter inside.

Acura MDX 2007

## Worst of the Worst

BMW 7 Series
BMW X5 (6-cyl.)
Chevrolet Uplander
Chrysler PT Cruiser
Chrysler Town & Country
Dodge Caravan
Dodge Grand Caravan
Dodge Journey
Dodge Ram 2500 (diesel)
Ford Explorer (V6, 4WD)
Ford F-250 (diesel)
GMC Acadia
Jeep Wrangler (4-door)
Kia Sorento (V6)
Mercedes-Benz GL-Class
Mini Cooper S
Nissan Armada
Saturn Outlook
Saturn Relay
Volkswagen Touareg

# RELIABLE USED CARS FOR EVERY BUDGET

As owners hold on to their vehicles longer, fewer late-model used cars are available for sale. The result: higher prices and a limited supply of reliable vehicles that have low miles. But there are still a large number of good buys to be found. These lists show 2003 through 2012 vehicles, in four price categories, that tested well when new and have had above-average reliability. Try to buy the newest vehicle that your budget allows so that you can get the most up-to-date safety features. To help, we show the first year each model offered electronic stability control (ESC), a proven lifesaver, as a standard or optional feature.

| Make & model | Under $10,000 | $10,000-$15,000 | $15,000-$20,000 | $20,000-$25,000 | ESC ('03-12) | |
|---|---|---|---|---|---|---|
| | | | | | Opt. from | Std. from |
| **SMALL CARS** | | | | | | |
| Ford Focus (hatchback/wagon) | '05-07 | – | – | – | '03, '09 | '10 |
| Ford Focus (sedan) | '05, '07-08 | '09-11 | – | – | '03, '09 | '10 |
| Honda Civic (sedan) | '03-07 | '08-11 | – | – | '09 | '12 |
| Honda Fit | '07-08 | '09-11 | '12 | – | '09 | '11 |
| Hyundai Elantra (sedan) | '07-08 | '09-10 | '11-12 | – | '08 | '11 |
| Kia Forte | – | '10, '12 | – | – | – | all |
| Kia Soul | – | '10 | – | – | – | all |
| Mazda2 | – | '11 | – | – | – | all |
| Mazda3 | '06 | '08-11 | '12 | – | '07 | '11 |
| Nissan Leaf | – | – | '11 | – | – | all |
| Nissan Sentra | '06 | '09-10 | – | – | '10 | '11 |
| Pontiac Vibe | '03-09 | '10 | – | – | '05 | '09 |
| Scion xB | '04-06 | '08-11 | '12 | – | – | all |
| Scion xD | – | '08, '10 | – | – | '08 | '10 |
| Subaru Impreza (sedan, nonturbo) | – | '09 | '10-12 | – | '08 | '09 |
| Subaru Impreza (wagon, nonturbo) | '05-06 | '07-08 | '10-11 | '12 | '08 | '09 |
| Suzuki SX4 | '08 | – | – | – | '07 | '12 |
| Toyota Corolla | '03-08 | '09-11 | '12 | – | '05 | '10 |
| Toyota Matrix | '03-07 | '08-10 | – | – | '05 | '10 |
| Toyota Prius | '03-06 | '07-08 | '09-11 | '12 | '04 | '10 |

| Make & model | Under $10,000 | $10,000-$15,000 | $15,000-$20,000 | $20,000-$25,000 | ESC ('03-12) | |
|---|---|---|---|---|---|---|
| | | | | | Opt. from | Std. from |
| **SMALL CARS** continued | | | | | | |
| **Volkswagen Golf** | – | – | '10-12 | – | '03 | '10 |
| **Volkswagen Rabbit** | '07 | '09 | – | – | '07 | '09 |
| **MIDSIZED AND LARGE SEDANS** | | | | | | |
| **Acura RL** | '04 | '05 | '06-07 | '08 | – | all |
| **Acura TL** | – | '05-06 | '07-08 | '09 | '03 | '04 |
| **Acura TSX** | '04 | '05-07 | '08 | '10-11 | – | all |
| **Audi A6 (V6)** | – | '05-06 | '07 | – | – | all |
| **BMW 328i** | – | – | – | '09 | – | all |
| **Cadillac CTS (V6)** | – | – | – | '10 | '03 | '08 |
| **Cadillac DTS** | – | – | – | '10 | '03 | '08 |
| **Chevrolet Malibu (4-cyl.)** | – | '11 | '12 | – | '08 | '09 |
| **Ford Fusion (4-cyl.)** | '08 | '09 | '12 | – | '09 | '10 |
| **Ford Fusion (V6, FWD)** | '06-07 | '08-09 | – | – | '09 | '10 |
| **Ford Fusion Hybrid** | – | – | '10-11 | '12 | – | all |
| **Honda Accord (4-cyl.)** | '03-05 | '06-07 | '10-12 | – | – | '08 |
| **Honda Accord (V6)** | '03-04 | '05-07 | '11 | '12 | – | '06 |
| **Honda Accord Hybrid** | – | '05-07 | – | – | – | '06 |
| **Hyundai Azera** | – | '07 | – | '11 | – | all |
| **Hyundai Sonata (4-cyl.)** | '06, '08 | '09 | – | – | – | '06 |
| **Hyundai Sonata (V6)** | '05 | '08, '10 | – | – | – | '06 |
| **Infiniti G (sedan)** | – | '04-06 | '07-08 | '09 | – | '03 |
| **Infiniti M** | – | – | '06-07 | '08 | – | all |
| **Kia Optima (4-cyl.)** | – | – | '11 | – | '06 | '10 |
| **Lexus ES** | – | '03-06 | '07 | '08-09 | '03 | '07 |
| **Lexus GS** | – | '03-04 | '06 | '07 | – | all |
| **Lexus IS (sedan, RWD)** | '03 | '04-05 | '06-07 | '08-09 | '03 | '06 |
| **Lexus LS** | – | – | '03-05 | '06 | – | all |
| **Lincoln MKZ (FWD)** | – | '07-08 | '09-10 | '11 | – | '09 |
| **Mazda 6** | – | '08, '10-11 | – | – | '05 | '09 |
| **Mercedes-Benz C-Class (V6)** | – | '05, '07 | – | '08-09 | – | all |
| **Mercedes-Benz E-Class (sedan, V6)** | – | '03 | '07 | '08 | – | all |
| **Mercury Milan (4-cyl.)** | '08 | '09 | – | – | '09 | '10 |
| **Mercury Milan (V6, FWD)** | '06-08 | '09 | – | – | '09 | '10 |

| Make & model | Under $10,000 | $10,000-$15,000 | $15,000-$20,000 | $20,000-$25,000 | ESC ('03-12) Opt. from | Std. from |
|---|---|---|---|---|---|---|
| **MIDSIZED AND LARGE SEDANS** continued | | | | | | |
| **Mercury Milan Hybrid** | – | – | '10-11 | – | – | all |
| **Nissan Altima (4-cyl.)** | '05-06 | '07, '10 | '11-12 | – | – | '10 |
| **Nissan Altima (V6)** | – | '06-07 | '08, '10 | – | '07 | '10 |
| **Nissan Altima Hybrid** | – | '07-10 | – | – | – | all |
| **Nissan Maxima** | – | '08 | '09 | '10-12 | '04 | '09 |
| **Subaru Legacy (4-cyl.)** | – | '09 | '10-11 | '12 | '07 | '09 |
| **Toyota Avalon** | '03-04 | '05-07 | '08-09 | '10 | '03 | '09 |
| **Toyota Camry (4-cyl.)** | '03-06 | '07-09 | '10-12 | – | '05 | '10 |
| **Toyota Camry (V6)** | '03-05 | '06-08 | '09-11 | '12 | '03 | '10 |
| **Toyota Camry Hybrid** | | '07-08 | '09-11 | '12 | – | all |
| **Volvo S60** | '03 | '05-07 | – | – | '03 | '07 |
| **SPORTS AND SPORTY CARS/CONVERTIBLES** | | | | | | |
| **BMW 328Ci** | – | – | – | '08-09 | – | all |
| **BMW Z4** | – | '03-04 | '06 | '07 | – | all |
| **Chevrolet Corvette** | – | – | '03 | '04 | – | all |
| **Ford Mustang (V6)** | '03-04 | – | '10 | – | – | '10 |
| **Ford Mustang (V8)** | '04 | '05-06 | '07-08 | '10 | – | '10 |
| **Honda Civic Si** | – | – | '09-10 | – | – | '07 |
| **Honda S2000** | – | '03-04 | '05-07 | – | – | '06 |
| **Lexus SC** | – | – | '03-04 | – | – | all |
| **Mazda MX-5 Miata** | '03-04 | '06-07 | '08-09 | '11 | '06 | '12 |
| **Nissan 350Z** | – | '04, '06 | '07 | – | '03 | '10 |
| **Porsche Boxster** | – | – | '03 | '06 | – | all |
| **Scion tC** | '05 | '07-08 | – | – | – | '11 |
| **WAGONS AND MINIVANS** | | | | | | |
| **Honda Accord Crosstour** | – | – | – | '10-12 | – | all |
| **Subaru Outback (4-cyl.)** | – | – | '08-10 | '11 | '07 | '09 |
| **Subaru Outback (6-cyl.)** | – | – | – | '09-10 | '03 | '07 |
| **Toyota Sienna (FWD)** | '03 | '04-06 | '07-09 | '10-11 | '03 | '08 |
| **Toyota Venza (V6)** | – | – | | '09-10 | – | all |
| **Volvo XC70** | '04 | – | '08 | '09 | '03 | '07 |

| Make & model | Under $10,000 | $10,000-$15,000 | $15,000-$20,000 | $20,000-$25,000 | ESC ('03-12) | |
|---|---|---|---|---|---|---|
| | | | | | Opt. from | Std. from |
| **SMALL SUVs** | | | | | | |
| **Acura RDX** | – | – | '07-08 | – | – | all |
| **Ford Escape Hybrid** | '05-06 | – | '09 | '10-11 | – | '09 |
| **Honda CR-V** | '03-04 | '05-07 | '08-09 | '10-12 | – | '05 |
| **Hyundai Tucson** | – | '08 | '09 | – | – | all |
| **Kia Sportage** | '06 | '07 | '11 | '12 | – | '05 |
| **Mercury Mariner Hybrid** | '06 | | '09-10 | '11 | – | '09 |
| **Mitsubishi Outlander** | – | '07-09 | '11 | – | – | '07 |
| **Mitsubishi Outlander Sport** | – | '11 | – | – | – | all |
| **Nissan Rogue** | – | '09 | '10-12 | – | – | all |
| **Subaru Forester (nonturbo)** | – | – | '08-10 | '11 | '07 | '09 |
| **Subaru Forester (turbo)** | – | – | – | '10-11 | '07 | '09 |
| **Toyota RAV4 (4-cyl.)** | '03-04 | '05-08 | '09-11 | '12 | – | '04 |
| **Toyota RAV4 (V6)** | – | '08 | '09-11 | '12 | – | all |
| **MIDSIZED AND LARGE SUVs** | | | | | | |
| **Acura MDX** | – | '04-05 | '06 | '07-08 | – | '03 |
| **Honda Pilot** | '03 | '04-06 | '07-08 | '09 | '05 | '06 |
| **Infiniti FX** | – | '03-04 | '05-06 | '07-08 | – | all |
| **Lexus GX** | – | – | '03-04 | '05-07 | – | all |
| **Lexus RX** | – | '03 | '04-07 | '08 | – | all |
| **Lexus RX Hybrid** | – | – | '06 | 07-08 | – | all |
| **Mazda CX-9** | – | – | '09 | '10-11 | – | all |
| **Nissan Murano** | – | – | – | '11 | '03 | '09 |
| **Subaru B9 Tribeca** | – | '06 | '07 | – | – | '08 |
| **Toyota 4Runner (V6)** | | '03-05 | 06-07 | '08-09 | – | all |
| **Toyota Highlander (V6)** | '03 | '04-07 | – | '08-09 | '03 | '04 |
| **Toyota Highlander Hybrid** | – | '06 | '07 | '08 | – | all |
| **Toyota Sequoia** | – | '03-05 | '06 | – | – | all |
| **PICKUP TRUCKS** | | | | | | |
| **Honda Ridgeline** | – | – | '06-08 | '09-10 | – | all |
| **Nissan Frontier** | '03 | '04 | '09 | '11 | '03 | '12 |
| **Toyota Tacoma (V6, 4WD)** | – | '03 | '04-06 | '07-09 | '04 | '09 |
| **Toyota Tundra (V8, 4WD)** | – | '03-04 | '05-06 | '07 | '04 | '07 |

# USED CARS TO AVOID

**These 2003 to 2012 models have a record of below-average overall reliability. They're listed alphabetically by make and model.**

**Audi** A3 '06; A4 (4-cyl.) '03-06, '09; A6 (V6) '03, '10; Q5 (3.2) '09-10; S4 '11; TT '08

**BMW** 135i '08; 325Ci '06; 325i '03-06; 330Ci '06; 330i '03-04; 335Ci '08; 335i '07-08; 5 Series (6-cyl., nonturbo) '03, '06-08; 5 Series (V8) '07; 535i '08-10; 7 Series '06, '08, '12; X3 (turbo) '11-12; X5 (6-cyl.) '03, '05-06, '08, '11; Z4 '08

**Buick** Enclave '08-10; LaCrosse (4-cyl.) '12; LaCrosse (V6) '08-10, '12; Lucerne '09-10; Regal '11; Rendezvous '03, '05; Verano '12

**Cadillac** CTS (V6, AWD) '08-09; CTS (V6, RWD) '03, '05-06; CTS-V '11; DeVille '03-04; DTS '06; Escalade '07-08; SRX '04, '06-07, '09-10; STS '07-08

**Chevrolet** Astro '03; Avalanche '04-09; Aveo '07, '09; Blazer '03; Camaro '11; Cavalier '05; Cobalt '06-08; Colorado '09-12; Corvette '05, '09-10, '12; Cruze '11; Equinox (4-cyl.) '10-11; Equinox (V6) '05-06; HHR '06, '08-10; Impala '03-09, '12; Malibu (4-cyl.) '06-08; Malibu (V6) '03, '07-08; Monte Carlo '03; S-10 Pickup '03; Silverado 1500 (V6) '08; Silverado 1500 (V8, 2WD) '09; Silverado 1500 (V8, 4WD) '04-06, '10; Silverado 2500 (turbodiesel) '11-12; Suburban '04-09, '12; Tahoe '07-09; TrailBlazer (6-cyl.) '05-08; TrailBlazer (V8) '03, '06-07; Traverse '09; Uplander '05-08; Venture '05

Buick LaCrosse (2012)

**Chrysler** 200 Sedan '12; 300 (V8) '11; Pacifica '04, '06-08; PT Cruiser (nonturbo) '03-09; PT Cruiser (turbo) '03-06; Sebring Convertible '04, '06; Sebring Sedan '04-06; Town & Country '03-12; Voyager '03

**Dodge** Avenger '08; Caliber '07-08; Caravan '03-07; Challenger '11-12; Charger '08, '11-12; Dakota '05-07; Durango (V8) '11; Grand Caravan '03-12; Journey '09-12; Magnum '06; Ram 1500 (V8) '07, '11; Ram 2500 (turbodiesel) '06-11; Stratus '04-06

Ford Edge (2011)

**Ford** Edge '11-12; Escape (4-cyl.) '10; Escape (V6) '07, '09; Expedition '09; Explorer (V6, 2WD) '04, '06, '11-12; Explorer (V6, 4WD) '03-06, '09, '11-12; Explorer (V8) '03-04, '06-07; Explorer Sport Trac '07; F-150 (V6) '12; F-150 EcoBoost '11; F-250 '06, '11; F-250 (turbodiesel) '04-08, '10-12; Fiesta '11-12; Flex '09-11; Flex EcoBoost '10-11; Focus '12; Freestar '04-05; Fusion (V6, AWD) '10-11; Mustang '12; Taurus SHO '10-11; Taurus Wagon '04; Taurus X '08; Windstar '03

**GMC** Acadia '07-10; Canyon '09-12; Envoy (6-cyl.) '05-08; Envoy (V8) '03, '06-07; S-15 Sonoma '03; Safari '03; Sierra 1500

(V6) '08; Sierra 1500 (V8, 2WD) '09; Sierra 1500 (V8, 4WD) '04-06, '10; Sierra 2500 (turbodiesel) '11-12; Terrain (4-cyl.) '10-11; Yukon '07-09; Yukon XL '04-09, '12

**Honda** Civic Hybrid '09

**Hummer** H3 '06

**Hyundai** Elantra Touring '10-11; Entourage '07; Genesis Coupe '10; Genesis Sedan '12; Santa Fe (V6) '10; Sonata (turbo) '11-12; Sonata Hybrid '11; Veracruz '08

**Infiniti** G Convertible '11

**Jaguar** XF '09-10; XJ '04, '11

**Jeep** Commander '06; Compass '07, '11; Grand Cherokee (V6) '03-07, '11; Grand Cherokee (V8) '03, '11; Liberty '05-08, '10-11; Patriot '07-08; Wrangler (2-door) '06-08; Wrangler (4-door) '07-11

**Kia** Optima (turbo) '11; Rondo '08; Sedona '03-08; Sorento (4-cyl.) '11; Sorento (V6) '04-06, '08, '11

**Land Rover** LR3 '06

**Lexus** GX '12; LS '12

**Lincoln** Aviator '03; LS '04; MKS '09; MKT '10; MKX '11-12; MKZ Hybrid '12; Town Car '10

**Mazda** CX-7 '07-08; MPV '03; RX-8 '04; Tribute (4-cyl.) '10; Tribute (V6) '09; Speed3 '08; 5 '06-09

Hummer H2 (2006)

Jeep Compass (2011)

**Mercedes-Benz** CLK '05; E-Class Convertible '11; GL-Class '07-08, '10-12; M-Class '06, '12; SL '03; SLK '07

**Mercury** Mariner (4-cyl.) '10; Mariner (V6) '07, '09; Milan (V6, AWD) '10-11; Monterey '04-05; Mountaineer (V6, 2WD) '04, '06; Mountaineer (V6, 4WD) '03-06, '09; Mountaineer (V8) '03-04, '06-07; Sable Wagon '04

**Mini** Cooper (except S) '03-07, '09; Cooper S '03, '05-11; Cooper Clubman S '08-09; Cooper Countryman '11-12

**Mitsubishi** Endeavor '04

**Nissan** Armada '10-11; Juke '11; Maxima '06; Murano '03, '05-06; Pathfinder '05-06; Quest '04-05, '07; Titan '04, '11; Versa Sedan '12; Xterra '05-06

**Pontiac** Bonneville '03; G6 Coupe & Convertible '07; G6 Sedan '06-08; G8 '09; Grand Am '03; Grand Prix '03, '05, '07-08; Montana '05; Montana SV6 '05-06; Solstice '08; Sunfire '05; Torrent '06

**Porsche** 911 '07-08; Cayenne '11-12; Cayman '08

**Saab** 9-3 '04; 9-5 '03

**Saturn** Aura '08; Outlook '07-09; Relay '05-07; Sky '08; Vue '03, '08

**Smart** ForTwo '08

**Subaru** Baja '05; Impreza WRX/STi '06, '08; Legacy (4-cyl.) '03; Legacy (turbo) '05-06; Outback (4-cyl.) '03-04; Outback (turbo) '05-06

**Toyota** Tacoma (4-cyl., 4WD) '10

**Volkswagen** Eos '08; Golf TDI '10; GTI '07-11; Jetta Sedan (4-cyl.) '03, '11; Jetta Sedan (5-cyl.) '06, '11-12; New Beetle '03-05, '07-08; Beetle '12; Passat (4-cyl.) '03-07, '10; Passat (V6) '03-04, '06; Passat TDI '05; Tiguan '09; Touareg '04, '11-12

**Volvo** C30 '11; C70 '11; XC60 '10; XC90 (6-cyl.) '04, '10

# DETAILED AUTO RELIABILITY

The charts on the following pages give you a model's complete reliability picture for both its used versions (2007 through 2012) and the new one currently on sale. These detailed reliability Ratings are based on our 2012 Annual Car Reliability Survey, for which we received responses on 1.2 million vehicles.

The Annual Car Reliability Survey is sent to subscribers of CONSUMER REPORTS and ConsumerReports.org. Respondents reported on any serious problems they had with their vehicles in any of the trouble spots included in the following charts, during the previous 12 months. These were considered serious because of cost, failure, safety, or downtime. Because high-mileage vehicles tend to have more problems than low-mileage ones, problem rates are standardized to minimize differences related to mileage. The 2012 models were generally less than six months old at the time of the survey and had been driven an average of about 3,000 miles. Models with insufficient data are noted with a column of asterisks (*).

## How to use the charts

### MAJOR REDESIGNS

A model year in **bold** identifies the year the model was introduced or underwent a major redesign.

### TROUBLE SPOTS

To assess a used car in more detail, look at the individual Ratings for each of the 17 trouble spots. They will pinpoint a model's strengths and weaknesses. Ratings are based on the percentage of survey respondents who reported problems for that trouble spot, compared with the average of all vehicles for that year.

Models that score a ● are not necessarily unreliable, but they have a higher problem rate than the average model. Similarly, models that score a ⊜ are not necessarily problem-free, but they had relatively few problems compared with other models.

Because problem rates in some trouble spots are very low, we do not assign a ● or ◒ unless the model's problem rate exceeds 3 percent. If a problem rate is below 2 percent, it will be assigned a ⊖; below 1 percent, it will be assigned a ⊜.

**Average Problem Rates**

| TROUBLE SPOTS | 07 | 08 | 09 | 10 | 11 | 12 |
|---|---|---|---|---|---|---|
| Engine, Major | 2 | 1 | 1 | <1 | <1 | <1 |
| Engine, Minor | 3 | 2 | 1 | 1 | 1 | <1 |
| Engine, Cooling | 2 | 1 | 1 | 1 | <1 | <1 |
| Trans., Major | 1 | 1 | 1 | 1 | <1 | <1 |
| Trans., Minor | 2 | 1 | 1 | 1 | 1 | 1 |
| Drive System | 3 | 2 | 1 | 1 | 1 | <1 |
| Fuel System | 5 | 4 | 3 | 2 | 2 | 1 |
| Electrical | 4 | 3 | 3 | 2 | 1 | <1 |
| Climate System | 4 | 3 | 2 | 2 | 1 | <1 |
| Suspension | 6 | 4 | 2 | 2 | 1 | <1 |
| Brakes | 8 | 6 | 5 | 3 | 1 | 1 |
| Exhaust | 1 | 1 | 1 | <1 | <1 | <1 |
| Paint/Trim | 4 | 3 | 2 | 2 | 1 | 1 |
| Body Integrity | 5 | 5 | 4 | 4 | 3 | 2 |
| Body Hardware | 6 | 6 | 5 | 3 | 3 | 1 |
| Power Equip. | 4 | 3 | 3 | 2 | 1 | 1 |
| Audio System | 3 | 3 | 3 | 3 | 3 | 2 |
| USED CAR VERDICTS | | | | | | |
| NEW CAR PREDICTION | | | | | | |

### USED CAR VERDICTS

To check the overall reliability of a used car, look at the Used Car Verdict. This Rating shows whether the model had more or fewer problems overall than the average model of that year.

The verdict is calculated from the total number of problems reported by subscribers in all trouble spots. Our calculations give extra weight to problems with major engine and transmission systems, the cooling system, and the drive system because they can be serious and expensive to repair.

## NEW CAR PREDICTIONS

To determine the New Car Prediction, we averaged a model's Used Car Verdict for the most recent three years, provided the vehicle did not change significantly in that time and wasn't redesigned for 2013. We have found that several model years' data are a better predictor than the single most recent model year.

One or two years' data may be used if the model was redesigned in 2012 or 2011, or if there were insufficient data for more years. Sometimes we include a prediction for a model that is new or has been redesigned, provided its reliability history or the manufacturer's track record has been consistently above average. "NA" means there were insufficient data for a prediction.

## WHAT THE TROUBLE SPOTS INCLUDE

**Engine, major:** Engine rebuild or replacement, cylinder head, head gasket, turbo or supercharger, timing chain or timing belt.

**Engine, minor:** Oil leaks, accessory belts and pulleys, engine mounts, engine knock or ping.

**Engine, cooling:** Radiator, cooling fan, antifreeze leaks, water pump, thermostat, overheating.

**Transmission, major:** Transmission rebuild or replacement, torque converter, premature clutch replacement.

**Transmission, minor:** Gear selector or linkage, coolers and lines, rough shifting, slipping transmission, leaks, transmission computer, transmission sensor or solenoid, clutch adjustment, hydraulics (clutch master or slave cylinder).

**Drive system:** Driveshaft or axle, CV joint, wheel bearing(s), differential, transfer case, 4WD/AWD components, driveline vibration, electrical failure.

**Fuel system:** Check engine light, sensors (includes O2 or oxygen sensor), emission control devices (includes EGR), engine computer, fuel cap, fuel gauge/sender, fuel injection system, fuel pump, fuel leaks, stalling or hesitation.

**Electrical:** Alternator, starter, hybrid battery and related systems, regular battery, battery cables, engine harness, coil, ignition switch, electronic ignition, distributor or rotor failure, spark plugs and wires failure.

**Climate system:** Blower (fan) motor, A/C compressor, condenser, evaporator, heater system, automatic climate control, refrigerant leakage, electrical failure.

**Suspension:** Shocks or struts, ball joints, tie rods, wheel bearings, alignment, steering linkage (includes rack and pinion), power steering, wheel balance, springs or torsion bars, bushings, electronic or air suspension.

**Brakes:** Premature wear, pulsation or vibration, squeaking, master cylinder, calipers, antilock brake system (ABS), parking brake, brake failure.

**Exhaust:** Muffler, pipes, catalytic converter, exhaust manifold, leaks.

**Paint/trim:** Paint (fading, chalking, cracking, peeling), loose exterior trim or moldings, rust.

**Body integrity:** Squeaks or rattles, seals and/or weather stripping, air or water leaks, loose interior trim and moldings, wind noise.

**Body hardware:** Windows, locks and latches, tailgate, hatch or trunk, doors or sliding doors, mirrors, seat controls, safety belts, sunroof, convertible top, glass defect.

**Power equipment and accessories:** Cruise control, clock, warning lights, body control module, keyless entry, wiper motor or washer, tire pressure monitor, interior or exterior light, horn, gauges, 12V power plug, alarm or security system.

**Audio system:** Audio systems, entertainment systems, navigation system, backup camera/sensors, communication system.

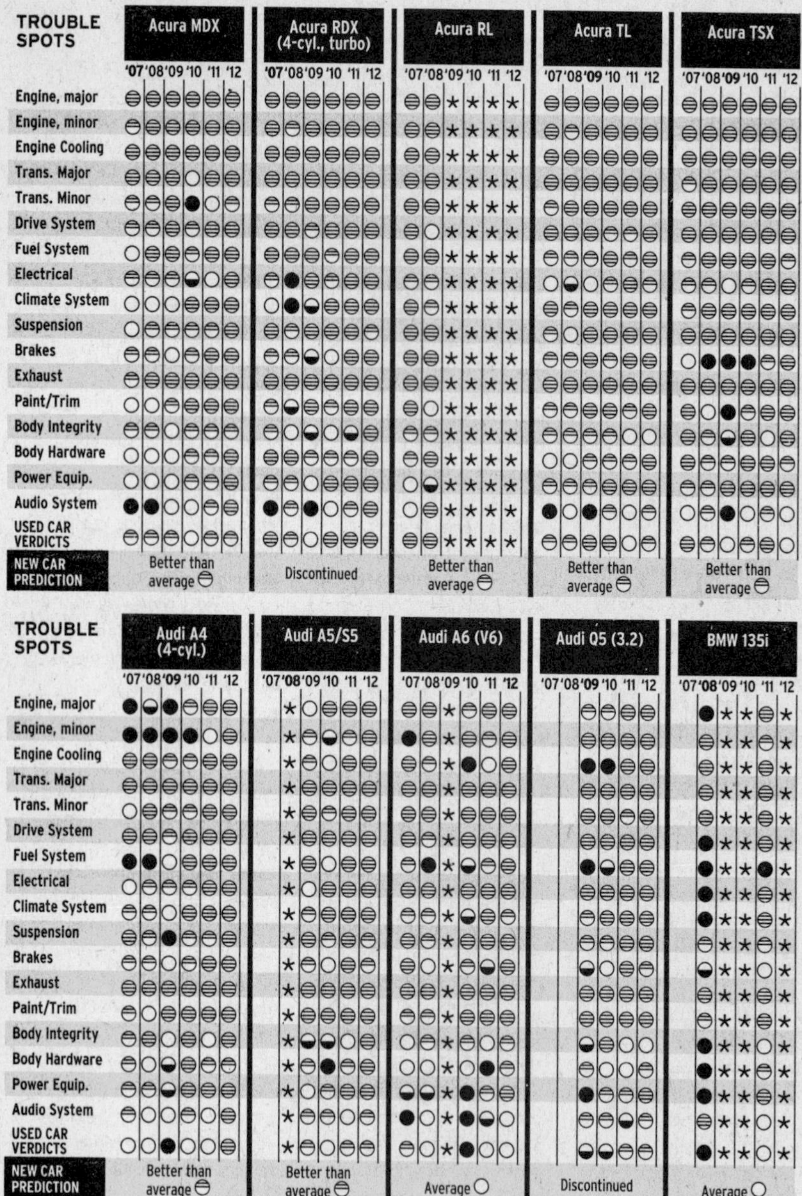
TROUBLE SPOTS
Acura MDX
Acura RDX (4-cyl., turbo)
Acura RL
Acura TL
Acura TSX
'07 '08 '09 '10 '11 '12
Engine, major
Engine, minor
Engine Cooling
Trans. Major
Trans. Minor
Drive System
Fuel System
Electrical
Climate System
Suspension
Brakes
Exhaust
Paint/Trim
Body Integrity
Body Hardware
Power Equip.
Audio System
USED CAR VERDICTS
NEW CAR PREDICTION
Better than average
Discontinued
Better than average
Better than average
Better than average
TROUBLE SPOTS
Audi A4 (4-cyl.)
Audi A5/S5
Audi A6 (V6)
Audi Q5 (3.2)
BMW 135i
'07 '08 '09 '10 '11 '12
Engine, major
Engine, minor
Engine Cooling
Trans. Major
Trans. Minor
Drive System
Fuel System
Electrical
Climate System
Suspension
Brakes
Exhaust
Paint/Trim
Body Integrity
Body Hardware
Power Equip.
Audio System
USED CAR VERDICTS
NEW CAR PREDICTION
Better than average
Better than average
Average
Discontinued
Average

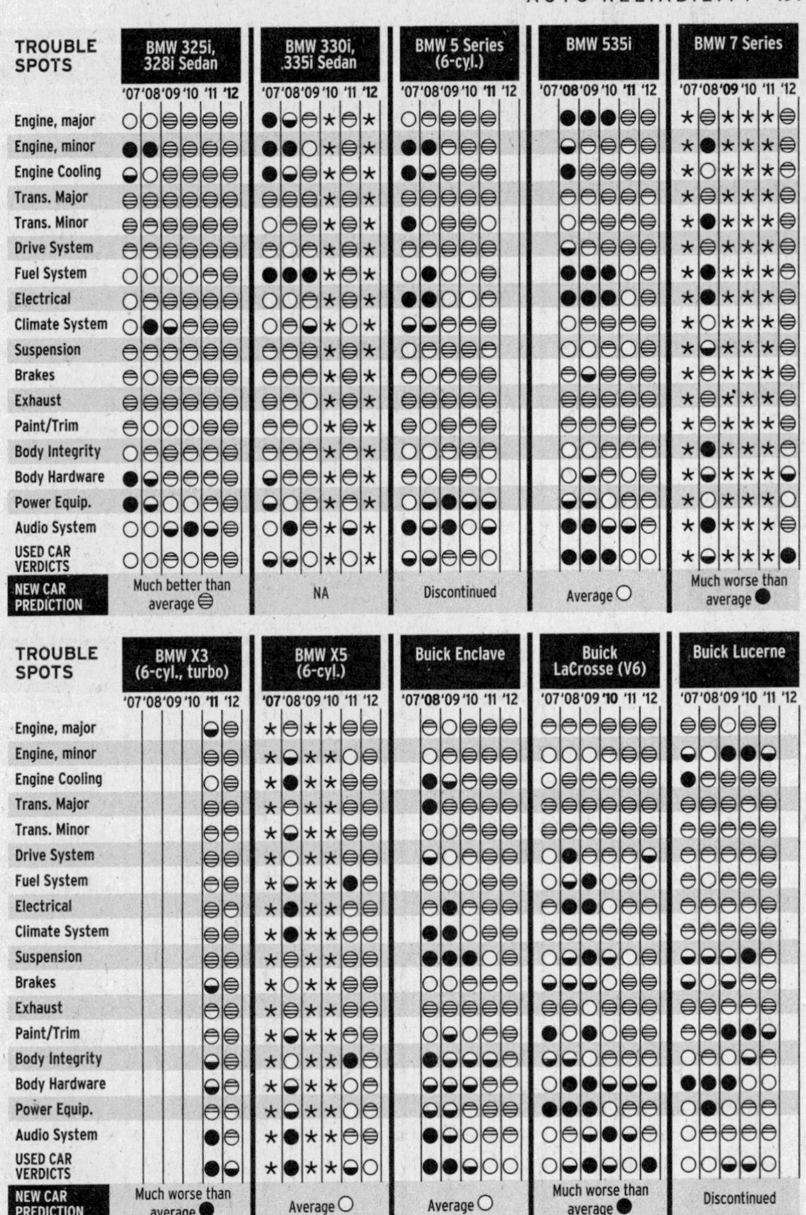
TROUBLE SPOTS
BMW 325i, 328i Sedan
BMW 330i, 335i Sedan
BMW 5 Series (6-cyl.)
BMW 535i
BMW 7 Series
'07 '08 '09 '10 '11 '12
Engine, major
Engine, minor
Engine Cooling
Trans. Major
Trans. Minor
Drive System
Fuel System
Electrical
Climate System
Suspension
Brakes
Exhaust
Paint/Trim
Body Integrity
Body Hardware
Power Equip.
Audio System
USED CAR VERDICTS
NEW CAR PREDICTION
Much better than average
NA
Discontinued
Average
Much worse than average
TROUBLE SPOTS
BMW X3 (6-cyl., turbo)
BMW X5 (6-cyl.)
Buick Enclave
Buick LaCrosse (V6)
Buick Lucerne
'07 '08 '09 '10 '11 '12
Engine, major
Engine, minor
Engine Cooling
Trans. Major
Trans. Minor
Drive System
Fuel System
Electrical
Climate System
Suspension
Brakes
Exhaust
Paint/Trim
Body Integrity
Body Hardware
Power Equip.
Audio System
USED CAR VERDICTS
NEW CAR PREDICTION
Much worse than average
Average
Average
Much worse than average
Discontinued

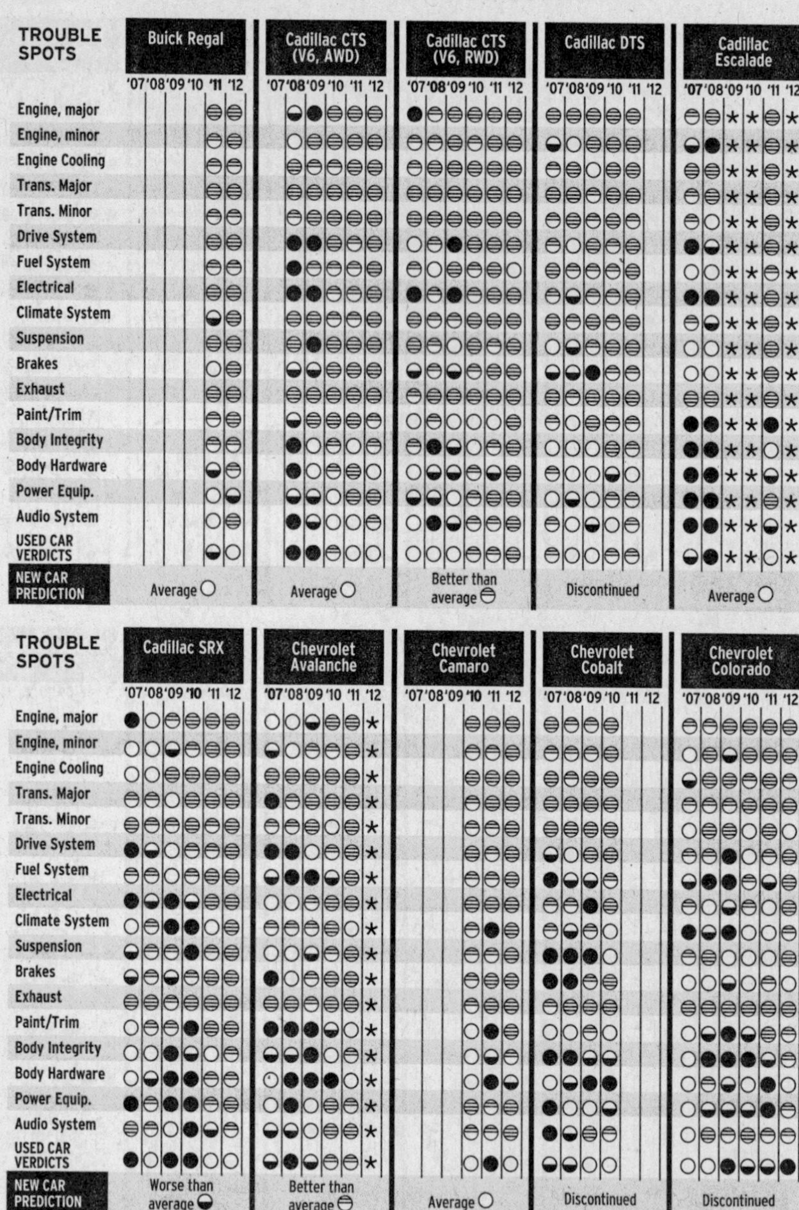
TROUBLE SPOTS
Buick Regal
Cadillac CTS (V6, AWD)
Cadillac CTS (V6, RWD)
Cadillac DTS
Cadillac Escalade
'07 '08 '09 '10 '11 '12
Engine, major
Engine, minor
Engine Cooling
Trans. Major
Trans. Minor
Drive System
Fuel System
Electrical
Climate System
Suspension
Brakes
Exhaust
Paint/Trim
Body Integrity
Body Hardware
Power Equip.
Audio System
USED CAR VERDICTS
NEW CAR PREDICTION
Average
Average
Better than average
Discontinued
Average
TROUBLE SPOTS
Cadillac SRX
Chevrolet Avalanche
Chevrolet Camaro
Chevrolet Cobalt
Chevrolet Colorado
'07 '08 '09 '10 '11 '12
Engine, major
Engine, minor
Engine Cooling
Trans. Major
Trans. Minor
Drive System
Fuel System
Electrical
Climate System
Suspension
Brakes
Exhaust
Paint/Trim
Body Integrity
Body Hardware
Power Equip.
Audio System
USED CAR VERDICTS
NEW CAR PREDICTION
Worse than average
Better than average
Average
Discontinued
Discontinued

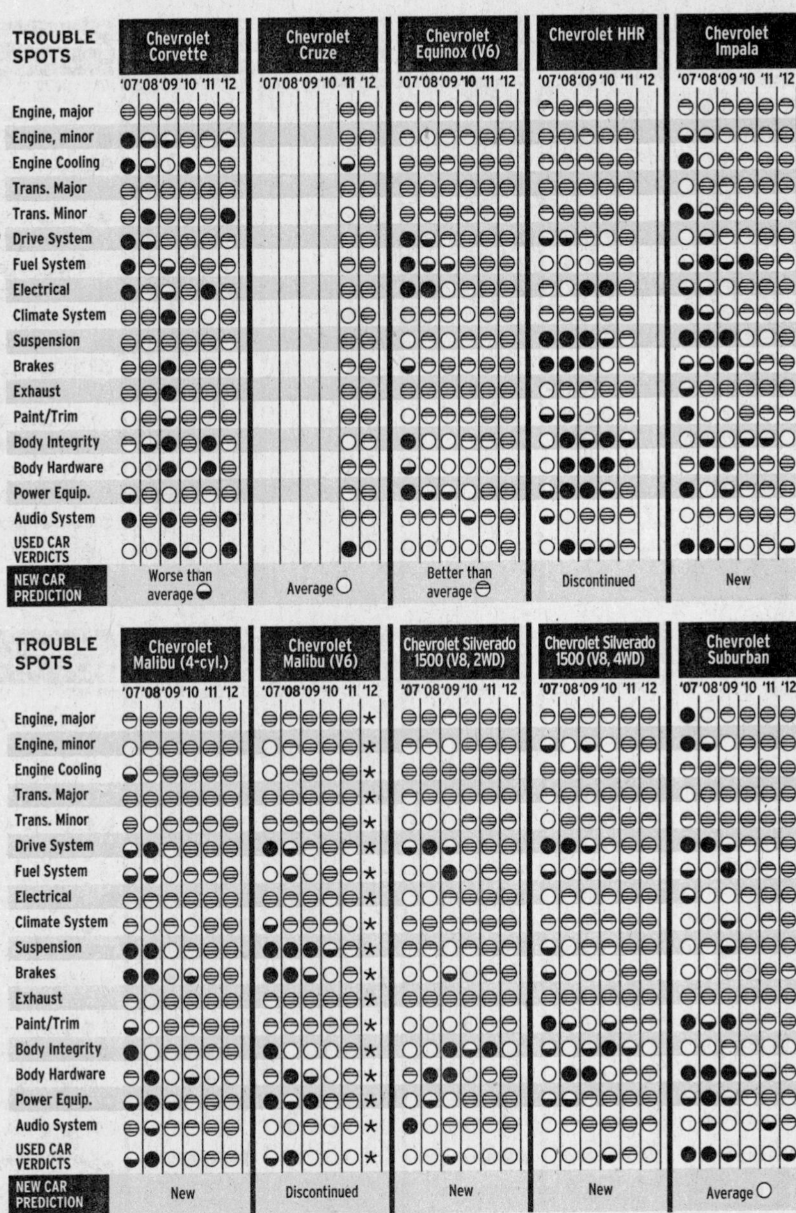
TROUBLE SPOTS
Chevrolet Corvette
Chevrolet Cruze
Chevrolet Equinox (V6)
Chevrolet HHR
Chevrolet Impala
'07 '08 '09 '10 '11 '12
Engine, major
Engine, minor
Engine Cooling
Trans. Major
Trans. Minor
Drive System
Fuel System
Electrical
Climate System
Suspension
Brakes
Exhaust
Paint/Trim
Body Integrity
Body Hardware
Power Equip.
Audio System
USED CAR VERDICTS
NEW CAR PREDICTION
Worse than average
Average
Better than average
Discontinued
New
TROUBLE SPOTS
Chevrolet Malibu (4-cyl.)
Chevrolet Malibu (V6)
Chevrolet Silverado 1500 (V8, 2WD)
Chevrolet Silverado 1500 (V8, 4WD)
Chevrolet Suburban
'07 '08 '09 '10 '11 '12
Engine, major
Engine, minor
Engine Cooling
Trans. Major
Trans. Minor
Drive System
Fuel System
Electrical
Climate System
Suspension
Brakes
Exhaust
Paint/Trim
Body Integrity
Body Hardware
Power Equip.
Audio System
USED CAR VERDICTS
NEW CAR PREDICTION
New
Discontinued
New
New
Average

| TROUBLE SPOTS | Chevrolet Tahoe '07 | '08 | '09 | '10 | '11 | '12 |
|---|---|---|---|---|---|---|
| Engine, major | ⊖ | ⊜ | ⊜ | ⊜ | ⊜ | ⊜ |
| Engine, minor | ◒ | ⊖ | ○ | ⊖ | ⊜ | ⊖ |
| Engine Cooling | ⊜ | ⊜ | ⊜ | ⊜ | ⊜ | ⊜ |
| Trans. Major | ○ | ⊜ | ⊜ | ⊜ | ⊜ | ⊜ |
| Trans. Minor | ○ | ⊜ | ⊜ | ⊜ | ⊜ | ⊜ |
| Drive System | ● | ◒ | ◒ | ⊖ | ⊜ | ⊜ |
| Fuel System | ○ | ⊖ | ◒ | ◒ | ⊜ | ⊜ |
| Electrical | ◒ | ◒ | ◒ | ⊖ | ⊜ | ⊜ |
| Climate System | ⊖ | ○ | ⊖ | ⊖ | ⊜ | ⊜ |
| Suspension | ○ | ⊖ | ⊖ | ⊖ | ⊜ | ⊜ |
| Brakes | ○ | ○ | ⊖ | ⊖ | ⊜ | ⊜ |
| Exhaust | ⊜ | ⊜ | ⊜ | ⊜ | ⊜ | ⊜ |
| Paint/Trim | ● | ◒ | ● | ○ | ⊖ | ⊜ |
| Body Integrity | ○ | ○ | ○ | ○ | ○ | ⊖ |
| Body Hardware | ● | ● | ● | ◒ | ○ | ⊜ |
| Power Equip. | ● | ● | ● | ⊖ | ⊖ | ⊜ |
| Audio System | ○ | ○ | ○ | ⊖ | ⊖ | ⊜ |
| USED CAR VERDICTS | ◒ | ◒ | ◒ | ○ | ⊜ | ⊜ |
| NEW CAR PREDICTION | Average ○ | | | | | |

| TROUBLE SPOTS | Chevrolet TrailBlazer (6-cyl.) '07 | '08 | '09 | '10 | '11 | '12 |
|---|---|---|---|---|---|---|
| Engine, major | ○ | ⊜ | ⊜ | | | |
| Engine, minor | ● | ○ | ◒ | | | |
| Engine Cooling | ○ | ⊖ | ⊜ | | | |
| Trans. Major | ⊜ | ⊜ | ⊜ | | | |
| Trans. Minor | ⊖ | ⊖ | ○ | | | |
| Drive System | ● | ● | ● | | | |
| Fuel System | ● | ● | ○ | | | |
| Electrical | ◒ | ○ | ● | | | |
| Climate System | ○ | ⊖ | ◒ | | | |
| Suspension | ○ | ○ | ⊖ | | | |
| Brakes | ⊖ | ⊖ | ⊜ | | | |
| Exhaust | ⊜ | ◒ | ⊖ | | | |
| Paint/Trim | ○ | ◒ | ⊖ | | | |
| Body Integrity | ◒ | ◒ | ⊖ | | | |
| Body Hardware | ● | ● | ○ | | | |
| Power Equip. | ● | ● | ◒ | | | |
| Audio System | ⊖ | ⊖ | ⊜ | | | |
| USED CAR VERDICTS | ◒ | ◒ | ○ | | | |
| NEW CAR PREDICTION | Discontinued | | | | | |

| TROUBLE SPOTS | Chevrolet Traverse '07 | '08 | '09 | '10 | '11 | '12 |
|---|---|---|---|---|---|---|
| Engine, major | | | ● | ⊜ | ⊜ | ⊜ |
| Engine, minor | | | ⊖ | ⊜ | ⊜ | ⊜ |
| Engine Cooling | | | ⊖ | ⊜ | ⊜ | ⊜ |
| Trans. Major | | | ⊜ | ⊜ | ⊜ | ⊜ |
| Trans. Minor | | | ⊖ | ⊖ | ⊜ | ⊜ |
| Drive System | | | ○ | ⊜ | ⊜ | ⊜ |
| Fuel System | | | ◒ | ○ | ⊖ | ⊜ |
| Electrical | | | ○ | ⊖ | ⊜ | ⊜ |
| Climate System | | | ● | ○ | ⊜ | ⊜ |
| Suspension | | | ● | ● | ○ | ⊜ |
| Brakes | | | ⊖ | ⊖ | ⊖ | ⊜ |
| Exhaust | | | ⊜ | ⊜ | ⊜ | ⊜ |
| Paint/Trim | | | ◒ | ◒ | ⊖ | ⊜ |
| Body Integrity | | | ⊖ | ○ | ⊖ | ⊖ |
| Body Hardware | | | ◒ | ○ | ○ | ⊖ |
| Power Equip. | | | ○ | ⊖ | ⊜ | ⊜ |
| Audio System | | | ◒ | ○ | ⊜ | ⊜ |
| USED CAR VERDICTS | | | ● | ○ | ○ | ⊖ |
| NEW CAR PREDICTION | Average ○ | | | | | |

| TROUBLE SPOTS | Chevrolet Volt '07 | '08 | '09 | '10 | '11 | '12 |
|---|---|---|---|---|---|---|
| Engine, major | | | | | ⊜ | ⊜ |
| Engine, minor | | | | | ⊜ | ⊜ |
| Engine Cooling | | | | | ⊖ | ⊜ |
| Trans. Major | | | | | ⊖ | ⊜ |
| Trans. Minor | | | | | ⊜ | ⊜ |
| Drive System | | | | | ⊜ | ⊜ |
| Fuel System | | | | | ⊖ | ⊜ |
| Electrical | | | | | ⊖ | ○ |
| Climate System | | | | | ⊜ | ⊜ |
| Suspension | | | | | ⊖ | ⊜ |
| Brakes | | | | | ⊜ | ⊜ |
| Exhaust | | | | | ⊜ | ⊜ |
| Paint/Trim | | | | | ⊜ | ⊜ |
| Body Integrity | | | | | ⊜ | ⊖ |
| Body Hardware | | | | | ⊜ | ⊜ |
| Power Equip. | | | | | ⊜ | ⊜ |
| Audio System | | | | | ⊜ | ⊜ |
| USED CAR VERDICTS | | | | | ⊖ | ⊖ |
| NEW CAR PREDICTION | Better than average ⊖ | | | | | |

| TROUBLE SPOTS | Chrysler 300 (V6) '07 | '08 | '09 | '10 | '11 | '12 |
|---|---|---|---|---|---|---|
| Engine, major | ⊜ | ⊜ | ★ | ⊖ | ⊜ | ⊜ |
| Engine, minor | ● | ⊖ | ★ | ⊜ | ⊜ | ⊖ |
| Engine Cooling | ⊜ | ⊜ | ★ | ⊜ | ⊜ | ⊜ |
| Trans. Major | ⊜ | ⊜ | ★ | ⊜ | ⊜ | ⊜ |
| Trans. Minor | ● | ⊖ | ★ | ⊜ | ⊜ | ⊜ |
| Drive System | ○ | ⊖ | ★ | ⊖ | ⊜ | ⊜ |
| Fuel System | ○ | ⊜ | ★ | ⊖ | ⊜ | ⊜ |
| Electrical | ⊜ | ⊜ | ★ | ⊖ | ⊖ | ⊜ |
| Climate System | ○ | ○ | ★ | ○ | ⊜ | ○ |
| Suspension | ● | ○ | ★ | ⊜ | ⊖ | ⊜ |
| Brakes | ◒ | ○ | ★ | ◒ | ⊖ | ⊜ |
| Exhaust | ⊜ | ⊜ | ★ | ⊜ | ⊜ | ⊜ |
| Paint/Trim | ○ | ○ | ★ | ◒ | ◒ | ⊜ |
| Body Integrity | ⊜ | ⊜ | ★ | ⊜ | ◒ | ⊜ |
| Body Hardware | ⊜ | ⊖ | ★ | ○ | ⊜ | ⊜ |
| Power Equip. | ⊜ | ⊖ | ★ | ● | ⊜ | ⊜ |
| Audio System | ⊖ | ○ | ★ | ◒ | ⊜ | ⊖ |
| USED CAR VERDICTS | ○ | ⊖ | ★ | ○ | ⊖ | ○ |
| NEW CAR PREDICTION | Average ○ | | | | | |

| TROUBLE SPOTS | Chrysler 300 (V8) '07 | '08 | '09 | '10 | '11 | '12 |
|---|---|---|---|---|---|---|
| Engine, major | ⊖ | ⊖ | ★ | ★ | ● | ★ |
| Engine, minor | ○ | ⊖ | ★ | ★ | ⊜ | ★ |
| Engine Cooling | ⊖ | ◒ | ★ | ★ | ⊜ | ★ |
| Trans. Major | ⊖ | ⊜ | ★ | ★ | ⊜ | ★ |
| Trans. Minor | ● | ○ | ★ | ★ | ⊜ | ★ |
| Drive System | ⊖ | ◒ | ★ | ★ | ● | ★ |
| Fuel System | ○ | ○ | ★ | ★ | ⊜ | ★ |
| Electrical | ⊖ | ⊖ | ★ | ★ | ⊖ | ★ |
| Climate System | ○ | ○ | ★ | ★ | ● | ★ |
| Suspension | ○ | ◒ | ★ | ★ | ⊜ | ★ |
| Brakes | ○ | ○ | ★ | ★ | ⊜ | ★ |
| Exhaust | ⊜ | ⊖ | ★ | ★ | ⊜ | ★ |
| Paint/Trim | ⊖ | ⊖ | ★ | ★ | ● | ★ |
| Body Integrity | ⊖ | ⊖ | ★ | ★ | ⊖ | ★ |
| Body Hardware | ○ | ◒ | ★ | ★ | ● | ★ |
| Power Equip. | ○ | ⊜ | ★ | ★ | ⊜ | ★ |
| Audio System | ● | ◒ | ★ | ★ | ⊖ | ★ |
| USED CAR VERDICTS | ○ | ○ | ★ | ★ | ● | ★ |
| NEW CAR PREDICTION | Much worse than average ● | | | | | |

| TROUBLE SPOTS | Chrysler PT Cruiser (non-turbo) '07 | '08 | '09 | '10 | '11 | '12 |
|---|---|---|---|---|---|---|
| Engine, major | ○ | ⊜ | ⊖ | ★ | | |
| Engine, minor | ● | ○ | ⊖ | ★ | | |
| Engine Cooling | ○ | ○ | ● | ★ | | |
| Trans. Major | ○ | ○ | ⊜ | ★ | | |
| Trans. Minor | ○ | ⊖ | ⊖ | ★ | | |
| Drive System | ◒ | ○ | ⊖ | ★ | | |
| Fuel System | ● | ⊖ | ◒ | ★ | | |
| Electrical | ● | ○ | ◒ | ★ | | |
| Climate System | ● | ● | ● | ★ | | |
| Suspension | ● | ● | ● | ★ | | |
| Brakes | ◒ | ◒ | ● | ★ | | |
| Exhaust | ⊜ | ⊜ | ⊜ | ★ | | |
| Paint/Trim | ◒ | ○ | ⊖ | ★ | | |
| Body Integrity | ○ | ○ | ⊖ | ★ | | |
| Body Hardware | ◒ | ⊖ | ⊖ | ★ | | |
| Power Equip. | ◒ | ◒ | ○ | ★ | | |
| Audio System | ⊖ | ⊜ | ⊖ | ★ | | |
| USED CAR VERDICTS | ● | ◒ | ◒ | ★ | | |
| NEW CAR PREDICTION | Discontinued | | | | | |

| TROUBLE SPOTS | Chrysler Sebring/200 Sedan '07 | '08 | '09 | '10 | '11 | '12 |
|---|---|---|---|---|---|---|
| Engine, major | ⊜ | ★ | ★ | ★ | ⊜ | ⊜ |
| Engine, minor | ⊜ | ★ | ★ | ★ | ⊜ | ⊜ |
| Engine Cooling | ⊖ | ★ | ★ | ★ | ⊜ | ⊜ |
| Trans. Major | ⊜ | ★ | ★ | ★ | ⊜ | ⊜ |
| Trans. Minor | ● | ★ | ★ | ★ | ○ | ○ |
| Drive System | ◒ | ★ | ★ | ★ | ⊖ | ⊜ |
| Fuel System | ⊖ | ★ | ★ | ★ | ⊜ | ⊖ |
| Electrical | ⊖ | ★ | ★ | ★ | ⊜ | ⊜ |
| Climate System | ⊜ | ★ | ★ | ★ | ⊜ | ⊜ |
| Suspension | ◒ | ★ | ★ | ★ | ⊖ | ⊜ |
| Brakes | ● | ★ | ★ | ★ | ⊜ | ⊜ |
| Exhaust | ⊜ | ★ | ★ | ★ | ⊜ | ⊜ |
| Paint/Trim | ⊖ | ★ | ★ | ★ | ⊜ | ⊖ |
| Body Integrity | ⊖ | ★ | ★ | ★ | ⊖ | ○ |
| Body Hardware | ⊜ | ★ | ★ | ★ | ⊖ | ○ |
| Power Equip. | ● | ★ | ★ | ★ | ⊖ | ⊜ |
| Audio System | ⊜ | ★ | ★ | ★ | ⊖ | ⊜ |
| USED CAR VERDICTS | ○ | ★ | ★ | ★ | ○ | ● |
| NEW CAR PREDICTION | Worse than average ◒ | | | | | |

| TROUBLE SPOTS | Chrysler Town & Country '07 | '08 | '09 | '10 | '11 | '12 |
|---|---|---|---|---|---|---|
| Engine, major | ⊜ | ⊖ | ⊜ | ⊜ | ⊜ | ⊜ |
| Engine, minor | ◒ | ◒ | ○ | ⊜ | ⊜ | ⊜ |
| Engine Cooling | ◒ | ○ | ⊜ | ⊜ | ⊜ | ⊜ |
| Trans. Major | ⊖ | ⊖ | ⊖ | ⊜ | ⊜ | ⊜ |
| Trans. Minor | ⊖ | ◒ | ◒ | ○ | ● | ○ |
| Drive System | ⊖ | ◒ | ○ | ⊖ | ⊖ | ⊜ |
| Fuel System | ● | ○ | ○ | ○ | ○ | ⊜ |
| Electrical | ◒ | ○ | ◒ | ◒ | ⊖ | ⊜ |
| Climate System | ● | ● | ● | ⊖ | ⊜ | ⊜ |
| Suspension | ◒ | ● | ◒ | ○ | ⊖ | ⊜ |
| Brakes | ● | ● | ● | ● | ● | ⊖ |
| Exhaust | ⊖ | ⊜ | ⊜ | ⊜ | ⊜ | ⊜ |
| Paint/Trim | ● | ○ | ○ | ⊖ | ⊖ | ⊜ |
| Body Integrity | ● | ● | ● | ● | ● | ○ |
| Body Hardware | ● | ● | ● | ● | ◒ | ○ |
| Power Equip. | ● | ● | ● | ◒ | ○ | ⊖ |
| Audio System | ○ | ◒ | ◒ | ⊖ | ○ | ○ |
| USED CAR VERDICTS | ● | ● | ● | ● | ● | ● |
| NEW CAR PREDICTION | Much worse than average ● | | | | | |

| TROUBLE SPOTS | Dodge Caliber '07 | '08 | '09 | '10 | '11 | '12 |
|---|---|---|---|---|---|---|
| Engine, major | ⊜ | ⊜ | ⊜ | ★ | ★ | ★ |
| Engine, minor | ⊖ | ⊖ | ⊜ | ★ | ★ | ★ |
| Engine Cooling | ⊖ | ⊖ | ⊖ | ★ | ★ | ★ |
| Trans. Major | ⊖ | ○ | ⊜ | ★ | ★ | ★ |
| Trans. Minor | ◒ | ⊜ | ⊖ | ★ | ★ | ★ |
| Drive System | ● | ⊖ | ⊖ | ★ | ★ | ★ |
| Fuel System | ○ | ⊖ | ⊜ | ★ | ★ | ★ |
| Electrical | ● | ◒ | ⊖ | ★ | ★ | ★ |
| Climate System | ⊖ | ◒ | ⊖ | ★ | ★ | ★ |
| Suspension | ● | ● | ● | ★ | ★ | ★ |
| Brakes | ◒ | ● | ● | ★ | ★ | ★ |
| Exhaust | ⊜ | ⊜ | ⊜ | ★ | ★ | ★ |
| Paint/Trim | ● | ● | ◒ | ★ | ★ | ★ |
| Body Integrity | ◒ | ◒ | ◒ | ★ | ★ | ★ |
| Body Hardware | ⊖ | ⊖ | ⊜ | ★ | ★ | ★ |
| Power Equip. | ◒ | ◒ | ◒ | ★ | ★ | ★ |
| Audio System | ⊖ | ⊖ | ◒ | ★ | ★ | ★ |
| USED CAR VERDICTS | ◒ | ◒ | ○ | ★ | ★ | ★ |
| NEW CAR PREDICTION | Discontinued | | | | | |

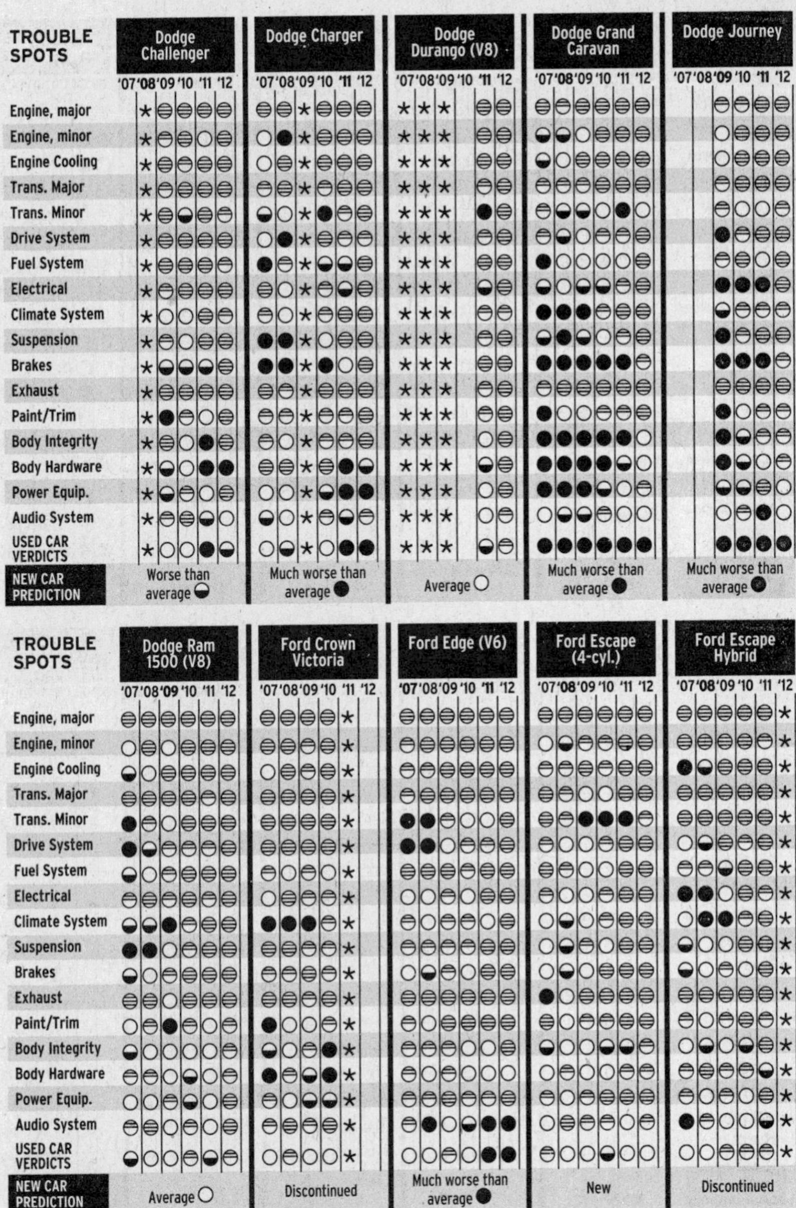
TROUBLE SPOTS
Dodge Challenger
Dodge Charger
Dodge Durango (V8)
Dodge Grand Caravan
Dodge Journey
'07 '08 '09 '10 '11 '12
Engine, major
Engine, minor
Engine Cooling
Trans. Major
Trans. Minor
Drive System
Fuel System
Electrical
Climate System
Suspension
Brakes
Exhaust
Paint/Trim
Body Integrity
Body Hardware
Power Equip.
Audio System
USED CAR VERDICTS
NEW CAR PREDICTION
Worse than average
Much worse than average
Average
Much worse than average
Much worse than average
TROUBLE SPOTS
Dodge Ram 1500 (V8)
Ford Crown Victoria
Ford Edge (V6)
Ford Escape (4-cyl.)
Ford Escape Hybrid
'07 '08 '09 '10 '11 '12
Engine, major
Engine, minor
Engine Cooling
Trans. Major
Trans. Minor
Drive System
Fuel System
Electrical
Climate System
Suspension
Brakes
Exhaust
Paint/Trim
Body Integrity
Body Hardware
Power Equip.
Audio System
USED CAR VERDICTS
NEW CAR PREDICTION
Average
Discontinued
Much worse than average
New
Discontinued

## TROUBLE SPOTS

| Ford Expedition | '07 | '08 | '09 | '10 | '11 | '12 |
|---|---|---|---|---|---|---|
| Engine, major | ⊜ | ⊜ | ○ | ⊜ | ⊜ | ⊜ |
| Engine, minor | ⊜ | ⊖ | ⊜ | ⊜ | ⊜ | ⊜ |
| Engine Cooling | ⊜ | ⊜ | ⊜ | ⊜ | ⊜ | ⊜ |
| Trans. Major | ⊖ | ⊜ | ⊜ | ⊜ | ⊜ | ⊜ |
| Trans. Minor | ◒ | ● | ○ | ○ | ⊖ | ⊜ |
| Drive System | ○ | ⊖ | ○ | ⊖ | ⊖ | ⊜ |
| Fuel System | ⊖ | ⊜ | ○ | ⊜ | ⊜ | ⊜ |
| Electrical | ○ | ○ | ○ | ⊖ | ⊜ | ⊜ |
| Climate System | ◒ | ◒ | ● | ◒ | ⊖ | ⊜ |
| Suspension | ⊖ | ⊖ | ⊜ | ○ | ⊖ | ⊜ |
| Brakes | ○ | ○ | ◒ | ○ | ⊖ | ⊜ |
| Exhaust | ⊜ | ⊜ | ⊜ | ⊜ | ⊜ | ⊜ |
| Paint/Trim | ● | ● | ◒ | ○ | ⊖ | ⊖ |
| Body Integrity | ○ | ⊖ | ○ | ◒ | ⊖ | ⊖ |
| Body Hardware | ● | ● | ● | ○ | ⊖ | ⊖ |
| Power Equip. | ⊖ | ○ | ● | ⊜ | ⊜ | ⊖ |
| Audio System | ● | ◒ | ● | ○ | ○ | ⊖ |
| USED CAR VERDICTS | ○ | ○ | ◒ | ○ | ○ | ○ |
| NEW CAR PREDICTION | Average ○ | | | | | |

| Ford Explorer (V6, 4WD) | '07 | '08 | '09 | '10 | '11 | '12 |
|---|---|---|---|---|---|---|
| Engine, major | ⊜ | ⊜ | ⊜ | ⊜ | ⊜ | ⊜ |
| Engine, minor | ⊖ | ⊖ | ⊖ | ⊜ | ⊜ | ⊜ |
| Engine Cooling | ● | ⊖ | ○ | ⊖ | ● | ⊖ |
| Trans. Major | ⊖ | ⊖ | ⊜ | ⊜ | ⊜ | ⊜ |
| Trans. Minor | ◒ | ○ | ○ | ⊜ | ⊖ | ⊜ |
| Drive System | ○ | ○ | ◒ | ⊜ | ⊖ | ⊜ |
| Fuel System | ○ | ⊖ | ⊖ | ○ | ⊜ | ⊜ |
| Electrical | ○ | ○ | ○ | ⊜ | ⊖ | ⊜ |
| Climate System | ○ | ◒ | ○ | ⊖ | ● | ⊖ |
| Suspension | ⊖ | ○ | ○ | ⊖ | ⊜ | ⊜ |
| Brakes | ○ | ⊖ | ○ | ⊖ | ○ | ⊜ |
| Exhaust | ⊜ | ⊜ | ⊜ | ⊜ | ⊜ | ⊜ |
| Paint/Trim | ⊖ | ○ | ● | ⊜ | ○ | ⊖ |
| Body Integrity | ⊖ | ⊜ | ● | ◒ | ● | ○ |
| Body Hardware | ○ | ○ | ⊜ | ⊖ | ● | ○ |
| Power Equip. | ○ | ◒ | ○ | ⊜ | ○ | ⊜ |
| Audio System | ⊖ | ○ | ⊜ | ○ | ● | ● |
| USED CAR VERDICTS | ○ | ○ | ◒ | ○ | ● | ● |
| NEW CAR PREDICTION | Much worse than average ● | | | | | |

| Ford F-150 (V6) | '07 | '08 | '09 | '10 | '11 | '12 |
|---|---|---|---|---|---|---|
| Engine, major | ⊖ | ⊜ | ⊖ | ⊜ | ⊜ | ⊜ |
| Engine, minor | ⊖ | ○ | ○ | ⊜ | ⊜ | ⊜ |
| Engine Cooling | ⊜ | ⊖ | ⊜ | ⊜ | ⊜ | ⊜ |
| Trans. Major | ⊖ | ○ | ⊖ | ⊜ | ⊜ | ⊜ |
| Trans. Minor | ○ | ⊖ | ◒ | ○ | ⊖ | ⊖ |
| Drive System | ○ | ⊜ | ⊜ | ⊖ | ⊜ | ⊜ |
| Fuel System | ○ | ⊜ | ○ | ⊜ | ⊜ | ⊖ |
| Electrical | ◒ | ○ | ⊖ | ⊖ | ⊜ | ⊜ |
| Climate System | ⊖ | ● | ○ | ⊜ | ⊜ | ⊜ |
| Suspension | ○ | ⊜ | ⊖ | ⊜ | ⊜ | ⊜ |
| Brakes | ○ | ○ | ⊖ | ⊖ | ⊜ | ⊜ |
| Exhaust | ⊜ | ⊜ | ⊖ | ⊜ | ⊜ | ⊜ |
| Paint/Trim | ◒ | ○ | ⊖ | ◒ | ⊖ | ⊖ |
| Body Integrity | ○ | ⊖ | ◒ | ○ | ⊖ | ○ |
| Body Hardware | ○ | ⊖ | ● | ⊜ | ⊖ | ⊜ |
| Power Equip. | ⊖ | ⊜ | ◒ | ⊖ | ⊜ | ⊖ |
| Audio System | ⊜ | ⊜ | ⊖ | ○ | ⊖ | ⊜ |
| USED CAR VERDICTS | ○ | ⊖ | ○ | ⊖ | ⊜ | ◒ |
| NEW CAR PREDICTION | Average ○ | | | | | |

| Ford F-150 (V8, 4WD) | '07 | '08 | '09 | '10 | '11 | '12 |
|---|---|---|---|---|---|---|
| Engine, major | ⊖ | ⊖ | ⊜ | ⊜ | ⊜ | ⊜ |
| Engine, minor | ⊖ | ⊜ | ⊖ | ⊜ | ⊜ | ⊜ |
| Engine Cooling | ⊜ | ⊜ | ⊜ | ⊜ | ⊜ | ⊜ |
| Trans. Major | ⊖ | ⊜ | ⊜ | ⊜ | ⊜ | ⊜ |
| Trans. Minor | ⊖ | ○ | ● | ◒ | ⊖ | ⊜ |
| Drive System | ● | ◒ | ⊖ | ○ | ⊖ | ⊖ |
| Fuel System | ⊖ | ⊖ | ⊖ | ⊜ | ⊜ | ⊜ |
| Electrical | ○ | ○ | ⊜ | ⊜ | ⊜ | ⊜ |
| Climate System | ○ | ● | ◒ | ⊖ | ⊜ | ⊜ |
| Suspension | ○ | ○ | ◒ | ⊖ | ⊜ | ⊜ |
| Brakes | ◒ | ○ | ○ | ⊖ | ⊜ | ⊜ |
| Exhaust | ⊖ | ⊖ | ⊜ | ⊜ | ⊜ | ⊜ |
| Paint/Trim | ○ | ○ | ○ | ○ | ⊜ | ⊜ |
| Body Integrity | ⊖ | ⊖ | ○ | ○ | ⊖ | ⊜ |
| Body Hardware | ⊖ | ○ | ◒ | ○ | ○ | ⊖ |
| Power Equip. | ⊖ | ⊖ | ⊖ | ⊖ | ⊜ | ⊜ |
| Audio System | ⊖ | ⊖ | ⊖ | ○ | ◒ | ⊖ |
| USED CAR VERDICTS | ○ | ○ | ○ | ○ | ○ | ○ |
| NEW CAR PREDICTION | Average ○ | | | | | |

| Ford F-250 (turbodiesel) | '07 | '08 | '09 | '10 | '11 | '12 |
|---|---|---|---|---|---|---|
| Engine, major | ● | ○ | * | ⊖ | ⊜ | ⊖ |
| Engine, minor | ● | ● | * | ○ | ⊖ | ⊖ |
| Engine Cooling | ○ | ● | * | ○ | ⊖ | ⊜ |
| Trans. Major | ⊜ | ⊜ | * | ⊜ | ⊜ | ⊜ |
| Trans. Minor | ⊖ | ⊜ | * | ⊜ | ● | ⊖ |
| Drive System | ◒ | ○ | * | ⊖ | ○ | ⊜ |
| Fuel System | ● | ● | * | ● | ● | ◒ |
| Electrical | ● | ○ | * | ⊖ | ⊜ | ⊜ |
| Climate System | ◒ | ○ | * | ● | ⊜ | ⊖ |
| Suspension | ○ | ○ | * | ⊜ | ⊖ | ⊜ |
| Brakes | ○ | ○ | * | ⊜ | ⊜ | ⊜ |
| Exhaust | ⊖ | ● | * | ⊖ | ⊜ | ⊜ |
| Paint/Trim | ○ | ⊖ | * | ⊖ | ⊖ | ⊜ |
| Body Integrity | ⊖ | ⊖ | * | ○ | ○ | ⊖ |
| Body Hardware | ⊖ | ⊜ | * | ⊖ | ⊜ | ⊜ |
| Power Equip. | ○ | ⊖ | * | ⊖ | ⊖ | ⊜ |
| Audio System | ⊖ | ○ | * | ⊖ | ○ | ○ |
| USED CAR VERDICTS | ● | ● | * | ◒ | ● | ◒ |
| NEW CAR PREDICTION | Much worse than average ● | | | | | |

## TROUBLE SPOTS

| Ford Fiesta | '07 | '08 | '09 | '10 | '11 | '12 |
|---|---|---|---|---|---|---|
| Engine, major | | | | | ⊜ | ⊜ |
| Engine, minor | | | | | ⊖ | ⊜ |
| Engine Cooling | | | | | ⊜ | ⊜ |
| Trans. Major | | | | | ⊖ | ⊖ |
| Trans. Minor | | | | | ● | ○ |
| Drive System | | | | | ⊜ | ⊜ |
| Fuel System | | | | | ⊖ | ⊜ |
| Electrical | | | | | ⊖ | ⊜ |
| Climate System | | | | | ⊜ | ⊜ |
| Suspension | | | | | ⊜ | ⊜ |
| Brakes | | | | | ⊜ | ⊜ |
| Exhaust | | | | | ⊜ | ⊜ |
| Paint/Trim | | | | | ○ | ⊜ |
| Body Integrity | | | | | ○ | ⊜ |
| Body Hardware | | | | | ○ | ⊜ |
| Power Equip. | | | | | ⊖ | ⊜ |
| Audio System | | | | | ◒ | ◒ |
| USED CAR VERDICTS | | | | | ◒ | ◒ |
| NEW CAR PREDICTION | Worse than average ◒ | | | | | |

| Ford Flex | '07 | '08 | '09 | '10 | '11 | '12 |
|---|---|---|---|---|---|---|
| Engine, major | | | ⊜ | ⊜ | ⊜ | ⊜ |
| Engine, minor | | | ⊜ | ⊜ | ⊜ | ⊜ |
| Engine Cooling | | | ⊜ | ⊜ | ◒ | ⊜ |
| Trans. Major | | | ⊜ | ⊜ | ⊜ | ⊜ |
| Trans. Minor | | | ◒ | ⊖ | ⊜ | ⊜ |
| Drive System | | | ⊖ | ⊜ | ⊜ | ⊜ |
| Fuel System | | | ⊖ | ○ | ⊜ | ⊜ |
| Electrical | | | ⊖ | ⊜ | ⊜ | ⊜ |
| Climate System | | | ○ | ○ | ◒ | ⊜ |
| Suspension | | | ○ | ◒ | ⊜ | ⊜ |
| Brakes | | | ● | ● | ○ | ⊜ |
| Exhaust | | | ⊜ | ⊜ | ⊜ | ⊜ |
| Paint/Trim | | | ● | ○ | ○ | ⊖ |
| Body Integrity | | | ◒ | ● | ● | ⊜ |
| Body Hardware | | | ◒ | ● | ⊖ | ⊖ |
| Power Equip. | | | ⊖ | ⊜ | ⊖ | ⊜ |
| Audio System | | | ◒ | ◒ | ◒ | ○ |
| USED CAR VERDICTS | | | ◒ | ◒ | ◒ | ⊖ |
| NEW CAR PREDICTION | Average ○ | | | | | |

| Ford Focus Sedan | '07 | '08 | '09 | '10 | '11 | '12 |
|---|---|---|---|---|---|---|
| Engine, major | ⊜ | ⊜ | ⊜ | ⊜ | ⊜ | ⊜ |
| Engine, minor | ⊖ | ◒ | ○ | ⊜ | ⊜ | ⊜ |
| Engine Cooling | ⊜ | ⊜ | ⊜ | ⊜ | ⊜ | ⊜ |
| Trans. Major | ⊖ | ⊜ | ⊜ | ⊜ | ⊜ | ⊜ |
| Trans. Minor | ⊖ | ⊜ | ⊜ | ⊜ | ⊜ | ● |
| Drive System | ⊜ | ○ | ⊜ | ⊜ | ⊜ | ⊜ |
| Fuel System | ⊜ | ⊜ | ⊜ | ○ | ⊜ | ⊜ |
| Electrical | ○ | ⊖ | ⊖ | ⊖ | ⊜ | ⊜ |
| Climate System | ○ | ○ | ⊜ | ⊖ | ⊜ | ⊜ |
| Suspension | ○ | ◒ | ● | ○ | ⊖ | ⊜ |
| Brakes | ○ | ⊖ | ○ | ⊖ | ⊜ | ⊜ |
| Exhaust | ⊜ | ⊜ | ⊜ | ⊜ | ⊜ | ⊜ |
| Paint/Trim | ⊖ | ⊖ | ○ | ⊖ | ⊜ | ⊜ |
| Body Integrity | ◒ | ● | ● | ◒ | ○ | ⊖ |
| Body Hardware | ○ | ⊖ | ⊜ | ⊖ | ⊜ | ⊖ |
| Power Equip. | ⊖ | ⊜ | ⊜ | ⊖ | ⊜ | ⊜ |
| Audio System | ⊖ | ⊜ | ⊖ | ⊖ | ○ | ● |
| USED CAR VERDICTS | ⊖ | ⊖ | ⊖ | ⊖ | ⊜ | ● |
| NEW CAR PREDICTION | Much worse than average ● | | | | | |

| Ford Fusion (4-cyl.) | '07 | '08 | '09 | '10 | '11 | '12 |
|---|---|---|---|---|---|---|
| Engine, major | ⊜ | ⊜ | ⊜ | ⊜ | ⊜ | ⊜ |
| Engine, minor | ○ | ⊖ | ⊜ | ⊜ | ⊜ | ⊜ |
| Engine Cooling | ● | ⊜ | ⊜ | ⊜ | ⊜ | ⊜ |
| Trans. Major | ⊜ | ⊜ | ⊜ | ○ | ⊜ | ⊜ |
| Trans. Minor | ⊖ | ⊜ | ⊜ | ● | ◒ | ⊖ |
| Drive System | ⊜ | ⊜ | ⊜ | ⊖ | ⊜ | ⊜ |
| Fuel System | ○ | ⊖ | ⊜ | ⊖ | ⊖ | ⊜ |
| Electrical | ○ | ⊖ | ○ | ○ | ⊜ | ⊜ |
| Climate System | ○ | ⊜ | ⊜ | ⊖ | ⊜ | ⊜ |
| Suspension | ⊜ | ⊖ | ⊜ | ⊜ | ⊖ | ⊜ |
| Brakes | ○ | ○ | ○ | ○ | ⊖ | ⊜ |
| Exhaust | ⊜ | ⊜ | ⊜ | ⊜ | ⊜ | ⊜ |
| Paint/Trim | ⊖ | ⊖ | ⊖ | ⊖ | ⊜ | ⊜ |
| Body Integrity | ⊖ | ⊜ | ⊖ | ⊖ | ⊖ | ⊜ |
| Body Hardware | ⊖ | ○ | ⊖ | ⊖ | ⊖ | ⊖ |
| Power Equip. | ⊜ | ⊜ | ⊜ | ⊜ | ⊖ | ⊜ |
| Audio System | ⊖ | ○ | ⊖ | ⊖ | ⊜ | ⊖ |
| USED CAR VERDICTS | ○ | ⊜ | ⊜ | ○ | ○ | ⊖ |
| NEW CAR PREDICTION | New | | | | | |

| Ford Fusion Hybrid | '07 | '08 | '09 | '10 | '11 | '12 |
|---|---|---|---|---|---|---|
| Engine, major | | | | ⊜ | ⊜ | ⊜ |
| Engine, minor | | | | ⊜ | ⊜ | ⊜ |
| Engine Cooling | | | | ⊜ | ⊜ | ⊜ |
| Trans. Major | | | | ⊜ | ⊜ | ⊜ |
| Trans. Minor | | | | ⊜ | ⊜ | ⊜ |
| Drive System | | | | ⊜ | ⊜ | ⊜ |
| Fuel System | | | | ⊖ | ⊜ | ⊜ |
| Electrical | | | | ○ | ⊖ | ⊜ |
| Climate System | | | | ⊖ | ⊜ | ⊜ |
| Suspension | | | | ⊜ | ⊜ | ⊜ |
| Brakes | | | | ○ | ⊖ | ⊜ |
| Exhaust | | | | ⊜ | ⊜ | ⊜ |
| Paint/Trim | | | | ⊖ | ⊜ | ⊜ |
| Body Integrity | | | | ⊜ | ⊜ | ⊜ |
| Body Hardware | | | | ⊖ | ⊜ | ⊖ |
| Power Equip. | | | | ⊖ | ⊜ | ⊜ |
| Audio System | | | | ○ | ○ | ○ |
| USED CAR VERDICTS | | | | ⊖ | ⊜ | ⊜ |
| NEW CAR PREDICTION | New | | | | | |

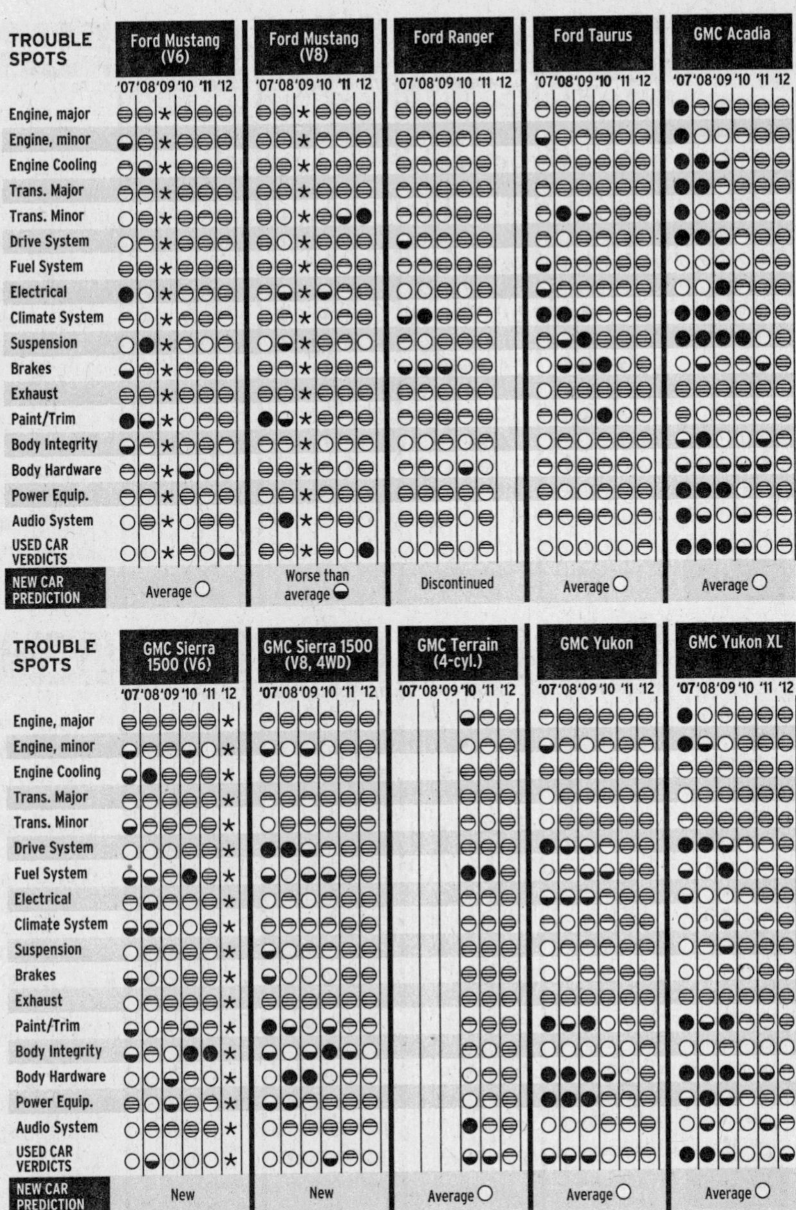
TROUBLE SPOTS
Ford Mustang (V6)
Ford Mustang (V8)
Ford Ranger
Ford Taurus
GMC Acadia
'07 '08 '09 '10 '11 '12
Engine, major
Engine, minor
Engine Cooling
Trans. Major
Trans. Minor
Drive System
Fuel System
Electrical
Climate System
Suspension
Brakes
Exhaust
Paint/Trim
Body Integrity
Body Hardware
Power Equip.
Audio System
USED CAR VERDICTS
NEW CAR PREDICTION
Average
Worse than average
Discontinued
Average
Average
TROUBLE SPOTS
GMC Sierra 1500 (V6)
GMC Sierra 1500 (V8, 4WD)
GMC Terrain (4-cyl.)
GMC Yukon
GMC Yukon XL
'07 '08 '09 '10 '11 '12
Engine, major
Engine, minor
Engine Cooling
Trans. Major
Trans. Minor
Drive System
Fuel System
Electrical
Climate System
Suspension
Brakes
Exhaust
Paint/Trim
Body Integrity
Body Hardware
Power Equip.
Audio System
USED CAR VERDICTS
NEW CAR PREDICTION
New
New
Average
Average
Average

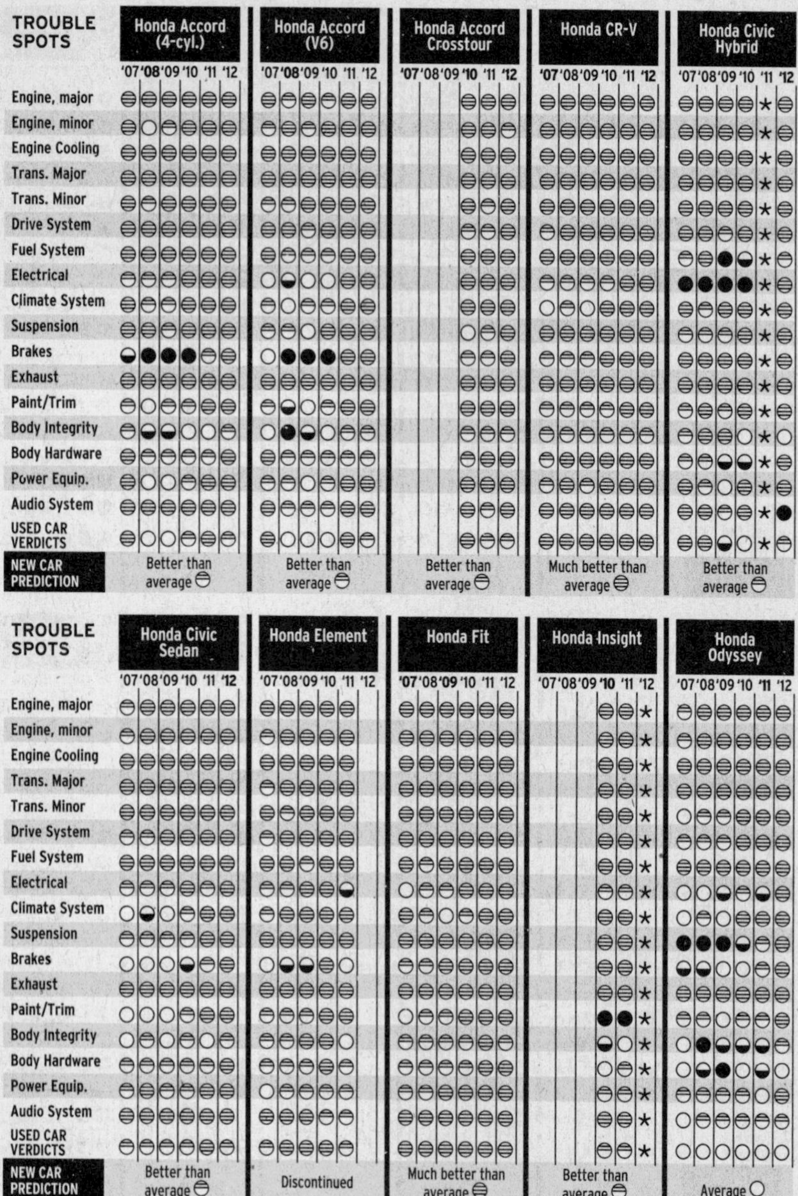
TROUBLE SPOTS
Honda Accord (4-cyl.)
Honda Accord (V6)
Honda Accord Crosstour
Honda CR-V
Honda Civic Hybrid
'07 '08 '09 '10 '11 '12
Engine, major
Engine, minor
Engine Cooling
Trans. Major
Trans. Minor
Drive System
Fuel System
Electrical
Climate System
Suspension
Brakes
Exhaust
Paint/Trim
Body Integrity
Body Hardware
Power Equip.
Audio System
USED CAR VERDICTS
NEW CAR PREDICTION
Better than average
Better than average
Better than average
Much better than average
Better than average
TROUBLE SPOTS
Honda Civic Sedan
Honda Element
Honda Fit
Honda Insight
Honda Odyssey
'07 '08 '09 '10 '11 '12
Engine, major
Engine, minor
Engine Cooling
Trans. Major
Trans. Minor
Drive System
Fuel System
Electrical
Climate System
Suspension
Brakes
Exhaust
Paint/Trim
Body Integrity
Body Hardware
Power Equip.
Audio System
USED CAR VERDICTS
NEW CAR PREDICTION
Better than average
Discontinued
Much better than average
Better than average
Average

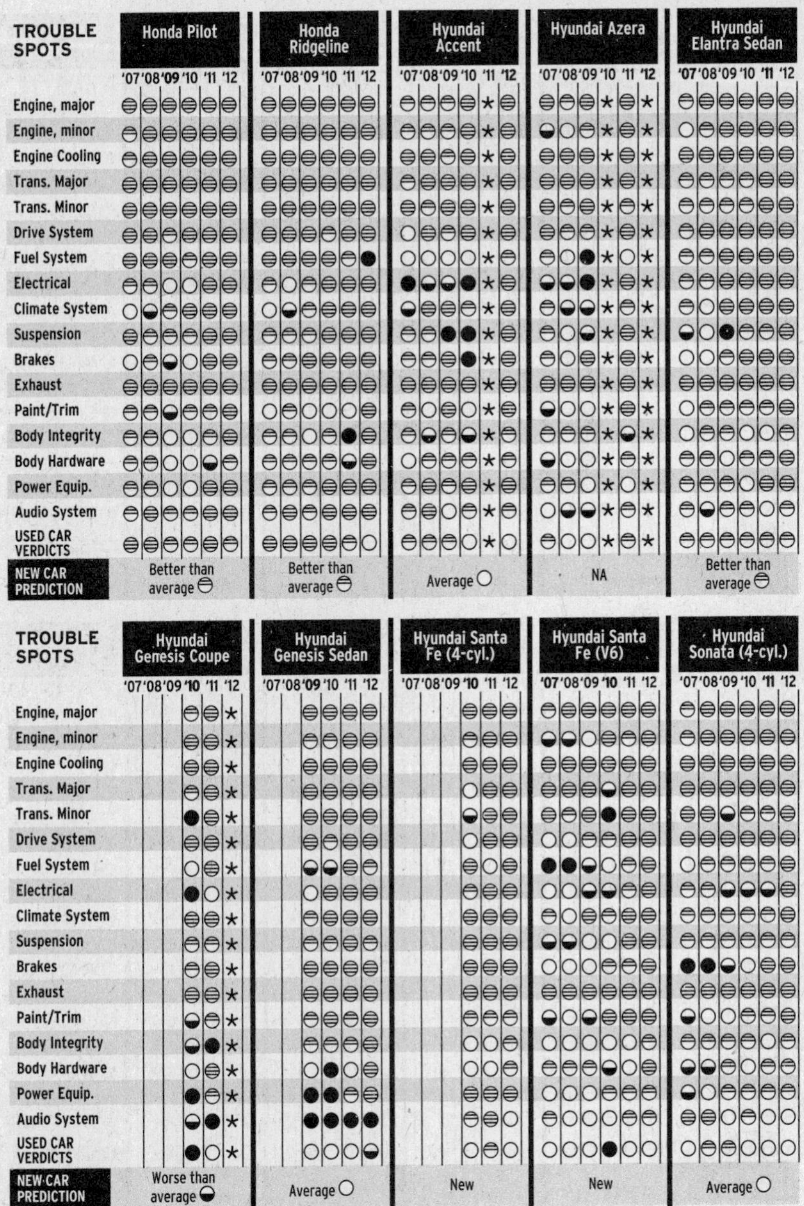
TROUBLE SPOTS
Honda Pilot
Honda Ridgeline
Hyundai Accent
Hyundai Azera
Hyundai Elantra Sedan
'07 '08 '09 '10 '11 '12
Engine, major
Engine, minor
Engine Cooling
Trans. Major
Trans. Minor
Drive System
Fuel System
Electrical
Climate System
Suspension
Brakes
Exhaust
Paint/Trim
Body Integrity
Body Hardware
Power Equip.
Audio System
USED CAR VERDICTS
NEW CAR PREDICTION
Better than average
Better than average
Average
NA
Better than average
TROUBLE SPOTS
Hyundai Genesis Coupe
Hyundai Genesis Sedan
Hyundai Santa Fe (4-cyl.)
Hyundai Santa Fe (V6)
Hyundai Sonata (4-cyl.)
'07 '08 '09 '10 '11 '12
Engine, major
Engine, minor
Engine Cooling
Trans. Major
Trans. Minor
Drive System
Fuel System
Electrical
Climate System
Suspension
Brakes
Exhaust
Paint/Trim
Body Integrity
Body Hardware
Power Equip.
Audio System
USED CAR VERDICTS
NEW-CAR PREDICTION
Worse than average
Average
New
New
Average

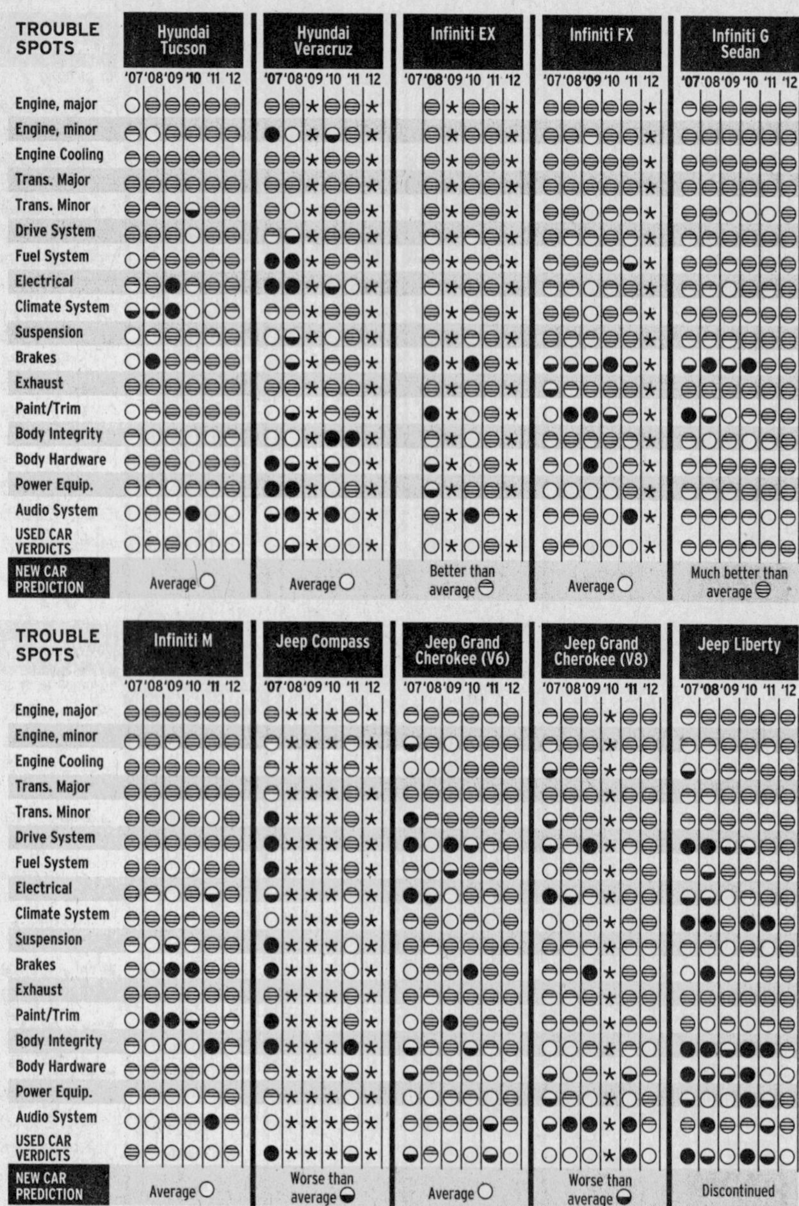

## TROUBLE SPOTS

| TROUBLE SPOTS | Hyundai Tucson '07 | '08 | '09 | **'10** | '11 | '12 | Hyundai Veracruz **'07** | '08 | '09 | '10 | '11 | '12 |
|---|---|---|---|---|---|---|---|---|---|---|---|---|
| Engine, major | ○ | ⊜ | ⊜ | ⊜ | ⊜ | ⊜ | ⊜ | ⊜ | ★ | ⊜ | ⊜ | ★ |
| Engine, minor | ⊖ | ○ | ⊜ | ⊜ | ⊜ | ⊜ | ● | ○ | ★ | ◒ | ⊜ | ★ |
| Engine Cooling | ⊖ | ⊜ | ⊜ | ⊜ | ⊜ | ⊜ | ⊜ | ⊜ | ★ | ⊜ | ⊜ | ★ |
| Trans. Major | ⊜ | ⊜ | ⊜ | ⊜ | ⊜ | ⊜ | ⊜ | ⊜ | ★ | ⊜ | ⊜ | ★ |
| Trans. Minor | ⊜ | ⊖ | ⊜ | ◒ | ⊜ | ⊜ | ⊜ | ○ | ★ | ⊜ | ⊜ | ★ |
| Drive System | ⊜ | ⊜ | ⊜ | ○ | ⊜ | ⊜ | ⊖ | ◒ | ★ | ⊜ | ⊜ | ★ |
| Fuel System | ○ | ⊖ | ⊜ | ⊜ | ⊖ | ⊜ | ● | ● | ★ | ⊜ | ⊖ | ★ |
| Electrical | ⊖ | ⊜ | ● | ⊖ | ⊜ | ⊜ | ● | ● | ★ | ◒ | ○ | ★ |
| Climate System | ◒ | ◒ | ● | ○ | ○ | ⊖ | ⊖ | ⊖ | ★ | ⊜ | ⊜ | ★ |
| Suspension | ○ | ⊖ | ⊜ | ⊖ | ⊖ | ⊜ | ○ | ◒ | ★ | ○ | ⊜ | ★ |
| Brakes | ○ | ● | ⊜ | ⊖ | ⊜ | ⊜ | ○ | ◒ | ★ | ⊖ | ⊜ | ★ |
| Exhaust | ⊜ | ⊜ | ⊜ | ⊜ | ⊜ | ⊜ | ⊜ | ⊜ | ★ | ⊜ | ⊜ | ★ |
| Paint/Trim | ○ | ⊖ | ⊜ | ⊜ | ⊜ | ⊜ | ○ | ◒ | ★ | ⊖ | ⊜ | ★ |
| Body Integrity | ⊖ | ○ | ⊖ | ○ | ○ | ⊖ | ○ | ○ | ★ | ● | ● | ★ |
| Body Hardware | ⊖ | ⊜ | ⊜ | ○ | ⊜ | ⊜ | ● | ◒ | ★ | ◒ | ○ | ★ |
| Power Equip. | ⊖ | ⊖ | ○ | ⊖ | ⊜ | ⊜ | ● | ● | ★ | ○ | ⊜ | ★ |
| Audio System | ○ | ⊖ | ⊖ | ● | ○ | ○ | ◒ | ● | ★ | ● | ○ | ★ |
| USED CAR VERDICTS | ○ | ⊖ | ⊜ | ○ | ○ | ○ | ○ | ◒ | ★ | ○ | ○ | ★ |
| NEW CAR PREDICTION | Average ○ | | | | | | Average ○ | | | | | |

| TROUBLE SPOTS | Infiniti EX '07 | **'08** | '09 | '10 | '11 | '12 | Infiniti FX '07 | '08 | **'09** | '10 | '11 | '12 | Infiniti G Sedan **'07** | '08 | '09 | '10 | '11 | '12 |
|---|---|---|---|---|---|---|---|---|---|---|---|---|---|---|---|---|---|---|
| Engine, major | | ⊜ | ★ | ⊜ | ⊜ | ★ | ⊜ | ⊜ | ⊜ | ⊜ | ⊜ | ★ | ⊖ | ⊜ | ⊜ | ⊜ | ⊜ | ⊜ |
| Engine, minor | | ⊜ | ★ | ⊜ | ⊜ | ★ | ⊜ | ⊜ | ⊖ | ⊜ | ⊖ | ★ | ⊜ | ⊜ | ⊜ | ⊜ | ⊜ | ⊜ |
| Engine Cooling | | ⊜ | ★ | ⊜ | ⊜ | ★ | ⊜ | ⊜ | ⊜ | ⊜ | ⊜ | ★ | ⊜ | ⊜ | ⊜ | ⊜ | ⊜ | ⊜ |
| Trans. Major | | ⊜ | ★ | ⊜ | ⊜ | ★ | ⊜ | ⊜ | ⊜ | ⊜ | ⊜ | ★ | ⊜ | ⊜ | ⊜ | ⊜ | ⊜ | ⊜ |
| Trans. Minor | | ⊜ | ★ | ⊜ | ⊜ | ★ | ⊜ | ⊜ | ○ | ⊖ | ⊖ | ★ | ⊜ | ⊜ | ○ | ○ | ○ | ⊜ |
| Drive System | | ⊖ | ★ | ⊖ | ⊜ | ★ | ⊜ | ⊖ | ⊖ | ⊜ | ⊖ | ★ | ⊖ | ⊖ | ⊜ | ⊜ | ⊜ | ⊜ |
| Fuel System | | ⊖ | ★ | ⊖ | ⊖ | ★ | ⊖ | ⊜ | ⊜ | ⊖ | ◒ | ★ | ⊜ | ⊜ | ⊖ | ⊜ | ⊜ | ⊜ |
| Electrical | | ⊖ | ★ | ⊜ | ⊜ | ★ | ⊖ | ⊖ | ○ | ⊖ | ⊜ | ★ | ⊖ | ⊖ | ○ | ⊜ | ⊖ | ⊜ |
| Climate System | | ⊜ | ★ | ⊖ | ⊜ | ★ | ⊜ | ⊜ | ○ | ⊜ | ⊖ | ★ | ⊖ | ⊜ | ⊜ | ⊖ | ⊜ | ⊜ |
| Suspension | | ⊖ | ★ | ⊖ | ⊜ | ★ | ⊜ | ⊖ | ⊖ | ⊜ | ⊜ | ★ | ⊖ | ⊖ | ⊖ | ⊜ | ⊜ | ⊜ |
| Brakes | | ● | ★ | ● | ⊜ | ★ | ◒ | ◒ | ◒ | ● | ◒ | ★ | ◒ | ● | ◒ | ● | ⊜ | ⊜ |
| Exhaust | | ⊜ | ★ | ⊜ | ⊜ | ★ | ◒ | ⊖ | ⊜ | ⊜ | ⊜ | ★ | ⊜ | ⊜ | ⊜ | ⊜ | ⊜ | ⊜ |
| Paint/Trim | | ● | ★ | ○ | ⊜ | ★ | ○ | ● | ● | ◒ | ⊖ | ★ | ● | ◒ | ○ | ⊖ | ⊜ | ⊜ |
| Body Integrity | | ⊖ | ★ | ○ | ⊜ | ★ | ⊖ | ⊜ | ⊖ | ⊜ | ⊖ | ★ | ⊖ | ○ | ⊖ | ○ | ⊖ | ⊜ |
| Body Hardware | | ◒ | ★ | ○ | ⊜ | ★ | ⊖ | ○ | ● | ○ | ⊖ | ★ | ⊖ | ⊖ | ⊜ | ⊜ | ⊜ | ⊜ |
| Power Equip. | | ◒ | ★ | ⊜ | ⊜ | ★ | ○ | ○ | ○ | ○ | ⊜ | ★ | ⊖ | ⊖ | ⊖ | ⊜ | ⊜ | ⊜ |
| Audio System | | ⊜ | ★ | ● | ⊖ | ★ | ⊖ | ⊖ | ⊜ | ○ | ● | ★ | ⊖ | ⊖ | ⊖ | ⊖ | ○ | ⊖ |
| USED CAR VERDICTS | | ○ | ★ | ○ | ⊜ | ★ | ⊜ | ⊖ | ○ | ○ | ○ | ★ | ⊜ | ⊖ | ⊖ | ⊖ | ⊖ | ⊜ |
| NEW CAR PREDICTION | Better than average ⊖ | | | | | | Average ○ | | | | | | Much better than average ⊜ | | | | | |

## TROUBLE SPOTS

| TROUBLE SPOTS | Infiniti M '07 | '08 | '09 | '10 | **'11** | '12 | Jeep Compass **'07** | '08 | '09 | '10 | '11 | '12 |
|---|---|---|---|---|---|---|---|---|---|---|---|---|
| Engine, major | ⊜ | ⊜ | ⊜ | ⊜ | ⊜ | ⊜ | ⊜ | ★ | ★ | ★ | ⊖ | ★ |
| Engine, minor | ⊖ | ⊜ | ⊖ | ⊜ | ⊜ | ⊜ | ⊖ | ★ | ★ | ★ | ⊖ | ★ |
| Engine Cooling | ⊜ | ⊜ | ⊜ | ⊜ | ⊜ | ⊜ | ⊖ | ★ | ★ | ★ | ⊖ | ★ |
| Trans. Major | ⊜ | ⊜ | ⊜ | ⊜ | ⊜ | ⊜ | ⊖ | ★ | ★ | ★ | ⊜ | ★ |
| Trans. Minor | ⊜ | ⊜ | ○ | ⊜ | ○ | ⊜ | ● | ★ | ★ | ★ | ⊜ | ★ |
| Drive System | ⊜ | ⊜ | ⊜ | ⊜ | ⊜ | ⊜ | ● | ★ | ★ | ★ | ⊜ | ★ |
| Fuel System | ⊜ | ⊜ | ○ | ○ | ⊜ | ⊜ | ● | ★ | ★ | ★ | ⊜ | ★ |
| Electrical | ⊜ | ⊖ | ○ | ⊜ | ◒ | ⊜ | ◒ | ★ | ★ | ★ | ⊖ | ★ |
| Climate System | ⊖ | ⊜ | ⊜ | ⊖ | ⊜ | ⊜ | ○ | ★ | ★ | ★ | ⊜ | ★ |
| Suspension | ⊖ | ○ | ◒ | ⊖ | ⊜ | ⊜ | ● | ★ | ★ | ★ | ○ | ★ |
| Brakes | ⊖ | ○ | ● | ● | ⊜ | ⊜ | ● | ★ | ★ | ★ | ○ | ★ |
| Exhaust | ⊜ | ⊜ | ⊜ | ⊜ | ⊜ | ⊜ | ⊜ | ★ | ★ | ★ | ⊜ | ★ |
| Paint/Trim | ○ | ● | ● | ◒ | ⊜ | ⊖ | ● | ★ | ★ | ★ | ⊜ | ★ |
| Body Integrity | ⊖ | ○ | ○ | ○ | ● | ⊖ | ● | ★ | ★ | ★ | ● | ★ |
| Body Hardware | ⊖ | ⊖ | ⊖ | ⊖ | ○ | ⊖ | ⊖ | ★ | ★ | ★ | ◒ | ★ |
| Power Equip. | ⊖ | ⊖ | ⊖ | ○ | ⊖ | ⊜ | ⊖ | ★ | ★ | ★ | ○ | ★ |
| Audio System | ○ | ○ | ⊖ | ⊖ | ● | ⊖ | ○ | ★ | ★ | ★ | ⊖ | ★ |
| USED CAR VERDICTS | ⊜ | ⊖ | ○ | ○ | ○ | ⊖ | ● | ★ | ★ | ★ | ◒ | ★ |
| NEW CAR PREDICTION | Average ○ | | | | | | Worse than average ◒ | | | | | |

| TROUBLE SPOTS | Jeep Grand Cherokee (V6) '07 | '08 | '09 | '10 | **'11** | '12 | Jeep Grand Cherokee (V8) '07 | '08 | '09 | '10 | **'11** | '12 | Jeep Liberty '07 | **'08** | '09 | '10 | '11 | '12 |
|---|---|---|---|---|---|---|---|---|---|---|---|---|---|---|---|---|---|---|
| Engine, major | ⊖ | ⊜ | ⊖ | ⊜ | ⊖ | ⊜ | ⊖ | ⊜ | ⊜ | ★ | ⊜ | ⊜ | ⊖ | ⊜ | ⊜ | ⊜ | ⊜ | ⊜ |
| Engine, minor | ◒ | ⊜ | ○ | ⊜ | ⊜ | ⊜ | ⊖ | ⊜ | ⊜ | ★ | ⊜ | ⊜ | ⊖ | ⊖ | ⊜ | ⊜ | ⊖ | ⊜ |
| Engine Cooling | ○ | ○ | ○ | ⊜ | ⊜ | ⊜ | ◒ | ⊖ | ⊜ | ★ | ⊖ | ⊜ | ◒ | ○ | ⊖ | ⊖ | ⊜ | ⊜ |
| Trans. Major | ⊜ | ⊜ | ⊜ | ⊜ | ⊜ | ⊜ | ⊜ | ⊜ | ⊜ | ★ | ⊜ | ⊜ | ⊖ | ⊖ | ⊜ | ⊜ | ⊜ | ⊜ |
| Trans. Minor | ● | ⊖ | ⊜ | ⊜ | ⊜ | ⊜ | ◒ | ⊖ | ⊖ | ★ | ⊖ | ⊜ | ⊖ | ⊖ | ⊜ | ⊖ | ⊖ | ⊜ |
| Drive System | ● | ○ | ● | ◒ | ⊖ | ⊜ | ◒ | ⊖ | ● | ★ | ⊖ | ⊜ | ● | ● | ◒ | ◒ | ⊜ | ⊜ |
| Fuel System | ⊖ | ○ | ◒ | ⊜ | ⊜ | ⊜ | ○ | ⊖ | ⊖ | ★ | ⊖ | ⊜ | ⊖ | ◒ | ⊜ | ⊖ | ⊖ | ⊜ |
| Electrical | ● | ◒ | ○ | ⊜ | ⊖ | ⊜ | ● | ◒ | ⊖ | ★ | ⊜ | ⊜ | ◒ | ◒ | ○ | ⊖ | ⊜ | ⊜ |
| Climate System | ⊖ | ⊜ | ○ | ⊖ | ○ | ⊜ | ○ | ○ | ⊖ | ★ | ⊖ | ⊜ | ● | ● | ⊜ | ● | ● | ⊜ |
| Suspension | ⊜ | ⊖ | ⊜ | ⊜ | ⊜ | ⊜ | ⊜ | ⊖ | ⊖ | ★ | ⊖ | ⊖ | ⊖ | ⊖ | ○ | ⊜ | ○ | ⊜ |
| Brakes | ○ | ⊖ | ⊖ | ● | ⊜ | ⊜ | ⊖ | ⊖ | ● | ★ | ⊜ | ⊜ | ○ | ● | ⊖ | ⊖ | ⊜ | ⊜ |
| Exhaust | ⊜ | ⊖ | ⊜ | ⊜ | ⊜ | ⊜ | ⊖ | ⊖ | ⊜ | ★ | ⊜ | ⊜ | ⊜ | ⊜ | ⊜ | ⊜ | ⊜ | ⊜ |
| Paint/Trim | ○ | ⊜ | ● | ⊜ | ⊖ | ⊜ | ⊖ | ⊜ | ⊖ | ★ | ⊖ | ⊖ | ⊜ | ○ | ⊖ | ○ | ⊖ | ⊜ |
| Body Integrity | ◒ | ⊖ | ⊜ | ◒ | ⊖ | ⊜ | ○ | ○ | ⊖ | ★ | ⊖ | ○ | ● | ● | ◒ | ● | ● | ⊖ |
| Body Hardware | ◒ | ⊖ | ⊖ | ⊖ | ○ | ⊖ | ◒ | ○ | ⊖ | ★ | ◒ | ⊖ | ● | ◒ | ◒ | ● | ○ | ○ |
| Power Equip. | ○ | ○ | ⊖ | ⊖ | ○ | ⊜ | ◒ | ⊖ | ○ | ★ | ○ | ⊜ | ◒ | ○ | ○ | ● | ◒ | ⊜ |
| Audio System | ⊖ | ⊖ | ⊖ | ⊖ | ◒ | ⊖ | ◒ | ● | ● | ★ | ● | ⊖ | ⊜ | ● | ⊜ | ⊖ | ◒ | ⊜ |
| USED CAR VERDICTS | ◒ | ⊖ | ○ | ○ | ◒ | ○ | ○ | ○ | ○ | ★ | ● | ○ | ● | ◒ | ○ | ● | ◒ | ○ |
| NEW CAR PREDICTION | Average ○ | | | | | | Worse than average ◒ | | | | | | Discontinued | | | | | |

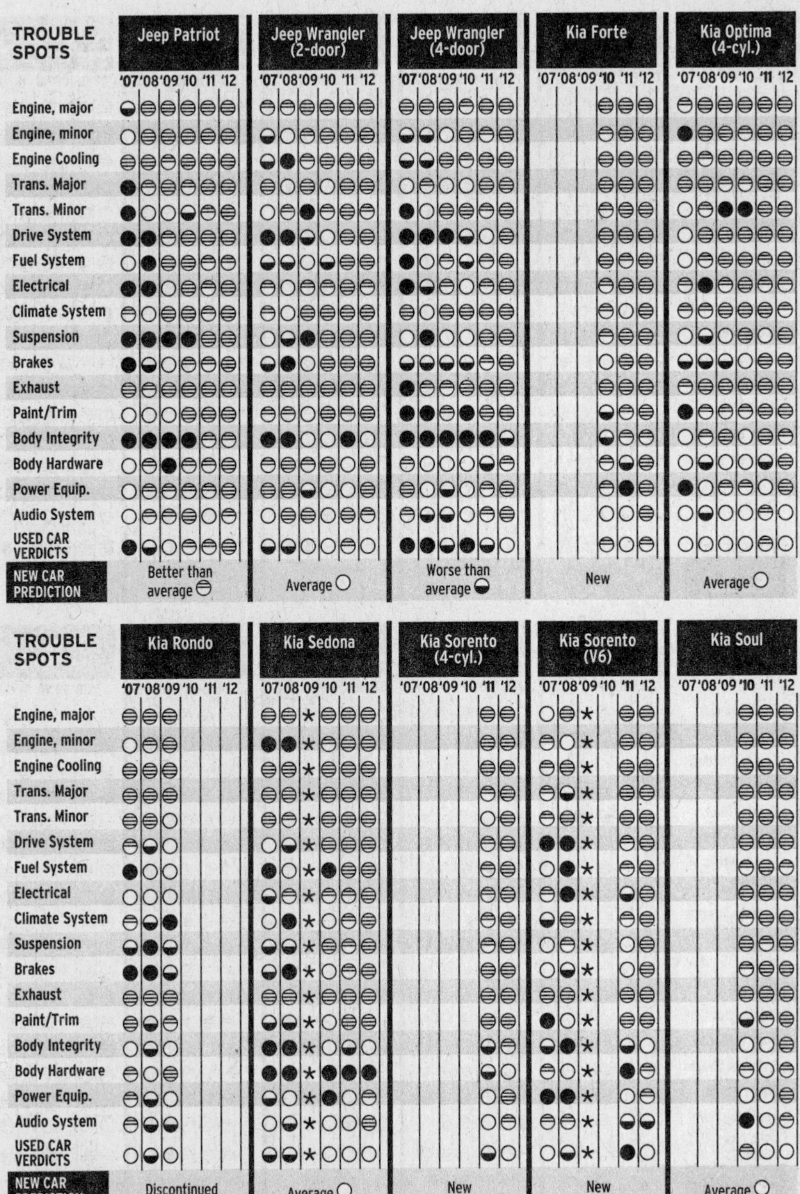

**TROUBLE SPOTS**

| Jeep Patriot | '07 | '08 | '09 | '10 | '11 | '12 |
|---|---|---|---|---|---|---|
| Engine, major | ◒ | ⊜ | ⊜ | ⊜ | ⊜ | ⊜ |
| Engine, minor | ○ | ⊜ | ⊜ | ⊜ | ⊜ | ⊜ |
| Engine Cooling | ⊜ | ⊜ | ⊖ | ⊜ | ⊜ | ⊜ |
| Trans. Major | ● | ⊖ | ⊜ | ⊖ | ⊜ | ⊜ |
| Trans. Minor | ● | ○ | ○ | ◒ | ⊖ | ⊜ |
| Drive System | ● | ● | ⊖ | ⊜ | ⊜ | ⊜ |
| Fuel System | ○ | ● | ⊜ | ⊜ | ⊖ | ⊖ |
| Electrical | ● | ● | ○ | ⊜ | ⊖ | ⊜ |
| Climate System | ⊖ | ○ | ⊜ | ⊜ | ⊖ | ⊜ |
| Suspension | ● | ● | ● | ● | ⊜ | ⊜ |
| Brakes | ● | ◒ | ○ | ⊖ | ⊖ | ⊜ |
| Exhaust | ⊜ | ⊖ | ⊜ | ⊜ | ⊜ | ⊜ |
| Paint/Trim | ○ | ○ | ○ | ⊜ | ⊜ | ⊜ |
| Body Integrity | ● | ● | ● | ● | ⊖ | ⊖ |
| Body Hardware | ○ | ⊖ | ● | ⊖ | ⊖ | ⊜ |
| Power Equip. | ○ | ⊖ | ⊖ | ⊖ | ⊖ | ⊜ |
| Audio System | ○ | ⊜ | ⊖ | ⊜ | ○ | ⊖ |
| USED CAR VERDICTS | ● | ◒ | ○ | ⊜ | ⊜ | ⊜ |
| NEW CAR PREDICTION | Better than average ⊖ | | | | | |

| Jeep Wrangler (2-door) | '07 | '08 | '09 | '10 | '11 | '12 |
|---|---|---|---|---|---|---|
| Engine, major | ⊖ | ⊖ | ⊜ | ⊜ | ⊜ | ⊜ |
| Engine, minor | ◒ | ○ | ⊖ | ⊜ | ⊜ | ⊜ |
| Engine Cooling | ◒ | ● | ⊖ | ⊜ | ⊜ | ⊜ |
| Trans. Major | ⊜ | ○ | ⊜ | ○ | ⊜ | ⊜ |
| Trans. Minor | ○ | ⊖ | ● | ⊖ | ⊜ | ⊖ |
| Drive System | ● | ● | ◒ | ○ | ⊜ | ⊜ |
| Fuel System | ◒ | ◒ | ○ | ◒ | ⊜ | ⊜ |
| Electrical | ⊖ | ○ | ⊖ | ⊜ | ⊜ | ⊖ |
| Climate System | ⊖ | ○ | ⊜ | ⊜ | ⊜ | ⊜ |
| Suspension | ○ | ◒ | ● | ⊜ | ⊜ | ⊜ |
| Brakes | ◒ | ● | ○ | ⊜ | ⊜ | ⊜ |
| Exhaust | ⊜ | ⊜ | ⊜ | ⊜ | ⊜ | ⊜ |
| Paint/Trim | ⊖ | ⊖ | ○ | ⊜ | ⊖ | ⊜ |
| Body Integrity | ● | ● | ○ | ○ | ● | ○ |
| Body Hardware | ⊖ | ⊜ | ⊖ | ⊜ | ○ | ⊜ |
| Power Equip. | ⊜ | ⊜ | ◒ | ○ | ○ | ⊜ |
| Audio System | ○ | ⊜ | ⊜ | ○ | ⊜ | ⊖ |
| USED CAR VERDICTS | ◒ | ◒ | ○ | ○ | ⊜ | ○ |
| NEW CAR PREDICTION | Average ○ | | | | | |

| Jeep Wrangler (4-door) | '07 | '08 | '09 | '10 | '11 | '12 |
|---|---|---|---|---|---|---|
| Engine, major | ⊜ | ⊜ | ⊜ | ⊖ | ⊜ | ⊜ |
| Engine, minor | ◒ | ◒ | ○ | ⊜ | ⊖ | ⊜ |
| Engine Cooling | ◒ | ◒ | ⊜ | ⊖ | ⊜ | ⊜ |
| Trans. Major | ○ | ⊖ | ○ | ○ | ⊜ | ⊜ |
| Trans. Minor | ● | ○ | ⊜ | ⊜ | ⊖ | ⊜ |
| Drive System | ● | ● | ● | ◒ | ○ | ⊜ |
| Fuel System | ● | ○ | ⊖ | ◒ | ⊖ | ⊜ |
| Electrical | ● | ◒ | ⊖ | ○ | ⊖ | ⊜ |
| Climate System | ⊜ | ○ | ⊜ | ⊜ | ⊜ | ⊜ |
| Suspension | ○ | ● | ○ | ○ | ⊜ | ⊜ |
| Brakes | ◒ | ◒ | ◒ | ◒ | ⊖ | ⊜ |
| Exhaust | ● | ⊖ | ⊖ | ⊜ | ⊜ | ⊜ |
| Paint/Trim | ● | ● | ⊖ | ● | ⊜ | ⊜ |
| Body Integrity | ● | ● | ● | ● | ● | ◒ |
| Body Hardware | ⊖ | ○ | ○ | ○ | ◒ | ⊖ |
| Power Equip. | ⊜ | ○ | ◒ | ○ | ⊖ | ⊜ |
| Audio System | ⊖ | ◒ | ◒ | ○ | ⊖ | ⊜ |
| USED CAR VERDICTS | ● | ● | ◒ | ● | ◒ | ○ |
| NEW CAR PREDICTION | Worse than average ◒ | | | | | |

| Kia Forte | '07 | '08 | '09 | '10 | '11 | '12 |
|---|---|---|---|---|---|---|
| Engine, major | | | | ⊜ | ⊜ | ⊜ |
| Engine, minor | | | | ⊖ | ⊜ | ⊜ |
| Engine Cooling | | | | ⊜ | ⊜ | ⊜ |
| Trans. Major | | | | ⊜ | ⊜ | ⊜ |
| Trans. Minor | | | | ⊖ | ⊜ | ⊜ |
| Drive System | | | | ⊜ | ⊜ | ⊜ |
| Fuel System | | | | ⊜ | ⊖ | ⊜ |
| Electrical | | | | ⊖ | ⊜ | ⊜ |
| Climate System | | | | ⊖ | ○ | ⊜ |
| Suspension | | | | ⊖ | ⊜ | ⊜ |
| Brakes | | | | ○ | ⊜ | ⊜ |
| Exhaust | | | | ⊜ | ⊜ | ⊜ |
| Paint/Trim | | | | ◒ | ⊖ | ⊜ |
| Body Integrity | | | | ◒ | ⊖ | ⊖ |
| Body Hardware | | | | ⊖ | ◒ | ⊜ |
| Power Equip. | | | | ⊖ | ● | ⊜ |
| Audio System | | | | ○ | ○ | ⊜ |
| USED CAR VERDICTS | | | | ⊜ | ○ | ⊖ |
| NEW CAR PREDICTION | New | | | | | |

| Kia Optima (4-cyl.) | '07 | '08 | '09 | '10 | '11 | '12 |
|---|---|---|---|---|---|---|
| Engine, major | ⊖ | ⊜ | ⊜ | ⊜ | ⊜ | ⊜ |
| Engine, minor | ● | ⊜ | ⊜ | ⊖ | ⊜ | ⊜ |
| Engine Cooling | ⊜ | ⊖ | ⊜ | ⊜ | ⊜ | ⊜ |
| Trans. Major | ⊜ | ⊜ | ⊖ | ⊖ | ⊜ | ⊜ |
| Trans. Minor | ○ | ⊖ | ● | ● | ⊜ | ⊜ |
| Drive System | ○ | ⊜ | ⊜ | ⊜ | ⊜ | ⊜ |
| Fuel System | ○ | ⊖ | ⊜ | ⊜ | ⊖ | ⊜ |
| Electrical | ⊖ | ● | ⊖ | ⊜ | ⊖ | ⊖ |
| Climate System | ⊖ | ⊖ | ⊜ | ⊜ | ⊜ | ⊖ |
| Suspension | ○ | ◒ | ○ | ⊜ | ○ | ⊜ |
| Brakes | ◒ | ◒ | ◒ | ○ | ⊜ | ⊜ |
| Exhaust | ⊖ | ⊜ | ⊜ | ⊜ | ⊜ | ⊜ |
| Paint/Trim | ● | ⊖ | ⊖ | ⊖ | ⊜ | ⊜ |
| Body Integrity | ○ | ⊖ | ⊜ | ○ | ⊜ | ⊖ |
| Body Hardware | ○ | ◒ | ○ | ○ | ◒ | ⊜ |
| Power Equip. | ● | ○ | ⊜ | ⊖ | ○ | ⊜ |
| Audio System | ○ | ◒ | ○ | ○ | ⊖ | ○ |
| USED CAR VERDICTS | ○ | ○ | ○ | ○ | ⊜ | ○ |
| NEW CAR PREDICTION | Average ○ | | | | | |

**TROUBLE SPOTS**

| Kia Rondo | '07 | '08 | '09 | '10 | '11 | '12 |
|---|---|---|---|---|---|---|
| Engine, major | ⊜ | ⊜ | ⊜ | | | |
| Engine, minor | ○ | ⊖ | ⊜ | | | |
| Engine Cooling | ⊜ | ⊜ | ⊜ | | | |
| Trans. Major | ⊜ | ⊜ | ⊜ | | | |
| Trans. Minor | ⊜ | ⊜ | ○ | | | |
| Drive System | ⊖ | ◒ | ○ | | | |
| Fuel System | ● | ○ | ○ | | | |
| Electrical | ○ | ○ | ○ | | | |
| Climate System | ⊖ | ◒ | ● | | | |
| Suspension | ◒ | ● | ◒ | | | |
| Brakes | ● | ● | ◒ | | | |
| Exhaust | ⊜ | ⊜ | ⊜ | | | |
| Paint/Trim | ⊜ | ◒ | ⊖ | | | |
| Body Integrity | ○ | ◒ | ○ | | | |
| Body Hardware | ⊖ | ○ | ⊜ | | | |
| Power Equip. | ⊖ | ◒ | ○ | | | |
| Audio System | ⊖ | ◒ | ◒ | | | |
| USED CAR VERDICTS | ○ | ◒ | ○ | | | |
| NEW CAR PREDICTION | Discontinued | | | | | |

| Kia Sedona | '07 | '08 | '09 | '10 | '11 | '12 |
|---|---|---|---|---|---|---|
| Engine, major | ⊜ | ⊜ | * | ⊜ | ⊜ | ⊜ |
| Engine, minor | ● | ● | * | ⊖ | ⊜ | ⊜ |
| Engine Cooling | ⊜ | ⊜ | * | ⊜ | ⊜ | ⊜ |
| Trans. Major | ⊜ | ⊜ | * | ⊜ | ⊜ | ⊜ |
| Trans. Minor | ⊜ | ⊖ | * | ⊜ | ⊜ | ⊜ |
| Drive System | ○ | ◒ | * | ⊜ | ⊜ | ⊜ |
| Fuel System | ● | ○ | * | ● | ⊜ | ⊜ |
| Electrical | ◒ | ⊖ | * | ⊖ | ⊖ | ⊜ |
| Climate System | ○ | ● | * | ○ | ⊖ | ⊜ |
| Suspension | ◒ | ◒ | * | ⊜ | ⊖ | ⊜ |
| Brakes | ◒ | ● | * | ○ | ⊖ | ⊜ |
| Exhaust | ⊜ | ⊜ | * | ⊜ | ⊜ | ⊜ |
| Paint/Trim | ◒ | ◒ | * | ○ | ⊜ | ⊜ |
| Body Integrity | ● | ● | * | ○ | ◒ | ○ |
| Body Hardware | ● | ● | * | ● | ● | ● |
| Power Equip. | ◒ | ○ | * | ● | ○ | ⊖ |
| Audio System | ○ | ◒ | * | ○ | ○ | ⊜ |
| USED CAR VERDICTS | ◒ | ◒ | * | ○ | ○ | ○ |
| NEW CAR PREDICTION | Average ○ | | | | | |

| Kia Sorento (4-cyl.) | '07 | '08 | '09 | '10 | '11 | '12 |
|---|---|---|---|---|---|---|
| Engine, major | | | | | ⊜ | ⊜ |
| Engine, minor | | | | | ⊜ | ⊜ |
| Engine Cooling | | | | | ⊜ | ⊜ |
| Trans. Major | | | | | ⊖ | ⊜ |
| Trans. Minor | | | | | ○ | ⊜ |
| Drive System | | | | | ⊖ | ⊜ |
| Fuel System | | | | | ⊖ | ⊜ |
| Electrical | | | | | ⊖ | ⊜ |
| Climate System | | | | | ⊖ | ⊜ |
| Suspension | | | | | ⊖ | ⊜ |
| Brakes | | | | | ⊜ | ⊜ |
| Exhaust | | | | | ⊜ | ⊜ |
| Paint/Trim | | | | | ⊜ | ⊜ |
| Body Integrity | | | | | ◒ | ⊖ |
| Body Hardware | | | | | ◒ | ○ |
| Power Equip. | | | | | ○ | ⊜ |
| Audio System | | | | | ○ | ⊖ |
| USED CAR VERDICTS | | | | | ◒ | ○ |
| NEW CAR PREDICTION | New | | | | | |

| Kia Sorento (V6) | '07 | '08 | '09 | '10 | '11 | '12 |
|---|---|---|---|---|---|---|
| Engine, major | ○ | ⊜ | * | | ⊜ | ⊜ |
| Engine, minor | ⊖ | ○ | * | | ⊜ | ⊜ |
| Engine Cooling | ⊖ | ⊜ | * | | ⊜ | ⊜ |
| Trans. Major | ⊖ | ◒ | * | | ⊜ | ⊜ |
| Trans. Minor | ⊖ | ⊜ | * | | ⊜ | ⊜ |
| Drive System | ● | ● | * | | ⊖ | ⊜ |
| Fuel System | ○ | ● | * | | ⊖ | ⊜ |
| Electrical | ⊖ | ● | * | | ◒ | ⊜ |
| Climate System | ◒ | ⊜ | * | | ⊖ | ⊜ |
| Suspension | ○ | ⊖ | * | | ○ | ⊜ |
| Brakes | ○ | ◒ | * | | ○ | ⊜ |
| Exhaust | ⊜ | ⊜ | * | | ⊜ | ⊜ |
| Paint/Trim | ● | ○ | * | | ⊜ | ⊜ |
| Body Integrity | ◒ | ● | * | | ◒ | ○ |
| Body Hardware | ⊖ | ○ | * | | ● | ⊖ |
| Power Equip. | ● | ● | * | | ○ | ⊖ |
| Audio System | ⊖ | ⊜ | * | | ◒ | ◒ |
| USED CAR VERDICTS | ○ | ◒ | * | | ● | ○ |
| NEW CAR PREDICTION | New | | | | | |

| Kia Soul | '07 | '08 | '09 | '10 | '11 | '12 |
|---|---|---|---|---|---|---|
| Engine, major | | | | ⊜ | ⊜ | ⊜ |
| Engine, minor | | | | ⊜ | ⊜ | ⊜ |
| Engine Cooling | | | | ⊜ | ⊜ | ⊜ |
| Trans. Major | | | | ⊜ | ⊜ | ⊜ |
| Trans. Minor | | | | ⊜ | ⊜ | ⊜ |
| Drive System | | | | ⊜ | ⊜ | ⊜ |
| Fuel System | | | | ⊖ | ⊜ | ⊖ |
| Electrical | | | | ⊜ | ⊜ | ⊜ |
| Climate System | | | | ⊖ | ⊜ | ⊜ |
| Suspension | | | | ⊜ | ⊖ | ⊜ |
| Brakes | | | | ⊖ | ⊜ | ⊜ |
| Exhaust | | | | ⊜ | ⊜ | ⊜ |
| Paint/Trim | | | | ◒ | ⊖ | ⊜ |
| Body Integrity | | | | ○ | ○ | ⊜ |
| Body Hardware | | | | ⊖ | ○ | ⊖ |
| Power Equip. | | | | ○ | ○ | ⊜ |
| Audio System | | | | ● | ○ | ⊖ |
| USED CAR VERDICTS | | | | ⊖ | ○ | ○ |
| NEW CAR PREDICTION | Average ○ | | | | | |

## TROUBLE SPOTS

### Kia Sportage

| TROUBLE SPOTS | '07 | '08 | '09 | '10 | '11 | '12 |
|---|---|---|---|---|---|---|
| Engine, major | ⊜ | ⊖ | ⊜ | * | ⊜ | ⊜ |
| Engine, minor | ○ | ○ | ⊜ | * | ⊜ | ⊜ |
| Engine Cooling | ⊜ | ⊖ | ⊜ | * | ⊜ | ⊜ |
| Trans. Major | ⊖ | ⊜ | ⊜ | * | ⊜ | ⊜ |
| Trans. Minor | ⊜ | ⊜ | ⊖ | * | ⊜ | ⊜ |
| Drive System | ⊖ | ◒ | ⊜ | * | ⊜ | ⊜ |
| Fuel System | ⊖ | ⊖ | ⊖ | * | ⊜ | ⊜ |
| Electrical | ⊜ | ⊖ | ○ | * | ⊜ | ⊜ |
| Climate System | ○ | ● | ◒ | * | ⊖ | ⊜ |
| Suspension | ⊖ | ⊖ | ⊜ | * | ⊜ | ⊜ |
| Brakes | ◒ | ● | ⊖ | * | ⊜ | ⊜ |
| Exhaust | ⊜ | ⊜ | ⊜ | * | ⊜ | ⊜ |
| Paint/Trim | ⊖ | ○ | ● | * | ⊖ | ⊜ |
| Body Integrity | ○ | ⊖ | ○ | * | ○ | ⊖ |
| Body Hardware | ⊖ | ⊜ | ⊖ | * | ⊖ | ⊜ |
| Power Equip. | ○ | ⊜ | ◒ | * | ⊖ | ⊜ |
| Audio System | ⊜ | ○ | ◒ | * | ○ | ⊖ |
| USED CAR VERDICTS | ⊖ | ○ | ○ | * | ⊖ | ⊜ |
| NEW CAR PREDICTION | Much better than average ⊜ | | | | | |

### Lexus CT 200h

| TROUBLE SPOTS | '07 | '08 | '09 | '10 | '11 | '12 |
|---|---|---|---|---|---|---|
| Engine, major | | | | | ⊜ | ⊜ |
| Engine, minor | | | | | ⊜ | ⊜ |
| Engine Cooling | | | | | ⊜ | ⊜ |
| Trans. Major | | | | | ⊜ | ⊜ |
| Trans. Minor | | | | | ⊜ | ⊜ |
| Drive System | | | | | ⊜ | ⊜ |
| Fuel System | | | | | ⊜ | ⊜ |
| Electrical | | | | | ⊜ | ⊜ |
| Climate System | | | | | ⊜ | ⊜ |
| Suspension | | | | | ⊜ | ⊜ |
| Brakes | | | | | ⊜ | ⊜ |
| Exhaust | | | | | ⊜ | ⊜ |
| Paint/Trim | | | | | ⊖ | ⊖ |
| Body Integrity | | | | | ⊖ | ⊜ |
| Body Hardware | | | | | ⊜ | ⊜ |
| Power Equip. | | | | | ⊜ | ⊜ |
| Audio System | | | | | ⊜ | ⊜ |
| USED CAR VERDICTS | | | | | ⊜ | ⊜ |
| NEW CAR PREDICTION | Much better than average ⊜ | | | | | |

### Lexus ES

| TROUBLE SPOTS | '07 | '08 | '09 | '10 | '11 | '12 |
|---|---|---|---|---|---|---|
| Engine, major | ⊖ | ⊜ | ⊜ | ⊜ | ⊜ | ⊜ |
| Engine, minor | ⊖ | ⊜ | ⊜ | ⊜ | ⊜ | ⊜ |
| Engine Cooling | ⊖ | ⊜ | ⊜ | ⊜ | ⊜ | ⊜ |
| Trans. Major | ⊜ | ⊜ | ⊜ | ⊜ | ⊜ | ⊜ |
| Trans. Minor | ⊜ | ⊜ | ⊜ | ⊜ | ⊜ | ⊜ |
| Drive System | ⊜ | ⊜ | ⊜ | ⊜ | ⊜ | ⊜ |
| Fuel System | ⊜ | ⊜ | ⊜ | ⊜ | ⊜ | ⊜ |
| Electrical | ⊖ | ⊜ | ⊖ | ⊜ | ⊜ | ⊜ |
| Climate System | ⊜ | ⊜ | ⊜ | ⊜ | ⊜ | ⊜ |
| Suspension | ⊜ | ⊜ | ⊜ | ⊜ | ⊜ | ⊜ |
| Brakes | ○ | ○ | ○ | ⊜ | ⊜ | ⊜ |
| Exhaust | ⊜ | ⊜ | ⊜ | ⊜ | ⊜ | ⊜ |
| Paint/Trim | ○ | ◒ | ⊖ | ○ | ⊜ | ⊜ |
| Body Integrity | ⊜ | ⊜ | ⊜ | ⊜ | ⊜ | ⊜ |
| Body Hardware | ⊖ | ⊜ | ⊜ | ⊜ | ⊜ | ⊜ |
| Power Equip. | ⊜ | ⊜ | ⊜ | ⊜ | ⊜ | ⊜ |
| Audio System | ○ | ⊖ | ⊖ | ⊜ | ⊜ | ⊜ |
| USED CAR VERDICTS | ⊜ | ⊜ | ⊜ | ⊜ | ⊜ | ⊜ |
| NEW CAR PREDICTION | Better than average ⊖ | | | | | |

### Lexus GS

| TROUBLE SPOTS | '07 | '08 | '09 | '10 | '11 | '13 |
|---|---|---|---|---|---|---|
| Engine, major | ⊖ | ⊜ | ⊜ | ⊖ | ⊜ | ⊜ |
| Engine, minor | ⊖ | ⊜ | ⊜ | ⊜ | ⊜ | ⊜ |
| Engine Cooling | ⊖ | ⊜ | ⊜ | ⊜ | ⊜ | ⊜ |
| Trans. Major | ⊜ | ⊜ | ⊜ | ⊜ | ⊜ | ⊜ |
| Trans. Minor | ⊜ | ⊜ | ⊜ | ⊜ | ⊜ | ⊜ |
| Drive System | ⊜ | ⊜ | ⊜ | ⊜ | ⊜ | ⊜ |
| Fuel System | ⊖ | ⊜ | ⊖ | ⊖ | ⊜ | ⊜ |
| Electrical | ⊖ | ⊖ | ⊖ | ⊜ | ⊜ | ⊜ |
| Climate System | ⊜ | ⊜ | ○ | ⊜ | ⊜ | ⊜ |
| Suspension | ⊖ | ⊖ | ⊖ | ⊜ | ⊖ | ⊜ |
| Brakes | ● | ◒ | ⊖ | ◒ | ⊜ | ⊜ |
| Exhaust | ⊜ | ⊜ | ⊜ | ⊜ | ⊜ | ⊜ |
| Paint/Trim | ⊖ | ⊖ | ⊖ | ○ | ⊖ | ⊜ |
| Body Integrity | ◒ | ⊖ | ⊖ | ⊖ | ⊜ | ⊜ |
| Body Hardware | ○ | ⊜ | ⊜ | ⊜ | ⊜ | ⊜ |
| Power Equip. | ○ | ⊖ | ○ | ○ | ⊜ | ⊜ |
| Audio System | ○ | ○ | ⊜ | ◒ | ◒ | ◒ |
| USED CAR VERDICTS | ⊖ | ⊖ | ⊜ | ⊖ | ⊜ | ⊖ |
| NEW CAR PREDICTION | Better than average ⊖ | | | | | |

### Lexus GX

| TROUBLE SPOTS | '07 | '08 | '09 | '10 | '11 | '12 |
|---|---|---|---|---|---|---|
| Engine, major | ⊜ | ⊜ | * | ⊜ | ⊖ | ⊜ |
| Engine, minor | ⊜ | ⊜ | * | ⊜ | ⊜ | ⊜ |
| Engine Cooling | ⊜ | ⊜ | * | ⊜ | ⊜ | ⊜ |
| Trans. Major | ⊜ | ⊜ | * | ⊜ | ⊜ | ⊜ |
| Trans. Minor | ⊖ | ⊜ | * | ⊜ | ⊜ | ⊜ |
| Drive System | ○ | ○ | * | ⊜ | ⊜ | ⊖ |
| Fuel System | ⊜ | ⊜ | * | ⊖ | ⊜ | ⊖ |
| Electrical | ○ | ⊖ | * | ⊜ | ⊜ | ⊜ |
| Climate System | ⊜ | ⊜ | * | ⊖ | ⊜ | ⊜ |
| Suspension | ⊜ | ⊜ | * | ⊜ | ⊖ | ⊖ |
| Brakes | ⊖ | ⊖ | * | ⊖ | ○ | ⊜ |
| Exhaust | ⊜ | ⊜ | * | ⊜ | ⊜ | ⊜ |
| Paint/Trim | ⊜ | ⊖ | * | ⊖ | ⊜ | ○ |
| Body Integrity | ⊜ | ⊖ | * | ⊖ | ⊜ | ○ |
| Body Hardware | ⊖ | ⊜ | * | ⊜ | ⊖ | ⊜ |
| Power Equip. | ⊜ | ⊜ | * | ⊜ | ⊜ | ⊜ |
| Audio System | ⊖ | ⊖ | * | ○ | ○ | ⊖ |
| USED CAR VERDICTS | ⊜ | ⊜ | * | ⊜ | ⊖ | ● |
| NEW CAR PREDICTION | Average ○ | | | | | |

## TROUBLE SPOTS

### Lexus HS 250h

| TROUBLE SPOTS | '07 | '08 | '09 | '10 | '11 | '12 |
|---|---|---|---|---|---|---|
| Engine, major | | | | ⊜ | ⊜ | * |
| Engine, minor | | | | ⊜ | ⊜ | * |
| Engine Cooling | | | | ⊜ | ⊜ | * |
| Trans. Major | | | | ⊜ | ⊜ | * |
| Trans. Minor | | | | ⊜ | ⊜ | * |
| Drive System | | | | ⊜ | ⊜ | * |
| Fuel System | | | | ⊜ | ⊖ | * |
| Electrical | | | | ⊜ | ⊜ | * |
| Climate System | | | | ⊜ | ⊜ | * |
| Suspension | | | | ⊜ | ⊜ | * |
| Brakes | | | | ⊖ | ⊜ | * |
| Exhaust | | | | ⊜ | ⊜ | * |
| Paint/Trim | | | | ○ | ⊜ | * |
| Body Integrity | | | | ⊖ | ⊜ | * |
| Body Hardware | | | | ⊜ | ⊖ | * |
| Power Equip. | | | | ⊜ | ⊜ | * |
| Audio System | | | | ⊜ | ⊜ | * |
| USED CAR VERDICTS | | | | ⊜ | ⊜ | * |
| NEW CAR PREDICTION | Discontinued | | | | | |

### Lexus IS Sedan (RWD)

| TROUBLE SPOTS | '07 | '08 | '09 | '10 | '11 | '12 |
|---|---|---|---|---|---|---|
| Engine, major | ○ | ⊖ | ⊖ | ⊜ | ⊜ | ⊜ |
| Engine, minor | ○ | ⊖ | ⊜ | ⊜ | ⊜ | ⊜ |
| Engine Cooling | ⊖ | ⊖ | ⊜ | ⊜ | ⊜ | ⊜ |
| Trans. Major | ⊜ | ⊜ | ⊜ | ⊜ | ⊜ | ⊜ |
| Trans. Minor | ⊜ | ⊜ | ⊜ | ⊜ | ⊜ | ⊜ |
| Drive System | ⊜ | ⊜ | ⊜ | ⊜ | ⊜ | ⊜ |
| Fuel System | ⊖ | ⊖ | ⊖ | ⊜ | ⊜ | ⊜ |
| Electrical | ⊖ | ○ | ⊜ | ⊖ | ⊜ | ⊜ |
| Climate System | ⊖ | ⊜ | ○ | ○ | ⊜ | ⊜ |
| Suspension | ⊖ | ⊖ | ○ | ⊜ | ⊜ | ⊜ |
| Brakes | ○ | ● | ⊖ | ⊜ | ⊜ | ⊜ |
| Exhaust | ⊜ | ⊜ | ⊜ | ⊜ | ⊜ | ⊜ |
| Paint/Trim | ○ | ⊜ | ⊜ | ⊜ | ⊜ | ⊖ |
| Body Integrity | ⊖ | ⊖ | ⊜ | ⊖ | ○ | ⊜ |
| Body Hardware | ⊖ | ⊜ | ⊖ | ⊜ | ⊖ | ⊜ |
| Power Equip. | ⊖ | ○ | ⊖ | ⊜ | ⊜ | ⊜ |
| Audio System | ● | ○ | ⊜ | ⊜ | ⊜ | ⊜ |
| USED CAR VERDICTS | ⊖ | ⊖ | ⊜ | ⊜ | ⊜ | ⊜ |
| NEW CAR PREDICTION | Much better than average ⊜ | | | | | |

### Lexus LS

| TROUBLE SPOTS | '07 | '08 | '09 | '10 | '11 | '12 |
|---|---|---|---|---|---|---|
| Engine, major | ⊖ | ○ | ⊜ | ⊜ | ⊜ | ⊜ |
| Engine, minor | ⊖ | ⊖ | ⊜ | ⊜ | ⊜ | ⊜ |
| Engine Cooling | ⊖ | ⊜ | ⊜ | ⊜ | ⊜ | ⊜ |
| Trans. Major | ⊜ | ⊜ | ⊜ | ⊜ | ⊜ | ⊜ |
| Trans. Minor | ⊜ | ⊖ | ⊖ | ⊜ | ⊜ | ⊜ |
| Drive System | ⊜ | ⊖ | ⊜ | ⊜ | ⊜ | ⊖ |
| Fuel System | ⊜ | ⊜ | ⊜ | ⊜ | ⊜ | ⊜ |
| Electrical | ⊖ | ⊖ | ⊖ | ⊜ | ⊜ | ⊜ |
| Climate System | ⊜ | ○ | ⊖ | ⊜ | ⊜ | ⊜ |
| Suspension | ⊜ | ⊖ | ⊖ | ○ | ○ | ⊜ |
| Brakes | ○ | ◒ | ○ | ○ | ⊖ | ○ |
| Exhaust | ⊜ | ⊜ | ⊜ | ⊜ | ⊜ | ⊜ |
| Paint/Trim | ⊖ | ⊖ | ⊜ | ⊖ | ⊜ | ⊜ |
| Body Integrity | ◒ | ○ | ○ | ⊖ | ⊜ | ○ |
| Body Hardware | ⊖ | ⊖ | ⊖ | ⊜ | ⊜ | ⊜ |
| Power Equip. | ⊖ | ⊜ | ⊜ | ⊜ | ⊜ | ⊜ |
| Audio System | ● | ◒ | ● | ○ | ⊖ | ⊖ |
| USED CAR VERDICTS | ⊖ | ⊖ | ⊖ | ⊜ | ⊖ | ◒ |
| NEW CAR PREDICTION | Better than average ⊖ | | | | | |

### Lexus RX

| TROUBLE SPOTS | '07 | '08 | '09 | '10 | '11 | '12 |
|---|---|---|---|---|---|---|
| Engine, major | ⊜ | ⊜ | ⊜ | ⊜ | ⊜ | ⊜ |
| Engine, minor | ⊖ | ⊜ | ⊖ | ⊜ | ⊜ | ⊜ |
| Engine Cooling | ⊖ | ⊜ | ⊜ | ⊜ | ⊜ | ⊜ |
| Trans. Major | ⊜ | ⊜ | ⊜ | ⊜ | ⊜ | ⊜ |
| Trans. Minor | ⊜ | ⊜ | ⊜ | ⊜ | ⊜ | ⊜ |
| Drive System | ⊖ | ⊜ | ⊜ | ⊜ | ⊜ | ⊜ |
| Fuel System | ⊖ | ⊜ | ⊜ | ⊜ | ⊜ | ⊜ |
| Electrical | ○ | ○ | ○ | ⊜ | ⊜ | ⊜ |
| Climate System | ⊖ | ⊖ | ⊜ | ⊜ | ⊜ | ⊜ |
| Suspension | ⊖ | ⊖ | ⊖ | ⊖ | ⊜ | ⊜ |
| Brakes | ⊖ | ⊖ | ⊖ | ⊜ | ⊜ | ⊜ |
| Exhaust | ⊜ | ⊜ | ⊜ | ⊜ | ⊜ | ⊜ |
| Paint/Trim | ○ | ⊖ | ⊜ | ⊖ | ⊜ | ⊜ |
| Body Integrity | ○ | ⊖ | ○ | ⊖ | ⊖ | ⊖ |
| Body Hardware | ⊖ | ⊖ | ⊜ | ⊖ | ⊜ | ⊜ |
| Power Equip. | ⊖ | ⊖ | ⊜ | ⊜ | ⊜ | ⊜ |
| Audio System | ○ | ⊖ | ○ | ○ | ⊖ | ⊖ |
| USED CAR VERDICTS | ⊖ | ⊜ | ⊜ | ⊜ | ⊜ | ⊜ |
| NEW CAR PREDICTION | Much better than average ⊜ | | | | | |

### Lexus RX Hybrid

| TROUBLE SPOTS | '07 | '08 | '09 | '10 | '11 | '12 |
|---|---|---|---|---|---|---|
| Engine, major | ⊜ | ⊜ | | ⊜ | ⊜ | ⊜ |
| Engine, minor | ⊜ | ⊜ | | ⊜ | ⊜ | ⊜ |
| Engine Cooling | ⊜ | ⊜ | | ⊜ | ⊜ | ⊜ |
| Trans. Major | ⊜ | ⊜ | | ⊜ | ⊜ | ⊜ |
| Trans. Minor | ⊜ | ⊜ | | ⊜ | ⊜ | ⊜ |
| Drive System | ⊜ | ⊜ | | ⊜ | ⊜ | ⊜ |
| Fuel System | ⊜ | ⊜ | | ⊖ | ⊜ | ⊜ |
| Electrical | ◒ | ○ | | ⊖ | ⊜ | ⊜ |
| Climate System | ⊖ | ⊜ | | ⊜ | ⊜ | ⊜ |
| Suspension | ⊜ | ⊖ | | ⊖ | ⊜ | ⊜ |
| Brakes | ⊜ | ⊜ | | ⊖ | ⊜ | ⊜ |
| Exhaust | ⊜ | ⊜ | | ⊜ | ⊜ | ⊜ |
| Paint/Trim | ⊖ | ⊜ | | ⊜ | ⊜ | ⊜ |
| Body Integrity | ⊜ | ⊖ | | ⊖ | ⊖ | ⊜ |
| Body Hardware | ⊖ | ⊖ | | ⊜ | ⊜ | ⊜ |
| Power Equip. | ⊖ | ⊖ | | ⊜ | ⊖ | ⊜ |
| Audio System | ○ | ⊖ | | ○ | ○ | ⊖ |
| USED CAR VERDICTS | ⊜ | ⊜ | | ⊜ | ⊜ | ⊜ |
| NEW CAR PREDICTION | Much better than average ⊜ | | | | | |

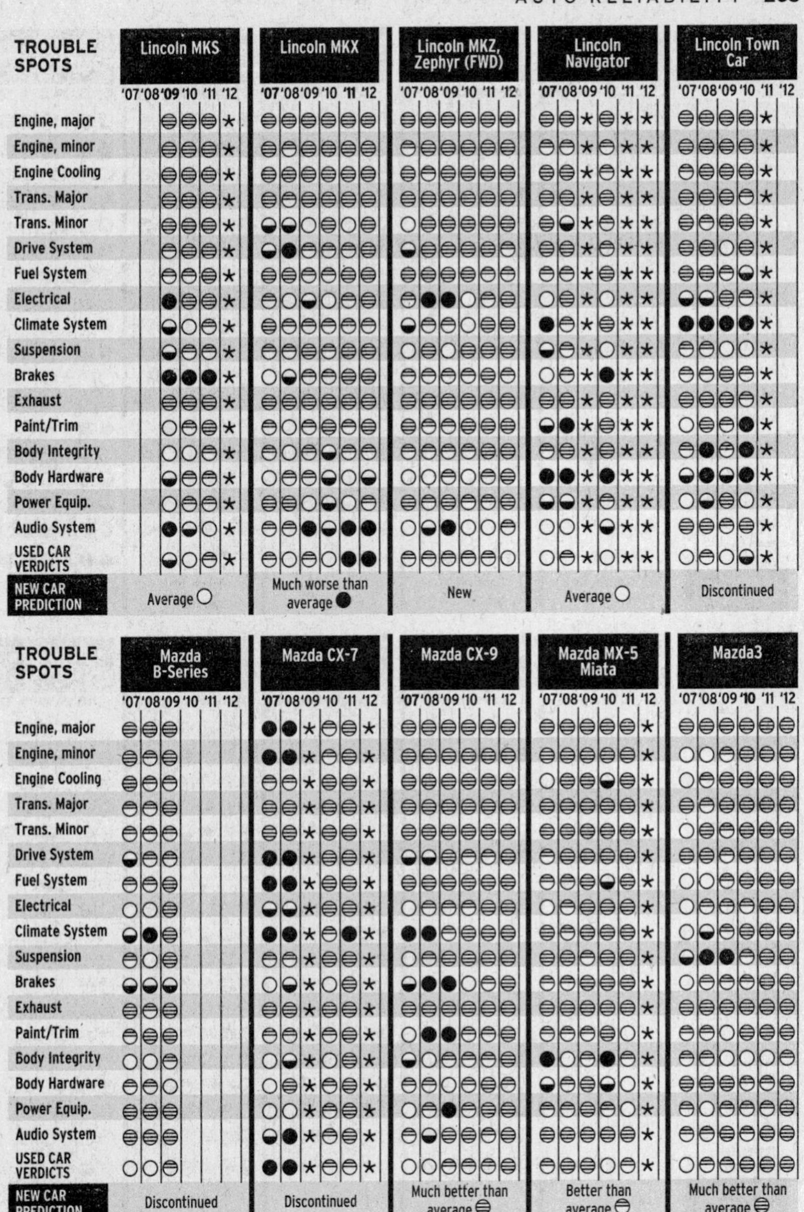

| TROUBLE SPOTS | Lincoln MKS '07 | '08 | '09 | '10 | '11 | '12 |
|---|---|---|---|---|---|---|
| Engine, major | | | ⊜ | ⊜ | ⊜ | * |
| Engine, minor | | | ⊜ | ⊜ | ⊜ | * |
| Engine Cooling | | | ⊜ | ⊜ | ⊜ | * |
| Trans. Major | | | ⊜ | ⊜ | ⊜ | * |
| Trans. Minor | | | ⊜ | ⊜ | ⊜ | * |
| Drive System | | | ⊖ | ⊜ | ⊜ | * |
| Fuel System | | | ⊖ | ⊖ | ⊜ | * |
| Electrical | | | ● | ⊜ | ⊜ | * |
| Climate System | | | ◒ | ○ | ⊖ | * |
| Suspension | | | ◒ | ⊖ | ⊖ | * |
| Brakes | | | ● | ● | ● | * |
| Exhaust | | | ⊜ | ⊜ | ⊜ | * |
| Paint/Trim | | | ○ | ⊖ | ⊜ | * |
| Body Integrity | | | ○ | ○ | ⊖ | * |
| Body Hardware | | | ◒ | ⊖ | ⊖ | * |
| Power Equip. | | | ○ | ⊜ | ⊖ | * |
| Audio System | | | ● | ◒ | ○ | * |
| USED CAR VERDICTS | | | ◒ | ○ | ⊖ | * |
| NEW CAR PREDICTION | Average ○ | | | | | |

| TROUBLE SPOTS | Lincoln MKX '07 | '08 | '09 | '10 | '11 | '12 |
|---|---|---|---|---|---|---|
| Engine, major | ⊜ | ⊜ | ⊜ | ⊜ | ⊜ | ⊜ |
| Engine, minor | ⊜ | ⊖ | ⊜ | ⊜ | ⊜ | ⊜ |
| Engine Cooling | ⊜ | ⊜ | ⊜ | ⊜ | ⊜ | ⊜ |
| Trans. Major | ⊜ | ⊖ | ⊜ | ⊜ | ⊜ | ⊜ |
| Trans. Minor | ◒ | ◒ | ○ | ⊜ | ○ | ⊜ |
| Drive System | ◒ | ● | ⊖ | ⊖ | ⊖ | ⊜ |
| Fuel System | ⊜ | ⊜ | ⊖ | ⊖ | ⊜ | ⊜ |
| Electrical | ⊖ | ○ | ◒ | ○ | ⊖ | ⊜ |
| Climate System | ⊜ | ⊖ | ⊖ | ⊖ | ⊖ | ⊖ |
| Suspension | ⊖ | ⊖ | ⊜ | ⊖ | ⊜ | ⊜ |
| Brakes | ○ | ◒ | ⊖ | ⊖ | ⊜ | ⊜ |
| Exhaust | ⊜ | ⊜ | ⊜ | ⊜ | ⊜ | ⊜ |
| Paint/Trim | ⊜ | ○ | ⊖ | ⊜ | ⊖ | ⊜ |
| Body Integrity | ⊖ | ○ | ⊖ | ◒ | ⊖ | ⊖ |
| Body Hardware | ○ | ⊜ | ⊖ | ◒ | ○ | ◒ |
| Power Equip. | ⊜ | ⊜ | ○ | ◒ | ○ | ⊖ |
| Audio System | ⊖ | ⊖ | ● | ◒ | ● | ● |
| USED CAR VERDICTS | ⊖ | ○ | ⊖ | ○ | ● | ● |
| NEW CAR PREDICTION | Much worse than average ● | | | | | |

| TROUBLE SPOTS | Lincoln MKZ, Zephyr (FWD) '07 | '08 | '09 | '10 | '11 | '12 |
|---|---|---|---|---|---|---|
| Engine, major | ⊜ | ⊜ | ⊜ | ⊜ | ⊜ | ⊜ |
| Engine, minor | ⊖ | ⊜ | ⊜ | ⊜ | ⊜ | ⊜ |
| Engine Cooling | ⊜ | ⊖ | ⊜ | ⊜ | ⊜ | ⊜ |
| Trans. Major | ⊜ | ⊜ | ⊜ | ⊜ | ⊜ | ⊜ |
| Trans. Minor | ○ | ⊜ | ⊜ | ⊜ | ⊜ | ⊜ |
| Drive System | ◒ | ⊜ | ⊜ | ⊜ | ⊜ | ⊖ |
| Fuel System | ⊜ | ⊜ | ⊜ | ⊜ | ⊖ | ⊖ |
| Electrical | ⊖ | ● | ● | ○ | ⊖ | ⊜ |
| Climate System | ◒ | ⊖ | ⊖ | ○ | ⊜ | ⊜ |
| Suspension | ○ | ⊜ | ○ | ⊜ | ⊜ | ⊜ |
| Brakes | ⊖ | ⊖ | ⊖ | ⊜ | ⊜ | ⊖ |
| Exhaust | ⊜ | ⊜ | ⊜ | ⊜ | ⊜ | ⊜ |
| Paint/Trim | ⊜ | ⊖ | ⊖ | ⊜ | ⊜ | ⊜ |
| Body Integrity | ⊖ | ⊖ | ⊖ | ⊖ | ⊜ | ⊜ |
| Body Hardware | ○ | ○ | ⊖ | ○ | ⊖ | ⊜ |
| Power Equip. | ⊜ | ⊖ | ⊜ | ⊖ | ⊖ | ⊜ |
| Audio System | ○ | ◒ | ● | ○ | ○ | ⊖ |
| USED CAR VERDICTS | ⊖ | ⊖ | ⊖ | ⊖ | ⊖ | ○ |
| NEW CAR PREDICTION | New | | | | | |

| TROUBLE SPOTS | Lincoln Navigator '07 | '08 | '09 | '10 | '11 | '12 |
|---|---|---|---|---|---|---|
| Engine, major | ⊜ | ⊜ | * | ⊜ | * | * |
| Engine, minor | ⊖ | ⊖ | * | ⊖ | * | * |
| Engine Cooling | ⊜ | ⊜ | * | ⊖ | * | * |
| Trans. Major | ⊜ | ⊜ | * | ⊜ | * | * |
| Trans. Minor | ⊜ | ◒ | * | ⊖ | * | * |
| Drive System | ⊜ | ⊜ | * | ⊖ | * | * |
| Fuel System | ⊖ | ⊖ | * | ⊜ | * | * |
| Electrical | ○ | ⊜ | * | ○ | * | * |
| Climate System | ● | ⊖ | * | ⊜ | * | * |
| Suspension | ◒ | ⊖ | * | ○ | * | * |
| Brakes | ○ | ⊖ | * | ● | * | * |
| Exhaust | ⊜ | ⊜ | * | ⊜ | * | * |
| Paint/Trim | ◒ | ● | * | ⊜ | * | * |
| Body Integrity | ⊖ | ⊜ | * | ⊜ | * | * |
| Body Hardware | ● | ● | * | ● | * | * |
| Power Equip. | ◒ | ◒ | * | ⊖ | * | * |
| Audio System | ○ | ○ | * | ◒ | * | * |
| USED CAR VERDICTS | ○ | ⊖ | * | ○ | * | * |
| NEW CAR PREDICTION | Average ○ | | | | | |

| TROUBLE SPOTS | Lincoln Town Car '07 | '08 | '09 | '10 | '11 | '12 |
|---|---|---|---|---|---|---|
| Engine, major | ⊜ | ⊜ | ⊜ | ⊜ | * | |
| Engine, minor | ⊜ | ⊜ | ⊜ | ⊜ | * | |
| Engine Cooling | ⊖ | ⊜ | ⊜ | ⊜ | * | |
| Trans. Major | ⊜ | ⊜ | ⊜ | ⊖ | * | |
| Trans. Minor | ⊜ | ⊖ | ⊜ | ⊜ | * | |
| Drive System | ⊜ | ⊜ | ○ | ⊜ | * | |
| Fuel System | ⊜ | ⊜ | ⊖ | ◒ | * | |
| Electrical | ◒ | ◒ | ⊜ | ⊖ | * | |
| Climate System | ● | ● | ● | ● | * | |
| Suspension | ⊖ | ⊖ | ○ | ○ | * | |
| Brakes | ⊖ | ⊖ | ⊜ | ⊖ | * | |
| Exhaust | ⊜ | ⊜ | ⊜ | ⊖ | * | |
| Paint/Trim | ○ | ⊜ | ⊖ | ● | * | |
| Body Integrity | ⊖ | ● | ⊖ | ● | * | |
| Body Hardware | ◒ | ● | ◒ | ● | * | |
| Power Equip. | ○ | ◒ | ⊜ | ○ | * | |
| Audio System | ⊜ | ⊜ | ⊖ | ⊜ | * | |
| USED CAR VERDICTS | ○ | ⊖ | ○ | ◒ | * | |
| NEW CAR PREDICTION | Discontinued | | | | | |

| TROUBLE SPOTS | Mazda B-Series '07 | '08 | '09 | '10 | '11 | '12 |
|---|---|---|---|---|---|---|
| Engine, major | ⊜ | ⊜ | ⊜ | | | |
| Engine, minor | ⊜ | ⊖ | ⊜ | | | |
| Engine Cooling | ⊜ | ⊖ | ⊖ | | | |
| Trans. Major | ⊖ | ⊖ | ⊜ | | | |
| Trans. Minor | ⊖ | ⊖ | ⊖ | | | |
| Drive System | ◒ | ⊖ | ⊖ | | | |
| Fuel System | ⊖ | ⊖ | ⊜ | | | |
| Electrical | ○ | ○ | ⊜ | | | |
| Climate System | ◒ | ● | ⊜ | | | |
| Suspension | ⊖ | ○ | ⊜ | | | |
| Brakes | ◒ | ◒ | ◒ | | | |
| Exhaust | ⊜ | ⊖ | ⊜ | | | |
| Paint/Trim | ⊖ | ⊜ | ⊜ | | | |
| Body Integrity | ○ | ○ | ⊖ | | | |
| Body Hardware | ⊖ | ⊖ | ○ | | | |
| Power Equip. | ⊜ | ⊜ | ⊜ | | | |
| Audio System | ⊜ | ⊜ | ⊜ | | | |
| USED CAR VERDICTS | ○ | ○ | ⊖ | | | |
| NEW CAR PREDICTION | Discontinued | | | | | |

| TROUBLE SPOTS | Mazda CX-7 '07 | '08 | '09 | '10 | '11 | '12 |
|---|---|---|---|---|---|---|
| Engine, major | ● | ● | * | ⊖ | ⊜ | * |
| Engine, minor | ● | ● | * | ⊖ | ⊜ | * |
| Engine Cooling | ⊖ | ⊖ | * | ⊜ | ⊜ | * |
| Trans. Major | ⊜ | ⊜ | * | ⊜ | ⊜ | * |
| Trans. Minor | ⊜ | ⊜ | * | ⊜ | ⊜ | * |
| Drive System | ● | ● | * | ⊜ | ⊜ | * |
| Fuel System | ● | ● | * | ⊜ | ⊜ | * |
| Electrical | ◒ | ◒ | * | ⊜ | ⊜ | * |
| Climate System | ● | ● | * | ⊖ | ● | * |
| Suspension | ⊖ | ⊖ | * | ⊜ | ⊜ | * |
| Brakes | ○ | ◒ | * | ○ | ⊜ | * |
| Exhaust | ⊜ | ⊜ | * | ⊜ | ⊜ | * |
| Paint/Trim | ⊖ | ⊖ | * | ⊖ | ⊜ | * |
| Body Integrity | ○ | ◒ | * | ○ | ⊜ | * |
| Body Hardware | ○ | ⊜ | * | ⊖ | ⊜ | * |
| Power Equip. | ○ | ○ | * | ⊖ | ⊜ | * |
| Audio System | ◒ | ● | * | ⊖ | ⊜ | * |
| USED CAR VERDICTS | ● | ● | * | ⊖ | ⊖ | * |
| NEW CAR PREDICTION | Discontinued | | | | | |

| TROUBLE SPOTS | Mazda CX-9 '07 | '08 | '09 | '10 | '11 | '12 |
|---|---|---|---|---|---|---|
| Engine, major | ⊜ | ⊜ | ⊜ | ⊜ | ⊜ | ⊜ |
| Engine, minor | ⊜ | ⊜ | ⊜ | ⊜ | ⊜ | ⊜ |
| Engine Cooling | ⊜ | ⊜ | ⊜ | ⊜ | ⊜ | ⊜ |
| Trans. Major | ⊜ | ⊜ | ⊜ | ⊜ | ⊜ | ⊜ |
| Trans. Minor | ⊜ | ⊜ | ⊜ | ⊜ | ⊜ | ⊜ |
| Drive System | ◒ | ◒ | ⊜ | ⊖ | ⊖ | ⊜ |
| Fuel System | ⊜ | ⊜ | ⊜ | ⊜ | ⊜ | ⊜ |
| Electrical | ○ | ⊖ | ⊖ | ⊖ | ⊜ | ⊜ |
| Climate System | ● | ● | ⊖ | ⊜ | ⊜ | ⊜ |
| Suspension | ○ | ⊖ | ⊜ | ⊜ | ⊜ | ⊜ |
| Brakes | ◒ | ● | ● | ○ | ⊖ | ⊜ |
| Exhaust | ⊜ | ⊜ | ⊜ | ⊜ | ⊜ | ⊜ |
| Paint/Trim | ○ | ● | ● | ⊖ | ⊖ | ⊜ |
| Body Integrity | ◒ | ○ | ⊖ | ⊖ | ⊖ | ⊜ |
| Body Hardware | ⊖ | ⊖ | ○ | ⊖ | ⊜ | ⊖ |
| Power Equip. | ○ | ⊖ | ● | ⊖ | ⊜ | ⊜ |
| Audio System | ⊖ | ◒ | ⊜ | ⊜ | ⊖ | ⊜ |
| USED CAR VERDICTS | ○ | ○ | ⊖ | ⊖ | ⊖ | ⊜ |
| NEW CAR PREDICTION | Much better than average ⊜ | | | | | |

| TROUBLE SPOTS | Mazda MX-5 Miata '07 | '08 | '09 | '10 | '11 | '12 |
|---|---|---|---|---|---|---|
| Engine, major | ⊜ | ⊜ | ⊜ | ⊜ | ⊜ | * |
| Engine, minor | ⊜ | ⊜ | ⊜ | ⊜ | ⊜ | * |
| Engine Cooling | ○ | ⊜ | ⊜ | ◒ | ⊜ | * |
| Trans. Major | ⊜ | ⊜ | ⊜ | ⊜ | ⊜ | * |
| Trans. Minor | ⊜ | ⊜ | ⊜ | ⊜ | ⊜ | * |
| Drive System | ⊖ | ⊜ | ⊜ | ⊜ | ⊜ | * |
| Fuel System | ⊖ | ⊖ | ⊜ | ◒ | ⊜ | * |
| Electrical | ○ | ⊖ | ⊜ | ⊜ | ⊜ | * |
| Climate System | ⊜ | ⊖ | ⊜ | ⊜ | ⊜ | * |
| Suspension | ⊜ | ⊜ | ⊖ | ⊜ | ⊜ | * |
| Brakes | ⊖ | ⊖ | ⊜ | ⊜ | ⊜ | * |
| Exhaust | ⊜ | ⊜ | ⊜ | ⊜ | ⊜ | * |
| Paint/Trim | ⊖ | ⊖ | ⊖ | ⊜ | ○ | * |
| Body Integrity | ● | ○ | ⊖ | ● | ⊖ | * |
| Body Hardware | ◒ | ⊖ | ⊜ | ◒ | ○ | * |
| Power Equip. | ⊖ | ⊖ | ⊜ | ⊖ | ○ | * |
| Audio System | ⊜ | ⊜ | ⊜ | ⊜ | ⊜ | * |
| USED CAR VERDICTS | ⊖ | ⊜ | ⊜ | ○ | ⊖ | * |
| NEW CAR PREDICTION | Better than average ⊖ | | | | | |

| TROUBLE SPOTS | Mazda3 '07 | '08 | '09 | '10 | '11 | '12 |
|---|---|---|---|---|---|---|
| Engine, major | ⊜ | ⊜ | ⊜ | ⊜ | ⊜ | ⊜ |
| Engine, minor | ○ | ○ | ⊖ | ⊜ | ⊜ | ⊜ |
| Engine Cooling | ○ | ⊖ | ⊜ | ⊜ | ⊜ | ⊜ |
| Trans. Major | ⊜ | ⊖ | ⊜ | ⊜ | ⊜ | ⊜ |
| Trans. Minor | ○ | ⊜ | ⊖ | ⊜ | ⊜ | ⊜ |
| Drive System | ⊜ | ⊜ | ⊖ | ⊜ | ⊜ | ⊜ |
| Fuel System | ○ | ○ | ⊖ | ⊜ | ⊜ | ⊜ |
| Electrical | ○ | ⊖ | ⊖ | ⊖ | ⊜ | ⊜ |
| Climate System | ○ | ◒ | ⊖ | ⊜ | ⊜ | ⊜ |
| Suspension | ◒ | ● | ● | ⊖ | ⊜ | ⊜ |
| Brakes | ○ | ⊖ | ⊖ | ⊖ | ⊜ | ⊜ |
| Exhaust | ⊜ | ⊜ | ⊜ | ⊜ | ⊜ | ⊜ |
| Paint/Trim | ⊖ | ⊖ | ○ | ⊜ | ⊜ | ⊜ |
| Body Integrity | ⊖ | ⊖ | ○ | ○ | ○ | ⊖ |
| Body Hardware | ⊜ | ⊜ | ⊜ | ⊖ | ⊖ | ⊜ |
| Power Equip. | ⊖ | ○ | ⊜ | ⊖ | ⊖ | ⊜ |
| Audio System | ⊖ | ⊖ | ⊜ | ⊖ | ⊜ | ⊜ |
| USED CAR VERDICTS | ○ | ⊖ | ⊖ | ⊜ | ⊜ | ⊜ |
| NEW CAR PREDICTION | Much better than average ⊜ | | | | | |

**TROUBLE SPOTS**

| Mazda5 | '07 | '08 | '09 | '10 | '11 | '12 |
|---|---|---|---|---|---|---|
| Engine, major | ⊜ | ⊜ | ⊜ | ⊜ | | ⊜ |
| Engine, minor | ◒ | ○ | ○ | ⊜ | | ⊜ |
| Engine Cooling | ⊖ | ○ | ⊜ | ⊜ | | ⊜ |
| Trans. Major | ⊖ | ⊖ | ⊖ | ⊜ | | ⊜ |
| Trans. Minor | ⊜ | ⊜ | ⊜ | ⊜ | | ⊜ |
| Drive System | ⊖ | ⊖ | ⊖ | ⊜ | | ⊜ |
| Fuel System | ○ | ○ | ◒ | ⊖ | | ⊜ |
| Electrical | ○ | ⊖ | ⊜ | ⊜ | | ⊜ |
| Climate System | ○ | ⊖ | ⊖ | ⊖ | | ⊜ |
| Suspension | ● | ● | ● | ● | | ⊜ |
| Brakes | ● | ● | ● | ◒ | | ⊜ |
| Exhaust | ⊖ | ⊜ | ⊜ | ⊜ | | ⊜ |
| Paint/Trim | ◒ | ○ | ○ | ⊖ | | ⊜ |
| Body Integrity | ● | ◒ | ● | ◒ | | ⊜ |
| Body Hardware | ○ | ⊖ | ⊖ | ⊜ | | ⊜ |
| Power Equip. | ⊖ | ⊖ | ○ | ⊜ | | ⊖ |
| Audio System | ○ | ⊖ | ⊖ | ⊖ | | ⊜ |
| USED CAR VERDICTS | ◒ | ◒ | ◒ | ○ | | ⊜ |
| NEW CAR PREDICTION | Much better than average ⊜ | | | | | |

| Mazda6 | '07 | '08 | '09 | '10 | '11 | '12 |
|---|---|---|---|---|---|---|
| Engine, major | ◒ | ⊜ | ⊜ | ⊜ | ⊜ | ★ |
| Engine, minor | ○ | ◒ | ⊜ | ⊜ | ⊜ | ★ |
| Engine Cooling | ◒ | ⊜ | ⊜ | ⊜ | ⊜ | ★ |
| Trans. Major | ⊖ | ⊜ | ⊜ | ⊜ | ⊜ | ★ |
| Trans. Minor | ⊖ | ⊜ | ⊜ | ⊜ | ⊜ | ★ |
| Drive System | ⊖ | ⊜ | ⊜ | ⊜ | ⊜ | ★ |
| Fuel System | ○ | ⊜ | ⊜ | ⊖ | ⊜ | ★ |
| Electrical | ○ | ○ | ● | ○ | ⊜ | ★ |
| Climate System | ○ | ⊖ | ⊖ | ⊖ | ⊜ | ★ |
| Suspension | ○ | ⊖ | ⊖ | ⊜ | ⊜ | ★ |
| Brakes | ◒ | ⊖ | ○ | ● | ⊖ | ★ |
| Exhaust | ⊜ | ⊜ | ⊜ | ⊖ | ⊜ | ★ |
| Paint/Trim | ◒ | ○ | ⊜ | ⊖ | ⊜ | ★ |
| Body Integrity | ○ | ⊖ | ◒ | ◒ | ○ | ★ |
| Body Hardware | ⊖ | ⊜ | ● | ○ | ⊖ | ★ |
| Power Equip. | ⊖ | ⊖ | ● | ⊖ | ⊜ | ★ |
| Audio System | ⊜ | ⊜ | ⊖ | ⊖ | ⊜ | ★ |
| USED CAR VERDICTS | ○ | ⊖ | ○ | ⊖ | ⊖ | ★ |
| NEW CAR PREDICTION | Better than average ⊖ | | | | | |

| Mercedes-Benz C-Class (V6) | '07 | '08 | '09 | '10 | '11 | '12 |
|---|---|---|---|---|---|---|
| Engine, major | ⊜ | ⊜ | ⊜ | ⊜ | ⊜ | ⊜ |
| Engine, minor | ◒ | ○ | ⊜ | ⊜ | ⊜ | ⊜ |
| Engine Cooling | ⊖ | ⊜ | ⊜ | ⊜ | ⊜ | ⊜ |
| Trans. Major | ⊜ | ⊜ | ⊜ | ⊜ | ⊜ | ⊜ |
| Trans. Minor | ◒ | ⊜ | ⊖ | ⊖ | ⊜ | ⊜ |
| Drive System | ⊖ | ⊖ | ⊜ | ⊜ | ⊜ | ⊜ |
| Fuel System | ⊖ | ⊖ | ⊖ | ⊜ | ⊜ | ⊜ |
| Electrical | ⊜ | ⊖ | ⊖ | ⊜ | ⊖ | ⊜ |
| Climate System | ⊜ | ⊖ | ⊖ | ⊖ | ⊜ | ⊜ |
| Suspension | ⊜ | ⊜ | ○ | ○ | ⊖ | ⊜ |
| Brakes | ⊖ | ⊖ | ⊖ | ⊖ | ⊖ | ⊜ |
| Exhaust | ⊜ | ⊜ | ⊜ | ⊜ | ⊜ | ⊜ |
| Paint/Trim | ⊜ | ⊖ | ⊖ | ◒ | ⊜ | ⊜ |
| Body Integrity | ⊖ | ⊖ | ⊖ | ○ | ⊜ | ⊜ |
| Body Hardware | ⊖ | ⊖ | ○ | ⊖ | ○ | ⊜ |
| Power Equip. | ⊖ | ○ | ◒ | ⊜ | ⊖ | ⊜ |
| Audio System | ◒ | ◒ | ◒ | ○ | ⊜ | ○ |
| USED CAR VERDICTS | ⊖ | ⊖ | ⊖ | ⊖ | ○ | ⊖ |
| NEW CAR PREDICTION | Better than average ⊖ | | | | | |

| Mercedes-Benz E-Class Sedan (V6) | '07 | '08 | '09 | '10 | '11 | '12 |
|---|---|---|---|---|---|---|
| Engine, major | ⊖ | ⊖ | ⊜ | ⊜ | ⊜ | ⊜ |
| Engine, minor | ◒ | ⊖ | ⊖ | ⊜ | ⊜ | ⊜ |
| Engine Cooling | ⊜ | ⊜ | ⊜ | ⊜ | ⊜ | ⊜ |
| Trans. Major | ⊖ | ⊜ | ⊜ | ⊜ | ⊜ | ⊜ |
| Trans. Minor | ● | ⊖ | ● | ⊖ | ⊜ | ⊜ |
| Drive System | ⊖ | ⊖ | ⊖ | ⊜ | ⊜ | ⊜ |
| Fuel System | ◒ | ⊖ | ○ | ⊖ | ⊖ | ⊖ |
| Electrical | ○ | ⊖ | ⊖ | ● | ○ | ⊜ |
| Climate System | ○ | ◒ | ⊖ | ⊜ | ⊜ | ⊜ |
| Suspension | ⊖ | ○ | ⊖ | ⊖ | ⊜ | ⊜ |
| Brakes | ⊖ | ⊖ | ⊖ | ⊜ | ⊖ | ⊜ |
| Exhaust | ⊜ | ⊜ | ⊜ | ⊜ | ⊜ | ⊜ |
| Paint/Trim | ⊖ | ⊜ | ⊜ | ⊖ | ⊜ | ⊜ |
| Body Integrity | ⊖ | ⊜ | ⊖ | ○ | ⊜ | ⊜ |
| Body Hardware | ⊖ | ⊜ | ⊖ | ⊖ | ◒ | ⊜ |
| Power Equip. | ⊜ | ⊖ | ◒ | ◒ | ⊖ | ⊜ |
| Audio System | ● | ◒ | ● | ● | ⊖ | ⊜ |
| USED CAR VERDICTS | ⊖ | ⊖ | ○ | ○ | ○ | ⊜ |
| NEW CAR PREDICTION | Better than average ⊖ | | | | | |

| Mercedes-Benz GL-Class | '07 | '08 | '09 | '10 | '11 | '12 |
|---|---|---|---|---|---|---|
| Engine, major | ◒ | ⊖ | ★ | ⊜ | ⊜ | ⊜ |
| Engine, minor | ● | ● | ★ | ◒ | ⊜ | ⊜ |
| Engine Cooling | ○ | ⊖ | ★ | ⊜ | ⊜ | ○ |
| Trans. Major | ● | ⊖ | ★ | ⊜ | ⊜ | ⊜ |
| Trans. Minor | ◒ | ○ | ★ | ○ | ⊖ | ⊜ |
| Drive System | ● | ● | ★ | ⊖ | ⊖ | ○ |
| Fuel System | ○ | ● | ★ | ● | ● | ○ |
| Electrical | ○ | ● | ★ | ⊖ | ○ | ⊖ |
| Climate System | ⊜ | ⊖ | ★ | ⊜ | ⊖ | ⊜ |
| Suspension | ● | ● | ★ | ● | ◒ | ⊜ |
| Brakes | ○ | ○ | ★ | ◒ | ○ | ⊜ |
| Exhaust | ⊜ | ⊜ | ★ | ⊜ | ⊜ | ⊖ |
| Paint/Trim | ● | ● | ★ | ⊖ | ⊜ | ○ |
| Body Integrity | ⊖ | ◒ | ★ | ⊖ | ⊜ | ⊜ |
| Body Hardware | ◒ | ● | ★ | ◒ | ● | ◒ |
| Power Equip. | ◒ | ● | ★ | ⊖ | ⊖ | ○ |
| Audio System | ◒ | ● | ★ | ● | ● | ○ |
| USED CAR VERDICTS | ● | ● | ★ | ● | ● | ● |
| NEW CAR PREDICTION | New | | | | | |

**TROUBLE SPOTS**

| Mercedes-Benz GLK | '07 | '08 | '09 | '10 | '11 | '12 |
|---|---|---|---|---|---|---|
| Engine, major | | | | ⊜ | ⊜ | ⊜ |
| Engine, minor | | | | ⊖ | ⊜ | ⊜ |
| Engine Cooling | | | | ⊜ | ⊜ | ⊖ |
| Trans. Major | | | | ⊜ | ⊜ | ⊜ |
| Trans. Minor | | | | ⊜ | ⊜ | ⊜ |
| Drive System | | | | ⊖ | ⊜ | ⊜ |
| Fuel System | | | | ⊖ | ⊜ | ⊜ |
| Electrical | | | | ⊖ | ⊜ | ⊜ |
| Climate System | | | | ⊖ | ⊜ | ⊜ |
| Suspension | | | | ⊜ | ⊜ | ⊜ |
| Brakes | | | | ⊜ | ⊖ | ⊜ |
| Exhaust | | | | ⊜ | ⊜ | ⊜ |
| Paint/Trim | | | | ⊜ | ⊖ | ⊜ |
| Body Integrity | | | | ⊜ | ⊖ | ⊖ |
| Body Hardware | | | | ◒ | ○ | ⊖ |
| Power Equip. | | | | ● | ○ | ⊜ |
| Audio System | | | | ⊖ | ⊖ | ⊜ |
| USED CAR VERDICTS | | | | ○ | ⊖ | ○ |
| NEW CAR PREDICTION | Average ○ | | | | | |

| Mercedes-Benz M-Class | '07 | '08 | '09 | '10 | '11 | '12 |
|---|---|---|---|---|---|---|
| Engine, major | ⊖ | ⊜ | ⊜ | ⊜ | ⊜ | ⊜ |
| Engine, minor | ● | ● | ⊜ | ⊜ | ⊜ | ⊜ |
| Engine Cooling | ⊜ | ⊖ | ⊖ | ⊜ | ⊜ | ⊜ |
| Trans. Major | ○ | ⊜ | ⊜ | ⊖ | ⊜ | ⊜ |
| Trans. Minor | ◒ | ⊖ | ⊜ | ⊜ | ⊜ | ⊜ |
| Drive System | ⊖ | ⊖ | ◒ | ⊜ | ⊜ | ⊜ |
| Fuel System | ⊜ | ○ | ⊖ | ⊖ | ⊜ | ⊜ |
| Electrical | ⊖ | ⊖ | ○ | ⊖ | ⊜ | ⊜ |
| Climate System | ⊖ | ○ | ⊖ | ⊜ | ⊖ | ⊜ |
| Suspension | ○ | ● | ◒ | ⊖ | ⊖ | ⊜ |
| Brakes | ○ | ○ | ⊖ | ○ | ⊖ | ⊜ |
| Exhaust | ⊜ | ⊜ | ⊜ | ⊜ | ⊜ | ⊜ |
| Paint/Trim | ● | ● | ◒ | ⊖ | ⊜ | ⊜ |
| Body Integrity | ○ | ⊖ | ⊖ | ○ | ⊖ | ○ |
| Body Hardware | ● | ◒ | ◒ | ○ | ● | ○ |
| Power Equip. | ◒ | ◒ | ○ | ⊖ | ⊖ | ⊖ |
| Audio System | ◒ | ⊖ | ● | ○ | ○ | ⊖ |
| USED CAR VERDICTS | ○ | ○ | ○ | ⊖ | ○ | ◒ |
| NEW CAR PREDICTION | Worse than average ◒ | | | | | |

| Mercury Grand Marquis | '07 | '08 | '09 | '10 | '11 | '12 |
|---|---|---|---|---|---|---|
| Engine, major | ⊜ | ⊜ | ⊜ | ⊜ | ★ | |
| Engine, minor | ⊜ | ⊜ | ⊖ | ⊜ | ★ | |
| Engine Cooling | ○ | ⊜ | ⊖ | ⊜ | ★ | |
| Trans. Major | ⊜ | ⊜ | ⊜ | ⊜ | ★ | |
| Trans. Minor | ⊜ | ⊜ | ⊜ | ⊜ | ★ | |
| Drive System | ⊜ | ⊜ | ⊜ | ⊜ | ★ | |
| Fuel System | ⊖ | ○ | ⊖ | ○ | ★ | |
| Electrical | ○ | ⊜ | ⊖ | ⊖ | ★ | |
| Climate System | ● | ● | ● | ⊖ | ★ | |
| Suspension | ⊜ | ⊜ | ⊖ | ⊖ | ★ | |
| Brakes | ⊖ | ⊖ | ⊜ | ⊖ | ★ | |
| Exhaust | ⊜ | ⊜ | ⊖ | ⊜ | ★ | |
| Paint/Trim | ● | ○ | ○ | ⊖ | ★ | |
| Body Integrity | ◒ | ○ | ⊖ | ● | ★ | |
| Body Hardware | ● | ⊖ | ◒ | ● | ★ | |
| Power Equip. | ⊖ | ○ | ◒ | ◒ | ★ | |
| Audio System | ⊖ | ⊜ | ⊖ | ⊜ | ★ | |
| USED CAR VERDICTS | ○ | ⊖ | ○ | ○ | ★ | |
| NEW CAR PREDICTION | Discontinued | | | | | |

| Mercury Mariner (V6) | '07 | '08 | '09 | '10 | '11 | '12 |
|---|---|---|---|---|---|---|
| Engine, major | ⊖ | ⊜ | ○ | ⊜ | ⊜ | |
| Engine, minor | ⊖ | ⊖ | ⊖ | ⊜ | ⊖ | |
| Engine Cooling | ⊜ | ⊜ | ⊜ | ⊜ | ⊜ | |
| Trans. Major | ● | ○ | ◒ | ○ | ⊜ | |
| Trans. Minor | ⊖ | ○ | ● | ◒ | ⊖ | |
| Drive System | ● | ○ | ● | ⊖ | ⊜ | |
| Fuel System | ⊜ | ⊖ | ◒ | ○ | ⊖ | |
| Electrical | ⊖ | ⊖ | ○ | ⊖ | ⊜ | |
| Climate System | ○ | ◒ | ◒ | ⊖ | ⊜ | |
| Suspension | ○ | ◒ | ◒ | ⊖ | ⊖ | |
| Brakes | ● | ◒ | ⊖ | ⊖ | ⊖ | |
| Exhaust | ⊖ | ⊜ | ⊜ | ⊜ | ⊜ | |
| Paint/Trim | ○ | ◒ | ⊖ | ⊖ | ⊜ | |
| Body Integrity | ● | ● | ◒ | ◒ | ○ | |
| Body Hardware | ◒ | ⊖ | ○ | ⊖ | ⊜ | |
| Power Equip. | ○ | ⊜ | ⊖ | ⊜ | ⊜ | |
| Audio System | ◒ | ⊜ | ⊜ | ○ | ○ | |
| USED CAR VERDICTS | ◒ | ○ | ● | ○ | ○ | |
| NEW CAR PREDICTION | Discontinued | | | | | |

| Mercury Milan (V6, FWD) | '07 | '08 | '09 | '10 | '11 | '12 |
|---|---|---|---|---|---|---|
| Engine, major | ⊜ | ⊜ | ⊜ | ⊜ | ⊜ | |
| Engine, minor | ⊜ | ⊖ | ⊜ | ⊖ | ⊜ | |
| Engine Cooling | ⊜ | ⊜ | ⊜ | ⊜ | ⊜ | |
| Trans. Major | ⊜ | ⊜ | ⊜ | ⊖ | ⊜ | |
| Trans. Minor | ⊜ | ⊜ | ⊜ | ◒ | ○ | |
| Drive System | ⊜ | ⊜ | ⊜ | ⊖ | ⊜ | |
| Fuel System | ⊜ | ⊜ | ⊜ | ◒ | ○ | |
| Electrical | ○ | ◒ | ○ | ◒ | ⊖ | |
| Climate System | ○ | ⊖ | ⊖ | ⊖ | ⊜ | |
| Suspension | ⊖ | ⊜ | ⊜ | ⊜ | ⊜ | |
| Brakes | ⊖ | ⊖ | ○ | ○ | ⊖ | |
| Exhaust | ⊜ | ⊜ | ⊜ | ⊜ | ⊜ | |
| Paint/Trim | ⊖ | ⊖ | ⊜ | ⊖ | ⊜ | |
| Body Integrity | ⊖ | ⊜ | ⊖ | ⊖ | ⊜ | |
| Body Hardware | ⊖ | ⊖ | ⊖ | ○ | ⊜ | |
| Power Equip. | ⊜ | ⊖ | ⊜ | ⊖ | ⊜ | |
| Audio System | ⊖ | ○ | ⊜ | ⊖ | ○ | |
| USED CAR VERDICTS | ⊜ | ⊜ | ⊜ | ○ | ○ | |
| NEW CAR PREDICTION | Discontinued | | | | | |

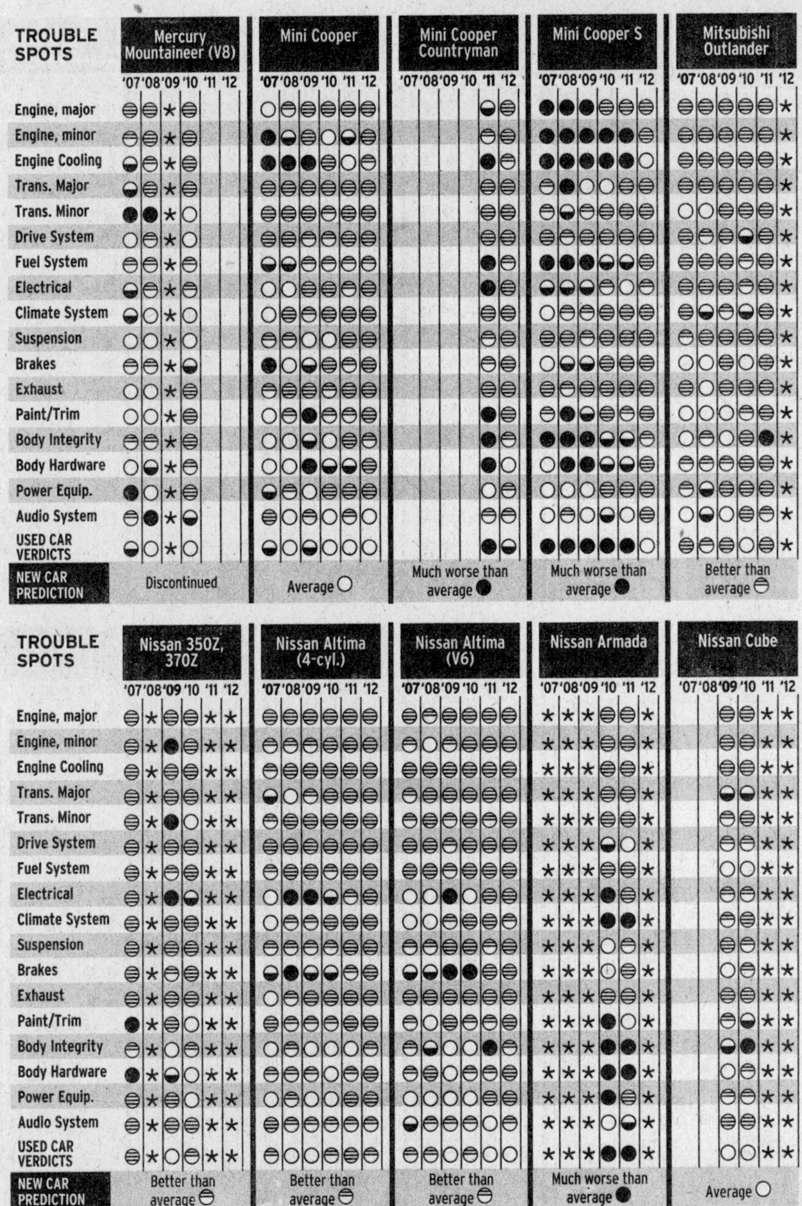
TROUBLE SPOTS
Mercury Mountaineer (V8)
Mini Cooper
Mini Cooper Countryman
Mini Cooper S
Mitsubishi Outlander
'07 '08 '09 '10 '11 '12
Engine, major
Engine, minor
Engine Cooling
Trans. Major
Trans. Minor
Drive System
Fuel System
Electrical
Climate System
Suspension
Brakes
Exhaust
Paint/Trim
Body Integrity
Body Hardware
Power Equip.
Audio System
USED CAR VERDICTS
NEW CAR PREDICTION
Discontinued
Average
Much worse than average
Much worse than average
Better than average
TROUBLE SPOTS
Nissan 350Z, 370Z
Nissan Altima (4-cyl.)
Nissan Altima (V6)
Nissan Armada
Nissan Cube
'07 '08 '09 '10 '11 '12
Engine, major
Engine, minor
Engine Cooling
Trans. Major
Trans. Minor
Drive System
Fuel System
Electrical
Climate System
Suspension
Brakes
Exhaust
Paint/Trim
Body Integrity
Body Hardware
Power Equip.
Audio System
USED CAR VERDICTS
NEW CAR PREDICTION
Better than average
Better than average
Better than average
Much worse than average
Average

| TROUBLE SPOTS | Nissan Frontier '07 | '08 | '09 | '10 | '11 | '12 | Nissan Juke '07 | '08 | '09 | '10 | **'11** | '12 | Nissan Leaf '07 | '08 | '09 | '10 | **'11** | '12 |
|---|---|---|---|---|---|---|---|---|---|---|---|---|---|---|---|---|---|---|
| Engine, major | ○ | ⊜ | ⊜ | ⊜ | ⊜ | ⊜ | | | | | ○ | ⊜ | | | | | ⊜ | ⊜ |
| Engine, minor | ⊖ | ⊜ | ⊖ | ⊜ | ⊜ | ⊖ | | | | | ⊜ | ⊜ | | | | | ⊜ | ⊜ |
| Engine Cooling | ⊖ | ⊜ | ⊜ | ⊜ | ⊜ | ⊜ | | | | | ⊜ | ⊜ | | | | | ⊜ | ⊜ |
| Trans. Major | ⊖ | ⊜ | ⊜ | ⊜ | ⊜ | ⊜ | | | | | ⊜ | ⊜ | | | | | ⊜ | ⊜ |
| Trans. Minor | ⊖ | ⊜ | ⊖ | ⊜ | ⊖ | ⊜ | | | | | ⊜ | ⊜ | | | | | ⊜ | ⊜ |
| Drive System | ○ | ○ | ⊖ | ⊖ | ⊖ | ⊜ | | | | | ⊜ | ⊜ | | | | | ⊜ | ⊜ |
| Fuel System | ● | ◒ | ⊖ | ○ | ⊜ | ⊜ | | | | | ● | ⊜ | | | | | ⊜ | ⊜ |
| Electrical | ⊖ | ◒ | ○ | ⊖ | ⊜ | ⊜ | | | | | ⊖ | ⊖ | | | | | ⊜ | ○ |
| Climate System | ⊖ | ⊖ | ⊖ | ⊜ | ⊜ | ⊜ | | | | | ⊖ | ⊜ | | | | | ⊜ | ⊜ |
| Suspension | ⊖ | ⊖ | ⊜ | ⊜ | ⊜ | ⊖ | | | | | ⊖ | ⊜ | | | | | ⊜ | ⊜ |
| Brakes | ⊜ | ⊖ | ◒ | ● | ⊖ | ⊜ | | | | | ⊜ | ⊜ | | | | | ⊜ | ⊜ |
| Exhaust | ⊜ | ⊖ | ⊜ | ⊜ | ⊜ | ⊜ | | | | | ⊜ | ⊜ | | | | | ⊜ | ⊜ |
| Paint/Trim | ⊖ | ◒ | ◒ | ○ | ⊖ | ⊜ | | | | | ⊜ | ⊜ | | | | | ⊜ | ⊜ |
| Body Integrity | ◒ | ◒ | ⊖ | ○ | ⊖ | ⊖ | | | | | ● | ⊖ | | | | | ⊜ | ⊜ |
| Body Hardware | ⊖ | ⊜ | ⊜ | ⊖ | ⊖ | ⊖ | | | | | ◒ | ⊜ | | | | | ⊜ | ⊜ |
| Power Equip. | ○ | ○ | ○ | ⊜ | ⊖ | ⊖ | | | | | ⊜ | ⊜ | | | | | ⊜ | ⊜ |
| Audio System | ⊜ | ⊜ | ⊜ | ⊜ | ⊜ | ⊜ | | | | | ⊖ | ⊜ | | | | | ⊜ | ⊜ |
| USED CAR VERDICTS | ○ | ○ | ⊖ | ○ | ⊖ | ○ | | | | | ● | ⊜ | | | | | ⊜ | ○ |
| NEW CAR PREDICTION | Better than average ⊖ | | | | | | Average ○ | | | | | | Much better than average ⊜ | | | | | |

| TROUBLE SPOTS | Nissan Maxima '07 | '08 | **'09** | '10 | '11 | '12 | Nissan Murano '07 | '08 | **'09** | '10 | '11 | '12 |
|---|---|---|---|---|---|---|---|---|---|---|---|---|
| Engine, major | ○ | ⊜ | ⊜ | ⊜ | ⊜ | ⊜ | ⊜ | | ○ | ⊜ | ⊜ | ⊜ |
| Engine, minor | ⊖ | ○ | ⊜ | ⊜ | ⊜ | ⊜ | ● | | ⊜ | ⊜ | ⊜ | ⊜ |
| Engine Cooling | ⊖ | ⊜ | ⊜ | ⊜ | ⊜ | ⊜ | ⊜ | | ⊜ | ⊜ | ⊜ | ⊜ |
| Trans. Major | ○ | ⊜ | ⊜ | ⊜ | ⊜ | ⊜ | ⊖ | | ⊜ | ⊜ | ⊜ | ⊜ |
| Trans. Minor | ⊜ | ⊜ | ⊜ | ⊜ | ⊜ | ⊜ | ⊖ | | ⊜ | ⊖ | ⊜ | ⊜ |
| Drive System | ⊜ | ⊖ | ⊜ | ⊜ | ⊜ | ⊜ | ○ | | ○ | ○ | ⊜ | ⊜ |
| Fuel System | ⊖ | ⊜ | ⊜ | ⊜ | ⊜ | ⊜ | ○ | | ⊖ | ⊜ | ⊜ | ⊜ |
| Electrical | ○ | ◒ | ● | ● | ⊖ | ⊜ | ○ | | ○ | ⊖ | ⊜ | ⊜ |
| Climate System | ● | ⊖ | ⊜ | ⊜ | ⊜ | ⊜ | ⊖ | | ⊜ | ⊜ | ⊜ | ⊜ |
| Suspension | ⊖ | ⊖ | ◒ | ⊖ | ⊖ | ⊜ | ● | | ⊖ | ⊜ | ⊜ | ⊜ |
| Brakes | ◒ | ○ | ⊖ | ⊖ | ⊜ | ⊜ | ● | | ⊖ | ⊖ | ⊜ | ⊜ |
| Exhaust | ⊜ | ⊖ | ⊜ | ⊜ | ⊜ | ⊜ | ⊖ | | ⊜ | ⊜ | ⊜ | ⊜ |
| Paint/Trim | ◒ | ● | ⊖ | ⊖ | ⊜ | ⊜ | ⊖ | | ⊜ | ⊜ | ⊜ | ⊜ |
| Body Integrity | ⊖ | ○ | ○ | ○ | ◒ | ⊜ | ○ | | ○ | ○ | ◒ | ⊖ |
| Body Hardware | ⊖ | ⊖ | ○ | ⊖ | ◒ | ⊜ | ○ | | ○ | ⊖ | ⊖ | ⊜ |
| Power Equip. | ◒ | ● | ● | ⊖ | ⊖ | ⊜ | ○ | | ○ | ⊜ | ⊖ | ⊜ |
| Audio System | ○ | ○ | ⊖ | ⊖ | ○ | ⊜ | ⊜ | | ⊜ | ○ | ⊖ | ⊜ |
| USED CAR VERDICTS | ○ | ⊖ | ⊖ | ⊖ | ⊖ | ⊜ | ○ | | ○ | ○ | ⊜ | ⊜ |
| NEW CAR PREDICTION | Better than average ⊖ | | | | | | Better than average ⊖ | | | | | |

| TROUBLE SPOTS | Nissan Pathfinder '07 | '08 | '09 | '10 | '11 | '12 | Nissan Quest '07 | '08 | '09 | '10 | **'11** | '12 |
|---|---|---|---|---|---|---|---|---|---|---|---|---|
| Engine, major | ◒ | ○ | ★ | ⊜ | ⊜ | ★ | ● | ★ | ★ | | ⊜ | ★ |
| Engine, minor | ⊜ | ⊖ | ★ | ⊜ | ⊜ | ★ | ● | ★ | ★ | | ⊜ | ★ |
| Engine Cooling | ◒ | ⊜ | ★ | ⊜ | ⊜ | ★ | ○ | ★ | ★ | | ⊜ | ★ |
| Trans. Major | ● | ⊜ | ★ | ⊜ | ⊜ | ★ | ⊖ | ★ | ★ | | ⊜ | ★ |
| Trans. Minor | ⊜ | ⊖ | ★ | ⊜ | ⊜ | ★ | ⊜ | ★ | ★ | | ⊜ | ★ |
| Drive System | ⊜ | ⊖ | ★ | ⊖ | ⊜ | ★ | ◒ | ★ | ★ | | ⊜ | ★ |
| Fuel System | ● | ◒ | ★ | ◒ | ⊜ | ★ | ⊖ | ★ | ★ | | ● | ★ |
| Electrical | ◒ | ◒ | ★ | ● | ⊜ | ★ | ⊜ | ★ | ★ | | ⊜ | ★ |
| Climate System | ◒ | ◒ | ★ | ⊖ | ◒ | ★ | ● | ★ | ★ | | ⊖ | ★ |
| Suspension | ⊜ | ⊖ | ★ | ⊖ | ○ | ★ | ◒ | ★ | ★ | | ⊜ | ★ |
| Brakes | ○ | ○ | ★ | ● | ◒ | ★ | ● | ★ | ★ | | ⊜ | ★ |
| Exhaust | ⊖ | ⊜ | ★ | ⊖ | ⊜ | ★ | ⊜ | ★ | ★ | | ⊜ | ★ |
| Paint/Trim | ○ | ⊖ | ★ | ⊖ | ⊜ | ★ | ◒ | ★ | ★ | | ⊜ | ★ |
| Body Integrity | ○ | ◒ | ★ | ◒ | ⊖ | ★ | ◒ | ★ | ★ | | ⊖ | ★ |
| Body Hardware | ◒ | ⊖ | ★ | ● | ⊖ | ★ | ● | ★ | ★ | | ◒ | ★ |
| Power Equip. | ○ | ○ | ★ | ⊖ | ⊜ | ★ | ● | ★ | ★ | | ⊜ | ★ |
| Audio System | ⊜ | ⊖ | ★ | ⊖ | ⊖ | ★ | ◒ | ★ | ★ | | ● | ★ |
| USED CAR VERDICTS | ○ | ○ | ★ | ○ | ⊖ | ★ | ● | ★ | ★ | | ○ | ★ |
| NEW CAR PREDICTION | New | | | | | | Average ○ | | | | | |

| TROUBLE SPOTS | Nissan Rogue '07 | **'08** | '09 | '10 | '11 | '12 | Nissan Sentra **'07** | '08 | '09 | '10 | '11 | '12 | Nissan Titan '07 | '08 | '09 | '10 | '11 | '12 |
|---|---|---|---|---|---|---|---|---|---|---|---|---|---|---|---|---|---|---|
| Engine, major | | ⊜ | ⊜ | ⊜ | ⊜ | ⊜ | ⊖ | ○ | ⊜ | ⊜ | ⊜ | ⊜ | ⊜ | ⊜ | ★ | ⊜ | ⊜ | ★ |
| Engine, minor | | ⊖ | ⊜ | ⊜ | ⊜ | ⊜ | ● | ⊜ | ⊖ | ⊜ | ⊜ | ⊜ | ⊜ | ⊖ | ★ | ⊜ | ⊜ | ★ |
| Engine Cooling | | ⊜ | ⊜ | ⊜ | ⊜ | ⊜ | ⊜ | ⊖ | ⊜ | ⊜ | ⊜ | ⊜ | ◒ | ⊖ | ★ | ⊜ | ⊜ | ★ |
| Trans. Major | | ○ | ⊖ | ⊜ | ⊜ | ⊜ | ⊖ | ⊜ | ⊜ | ⊜ | ⊜ | ⊜ | ⊜ | ⊜ | ★ | ⊜ | ⊜ | ★ |
| Trans. Minor | | ⊖ | ⊖ | ⊜ | ⊜ | ⊜ | ⊖ | ⊜ | ⊜ | ⊜ | ⊖ | ⊜ | ○ | ⊜ | ★ | ⊜ | ⊜ | ★ |
| Drive System | | ○ | ⊜ | ⊜ | ⊜ | ⊜ | ⊖ | ⊖ | ⊜ | ⊖ | ⊜ | ⊜ | ● | ● | ★ | ⊖ | ○ | ★ |
| Fuel System | | ◒ | ○ | ⊖ | ⊖ | ⊜ | ⊜ | ⊖ | ⊖ | ○ | ⊜ | ⊖ | ⊖ | ○ | ★ | ⊖ | ⊜ | ★ |
| Electrical | | ⊖ | ⊖ | ⊜ | ⊜ | ⊜ | ⊖ | ○ | ⊜ | ⊖ | ⊖ | ⊜ | ⊖ | ⊖ | ★ | ⊖ | ○ | ★ |
| Climate System | | ⊖ | ⊖ | ⊖ | ⊜ | ⊜ | ⊜ | ◒ | ○ | ⊖ | ⊖ | ⊖ | ● | ⊖ | ★ | ● | ● | ★ |
| Suspension | | ⊖ | ⊜ | ⊜ | ⊜ | ⊜ | ◒ | ○ | ⊖ | ○ | ○ | ⊜ | ⊖ | ○ | ★ | ⊜ | ○ | ★ |
| Brakes | | ○ | ○ | ⊖ | ⊖ | ⊜ | ○ | ◒ | ◒ | ○ | ◒ | ⊜ | ● | ● | ★ | ⊜ | ⊜ | ★ |
| Exhaust | | ⊜ | ⊜ | ⊜ | ⊜ | ⊜ | ◒ | ◒ | ⊖ | ⊜ | ⊜ | ⊜ | ◒ | ● | ★ | ⊜ | ⊜ | ★ |
| Paint/Trim | | ○ | ⊜ | ⊖ | ⊜ | ⊜ | ○ | ◒ | ◒ | ⊖ | ○ | ⊜ | ○ | ◒ | ★ | ● | ⊖ | ★ |
| Body Integrity | | ◒ | ○ | ○ | ○ | ⊖ | ○ | ○ | ◒ | ⊖ | ○ | ⊖ | ○ | ◒ | ★ | ● | ● | ★ |
| Body Hardware | | ⊖ | ⊖ | ⊜ | ⊜ | ⊜ | ⊖ | ◒ | ⊖ | ⊖ | ◒ | ○ | ○ | ○ | ★ | ○ | ◒ | ★ |
| Power Equip. | | ⊖ | ◒ | ⊖ | ⊜ | ⊜ | ○ | ○ | ○ | ⊖ | ◒ | ⊜ | ○ | ⊖ | ★ | ● | ⊖ | ★ |
| Audio System | | ⊜ | ⊜ | ⊜ | ⊖ | ⊖ | ⊖ | ⊖ | ⊖ | ⊖ | ⊖ | ⊖ | ⊖ | ○ | ★ | ⊖ | ○ | ★ |
| USED CAR VERDICTS | | ○ | ⊖ | ⊜ | ⊖ | ⊖ | ○ | ○ | ⊖ | ⊖ | ○ | ○ | ○ | ○ | ★ | ○ | ● | ★ |
| NEW CAR PREDICTION | Better than average ⊖ | | | | | | New | | | | | | Worse than average ◒ | | | | | |

| TROUBLE SPOTS | Nissan Versa Hatchback | | | | | | Nissan Xterra | | | | | | Pontiac Vibe | | | | | |
|---|---|---|---|---|---|---|---|---|---|---|---|---|---|---|---|---|---|---|
| | **'07** | '08 | '09 | '10 | '11 | '12 | '07 | '08 | '09 | '10 | '11 | '12 | '07 | '08 | **'09** | '10 | '11 | '12 |
| Engine, major | ⊜ | ⊜ | ⊜ | ⊜ | ⊜ | ★ | ○ | ⊜ | ⊖ | ⊜ | ⊜ | ★ | ⊜ | ⊜ | ⊜ | ⊜ | | |
| Engine, minor | ⊖ | ⊖ | ⊖ | ⊜ | ⊜ | ★ | ⊖ | ⊜ | ⊜ | ⊜ | ⊜ | ★ | ⊜ | ⊖ | ⊜ | ⊜ | | |
| Engine Cooling | ⊜ | ⊜ | ⊜ | ⊜ | ⊜ | ★ | ⊖ | ⊜ | ⊖ | ⊜ | ⊜ | ★ | ○ | ⊖ | ⊜ | ⊜ | | |
| Trans. Major | ⊖ | ⊜ | ⊖ | ⊖ | ⊜ | ★ | ○ | ⊖ | ⊜ | ⊖ | ⊜ | ★ | ⊜ | ⊜ | ⊜ | ⊜ | | |
| Trans. Minor | ⊜ | ⊜ | ⊜ | ⊜ | ⊜ | ★ | ⊜ | ⊜ | ⊜ | ⊖ | ⊜ | ★ | ⊖ | ⊜ | ⊜ | ⊖ | | |
| Drive System | ⊜ | ⊜ | ⊜ | ⊜ | ⊜ | ★ | ⊖ | ○ | ⊖ | ○ | ⊖ | ★ | ⊜ | ⊜ | ⊜ | ⊜ | | |
| Fuel System | ◒ | ⊖ | ⊖ | ⊜ | ⊜ | ★ | ● | ○ | ⊖ | ⊜ | ⊜ | ★ | ⊖ | ⊖ | ⊖ | ⊜ | | |
| Electrical | ⊜ | ⊖ | ○ | ⊜ | ⊜ | ★ | ⊖ | ⊖ | ⊖ | ⊖ | ⊜ | ★ | ⊖ | ⊜ | ⊜ | ⊜ | | |
| Climate System | ○ | ● | ⊖ | ⊜ | ○ | ★ | ⊖ | ⊜ | ⊜ | ⊖ | ⊜ | ★ | ⊖ | ⊜ | ⊜ | ⊜ | | |
| Suspension | ⊖ | ○ | ⊖ | ⊖ | ⊜ | ★ | ⊖ | ⊖ | ⊜ | ⊖ | ⊜ | ★ | ⊜ | ⊜ | ⊖ | ⊖ | | |
| Brakes | ⊖ | ○ | ○ | ⊖ | ○ | ★ | ⊖ | ⊖ | ⊖ | ◒ | ⊜ | ★ | ○ | ⊖ | ○ | ○ | | |
| Exhaust | ● | ● | ⊜ | ⊜ | ⊜ | ★ | ⊖ | ⊜ | ⊜ | ⊜ | ⊜ | ★ | ⊜ | ⊜ | ⊜ | ⊜ | | |
| Paint/Trim | ◒ | ● | ● | ◒ | ⊖ | ★ | ⊖ | ◒ | ● | ○ | ⊜ | ★ | ⊖ | ○ | ○ | ⊖ | | |
| Body Integrity | ◒ | ○ | ◒ | ◒ | ○ | ★ | ⊖ | ○ | ● | ○ | ○ | ★ | ⊜ | ⊖ | ○ | ◒ | | |
| Body Hardware | ⊖ | ⊖ | ○ | ○ | ○ | ★ | ⊜ | ⊜ | ○ | ○ | ⊖ | ★ | ⊜ | ⊜ | ⊖ | ⊜ | | |
| Power Equip. | ● | ◒ | ● | ○ | ⊖ | ★ | ◒ | ◒ | ⊜ | ⊜ | ⊜ | ★ | ⊜ | ⊜ | ⊖ | ⊜ | | |
| Audio System | ⊜ | ⊖ | ⊜ | ⊜ | ⊖ | ★ | ○ | ⊜ | ⊖ | ⊜ | ⊜ | ★ | ⊖ | ⊖ | ◒ | ⊖ | | |
| USED CAR VERDICTS | ○ | ○ | ○ | ○ | ⊖ | ★ | ○ | ⊖ | ○ | ○ | ⊖ | ★ | ⊜ | ⊜ | ⊖ | ⊜ | | |
| NEW CAR PREDICTION | New | | | | | | Average ○ | | | | | | Discontinued | | | | | |

| TROUBLE SPOTS | Porsche 911 | | | | | | Porsche Boxster | | | | | |
|---|---|---|---|---|---|---|---|---|---|---|---|---|
| | '07 | '08 | '09 | '10 | '11 | **'12** | '07 | '08 | '09 | '10 | '11 | '12 |
| Engine, major | ⊜ | ○ | ⊜ | ★ | ★ | ★ | ⊜ | ⊜ | ★ | ★ | ★ | ★ |
| Engine, minor | ● | ● | ○ | ★ | ★ | ★ | ⊜ | ⊜ | ★ | ★ | ★ | ★ |
| Engine Cooling | ● | ◒ | ⊜ | ★ | ★ | ★ | ⊜ | ⊜ | ★ | ★ | ★ | ★ |
| Trans. Major | ⊜ | ⊜ | ○ | ★ | ★ | ★ | ⊜ | ⊜ | ★ | ★ | ★ | ★ |
| Trans. Minor | ⊖ | ⊜ | ⊜ | ★ | ★ | ★ | ⊜ | ⊜ | ★ | ★ | ★ | ★ |
| Drive System | ⊜ | ⊜ | ⊜ | ★ | ★ | ★ | ⊜ | ⊜ | ★ | ★ | ★ | ★ |
| Fuel System | ● | ● | ● | ★ | ★ | ★ | ⊖ | ⊜ | ★ | ★ | ★ | ★ |
| Electrical | ● | ⊜ | ⊜ | ★ | ★ | ★ | ○ | ⊖ | ★ | ★ | ★ | ★ |
| Climate System | ○ | ⊜ | ⊜ | ★ | ★ | ★ | ⊜ | ⊜ | ★ | ★ | ★ | ★ |
| Suspension | ⊜ | ● | ⊜ | ★ | ★ | ★ | ⊜ | ● | ★ | ★ | ★ | ★ |
| Brakes | ⊖ | ◒ | ⊜ | ★ | ★ | ★ | ⊜ | ⊜ | ★ | ★ | ★ | ★ |
| Exhaust | ⊜ | ⊜ | ⊖ | ★ | ★ | ★ | ⊜ | ⊜ | ★ | ★ | ★ | ★ |
| Paint/Trim | ○ | ● | ⊜ | ★ | ★ | ★ | ⊜ | ⊜ | ★ | ★ | ★ | ★ |
| Body Integrity | ⊜ | ● | ⊖ | ★ | ★ | ★ | ⊖ | ⊜ | ★ | ★ | ★ | ★ |
| Body Hardware | ⊖ | ● | ⊜ | ★ | ★ | ★ | ⊖ | ⊜ | ★ | ★ | ★ | ★ |
| Power Equip. | ⊜ | ⊖ | ⊜ | ★ | ★ | ★ | ⊜ | ⊜ | ★ | ★ | ★ | ★ |
| Audio System | ⊜ | ○ | ○ | ★ | ★ | ★ | ○ | ⊜ | ★ | ★ | ★ | ★ |
| USED CAR VERDICTS | ◒ | ● | ⊖ | ★ | ★ | ★ | ⊜ | ⊜ | ★ | ★ | ★ | ★ |
| NEW CAR PREDICTION | NA | | | | | | New | | | | | |

| TROUBLE SPOTS | Porsche Cayenne | | | | | | Saturn Aura | | | | | | Saturn Outlook | | | | | |
|---|---|---|---|---|---|---|---|---|---|---|---|---|---|---|---|---|---|---|
| | '07 | **'08** | '09 | '10 | **'11** | '12 | **'07** | '08 | '09 | '10 | '11 | '12 | **'07** | '08 | '09 | '10 | '11 | '12 |
| Engine, major | | ○ | ★ | ★ | ⊜ | ⊜ | ○ | ⊜ | ⊜ | | | | ● | ⊖ | ◒ | | | |
| Engine, minor | | ⊖ | ★ | ★ | ○ | ⊖ | ○ | ⊖ | ⊜ | | | | ● | ○ | ○ | | | |
| Engine Cooling | | ○ | ★ | ★ | ⊖ | ⊜ | ○ | ⊜ | ⊜ | | | | ● | ● | ◒ | | | |
| Trans. Major | | ⊜ | ★ | ★ | ⊜ | ⊜ | ⊜ | ⊜ | ⊜ | | | | ● | ● | ⊖ | | | |
| Trans. Minor | | ⊖ | ★ | ★ | ⊖ | ⊜ | ⊖ | ○ | ⊖ | | | | ● | ○ | ● | | | |
| Drive System | | ● | ★ | ★ | ⊖ | ⊜ | ⊖ | ◒ | ⊜ | | | | ● | ● | ◒ | | | |
| Fuel System | | ● | ★ | ★ | ⊖ | ⊖ | ◒ | ⊖ | ⊖ | | | | ○ | ○ | ◒ | | | |
| Electrical | | ⊖ | ★ | ★ | ⊜ | ⊜ | ⊖ | ⊖ | ○ | | | | ○ | ○ | ● | | | |
| Climate System | | ⊖ | ★ | ★ | ○ | ⊜ | ⊜ | ⊖ | ○ | | | | ● | ● | ● | | | |
| Suspension | | ⊜ | ★ | ★ | ⊜ | ⊜ | ● | ● | ● | | | | ● | ● | ● | | | |
| Brakes | | ⊖ | ★ | ★ | ⊖ | ⊜ | ● | ● | ◒ | | | | ○ | ◒ | ⊖ | | | |
| Exhaust | | ⊜ | ★ | ★ | ⊜ | ⊜ | ○ | ⊜ | ⊜ | | | | ⊜ | ⊜ | ⊜ | | | |
| Paint/Trim | | ○ | ★ | ★ | ⊜ | ⊜ | ⊖ | ○ | ○ | | | | ⊜ | ○ | ⊖ | | | |
| Body Integrity | | ⊖ | ★ | ★ | ⊖ | ⊜ | ⊖ | ◒ | ⊖ | | | | ◒ | ● | ○ | | | |
| Body Hardware | | ⊖ | ★ | ★ | ○ | ⊖ | ⊖ | ● | ◒ | | | | ◒ | ◒ | ◒ | | | |
| Power Equip. | | ○ | ★ | ★ | ⊖ | ⊖ | ● | ● | ● | | | | ● | ● | ● | | | |
| Audio System | | ⊖ | ★ | ★ | ○ | ○ | ○ | ○ | ○ | | | | ● | ◒ | ○ | | | |
| USED CAR VERDICTS | | ○ | ★ | ★ | ◒ | ◒ | ○ | ◒ | ○ | | | | ● | ● | ● | | | |
| NEW CAR PREDICTION | Worse than average ◒ | | | | | | Discontinued | | | | | | Discontinued | | | | | |

| TROUBLE SPOTS | Saturn Vue (V6) | | | | | | Scion xB | | | | | |
|---|---|---|---|---|---|---|---|---|---|---|---|---|
| | '07 | **'08** | '09 | '10 | '11 | '12 | '07 | **'08** | '09 | '10 | '11 | '12 |
| Engine, major | ⊜ | ⊜ | ◒ | | | | | ⊜ | ⊜ | ⊜ | ⊜ | ⊜ |
| Engine, minor | ⊜ | ○ | ○ | | | | | ⊖ | ⊜ | ⊜ | ⊜ | ⊜ |
| Engine Cooling | ⊜ | ○ | ⊖ | | | | | ● | ◒ | ⊜ | ⊜ | ⊜ |
| Trans. Major | ⊖ | ◒ | ⊜ | | | | | ⊜ | ⊜ | ⊜ | ⊜ | ⊜ |
| Trans. Minor | ◒ | ○ | ⊖ | | | | | ⊜ | ⊖ | ⊜ | ⊜ | ⊜ |
| Drive System | ○ | ◒ | ⊜ | | | | | ⊜ | ⊜ | ⊜ | ⊜ | ⊜ |
| Fuel System | ⊜ | ○ | ◒ | | | | | ⊖ | ⊜ | ⊜ | ⊜ | ⊜ |
| Electrical | ⊖ | ● | ⊖ | | | | | ○ | ○ | ⊜ | ⊜ | ⊜ |
| Climate System | ◒ | ● | ● | | | | | ⊜ | ⊜ | ⊜ | ⊜ | ⊜ |
| Suspension | ◒ | ● | ◒ | | | | | ⊜ | ⊖ | ⊖ | ⊜ | ⊖ |
| Brakes | ◒ | ⊖ | ○ | | | | | ◒ | ◒ | ⊖ | ⊖ | ⊜ |
| Exhaust | ⊜ | ⊜ | ⊖ | | | | | ⊜ | ⊜ | ⊜ | ⊜ | ⊜ |
| Paint/Trim | ○ | ◒ | ⊜ | | | | | ◒ | ⊖ | ⊜ | ⊜ | ⊜ |
| Body Integrity | ● | ○ | ● | | | | | ⊖ | ⊖ | ⊖ | ○ | ⊜ |
| Body Hardware | ⊜ | ◒ | ⊖ | | | | | ⊜ | ⊖ | ⊜ | ⊖ | ⊖ |
| Power Equip. | ⊖ | ◒ | ○ | | | | | ⊜ | ⊜ | ⊖ | ⊜ | ⊖ |
| Audio System | ○ | ○ | ⊜ | | | | | ⊜ | ○ | ○ | ⊖ | ⊜ |
| USED CAR VERDICTS | ○ | ● | ○ | | | | | ⊖ | ⊖ | ⊜ | ⊜ | ⊜ |
| NEW CAR PREDICTION | Discontinued | | | | | | Much better than average ⊜ | | | | | |

## TROUBLE SPOTS

| Scion xD | '07 | '08 | '09 | '10 | '11 | '12 |
|---|---|---|---|---|---|---|
| Engine, major | | ⊜ | ⊜ | ⊜ | * | * |
| Engine, minor | | ⊜ | ⊜ | ⊜ | * | * |
| Engine Cooling | | ● | ◒ | ⊜ | * | * |
| Trans. Major | | ⊜ | ⊜ | ⊜ | * | * |
| Trans. Minor | | ⊜ | ⊖ | ⊜ | * | * |
| Drive System | | ⊜ | ⊜ | ⊜ | * | * |
| Fuel System | | ⊖ | ⊜ | ⊖ | * | * |
| Electrical | | ⊖ | ⊖ | ⊜ | * | * |
| Climate System | | ⊜ | ⊜ | ⊜ | * | * |
| Suspension | | ⊜ | ⊖ | ⊜ | * | * |
| Brakes | | ○ | ◒ | ○ | * | * |
| Exhaust | | ⊜ | ⊜ | ⊜ | * | * |
| Paint/Trim | | ⊜ | ● | ⊜ | * | * |
| Body Integrity | | ⊖ | ◒ | ⊖ | * | * |
| Body Hardware | | ⊜ | ⊖ | ⊜ | * | * |
| Power Equip. | | ⊜ | ⊜ | ⊜ | * | * |
| Audio System | | ⊜ | ○ | ⊜ | * | * |
| USED CAR VERDICTS | | ⊖ | ○ | ⊜ | * | * |
| NEW CAR PREDICTION | Much better than average ⊜ | | | | | |

| Smart ForTwo | '07 | '08 | '09 | '10 | '11 | '12 |
|---|---|---|---|---|---|---|
| Engine, major | | ◒ | ⊜ | * | * | * |
| Engine, minor | | ⊖ | ⊜ | * | * | * |
| Engine Cooling | | ⊜ | ⊜ | * | * | * |
| Trans. Major | | ◒ | ⊜ | * | * | * |
| Trans. Minor | | ● | ◒ | * | * | * |
| Drive System | | ◒ | ⊜ | * | * | * |
| Fuel System | | ◒ | ● | * | * | * |
| Electrical | | ● | ⊖ | * | * | * |
| Climate System | | ● | ◒ | * | * | * |
| Suspension | | ⊖ | ⊜ | * | * | * |
| Brakes | | ⊖ | ⊖ | * | * | * |
| Exhaust | | ○ | ⊖ | * | * | * |
| Paint/Trim | | ⊜ | ⊜ | * | * | * |
| Body Integrity | | ○ | ⊜ | * | * | * |
| Body Hardware | | ● | ○ | * | * | * |
| Power Equip. | | ⊖ | ◒ | * | * | * |
| Audio System | | ⊜ | ⊖ | * | * | * |
| USED CAR VERDICTS | | ◒ | ⊖ | * | * | * |
| NEW CAR PREDICTION | NA | | | | | |

| Subaru B9 Tribeca, Tribeca | '07 | '08 | '09 | '10 | '11 | '12 |
|---|---|---|---|---|---|---|
| Engine, major | ○ | ⊜ | ⊜ | * | * | * |
| Engine, minor | ◒ | ⊖ | ⊜ | * | * | * |
| Engine Cooling | ⊜ | ⊜ | ⊜ | * | * | * |
| Trans. Major | ⊜ | ⊖ | ⊖ | * | * | * |
| Trans. Minor | ⊜ | ○ | ◒ | * | * | * |
| Drive System | ○ | ◒ | ○ | * | * | * |
| Fuel System | ○ | ⊜ | ⊜ | * | * | * |
| Electrical | ⊜ | ◒ | ⊖ | * | * | * |
| Climate System | ⊖ | ⊖ | ○ | * | * | * |
| Suspension | ○ | ● | ⊖ | * | * | * |
| Brakes | ⊖ | ○ | ⊖ | * | * | * |
| Exhaust | ⊜ | ⊜ | ⊜ | * | * | * |
| Paint/Trim | ⊜ | ⊜ | ⊜ | * | * | * |
| Body Integrity | ○ | ○ | ⊖ | * | * | * |
| Body Hardware | ⊖ | ⊖ | ⊜ | * | * | * |
| Power Equip. | ○ | ● | ● | * | * | * |
| Audio System | ○ | ● | ◒ | * | * | * |
| USED CAR VERDICTS | ⊖ | ○ | ○ | * | * | * |
| NEW CAR PREDICTION | NA | | | | | |

| Subaru Forester (non-turbo) | '07 | '08 | '09 | '10 | '11 | '12 |
|---|---|---|---|---|---|---|
| Engine, major | ◒ | ⊜ | ⊜ | ⊜ | ⊜ | ⊜ |
| Engine, minor | ○ | ⊖ | ⊜ | ⊜ | ⊜ | ⊜ |
| Engine Cooling | ⊜ | ⊜ | ⊜ | ⊜ | ⊜ | ⊜ |
| Trans. Major | ⊖ | ⊜ | ⊜ | ⊜ | ⊜ | ⊜ |
| Trans. Minor | ○ | ⊜ | ⊜ | ⊜ | ⊜ | ⊜ |
| Drive System | ⊖ | ⊖ | ⊜ | ⊜ | ⊜ | ⊜ |
| Fuel System | ◒ | ○ | ⊖ | ⊖ | ⊜ | ⊖ |
| Electrical | ○ | ⊜ | ⊖ | ⊜ | ⊜ | ⊜ |
| Climate System | ⊖ | ○ | ⊖ | ⊜ | ⊜ | ⊜ |
| Suspension | ○ | ○ | ⊖ | ⊜ | ⊜ | ⊜ |
| Brakes | ⊖ | ○ | ○ | ⊖ | ⊜ | ⊜ |
| Exhaust | ○ | ⊜ | ⊜ | ⊜ | ⊜ | ⊜ |
| Paint/Trim | ⊖ | ○ | ○ | ⊖ | ⊖ | ⊜ |
| Body Integrity | ○ | ○ | ○ | ○ | ○ | ⊖ |
| Body Hardware | ⊖ | ⊖ | ⊖ | ⊖ | ⊖ | ○ |
| Power Equip. | ⊖ | ○ | ⊖ | ⊜ | ⊜ | ⊜ |
| Audio System | ⊖ | ⊜ | ⊖ | ⊜ | ⊖ | ⊜ |
| USED CAR VERDICTS | ○ | ⊖ | ⊖ | ⊜ | ⊖ | ○ |
| NEW CAR PREDICTION | Better than average ⊖ | | | | | |

| Subaru Forester (turbo) | '07 | '08 | '09 | '10 | '11 | '12 |
|---|---|---|---|---|---|---|
| Engine, major | * | * | ◒ | ⊜ | ⊜ | * |
| Engine, minor | * | * | ⊜ | ⊜ | ⊜ | * |
| Engine Cooling | * | * | ⊜ | ⊜ | ⊜ | * |
| Trans. Major | * | * | ⊖ | ⊖ | ⊜ | * |
| Trans. Minor | * | * | ⊜ | ⊜ | ⊜ | * |
| Drive System | * | * | ⊜ | ⊜ | ⊜ | * |
| Fuel System | * | * | ○ | ⊖ | ⊜ | * |
| Electrical | * | * | ⊜ | ⊜ | ⊜ | * |
| Climate System | * | * | ○ | ⊖ | ⊜ | * |
| Suspension | * | * | ⊖ | ⊜ | ⊜ | * |
| Brakes | * | * | ⊖ | ⊖ | ⊜ | * |
| Exhaust | * | * | ⊜ | ⊜ | ⊜ | * |
| Paint/Trim | * | * | ⊖ | ○ | ⊜ | * |
| Body Integrity | * | * | ◒ | ⊖ | ⊜ | * |
| Body Hardware | * | * | ⊖ | ⊜ | ⊖ | * |
| Power Equip. | * | * | ○ | ⊖ | ⊜ | * |
| Audio System | * | * | ⊖ | ⊜ | ○ | * |
| USED CAR VERDICTS | * | * | ○ | ⊜ | ⊜ | * |
| NEW CAR PREDICTION | Better than average ⊖ | | | | | |

## TROUBLE SPOTS

| Subaru Impreza Sedan | '07 | '08 | '09 | '10 | '11 | '12 |
|---|---|---|---|---|---|---|
| Engine, major | * | ⊖ | ⊜ | ⊜ | ⊜ | ⊜ |
| Engine, minor | * | ⊜ | ⊜ | ⊜ | ⊜ | ⊜ |
| Engine Cooling | * | ⊜ | ⊜ | ⊜ | ⊜ | ⊜ |
| Trans. Major | * | ⊜ | ⊜ | ⊜ | ⊜ | ⊜ |
| Trans. Minor | * | ⊜ | ⊜ | ⊜ | ⊜ | ⊜ |
| Drive System | * | ⊖ | ⊜ | ⊜ | ⊜ | ⊜ |
| Fuel System | * | ⊖ | ○ | ⊖ | ⊜ | ⊜ |
| Electrical | * | ⊜ | ⊜ | ⊖ | ⊜ | ⊜ |
| Climate System | * | ◒ | ⊜ | ⊜ | ⊜ | ⊜ |
| Suspension | * | ⊖ | ⊜ | ⊜ | ⊜ | ⊖ |
| Brakes | * | ● | ◒ | ⊖ | ⊖ | ⊜ |
| Exhaust | * | ⊜ | ⊖ | ⊜ | ⊜ | ⊜ |
| Paint/Trim | * | ● | ○ | ○ | ⊖ | ⊜ |
| Body Integrity | * | ⊖ | ○ | ⊜ | ● | ⊜ |
| Body Hardware | * | ⊖ | ⊖ | ⊖ | ⊜ | ⊜ |
| Power Equip. | * | ○ | ⊖ | ○ | ⊖ | ⊜ |
| Audio System | * | ○ | ⊜ | ⊜ | ⊖ | ⊜ |
| USED CAR VERDICTS | * | ○ | ⊜ | ⊜ | ⊖ | ⊜ |
| NEW CAR PREDICTION | Much better than average ⊜ | | | | | |

| Subaru Impreza WRX/STi | '07 | '08 | '09 | '10 | '11 | '12 |
|---|---|---|---|---|---|---|
| Engine, major | * | ◒ | ○ | * | ⊖ | ⊜ |
| Engine, minor | * | ○ | ⊖ | * | ⊜ | ⊜ |
| Engine Cooling | * | ⊜ | ⊜ | * | ⊜ | ⊜ |
| Trans. Major | * | ● | ● | * | ⊜ | ⊜ |
| Trans. Minor | * | ● | ⊜ | * | ⊖ | ⊜ |
| Drive System | * | ⊜ | ⊜ | * | ⊜ | ⊜ |
| Fuel System | * | ● | ⊖ | * | ⊖ | ⊖ |
| Electrical | * | ⊜ | ⊜ | * | ⊜ | ⊜ |
| Climate System | * | ● | ◒ | * | ⊜ | ⊜ |
| Suspension | * | ○ | ○ | * | ⊜ | ⊜ |
| Brakes | * | ○ | ⊖ | * | ⊜ | ⊜ |
| Exhaust | * | ⊜ | ⊜ | * | ⊜ | ⊜ |
| Paint/Trim | * | ● | ● | * | ◒ | ○ |
| Body Integrity | * | ⊖ | ○ | * | ◒ | ◒ |
| Body Hardware | * | ⊜ | ⊖ | * | ○ | ⊜ |
| Power Equip. | * | ⊜ | ⊜ | * | ○ | ⊖ |
| Audio System | * | ⊜ | ⊖ | * | ⊖ | ◒ |
| USED CAR VERDICTS | * | ◒ | ○ | * | ○ | ○ |
| NEW CAR PREDICTION | Average ○ | | | | | |

| Subaru Impreza Wagon & Hatchback | '07 | '08 | '09 | '10 | '11 | '12 |
|---|---|---|---|---|---|---|
| Engine, major | ○ | ⊜ | ⊜ | ⊜ | ⊜ | ⊜ |
| Engine, minor | ⊖ | ○ | ⊜ | ⊜ | ⊜ | ⊜ |
| Engine Cooling | ⊜ | ⊜ | ⊜ | ⊜ | ⊜ | ⊜ |
| Trans. Major | ⊖ | ⊜ | ⊜ | ⊜ | ⊜ | ⊜ |
| Trans. Minor | ◒ | ⊜ | ⊜ | ⊜ | ⊜ | ⊜ |
| Drive System | ○ | ⊜ | ⊜ | ⊜ | ⊜ | ⊜ |
| Fuel System | ⊖ | ⊖ | ⊖ | ⊜ | ⊜ | ⊜ |
| Electrical | ⊖ | ⊜ | ⊖ | ⊜ | ⊜ | ⊜ |
| Climate System | ⊜ | ○ | ⊖ | ⊜ | ⊖ | ⊜ |
| Suspension | ⊖ | ⊖ | ⊖ | ⊜ | ⊜ | ⊜ |
| Brakes | ○ | ◒ | ○ | ⊖ | ⊜ | ⊜ |
| Exhaust | ○ | ⊜ | ⊜ | ⊜ | ⊜ | ⊜ |
| Paint/Trim | ⊜ | ● | ● | ● | ⊜ | ⊜ |
| Body Integrity | ⊖ | ○ | ● | ● | ⊖ | ◒ |
| Body Hardware | ⊜ | ⊖ | ⊖ | ⊜ | ⊜ | ⊜ |
| Power Equip. | ○ | ⊖ | ○ | ⊜ | ○ | ⊜ |
| Audio System | ⊖ | ⊜ | ○ | ⊖ | ⊖ | ⊜ |
| USED CAR VERDICTS | ⊖ | ⊖ | ○ | ⊜ | ⊖ | ⊜ |
| NEW CAR PREDICTION | Much better than average ⊜ | | | | | |

| Subaru Legacy (4-cyl.) | '07 | '08 | '09 | '10 | '11 | '12 |
|---|---|---|---|---|---|---|
| Engine, major | ● | ⊖ | ⊜ | ⊜ | ⊜ | ⊜ |
| Engine, minor | ● | ○ | ⊜ | ⊜ | ⊜ | ⊜ |
| Engine Cooling | ⊜ | ⊖ | ⊜ | ⊜ | ⊜ | ⊜ |
| Trans. Major | ○ | ⊜ | ⊜ | ⊜ | ⊜ | ⊜ |
| Trans. Minor | ⊖ | ⊜ | ⊖ | ⊜ | ⊜ | ⊜ |
| Drive System | ⊖ | ⊖ | ⊜ | ⊜ | ⊜ | ⊜ |
| Fuel System | ⊖ | ⊖ | ⊜ | ⊜ | ⊜ | ⊜ |
| Electrical | ○ | ⊜ | ⊜ | ⊜ | ⊜ | ⊜ |
| Climate System | ⊜ | ◒ | ⊜ | ⊜ | ⊖ | ⊜ |
| Suspension | ○ | ◒ | ⊖ | ⊖ | ⊜ | ⊜ |
| Brakes | ◒ | ◒ | ⊜ | ⊜ | ⊖ | ⊖ |
| Exhaust | ⊖ | ○ | ⊜ | ⊜ | ⊜ | ⊜ |
| Paint/Trim | ○ | ○ | ⊖ | ⊖ | ⊜ | ⊜ |
| Body Integrity | ○ | ◒ | ⊖ | ⊜ | ⊖ | ⊜ |
| Body Hardware | ○ | ⊖ | ⊜ | ⊖ | ○ | ⊖ |
| Power Equip. | ⊖ | ○ | ⊖ | ⊖ | ⊖ | ⊜ |
| Audio System | ⊖ | ⊖ | ⊜ | ○ | ⊖ | ⊜ |
| USED CAR VERDICTS | ○ | ○ | ⊜ | ⊜ | ⊖ | ⊖ |
| NEW CAR PREDICTION | Better than average ⊖ | | | | | |

| Subaru Outback (4-cyl.) | '07 | '08 | '09 | '10 | '11 | '12 |
|---|---|---|---|---|---|---|
| Engine, major | ● | ⊜ | ⊜ | ⊜ | ⊜ | ⊜ |
| Engine, minor | ● | ⊖ | ⊖ | ⊜ | ⊜ | ⊜ |
| Engine Cooling | ⊜ | ⊜ | ⊜ | ⊜ | ⊜ | ⊜ |
| Trans. Major | ⊖ | ⊜ | ⊜ | ⊜ | ⊜ | ⊜ |
| Trans. Minor | ⊖ | ⊜ | ⊜ | ⊜ | ⊜ | ⊜ |
| Drive System | ● | ○ | ⊖ | ⊜ | ⊜ | ⊜ |
| Fuel System | ⊖ | ⊖ | ⊜ | ⊖ | ⊜ | ⊜ |
| Electrical | ○ | ⊖ | ○ | ⊜ | ⊜ | ⊜ |
| Climate System | ⊜ | ⊖ | ⊖ | ⊜ | ⊜ | ⊜ |
| Suspension | ○ | ○ | ⊖ | ⊜ | ⊜ | ⊜ |
| Brakes | ○ | ○ | ⊖ | ⊜ | ⊜ | ⊜ |
| Exhaust | ⊖ | ○ | ⊜ | ⊜ | ⊜ | ⊜ |
| Paint/Trim | ⊖ | ⊖ | ⊖ | ⊜ | ⊜ | ⊜ |
| Body Integrity | ⊖ | ⊖ | ○ | ⊖ | ⊖ | ⊜ |
| Body Hardware | ⊖ | ⊖ | ⊖ | ⊖ | ○ | ⊖ |
| Power Equip. | ○ | ⊖ | ⊖ | ⊖ | ⊖ | ⊜ |
| Audio System | ⊖ | ⊖ | ⊖ | ⊖ | ⊖ | ⊖ |
| USED CAR VERDICTS | ○ | ⊖ | ⊖ | ⊜ | ⊖ | ⊖ |
| NEW CAR PREDICTION | Much better than average ⊜ | | | | | |

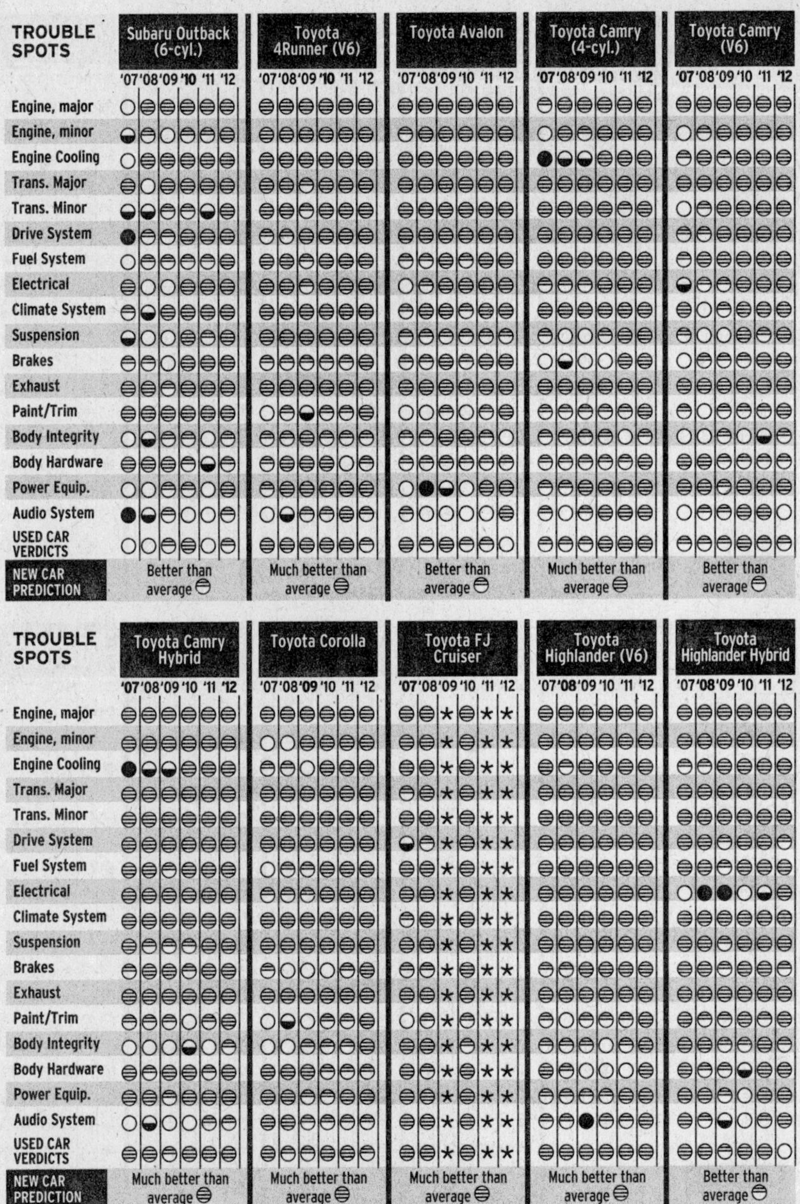
TROUBLE SPOTS
Subaru Outback (6-cyl.)
Toyota 4Runner (V6)
Toyota Avalon
Toyota Camry (4-cyl.)
Toyota Camry (V6)
'07 '08 '09 '10 '11 '12
Engine, major
Engine, minor
Engine Cooling
Trans. Major
Trans. Minor
Drive System
Fuel System
Electrical
Climate System
Suspension
Brakes
Exhaust
Paint/Trim
Body Integrity
Body Hardware
Power Equip.
Audio System
USED CAR VERDICTS
NEW CAR PREDICTION
Better than average
Much better than average
Better than average
Much better than average
Better than average
TROUBLE SPOTS
Toyota Camry Hybrid
Toyota Corolla
Toyota FJ Cruiser
Toyota Highlander (V6)
Toyota Highlander Hybrid
'07 '08 '09 '10 '11 '12
Engine, major
Engine, minor
Engine Cooling
Trans. Major
Trans. Minor
Drive System
Fuel System
Electrical
Climate System
Suspension
Brakes
Exhaust
Paint/Trim
Body Integrity
Body Hardware
Power Equip.
Audio System
USED CAR VERDICTS
NEW CAR PREDICTION
Much better than average
Much better than average
Much better than average
Much better than average
Better than average

**Toyota Matrix**

| TROUBLE SPOTS | '07 | '08 | '09 | '10 | '11 | '12 |
|---|---|---|---|---|---|---|
| Engine, major | ⊖ | ⊜ | ⊜ | ⊜ | ★ | ★ |
| Engine, minor | ○ | ○ | ⊜ | ⊜ | ★ | ★ |
| Engine Cooling | ⊖ | ⊜ | ⊜ | ⊜ | ★ | ★ |
| Trans. Major | ⊖ | ⊜ | ⊜ | ⊜ | ★ | ★ |
| Trans. Minor | ⊖ | ⊜ | ⊜ | ⊜ | ★ | ★ |
| Drive System | ⊜ | ⊜ | ⊜ | ⊜ | ★ | ★ |
| Fuel System | ○ | ⊖ | ⊖ | ⊜ | ★ | ★ |
| Electrical | ⊖ | ⊜ | ⊖ | ⊜ | ★ | ★ |
| Climate System | ⊜ | ⊜ | ⊜ | ⊖ | ★ | ★ |
| Suspension | ⊜ | ⊖ | ⊖ | ⊜ | ★ | ★ |
| Brakes | ⊖ | ⊖ | ○ | ⊖ | ★ | ★ |
| Exhaust | ⊖ | ⊜ | ⊜ | ⊜ | ★ | ★ |
| Paint/Trim | ○ | ⊖ | ◒ | ⊖ | ★ | ★ |
| Body Integrity | ○ | ○ | ○ | ⊖ | ★ | ★ |
| Body Hardware | ⊜ | ⊜ | ⊖ | ⊖ | ★ | ★ |
| Power Equip. | ⊜ | ⊖ | ⊜ | ⊖ | ★ | ★ |
| Audio System | ⊖ | ⊜ | ○ | ⊜ | ★ | ★ |
| USED CAR VERDICTS | ⊖ | ⊜ | ⊖ | ⊜ | ★ | ★ |
| NEW CAR PREDICTION | Much better than average ⊜ | | | | | |

**Toyota Prius**

| TROUBLE SPOTS | '07 | '08 | '09 | '10 | '11 | '12 |
|---|---|---|---|---|---|---|
| Engine, major | ⊜ | ⊜ | ⊜ | ⊜ | ⊜ | ⊜ |
| Engine, minor | ⊜ | ⊜ | ⊜ | ⊜ | ⊜ | ⊜ |
| Engine Cooling | ◒ | ⊖ | ⊜ | ⊜ | ⊜ | ⊜ |
| Trans. Major | ⊜ | ⊜ | ⊜ | ⊜ | ⊜ | ⊜ |
| Trans. Minor | ⊜ | ⊜ | ⊜ | ⊜ | ⊜ | ⊜ |
| Drive System | ⊜ | ⊜ | ⊜ | ⊜ | ⊜ | ⊜ |
| Fuel System | ⊜ | ⊜ | ⊜ | ⊜ | ⊜ | ⊜ |
| Electrical | ○ | ◒ | ◒ | ⊖ | ⊜ | ⊜ |
| Climate System | ⊜ | ⊜ | ⊜ | ⊜ | ⊜ | ⊜ |
| Suspension | ⊜ | ⊜ | ⊜ | ⊜ | ⊜ | ⊜ |
| Brakes | ⊜ | ⊜ | ⊜ | ⊖ | ⊜ | ⊜ |
| Exhaust | ⊜ | ⊜ | ⊜ | ⊜ | ⊜ | ⊜ |
| Paint/Trim | ⊜ | ⊖ | ⊜ | ⊜ | ⊜ | ⊜ |
| Body Integrity | ⊖ | ⊖ | ⊖ | ⊖ | ⊖ | ⊜ |
| Body Hardware | ⊜ | ⊜ | ⊜ | ⊜ | ⊜ | ⊜ |
| Power Equip. | ◒ | ○ | ⊖ | ⊜ | ⊜ | ⊜ |
| Audio System | ⊖ | ⊖ | ⊖ | ⊖ | ⊖ | ⊖ |
| USED CAR VERDICTS | ⊜ | ⊜ | ⊜ | ⊜ | ⊜ | ⊜ |
| NEW CAR PREDICTION | Much better than average ⊜ | | | | | |

**Toyota RAV4 (4-cyl.)**

| TROUBLE SPOTS | '07 | '08 | '09 | '10 | '11 | '12 |
|---|---|---|---|---|---|---|
| Engine, major | ⊜ | ⊜ | ⊜ | ⊜ | ⊜ | ⊜ |
| Engine, minor | ○ | ⊖ | ⊜ | ⊜ | ⊜ | ⊜ |
| Engine Cooling | ◒ | ◒ | ⊜ | ⊜ | ⊜ | ⊜ |
| Trans. Major | ⊜ | ⊜ | ⊜ | ⊜ | ⊜ | ⊜ |
| Trans. Minor | ⊜ | ⊜ | ⊜ | ⊜ | ⊜ | ⊜ |
| Drive System | ⊖ | ⊜ | ⊜ | ⊜ | ⊜ | ⊜ |
| Fuel System | ⊖ | ⊖ | ⊜ | ⊜ | ⊜ | ⊜ |
| Electrical | ⊖ | ⊖ | ⊖ | ⊖ | ⊜ | ⊜ |
| Climate System | ⊜ | ⊜ | ⊜ | ⊜ | ⊜ | ⊜ |
| Suspension | ○ | ⊖ | ⊜ | ⊜ | ⊜ | ⊜ |
| Brakes | ○ | ○ | ⊖ | ⊖ | ⊜ | ⊜ |
| Exhaust | ⊜ | ⊜ | ⊜ | ⊜ | ⊜ | ⊜ |
| Paint/Trim | ⊖ | ⊖ | ⊜ | ⊜ | ⊜ | ⊜ |
| Body Integrity | ○ | ⊖ | ⊖ | ⊜ | ⊖ | ⊜ |
| Body Hardware | ⊜ | ⊜ | ⊜ | ⊜ | ⊜ | ⊜ |
| Power Equip. | ⊖ | ⊜ | ⊜ | ⊜ | ⊜ | ⊜ |
| Audio System | ⊜ | ⊜ | ⊜ | ⊖ | ⊜ | ⊜ |
| USED CAR VERDICTS | ⊖ | ⊖ | ⊜ | ⊜ | ⊜ | ⊜ |
| NEW CAR PREDICTION | Better than average ⊖ | | | | | |

**Toyota RAV4 (V6)**

| TROUBLE SPOTS | '07 | '08 | '09 | '10 | '11 | '12 |
|---|---|---|---|---|---|---|
| Engine, major | ⊜ | ⊜ | ⊜ | ⊜ | ⊜ | ⊜ |
| Engine, minor | ⊖ | ⊖ | ⊜ | ⊜ | ⊜ | ⊜ |
| Engine Cooling | ● | ◒ | ⊖ | ⊜ | ⊜ | ⊜ |
| Trans. Major | ⊜ | ⊜ | ⊜ | ⊜ | ⊜ | ⊜ |
| Trans. Minor | ⊜ | ⊜ | ⊜ | ⊜ | ⊜ | ⊜ |
| Drive System | ○ | ⊖ | ⊜ | ⊜ | ⊜ | ⊜ |
| Fuel System | ⊖ | ⊖ | ⊜ | ⊖ | ⊜ | ⊜ |
| Electrical | ○ | ○ | ⊖ | ⊖ | ⊜ | ⊜ |
| Climate System | ⊜ | ⊜ | ⊜ | ⊜ | ⊜ | ⊜ |
| Suspension | ○ | ⊖ | ⊜ | ⊜ | ⊜ | ⊜ |
| Brakes | ○ | ○ | ○ | ⊖ | ⊜ | ⊜ |
| Exhaust | ⊖ | ⊜ | ⊜ | ⊜ | ⊜ | ⊜ |
| Paint/Trim | ⊖ | ⊖ | ⊖ | ⊜ | ⊜ | ⊜ |
| Body Integrity | ○ | ⊖ | ⊖ | ⊖ | ⊖ | ⊜ |
| Body Hardware | ⊜ | ⊜ | ⊜ | ⊜ | ⊖ | ⊜ |
| Power Equip. | ⊜ | ⊜ | ⊖ | ⊜ | ⊜ | ⊜ |
| Audio System | ⊖ | ⊖ | ⊖ | ⊖ | ⊖ | ⊜ |
| USED CAR VERDICTS | ○ | ⊖ | ⊖ | ⊜ | ⊜ | ⊜ |
| NEW CAR PREDICTION | Discontinued | | | | | |

**Toyota Sequoia**

| TROUBLE SPOTS | '07 | '08 | '09 | '10 | '11 | '12 |
|---|---|---|---|---|---|---|
| Engine, major | ⊜ | ⊜ | | ⊜ | ⊜ | ★ |
| Engine, minor | ⊖ | ⊖ | | ⊜ | ⊜ | ★ |
| Engine Cooling | ⊖ | ⊖ | | ⊜ | ⊜ | ★ |
| Trans. Major | ⊜ | ⊜ | | ⊜ | ⊜ | ★ |
| Trans. Minor | ⊖ | ⊖ | | ⊜ | ⊜ | ★ |
| Drive System | ○ | ⊖ | | ⊜ | ⊜ | ★ |
| Fuel System | ⊜ | ⊖ | | ⊜ | ⊜ | ★ |
| Electrical | ⊖ | ⊖ | | ⊜ | ⊜ | ★ |
| Climate System | ⊜ | ⊜ | | ⊖ | ⊜ | ★ |
| Suspension | ⊜ | ⊜ | | ⊜ | ⊜ | ★ |
| Brakes | ○ | ⊖ | | ○ | ⊜ | ★ |
| Exhaust | ⊜ | ⊜ | | ⊜ | ⊜ | ★ |
| Paint/Trim | ○ | ⊖ | | ⊖ | ⊜ | ★ |
| Body Integrity | ⊖ | ⊖ | | ⊜ | ⊜ | ★ |
| Body Hardware | ● | ⊖ | | ○ | ○ | ★ |
| Power Equip. | ◒ | ⊖ | | ⊖ | ⊜ | ★ |
| Audio System | ○ | ◒ | | ⊖ | ⊖ | ★ |
| USED CAR VERDICTS | ○ | ⊖ | | ⊜ | ⊜ | ○ |
| NEW CAR PREDICTION | Much better than average ⊜ | | | | | |

**Toyota Sienna (AWD)**

| TROUBLE SPOTS | '07 | '08 | '09 | '10 | '11 | '12 |
|---|---|---|---|---|---|---|
| Engine, major | ○ | ⊜ | ⊜ | ⊖ | ⊜ | ⊜ |
| Engine, minor | ○ | ⊜ | ⊜ | ⊖ | ⊜ | ⊜ |
| Engine Cooling | ◒ | ⊜ | ⊜ | ⊜ | ⊜ | ⊜ |
| Trans. Major | ⊖ | ⊜ | ⊜ | ⊖ | ⊜ | ⊜ |
| Trans. Minor | ⊜ | ⊜ | ⊜ | ⊜ | ⊜ | ⊜ |
| Drive System | ⊖ | ○ | ◒ | ⊖ | ⊜ | ⊖ |
| Fuel System | ⊜ | ⊖ | ⊜ | ⊜ | ⊜ | ⊜ |
| Electrical | ⊖ | ○ | ○ | ⊜ | ⊜ | ⊜ |
| Climate System | ◒ | ○ | ○ | ⊖ | ⊜ | ⊜ |
| Suspension | ⊖ | ⊖ | ⊖ | ⊜ | ⊜ | ⊜ |
| Brakes | ◒ | ○ | ◒ | ◒ | ⊜ | ⊜ |
| Exhaust | ⊖ | ⊜ | ⊜ | ⊜ | ⊜ | ⊜ |
| Paint/Trim | ○ | ○ | ○ | ⊖ | ⊖ | ⊖ |
| Body Integrity | ⊖ | ◒ | ○ | ○ | ◒ | ○ |
| Body Hardware | ○ | ○ | ○ | ● | ● | ◒ |
| Power Equip. | ◒ | ◒ | ○ | ○ | ⊖ | ⊜ |
| Audio System | ● | ◒ | ◒ | ◒ | ⊖ | ⊖ |
| USED CAR VERDICTS | ○ | ○ | ○ | ○ | ○ | ○ |
| NEW CAR PREDICTION | Average ○ | | | | | |

**Toyota Sienna (FWD)**

| TROUBLE SPOTS | '07 | '08 | '09 | '10 | '11 | '12 |
|---|---|---|---|---|---|---|
| Engine, major | ⊜ | ⊜ | ⊜ | ⊜ | ⊜ | ⊜ |
| Engine, minor | ⊖ | ⊖ | ⊜ | ⊜ | ⊜ | ⊜ |
| Engine Cooling | ⊜ | ⊜ | ⊜ | ⊜ | ⊜ | ⊜ |
| Trans. Major | ⊖ | ⊜ | ⊜ | ⊖ | ⊜ | ⊜ |
| Trans. Minor | ⊖ | ⊜ | ⊜ | ⊜ | ⊜ | ⊜ |
| Drive System | ⊜ | ⊖ | ⊜ | ⊜ | ⊜ | ⊜ |
| Fuel System | ⊖ | ⊖ | ⊖ | ⊜ | ⊜ | ⊜ |
| Electrical | ⊖ | ⊖ | ○ | ⊖ | ⊜ | ⊜ |
| Climate System | ⊖ | ○ | ⊖ | ⊜ | ⊜ | ⊜ |
| Suspension | ⊖ | ⊖ | ⊖ | ⊜ | ⊜ | ⊜ |
| Brakes | ⊖ | ○ | ⊖ | ⊖ | ⊜ | ⊜ |
| Exhaust | ⊜ | ⊜ | ⊜ | ⊜ | ⊜ | ⊜ |
| Paint/Trim | ○ | ◒ | ○ | ⊖ | ⊖ | ⊜ |
| Body Integrity | ⊖ | ⊖ | ○ | ○ | ◒ | ○ |
| Body Hardware | ◒ | ○ | ○ | ○ | ● | ○ |
| Power Equip. | ○ | ⊖ | ⊖ | ⊖ | ⊜ | ⊜ |
| Audio System | ● | ◒ | ⊖ | ⊖ | ⊖ | ⊖ |
| USED CAR VERDICTS | ⊖ | ⊖ | ⊖ | ⊖ | ⊖ | ⊖ |
| NEW CAR PREDICTION | Better than average ⊖ | | | | | |

**Toyota Tacoma (V6, 2WD)**

| TROUBLE SPOTS | '07 | '08 | '09 | '10 | '11 | '12 |
|---|---|---|---|---|---|---|
| Engine, major | ⊜ | ⊜ | ⊜ | ⊜ | ⊜ | ⊜ |
| Engine, minor | ⊜ | ⊜ | ⊖ | ⊜ | ⊜ | ⊜ |
| Engine Cooling | ⊜ | ⊜ | ⊜ | ⊜ | ⊜ | ⊜ |
| Trans. Major | ⊜ | ⊜ | ⊜ | ⊜ | ⊜ | ⊜ |
| Trans. Minor | ⊖ | ⊜ | ○ | ⊖ | ○ | ⊜ |
| Drive System | ○ | ⊜ | ⊖ | ⊜ | ⊜ | ⊜ |
| Fuel System | ⊜ | ⊜ | ⊜ | ⊜ | ⊜ | ⊜ |
| Electrical | ⊖ | ⊖ | ⊖ | ⊜ | ⊜ | ⊜ |
| Climate System | ○ | ⊖ | ⊖ | ● | ● | ⊖ |
| Suspension | ⊖ | ⊜ | ⊖ | ⊖ | ⊜ | ⊜ |
| Brakes | ⊜ | ⊜ | ⊖ | ○ | ⊖ | ⊜ |
| Exhaust | ⊜ | ⊜ | ⊜ | ⊜ | ⊜ | ⊜ |
| Paint/Trim | ⊖ | ⊜ | ⊖ | ⊖ | ⊜ | ⊜ |
| Body Integrity | ⊖ | ⊖ | ○ | ◒ | ● | ○ |
| Body Hardware | ⊜ | ⊜ | ⊜ | ⊖ | ⊜ | ⊖ |
| Power Equip. | ◒ | ⊖ | ○ | ⊜ | ⊖ | ⊜ |
| Audio System | ⊖ | ⊜ | ● | ○ | ⊖ | ⊜ |
| USED CAR VERDICTS | ⊜ | ⊜ | ⊖ | ⊖ | ⊖ | ⊜ |
| NEW CAR PREDICTION | Better than average ⊖ | | | | | |

**Toyota Tacoma (V6, 4WD)**

| TROUBLE SPOTS | '07 | '08 | '09 | '10 | '11 | '12 |
|---|---|---|---|---|---|---|
| Engine, major | ⊜ | ⊜ | ⊜ | ⊜ | ⊜ | ⊜ |
| Engine, minor | ⊖ | ⊜ | ⊜ | ⊜ | ⊜ | ⊜ |
| Engine Cooling | ⊖ | ⊜ | ⊜ | ⊜ | ⊜ | ⊜ |
| Trans. Major | ⊜ | ⊜ | ⊜ | ⊜ | ⊜ | ⊜ |
| Trans. Minor | ⊖ | ⊜ | ⊖ | ⊖ | ⊜ | ⊜ |
| Drive System | ◒ | ⊖ | ○ | ⊖ | ⊜ | ⊜ |
| Fuel System | ⊜ | ⊜ | ⊜ | ⊜ | ⊜ | ⊜ |
| Electrical | ⊖ | ⊜ | ⊜ | ⊖ | ⊜ | ⊜ |
| Climate System | ○ | ○ | ⊖ | ● | ● | ⊖ |
| Suspension | ⊖ | ⊜ | ⊖ | ⊖ | ⊖ | ⊜ |
| Brakes | ⊖ | ⊜ | ⊜ | ⊖ | ⊖ | ⊜ |
| Exhaust | ⊜ | ⊜ | ⊜ | ⊜ | ⊜ | ⊜ |
| Paint/Trim | ○ | ⊜ | ⊖ | ◒ | ○ | ⊖ |
| Body Integrity | ⊖ | ○ | ○ | ○ | ◒ | ○ |
| Body Hardware | ⊜ | ⊜ | ⊜ | ⊖ | ⊖ | ⊜ |
| Power Equip. | ○ | ⊖ | ⊜ | ⊜ | ⊜ | ⊜ |
| Audio System | ⊖ | ⊜ | ● | ○ | ⊖ | ⊖ |
| USED CAR VERDICTS | ⊖ | ⊜ | ⊜ | ○ | ○ | ⊖ |
| NEW CAR PREDICTION | Average ○ | | | | | |

**Toyota Tundra (V8, 2WD)**

| TROUBLE SPOTS | '07 | '08 | '09 | '10 | '11 | '12 |
|---|---|---|---|---|---|---|
| Engine, major | ⊜ | ⊜ | ★ | ⊜ | ⊜ | ⊜ |
| Engine, minor | ○ | ◒ | ★ | ⊖ | ⊜ | ⊜ |
| Engine Cooling | ● | ⊖ | ★ | ⊜ | ⊜ | ⊜ |
| Trans. Major | ⊜ | ⊜ | ★ | ⊜ | ⊜ | ⊜ |
| Trans. Minor | ○ | ⊖ | ★ | ⊖ | ⊜ | ⊜ |
| Drive System | ○ | ○ | ★ | ⊖ | ⊜ | ⊜ |
| Fuel System | ⊖ | ⊜ | ★ | ⊜ | ⊜ | ⊜ |
| Electrical | ⊜ | ⊖ | ★ | ⊜ | ⊜ | ⊜ |
| Climate System | ⊖ | ⊖ | ★ | ⊜ | ⊜ | ⊜ |
| Suspension | ⊜ | ⊖ | ★ | ⊖ | ⊜ | ⊜ |
| Brakes | ⊖ | ⊖ | ★ | ⊜ | ⊜ | ⊜ |
| Exhaust | ⊜ | ⊜ | ★ | ⊜ | ⊜ | ⊜ |
| Paint/Trim | ○ | ○ | ★ | ○ | ⊜ | ⊖ |
| Body Integrity | ⊖ | ⊖ | ★ | ⊜ | ⊜ | ⊜ |
| Body Hardware | ⊜ | ⊜ | ★ | ⊖ | ⊖ | ⊖ |
| Power Equip. | ⊜ | ⊜ | ★ | ⊜ | ⊜ | ⊜ |
| Audio System | ◒ | ◒ | ★ | ⊜ | ⊜ | ⊖ |
| USED CAR VERDICTS | ⊖ | ⊖ | ★ | ⊖ | ⊜ | ⊜ |
| NEW CAR PREDICTION | Much better than average ⊜ | | | | | |

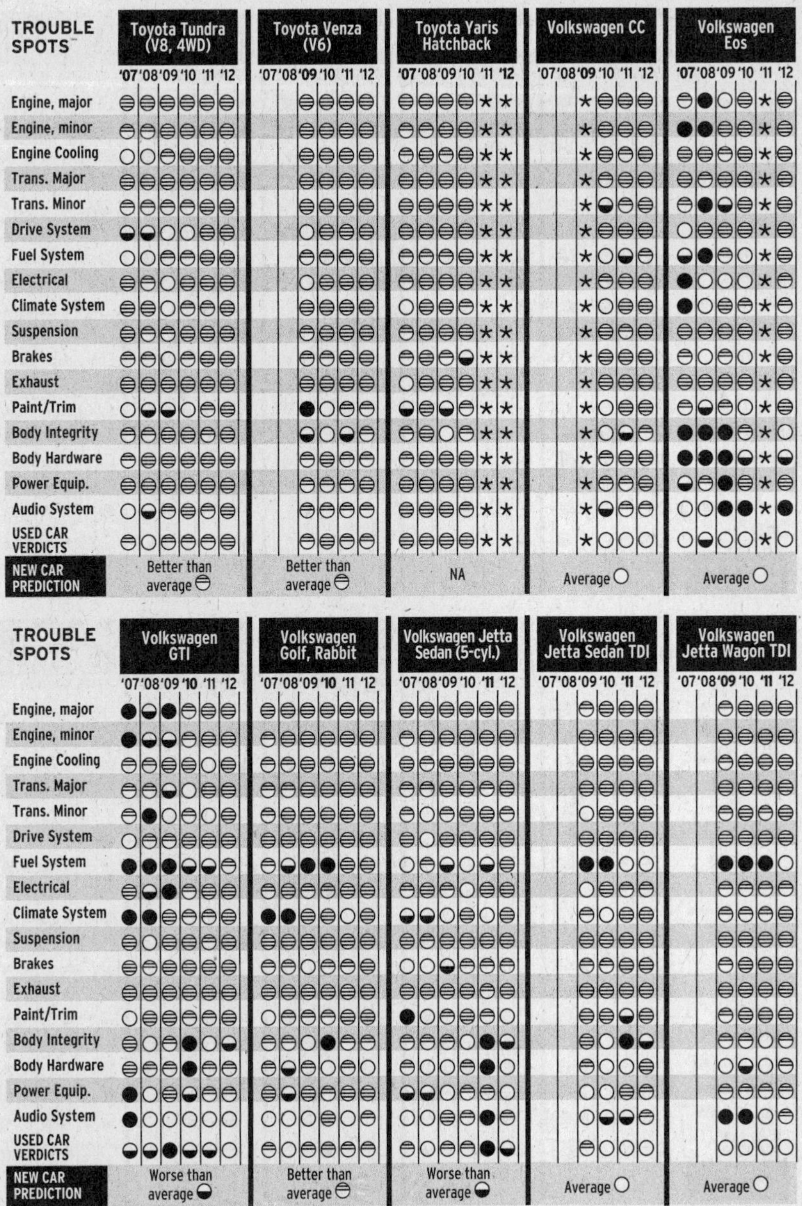
TROUBLE SPOTS
Toyota Tundra (V8, 4WD)
Toyota Venza (V6)
Toyota Yaris Hatchback
Volkswagen CC
Volkswagen Eos
'07 '08 '09 '10 '11 '12
Engine, major
Engine, minor
Engine Cooling
Trans. Major
Trans. Minor
Drive System
Fuel System
Electrical
Climate System
Suspension
Brakes
Exhaust
Paint/Trim
Body Integrity
Body Hardware
Power Equip.
Audio System
USED CAR VERDICTS
NEW CAR PREDICTION
Better than average
Better than average
NA
Average
Average
TROUBLE SPOTS
Volkswagen GTI
Volkswagen Golf, Rabbit
Volkswagen Jetta Sedan (5-cyl.)
Volkswagen Jetta Sedan TDI
Volkswagen Jetta Wagon TDI
'07 '08 '09 '10 '11 '12
Engine, major
Engine, minor
Engine Cooling
Trans. Major
Trans. Minor
Drive System
Fuel System
Electrical
Climate System
Suspension
Brakes
Exhaust
Paint/Trim
Body Integrity
Body Hardware
Power Equip.
Audio System
USED CAR VERDICTS
NEW CAR PREDICTION
Worse than average
Better than average
Worse than average
Average
Average

## TROUBLE SPOTS

| TROUBLE SPOTS | Volkswagen New Beetle, Beetle '07 | '08 | '09 | '10 | '11 | '12 |
|---|---|---|---|---|---|---|
| Engine, major | ⊜ | ⊜ | ⊜ | ⊜ | | ⊜ |
| Engine, minor | ⊖ | ⊖ | ⊜ | ⊜ | | ⊜ |
| Engine Cooling | ● | ● | ⊜ | ⊖ | | ⊜ |
| Trans. Major | ⊜ | ⊜ | ○ | ⊜ | | ⊜ |
| Trans. Minor | ○ | ⊜ | ⊜ | ⊜ | | ⊜ |
| Drive System | ○ | ● | ⊜ | ⊜ | | ⊜ |
| Fuel System | ● | ● | ⊜ | ⊜ | | ◒ |
| Electrical | ○ | ⊖ | ⊜ | ◒ | | ⊜ |
| Climate System | ● | ⊜ | ◒ | ◒ | | ⊜ |
| Suspension | ⊖ | ● | ⊜ | ⊜ | | ⊜ |
| Brakes | ⊖ | ⊖ | ⊜ | ⊜ | | ⊜ |
| Exhaust | ⊜ | ◒ | ⊜ | ⊖ | | ⊜ |
| Paint/Trim | ◒ | ● | ⊜ | ⊖ | | ⊜ |
| Body Integrity | ● | ○ | ● | ● | | ◒ |
| Body Hardware | ● | ● | ● | ● | | ● |
| Power Equip. | ● | ● | ⊜ | ● | | ⊜ |
| Audio System | ● | ⊜ | ⊖ | ⊖ | | ⊜ |
| USED CAR VERDICTS | ◒ | ● | ⊖ | ○ | | ● |
| NEW CAR PREDICTION | Much worse than average ● | | | | | |

| TROUBLE SPOTS | Volkswagen Passat (4-cyl., 5-cyl.) '07 | '08 | '09 | '10 | '11 | '12 |
|---|---|---|---|---|---|---|
| Engine, major | ● | ○ | ⊜ | ⊜ | | ⊜ |
| Engine, minor | ● | ● | ⊜ | ⊜ | | ⊜ |
| Engine Cooling | ⊖ | ⊜ | ● | ○ | | ⊜ |
| Trans. Major | ⊜ | ⊜ | ⊜ | ◒ | | ⊜ |
| Trans. Minor | ⊖ | ⊖ | ⊜ | ⊖ | | ⊜ |
| Drive System | ● | ⊖ | ⊜ | ⊜ | | ⊜ |
| Fuel System | ● | ● | ● | ○ | | ⊜ |
| Electrical | ● | ◒ | ⊜ | ⊖ | | ⊜ |
| Climate System | ● | ○ | ⊖ | ⊜ | | ⊖ |
| Suspension | ⊖ | ⊖ | ⊖ | ⊖ | | ⊜ |
| Brakes | ○ | ⊖ | ○ | ⊜ | | ⊜ |
| Exhaust | ○ | ⊜ | ⊖ | ⊜ | | ⊜ |
| Paint/Trim | ○ | ○ | ⊖ | ⊖ | | ⊜ |
| Body Integrity | ⊖ | ⊜ | ⊖ | ⊖ | | ⊜ |
| Body Hardware | ◒ | ○ | ⊖ | ◒ | | ○ |
| Power Equip. | ◒ | ◒ | ○ | ⊖ | | ⊜ |
| Audio System | ⊖ | ⊖ | ⊖ | ● | | ⊜ |
| USED CAR VERDICTS | ● | ○ | ○ | ◒ | | ⊖ |
| NEW CAR PREDICTION | Better than average ⊖ | | | | | |

| TROUBLE SPOTS | Volkswagen Tiguan '07 | '08 | '09 | '10 | '11 | '12 |
|---|---|---|---|---|---|---|
| Engine, major | | | ⊖ | ⊜ | ⊜ | ⊜ |
| Engine, minor | | | ⊖ | ⊖ | ⊜ | ⊜ |
| Engine Cooling | | | ◒ | ⊖ | ⊜ | ⊜ |
| Trans. Major | | | ⊜ | ⊜ | ⊜ | ⊜ |
| Trans. Minor | | | ⊖ | ⊜ | ⊜ | ⊜ |
| Drive System | | | ⊜ | ⊜ | ⊜ | ⊜ |
| Fuel System | | | ● | ◒ | ○ | ⊜ |
| Electrical | | | ◒ | ⊜ | ⊜ | ⊖ |
| Climate System | | | ○ | ⊜ | ⊜ | ⊖ |
| Suspension | | | ○ | ⊖ | ⊜ | ⊜ |
| Brakes | | | ○ | ○ | ○ | ⊜ |
| Exhaust | | | ⊖ | ⊜ | ⊜ | ⊜ |
| Paint/Trim | | | ⊜ | ○ | ⊖ | ⊜ |
| Body Integrity | | | ○ | ○ | ⊖ | ⊖ |
| Body Hardware | | | ⊖ | ◒ | ⊖ | ⊜ |
| Power Equip. | | | ● | ○ | ○ | ⊖ |
| Audio System | | | ○ | ○ | ◒ | ○ |
| USED CAR VERDICTS | | | ◒ | ○ | ○ | ○ |
| NEW CAR PREDICTION | Average ○ | | | | | |

| TROUBLE SPOTS | Volkswagen Touareg '07 | '08 | '09 | '10 | '11 | '12 |
|---|---|---|---|---|---|---|
| Engine, major | * | * | * | * | ⊜ | ⊜ |
| Engine, minor | * | * | * | * | ⊜ | ⊜ |
| Engine Cooling | * | * | * | * | ⊜ | ⊜ |
| Trans. Major | * | * | * | * | ⊜ | ⊜ |
| Trans. Minor | * | * | * | * | ⊜ | ⊜ |
| Drive System | * | * | * | * | ⊜ | ⊜ |
| Fuel System | * | * | * | * | ● | ● |
| Electrical | * | * | * | * | ⊜ | ⊜ |
| Climate System | * | * | * | * | ○ | ⊜ |
| Suspension | * | * | * | * | ○ | ⊖ |
| Brakes | * | * | * | * | ● | ⊖ |
| Exhaust | * | * | * | * | ⊜ | ⊜ |
| Paint/Trim | * | * | * | * | ⊖ | ⊜ |
| Body Integrity | * | * | * | * | ⊖ | ◒ |
| Body Hardware | * | * | * | * | ● | ⊜ |
| Power Equip. | * | * | * | * | ⊖ | ⊜ |
| Audio System | * | * | * | * | ◒ | ⊖ |
| USED CAR VERDICTS | * | * | * | * | ● | ◒ |
| NEW CAR PREDICTION | Much worse than average ● | | | | | |

| TROUBLE SPOTS | Volvo C70 '07 | '08 | '09 | '10 | '11 | '12 |
|---|---|---|---|---|---|---|
| Engine, major | ○ | ⊜ | * | * | ⊜ | * |
| Engine, minor | ⊖ | ⊜ | * | * | ⊜ | * |
| Engine Cooling | ⊜ | ⊜ | * | * | ⊜ | * |
| Trans. Major | ⊜ | ○ | * | * | ⊜ | * |
| Trans. Minor | ◒ | ⊜ | * | * | ⊜ | * |
| Drive System | ⊖ | ⊜ | * | * | ○ | * |
| Fuel System | ◒ | ⊜ | * | * | ◒ | * |
| Electrical | ● | ⊜ | * | * | ⊖ | * |
| Climate System | ○ | ⊖ | * | * | ◒ | * |
| Suspension | ○ | ● | * | * | ● | * |
| Brakes | ○ | ○ | * | * | ● | * |
| Exhaust | ⊜ | ⊜ | * | * | ⊜ | * |
| Paint/Trim | ○ | ⊜ | * | * | ○ | * |
| Body Integrity | ◒ | ● | * | * | ● | * |
| Body Hardware | ○ | ○ | * | * | ● | * |
| Power Equip. | ○ | ◒ | * | * | ⊖ | * |
| Audio System | ● | ⊖ | * | * | ⊖ | * |
| USED CAR VERDICTS | ○ | ○ | * | * | ● | * |
| NEW CAR PREDICTION | Much worse than average ● | | | | | |

## TROUBLE SPOTS

| TROUBLE SPOTS | Volvo S60 '07 | '08 | '09 | '10 | '11 | '12 |
|---|---|---|---|---|---|---|
| Engine, major | ⊜ | ⊜ | * | | * | ⊜ |
| Engine, minor | ⊖ | ○ | * | | * | ⊜ |
| Engine Cooling | ○ | ⊖ | * | | * | ⊜ |
| Trans. Major | ⊖ | ⊜ | * | | * | ⊜ |
| Trans. Minor | ⊜ | ⊜ | * | | * | ⊜ |
| Drive System | ⊜ | ⊖ | * | | * | ⊜ |
| Fuel System | ○ | ⊖ | * | | * | ⊜ |
| Electrical | ⊖ | ◒ | * | | * | ⊜ |
| Climate System | ⊖ | ⊖ | * | | * | ⊜ |
| Suspension | ◒ | ⊖ | * | | * | ⊜ |
| Brakes | ◒ | ⊖ | * | | * | ⊜ |
| Exhaust | ⊜ | ⊖ | * | | * | ⊜ |
| Paint/Trim | ⊜ | ⊖ | * | | * | ⊜ |
| Body Integrity | ⊖ | ⊜ | * | | * | ⊖ |
| Body Hardware | ⊖ | ◒ | * | | * | ⊖ |
| Power Equip. | ○ | ◒ | * | | * | ⊜ |
| Audio System | ○ | ◒ | * | | * | ⊖ |
| USED CAR VERDICTS | ⊖ | ○ | * | | * | ○ |
| NEW CAR PREDICTION | Average ○ | | | | | |

| TROUBLE SPOTS | Volvo S80 (6-cyl.) '07 | '08 | '09 | '10 | '11 | '12 |
|---|---|---|---|---|---|---|
| Engine, major | ⊜ | ⊜ | * | ⊜ | * | * |
| Engine, minor | ⊖ | ⊜ | * | ⊜ | * | * |
| Engine Cooling | ⊖ | ⊜ | * | ⊜ | * | * |
| Trans. Major | ⊜ | ⊜ | * | ⊜ | * | * |
| Trans. Minor | ⊜ | ⊜ | * | ⊜ | * | * |
| Drive System | ⊜ | ⊜ | * | ⊜ | * | * |
| Fuel System | ⊖ | ⊖ | * | ○ | * | * |
| Electrical | ○ | ◒ | * | ◒ | * | * |
| Climate System | ⊖ | ⊜ | * | ⊜ | * | * |
| Suspension | ◒ | ⊜ | * | ○ | * | * |
| Brakes | ⊖ | ⊖ | * | ⊖ | * | * |
| Exhaust | ⊜ | ⊜ | * | ⊜ | * | * |
| Paint/Trim | ○ | ⊜ | * | ○ | * | * |
| Body Integrity | ⊖ | ⊖ | * | ○ | * | * |
| Body Hardware | ⊖ | ⊜ | * | ● | * | * |
| Power Equip. | ⊜ | ⊜ | * | ⊖ | * | * |
| Audio System | ○ | ● | * | ○ | * | * |
| USED CAR VERDICTS | ⊖ | ⊜ | * | ⊖ | * | * |
| NEW CAR PREDICTION | Better than average ⊖ | | | | | |

| TROUBLE SPOTS | Volvo XC60 '07 | '08 | '09 | '10 | '11 | '12 |
|---|---|---|---|---|---|---|
| Engine, major | | | | ⊜ | ⊜ | ⊜ |
| Engine, minor | | | | ⊖ | ⊜ | ⊜ |
| Engine Cooling | | | | ⊜ | ⊜ | ⊜ |
| Trans. Major | | | | ⊜ | ⊜ | ⊜ |
| Trans. Minor | | | | ⊜ | ⊜ | ⊜ |
| Drive System | | | | ○ | ⊜ | ⊜ |
| Fuel System | | | | ⊖ | ⊜ | ⊜ |
| Electrical | | | | ● | ⊜ | ⊜ |
| Climate System | | | | ⊖ | ⊜ | ⊜ |
| Suspension | | | | ○ | ⊜ | ⊜ |
| Brakes | | | | ⊖ | ⊖ | ⊜ |
| Exhaust | | | | ⊜ | ⊜ | ⊜ |
| Paint/Trim | | | | ○ | ⊜ | ⊜ |
| Body Integrity | | | | ○ | ⊖ | ⊖ |
| Body Hardware | | | | ○ | ○ | ⊖ |
| Power Equip. | | | | ⊜ | ○ | ⊖ |
| Audio System | | | | ● | ● | ○ |
| USED CAR VERDICTS | | | | ◒ | ○ | ○ |
| NEW CAR PREDICTION | Average ○ | | | | | |

| TROUBLE SPOTS | Volvo XC70 '07 | '08 | '09 | '10 | '11 | '12 |
|---|---|---|---|---|---|---|
| Engine, major | ⊖ | ⊜ | ⊜ | ⊜ | ○ | ⊜ |
| Engine, minor | ⊖ | ⊖ | ⊜ | ◒ | ⊜ | ⊜ |
| Engine Cooling | ● | ⊜ | ⊜ | ⊜ | ⊜ | ⊜ |
| Trans. Major | ⊜ | ⊜ | ⊜ | ⊜ | ⊜ | ⊜ |
| Trans. Minor | ⊜ | ⊜ | ⊜ | ⊜ | ⊜ | ⊜ |
| Drive System | ○ | ⊜ | ⊜ | ⊜ | ⊜ | ⊜ |
| Fuel System | ⊖ | ⊖ | ○ | ⊜ | ⊖ | ⊖ |
| Electrical | ○ | ○ | ⊖ | ⊖ | ⊖ | ⊜ |
| Climate System | ⊖ | ○ | ◒ | ⊖ | ⊜ | ⊜ |
| Suspension | ◒ | ⊖ | ○ | ⊜ | ⊜ | ⊜ |
| Brakes | ○ | ⊖ | ⊖ | ⊜ | ⊜ | ⊜ |
| Exhaust | ⊖ | ⊜ | ⊜ | ⊜ | ⊜ | ⊜ |
| Paint/Trim | ⊜ | ○ | ⊜ | ⊖ | ⊜ | ⊜ |
| Body Integrity | ⊜ | ⊖ | ⊖ | ⊜ | ⊜ | ⊖ |
| Body Hardware | ○ | ⊖ | ⊜ | ◒ | ○ | ⊜ |
| Power Equip. | ○ | ◒ | ◒ | ⊜ | ⊖ | ⊜ |
| Audio System | ○ | ● | ○ | ⊜ | ○ | ○ |
| USED CAR VERDICTS | ○ | ⊖ | ⊖ | ⊖ | ○ | ○ |
| NEW CAR PREDICTION | Better than average ⊖ | | | | | |

| TROUBLE SPOTS | Volvo XC90 (6-cyl.) '07 | '08 | '09 | '10 | '11 | '12 |
|---|---|---|---|---|---|---|
| Engine, major | ⊜ | ⊜ | * | ⊖ | * | * |
| Engine, minor | ○ | ○ | * | ⊜ | * | * |
| Engine Cooling | ⊜ | ⊜ | * | ⊖ | * | * |
| Trans. Major | ⊖ | ⊜ | * | ⊜ | * | * |
| Trans. Minor | ⊖ | ⊖ | * | ⊜ | * | * |
| Drive System | ● | ⊖ | * | ○ | * | * |
| Fuel System | ⊖ | ⊖ | * | ⊜ | * | * |
| Electrical | ⊖ | ○ | * | ◒ | * | * |
| Climate System | ● | ● | * | ⊜ | * | * |
| Suspension | ⊖ | ⊖ | * | ⊖ | * | * |
| Brakes | ○ | ○ | * | ⊖ | * | * |
| Exhaust | ⊜ | ⊜ | * | ⊜ | * | * |
| Paint/Trim | ◒ | ⊖ | * | ○ | * | * |
| Body Integrity | ◒ | ⊖ | * | ⊖ | * | * |
| Body Hardware | ● | ○ | * | ○ | * | * |
| Power Equip. | ● | ○ | * | ◒ | * | * |
| Audio System | ◒ | ● | * | ● | * | * |
| USED CAR VERDICTS | ○ | ○ | * | ◒ | * | * |
| NEW CAR PREDICTION | Worse than average ◒ | | | | | |

# Quick Guide TIRES

**Tires have a direct impact on your car's handling, braking, ride comfort, and fuel economy. More important, the cornering grip, braking distances, and resistance to hydroplaning affect your safety on the road.**

**Shopping tip**

Remember that if you buy your tires online, you may have to pay for shipping, and also pay for mounting and balancing when the mail-order tires arrive.

Scan this or see how, page 11

For more buying advice, go to *ConsumerReports.org/tires*

### Types and features

*All-season*—These are the tires that come standard on many cars, minivans, and SUVs.

• Best for: Year-round traction, long tread life, and a comfortable ride. But they typically lack the precise handling and grip of performance tires.

• Speed ratings: Most are S (112 mph) or T (118 mph).

• Tread-wear warranty: None or 40,000 to 100,000 miles.

*Performance all-season*—These come standard on newer cars.

• Best for: Improved handling and grip over all-season tires on wet and dry pavement. But they often have shorter tread wear than many all-season tires.

• Speed ratings: H (130 mph), V (149 mph).

• Tread-wear warranty: None or 40,000 to 70,000 miles.

*Ultra-high performance all-season*—Found on sports cars, sports sedans, and some lower-priced sporty models.

• Best for: Wet and dry braking and handling. But they trade winter performance for ultimate warm-weather grip.

• Speed ratings: Z (more than 149 mph), W (168 mph), Y (186 mph).

• Tread-wear warranty: None or 30,000 to 40,000 miles.

*Ultra-high performance summer*—Found mostly on high-performance sports cars and sports sedans.

• Best for: Wet and dry braking and handling. But they are not suited for use in winter conditions.

• Speed ratings: Z (more than 149 mph), W (168 mph), Y (186 mph).

• Tread-wear warranty: Typically none.

*Winter*—Specially made for use in freezing temperatures and on snow and ice.

• Best for: Maintaining traction on snow and ice. But fast wear and so-so wet and dry braking make them suitable only for cold-weather use.

• Speed ratings: Q (99 mph and higher).

• Tread-wear warranty: Typically none.

*SUV/Pickup*—Designed for the rigors of truck use.

• Best for: All-terrain models are designed for on-road and light-duty off-pavement use; all-season models are made primarily for on-road use. But some automakers recommend staying with whatever type of tire came with your vehicle.

• Speed ratings: S (112 mph and higher).

• Tread-wear warranty: None or 40,000 to 70,000 miles.

Within types, in performance order.

| Recommended | Brand & model | Overall score (0–100; P \| F \| G \| VG \| E) | Three-season driving: Dry braking | Three-season driving: Wet braking | Three-season driving: Handling | Three-season driving: Hydroplaning | Winter driving: Snow traction | Winter driving: Ice braking | Comfort: Ride | Comfort: Noise | Rolling resistance | Tread life |
|---|---|---|---|---|---|---|---|---|---|---|---|---|
| **ALL-SEASON T-SPEED RATED** | | | | | | | | | | | | |
| ✔ | **Michelin** Defender | 70 | VG | VG | VG | VG | G | G | G | VG | VG | E |
| ✔ | **Continental** ProContact EcoPlus | 68 | VG | E | VG | VG | VG | G | VG | VG | VG | VG |
| ✔ | **Goodyear** Assurance TripleTred All-Season | 66 | VG | E | VG | VG | G | F | G | G | VG | E |
| ✔ | **Pirelli** P4 Four Seasons | 64 | VG | VG | VG | VG | G | F | VG | VG | G | E |
| | **Michelin** Energy Saver A/S | 64 | VG | VG | G | VG | G | F | VG | VG | E | G |
| ✔ | **Yokohama** Avid Ascend | 64 | VG | VG | G | VG | G | F | VG | E | VG | E |
| | **Uniroyal** Tiger Paw Touring | 62 | VG | VG | VG | VG | F | F | VG | G | G | G |
| | **Falken** Sincera Touring SN211 | 62 | VG | VG | G | VG | G | F | VG | VG | G | G |
| | **Cooper** CS4 Touring | 60 | VG | G | G | VG | VG | F | VG | G | G | G |
| | **Hankook** Optima H727 | 60 | G | VG | G | VG | VG | G | VG | G | G | G |
| | **Firestone** FR710 | 60 | VG | VG | VG | G | F | G | VG | G | G | G |
| | **Yokohama** Avid Touring-S | 58 | VG | G | G | VG | VG | F | VG | VG | VG | VG |
| | **Cooper** GFE | 58 | VG | VG | G | VG | G | F | VG | G | E | F |
| | **Kumho** Solus KR21 | 56 | VG | G | G | VG | VG | F | VG | VG | G | F |
| | **Firestone** Precision Touring | 56 | VG | VG | G | G | G | F | VG | VG | G | G |
| | **Toyo** Extensa A/S | 56 | G | G | G | G | VG | F | G | VG | F | VG |
| | **Maxxis** MA-T1 Escapade | 54 | VG | VG | G | VG | F | F | G | G | G | G |
| | **Firestone** Affinity Touring | 54 | VG | VG | G | G | G | G | G | VG | G | G |
| | **Sumitomo** HTR T4 | 52 | VG | G | G | VG | G | F | G | VG | VG | F |
| | **Kelly** Explorer Plus | 50 | G | G | G | G | VG | F | G | F | VG | G |

**Ratings Key** Better ←→ Worse: E, VG, G, F, P  ✔ Recommended

## Quick Picks

**ALL SEASON TIRES T-SPEED RATED**
**Best for all-weather performance:**

Michelin Defender
Continental ProContact EcoPlus

**Best balance of three-season performance and long tread life:**

Michelin Defender
Goodyear Assurance TripleTred All-Season
Pirelli P4 Four Seasons
Yokohama Avid Ascend

**Within types, in performance order.**

| Recommended | Brand & model | Overall score (0–100; P \| F \| G \| VG \| E) | Three-season driving: Dry braking | Wet braking | Handling | Hydroplaning | Winter driving: Snow traction | Ice braking | Comfort: Ride | Noise | Rolling resistance | Tread life |
|---|---|---|---|---|---|---|---|---|---|---|---|---|
| | **PERFORMANCE ALL-SEASON H-SPEED RATED** | | | | | | | | | | | |
| ✔ | **Michelin** Primacy MXV4 | 70 | ⊖ | ⊖ | ⊖ | ○ | ⊖ | ○ | ⊖ | ⊖ | ⊜ | ⊖ |
| ✔ | **Continental** PureContact | 68 | ⊖ | ⊜ | ⊖ | ○ | ○ | ○ | ⊖ | ⊖ | ⊖ | ⊖ |
| | **Nexen** CP672 | 66 | ⊖ | ⊖ | ⊖ | ○ | ○ | ◒ | ⊖ | ⊖ | ⊖ | ⊖ |
| | **Pirelli** P7 Cinturato A/S | 64 | ⊖ | ⊖ | ⊖ | ⊖ | ⊖ | ◒ | ⊖ | ⊖ | ⊖ | ◒ |
| | **Michelin** Pilot Exalto A/S | 64 | ⊖ | ⊜ | ○ | ⊖ | ○ | ◒ | ⊖ | ⊖ | ○ | ◒ |
| | **BFGoodrich** Advantage T/A | 62 | ⊖ | ⊖ | ⊖ | ⊖ | ○ | ◒ | ○ | ⊖ | ○ | ○ |
| | **Dunlop** SP Sport 7000 A/S | 60 | ⊖ | ⊜ | ○ | ⊖ | ◒ | ◒ | ⊖ | ⊖ | ⊜ | ◒ |
| | **Cooper** CS4 Touring | 58 | ⊖ | ⊖ | ○ | ⊖ | ○ | ◒ | ⊖ | ⊖ | ○ | ◒ |
| | **Fuzion** Touring | 58 | ⊖ | ○ | ○ | ○ | ◒ | ○ | ⊖ | ○ | ⊖ | ⊖ |
| | **Falken** Ziex ZE912 | 58 | ⊜ | ⊖ | ⊖ | ⊖ | ◒ | ◒ | ○ | ○ | ○ | ◒ |
| | **Uniroyal** Tiger Paw Touring | 58 | ⊖ | ⊖ | ⊖ | ○ | ◒ | ○ | ○ | ○ | ○ | ○ |
| | **Kumho** Solus KH16 | 58 | ⊖ | ⊖ | ⊖ | ○ | ● | ◒ | ⊖ | ⊖ | ○ | ○ |
| | **Dunlop** Signature II | 58 | ⊖ | ○ | ○ | ○ | ⊖ | ○ | ⊖ | ○ | ○ | ○ |
| | **Sumitomo** HTR A/S P01 | 58 | ⊜ | ⊜ | ⊖ | ⊖ | ● | ● | ○ | ⊖ | ○ | ● |
| | **GT** Radial Champiro VP1 | 56 | ⊜ | ⊖ | ⊖ | ⊖ | ● | ◒ | ⊖ | ○ | ○ | ● |
| | **Yokohama** Avid ENVigor | 56 | ⊖ | ⊜ | ⊖ | ⊖ | ● | ● | ⊖ | ○ | ⊖ | ● |
| | **Firestone** Champion HR | 56 | ⊖ | ⊖ | ○ | ⊖ | ◒ | ○ | ⊖ | ○ | ◒ | ◒ |
| | **Firestone** Precision Sport | 54 | ⊖ | ⊖ | ⊖ | ⊖ | ● | ◒ | ⊖ | ⊖ | ◒ | ● |
| | **Bridgestone** Ecopia EP422 | 52 | ○ | ⊖ | ◒ | ○ | ○ | ○ | ⊖ | ⊖ | ⊜ | ○ |

**Ratings Key** Better ⟵⟶ Worse: ⊜ ⊖ ○ ◒ ●   ✔ **Recommended**

## Quick Picks

**PERFORMANCE ALL SEASON H-SPEED RATED**

**Best for all weather conditions:**

Michelin Primacy MXV4
Continental PureContact

**Within types, in performance order.**

| Recommended | Brand & model | Overall score (0–100; P \| F \| G \| VG \| E) | Three-season driving: Dry braking | Wet braking | Handling | Hydroplaning | Winter driving: Snow traction | Ice braking | Comfort: Ride | Noise | Rolling resistance | Tread life |
|---|---|---|---|---|---|---|---|---|---|---|---|---|
| | **PERFORMANCE ALL SEASON V-SPEED RATED** | | | | | | | | | | | |
| ✔ | **Continental** Pure Contact | 70 | ⊖ | ⊜ | ⊖ | ⊖ | ○ | ○ | ⊖ | ⊖ | ⊖ | ⊖ |
| | **Pirelli** P7 Cinturato A/S | 68 | ⊖ | ⊜ | ⊜ | ⊖ | ○ | ◒ | ⊖ | ⊖ | ○ | ◒ |
| ✔ | **Michelin** Primacy MXV4 | 66 | ⊖ | ⊜ | ⊖ | ○ | ○ | ○ | ⊖ | ⊖ | ○ | ⊜ |
| | **Michelin** Pilot Exalto A/S | 64 | ⊖ | ⊜ | ⊖ | ⊖ | ○ | ◒ | ⊖ | ⊖ | ○ | ○ |
| | **Nokian** eNTYRE | 64 | ⊖ | ⊖ | ⊖ | ○ | ⊖ | ○ | ⊖ | ⊖ | ○ | ○ |
| | **Goodyear** Assurance TripleTred All-Season | 64 | ⊖ | ⊜ | ⊖ | ⊖ | ◒ | ○ | ⊖ | ○ | ⊖ | ⊜ |
| | **Dunlop** SP Sport 5000 | 62 | ⊜ | ⊖ | ⊖ | ⊖ | ○ | ○ | ⊖ | ⊖ | ◒ | ◒ |
| | **Goodyear** Assurance ComforTred Touring | 62 | ○ | ○ | ○ | ⊖ | ⊜ | ○ | ⊖ | ⊖ | ⊖ | ⊜ |
| | **Bridgestone** Turanza Serenity Plus | 62 | ⊖ | ⊖ | ◒ | ⊖ | ○ | ○ | ⊖ | ⊖ | ⊖ | ⊖ |
| | **Dunlop** SP Sport 7000 A/S | 60 | ⊖ | ⊖ | ⊖ | ○ | ⊖ | ○ | ⊖ | ⊖ | ⊖ | ● |
| | **GT** Radial Champiro 228 | 60 | ⊜ | ⊜ | ⊖ | ⊖ | ● | ● | ○ | ⊖ | ○ | ◒ |
| | **BFGoodrich** Advantage T/A | 60 | ⊖ | ⊖ | ⊖ | ⊖ | ○ | ◒ | ○ | ⊖ | ○ | ○ |
| | **Cooper** CS4 Touring | 60 | ⊖ | ⊖ | ⊖ | ⊖ | ○ | ◒ | ⊖ | ⊖ | ○ | ○ |
| | **Sumitomo** HTR A/S P01 | 60 | ⊜ | ⊜ | ⊖ | ⊖ | ● | ◒ | ○ | ⊖ | ○ | ◒ |
| | **Yokohama** YK580 | 58 | ⊖ | ○ | ○ | ○ | ○ | ◒ | ⊖ | ⊖ | ⊖ | ⊖ |
| | **Kumho** Ecsta LX Platinum | 56 | ⊖ | ⊖ | ⊖ | ⊖ | ● | ◒ | ⊖ | ⊖ | ⊖ | ◒ |
| | **Uniroyal** Tiger Paw Touring | 56 | ⊖ | ○ | ○ | ⊖ | ◒ | ◒ | ○ | ○ | ○ | ○ |
| | **Bridgestone** Turanza Serenity | 56 | ⊜ | ⊜ | ○ | ○ | ● | ◒ | ⊖ | ⊖ | ◒ | ◒ |
| | **Hankook** Optimo H426 | 56 | ⊖ | ⊜ | ○ | ⊖ | ● | ◒ | ○ | ⊖ | ⊖ | ◒ |
| | **Firestone** Firehawk Wide Oval AS | 56 | ⊖ | ⊖ | ○ | ⊖ | ○ | ◒ | ○ | ⊖ | ○ | ◒ |
| | **Bridgestone** Ecopia EP422 | 52 | ○ | ○ | ◒ | ○ | ○ | ○ | ⊖ | ⊖ | ⊜ | ○ |
| | **Yokohama** Avid ENVigor | 52 | ⊖ | ⊖ | ⊖ | ⊖ | ● | ● | ⊖ | ○ | ⊖ | ◒ |
| | **Toyo** Versado LX II | 52 | ⊖ | ⊖ | ○ | ⊖ | ● | ◒ | ○ | ◒ | ○ | ○ |

**Ratings Key** Better ⟷ Worse: ⊜ ⊖ ○ ◒ ●

✔ Recommended

## Quick Picks

**PERFORMANCE ALL SEASON V-SPEED RATED**

**Best for all-weather performance:**
Continental PureContact
Michelin Primacy MXV4

**Best balance of three-season performance and long tread life:**
Michelin Primacy MXV4

**Within types, in performance order.**

| Recommended | Brand & model | Overall score | Three-season driving: Dry braking | Dry handling | Wet braking | Wet handling | Hydroplaning | Winter driving: Snow traction | Ice braking | Comfort: Ride | Noise | Rolling resistance | Tread life |
|---|---|---|---|---|---|---|---|---|---|---|---|---|---|
| | **UHP ALL-SEASON** | | | | | | | | | | | | |
| ✓ | **Michelin** Pilot Sport A/S 3 | 76 | ⊜ | ⊜ | ⊖ | ⊖ | ⊖ | ○ | ○ | ⊖ | ⊖ | ○ | ⊖ |
| ✓ | **Goodyear** Eagle F1 Asymmetric All Season | 70 | ⊖ | ⊖ | ⊖ | ⊖ | ⊖ | ○ | ⊖ | ○ | ⊖ | ⊖ | ⊖ |
| | **Continental** Extreme Contact DWS | 66 | ⊖ | ⊜ | ⊖ | ⊖ | ⊜ | ● | ○ | ⊖ | ○ | ○ | ◒ |
| ✓ | **Hankook** Ventus S1 noble 2 | 66 | ⊖ | ⊖ | ⊖ | ⊖ | ⊜ | ○ | ○ | ⊖ | ⊖ | ⊖ | ◒ |
| | **BFGoodrich** g-Force Super Sport A/S | 66 | ⊜ | ⊜ | ⊖ | ⊖ | ⊖ | ○ | ◒ | ○ | ○ | ◒ | ○ |
| ✓ | **Pirelli** P Zero Nero All Season | 64 | ⊖ | ⊖ | ⊖ | ⊖ | ⊜ | ○ | ○ | ○ | ⊖ | ⊖ | ○ |
| ✓ | **Cooper** Zeon RS3-A | 64 | ⊖ | ⊖ | ⊖ | ⊖ | ⊖ | ○ | ○ | ⊖ | ○ | ⊖ | ○ |
| | **Uniroyal** Tiger Paw GTZ | 62 | ⊜ | ⊖ | ○ | ○ | ⊖ | ○ | ⊖ | ⊖ | ○ | ⊖ | ⊜ |
| | **General** G-Max AS-03 | 62 | ⊖ | ⊖ | ○ | ○ | ⊖ | ○ | ◒ | ⊖ | ◒ | ⊖ | ⊖ |
| | **Nexen** N7000 | 62 | ○ | ○ | ○ | ○ | ⊜ | ○ | ○ | ⊖ | ⊖ | ⊜ | ⊜ |
| | **Bridgestone** Potenza RE970AS Pole Position | 60 | ⊖ | ○ | ⊖ | ⊖ | ⊖ | ◒ | ○ | ◒ | ○ | ○ | ○ |
| | **Sumitomo** HTR A/S P01 | 58 | ⊖ | ⊖ | ○ | ○ | ⊖ | ○ | ◒ | ⊖ | ⊖ | ○ | ○ |
| | **Kumho** Ecsta 4x | 58 | ⊖ | ⊖ | ○ | ○ | ⊜ | ◒ | ◒ | ⊖ | ⊖ | ○ | ○ |
| | **Nitto** Motivo | 56 | ⊖ | ○ | ◒ | ○ | ⊖ | ⊖ | ○ | ○ | ⊖ | ○ | ⊜ |
| | **Falken** Azenis PT722 A/S | 56 | ⊖ | ⊖ | ◒ | ◒ | ⊖ | ⊖ | ○ | ○ | ○ | ⊖ | ⊜ |
| | **Toyo** Proxes 4 Plus | 56 | ⊖ | ⊖ | ◒ | ◒ | ⊖ | ○ | ○ | ○ | ⊖ | ○ | ⊜ |
| | **Falken** Ziex ZE912 | 56 | ⊖ | ⊖ | ○ | ○ | ⊜ | ◒ | ● | ⊖ | ○ | ○ | ◒ |
| | **Maxxis** Victra MA-Z4S | 54 | ⊖ | ⊖ | ○ | ○ | ⊜ | ● | ● | ⊖ | ○ | ○ | ○ |
| | **Yokohama** Avid ENVigor | 52 | ○ | ⊖ | ○ | ○ | ⊜ | ● | ◒ | ⊖ | ○ | ⊖ | ⊖ |
| | **Firestone** Firehawk Wide Oval AS | 52 | ○ | ○ | ◒ | ○ | ⊜ | ○ | ○ | ⊖ | ⊖ | ⊖ | ○ |
| | **Fuzion** UHP | 52 | ⊖ | ○ | ○ | ○ | ⊖ | ○ | ○ | ○ | ◒ | ⊖ | ○ |

## Quick Picks

**UHP ALL-SEASON TIRES**

**Best for all-weather driving and tread life:**

Michelin Pilot Sport A/S 3
Goodyear Eagle F1 Asymmetric All Season

**Very good choices for all-weather driving:**

Hankook Ventus S1 noble 2
Pirelli P Zero Nero All Season
Cooper Zeon RS3-A

**Within types, in performance order.**

| Recommended | Brand & model | Overall score (0–100; P \| F \| G \| VG \| E) | Three Season Driving: Dry braking | Dry handling | Wet braking | Wet handling | Hydroplaning | Comfort: Ride | Noise | Rolling resistance | Tread life |
|---|---|---|---|---|---|---|---|---|---|---|---|
| | **UHP SUMMER** | | | | | | | | | | |
| ✓ | **Pirelli** P Zero | 78 | E | E | E | E | E | VG | VG | F | F |
| ✓ | **Michelin** Pilot Super Sport | 78 | E | E | VG | E | E | VG | VG | G | VG |
| ✓ | **Yokohama** ADVAN Sport V105 | 76 | E | E | E | VG | E | G | VG | G | G |
| ✓ | **Nokian** zLine | 76 | E | E | E | E | E | VG | VG | VG | G |
| ✓ | **Continental** Extreme Contact DW | 76 | E | E | E | VG | E | VG | VG | VG | F |
| ✓ | **Goodyear** Eagle F1 Asymmetric 2 | 74 | E | VG | E | E | E | G | VG | VG | F |
| ✓ | **Vredestein** Ultrac Vorti | 72 | E | VG | E | VG | E | VG | VG | G | G |
| | **Bridgestone** Potenza S-04 Pole Position | 70 | E | VG | E | VG | E | VG | F | F | F |
| | **Toyo** Proxes T1 Sport | 68 | E | E | VG | VG | E | VG | VG | F | P |
| | **Bridgestone** Potenza RE-11 | 66 | E | VG | VG | VG | E | VG | G | G | G |
| | **Bridgestone** Potenza RE760 Sport | 66 | E | VG | VG | VG | E | VG | E | F | G |
| | **Hankook** Ventus V12 evo | 66 | E | VG | VG | VG | E | G | G | VG | G |
| | **BFGoodrich** g-Force Sport COMP-2 | 66 | E | VG | VG | VG | E | G | P | F | G |
| | **GT** Radial Champiro UHP1 | 64 | E | E | VG | VG | VG | F | VG | G | F |
| | **Falken** Azenis FK-453 | 64 | VG | VG | VG | VG | E | VG | VG | G | F |
| | **Kumho** Ecsta LE Sport | 62 | E | VG | VG | VG | E | VG | VG | G | F |
| | **Yokohama** S.Drive | 62 | VG | VG | VG | VG | VG | G | G | G | F |
| | **Sumitomo** HTR ZIII | 62 | VG | VG | VG | VG | VG | G | G | G | F |
| | **Maxxis** Victra MA-Z1 | 60 | VG | VG | VG | VG | E | G | F | F | F |
| | **Cooper** Zeon RS3-S | 58 | VG | VG | G | VG | E | VG | F | G | F |
| | **Firestone** Firehawk Wide Oval Indy 500 | 56 | VG | VG | G | G | E | VG | VG | F | F |

## Quick Picks

**UHP SUMMER TIRES**

**Best performing tires:**

Pirelli P Zero
Michelin Pilot Super Sport
Yokohama ADVAN Sport V105
Nokian zLine
Continental Extreme Contact DW

**Very good choices:**

Goodyear Eagle F1 Asymmetric 2
Vredestein Ultrac Vorti

Within types, in performance order.

| Recommended | Brand & model | Overall score (0–100; P \| F \| G \| VG \| E) | Winter driving: Snow traction | Winter driving: Ice braking | Three-season driving: Dry braking | Three-season driving: Wet braking | Three-season driving: Handling | Three-season driving: Hydroplaning | Comfort: Ride | Comfort: Noise | Rolling resistance |
|---|---|---|---|---|---|---|---|---|---|---|---|
| **WINTER TIRES** | | | | | | | | | | | |
| ✔ | **Michelin** X-Ice Xi3 | 62 | E | E | P | P | F | F | VG | VG | E |
| ✔ | **Michelin** X-Ice Xi2 | 62 | E | E | P | P | G | F | VG | VG | VG |
| ✔ | **Hankook** Winter I*cept evo | 60 | VG | G | G | F | G | VG | VG | VG | VG |
| ✔ | **Pirelli** Winter 210 Sottozero Serie II | 58 | VG | F | G | G | G | E | VG | VG | G |
| ✔ | **Uniroyal** Tiger Paw Ice & Snow II | 58 | E | VG | F | F | F | G | G | P | VG |
| ✔ | **Bridgestone** Blizzak WS70 | 58 | E | VG | F | P | P | G | E | G | G |
| | **Nokian** Hakkapeliitta R | 58 | E | G | F | P | G | G | G | VG | VG |
| | **Goodyear** Ultra Grip Ice WRT | 58 | E | G | F | F | F | G | VG | F | G |
| | **BFGoodrich** Winter Slalom KSI | 56 | E | G | F | F | F | VG | VG | VG | VG |
| | **Continental** ExtremeWinterContact | 56 | E | VG | P | P | F | F | VG | VG | P |
| | **General** Altimax Arctic | 56 | E | G | P | F | F | G | VG | G | F |
| | **Hankook** Winter I*Pike | 54 | E | G | P | P | F | VG | VG | F | G |
| | **Falken** Espia EPZ | 54 | E | VG | F | P | P | F | VG | F | VG |
| | **Dunlop** Graspic DS-3 | 54 | VG | VG | P | P | F | F | G | G | VG |
| | **Yokohama** iceGuard ig20 | 50 | VG | G | P | P | P | F | VG | F | G |
| | **Firestone** Winterforce | 46 | VG | F | F | F | F | E | VG | F | G |

**Ratings Key** Better ⟷ Worse: E, VG, G, F, P

✔ **Recommended**

## Quick Picks

**WINTER TIRES**

**Best for severe winter driving conditions:**

Michelin X-Ice Xi3
Michelin X-Ice Xi2
Uniroyal Tiger Paw Ice & Snow II
Bridgestone Blizzak WS70

**Best for most driving conditions:**

Hankook Winter I*cept evo
Pirelli Winter 210 Sottozero Serie II

**Within types, in performance order.**

| Recommended | Brand & model | Overall score (0–100; P \| F \| G \| VG \| E) | Winter driving: Snow traction | Winter driving: Ice braking | Three-season driving: Dry braking | Three-season driving: Wet braking | Three-season driving: Handling | Three-season driving: Hydroplaning | Comfort: Ride | Comfort: Noise | Rolling resistance |
|---|---|---|---|---|---|---|---|---|---|---|---|
| | **PERFORMANCE WINTER** | | | | | | | | | | |
| ✔ | **Nokian** WR G3 | 66 | ⊖ | ⊖ | ○ | ○ | ⊖ | ⊖ | ⊖ | ○ | ⊖ |
| ✔ | **Michelin** Pilot Alpin PA4 | 66 | ⊖ | ⊖ | ◒ | ◒ | ⊖ | ⊖ | ⊖ | ○ | ⊖ |
| ✔ | **Nokian** Hakkapeliitta R2 | 64 | ⊜ | ⊜ | ● | ● | ◒ | ○ | ⊖ | ◒ | ⊜ |
| | **Hankook** Winter i*cept evo | 62 | ⊖ | ○ | ⊖ | ○ | ○ | ⊖ | ⊖ | ◒ | ○ |
| | **Dunlop** SP Winter Sport 4D | 62 | ⊖ | ⊖ | ◒ | ◒ | ◒ | ⊜ | ○ | ○ | ⊖ |
| | **Pirelli** Winter 240 Sottozero Series II | 60 | ⊜ | ⊖ | ◒ | ● | ◒ | ⊜ | ⊖ | ◒ | ⊖ |
| | **Vredestein** Wintrac Xtreme | 60 | ⊖ | ⊖ | ○ | ◒ | ○ | ⊖ | ⊖ | ● | ⊖ |
| | **Cooper** WeatherMaster Snow | 56 | ⊖ | ○ | ○ | ◒ | ○ | ⊖ | ⊖ | ◒ | ○ |

**Ratings Key** Better ⊜ ⊖ ○ ◒ ● Worse    ✔ Recommended

## Quick Picks

**PERFORMANCE WINTER TIRES**

**Best for most winter driving conditions:**

Nokian WR G3
Michelin Pilot Alpin PA4

**Best for severe winter driving conditions:**

Nokian Hakkapeliitta R2

**Within types, in performance order.**

| Recommended | Brand & model | Overall score (0–100; P \| F \| G \| VG \| E) | Three-season driving: Dry braking | Wet braking | Handling | Hydroplaning | Winter driving: Snow traction | Ice braking | Comfort: Ride | Noise | Rolling resistance | Tread life |
|---|---|---|---|---|---|---|---|---|---|---|---|---|
| | **ALL-SEASON TRUCK** | | | | | | | | | | | |
| ✔ | **Michelin** LTX M/S[2] | 72 | VG | VG | VG | E | VG | G | VG | VG | G | E |
| ✔ | **Michelin** X Radial LT[2] | 72 | VG | VG | VG | E | VG | G | G | VG | G | E |
| ✔ | **Continental** CrossContact LX20 EcoPlus | 72 | E | E | VG | VG | VG | G | VG | E | G | G |
| ✔ | **Michelin** Latitude Tour HP | 72 | E | E | G | VG | VG | G | VG | E | VG | G |
| ✔ | **Michelin** Latitude Tour | 72 | E | E | G | VG | VG | G | VG | E | G | E |
| | **Hankook** Dynapro HT | 70 | E | VG | VG | E | VG | G | VG | E | G | G |
| | **Nokian** WR G2 Sport Utility | 70 | VG | VG | VG | E | E | G | G | G | G | G |
| | **General** General Grabber HTS | 68 | E | E | G | VG | VG | G | VG | E | G | G |
| | **Goodyear** Wrangler SR-A | 66 | E | VG | G | VG | VG | G | VG | VG | VG | VG |
| | **Cooper** Discoverer CTS | 66 | E | VG | G | VG | VG | G | VG | VG | F | G |
| | **Nokian** HT Sport Utility | 66 | E | E | E | E | P | P | G | E | G | F |
| | **Bridgestone** Dueler H/L Alenza H | 66 | E | VG | VG | E | VG | F | VG | VG | P | F |
| | **Kumho** Road Venture APT KL51 | 64 | E | VG | VG | VG | F | F | VG | VG | G | F |
| | **Bridgestone** Dueler H/L Alenza T | 64 | E | VG | VG | VG | G | P | VG | G | F | G |
| | **BFGoodrich** Long Trail T/A Tour | 64 | E | VG | G | VG | VG | G | G | VG | F | G |
| | **Dunlop** Rover H/T | 64 | VG | G | G | G | E | VG | VG | VG | G | G |
| | **Maxxis** 750 Bravo H/T | 64 | E | VG | G | E | G | G | G | G | G | G |
| | **Firestone** Destination LE | 62 | E | VG | G | E | G | F | G | VG | F | F |
| | **Nexen** Roadian HT SUV | 62 | E | VG | VG | VG | F | F | G | VG | G | G |
| | **Toyo** Open Country H/T | 62 | VG | VG | G | VG | VG | F | G | VG | F | G |
| | **Uniroyal** Laredo Cross Country | 60 | E | VG | G | VG | F | G | VG | G | G | VG |
| | **Yokohama** Geolandar H/T-S G051 | 58 | E | VG | G | E | F | P | G | VG | P | F |
| | **Pirelli** Scorpion STR A | 56 | E | VG | VG | VG | P | P | G | VG | P | P |

## Quick Picks

**ALL-SEASON TRUCK TIRES**

**Best for most weather conditions:**

Michelin LTX M/S[2]
Michelin X Radial LT[2]
Continental CrossContact LX20 EcoPlus
Michelin Latitude Tour HP
Michelin Latitude Tour

**Within types, in performance order.**

| Recommended | Brand & model | Overall score (0–100; P \| F \| G \| VG \| E) | Three-season driving: Dry braking | Wet braking | Handling | Hydroplaning | Winter driving: Snow traction | Ice braking | Comfort: Ride | Noise | Rolling resistance | Tread life |
|---|---|---|---|---|---|---|---|---|---|---|---|---|
| | **ALL-TERRAIN TRUCK** | | | | | | | | | | | |
| ✔ | **Cooper** Discoverer A/T[3] | 66 | VG | VG | G | VG | E | F | VG | G | F | VG |
| ✔ | **Michelin** LTX A/T[2] | 64 | VG | VG | G | VG | VG | F | G | G | G | E |
| ✔ | **Hankook** Dynapro ATM | 64 | VG | VG | G | VG | E | G | G | F | G | VG |
| ✔ | **Kumho** Road Venture AT KL-78 | 64 | E | VG | G | VG | E | G | VG | G | F | F |
| ✔ | **Kumho** Road Venture SAT KL61 | 64 | E | VG | G | E | VG | P | G | VG | G | F |
| | **Bridgestone** Dueler A/T Revo 2 | 62 | E | VG | G | VG | VG | F | VG | VG | F | F |
| | **BFGoodrich** Rugged Terrain | 62 | E | VG | G | G | VG | F | G | G | F | VG |
| | **Pirelli** Scorpion ATR | 62 | E | VG | VG | VG | G | F | G | G | P | F |
| | **Toyo** Open Country A/T | 60 | VG | VG | G | E | VG | F | VG | G | F | G |
| | **Firestone** Destination A/T | 60 | E | VG | G | VG | VG | F | G | G | F | G |
| | **Bridgestone** Dueler APT IV | 60 | VG | VG | G | VG | VG | F | VG | G | F | G |
| | **Nexen** Roadian AT II | 60 | E | G | G | E | E | G | G | G | F | G |
| | **Yokohama** Geolandar A/T-S G012 | 60 | E | VG | G | E | G | P | VG | G | F | F |

## Quick Picks

**ALL-TERRAIN TRUCK TIRES**
**Best for most weather conditions:**
Cooper Discoverer A/T[3]
Michelin LTX A/T[2]
Hankook Dynapro ATM
Kumho Road Venture AT KL-78
Kumho Road Venture SAT KL61

**For longer tread life:**
Michelin LTX A/T[2]

## Guide to the Ratings

**Overall score** is based on 12 to 14 tests, with braking, handling, and hydroplaning resistance weighed most heavily for most tires. Snow traction and ice braking weigh more heavily for winter tires. **Braking** tests on dry and wet pavement are from 60 mph; and on ice, from 10 mph. **Handling**, in most cases, combines how well a tire did in wet and dry cornering grip, steering feel, and an emergency handling maneuver. Wet handling for UHP tires is evaluated by driving the car through a wet slalom course, and includes wet cornering grip. Dry handling for UHP tires combines the emergency handling maneuver, dry cornering grip, and steering feel. **Hydroplaning** denotes a tire's ability to resist skimming along the surface of standing water and causing loss of steering ability. **Snow traction** tests denote how far a vehicle has to travel to accelerate from 5 to 20 mph on flat, moderately packed snow. **Ride** and **noise** are evaluated subjectively, on rough and smooth roads. **Rolling resistance,** as measured on a dynamometer, is a factor in fuel economy. **Tread life** is an indicator of wear potential from CR's extended mixed driving test run on the government's tread wear course.

# Statement of Ownership, Management, and Circulation

(Required by 39 U.S.C. 3685)

1. Publication Title: Consumer Reports. 2. Publication No: 0010-7174. 3. Filing Date: August 22, 2013. 4. Issue Frequency: Monthly, except two issues in December. 5. No. of Issues Published Annually: 13. 6. Annual Subscription Price: $29. 7. Complete Mailing Address of Known Office of Publication: Consumer Reports Inc., 101 Truman Avenue, Yonkers, NY 10703-1057. 8. Complete Mailing Address of Headquarters or General Business Office of Publisher: Consumer Reports Inc., 101 Truman Avenue, Yonkers, NY 10703-1057. 9. Full Names and Complete Mailing Addresses of Publisher, Editor, and Managing Editor. Publisher: Consumer Reports Inc., 101 Truman Avenue, Yonkers, NY 10703-1057. President: James A. Guest; Interim Editor: Brent Diamond; Managing Editor: Robert Tiernan.

10. Owner: (If the publication is published by a nonprofit organization, its name and address must be stated.) Full Name: Consumer Reports Inc., a nonprofit organization. Complete Mailing Address: 101 Truman Avenue, Yonkers, NY 10703-1057. 11. Known Bondholders, Mortgagees, and Other Security Holders Owning or Holding 1 Percent or More of Total Amount of Bonds, Mortgages, or Other Securities. If none, so state: None. 12. For Completion by Nonprofit Organizations Authorized to Mail at Special Rates: The purpose, function, and nonprofit status of this organization and the exempt status for federal income tax purposes has not changed during preceding 12 months. 13. Publication title: Consumer Reports. 14. Issue Date for Circulation Data below: October 2013.

| 15. Extent and Nature of Circulation: Print Magazine, U.S. and Canada | Average no. copies each issue during past 12 mo. | No. copies of single issue published-nearest to filing date |
|---|---|---|
| A. Total no. of copies (net press run) | 4,432,806 | 4,397,746 |
| B. Paid circulation | | |
| 1. Mailed outside-county paid subscriptions stated on Form 3541 | 3,921,442 | 3,922,004 |
| 2. Mailed in-county paid subscriptions stated on Form 3541 | 0 | 0 |
| 3. Sales through dealers, carriers, street vendors, counter sales, and other non-USPS paid distribution | 96,608 | 80,000 |
| 4. Other classes mailed through the USPS | 0 | 0 |
| C. Total paid distribution (sum of 15b(1), (2), (3), and (4)) | 4,018,050 | 4,002,004 |
| D. 1. Free or Nominal Rate Outside-County Copies included on PS Form 3541 | 1,366 | 1,296 |
| 2. Free or Nominal Rate In-County included on PS form 3541 | 0 | 0 |
| 3. Free or Nominal Rate Copies Mailed at Other Classes Through the USPS (e.g. First-Class Mail) | 0 | 0 |
| 4. Free or Nominal Rate Distribution Outside the Mail (Carriers or other means) | 11,197 | 10,131 |
| E. Total free distribution (sum of 15d(1) and (4)) | 12,563 | 11,427 |
| F. Total distribution (sum of 15c and 15e) | 4,030,613 | 4,013,431 |
| G. Copies not distributed | 402,193 | 384,315 |
| H. TOTAL (sum of 15f and 15g) | 4,432,806 | 4,397,746 |
| I. Percent paid and/or requested circulation | 99.69% | 99.72% |

17. I certify that the statements made by me above are correct and complete.

Brent Diamond, VP and GM, Magazine and Newsletter Products

**CONSUMER REPORTS BUYING GUIDE 2014** VOLUME 78, No. 13

CONSUMER REPORTS magazine (ISSN 0010-7174) is published monthly, except twice in December, by CONSUMER REPORTS, 101 Truman Avenue, Yonkers, NY 10703-1057. Periodicals postage paid at Yonkers, NY, and at other mailing offices. Canadian postage paid at Mississauga, Ontario, Canada. Canadian publications registration no. 2665247-98, agreement number 40015148.  CR is a member of Consumers International. **Mailing lists:** CR rents or exchanges its customer postal list so it can be provided to other publications, companies, and nonprofit organizations. If you wish your name deleted from lists and rentals, send your address label with a request for deletion to CONSUMER REPORTS, P.O. Box 2127, Harlan, IA 51593-0316. **U.S. Postmaster:** Send address changes to P.O. Box 2109, Harlan, IA 51593-0298. If the Post Office alerts us that your magazines are undeliverable, we have no further obligation to fulfill your magazines unless we have a corrected address within two years. **Canada Post:** If copies are undeliverable, return to CONSUMER REPORTS, P.O. Box 1051, STN MAIN, Fort Erie, ON L2A 6C7. **Back issues:** Single copies of 12 preceding issues, $7.95 each; Buying Guide, $14.49 each (includes shipping and handling). Write Back Issues, CONSUMER REPORTS, Customer Relations, 101 Truman Ave., Yonkers, N.Y. 10703-1057.